I0900929

Dönitz's Crews

Dedicated photograph of Admiral Karl Dönitz postwar signed to one of his boys, Herbert Griephan, who had served on the U-504 and U-575. *Dedication is signed and dated March 29, 1972. Herbert Griephan died on January 20, 1999.*

Dönitz's Crews

Germany's U-Boat Sailors in World War II

French L. MacLean

Schiffer Military History
Atglen, PA

Book design by Robert Biondi.

Copyright © 2009 by French L. MacLean.
Library of Congress Catalog Number: 2009934123.

All rights reserved. No part of this work may be reproduced or used in any forms or by any means – graphic, electronic or mechanical, including photocopying or information storage and retrieval systems – without written permission from the publisher.

The scanning, uploading and distribution of this book or any part thereof via the Internet or via any other means without the permission of the publisher is illegal and punishable by law. Please purchase only authorized editions and do not participate in or encourage the electronic piracy of copyrighted materials.

"Schiffer," "Schiffer Publishing Ltd. & Design," and the "Design of pen and ink well" are registered trademarks of Schiffer Publishing, Ltd.

Printed in China.
ISBN: 978-0-7643-3356-9

We are always looking for people to write books on new and related subjects. If you have an idea for a book, please contact us at the address below.

Published by Schiffer Publishing Ltd.
4880 Lower Valley Road
Atglen, PA 19310
Phone: (610) 593-1777
FAX: (610) 593-2002
E-mail: Info@schifferbooks.com.
Visit our web site at: www.schifferbooks.com
Please write for a free catalog.
This book may be purchased from the publisher.
Please include $5.00 postage.
Try your bookstore first.

In Europe, Schiffer books are distributed by:
Bushwood Books
6 Marksbury Ave.
Kew Gardens, Surrey TW9 4JF
England
Phone: 44 (0)20 8392-8585
FAX: 44 (0)20 8392-9876
E-mail: info@bushwoodbooks.co.uk
www.bushwoodbooks.co.uk

CONTENTS

Appendices

Appreciation

The list increases with each passing book of the wonderful people I have known who helped on each latest effort. I'd like to thank my wife Olga, and my parents (especially my Mother who passed away last summer), for encouraging me to write and study subjects that interested me. I would like to thank all my friends for at least feigning interest in the subjects I undoubtedly have bored them to death over; special thanks goes to Hank Adams, Ray Embree, Lou DiMarco, Jack Pattison, Scott Pritchett and Tom Veve – all old Army buddies. Over the last ten years our neighbors, the Garretts and the Baldwins, have made living in Northern Virginia a true pleasure. Bob Biondi and the folks at Schiffer Publishing have made it easy to concentrate on just writing. That has its perils and Mrs. Marianne Driscoll has courageously served in the thankless role as the writing editor, attempting to make sense and good order of my frequent incomplete sentences and misspelled words – any errors you may see have been made when I overrode her good wisdom.

Concerning the actual subject matter, I would like to thank Herr Walter Wittig in Cuxhaven for graciously giving me an interview concerning his experiences on the *U-518*. I would also like to thank *Kapitän zur See* (a.D.) Peter Monte for showing me the various cubbyholes of the U-boat Archive & Museum in Cuxhaven. Finally, I offer a huge thank you to Herr Horst Bredow who has devoted his entire adult life in managing this unique resource of the U-boat Archive. For anyone with an interest in the subject, a visit to Cuxhaven is truly a dream come true.

Also in Germany I would like to thank our wonderful friends Manfred and Lucie Sommer and their entire family; their home in Heidelberg has been like a second home to us. I would also like to thank Thomas Huss, Andre Hüsken and Detlev Niemann for helping me find obscure military artifacts related to the subject without which this book would not be possible. Gabi Schmidt of Christian Schmidt Buchhandlung in Munich searched far and wide over the last several years to ensure I knew about every new U-boat book.

Seeing really great writers work their craft is an inspiration. In this regard I would like to thank Jak Mallmann Showell and Gordon Williamson for demonstrating what could be written about the U-boat war; by reading their works I found what niche I might be able to fill with this humble effort.

More thanks go to my good National War College friend, Mike Mahon. Currently a Navy Rear Admiral, he and his family have been wonderful friends and he has also encouraged me to write on a naval subject, which you see here.

I would like to thank all the wonderful people of Decatur, Illinois who have helped take care of my mother and father over the last several years; your friendship and medical assistance to them has made all the difference in the world.

And finally to Max and Benji; Benji, you have been the mischievous spark that makes life a hoot every day; Max, how I miss you so, my great friend.

French L. MacLean
Colonel (*Ret.*)

FOREWORD

I have always loved history, especially concerning World War II. Why that conflict has intrigued me may have several answers. First, my father – who has been and always will be my personal hero – fought in the war as an infantry private first class in the 1st Battalion, 39th Infantry Regiment, of the U.S. 9th Infantry Division in the Hürtgen Forest and the Battle of the Bulge, before being wounded and taken prisoner by the Germans. Although he has always been reluctant to discuss his experiences, it was possible to get bits and pieces of his recollections. Additionally, growing up in the 1950s and 1960s, I could not get enough of television accounts from the war from dramatized accounts such as *Combat* and the *Rat Patrol* to more factually-correct descriptions on the *Twentieth Century*. The big screen came through in a big way as well for those interested in the war and I must have seen *The Guns of Navaronne* and *The Longest Day* a dozen times, not to mention *The Dirty Dozen* and dozens more excellent movies. My mother, who taught me how to read before I attended kindergarten, sensed my keen, if narrow, interest and enrolled me in special children's summer reading programs, in which I probably attempted to read every book on the subject in the Peoria Public Library, while after the visits, on the walk home, my mother would buy me a blueberry or banana popsicle as a reward for reading a book each week. And on birthdays, Christmas and whenever my grandmother came over, I could count on getting a present of a newly published book on the war.

Historical artifacts have also interested me a great deal. Holding a medal from a past war always got my mind racing as to who might have done the heroic deed for which the decoration was presented. After graduating from West Point, my first Army assignment was in Germany in the mid-1970s and it was during these years that I discovered old German military award documents in off-the-beaten-path antique stores and flea markets. These documents actually told a small story, providing the name of the individual who won the award, the date and type of award and the organization of the soldier, as well as a signature by the awardee's commanding officer. In those days very few people were interested in the old papers, preferring the glitzier medals themselves, an easily identifiable German coalscuttle helmet or perhaps a dagger. But I liked the old documents and would spend hours poring over every facet of information contained on them. Sometimes, but not often, I would even run across a document or two for a U-boat sailor. Those documents, according to most local antique storeowners, were brought in during sales of estates of the parents of the U-boat men. I asked why that was so and was told that most of the submariners themselves had been killed in the war.

Over the next several decades I researched and wrote eight non-fiction history books on the war. For all of them, from German General Officer casualties to the Dirlewanger Brigade, to three books on the SS, to a two-volume set on *Luftwaffe* officer efficiency reports, I selected narrow topics that had not really been previously addressed by other books and authors. My rhetorical question to myself was always, "Why write the 150th book on D-Day?"

That question and obvious answer for me remained in force over the last ten years until I read an interesting set of numbers by Jak Mallmann Showell in several of his works. According to this author, a respected U-boat historian, of the 1,170 German U-boats constructed in the war, about 863 were put in operational use (the others were still in training or work-up) and, in theory, could have seen combat. Of these, 462 U-boats made contact and hit at least one target; but 401 attack submarines never hit a target at all. Of those 462 that did:

- 38 boats attacked and at least damaged 20 or more ships,
- 45 boats attacked and at least damaged between 11 and 19 ships,
- 72 boats attacked and at least damaged between 6 and 10 ships and
- 307 boats attacked and at least damaged between 1 and 5 ships.

Showell then postulated that these numbers showed that Germany had its naval priorities mistaken and instead of building such vast numbers of U-boats (half of which would sink nothing), the High Command should have provided more support to the U-boat effort to give the truly combat-effective boats and crews (perhaps the eighty-three proven "killer-boats" demonstrated in the top two categories above) superior technology; he also believed that wolf packs were not that effective – it was mainly just a few killer-boats that achieved success on their own. Conversely, Mallmann Showell demonstrated how many U-boats met their end in just their first week at war.

> *Dönitz's Crews*
> ***Maschinengefreiter* Wolfgang Hetschger**
> Born on January 10, 1924.
> Served in the engine room on the *U-227*.
> Spent 6 days at sea on a U-boat war patrol.
> Killed in action on April 30, 1943 in the North Atlantic.

I came up with a different conclusion, not about Germany's naval priorities, but on possibly writing another book, and decided that by researching and describing anecdotes about a few select boats – typically from the most-successful boats and also a few specialty boats or those that had unique experiences, as well – the reader could get an excellent overall picture of the men who sailed in Dönitz's force. One did not need to read about all 1,170 boats, especially when 2% of U-boat commanders sank 30% of all Allied shipping that fell to the U-boats. Additionally, I wanted to link the old papers on U-boat men with actual history, to show what could be done tracing an artifact and spending interesting hours finding hidden stories. Finally, most books on U-boat men concentrate on the boat commanders – clearly key personnel – but here was an opportunity to look at the ordinary seamen who responded to the commander's orders and actually made the boat function.

For an author, one temptation that must be avoided at all costs is to make "perfect" the enemy of "good enough." On any subject it is always possible to find one more piece of information that will make one's book incrementally better. But at some point the author must call it a day and submit the work for publication; the alternative is to write the best book that never gets published. To those who may say, "Why not include even more U-boat histories in this work?" I would explain it thusly; concentrating on just a few boats opened the possibility of finding and acquiring a manageable number of historical artifacts and photos on these selected boats to present in the book, which would add an important human dimension to the history – not to mention helping me remain in the good graces of my wife, who might view too many purchases of "old pictures and papers" with a less positive outlook!

The result lies before you; a subject that has been written about numerous times in many excellent books over the years, but perhaps in a format that is unique and interesting for the landlubber – of which I am one – more interested in what went on inside of the hearts and minds of men who fought far from home and how they lived, and often died, rather than what occurred inside the diesel engines or how the U-boat targeting optics functioned.

Sources, Foreword: Jak Mallmann Showell, *U-boat Warfare: The Evolution of the Wolf Pack*, Annapolis, Maryland: Naval Institute Press, 2002, 11.

Dönitz's boys on the U-373 relax after returning from a war patrol in August 1941 at Trondheim, Norway.
Officer in the white cap is the U-boat's skipper Paul-Karl Loeser, born April 26, 1915 in Berlin; he would survive the war. Immediately right of Loeser is Leutnant zur See Herbert Zeissler; he would later command the U-1192, U-140 and U-1194 and would also survive.

Dönitz's boys eat on their bunks on the U-373. *Photo from the estate of former Bootsmaat Walter Schüler.*

The U-boat war was a cruel war. *Dönitz's boys on the U-373 and merchant survivors on a life raft. There was no room for prisoners on a U-boat; the best they could do was give food, water and perhaps a blanket – not much protection against a cruel sea.*

Zum Andenken im Gebete

an unsern lieben Sohn, Bruder und Schwager

Kriegsfreiwilliger Masch.-Gefr.

Wolfgang Hetschger

geb. am 10. Januar 1924.

Er erlitt den Seemannstod bei seiner ersten Feindfahrt am 6. Mai 1943.

Mutter trockne Deine Tränen: —
Als mich rief der nasse Tod.
War bei Dir mein letztes Sehnen, —
Brich nicht, brich nicht, Mutterherz!

Liebe Eltern, Brüder, Schwägerinnen!
Tragt geduldig euren Schmerz!
Im Himmel sehn wir uns ja wieder,
Brich nicht, brich nicht, Vaterherz!

No place for youngsters. *Death Announcement for Maschinengefreiter Wolfgang Hetschger, age 19, and on his first patrol, who died with all his boatmates onboard the U-227 north of the Faeroes on April 30, 1943 (not May 6 as thought by the German Navy and shown on the card) during an Australian Hampden aircraft depth charge attack. The U-227 was on her first war patrol. Her skipper, Jürgen Kuntze, was 25; he also perished in the attack. Her attacker, Australian Flight Officer J.S. Freeth, was 22; he was killed in action three weeks later, one day after his 23rd birthday.*

Off to the Navy!

Dedication

This book is dedicated to the hundreds of thousands of sailors – both naval and merchant marine – of all nations who fought above, on and below the sea around the globe in World War II. More specifically, it is dedicated to the tens of thousands who perished during the conflict.

Quite clearly the book specifically memorializes the many German enlisted men who went to war in the U-boat force – a majority of which never returned to Germany. One might be tempted to say that these young men deserved the cold, painful fate that awaited them; for, in fact, the U-boat men like their brothers-in-arms in the *Luftwaffe* and Panzer forces were advancing an evil ideology that called for the deaths of tens of millions of innocents and the subjugation of much of the world in virtual slavery.

This author would submit that these sailors, airmen and soldiers were, in their own right, also victims of Nazism. Nazism took away their individual freedoms; it forced them to serve many years in harsh conditions away from their families; it eliminated any possibility of a negotiated end to the war, which in turn led to massive levels of destruction of German livelihood, the flattening of German cities from aerial attack displacing of millions of Germans from their homes, and fragmented the nation that would last more than forty years after the war.

Perhaps equally as insidious, National Socialism caused the eternal damnation in history of levels of bravery and self-sacrifice that would have been extolled in any other place and time.

But that is only one opinion and that view can be argued between scholars and laymen alike, each with a valid point of view. Perhaps to better illustrate my point, we can refer to Seaman Ernst Heinz Wehner. Ernst was born on February 18, 1922 in Dresden to a twenty-two year old single mother Elsa Wehner. Ernst grew up, went to school and joined the *Kriegsmarine*, entering the U-boat service at the beginning of the war. After completing his training, he appears to have served on the *U-581* until early 1942 when his boat was sunk by Allied anti-submarine forces. He wound up in a prisoner of war camp in Canada, just shy of his twentieth birthday.

A year before this event Ernst's mother died; she was only forty-one, but suffered from epilepsy, and appeared to have been in and out of hospitals during her young life. Ernst's grandfather (Elsa's father) Robert Wehner received a letter explaining her sudden death during a stay at one of these hospitals at Hartheim, Austria. The letter read:

February 13, 1941

Dear Mr. Wehner!
We regret that we have to inform you that your daughter Elsa Wehner has died unexpectedly on February 13 due to a severe epileptic attack. Her transfer to our institute represents a measure caused by the war and took place according to reasons in connection with the defense of our country.

Since our institute merely serves as a transit station for those sick persons who are to be transferred to another institute and the stay here merely serves for locating virus-bearers who again and again are among these sick people as is well-known, the respective local police in Hartheim, in agreement with the authorities concerned, have ordered comprehensive protection measures and according to Paragraph 22 of the Order for Fighting Communicable Diseases, the immediate incineration of the corpse and the disinfection of the personal belongings. An agreement by family members, etc., is not necessary in this case.

The remains, after having been disinfected, are retained for delivery to the heir, who must legitimize himself with a certificate issued by the respective authorities.

If you wish to have the urn placed in a particular cemetery – the transfer is being made at no cost – we request that you reply to us by adding the declaration of agreement by the respective cemetery administration. In case you do not send us this information within 14 days, we will arrange for disposal otherwise, as we would assume that you will forego the remains, if we do not receive information about this within the same time.

We are enclosing two death certificates, which you may use for possible presentation to authorities.

Heil Hitler!

[Signature illegible]

Unfortunately for Ernst Heinz Wehner, Robert Wehner and most unfortunately for Elsa Wehner, Hartheim was not a hospital in the true sense of the word. It was not dedicated to curing patients or relieving suffering; its staff did not subscribe to the Hippocratic Oath.

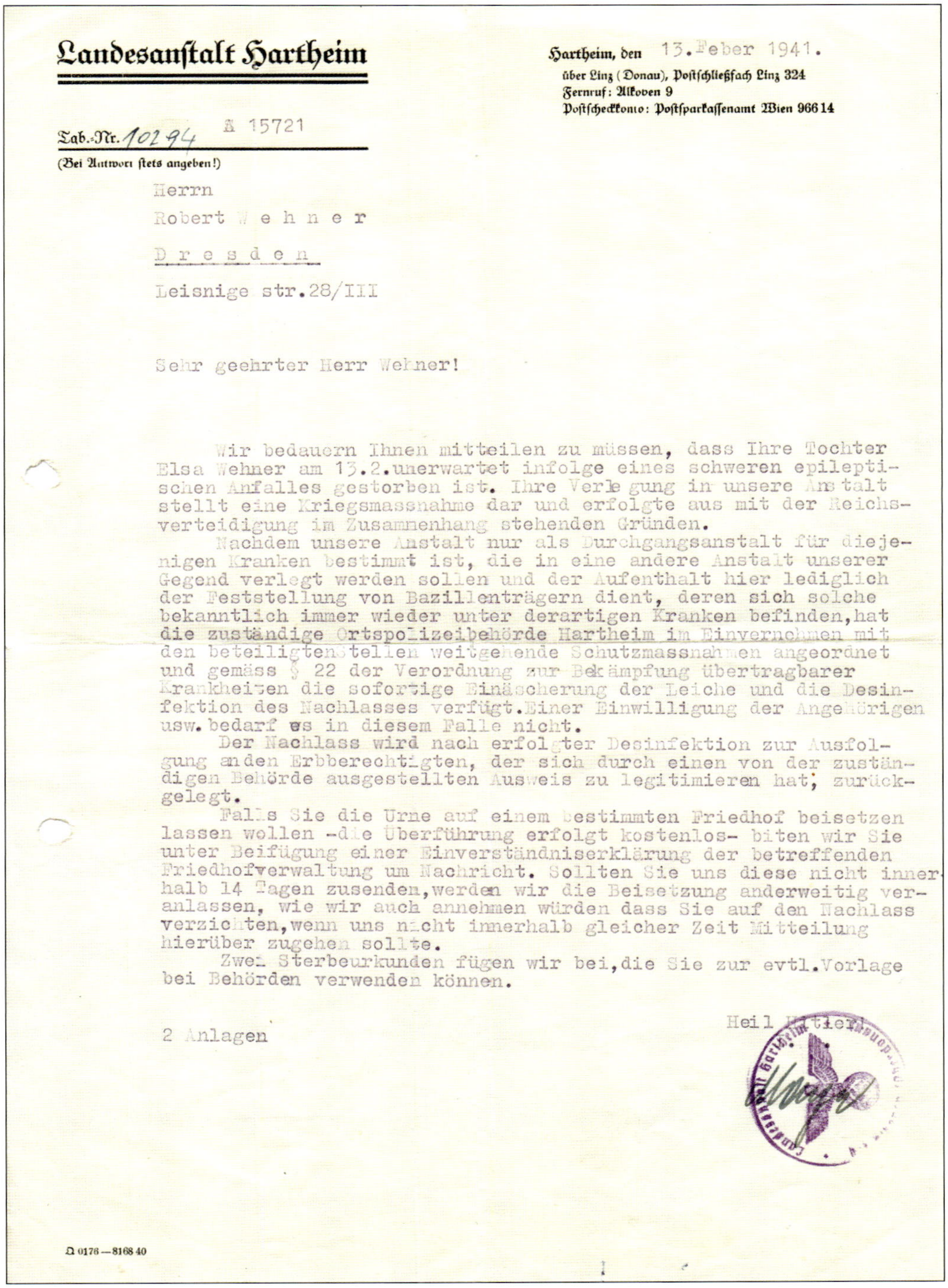

Landesanstalt Hartheim

Hartheim, den 13. Feber 1941.
über Linz (Donau), Postschließfach Linz 324
Fernruf: Alkoven 9
Postscheckkonto: Postsparkassenamt Wien 96614

Tab.-Nr. 10294 A 15721
(Bei Antwort stets angeben!)

Herrn
Robert Wehner
Dresden
Leisnige str. 28/III

Sehr geehrter Herr Wehner!

Wir bedauern Ihnen mitteilen zu müssen, dass Ihre Tochter Elsa Wehner am 13.2. unerwartet infolge eines schweren epileptischen Anfalles gestorben ist. Ihre Verlegung in unsere Anstalt stellt eine Kriegsmassnahme dar und erfolgte aus mit der Reichsverteidigung im Zusammenhang stehenden Gründen.

Nachdem unsere Anstalt nur als Durchgangsanstalt für diejenigen Kranken bestimmt ist, die in eine andere Anstalt unserer Gegend verlegt werden sollen und der Aufenthalt hier lediglich der Feststellung von Bazillenträgern dient, deren sich solche bekanntlich immer wieder unter derartigen Kranken befinden, hat die zuständige Ortspolizeibehörde Hartheim im Einvernehmen mit den beteiligten Stellen weitgehende Schutzmassnahmen angeordnet und gemäss § 22 der Verordnung zur Bekämpfung übertragbarer Krankheiten die sofortige Einäscherung der Leiche und die Desinfektion des Nachlasses verfügt. Einer Einwilligung der Angehörigen usw. bedarf es in diesem Falle nicht.

Der Nachlass wird nach erfolgter Desinfektion zur Ausfolgung an den Erbberechtigten, der sich durch einen von der zuständigen Behörde ausgestellten Ausweis zu legitimieren hat, zurückgelegt.

Falls Sie die Urne auf einem bestimmten Friedhof beisetzen lassen wollen - die Überführung erfolgt kostenlos - biten wir Sie unter Beifügung einer Einverständniserklärung der betreffenden Friedhofverwaltung um Nachricht. Sollten Sie uns diese nicht innerhalb 14 Tagen zusenden, werden wir die Beisetzung anderweitig veranlassen, wie wir auch annehmen würden dass Sie auf den Nachlass verzichten, wenn uns nicht innerhalb gleicher Zeit Mitteilung hierüber zugehen sollte.

Zwei Sterbeurkunden fügen wir bei, die Sie zur evtl. Vorlage bei Behörden verwenden können.

2 Anlagen

Heil Hitler!

D 0176—816840

Death Notification Letter from the Hartheim Action T4 euthanasia center to the Wehner family.

Hartheim was a euthanasia center; medical, police and SS personnel killed physically and mentally disabled patients by carbon monoxide gassing and lethal injection. Known as "Action T4," the program killed at least 18,269 people at Hartheim and tens of thousands more at several other euthanasia centers across Germany during the late 1930s and early 1940s. These victims were neither nefarious enemies of the government nor convicted of any crimes; their long-term care simply cost the state too much – additionally, Nazi racial experts did not desire that their substandard genetic traits be passed on to future generations. So Elsa Wehner had to die.

We do not know if Ernst Heinz Wehner comprehended the actual circumstances surrounding his mother's death at the hands of the state. What we do know is that while the young sailor was trying his best to defend Germany far from home – while enemy forces were trying to blow Wehner and his boat-mates into oblivion – the political leaders of his country were murdering his helpless mother and lying to his family back in Germany. Was he a victim? I think so.

Preface

Dönitz's crews were many things; they could be young, resourceful, courageous, stoic, ambitious, intelligent, confident, determined, chivalrous, tenacious and idealistic. They could also be nervous, cynical, depressed, frustrated, desperate and terrified. Sometimes they could be many of these characteristics in a single, short period of time from the ultimate high of sinking an enemy ship to moments later sitting inside a cold, wet, dark steel "coffin," during a rain of exploding depth charges, waiting for the one that would destroy their boat by crushing the hull and killing them instantly or causing their boat to sink uncontrollably to the bottom of the ocean, where they would choke to death on the toxic fumes emitted by broken batteries or – one by one – die by inches in the cold, wet darkness as their oxygen supply slowly ran out. Afraid – they all were, but in a U-boat you couldn't let your fear take control or the enemy would locate you immediately. Survival for all depended on perfect performance by every man.

Dönitz's Crews
***Obersteuermann* Walter Schuler**

Born on October 25, 1919 at Leipheim/Bavaria.
Joined the Navy on October 1, 1938; served on U-boats from December 1940 to May 1945.
Served as a flak gunner on the *U-373* and Navigator on the *U-1026*; wounded in action on July 24, 1943. Also served on the *U-80* and *UD-5*.
Awarded the U-boat War Badge on November 11, 1941; awarded the Iron Cross 2nd Class on April 21, 1942; awarded the Iron Cross 1st Class on April 16, 1943; awarded the U-boat Clasp in Bronze on November 21, 1944.
Spent 365 days at sea on U-boat war patrols.
Helped clear mines after the war on the minesweeper M-803; served in the postwar German Navy.
Died in 2002 at Kappeln am Schlei/Schleswig-Holstein.

Dönitz's crews were also very talented. The U-boat command looked for men with a technical background, especial mechanics and metal workers. Many U-boat men came from families where their fathers were civilian master craftsmen.

Young men without a certificate stating they had graduated from the Volksschule (elementary school) need not apply. The Navy was also not interested in men who had a criminal record; in the close confines of a U-boat no one wanted a thief in his midst. At the beginning of the war only 33% of those who volunteered for U-boat service were considered suitable and only 60% of these suitable men were eventually accepted into the program. Prospective U-boat sailors also needed to have good dental hygiene. Although some dental procedures could be accomplished on a U-boat on patrol, the visualization of a potentially difficult, lengthy tooth extraction – probably without the benefit of any type of anesthesia or a trained dentist – on a boat bucking in rough seas, could make even the "saltiest" battle-hardened Chief Petty Officer become queasy.

Dönitz's crews were not selfish concerning creature comforts. They had to be as the U-boats the Germans went to war with in 1939 were essentially World War I designs, lacking foresight and innovation especially in the area of crew comfort. On a Type VIIC U-boat, the most abundant type of submarine in the German Navy, for example, there were eight sleeping bunks for the boat's thirteen petty officers. The junior enlisted men – twenty-five in number – shared twelve sleeping bunks. The crews on the larger Type IXC boats considered these to be luxurious, as this type of boat had eight bunks for twelve petty officers and twenty-four bunks for some thirty-four junior enlisted men, but on any type of U-boat shared bunks meant "shared" head or body lice if even one crewmember was infested with the itchy rash-causing parasites when the patrol started. And, there was only one change of linen stowed for the entire voyage. The men in the forward torpedo room, referred to as "the Lords" (the nickname given to naval ratings) were cramped the worst, often sleeping on thin mats laid on top of oily stored torpedoes or fitfully resting in ad hoc hammocks. "The Lords" also had the onerous, but very important, task of inspecting the torpedoes every three days or so; this involved easing each "eel" out of its launch tube onto hoist rings where the torpedo mates would inspect battery charges, bearings and guidance systems – all of which were thickly coated with grease, which invariably slopped onto all the men.

In heavy seas, sleepers could be torn from their bunks and hammocks and thrown to the deck in an instant. When men could go to sleep, the German Navy's medical service concluded that much of the sleep was fitful and not deep enough (in part because some lights were always on) – the same diagnosis that any U-boat man could determine after just a few days aboard! Part of that fitful rest may have been caused by the size of the bunks; U-boat berths for both officers and men were four inches shorter and four inches narrower than standard berths on World War II U.S. Navy fleet submarines. Four inches does not seem like a lot, except when a man cannot fully stretch out to sleep and must awake after lying with muscles contracted in his legs and back – day after day in damp conditions.

Messing services were also Spartan. Most boats had a small galley with two hotplates to heat meals for a crew of forty-four to fifty-six men. However, in rough seas, for safety, the hotplates were not used and the food was thus served cold. As less than a quarter of the crew could actually eat their meals at proper tables, the rest of the crew sat on the hard, damp metal floor deck plates or on boxes, precariously balancing their dish and bowl on their knees in order to eat their meals quickly before the grease and gravy cooled and coagulated. The dishwasher on a U-boat was not a machine, but one of the sailors using warm seawater from the cooling system in the engine room – without detergent – often with a rag of "questionable appearance."

Lavatory facilities (heads in naval parlance) were even worse. Most U-boats had two small compartments but one was often used to store provisions, including food! The other head near the boat's stern thus had to service the entire crew of forty-six to sixty men. Paper was often not supplied. Flushing the toilet required a specific sequence of pulling levers, and operating them in the wrong order could result in the bowl's contents being sprayed over the user instead of flushing away. Additionally, the toilet could not be operated below a depth of about 80 feet due to the increased water pressure outside the U-boat. To add insult to injury, the operation of the appliance was extremely noisy and thus was prohibited during periods of silent running when the enemy was in close proximity – and that could last for many, many hours. Crewmen thus had to use buckets located in the various compartments. When surfaced the crew sometimes put a makeshift toilet seat over the side rail as long as the sea breezes were neither too strong nor from the wrong direction!

There were no showers or baths aboard the boats, so the men never undressed, changing underwear garments only when they became too unpleasant. On some war patrols in warmer water it might be possible to stop and allow part of the crew to take a quick swim in the ocean, but every lookout then had to keep his eyes peeled for patrolling enemy aircraft, while other men watched for marauding sharks. The extreme shortage of water also meant that little could be spared for shaving, and wartime photographs of men returning on a U-boat from patrol show many sailors with full beards.

Temperatures inside a U-boat varied, but none were quite comfortable, as no operational U-boats were provided with air conditioning, heating or cooling systems. In the Arctic and North Atlantic it could be quite cold and damp, while in the Caribbean, West Africa or Mediterranean overall temperatures inside a boat could reach 95°F, with the temperature in the engine room approaching 122°F; one U-boat commander reported that in the Gulf of Aden temperatures in the engine room hit 163°F! The humid air produced a squalid, oppressive, damp, greenhouse effect – along with an eerie fog that would sometimes form around the interior lights. Sweaty men, unable to bathe, in a cramped humid environment for perhaps eight weeks or more on patrol could make the atmosphere inside of a U-boat seem more foul than the stale air in the dirtiest athletic equipment-storage locker in a run-down gymnasium. No wonder that *eau de cologne* was ever-present, and that the crew had a particular term for the rank foulness – "U-boat stink."

Condensing moisture constantly dripped from overhead pipes, ducts and valves ruining maps and papers. This fetid atmosphere also affected the storage of food, which quickly started to mold and rot or take on a faintly diesel taste after only a few days at sea; salami could turn green and slimy in the humidity, which often approached 100%. At the start of a war patrol the boat was well-provisioned (the best rations of any in the German military services): fresh meat, fruit, eggs, vegetables and bread; occasionally large smoked hams hung from brackets in the control room, while empty hammocks were filled to overflow with fresh bread. The crew would consume these staples first as after only three weeks the loaves of black bread – the German sailor's staple food – would have a covering of fluffy white mold. The crew referred to the loaves at this point as "rabbits" and carefully ate only the center of each loaf. When this fresh food ran out, or when it became unpalatable, the crew switched to tinned food. However, often the captain did not want the wasted food or garbage to be dumped over the side as it could reveal a U-boat's presence in enemy waters, so the decomposing food sometimes had to be retained onboard for several additional days, or even longer, before being thrown over the side – giving the boat somewhat of a garbage-dump-aroma.

Smells from paint and diesel could give the men headaches, and sea-sickness could also be a problem. Whether the cause was fear, tainted food, rolling seas or the overall putrid odor in the boat, there was simply no decent place to vomit inside a U-boat. The aft head was too far away (and often occupied); men either heaved their stomach contents into "the diesel room pail" – which may already have been half-full – or where they stood or lay, which raised the unpleasant problem of how to eliminate this waste from the boat. In some instances sea-sickness became an induced rapid chain-reaction among the crew that completely fouled the boat, as vomit overcame the capacity of the heads and buckets. Often filthy water – and everything else – sloshed around the men's feet.

Diarrhea could also be a hindrance on a U-boat war patrol. On the "good" side, many men lost their appetite for prolonged periods. In all this uncomfortable living, veteran U-boat crewmen learned the following fundamental truth: "The secret of tranquility [aboard a U-boat] was getting used to the fact that, after all, there was no getting used to it."

Situational awareness was difficult for many of the crew. The constant, often painfully loud throbbing of the diesel engines made the men temporarily deaf and numbed their other senses. Most of the sailors had no idea where they were on the ocean; many even did not have a good sense of the time in the closed confines and artificial light inside the boat. Men returning from a war patrol often had "U-boat pallor" due to a lack of exposure to sunlight for many weeks. The low light level and orientation difficulties had other ramifications. U-boat interiors had hundreds of sharp, pointy, hard objects waiting to be run into by crewmen in a hurry during a crash-dive drill, an enemy attack or during the tossing of the boat in rough water while surfaced. Thus, many of Dönitz's crews would sport cuts and bruises – if they were lucky; bashed noses and broken ribs if they were not – until they developed a sixth sense of available "safe" space around them at all times.

Those crewmen designated to stand watch on the bridge could get some fresh air and sunlight. That was the positive aspect of standing watch. On the negative: watch personnel termed the bridge "the bathtub" because high seas rolling from the stern of the boat often filled the bridge platform with water that was one meter deep; often that water was just above freezing. In heavy seas the boat would sometimes roll thirty degrees to each side making a slippery deck even more hazardous. Many U-boats lost crewmen to the deep who were washed overboard; in one case an entire watch crew disappeared from the bridge of a U-boat in a heavy storm despite having safety belts to hold them fast. Even with heavy watch protective clothing, the often frigid North Atlantic water temperatures meant that most men would not survive even a few minutes over the side.

Until mid-1941, all U-boat sailors were true volunteers. As the war progressed and losses mounted, sailors serving in other branches of the Navy transferred to the submarine fleet. The average age of an enlisted U-boat sailor for much of the war was in the mid-twenties (junior men who were not yet petty officers averaged twenty or twenty-one), with the commander – often referred to as the "Old Man" – aged about twenty-seven. The mean age dropped slightly during the war; at the conclusion of the conflict U-boat commanders were often only twenty-four years old.

Service on a U-boat could age a man very quickly. Crewmen pulled watch four hours at a time, and four hours on the bridge of a surfaced boat, on a raging sea, in temperatures hovering at the freezing mark, occasionally in driving snow or sleet storms, could seem like an eternity – especially when frozen spray clawed the men's faces bloody as winds in the Arctic Circle, for example, sometimes exceeded one-hundred miles an hour and giant waves tried to violently rip the men off the slick bridge and carry them to the depths below. Given a different set of wartime circumstances – those that were less lethal – Dönitz's crews easily could have become Dönitz's old men. But the war did not go according to plan and unfortunately, most of Dönitz's crews would die as young men before they reached even middle age.

One of Dönitz's crews wrote a letter home just before his U-boat set sail on what would become her final mission. He wrote:

> "Dear loved ones! Should you learn one day that our boat has not come back, there is no need for you to keep up hope. We are blessed to be able to serve under such a marvelous commanding officer. We are agreed that none of us will fall into the hands of the British. We want to fight and win together; or else, if it cannot be helped, to die together."

This is their story.

Sources, Preface: Michael Gannon, *Black May: The Epic Story of the Allies Defeat of the German U-boats in May 1943*, New York: HarperCollins, 1998, 10; Michael Gannon, *Operation Drumbeat: The Dramatic True Story of Germany's First U-boat Attacks Along the American Coast in World War II*, New York: Harper & Row, 1990, 3, 4, 5, 49, 108, 109, 112, 312, 314, 439; Jak Mallmann Showell, *U-boat Warfare: The Evolution of the Wolf Pack*, Annapolis, Maryland: Naval Institute Press, 2002, 33, 35; Theodore P. Savas, Editor, *Silent Hunters: German U-boat Commanders of World War II*, Campbell, CA: Savas Publishing, 1997, 11; Jak Mallmann Showell, *Wolfpacks at War: The U Boat Experience in World War II*, Hersham, England: Ian Allan Publishing, 2002, 8, 10, 14, 45, 59; T.V. Tuleja, *Twilight of the Sea Gods*, New York: W.W. Norton & Company, 1958, 44, 45; Herbert A. Werner, *Iron Coffins*, New York: Holt, Rinehart and Winston, 1969, 14, 24, 71, 74, 102; Gordon Williamson, *Wolf Pack: The Story of the U-boat in World War II*, Oxford, England: Osprey Publishing, 2006, 145, 148, 149, 163, 166, 167; www.ubootwaffe.net; www.uboatarchive.net.

A confidant young member of Dönitz's crews is standing watch in rough weather. *Photo taken on the U-38 in 1939. All photos of the U-38 in this section are from a collection of pictures taken on the first war patrol of the U-38, August-September 1939, compiled by future German Cross in Gold winner Karl Bade.*

Dönitz's boys tending to the myriad of gauges and valves aboard a U-boat. *Photo taken on the U-38 in 1939.*

A pensive U-boat sailor on watch. *Photo taken on the U-38 in 1939.*

A U-boat's "barber" assists the Chief Engineer to get a "pirate's look." *Photo taken on the U-38 in 1939.*

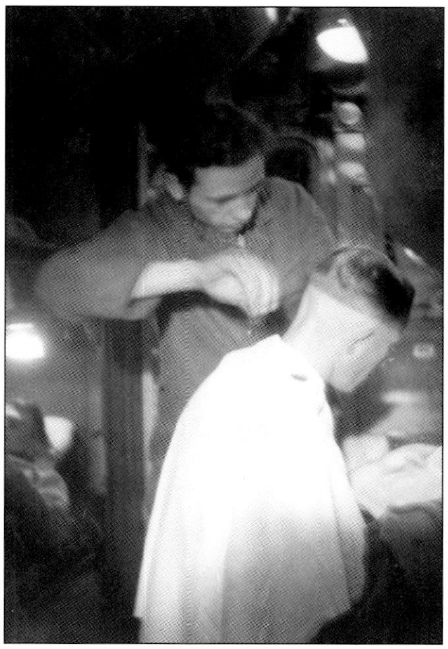

A more typical result obtained in the "barber's chair." *Photo taken on the U-38 in 1939.*

Emptying "the diesel room pail"? *Photo taken on the U-38 in 1939.*

Getting a little sun and a cigarette while on the conning tower. *Photo taken on the U-38 in 1939.*

Like sailors everywhere – mail-call. *Photo taken on the U-38 in 1939, probably September 18, 1939.*

The boat dog. *Photo taken on the U-459; sailor is Obermaat Müller. All the photos of the U-459 in this section came from the estate of a crewmember of the U-459.*

Four of Dönitz's boys on the U-618. *On December 28, 1943 the U-618 would rescue twenty-one men from certain death after the German destroyer Z27 was destroyed in a brutal fight with the British light cruisers HMS Glasgow and HMS Enterprise in the Bay of Biscay. The U-618 was later sunk with all hands on August 14, 1944 west of St. Nazaire by depth charges from the British frigates HMS Duckworth and HMS Essington, as well as depth charges from a British B-24 Liberator.*

It took a sense of humor to serve on a U-boat. *Here on the U-459, Oberbootsmann Johann Völz checks the U-boat's location using a sextant while an "assistant," the real navigator Obersteuermann Helmut Voigt uses his own technique!*

Sharing a sunny, pipe-smoking moment on the bridge. *Photo taken on the U-459; on the left is Korvettenkapitän Georg Wilamowitz-Möllendorf, the commander. On the U-459 his popularity amounted almost to hero-worship; he had a cheerful disposition and was a born humorist. When the U-459 was mortally damaged in the air attack, Wilamowitz-Möllendorf ordered every man into the water. He remained on the bridge and, having saluted his men as they pulled away in rubber dinghies, went below and set a scuttling charge, which destroyed the boat. He was never seen again by survivors, who believed that he made no attempt to save himself. On the right is the 3rd Watch Officer, probably Leutnant zur See Wolfgang von Kirschenbaum.*

In good spirits. *Photo from the U-459; from left to right appear to be: Obermaschinist Friedrich Hirth, 3rd Watch Officer – probably Leutnant zur See Wolfgang von Kirschenbaum, 2nd Watch Officer – an Oberleutnant zur See, Oberbootsmann Johann Völz, Obermaat Wilhelm Wetzel and the 2nd Funkmaat. Wetzel, born February 13, 1917, was killed in action on July 24, 1943 when the U-459 was sunk by two British Wellington aircraft off Cape Ortegal, Spain as was Völz; Hirth, the senior Chief Petty Officer in the engine room, was taken prisoner and survived the war. Kirschenbaum, born February 26, 1921, also was taken prisoner and survived the war.*

***A moment of serious discussion topside at sea.** Photo from the U-459; on the left is Obermaschinist Friedrich Hirth. On the right is Oberbootsmaat Edmund Friedrich. Friedrich, born on November 11, 1919, and killed in action on July 24, 1943.*

***Looking like he just got out of his bunk and wanting his first smoke of the day.** On the U-459, a smiling Obermaat Wilhelm Wetzel sits on the bridge.*

***On the bridge in heavy seas.** Photo taken on the U-459. On the left is the navigator Obersteuermann Helmut Voigt; on the right the 2nd Watch Officer – an Oberleutnant zur See. Helmut Voigt, born on December 18, 1911, was captured on July 24, 1943 and survived the war.*

***Whiling away the hours; two crewmen on the U-333 play chess.** Commanded for much of the war by Knight's Cross winner Kapitänleutnant Peter-Erich Cremer, she was sunk with all hands on July 31, 1944 in the North Atlantic west of the Scilly Islands by depth charges from the British sloop HMS Starling and frigate HMS Loch Killin. Photo is from the estate of a former crewmember of the U-333.*

Family portrait of the U-boat family Schüler. *Walter Schüler appears seated; he initially served on the battleship Schleswig-Holstein. He joined the U-373 in October 1941 and served on her as a flak gunner for twelve war patrols until he was wounded on July 24, 1943, when the U-373 was attacked by Avenger and Wildcat aircraft from the American escort carrier USS Santee; the attack killed two men and wounded seven. During this time he won an Iron Cross 1st Class for his actions during three enemy aircraft attacks in March 1943. After recovering, he served on the U-1025. He survived the war and died in 2002. The photos of the U-373 are from his estate. Photo taken in the spring of 1943; note U-boat War Badge, High Seas Fleet Badge, Iron Cross 2nd Class ribbon and Iron Cross 1st Class. It appears his two brothers were also U-boat sailors, while his father (to the left) was a Chief Petty Officer.*

One of the Schüler family. *Photo taken at La Rochelle shortly after conclusion of a war patrol; Schüler is wearing a tropical uniform.*

Whiling away the hours; crewmen on the U-373 play cards. *The U-373 was sunk on June 8, 1944 in the Bay of Biscay by a British B-24 Liberator aircraft, killing four men; forty-seven survived. Photo is from the estate of a former crewmember of the U-373.*

Celebrating a birthday in style. *Crewman on the U-373 with his birthday cake. Boat cooks often attempted to add a home touch with cakes on birthdays and holidays. Photo is from the estate of a former crewmember of the U-373.*

A good cook eats his own food. *Cook on the U-373 samples his creation in the tiny galley of the boat. Photo is from the estate of a former crewmember of the U-373.*

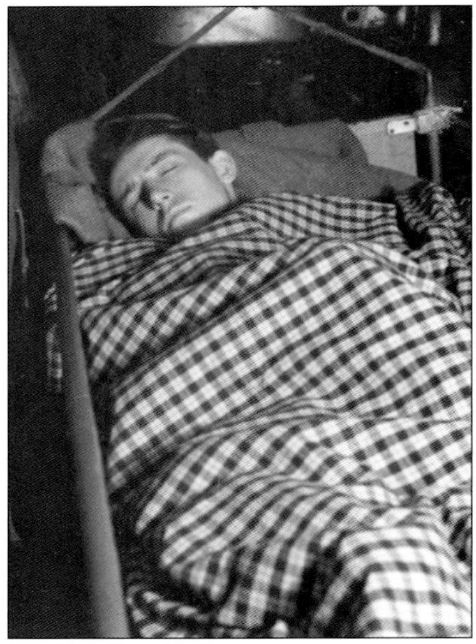

Catching forty winks. *Junior crewmen such as this one on the U-373 had to share bunks; while one man was on duty, the other slept in the bunk. Photo is from the estate of a former crewmember of the U-373.*

Crewmen of the U-65 relax at sea. *Photo was probably taken in late 1940 off the coast of Africa, during which the U-65 sank eight ships (47,794 tons). The British destroyer HMS Douglas sank the U-65 southeast of Iceland on April 28, 1941; all the men on the U-65 perished in the attack.*

Young sailor from the U-94. *The insignia on his lower arm appears to be that of an underwater sound detector. On August 28, 1942 an American aircraft damaged the U-boat with depth charges and the Canadian corvette HMCS Oakville sank her by ramming, killing nineteen; twenty-six men survived.*

Sailors on the U-256 load canned goods on their boat shortly before a war patrol. *Chief Petty Officer (center rear) is the boat's navigator/quartermaster who ensured no storage space was wasted. The photo was probably taken at Brest, France.*

Hot soup on the bridge of the U-333. *Kapitänleutnant with Knight's Cross is Peter-Erich Cremer, probably in late 1942 and in port. Photo is from the estate of a former crewmember of the U-333.*

Officer on the U-172 enjoys a sunny day in a straw hat. *The photo was taken in the summer of 1943 off the coast of Brazil; officer is probably Oberleutnant zur See Hermann Hoffmann. He later commanded the U-172, survived the war and died in 1982. Photo is from the estate of a former crewmember of the U-172.*

Crewman on the U-172 prepares a cake on July 6, 1943 at sea. *Cake was in celebration of the announcement by radio from the B.d.U. that Carl Emmermann, the commander of the U-boat, had been awarded the Oak Leaves to the Knight's Cross.*

Crewmen on the U-172 peruse the boat's "library." *Photo is from the estate of a former crewmember of the U-172.*

Young sailor during recruit training at Stralsund on May 10, 1940. *Youngster is probably Rudi Berghahn who went on to serve on the U-94. The U-94 was sunk in the Caribbean on August 27, 1942 but Berghahn had left the boat by that time.*

INTRODUCTION

It has been seventy years since the beginning of what would become the most significant event in the Twentieth Century, World War II in Europe. Despite thousands of excellent books and a few very good motion pictures – *The Boat* (*Das Boot*) comes to mind – it is hard to imagine what it was really like during perhaps the most pivotal campaign in that war, the Battle of the Atlantic. No less an authority than British Prime Minister Sir Winston Churchill declared as much when he wrote, "The only thing that ever really frightened me during the war was the U-boat peril." President Franklin Roosevelt was more colorful in his description of the U-boat scourge; in one "fireside chat" he called them the "rattlesnakes of the Atlantic." While other experts might offer differing views as to the nature of the undersea threat and the primacy of this theater of the war – certainly the struggle between Germany and the Soviet Union was titanic and crucial in many respects – it is a safe assumption that almost all scholars, professionally educated and other, would assert that the convoy versus U-boat Battle of the Atlantic certainly was a key contributor to the overall Allied victory in the war in Europe.

Numbers tell part of the story. The German Navy began the war on September 1, 1939 with just fifty-seven U-boats, far short of the 300 that Karl Dönitz, the commander of the U-boat force, felt was the minimum required to win the struggle. From the beginning of the war through its end on May 8, 1945 a further 1,113 U-boats were built and commissioned. Of this total of 1,170 craft, 863 became operational. Of this number of operational craft, 753 were destroyed – a rate of destruction of over 87%.

Those operational U-boats sank 148 Allied warships: three aircraft carriers, three escort aircraft carriers, two battleships, five light cruisers, thirty-four destroyers and eighteen destroyer escorts were among them. But it was the merchantmen – Dönitz's identified center of gravity of Great Britain's wartime economic system – that the U-boat wolves made their most serious predations. No less than 2,759 merchant ships – oil tankers, freighters, coal carriers, transports – went to the bottom due to U-boat torpedoes, gunfire or mines. This amounted to 14,119,413 tons of shipping.

Neither U-boat losses nor Allied sinkings occurred as a steady trend over the almost six-year conflict. Eminent German Navy scholar Jürgen Rohwer, examining key post-war summaries by former U-boat commanders and staff, determined that the undersea conflict transpired in eight phases, although this book proposes that an alternative method of tracking the U-boat war is that of nine sequential campaigns, slightly modifying Rohwer's description but not supplanting his excellent conclusions and logic. These subordinate campaigns were not envisioned as such at the start of the war by Dönitz; he viewed the struggle as a *la guerre de course*, a single, constant, cumulative destruction of the Allied merchant fleet, wherever they could be found, in such numbers that they could not be replaced, which would therefore lead to a negotiated surrender before the economic situation in Great Britain became untenable. Dönitz believed that England was dependent on seaborne supply for food and the import of raw materials, and cutting these sea lanes could never be accomplished by a surface fleet; only the U-boat could penetrate into the main areas of English sea commerce in spite of England's supremacy on the surface.

To place the following chapters of the book in strategic context, those nine campaigns, derived from a look back at what actually happened, are summarized as follows:

Campaign 1 (September 1939 to March 1940): A small number of operational U-boats (the average number of U-boats at sea for the month of December 1939, for example, was just eight), patrolling independently (not in wolf packs [more correctly pack tactics, *Rudeltaktik*]) in the North Sea, west of the British Isles and in the Bay of Biscay, sank a modest number (twenty-five in September alone) of Allied merchant ships traveling alone as the Allied convoy system was not well-organized. A single U-boat achieved perhaps the most significant U-boat victory of the entire war with the sinking of the *HMS Royal Oak* at Scapa Flow, but insufficient numbers of U-boats and the beginning of a period of torpedo failures prevented large-scale successes, while the Germans lost nineteen frontline U-boats.

Campaign 2 (April 1940 to June 1940): An unplanned (from Dönitz's point of view) diversion of the U-boat campaign away from Allied merchant shipping, when a large proportion of the U-boat fleet became engaged in tactical operations against Allied warships during the German invasion of Denmark, Norway, the Low Countries and France. Torpedo failures (in a nutshell, many ran too deep due to internal torpedo pressure balance chambers malfunctioning) prevented success against numerous British warships when all other circumstances favored their destruction. The U-boat arm lost six frontline boats during this period, averaging fourteen operational boats at sea for the month of April, eight for the month of May and eighteen for the month of June.

Campaign 3 (July 1940 to March 1941): With the German conquest of Norway and western France, the U-boat fleet gained new bases much closer to their main anti-merchant-shipping area of the Western Approaches to the British Isles. German successes began to rise as U-boats began operating in more efficient groups (wolf packs) against shipping that although was operating more in the convoy system, had too few escorts (with limited technical means – ASDIC at this point [sonar] could only acquire U-boats at 1,300 yards). This was because of the potential threat of a German seaborne invasion of Great Britain ("Operation Sea Lion") and the perceived necessity of the British Admiralty to keep a large number of Royal Navy warships in home waters to repel such an operation. German U-boat successes were many, highlighted by the battle for convoy HX-72 in September 1940, when U-boats sank eleven of the forty-one ships and the battle for convoy SC-7. This convoy, sailing from Sydney, Nova Scotia to Liverpool, saw twenty of thirty-five ships go to the bottom with no U-boats lost. U-boat successes spread from not only the eastern North Atlantic, but also to Allied ships off the western coast of Africa. U-boat crews referred to this period of the war as the "Happy Time," although thirteen frontline U-boats never returned to base. This phase ended on a down note as several highly-experienced and highly-successful U-boat commanders were killed in action or captured in March 1941; additionally, British air cover and an increase in surface escorts began to force the U-boats further west away from the area of the North Channel and Rockall Bank. The average number of U-boats at sea remained small; the high monthly average was just thirteen for this period. Ominously, in October 1940 there occurred the first sighting of a surfaced U-boat at night by radar mounted in a British aircraft.

Campaign 4 (April 1941 to December 1941): As the threat of German invasion of Great Britain subsided, the Royal Navy and Royal Air Force continued to deploy more assets to convoy protection forcing the U-boats to operate further west in the Atlantic to avoid enemy shore-based aircraft patrols. But this action, in turn, forced the British to escort convoys the entire breadth of the Atlantic from Newfoundland to Great Britain, a drain on Allied assets that was partly eased by escort assets from the United States. U-boat confirmed kills of merchantmen extended west to include a large number south of Greenland, although U-boat successes dropped off at the end of this period. Michael Gannon, another respected U-boat historian, credits this downturn to: a loss of several distinguished U-boat commanders, improved Allied signals intelligence and improvements in the convoy system that increased convoy speeds. Against Dönitz's wishes, the U-boat arm was ordered to send submarines into the Mediterranean Sea to stiffen the defenses (and Germany's ally Italy) there; twenty-one valuable boats initially left the North Atlantic, but scored immediately, sending the battleship *HMS Barham* to the bottom off the African coast. The campaign climaxed with the battle of convoy HG-76, thirty-two merchant ships sailing from Gibraltar to England under heavy anti-submarine escort that sank four U-boats and defeated a wolf pack for the first time, even though the pack sank an escort aircraft carrier, *HMS Audacity*. For Dönitz it was a significant psychological defeat and – although he would not publically state so – put his wolf pack theory into question. The *Kriegsmarine* lost twenty-eight frontline U-boats during these nine months, ten in December alone, but average monthly U-boats at sea strength rose to a high of thirty-eight in November. The British capture of the Enigma material and other code materials on the *U-110* on May 9, 1941 would prove to be a devastating blow to U-boat signal security for the duration of the war. In another key area, Dönitz concluded that air-sea coordination as he envisioned would never materialize; the lack of air reconnaissance would plague the U-boat fleet for the entire war.

Campaign 5 (January 1942 to June 1942): With the entrance of the United States into the war, Dönitz launched "Operation Drumbeat" to attack merchant shipping off the coast of Canada and the eastern seaboard of the United States. The plan was for attacking U-boats to strike first on the same day to gain a psychological advantage. Initial U-boat successes were quite high, so much so that U-boat crews referred to the period as the second "Happy Time." For five months there was virtually no organized resistance on the eastern seaboard to the U-boat threat. But the Americans learned from this error and instituted their own convoy system and the focus of effort of the U-boat fleet subsequently returned to the North Atlantic and a verdant new area of operation, the Caribbean Sea. In February 1942 there were twenty-four U-boats in Norway and twenty-one in the Mediterranean. Dönitz lost twenty-one frontline U-boats during this period.

Campaign 6 (July 1942 to May 1943): The high-water mark of U-boat operations in the war, the *Kriegsmarine* now had more than 300 boats in service. Far-ranging U-boats, utilizing "Milk Cow" resupply operations from special supply U-boats, struck vital oil transports coming out of the Gulf of Mexico and Maracaibo, Venezuela. In the North Atlantic U-boat groups would pick up convoys when they were beyond the range of land-based air cover, attack them in these air gaps and halt the attacks when the remnants of the convoys reached the next safe area; the plan then called for the same U-boats to conduct the same tactic against ships coming from the other direction across the Atlantic – in theory it was deadly. By November 1942, the U-boats were sinking almost 700,000 tons of Allied shipping per month. But Hitler's decision that month to concentrate U-boats against the Allied invasion of North Africa ("Operation Torch") caused another disruption to Dönitz's plan of winning in the North Atlantic. Nevertheless, U-boat successes in March 1943 seemed to spell the beginning of the end of the Allied existing convoy system, but Allied intelligence breakthroughs and increased convoy escort aircraft capability set the stage for a reversal of fortunes, which occurred in May. The campaign began with the largest convoy disaster of the war – the destruction of convoy PQ-17 enroute to northern Russia from Iceland. U-boats and *Luftwaffe* bombers sank twenty-four of thirty-five ships. The campaign climaxed with the battle for convoy ONS-5, a slow forty-two ship group heading from Great Britain to North America; on May 5 the convoy lost twelve ships but anti-submarine escorts sank six U-boats and severely damaged seven others from *Wolf Pack Fink* as ULTRA intelligence played a decisive role in portraying likely concentrations of U-boats. Depth charges also became more efficient.

Additionally, the Allies had perfected high frequency radio detection that could locate a transmitting U-boat to about twenty-five miles – not adequate to attack (at least initially), but sufficient for merchant ships to avoid. Historian Jürgen Rohwer stated that the outcome of convoy battles between June 1942 and May 1943 always depended on the efficient use of radio direction finding. Shore-based Allied attack aircraft also began to make their mark: B-24 Liberators given to British Coastal Command became the biggest aerial killer of U-boats during the war (followed by British Sunderlands and Vickers Wellingtons). Metox, a radar-detection piece of equipment on a U-boat, negated some of the Allied superiority as it could warn the crew that a radar set was operating not too far away. In March the Royal Navy established the first five Support Groups; with four to six anti-submarine vessels, once they located a U-boat their mission was to destroy it no matter where that took them in relation to any convoy. It was truly a bleak period; 156 frontline U-boats never returned to base – forty sank in May 1943 alone. Many U-boat men referred to the month as "Stalingrad at Sea." In short, the U-boats in operation were simply too old-fashioned to compete with the variety of newly-developed submarine countermeasures which in total had reached a critical mass. Dönitz begged Hitler for an increased allocation of 30,000 tons of steel for U-boat construction yards to step up construction to reach twenty-seven boats per month.

Campaign 7 (June 1943 to August 1943): Unaware of the exact causes for this reversal (one was improved ASDIC, which could now determine U-boat depth as well as range), but understanding that the fundamental dynamics had changed for the worse in the North Atlantic, Dönitz took a highly unusual step for a commander in wartime: he asked his subordinates if the U-boat war should continue in the North Atlantic and elsewhere. The U-boat chief started with his flotilla commanders and put the questions to them. He then asked that they put the issue to their individual U-boat commanders. The commanders in turn were to query their crews to the last seaman by secret ballot so that no one would be influenced by strong-willed personalities. The feedback was overwhelming; despite the odds, the crews wanted to continue the fight against the enemy even though they knew it might mean mounting casualties to the already alarming loss-rates.

With that mandate in hand, Dönitz first directed the U-boats to operate in distant areas to include the South Atlantic and the Indian Ocean – areas where anti-submarine forces (especially enemy air reconnaissance) were perceived to be weaker, while targets were still lucrative. But German losses continued with seventy-eight frontline U-boats going to the bottom. In hindsight the U-boats could not alter their tactics because they had no means to do so; the boats were stuck with the sole option of moving into a good firing position, firing one or more torpedoes and then trying to escape – they had no means at this point to patrol submerged and attack submerged day or night and were truly a hunted force. In Germany the design of the Walter Type XXI U-boat – a true submarine – was ready to begin production.

Campaign 8 (September 1943 to May 1944): During this campaign, the Germans introduced new equipment, including acoustic torpedoes (designed to home in on the cavitation noise of an escort warship's propeller running at ten to eighteen knots), radar warning sets and increased anti-aircraft armaments in an attempt to wrest the initiative from the Allies. The bulk of the fighting took place in the North Atlantic and along the Gibraltar-England shipping routes but these operations failed to give the German Navy the upper hand, while the U-boat arm lost a further 153 frontline boats.

Campaign 9 (June 1944 to May 1945): This could probably be called "The Snorkel Campaign" after the innovation that allowed U-boats to operate underwater using their diesel engines with a device that pulled in required air from above the water. There simply were not enough of these devices, nor the "miracle" Type XXI and XXIII U-boats. During the campaign, in August, the Germans moved most of the U-boats from French bases to Norway to avoid their capture as Allied ground forces closed in on these French ports; their ensuing reduced range of operations had come almost full circle from the heady days in 1940. Allied planes and ships destroyed 236 frontline U-boats in this time period.

It is to more significant numbers, though, which we must return before delving further into this story. For fifty years after the war, conventional wisdom has postulated that some 40,000 German sailors went on operations in the U-boat fleet, of which 30,000 perished in the fight, perhaps the highest loss rate – at 75% – of any major combat force in military history. The Allied merchant marine fleets also suffered grievous losses; the British Merchant Navy, for example, lost 32,952 men of a force of 185,000 during the war – most to U-boat attacks. Concerning just the young men who became U-boat commanders 1,418 passed all required training and qualified to assume command; of these 538 died in wartime operations and a further thirty-eight perished in training accidents.

In recent years the Internet site www.ubootwaffe.net, *Kriegsmarine* and U-boat history, has undertaken a superb massive effort to identify as many of those U-boat crewmen as possible. Historians Hubertus Weggelaar, Horst Schmeisser and Peter Schmid have, at last count, identified 58,312 U-boat-related individuals by name – the bulk of which actually served on the boats. The trio is still in progress collecting this valuable, unique information. Whatever the final number who served and the percentage of their loss, from the frozen Arctic Circle to the deadly Straits of Gibraltar and from the calm waters of the Caribbean Sea to the monsoon-lashed Indian Ocean, as a group Dönitz's crews stared death in the face and never flinched.

Note: A better description of a wolf pack is to compare it to the tines on a rake – it was more a linear formation, not a closely-packed group. The group of U-boats would spread out more or less in a line, some ten miles apart, perpendicular to the direction of the convoy's travel. When one of the boats spotted the anticipated convoy (the whole tactic depended on good intelligence and continuous communication), it would report its position, course and speed to the B.d.U. by radio, and the individual "tines" would then move laterally to the target's location. Additionally, the B.d.U. referred to the massing of boats as "groups" rather than wolf packs.

Sources, Introduction: G.H. Bennett, and R. Bennett, *Hitler's Admirals*, Annapolis, Maryland: Naval Institute Press, 2004, 59, 120; Chris Bishop, *Kriegsmarine U-boats 1939-45*, London: Amber Books, 2006, 19, 20, 21, 42, 75, 76, 110, 111, 184, 185, 186; Clay Blair, *Hitler's U-boat War: The Hunted, 1942-1945*, New York: Modern Library, 2000, ix; Philip A. Crowl, "Alfred Thayer Mahan: The Naval Historian," in *Makers of Modern Strategy from Machiavelli to the Nuclear Age*, edited by Peter Paret, Princeton, NJ: Princeton University Press, 1986, 444-477; Karl Dönitz, *Memoirs: Ten Years and Twenty Days*, translated by R.H. Stevens, Annapolis, Maryland: Da Capo Press, 1997, 486, 489, 490, 492, 493, 494; Michael Gannon, *Black May: The Epic Story of the Allies Defeat of the German U-boats in May 1943*, New York: HarperCollins, 1998, xxvii, 3, 4, 10, 57, 59, 62, 63, 64, 65, 69, 70, 73; Michael Gannon, *Operation Drumbeat: The Dramatic True Story of Germany's First U-boat Attacks Along the American Coast in World War II*, New York: Harper & Row, 1990, 87; Peter C. Hansen, *Execution for Duty: The Life, Trial & Murder of a U-boat Captain*, Barnsley, England: Pen & Sword Maritime, 2003, 67, 138; Günter Hessler, *The U-boat War in the Atlantic, 1939-1945, Volume 1-3*, London: Her Majesty's Stationery Office, 1989, Volume 1 – Diagram 7; Axel Niestlé, *German U-boat Losses during World War II*, Annapolis, Maryland: Naval Institute Press, 1998, 200, 201; David Westwood, *The U-boat War: The German Submarine Service and the Battle of the Atlantic, 1935-1945*, Philadelphia, PA: Casemate, 2005, 92, 111, 119, 126, 144, 146, 151, 157, 161, 179, 183, 192, 196, 259; www.ubootwaffe.net; www.uboatarchive.net; Interview with *Kapitän zur See* (Retired) Peter Monte, former German Navy (Bundesmarine) Attaché to Great Britain and Ireland at Cuxhaven, Germany on October 21, 2008.

A U-boot in rough seas under a foreboding sky. *Propaganda postcard early in the war.*

U-boat commander and lookouts stand watch. *Propaganda postcard early in the war.*

In the combat zone of the Atlantic. *Heinrich Hoffmann propaganda postcard early in the war.*

U-boat in the Atlantic. *Heinrich Hoffmann propaganda postcard early in the war.*

U-boat torpedo-man. *W. Willrich propaganda postcard early in the war.*

CHAPTER ONE

"THE FATHER OF THE U-BOATS" KARL DÖNITZ

Attack! Advance! Sink! Those words were the motto of the World War II German U-boat force and they quite adequately summarize the essence of the father of these U-boats, Karl Dönitz.

Karl Dönitz was a simple man, but also a man of great intellect and vision. Shaped by his multi-dimensional combat experience in World War I, in the inter-war years he was one of the visionary officers on a par with fellow Germans Heinz Guderian, Erich von Manstein and Kurt Student, as well as foreign military thinkers such as Charles De Gaulle, George Marshall, Henry "Hap" Arnold, Chester Nimitz, Mikhail Tukhachevsky, Liddell Hart and Isoroku Yamamoto. However, Dönitz was not just a brilliant theoretical thinker; he was an empathetic leader as well. Dönitz loved his U-boat boys and for the most part they admired him, referring to their admiral as "The Lion" and "Onkel Karl" (Uncle Karl). Sometimes referring to themselves as "Freikorps Dönitz," Dönitz's crews thought of themselves as a "navy within the Navy."

Karl Dönitz was born in Grünau near Berlin on September 16, 1891, the younger of two sons of an engineer with the prestigious Zeiss optical firm. His mother died when Karl was only four years old; his father moved the two boys to Jena, the Zeiss headquarters. Dönitz began his Imperial Navy (Kaiserliche Marine) career as a Sea Cadet in 1910 on the *SMS Hertha* spending a year on the ship before beginning officer training as a *Fähnrich zur See* with the Class of 1911. A year later he trained on the *SMS Württemberg* as a torpedo officer and later received artillery training before joining the complement of the light cruiser *SMS Breslau* as the ship's adjutant and a watch officer. The young Dönitz was admired by his superiors as reflected in this description from an officer efficiency report in 1913:

> "Charming, dashing, plucky ... especially good professional ability ... strength of judgment ... very good military appearance, socially very deft ... popular comrade, tactful messmate ... magnificent dash and great circumspection ... tough and brisk officer ... absolutely reliable ... always in good spirits ... taut, stern ... quick power of perception and blameless character ... iron willpower, goal-oriented certainty and unwearying toughness."

The beginning of World War I found Dönitz and the *SMS Breslau* and the battle cruiser *SMS Goeben* in the Mediterranean Sea. After bombarding shore targets in French Algeria, the pair of ships eluded a British task force of three battlecruisers, four armored cruisers, four light cruisers and sixteen destroyers – bent on their destruction. After a harrowing 1,200-mile, week-long journey, the two German ships reached neutral Constantinople, Turkey and were transferred to the Turkish Navy, influencing Turkey's subsequent decision to join the Central Powers as Germany's ally. *Leutnant zur See* Karl Dönitz received the Iron Cross 2nd Class three months later and wrote a book about his adventures, *The Voyages of the Breslau in the Black Sea*. He also found time to court and marry Ingeborg Weber, a fully-trained nurse and daughter of a German army general stationed in Turkey; the couple would later have a daughter and two sons.

With this valuable surface experience under his belt, Dönitz was selected the following year to be an aerial observer, serving in the Dardanelles, and subsequently became the commander of a seaplane base, experiences which undoubtedly broadened his career and outlook. In 1916 good fate struck a third time and *Oberleutnant zur See* Dönitz commenced U-boat training. In his initial undersea assignment, he spent eleven months in 1917 as a watch officer on the *U-39*, which was commanded by Germany's second-leading skipper Walter Forstmann. Dönitz on the *U-39* would make four war patrols and sink thirty-two ships. Dönitz ended the war with successive commands of the *UC-25* and the *UB-68*, torpedoing five enemy ships and winning the Knight's Cross of the House of Hohenzollern. Dönitz would be forced to scuttle his boat under heavy attack in 1918 and spend nine months as a British prisoner of war after the armistice, certainly not adding to his feeling toward the English. Later he would remark:

> "On one point I am quite certain – if at some time or other war comes, we shall find Britain on the side of the enemy."

After the war, Dönitz remained in the Navy (known as the *Reichsmarine*), but as the Versailles Treaty forbade Germany from possessing U-boats, Dönitz spent many assignments with torpedo boats as well as some key positions with the torpedo inspectorate and the training department. The experiences gained in both would serve him well in future years. However, it was not a foregone conclusion or master plan that Dönitz would later advance to become the chief of the undersea fleet. In 1935 Germany began to create a new small submarine flotilla, not previously allowed under the Treaty of

Versailles. But real-life problems conspired against the idea. The majority of men who had served in submarines in World War I were now too old, out of touch with developments or dead. Younger, vibrant Navy officers had no real experience to lead a flotilla and have the crews respect them. To be able to think in three dimensions, necessary for controlling future U-boat operations was a limiting factor; there were simply too few men with that characteristic, and many in the Naval High Command considered that the position would likely end in failure – for both the U-boat organization and the career of whomever was selected to lead it. Karl Dönitz, recently returned from a flag-showing tour around the world as the captain of the light cruiser *Emden*, received the call – assured that the assignment would be a temporary one and that he would later receive command of a more-prestigious surface ship. Dönitz accepted, and before events could happen to realize the promise made to him, the march toward war forced a change in plans. Dönitz also had limited control of many U-boat matters at the start of his tenure. His mission was to make the small U-boat flotilla into an effective combat force. The training flotilla did not come under his domain, nor did technical U-boat matters, which fell under the U-boat Office of the Supreme Naval command.

But the young officer did meet some interesting people during the period. Navy Admiral Wilhelm Canaris, who would later become the director of the Abwehr, the counter-intelligence department of the High Command of the Armed Forces, was Karl Dönitz's superior officer in the early 1930s. Canaris had this to say about the future U-boat chief in two official annual officer fitness reports:

> (November 1, 1931) "[He is] a very competent staff officer with thorough knowledge of all spheres. [He is] goal-conscious and systematic ... very deft in oral and written expression. Very intellectually animated and interested in all professional questions. Very ambitious and consequently asserts himself to obtain prestige, finding it difficult to subordinate himself and confine himself to his own work-sphere ... His strong temperament and inner verve frequently affected him with restlessness and, for his age, imbalance. Must therefore be brought to take things more calmly and not to set exaggerated demands, above all on himself ... Despite these limitations, I consider him an excellent officer whose character is not yet fully formed and who is in need of strong and benevolent leadership."
>
> (November 1, 1932) "Ambition and the endeavor to distinguish himself remain outstanding characteristics. Nevertheless they have no more exceeded the permissible measure. In his whole manner he has become essentially calmer and balanced. This is due in great part to an improvement in his health. A strong personality of great knowledge and ability, who will always give outstanding performances. This depends upon advancing this valuable officer as much as possible, although an eye must be kept on him to ensure he takes things calmly and does not place too high demands on himself and others."

Dönitz was not as praiseworthy of Canaris in return. After the war he said of the German spy master:

> "He was a man quite different from us. We used to say he had seven souls in his breast."

But Dönitz was also different from other officers in many respects as well. First, he was a voracious reader and pored over German World War I U-boat records, as well as every official and unofficial naval history of the war. He concluded that had the Kaiser authorized unrestricted U-boat warfare much earlier and had the Imperial Navy built more submarines instead of capital surface ships, Germany could have conducted a war-winning maritime blockade of Great Britain.

As he was building the U-boat arm in the mid-1930s at Kiel-Wik as a relatively junior officer, Dönitz made the intellectual leap from his conclusions from the past war to a forecast of the next, and viewed the impending struggle as a *la guerre de course*, a single, constant, cumulative destruction of the enemy merchant fleet in such numbers that they could not be replaced, which would therefore lead to a negotiated surrender before the economic situation in Great Britain – which Dönitz viewed as Germany's most likely opponent – forced Britannia to her knees. Additionally, he felt that a continuous high rate of losses might well lead to merchant seamen refusing to sail for fear of their own lives. In 1935 Dönitz stated:

> "The U-boat is wholly and essentially an attack weapon. Its great action radius makes it suitable for operations in distant enemy sea areas. In consequence of its low submerged and surface speed, its tactical mobility will therefore in essence be only stationary."

This view certainly went against much traditional naval thought, including Alfred Thayer Mahan, who believed that only by concentrating the fleet – and destroying the enemy's fleet – could a nation attempt to control the sea. Several German admirals concurred with these traditional thoughts and pushed for battleship development but, while the *Bismarck* and *Tirpitz* were certainly powerhouse designs, they were never decisive and a use of resources that Dönitz could have sorely used to make more underwater craft. (One of Dönitz's memos to the Naval Staff received the marginal note: "We do not want to become a navy of U-boats.") We do not know the views Dönitz had of Mahan; he made no mention in his memoirs, *Memoirs: Ten Years and Twenty Days*, of the American naval thinker.

Other German Navy strategists concurred with Dönitz's appreciation for submarine warfare, but desired to spread the U-boat fleet to distant theaters so as to dilute Allied anti-submarine assets. Dönitz did not concur with this latter caveat; he always believed that the North Atlantic was the decisive point in the U-boat war precisely because the bulk of Allied shipping could be found there, and if he could maintain at least relative superiority there, a concept that Nineteenth Century Prussian military thinker Carl von Clausewitz in his *On War* deemed required "the courage to retain the major part of one's forces united," and which, therefore, could require a "sacrifice [of] nonessentials for the sake of essentials," Germany could win the war. We also do not know if Dönitz studied Clausewitz; again there is no mention of the thinker in Dönitz's book, but we do know that Dönitz often fought to keep his U-boats concentrated in the North Atlantic.

Dönitz summed up his strategic feelings in April 1942, when he wrote:

> "The enemy's shipping constitutes one single, great entity. It is therefore immaterial where a ship is sunk. Once it has been destroyed, it has to be replaced by a new ship; and that's that. In the long run the result of the war will depend on the result of the race between sinkings and new construction. But the hub of both shipbuilding and the production of armaments lie in the United States. If, therefore, I go for the hub, and particularly the oil supplies, I am getting to the root of the evil."

This was a subtle change to Dönitz's thinking. At the beginning of the war he was focused on sinking ships enroute with goods to Great Britain; this was why he balked at stationing U-boats anywhere where they could not directly contribute to this goal. His original objective was to deny Great Britain the cargo on the ships sailing to her shores. He repeatedly told his subordinates that the U-boats' objective was to sink ships carrying goods, equipment and men <u>to</u> the British Isles. But now, after the United States entered the war on Great Britain's side, Dönitz concentrated on the ships themselves, and in his mind a ship was a ship. In hindsight this shift in strategy may have been fatal as it allowed his superior to micromanage Dönitz's efforts. It also went against the twin punches Dönitz had aimed at Great Britain; Dönitz's original plan of sinking ships in convoy proceeding to Great Britain caused not only the loss of the ship but the loss of the ship's contents.

Adolf Hitler weighed in with his own strategic thoughts during the war, based more on intuition then on any strategic readings he made or understood. An acknowledged amateur concerning sea strategy, he nevertheless directed that the U-boats be the first line of defense against potential Allied invasions against Norway and Western Europe – first lines that would sink Allied warships. Dönitz was not a backer of these schemes or of U-boats primarily engaging warships instead of merchant vessels, although the U-boat arm did achieve some spectacular successes in this arena.

It was a tall order; even in the North Atlantic the U-boats often fought at a great numerical disadvantage. In an attempt to overcome these numbers, Dönitz sought to imbue his crews with enthusiasm and a complete faith in the U-boat arm. Additionally he desired to instill in each man, regardless of rank, a spirit of selfless readiness to serve in a submarine. On February 5, 1943, he summed up his feelings on selfless service in the following remark:

> "Our honor lies in our duty-fulfillment and readiness for action. No one of us has the right to private life. The question for us is winning the war. We have to pursue this goal with fanatical devotion and the most ruthless determination to win."

Realistic training was Dönitz's goal; he demanded that U-boat crews in peacetime be confronted with every situation they would undoubtedly be confronted with in war. By thorough training, when these situations did later arise, his crews would be able to cope with them. As Dönitz once remarked:

> "For the lessons which one fails to learn in peace one pays a high price in war."

U-boat crews had to be equally at home on the surface and beneath the waves, for long periods of time, in all conditions of weather and seas. Crews had to be completely acclimatized to life aboard the boat, total familiarity with the sea under all conditions, and absolute precision in navigation – particularly astronomical navigation.

In the mid-1930s each U-boat crew carried out sixty-six practice surface attacks and an equal number of submerged attacks – with Dönitz coaching from inside the boat or from his command ship *Saar* – before firing their first practice torpedo. Other aspects of training fell under the category of "war readiness." These training blocks included:

- Conduct of the boat when in enemy waters;
- When to submerge in the face of a sighted enemy aircraft (referred to by U-boat men as "bees") or surface vessel;
- Attacking at periscope depth or with minimum use of the periscope;
- Maintaining contact and reaching a position ahead of the target;
- Action in the face of enemy defensive action;
- How to withdraw submerged at speed or slip away silently;
- Diving techniques;
- Defensive surface and anti-aircraft gunfire prior to emergency diving.

This was not a case of Dönitz ordering tough training from the comfort of his headquarters. At the beginning of his command he went to sea almost daily with one boat or another, putting crews in different stressful situations, measuring their performance and providing feedback to them on how they could improve. He shared the same food, work, hazards and hardships as the crew – this camaraderie would spread throughout the U-boat Arm for the duration of the war as bonds between officers and enlisted men became very strong. His concern was not confined to training; Dönitz believed in charismatic leadership and could be found on the docks greeting his returning U-boat crews and personally bestowing decorations on commanders and junior seamen alike. Whenever possible, he personally interviewed returning U-boat commanders to get a personal feel of their experiences. Dönitz even established a special U-boat train with the German railway system (known as the "B.d.U. Zug") on which his crews in France could expeditiously ride back to Germany for leave to see their loved ones.

Dönitz believed that in peacetime the ideal training period for U-boat crews was three years. The first year would consist of individual training, from introduction into the Navy to preliminary U-boat-specific training. The second year would be collective training, where the crews would train and live together. Once that was mastered, the U-boat crew and their boat would deploy to a U-boat station and train in some of the potential areas in which they would later fight.

The U-boat leader felt that a U-boat commander – in both torpedo attacks from the surface or from underwater – should close to within six-hundred meters before firing, a very short range, and contrary to the opinions at the U-boat school in the mid-1930s, where the commandant favored long-range submerged attacks. Dönitz countered that such proximity served two purposes: first, a shot at that range was bound to hit; any minor error in firing deflection would not have any effect until at much greater range. Second, even if the target ship saw the torpedo wake or was made aware of the U-boat's presence in some other manner, at that short range it would already be too late to take successful evasive action.

Dönitz championed night surface attacks for two major reasons: traveling on the surface the U-boat could keep up with most targets and move faster than some targets, both of which made firing positions easier to obtain. Second, the only part of a U-boat that was actually above the surface was the small conning tower, which was extremely difficult to see with the human eye at night. He believed the U-boat was a first-class torpedo-carrier, but a very poor gun platform due to its low freeboard and restricted field of vision. The very term U-boat, or submarine, in the 1930s and for most of World War II was a misnomer, however. U-boats could go underwater, but spent the most of their time on the surface. For the most part a U-boat cruised on the surface and fought on the surface – until 1944 a more accurate term for most U-boats was "submersible" or "diving" boat.

Dönitz's experiences on a U-boat in World War I, combined with an active mind, helped formulate his views on U-boat tactics. He considered it essential that a system of tactical cooperation and tactical leadership be established that would allow a large number of U-boats be concentrated to attack any given objective simultaneously; in his mind, a minimum of five U-boats would achieve critical mass against a convoy. This concept applied to individual high-value objectives, such as a particular enemy warship, as well as formations of warships or convoys or merchant ships – massed targets should be attacked by massed U-boats. The next conflict would feature massed targets, Dönitz believed, as the convoy system that had saved Great Britain in World War I would undoubtedly be used again if war occurred. Organizing the undersea fleet to attain this critical mass was a difficult proposition; Dönitz understood that at any given time one-third of his charges would be on combat operations, a second third would be in port refitting and another third would be enroute to or from their assigned operational areas.

Further compounding this difficulty, once in the fight due to its low height, a U-boat had a very restricted radius of vision. This, combined with its relatively slow speed – even surface speed – meant that U-boats were not suitable platforms for reconnaissance operations. This lack of speed also meant that U-boats were unsuitable for joint action with surface forces, although that concept would be attempted – unsuccessfully – in 1940 in the German invasion of Norway. U-boats were, in Dönitz's opinion, very suitable for mine-laying operations, since he could penetrate unseen into enemy coastal waters – where the sea traffic was heaviest – without arousing suspicion, and then could slip away unseen.

Dönitz's mid-war experiences may have had a negative impact on his thinking as well. Emerging technologies in the 1930s and early 1940s threatened to change the paradigm of submarine warfare. It appears that Dönitz may not have examined in detail German radar systems and formulated his opinion on radar's capabilities from the observations of others. In other technologies, however, he clearly understood their potential. Because the U-boat was such a poor reconnaissance asset, Dönitz supported the creation of a sea aviation component, which could ultimately give the U-boats "eyes in the sky" to find their targets. A sea-air arm was developed and was then incorporated into the *Luftwaffe,* but cooperation between the air force and Navy was slow to develop. Dönitz would later state that had the U-boat force had its own naval air arm in 1941, the outcome of the U-boat war could have been quite different. Dönitz blamed Hermann Göring, the head of the *Luftwaffe*, for these problems. For the most part – unlike Göring – Dönitz was quite correct and diplomatic in raising his concerns, but in 1944 he exploded in an argument with the chief airman:

> "I refuse to tolerate these criticisms of the Navy, Herr Reichsmarschall. You would be better advised to look to your own *Luftwaffe*, where there is ample scope for your activities!"

Dönitz believed that unlike surface warships, the fighting power of a U-boat did not increase in proportion to an increase in its size. In fact, larger submarines often experienced added problems once a certain size was exceeded. Submerging became lengthier (35 seconds for a Type IXB), and thus more vulnerable to attack. Controlling the boat at periscope level was riskier as a larger boat had a tendency to sometimes break the surface. Larger craft were less easy to maneuver and had larger turning circles. Finally, larger U-boats had larger silhouettes and were thus easier for the enemy to see.

Larger U-boats did have some advantages. Larger craft could carry more torpedoes, food and fuel and therefore had increased ranges of action to take the fight to the enemy into more areas. Bigger boats offered more space for the crew and thus improved living conditions.

In concluding his thoughts on the size of the craft, Dönitz believed that the ideal size of a U-boat was five-hundred tons displacement – most closely approximated by the Type VII U-boat. With four bow torpedo tubes and one stern, the craft could carry twelve to fourteen torpedoes. It had a very fast diving time – 28 seconds (by 30 seconds the boat would have 42 feet of water above its hull) – and was stable underwater.

On the surface the boat was relatively fast – sixteen knots – but its range at 6,200 miles was considered too short by Dönitz to reach and remain for a reasonable duration in all reaches of the Atlantic. The boats had subtle improvements from their World War I predecessors; for example, the pressure hull sections were now welded together rather than riveted. This gave the hull some critical elasticity, which mitigated the effects of depth-charge attacks, although at any depth of fifty meters or greater a hole in the pressure hull of even the size of a man's hand would be uncontrollable by the boat's pumps and inevitably lead to the flooding of the U-boat.

Dönitz believed that with three hundred sea-going U-boats he could successfully wage war against the shipping of the most likely enemy Germany would face, Great Britain. He arrived at this number by assuming that at any given moment one-hundred U-boats would be in port for overhaul with their crews receiving much-needed rest. Another one-hundred boats would be on their way to or from the theater of operations (most likely the North Atlantic), while another one-hundred would be actively engaged in operations against the enemy. Dönitz had a problem though. The German Navy long-term building program, often called the "Z-Plan," envisioned the completion of a total of 233 U-boats – but not until 1948.

If this lack of German U-boats at the start of World War II bothered Dönitz – and we know it did – he kept a stiff upper lip. On the first day of the war he sent the following message to his men:

> "We know our enemy. We have today the weapon [the U-boat] and a leadership that can face up to this enemy. The war will last a long time; but if each does his duty we will win. Now to your tasks!"

This duty would be complex, and Dönitz believed that such a number of boats in a theater of operations would require two levels of command. A land-based Commander-in-Chief U-boats could best provide broad operational and tactical control concerning searches for convoys and transfer of key information on weather, wind and enemy dispositions. The command of an actual attack would be delegated to a subordinate commander in one of the U-boats.

However, combat experience in 1939 and 1940 would cause Dönitz to change his thinking. In order to exercise adequate tactical command, the subordinate commander had to remain on the surface, but far away from the target convoy that he was not in range of its escorting aircraft. This placed the U-boat out of sight of the convoy and robbed him of personal observation from which to make key decisions. The paucity of U-boats also played a role; Dönitz felt he could not spare an attack boat for command and control duties. Dönitz felt, therefore, that he could direct the whole tactical operation from his headquarters ashore. As he instructed his U-boat commanders, Dönitz's control extended up to the moment of launching an attack, but not to the attack itself. For the actual attack each U-boat commander would act independently and base his decisions on his own initiative, training and determination.

There is some evidence that Dönitz also concluded that Type VII boats required a different style commander than the Type IX boats. Type VII boats operated for relatively short patrols in combat-intensive periods battling escorted convoys; this environment called for youth, aggressiveness, quick reactions and high optimism to attempt dangerous maneuvers. Type IX U-boats generally remained at sea for much longer periods of time and operated on their own; this required maturity, patience, endurance, experience, coolness under sustained pressure and independent judgment.

Dönitz found that his "on the spot knowledge" within this system worked quite well. He personally questioned each individual U-boat commander after his return to base, reviewing the boat's war diary line by line, and ensured that this information was passed to the entire fleet to maximize lessons learned. He also got a sense in this concentrated debriefing on a U-boat commander's fitness to conduct future missions. As a result, Dönitz concentrated more and more of his energy into controlling the central front of his U-boat war – the North Atlantic.

Dönitz developed a relatively simple command and control system to manage this U-boat war. During the peacetime years, he held the position Commander of U-boats (*Führer der Unterseeboote* [F.d.U.]). In October 1939 this position changed to Commander-in-Chief U-boats (*Befehlshaber der Unterseeboote* [B.d.U.]). Karl Dönitz would hold this position until February 1943. Doing the day-to-day operational control within the B.d.U. was the Chief, Operations Detachment (*Operationsabteilung* [B.d.U. op.]). *Konteradmiral* Eberhardt Godt held this position for the duration of the war, but Dönitz also kept a steady hand on the tiller in this organization. For example, in December 1943 he stated the following about where his place should be in the fight:

> "I must go to the front – that is where I belong. I must be with the troops. I must ever and always have an ear for my people."

> *Dönitz's Crews*
> ***Korvettenkapitän* Peter Lohmeyer**
> Born on January 2, 1911 in Zanzibar, East Africa.
> Joined the Navy in 1932.
> Served as a watch officer on the *U-19*; served as Commander of the *U-138* and *U-651*.
> Became a prisoner of war on June 29, 1941 when the *U-651* was sunk south of Iceland.
> Spent 109 days at sea on U-boat war patrols.
> Survived the war; released from prison camp on July 16, 1947.
> Died on May 28, 2002 in Schleswig.

To accomplish this, Dönitz occupied eleven different headquarters during the war from which he controlled the actions of his boats. But he needed assistance and for that Dönitz established several major regional U-boat commanders. Commander U-boats West (*Führer der Unterseeboote West* [F.d.U. West]) was established in July 1942, commanded by *Kapitän zur See* Hans-Rudolf Rösing until the end of the war, and in general he directed U-boat operations in the Atlantic from bases in France. F.d.U. West transferred its own headquarters from Angers, France to Bergen, Norway in August 1944 to avoid capture by Allied forces when they broke out of Normandy.

Commander U-boats Norway/North Sea (*Führer der Unterseeboote Norwegen/Nordsee* [F.d.U. Norwegen/Nordsee]) came into being in January 1943. *Kapitän zur See* Rudolf Peters commanded the organization until May 1944; *Fregattenkapitän* Reinhard Suhren assumed command in May 1944 and led the organization through the end of the war. This headquarters commanded two flotillas of U-boats in the Norway region and also directed operations against Allied convoys attempting to reach northern Russia.

Commander U-boats Italy/Mediterranean (*Führer der Unterseeboote Italien/Mittelmeer* [F.d.U. Italien/Mittelmeer]) was formed in November 1941 in Rome; it transferred in August 1943 to Toulon, France. *Korvettenkapitän* Victor Oehrn served in temporary command of this F.d.U. from November 1941 to February 1942. *Konteradmiral* Leo Kreisch then assumed command and held this position until January 1944, when he was replaced by *Kapitän zur See* Werner Hartmann who remained in charge until September 1944, when the command was dissolved. While all three commands made independent decisions, Dönitz was never far away in spirit or concern and maintained full awareness of the situation.

Even so, the German U-boat war was truly shaped by the decisions made by relatively young officers. One post-war author, and former U-boat crewman, termed the fight the "War of the Lieutenant Commanders," since "there was no place in it for older admirals and captains." Even this description does not fully capture the youthfulness of the officers in command of the U-boats; most skippers were not, in fact, lieutenant commanders but rather lieutenants and lieutenants junior grade. Opposing the young U-boat men were Allied escort commanders and their staffs, who were ten to twenty years their senior, and armed with command and control technology that was much superior to that of the submarines. Dönitz and his staff at the B.D.U. and various F.d.U. headquarters could only issue general guidance by radio and sit by and await results.

As to the submarines themselves, Dönitz loved the Type VII series of boats. Although they were comparatively small, they had a decent radius of action, a comparatively high number of torpedoes, were light and easy to handle, dove quickly, were difficult to be located by British early-war detection gear and were difficult to see at night – in short, boats with excellent all-around fighting capabilities. Their well-thought-out design was such that a Type VII U-boat could be effectively operated by a twelve-man shift. The Type IX boats were less maneuverable (and ten seconds slower in diving than the VIIs), in Dönitz's opinion, and more complicated to operate but this was balanced by a larger radius of action and increased torpedo capacity; Type IX U-boats required only sixteen men at a time to effectively operate them. The U-boat chief estimated that from ports in Germany his Type VII boats could operate as far as the north coast of Spain, while the Type IX craft could take the fight to the Straits of Gibraltar.

Speeds and the radius of action were somewhat deceptive, however. The bottom line was that you couldn't sail at high speed and maintain a long radius of action, and Dönitz was one of the few to truly understand this. For example, the Type VIIC boat had a top surface speed of just over twenty miles per hour. Its most economical surface cruising speed, using the diesel engines, was much lower at eleven miles an hour. The boat's captain, if he had patience could sail his U-boat about 9,500 nautical miles at this economical speed. However, if he was an impatient skipper and often took the boat to top speed, he would find his cruising range reduced to 3,250 nautical miles. Understanding battery life, which before the advent of the snorkel was the driving force for the electric motors, was equally critical. Submerged, a Type VIIC boat's top speed was about nine miles per hour, but this speed would exhaust the craft's batteries in a couple of hours. By keeping the submerged speed to 4 1/2 miles an hour, the U-boat commander could prolong battery life several-fold. It required an intelligent skipper, not just an aggressive one.

Becoming a naval officer required even more positive traits such as physical ability, courage, tenacity, leadership and the ability to react in an emergency. Prospective midshipmen underwent gymnastics tests – counter-intuitively, a young man who struggled to achieve a seventh chin-up was rated higher than one who easily did ten and then quit. To measure tenacity, a candidate was placed alone in a room and told to lift a heavy metal bar. As he did so, hidden observers switched on an increasing electric current running through the bar and measured how long the boy kept the bar raised – those who defied the shock and pain longest received the highest marks.

Karl Dönitz was a very intelligent man – a post-war intelligence test estimated he had an IQ of 138 – but he was a troubled leader. According to a post-war interview, Admiral Otto Schniewind recalled that in the winter of 1940-1941 Dönitz confided in him that U-boat warfare alone could not end the war victoriously against Great Britain, but the U-boat chief never let his doubts come out into the open. He was also not critical of Adolf Hitler, although with Hitler's neglect of emphasis on the sea service he had room to be. On August 10, 1943 Dönitz summed up his feelings on the Führer with the following words:

> "... What very poor little sausages we all are in comparison with the Führer; and that our knowledge, our vision of things outside our limited sphere is fragmentary. Anyone who believes he can do better than the Führer is foolish."

In part because of his loyalties, Dönitz was named as successor to Adolf Hitler, after the Führer's suicide in Berlin on April 30, 1945. But the admiral's heart remained at sea. Several days later, on May 4, 1945 Karl Dönitz sent his final wartime message to his U-boat boys. It read:

> "My U-boat men! Six years of U-boat war lie behind us. You have fought like lions. A crushing material superiority has forced us into a narrow area. A continuation of our fight from the remaining basis is no longer possible. U-boat men! Undefeated and spotless you lay down your arms after a heroic battle without equal. We remember in deep respect our fallen comrades, who have sealed with their death their loyalty to the Führer and Fatherland. Comrades! Preserve your U-boat spirit, with which you have fought courageously, stubbornly and imperturbably through the years for the good of the Fatherland. Long live Germany! Your Grand Admiral."

Karl Dönitz could be a hard man. After Hitler elevated him to the command of the entire German Navy in 1943, Dönitz dismissed many senior-level admirals – men whom Dönitz felt might not forcefully carry out his intent. The magnitude of the dismissals was so large that throughout the fleet the action was known as "The Great Seal Kill." Earlier in the war, when he could devote all his time to his U-boat duties, he was not hesitant in banishing U-boat commanders to non-sea duty if they did not measure up to his high standards. Later, he refused to commute the death sentences of two U-boat commanders found guilty of cowardice by Navy courts-martial and the officers were subsequently shot. But he could also be understanding; after the war *Konteradmiral* Eberhardt Godt, the Chief of the U-boat Operation's Detachment, explained that at the U-boat headquarters Dönitz had a private room with a desk and cot but little other furnishings. According to Godt, whenever Dönitz received confirmation that one of his boats had been destroyed, he would retire by himself to the room and think about the men of the crew, often appearing to have been overcome by his emotions when he emerged.

After the war, the Allies charged and convicted Karl Dönitz at Nürnberg of war crimes and sentenced him to ten years imprisonment. Released in 1956, he set about writing his life's story which was published under the title, *Memoirs: Ten Years and Twenty Days*. In the work, the old admiral painfully came to the conclusion that he had lost the Battle of the Atlantic in May of 1943, inferring that he had not recognized this conclusion at that time. Sending boat after boat with his boys into the cauldron after this point must have been crushing to the U-boat commander; during the war he reached the bitter conclusion privately that he had no alternative but to continue the undersea war. Dönitz recalled:

> "Germany was on the defensive on all fronts. The Army was engaged in a series of hard-fought defensive battles. The air-raids on Germany were becoming increasingly severe. Under these conditions what effect would the abandonment of the U-boat campaign have on our war situation as a whole? Could we afford to abandon it? Were we justified, in terms of our inferiority, in calling upon our submarines to continue the unequal struggled?"

Karl Dönitz had thirty-seven long years to reflect on these agonizing questions. He died on December 24, 1980 in Aumühle near Hamburg. Two thousand five-hundred mourners attended the funeral; many were his U-boat boys now men in their sixties. Veterans' groups laid wreaths at the site, with inscriptions such as "In Honor and Fidelity" and "Courage to the End."

We do not know what final words Karl Dönitz said before he died. However, his remarks at the funeral of U-boat Commander Wolfgang Lüth on May 15, 1945 give us a clue as to what his final thoughts might have been on that Christmas Eve some thirty-five years later. On that morning in 1945 at Lüth's funeral, Dönitz eulogized:

> "Wolfgang Lüth, we now take leave of you. It is not mine to describe your family's loss; we, your comrades, have lost a great warrior, a true and noble friend, and I a beloved member of the old guard of my U-Bootwaffe, to which my entire heart once belonged and belongs still ..."

These words and thoughts would have made perfect sense to Dönitz's crews.

Key dates in the *Kriegsmarine* career of Karl Dönitz

September 29, 1935	Named Commander, U-boat Flotilla *Weddigen*
October 1, 1935	Promoted to *Kapitän zur See* (Captain)
January 1, 1936	Named *Führer der Unterseeboote* (Commander U-boats)
January 28, 1939	Promoted to *Kommodore* (Commodore)
September 18, 1939	Awarded Clasp for the Iron Cross 2nd Class
October 1, 1939	Promoted to *Konteradmiral* (Rear Admiral)
October 17, 1939	Named *Befehlshaber der Unterseeboote* (Commander-in-Chief U-boats)
December 20, 1939	Awarded Clasp for the Iron Cross 1st Class
April 21, 1940	Awarded the Knight's Cross of the Iron Cross
September 1, 1940	Promoted to *Vizeadmiral* (Vice Admiral)
March 14, 1942	Promoted to Admiral (Admiral)
January 30, 1943	Promoted to *Großadmiral* (Grand Admiral; Admiral of the Fleet)
January 31, 1943	Named Commander-in-Chief *Kriegsmarine*
April 6, 1943	Awarded Oak Leaves to the Knight's Cross
May 1, 1945	Named Reichs President and Commander-in-Chief of the German Armed Forces

Sources, "Father of the U-boats:" G.H. Bennett, and R. Bennett, *Hitler's Admirals*, Annapolis, Maryland: Naval Institute Press, 2004, 59, 60, 93, 94, 95, 139; Clay Blair, *Hitler's U-boat War: The Hunters, 1939-1942*, New York: Random House, 1996, 35, 36, 43; Carl von Clausewitz, *On War*, edited and translated by Michael Howard and Peter Paret, Princeton, New Jersey: Princeton University Press, 1989, 196, 197; Philip A. Crowl, "Alfred Thayer Mahan: The Naval Historian," in *Makers of Modern Strategy from Machiavelli to the Nuclear Age*, edited by Peter Paret, Princeton, NJ: Princeton University Press, 1986, 444-477; Karl Dönitz, *Memoirs: Ten Years and Twenty Days*, translated by R.H. Stevens, Annapolis, Maryland: Da Capo Press, 1997, 13, 14, 15, 16, 26, 27, 28, 29, 32, 33, 37, 40, 41, 62, 63, 228, 301, 313, 406; Michael Gannon, *Black May: The Epic Story of the Allies Defeat of the German U-boats in May 1943*, New York: HarperCollins, 1998, 6, 7; Michael Gannon, *Operation Drumbeat: The Dramatic True Story of Germany's First U-boat Attacks Along the American Coast in World War II*, New York: Harper & Row, 1990, xix, 9, 19, 24, 52, 73, 74, 76, 81, 383; Peter C. Hansen, *Execution for Duty: The Life, Trial & Murder of a U-boat Captain*, Barnsley, England: Pen & Sword Maritime, 2003, 18, 25; Günter Hessler, *The U-boat War in the Atlantic, 1939-1945, Volume 1-3*, London: Her Majesty's Stationery Office, 1989, 5; Geoffrey Jones, *U-boat Aces*, Cerberus Publishing, Bristol, England, 2005, 41; Peter Padfield, *Dönitz: The Last Führer*, London: Victor Gollancz LTD., 1984, 42, 125, 130, 152, 188, 225, 270, 316, 339, 419; Theodore P. Savas, Editor, *Silent Hunters: German U-boat Commanders of World War II*, Campbell, CA: Savas Publishing, 1997, 28; Jak Mallmann Showell, *German Navy Handbook, 1939-1945*, Thrupp, England: Sutton Publishing, 1999, 142, 143; Jak Mallmann Showell, *Wolfpacks at War: The U Boat Experience in World War II*, Hersham, England: Ian Allan Publishing, 2002, 12; Jak Mallmann Showell, *U-boat Warfare: The Evolution of the Wolf Pack*, Annapolis, Maryland: Naval Institute Press, 2002, 7; Jordan Vause, *U-boat Ace: the story of Wolfgang Lüth*, Annapolis, Maryland: Naval Institute Press, 1990, 209; David Westwood, *The U-boat War: The German Submarine Service and the Battle of the Atlantic, 1935-1945*, Philadelphia, PA: Casemate, 2005, 33, 126, 154, 157, 158, 162, 170; www.ubootwaffe.net; www.uboatarchive.net; Interview with Horst Bredow, curator of the U-boat Archives & Museum and former crewmember on the *U-288* at Cuxhaven, Germany on October 22, 2008.

Admiral Karl Dönitz. *Signed postcard during the war.*

Dönitz's early U-boat "fleet." *U-boat Flotilla Weddigen and U-boat tender Saar (Dönitz's command ship); photo is probably from 1936.*

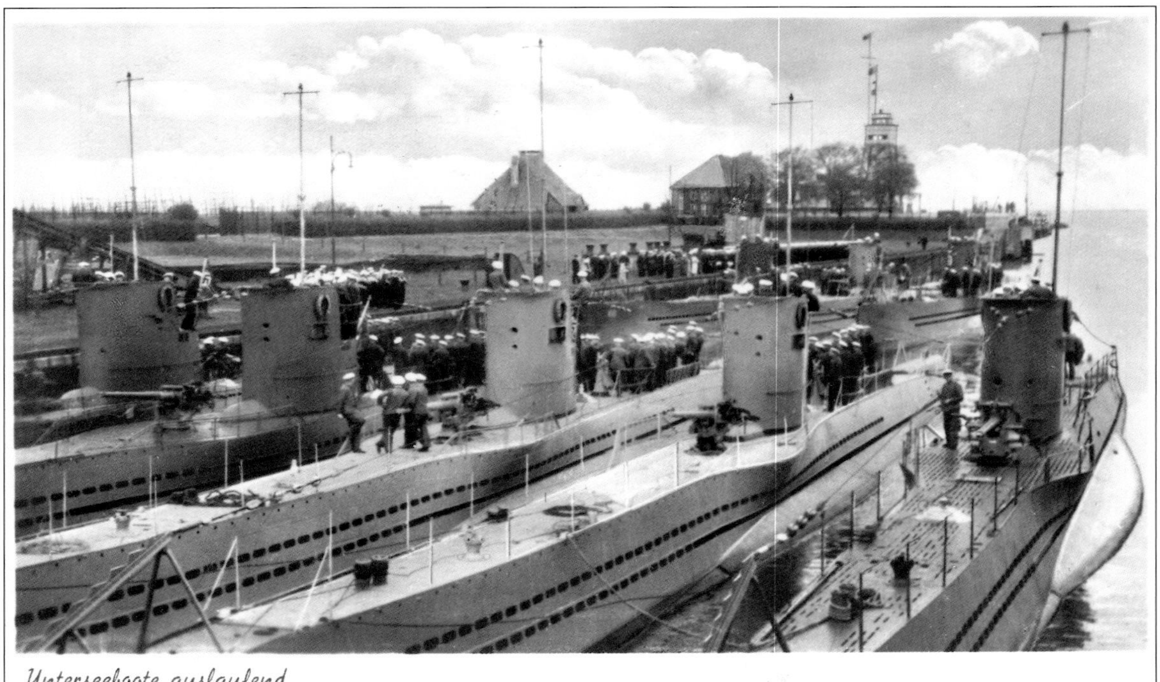

Early U-boats at peace at Wilhelmshaven. *Note that all personnel are wearing white caps. After the start of the war in 1939, generally only the U-boat commander would wear a white cap, the other crewmen would wear blue or (in the Mediterranean) khaki-colored headgear.*

Early Type IIB U-boats. *Identifiable are the U-10, U-13, U-18 and U-19. The surface ship on the right is probably the U-boat tender Donau. Photo probably taken in 1936 or 1937 at Kiel.*

Dönitz's boys on the bridge of the U-29 in 1939 before the war. *Men are still wearing the U-boat Flotilla Salzwedel cap band as well as their gray leather uniforms. Just after the start of the war, on September 17, 1939 the U-29 sank the British aircraft carrier HMS Courageous.*

U-25, U-27 and U-28 of the U-boat Flotilla Salzwedel next to the U-boat tender Saar. *Photo taken at Wilhelmshaven before the war.*

U-boats at Kiel in 1936.

U-19 breaks spray in the Baltic. *Photo taken in 1939; it belonged to Peter Lohmeyer, a watch officer on the U-19 during this period. Lohmeyer later commanded the U-651. He sank two enemy ships before the U-651 was sunk on June 29, 1941 by the British destroyers HMS Malcolm and HMS Scimitar, the corvettes HMS Arabis and HMS Violet and the minesweeper HMS Speedwell; he would remain a prisoner of war for over five years. Peter Lohmeyer died on May 28, 2002.*

The calm before the storm. *Peter Lohmeyer on the bridge of the U-19 having a cup of coffee. Photo taken in 1939.*

U-19. *Pre-war paint schemes for U-boats were light in color; this was quickly changed in late 1939. Photo was taken in 1939; it belonged to Peter Lohmeyer.*

View of the rear of the bridge of the U-19. *Photo was taken in 1939.*

U-boat officers stand at the rear of the bridge on the U-19. *There is a brisk wind causing the national flag to flutter almost straight. Photo was taken in 1939.*

Peter Lohmeyer in full dress uniform with his new bride in 1940. *Lohmeyer previously served with the Luftwaffe in the Spanish Civil War and received the Pilot's Badge and Spanish Cross, both visible here.*

Peter Lohmeyer at the pistol range firing a Luger. *Photo is a post-war copy of an original.*

Peter Lohmeyer (right) at 20-mm flak gun training.

Peter Lohmeyer looks through observation binoculars.
Photo is a post-war copy of an original.

Peter Lohmeyer's ship identification book dated 1940.

The German Navy Officers' School at Flensburg-Mürwik.
Photo from Peter Lohmeyer.

World War I U-boat hero Otto Weddigen. *Otto Weddigen was killed in action on March 18, 1915 in his U-29 while attempting to penetrate the British anchorage of Scapa Flow. The Kriegsmarine U-boat Flotilla Weddigen was named in his honor.*

Karl Dönitz as Commander-in-Chief of the German Navy.

Admiral Karl Dönitz reviews the troops in Berlin, March 12, 1944. *Ceremony was to honor the fallen soldiers, sailors and airmen.*

Admiral Karl Dönitz receives the pass-in-review of the troops in Berlin, March 12, 1944.

Admiral Dönitz awards Iron Crosses to his "boys." *The U-boat chief made a special effort to personally greet returning U-boat crews and participate in award ceremonies. The expressions in this photo show his presence meant a lot to the men.*

Admiral Dönitz (center) greets crew of U-105 as part of Knight's Cross award ceremony for commander of the boat Kapitänleutnant Georg Schewe. *Photo taken at Lorient, France on June 13, 1941. Photo from the estate of German Cross in Gold winner August Bischoff.*

9b

Im Namen
des Führers und Reichskanzlers

verleihe ich

dem Kapitän zur See
(Dienstgrad)

Kurt Slevogt
(Vor- und Zuname)

Kommandeur der Unterseebootsschule
(Marineteil)

für 25 jährige treue Dienste in der Wehrmacht die

Dienstauszeichnung I. bis IV. Klasse.

Berlin, den 2.Oktober 1936.

Der Reichskriegsminister
und Oberbefehlshaber der Wehrmacht
von Blomberg
Generalfeldmarschall

Kriegsmarine · Kommando der Marinestation der Ostsee
Dienststempel

Für die Richtigkeit

Boehte
(Name)

Korvettenkapitän,
(Dienstgrad und Dienststellung)
I.Adjutant des Kommandos der
Marinestation der Ostsee.

St.O.G.14192/36.

Admiral Dönitz visits U-boat men, dated August 1942. *Note variety of uniforms of the U-boat crews. Officer on the far left is a Knight's Cross winner; it appears to be Korevettenkapitän Wilhelm Schulz, which would indicate this is at the 6th U-boat Flotilla.*

Opposite
Armed Forces Long Service Award 1st through 4th Class document, October 2, 1936, to Kapitän zur See Kurt Slevogt, Commander of the U-boat School. *In 1936 Adolf Hitler instituted the award in recognition for loyal service in the Wehrmacht. The 4th Class was for four years service, 3rd Class for twelve years service, 2nd Class for eighteen years service and 1st Class for twenty-five years service. Document is signed by Korvettenkapitän Friedrich Bonte who was later posthumously awarded the Knight's Cross for commanding German destroyers at Narvik in April 1940. Slevogt commanded a U-boat in World War I; while Dönitz praised Slevogt in his memoirs, the two had philosophical differences concerning U-boat tactics. In 1939 Slevogt left the position and while he was promoted to admiral, he was retired in 1943; Kurt Slevogt died on July 23, 1957.*

Below
Armed Forces Long Service Award 3rd and 4th Class. *Award on the left in gold is the 3rd Class; that on the right in silver is the 4th Class.*

CHAPTER TWO

"JONAH"
U-38, U-68, U-170, U-171, U-437, AND U-3029
1939-1945

Service in the U-boats was extremely hazardous and became even more so as the war went on. Tens of thousands of Dönitz's men were killed in action or went missing, never to be seen again. Despite the dismal chances of survival, some U-boat sailors overcame the odds time and time again. Much like the Biblical character Jonah, these men seemingly were swallowed up by the war at sea only to be "vomited" back to safety and survival.

Dönitz's Crews
***Obersteuermann* Karl Bade**

Born on March 4, 1915.
Served on the *U-38*, *U-68*, *U-437* and *U-3029*.
Awarded the Iron Cross 2nd Class and U-boat War Badge on December 16, 1939; awarded the Iron Cross 1st Class on July 5, 1942; awarded the German Cross in Gold on May 9, 1944; awarded the U-boat Clasp in Bronze on October 18, 1944; awarded the U-boat Clasp in Silver on March 17, 1945.
Spent 724 days at sea on U-boat war patrols.
Survived the war and served in the post-war German Navy.
Lived in Kiel.

Obersteuermann Karl Bade was such a modern day Jonah. Born on March 4, 1915, he began his U-boat service on the *U-38*, a Type IX U-boat, before the war began. The German Navy ordered the boat to be built on July 29, 1936; engineers laid her keel at the shipyards of the Deutsche Schiff und Maschinenbau AG at Bremen on April 15, 1937. On August 9, 1938 the *U-38* was launched; after launching, the *U-38* – like every other new U-boat – went out for sea trials where everything that could be tested was thoroughly examined. This included all electrical and mechanical equipment; hull welds were tested by pressure dives; dive and trim tests established her seaworthiness. Declared ready, the *U-38* was commissioned on October 24, 1938 by her commander *Kapitänleutnant* Heinrich Liebe and joined the U-boat Flotilla *Hundius*.

The son of a German Army officer, Heinrich Liebe was born in Gotha on January 29, 1908 and joined the German Navy on April 5, 1927. After nine years in the surface forces, he joined the U-boats on September 30, 1935. After briefly commanding the *U-2*, he transferred to the *U-38*.

On August 19, 1939 the *U-38* departed Wilhelmshaven under the command of Heinrich Liebe for operations off Lisbon, Portugal. She hit two ships on this patrol. On September 6, 1939 at 7:44 a.m. off Portugal the *U-38* sank the British 7,242-ton *Manaar* carrying government stores from Liverpool to Calcutta, India with deck-gun fire and three torpedoes, killing seven, after the *Manaar* opened fire with her own deck-gun as the U-boat approached. At 1:50 p.m. on September 11, 1939 southwest of Ireland the *U-38* sank the British 9,456-ton tanker *Inverliffey*, carrying 13,000 tons of gasoline from Trinidad to Coryton, England, with torpedoes and gunfire. As the ship exploded, Liebe towed the ship's lifeboats to safety. The *U-38* returned to Wilhelmshaven on September 18, 1939. For his accomplishments, Heinrich Liebe received the Iron Cross 2nd Class on October 8, 1939.

While in port, the technicians overhauled the electric motors. Finally, on November 14, 1939 the *U-38* left Wilhelmshaven for her second war patrol for operations northwest of Norway. On December 7, 1939 at 5:09 p.m. the *U-38* he torpedoed and sank the British 4,460-ton *Thomas Walton* off central Norway; the ship, in ballast, went down with thirteen of her crew. Off the Norwegian coast at 8:49 a.m. on December 11, 1939 the *U-38* torpedoed and sank the Greek 4,708-ton *Garoufalia*; four men died in the attack. On December 13, 1939 at 3:33 p.m., still off the Norwegian coast, the *U-38* sank the British 4,101-ton freighter *Deptford*; thirty-two men died when the ship carrying 6,000 tons of iron ore form Narvik, Norway to Middlesbrough, England sank within five minutes. The *U-38* returned to Wilhelmshaven on December 16, 1939. That same day Karl Bade was awarded the U-boat War Badge and the Iron Cross 2nd Class for his performance on the patrol; the commander Heinrich Liebe also received the U-boat War Badge the same day.

After two months in port, the *U-38* departed Wilhelmshaven on February 26, 1940 for operations in the North West approaches; Heinrich Liebe had a good patrol and hit six enemy ships. But it started dangerously when on March 3, 1940 the *U-38* was forced to crash-dive when attacked by enemy aircraft that dropped several depth charges in the vicinity of the U-boat. There was damage and the following day machinists on the boat spent seventeen hours repairing three cylinders on the starboard engine. At 9:13 p.m. on March 9, 1940, twelve miles northeast of Tory Island, Ireland, the *U-38* fired a warning shot from her deck-gun at the Irish 216-ton fishing vessel *Leukos*. But the shot hit the vessel in the engine room and the ship exploded, killing her entire crew of eleven. On March 17, 1940 at 11:25 p.m. the *U-38* fired a spread of two torpedoes at the Danish 5,375-ton freighter *Argentina* northeast of Scotland. The ship, bound from Denmark to Las Palmas, Canary Islands, quickly sank taking all thirty-three men with her. At 1:05 a.m. northeast of Scotland the *U-38* torpedoed and sank the Danish 1,654-ton freighter *Algier* carrying general cargo from New York to Oslo; five men died in the attack. Liebe's next victim was hit at 3:26 a.m. on March 21, when the Danish 3,270-ton *Christiansborg*, heading from Philadelphia, Pennsylvania to Copenhagen, Denmark, was struck by a torpedo northeast of Scotland and broke in two. One man died in the attack that sent 4,107 tons of maize to the bottom. The following day enemy aircraft attacked the *U-38* dropping two depth charges near her as she submerged to safety. At 2:20 a.m. on March 26, 1940 the *U-38* torpedoed and sank the Norwegian 3,794-ton *Cometa* north of Scotland; the ship was carrying general cargo from Oslo, Norway to Buenos Aires, Argentina. Finally on April 2, 1940 at 12:21 a.m. Liebe torpedoed the Finnish 1,540-ton *Signe* north of Scotland, killing all nineteen men aboard. The *U-38* returned to Wilhelmshaven on April 5, 1940. The next day the commander Heinrich Liebe was awarded the Iron Cross 1st Class; interestingly, he recorded that the *U-38* had sailed 5,730 sea-miles on the surface during the patrol and just 738 sea-miles submerged.

But necessity caused a quick turnaround and the *U-38* left Wilhelmshaven on April 8, 1940 to support German operations in the invasion of Norway. Suffering torpedo problems – as did every boat on the operation – the *U-38* fired several torpedoes at the British heavy cruiser *HMS Effingham*, with no effect. Enemy forces attacked the *U-38* on several occasions during the patrol and by late April she was leaking – and more critically trailing – oil. The *U-38* returned two weeks later to Wilhelmshaven on April 27, 1940; she had spent 2,777 sea-miles surfaced and 426 sea-miles submerged.

For two months the *U-38* remained in port. Then on June 6, 1940 she departed for the North Atlantic. Liebe's first task was to land two Abwehr agents in Ireland to set up a weather-monitoring post to help observe impending weather approaching Europe; on the night of June 12-13 Liebe landed the pair at Brandon Bay, Ireland; the men were later apprehended and their fates remain unknown. Then the *U-38* took up her traditional role and sank six ships during the war patrol:

- On June 14, 1940 south of Ireland the *U-38* attacked the Greek 5,403-ton *Mount Myrto* carrying general cargo and timber from Galveston, Texas to London; while the deck-gun crew was firing at their target, the *U-38* accidentally dove leaving six men in the water but Liebe quickly surfaced and picked them up before a flying boat drove him under water. Four men on the *Mount Myrto* were not so fortunate and perished.
- At 1:01 a.m. on June 15, 1940, west of the Scilly Isles, the *U-38* torpedoed and sank the Canadian freighter 2,238-ton *Erik Boye*, sailing with convoy HX-47 with 3,568 tons of wheat from Halifax to England.
- Four minutes later at 1:05 a.m. on June 15, 1940 the *U-38* sank the Norwegian 9,973-ton tanker *Italia*, bound from Port Arthur, Texas to Manchester England with convoy HX-47; nineteen men died when the ship's cargo of 13,000 tons of aviation spirits exploded.
- On June 20, 1940 at 4:12 a.m., west of Brest, France, the *U-38* sank the Swedish 1,776-ton merchant *Tilia Gorthon* with torpedoes and deck-gun fire; ten men died when the ship, carrying coal, went to the bottom.
- At 5:53 p.m. on June 21, 1940 the *U-38* torpedoed and sank the Belgian 5,809-ton freighter *Luxembourg* carrying boiled beef, maize and sunflower seed from Buenos Aires, Argentina to Antwerp.
- On June 22, 1940 at 2:17 a.m. the *U-38* torpedoed and sank the Greek 5,154-ton *Neion*. Shortly after, the U-38's watch crew spotted an enemy destroyer and dove to safety.

The *U-38* arrived back at Wilhelmshaven after this highly-successful patrol on July 2, 1940. Remaining in port for almost a month, she then departed Wilhelmshaven on August 1, 1940 for operations west of Ireland. It started dangerously as on August 2 enemy aircraft attacked the U-boat with depth charges, but there was no damage. Three days later more enemy aircraft, lurking in low cloud cover, attacked the U-boat, again with no results. On August 7, 1940 at 11:40 p.m. west of Ireland the *U-38* torpedoed and sank the British 7,527-ton *Mohamed Ali El-Kebir*, a troopship on convoy HX-61 bound for Gibraltar; ninety-six men died. On August 11, 1940 at 3:19 p.m. the *U-38* sank the British 4,966-ton *Llanfair*, from convoy SL-41, bringing 7,800 tons of sugar from Freetown, Sierra Leone to Avonmouth, England; three crewmen died when the ship went down in eleven minutes. Enemy aircraft forced the *U-38* to crash-dive on August 18, August 19 and August 24. Finally, on August 31, 1940 northwest of Bloody Foreland, Ireland the *U-38* sank the British 2,508-ton *Har Zion*, a straggler from convoy OB-205 and carrying fertilizer from Liverpool, England to Savannah, Georgia; thirty-four men died in the attack – only one man survived. After four weeks at sea, the *U-38* arrived at her new home port of Lorient, France on September 3, 1940. Liebe calculated that during the war patrol the *U-38* traveled 5,887 sea-miles surfaced and 344 sea-miles submerged. During the patrol, Dönitz announced on August 14, 1940 that *Kapitänleutnant* Heinrich Liebe had earned the Knight's Cross for his cumulative accomplishments; Dönitz actually presented the award to Liebe on September 3, 1940.

The sailors of the *U-38* got to know their new home in France for about three weeks until September 25, 1940 when they departed on their next war patrol for operations in the North West approaches; it would be another successful operation. On board as well were two officers in training, *Kapitänleutnant* Hans-Georg Fischer and *Kapitänleutnant* Karl-Friedrich Merten. Success came quickly, but only after the starboard engine broke down on September 30. On October 1, 1940 at 6:47 a.m. west of Ireland operating on one engine, the *U-38* torpedoed and sank the unescorted British 14,172-ton *Highland Patriot* carrying 5,700 tons of general and refrigerated cargo from Buenos Aires, Argentina to Glasgow, Scotland; three crewmen died in the attack. The next day Liebe's machinists repaired the engine; time then went by until 9:57 a.m. on October 17, 1940 when the *U-38* attacked the Greek 3,554-ton freighter *Aenos*, a straggler from convoy SC-7, with torpedoes and deck-gun fire. Four men died when the ship sank northwest of Ireland, carrying 6,276 tons of wheat from Sorel, Canada to Manchester, England. The next day on October 18, 1940 the *U-38* damaged the British 3,670-ton *Carsbreck*, part of convoy SC-7. She would be sunk six days later by the *U-564*. On October 19, 1940 at 10:19 p.m. west of Ireland, the *U-38* torpedoed and sank the Dutch 6,856-ton *Bilderdijk* with convoy HX-79. The Dutch freighter was carrying 8,640 tons of grain and general cargo from Baltimore, Maryland to Liverpool, England. Four minutes later, the *U-38* sank the British 7,653-ton *Matheran*, also sailing with convoy HX-79. Nine men died on the ship carrying 3,000 tons of iron, 1,200 tons of zinc and general cargo from Halifax, Nova Scotia to Liverpool, England. With these accomplishments, the *U-38* set sail for home and arrived at Lorient on October 24, 1940.

At Lorient the men of the *U-38* were able to take leave as they did not again go out on patrol until December 18, 1940 when Liebe and the boat departed to again patrol the North West approaches. Again *Kapitänleutnant* Karl-Friedrich Merten accompanied the boat in a training status. South of Iceland on December 27, 1940 the *U-38* located the seriously damaged British 12,823-ton freighter *Waiotira*. Previously torpedoed by the *U-95*, the ship, carrying 7,000 tons of refrigerated cargo from Sydney, Nova Scotia to Great Britain, quickly sank. At 9:12 p.m. on December 31, 1940, still south of Iceland, the *U-38* torpedoed and sank the Swedish 3,760-ton *Valparaiso*, a member of convoy HX-97 sailing from Halifax, Nova Scotia to Glasgow, Scotland. The entire crew of thirty-five men perished in the freezing sea. On January 2, 1941 an enemy destroyer drove the *U-38* under and attacked with depth charges. On January 12, 1941 the *U-38* experienced problems with the ventilation system and had to surface to make repairs. Then the *U-38* returned to Lorient on January 22, 1941. It is likely that Karl Bade departed the *U-38* at this time as he was then assigned to the *U-68*, which was about to be commissioned by *Kapitänleutnant* Karl-Friedrich Merten, who undoubtedly asked for Bade to be assigned to the new boat after he observed the sailor during Merten's training patrols on the *U-38*. Merten, who was born on August 15, 1908 at Posen, West Prussia, was the son of the Lord Mayor of Elbing; earlier the senior Merten had been an Army lieutenant in the Kaiser's personal honor guard.

Life went on for the crew of the *U-38* and on April 9, 1941 the *U-38*, still under the command of Heinrich Liebe, departed Lorient for operations west of Africa to take advantage of her long range. It would be the *U-38*'s most successful patrol. Liebe would sink eight enemy ships, a total of 47,279 tons:

1. On May 4, 1941 at 6:29 p.m. the *U-38* began shelling the Swedish 5,230-ton freighter *Japan*, part of the dispersed convoy OB-310, carrying general cargo and coal northwest of Freetown, Sierra Leone. While firing the ninth round, the deck-gun exploded lightly injuring several of the crew; the *U-38* then sank the ship with a torpedo.
2. At 11:05 a.m. on May 5, 1941 the *U-38* torpedoed and sank the British 4,976-ton *Queen Maud* west of Freetown; part of the dispersed convoy OB-310, she was carrying 7,320 tons of coal and government stores from Cardiff, Wales to Alexandria, Egypt – one man died in the attack.
3. On May 23, 1941 at 7:51 p.m. the *U-38* torpedoed and sank the Dutch 6,622-ton *Berhala*, from the dispersed convoy OB-318 west of Freetown.
4. The next day (May 24) at 2:49 a.m., the *U-38* sank the British 4,362-ton *Vulcain* from the dispersed convoy OB-318. She was carrying 4,617 tons of coal to Freetown.
5. On May 29, 1941 at 11:50 p.m. the *U-38* sank the British 6,251-ton *Tabaristan* in just four minutes, killing twenty-one men. The ship was carrying 3,950 tons of ground nuts, 2,200 tons of pig iron and 560 tons of manganese ore from Capetown, South Africa to the United Kingdom when she went down southwest of Freetown.
6. The next day (May 30) at 1:11 p.m. the *U-38* torpedoed the British 6,181-ton *Empire Protector* carrying 2,250 tons of cotton, 4,200 tons of cotton seed and 1,252 tons of copper from Port Sudan, Egypt to London; five men died when the ship went to the bottom.
7. On May 31, 1941 at 12:24 a.m. the *U-38* sank the unescorted Norwegian 6,029-ton *Rinda* carrying 6,719 tons of general cargo (including cotton balls) from Haifa, Palestine and Table Bay, South Africa to the United Kingdom; thirteen men died in the attack.
8. On June 8, 1941 at 1:08 a.m. the *U-38* torpedoed and sank the unescorted British 7,628-ton *Kingston Hill* southwest of the Cape Verde Islands. The ship, bound from Glasgow, Scotland to Capetown, was carrying 8,300 tons of coal and 400 tons of general cargo; fourteen men died.

On June 10, 1941 the *U-38* received a radio message that Heinrich Liebe had been awarded the Oak Leaves to the Knight's Cross; he would receive the award on return from the patrol. Torpedoes expended, the *U-38* returned to Lorient on June 29, 1941. Heinrich Liebe then left the *U-38*; in his place came Heinrich Schuch. Liebe would spend the remainder of the war in various significant *Kriegsmarine* high-level staffs and ended the war as a *Fregattenkapitän*; he died at Eisenach on July 27, 1997. On August 6, 1941 Schuch took the *U-38* on her tenth war patrol to the North Atlantic. On August 18, 1941 at 2:50 a.m. southwest of Iceland, the *U-38* sank the unescorted Panamanian 1,700-ton *Longtaker* in under a minute; the ship, carrying timber and foodstuffs from the U.S. to Iceland, took twenty-four of her crew with her to the depths. The *U-38* returned to Lorient on September 14, 1941 after five and a half weeks on patrol. It would be her last victory. From October 15, 1941 to November 21, 1941, the *U-38* patrolled the North Atlantic before arriving at Bergen, Norway at the conclusion of the patrol. Two days later, the *U-38* departed Norway for Stettin and service in the training command for the rest of the war. The *U-38* was the tenth-most successful U-boat of the war.

Meanwhile Karl Bade had joined the *U-68*. A Type IXC U-boat, the *U-68* was ordered by the German Navy on August 7, 1939; shipyard engineers at the Deutsche Schiff und Maschinenbau AG at Bremen laid her keel on April 20, 1940. After *Kapitänleutnant* Karl-Friedrich Merten joined the process, the *U-68* was commissioned on February 11, 1941. The crew then spent four full months training and preparing for combat. On June 30, 1941 the *U-68* departed Kiel for her first war patrol that took the U-boat to operations south of Greenland. She was almost destroyed on July 5, 1941 when an enemy destroyer emerged from the fog and nearly rammed her. The U-68 finally arrived at Lorient, France on August 1, 1941; the next day Karl-Friedrich Merten was awarded the U-boat War Badge. Mertens estimated that the *U-68* sailed 6,416 sea-miles on the surface and only 96.3 sea-miles submerged. The *U-68* remained at Lorient until September 11, 1941 when she set sail for the South Atlantic. The U-boat would sink four enemy ships on the patrol. On September 22, 1941 at 2:22 a.m. the *U-68* torpedoed and sank the British 5,302-ton *Silverbelle*, sailing with convoy SL-87 from Freetown to Liverpool, southwest of the Canary Islands; she was loaded with 6,000 tons of phosphate and general cargo that included palm oil and cocoa beans.

Running low on supplies, the *U-68* was reprovisioned with fuel and seven torpedoes from the *U-67*. At 1:42 a.m. on October 22, 1941, the *U-68* crept into the Jamestown harbor at St. Helena Island and torpedoed the British 8,145-ton fleet oiler *Darkdale*. The ship, carrying 3,000 tons of fuel oil, 850 tons of aviation fuel and 500 tons of lubricating oil, took forty-one men with her when she sank. On October 28, 1941 at 3:43 a.m., the *U-68* torpedoed and sank the unescorted British 5,297-ton *Hazelside* six-hundred miles southeast of St. Helena. Her 3,476 tons of general cargo would never get to Durban, South Africa; two men died in the attack. Finally, at 6:54 a.m. on November 1, 1941 the *U-68* sank the British 4,953-ton *Bradford City* three-hundred miles west of Walvis Bay, South West Africa. While all crewmen on the ship survived, some 9,500 tons of sugar and rum did not. Again running low on supplies, the *U-68* refueled from the German supply ship *Python* and also received nine torpedoes. After fifteen weeks at sea, the *U-68* returned to Lorient on Christmas Day 1941; on the war patrol the *U-68* sailed 17,481 sea-miles on the surface and just 119 sea-miles submerged. Karl-Friedrich Merten received the Iron Cross 1st Class on December 30, 1941.

After holiday leaves at home, the crewmen of the *U-68* returned to Lorient and departed on February 11, 1942 for their third war patrol; they would go back to the west coast of Africa. During the two month patrol the *U-68* achieved the following results:

- On March 3, 1942 at 5:21 p.m. south of Freetown the *U-68* torpedoed and sank the British 7,366-ton *Helenus*. The ship, carrying 4,248 tons of rubber and 1,350 tons of copper from Penang, Malaya to Liverpool, England, sank with six of her crew.
- At 12:41 p.m. on March 8, 1942 thirty miles southwest of Grand Cess, Liberia the *U-68* sank the British 6,992-ton *Baluchistan* with torpedoes and deck-gun fire. Three men went down with the ship which was carrying dates from Basrah to Great Britain.
- On March 16, 1942 at 11:17 p.m. the *U-68* sank the unescorted British 3,386-ton freighter *Baron Newlands* six miles south of Cape Palmas, Liberia. Eighteen men died when the ship carrying 4,800 tons of manganese from Takoradi, Ghana to Freetown, Sierra Leone went to the bottom.
- At 1:26 p.m. on March 17, 1942, the *U-68* sank the British 4,917-ton *Scottish Prince* with torpedoes and deck-gun fire. The ship, carrying 6,000 tons of palm kernels, 600 tons of castor seed and 900 tons of pig iron from Calcutta, India to Great Britain, took one crewman with her when she went down.
- At 9:53 p.m on March 17, 1942 south of Cape Palmas, Liberia, the *U-68* torpedoed and sank the British 5,081-ton *Allende* bound from Calcutta, India to Great Britain; six men perished in the attack.
- At 6:35 a.m. on March 17, 1942 southwest of Cape Palmas, Liberia, the *U-68* damaged the British 5,755-ton *Ile de Batz* with a torpedo; the U-boat then sank the ship, carrying general cargo from Rangoon, Burma to Great Britain, with thirty-three high explosive rounds from her deck-gun. Four men died in the sinking.
- On March 30, 1942 at 10:43 p.m. the *U-68* used her last three torpedoes to sink the British 5,853-ton *Muncaster Castle* southwest of Monrovia, Liberia. The ship carrying several hundred passengers and general cargo from Glasgow, Scotland to Colombo, Ceylon, sank with a loss of life of twenty-four.

Her torpedoes expended, the *U-68* headed north and arrived at Lorient on April 13, 1942; she had spent 10,985 sea-miles on the surface and 237 sea-miles submerged. The U-boat spent one month in port and then departed Lorient on May 14, 1942 for operations in the Caribbean Sea. Leaking oil, the *U-68*, under cover of darkness, pulled in to the Spanish port of El Ferrol and found the German supply ship *Max Albrecht*, made repairs and took on fuel. The U-boat then headed west; the Caribbean would prove profitable for the boat. The action started on June 5, 1942 at 8:49 p.m. southwest of Puerto Rico when the *U-68* torpedoed and sank the American 6,693-ton tanker *LJ Drake* carrying 72,961 barrels of gasoline from Aruba to San Juan, Puerto Rico. The ship exploded and killed all forty men onboard.

Another tanker died southwest of Puerto Rico at 3:07 a.m on June 6, 1942 when the *U-68* torpedoed and sank the Panamanian 13,006-ton tanker *CO Stillman*. Carrying 125,812 barrels of fuel oil from Aruba to New York, the ship sank with three men. The *U-68* then moved to north of Panama and sank three ships on June 10, 1942. At 5:20 a.m. the U-boat torpedoed and sank the British 5,025-ton *Ardenvohr* headed from New York to the Panama Canal and then to Melbourne, Australia with munitions, tanks and guns, killing one crewman. At the same time the *U-68* sank the British 8,581-ton *Surrey* carrying more military cargo to Sydney, Australia – twelve men died in this attack. At 11:58 a.m. Merten sank the British 5,882-ton *Port Montreal*, also bound for the Panama Canal and Australia, and carrying 7,500 tons of ammunition and fourteen aircraft on deck. Two crewmen later died in lifeboats. On June 15, 1942 off the coast of Colombia, the *U-68* sank the French 9,242-ton tanker *Frimaire*; there were no survivors.

Finally on June 23, 1942 at 7:33 p.m. the *U-68* torpedoed and sank the Panamanian 2,345-ton tanker *Arriaga*, carrying fresh water from Baltimore to Aruba; one man died in the attack. Disaster almost struck on June 26 when an enemy flying boat was not seen in time by the bridge watch and dropped two depth charges near the boat; there were no fatal damages. The *U-68* then returned to Lorient where she arrived on July 10, 1942; on this war patrol the *U-68* sailed 11,490 sea-miles on the surface and 189 sea-miles submerged. It would be the last patrol for Karl Bade on the *U-68*; he received the Iron Cross 1st Class on July 5, 1942 and appears to have been reassigned about this time. During the voyage on June 13, 1942, Dönitz radioed the *U-68* to inform the commander and crew that Karl-Friedrich Merten had been awarded the Knight's Cross.

Karl-Friedrich Merten would make one additional patrol with the *U-68* and it would last almost four months. On August 20, 1942 the U-boat departed Lorient; for this voyage she would head for South Africa and it would be her most successful.

- On September 12, 1942 at 3:32 a.m. northeast of Ascension Island, the *U-68* sank the British 5,296-ton *Trevilley* carrying general and military cargo from Oban, Scotland to Beira, Mozambique, with torpedoes and deck-gun fire.
- On September 15, 1942 at 12:59 a.m. Merten sank the Dutch 6,861-ton *Breedijk* enroute from Madras, India to Freetown, Sierra Leone with tea, jute and pig iron.
- On October 8, 1942 the *U-68* sank four ships. At 2:31 a.m. she torpedoed and sank the Greek 3,598-ton *Koumoundouros* carrying 5,539 tons of maize; five men died. At 3:46 a.m. the *U-68* sank the Dutch 8,679-ton *Gaasterkerk* sailing in ballast from Alexandria, Egypt to New York. At 8:51 p.m. the *U-68* torpedoed the American 8,207-ton tanker *Swiftsure* carrying 70,000 barrels of diesel oil from Abadan, Iran to Capetown; the ship finally sank sixty-two hours later. At 10:02 p.m. the *U-68* torpedoed and sank the unescorted British 5,271-ton freighter *Sarthe* carrying 6,000 tons of bauxite and pinewood from Port Said, Egypt to Buenos Aires, Argentina.
- On October 9, 1942 Merten sank two ships. At 3:44 a.m. he sank the unescorted American 4,981-ton *Examelia* carrying 5,776 tons of chrome ore, jute and hemp from Colombo, Ceylon to Capetown. At 4:54 a.m. the *U-68* torpedoed and sank the Belgian 5,403-ton *Belgian Fighter* south of Capetown; five men died when the ship carrying general cargo from Abu Zenima, Egypt to Baltimore, Maryland went down.
- On November 6, 1942 at 9:36 p.m. the *U-68* torpedoed and sank the British 8,034-ton *City of Cairo* enroute from Capetown to Pernambuco, Brazil with 7,422 tons of pig iron, timber, wool, cotton, 2,000 boxes of silver coins and 150 passengers. Some 104 people died in the attack.

On November 16, 1942 B.d.U. informed the *U-68* that Karl-Friedrich Merten had been awarded the Oak Leaves to his Knight's Cross. Merten and the *U-68* arrived at Lorient on December 6, 1942; he calculated that on this patrol the *U-68* cruised 17,254 sea-miles on the surface and 553 sea-miles submerged. Merten became the acting commander of the 26th U-boat Training Flotilla at Pillau. The crewmen were sad to see him depart; the *U-68* had been a happy boat; Merten, always concerned about morale, had instituted one cold beer each week on Saturday for every crewman and the men looked forward to the day! On January 30, 1943 *Korvettenkapitän* Karl-Friedrich Merten received the U-boat War Badge with Diamonds. Later in the war he commanded the 24th U-boat Training Flotilla at Memel, where he trained future U-boat commanders using his own excellent combat experience. He survived the war and had a prosperous career in the shipyard and shipbuilding industry. Karl-Friedrich Merten died of cancer at Waldshut-Tiengen in Württemberg on May 2, 1993.

Oberleutnant zur See Albert Lauzemis then took command of the *U-68*. He would take the *U-68* on six war patrols, sinking six enemy ships for a total of 27,847 tons. On one patrol off Puerto Rico, American aircraft kept the U-boat submerged with continuous air attacks for 127 hours over six days. On another patrol, on June 14, 1943 four British Mosquito aircraft strafed the U-boat, wounding the commander and the 2nd Watch Officer and killing another crewman; after that close call the U-boat limped back to port. But her luck ran out on April 10, 1944 northwest of Madeira, Portugal. Avenger and Wildcat aircraft from the American escort aircraft carrier *USS Guadalcanal* found the U-boat and destroyed her with rockets and depth charges. Fifty-six men on the *U-68* perished; only one man survived. The *U-68* was the ninth-most successful U-boat of the war. At some point before the *U-68* made her last voyage, *Obersteuermann* Karl Bade joined the *U-437* as the navigator/quartermaster. The *U-437* was a Type VIIC boat; she was built in the F. Schichau GmbH shipyard at Danzig and commissioned on October 25, 1941. Her first commander, *Kapitänleutnant* Werner-Karl Schulz, operated the U-boat in the 6th U-boat Flotilla based at St. Nazaire. He would command the *U-437* for four war patrols; she did not sink any enemy ships. On December 21, 1942 *Kapitänleutnant* Hermann Lamby assumed command; with this change of command, it is very possible that Bade arrived at the boat then as well. Lamby would command the *U-437* for nine war patrols, some 205 days at sea. While he would not sink any ships, Lamby commanded the *U-437* with great distinction. On the night of April 29, 1943 a British Wellington bomber switched on its Leigh-Light and dropped six bombs on the surfaced boat. The boat was heavily damaged but made its way back to port.

A year later, on April 19, 1944, *Kapitänleutnant* Hermann Lamby received the German Cross in Gold. *Obermaschinenmaat* Friedrich Kowalewsky received a German Cross in Gold on May 3, 1944. Finally on May 9, 1944 *Kapitänleutnant* Carl Emmermann, Knight's Cross with Oak Leaves winner and Commander, 6th U-boat Flotilla, presented the German Cross in Gold to *Obersteuermann* Karl Bade at St. Nazaire, France. The German Cross in Gold was a special award when given to U-boat men. In other services it was often awarded for distinguished combat achievement, and could be given to a U-boat man for a single act of bravery as well. However, a more traditional reason for the award, especially concerning enlisted men, was as a measure to reward longevity – to qualify, a man must have served an aggregate total of 500 days at sea in the U-boat force. Given the dramatic casualty rates, accumulating 500 days at sea in a submarine was almost unthinkable and so those sailors who received the award were highly regarded.

On August 23, 1944 Lamby took the *U-437* from Bordeaux, France to Bergen, Norway as Allied ground troops approached the French port; she arrived at Bergen on September 21. The British Royal Air Force bombed the U-boat base at Bergen on October 4, 1944. The British bombs did not penetrate the heavily protected U-boat bunkers, but the *U-437* was berthed outside that night and was destroyed.

Hermann Lamby was then named to be the commander of the new Type XXI U-boat, *U-3029*, which would be commissioned at Bremen on February 5, 1945. Karl Bade, who had received the U-boat Front Clasp in Bronze on October 11, 1944 for his many patrols, went with Lamby to the new boat as her navigator/quartermaster. The *U-3029* would make no war patrols, but Karl Bade would receive the U-boat Front Clasp in Silver on March 17, 1945 for his service during the entire war in the submarine fleet.

Stabsobersteuermann Johannes Richter was another "Jonah." Born on August 7, 1914 at Kiel, Richter entered the German Navy on July 1, 1934. In 1935 he attended signal school at Flensburg-Mürwik. In 1936 his Navy duties as a signalman in support of the Olympics in Germany earned him the Commemorative Medal for the Olympic Games. Richter was aboard the destroyer *Hermann Schoemann* in 1938 as a *Signalmaat*. He remained on the destroyer through the beginning of the war, receiving the Commemorative Medal for 1 October 1938 (The Annexation of the Sudentenland) on October 17, 1939. In 1940 Richter attended U-boat training. From January 7, 1941 to June 12, 1941 *Signalobermaat* Johannes Richter completed a senior navigator's course (*Obersteuermannslehrgang*) at the Navigator's School (*Steuermannschule*) at Gotenhafen. Richter then joined the crew of the *U-171*. This Type IXC U-boat was launched on July 22, 1941 at the Deutsche Schiff und Maschinenbau AG shipyard at Bremen; she was commissioned on October 25, 1941 with twenty-seven-year-old *Oberleutnant zur See* Günther Pfeffer as her commander. Pfeffer earlier had been 1st Watch Officer to Knight's Cross winner Heinrich Bleichrodt on the *U-67*. From October 1941 to June 1942, the *U-171* was assigned to the 4th U-boat Training Flotilla at Stettin for training.

Dönitz's Crews

***Stabsobersteuermann* Johannes Richter**

Born on August 7, 1914 in Kiel.

Served as navigator/quartermaster on the *U-170* and *U-171*.

Awarded the Iron Cross 2nd Class on October 12, 1942; awarded the U-boat War Badge on October 12, 1942; awarded the Iron Cross 1st Class on December 28, 1943; awarded the U-boat Clasp in Bronze on December 5, 1944; awarded the German Cross in Gold on December 26, 1944.

Spent 511 days at sea on U-boat war patrols.

Survived the war; died July 3, 2005 in Bremen.

On June 17, 1942 the *U-171*, with Johannes Richter as her navigator, departed Kiel for her first war patrol bound for the Gulf of Mexico; she was now under the command of the 10th U-boat Flotilla. The *U-171* refueled north of Bermuda from the *U-460* on July 5 and passed through the Yucatan Channel into the Gulf of Mexico on July 22. Off the coast of Texas near Corpus Christi, at 9:45 a.m. on July 26, 1942 – after two previous torpedoes missed their target – two of the *U-171*'s "eels" slammed into the side of the 4,351-ton Mexican freighter *Oaxaca* carrying general cargo and telephone poles from New Orleans, Louisiana to Vera Cruz, Mexico. Six crewmen died when the ship sank. Pfeffer reported missing a tanker with two torpedoes on July 29; on July 29, 1942 the U-boat found a convoy but was driven under by a U.S. Coast Guard aircraft dropping depth charges.

At 7:50 a.m. on August 13, 1942 south of Isles Dernieres, Louisiana, the *U-171* torpedoed the American tanker *RM Parker Jr.* The tanker, which was in ballast and not loaded with oil, listed to port and the *U-171* surfaced and fired five rounds from her 105-mm deck-gun; the high-explosive rounds set the ship on fire and she sank in shallow water. On September 4, 1942 off the Mexican coast, the *U-171* made a frustrating attack against the Mexican 6,511-ton tanker *Amatlan*. In the early morning hours, Günther Pfeffer fired three spreads of two torpedoes each against the tanker sailing in ballast but all six torpedoes missed. After maneuvering, Pfeffer fired a seventh torpedo from a stern tube that finally hit the *Amatlan*, killing ten men; but the ship would not sink and Pfeffer had to fire three more torpedoes as a coup de grâce before she sank at about 4:30 a.m.

Her torpedoes dwindling, the *U-171* began her return to France sailing into the Caribbean Sea and then proceeded north through the Mona Passage west of Puerto Rico into the Atlantic. On September 24, 1942 the *U-171* refueled from the *U-461*. At 1:00 p.m. on October 9, 1942 the U-boat had transited the Bay of Biscay, and was ordered to rendezvous with a surface escort to complete the last part of her 115-day journey. Pfeffer was two hours early; whether Richter and the helmsman strayed slightly off course or whether there was unknown enemy ordinance on the prescribed route will never be known. Suddenly disaster struck when the U-boat hit a British mine. Twenty-two men died as the *U-171* quickly sank; thirty men, including Johannes Richter, and the U-boat's officers survived, when the surface escort arrived shortly thereafter, fished them out of the water and returned the survivors to land at a U-boat port in France where Johannes Richter, now an *Obersteuermann*, was awarded the U-boat War Badge and the Iron Cross 2nd Class on October 12, 1942.

B.d.U. then made an interesting decision. The survivors of the *U-171* were a cohesive, veteran crew. The *U-170*, a Type IXC/40 boat, had been launched on June 6, 1942 but had yet to be commissioned. Twenty-three survivors of the *U-171* accompanied *Kapitänleutnant* Günther Pfeffer to the new U-boat; the new crew commissioned the *U-170* at Bremen on January 19, 1943. Through May 26, 1943 the *U-170* and her crew were assigned to the 4th U-boat Training Flotilla at Stettin for additional training and preparation for combat. Johannes Richter assumed duties as the boat's navigator and quartermaster.

The U-boat departed Kiel on May 27, 1943 for her first war patrol to the area of the Azores and arrived at Lorient, France on July 9, 1943; the *U-170* sank no enemy ships as she had been diverted from that mission to serve as a provisional tanker for other U-boats during the patrol. During her return to Lorient, however, the *U-170* was in a group with the *U-535* and *U-536* on July 5 when the three surfaced boats were attacked by a British B-24 Liberator; the three U-boats put up a wall of flak that damaged the enemy aircraft, but the plane was able to destroy the *U-535* with all hands. The *U-170* remained in port until August 29, 1943 when she departed Lorient for a lengthy patrol to the South Atlantic off the coast of Brazil. Pfeffer met the *U-621* on September 6 to pick up a new radar detector and refueled from the *U-460* on September 13. On October 23, 1943 the *U-170* caught the 4,663-ton Brazilian freighter *Campos* off Brazil and sank her, killing sixteen of the crew. The *U-170* returned to Lorient on December 23, 1943. Johannes Richter was awarded the Iron Cross 1st Class on December 28, 1943.

After another lengthy overhaul, the *U-170* departed Lorient on February 9, 1944 for operations off Cape Hatteras, North Carolina, but Pfeffer had abysmal luck and the boat returned to Lorient on May 27, 1944. B.d.U. then assigned Günther Pfeffer to other duties and replaced him with the *U-170*'s 1st Watch Officer Hans-Gerold Hauber. At Lorient shipyard engineers fitted the U-boat with a snorkel; the boat departed Lorient on August 4, 1944 for operations off Dakar-Sierra Leone, Africa. For a month the *U-170* found no targets and Hauber decided to return to port; he was directed to take the boat to Norway, but Allied direction-finding operators located the U-boat's position and the U.S. Tenth Fleet took up the chase. On October 25, 1944 aircraft from the American escort aircraft carrier *USS Guadalcanal* found and damaged the *U-170*, but the U-boat escaped. Several days later Hauber reported firing two homing torpedoes at enemy destroyers, but no enemy ships were actually hit. The *U-170* reached Norway on November 30 and then arrived at Flensburg on December 4, 1944. The next day *Stabsobersteuermann* Johannes Richter received the U-boat Clasp in Bronze by order of the commander of the 33rd U-boat Flotilla *Korvettenkapitän* Günther Kuhnke.

The *U-170* would make no more war patrols, but many of her enlisted crew would be honored for distinguished service. On December 12, 1944, *Oberbootsmann* Rudolf Mühlbauer received the Knight's Cross for service on the *U-170* and his previous duties on the *U-123* (see "The Backbone of the Fleet.") On December 26, 1944 more crewmembers were recognized with the award of the German Cross in Gold. *Stabsobersteuermann* Johannes Richter, *Obermaschinist* Rudolf Lautz, *Oberbootsmannsmaat* Gerhard Rädel and *Maschinenmaat* Hans Lehnert received the prestigious award. All could be considered as performing "Jonah-like" feats. Johannes Richter survived the maelstrom of World War II; he died on July 3, 2005 shortly before his ninety-first birthday.

Known Crewmembers for the U-38

Adelhelm	*Funkgefreiter*
Andechser	
Asmus	*Funkgefreiter*
Bade, Karl	*Obermaschinist*
Bade, Karl-Franziskus	*Obersteuermann*
Bartels, Hermann	*Leutnant zur See*
Berg, Erich	*Obermechanikermaat*
Berg, Wilhelm	
Bitter, Georg von	*Oberleutnant zur See*
Bonacker, Arthur	*Obersteuermann*
Breinlinger, Siegfried	*Oberleutnant zur See*
Brüninghaus, Herbert	*Kapitänleutnant*
Buchholz, Helmut	*Leutnant zur See*
Dangschat, Günther	*Kapitänleutnant*
Dierks, Heinrich	*Oberleutnant (Ing)*
Eppen, Günter	*Kapitänleutnant*
Fischer, Hans-Georg	*Fregattenkapitän*
Freund, Herbert	
Gemeiner, Gerth	*Oberleutnant zur See*
Göing, Walter	*Kapitänleutnant*
Grünsiedel, Sepp	*Bootsmaat*
Hampel, Fritz	*Obermaat*
Hanschel	*Oberleutnant zur See*
Hennecke, Heinrich	*Obermaschinenmaat*
Junkers, Georg	*Leutnant zur See*
Keller, Siegfried	*Oberleutnant zur See*
Kranz, Fritz	
Kreglinger, Eduard	
Kretschmer, Heinz	*Obermaschinist*
Krüger, Ferdinand	
Krutin, Manfred	
Kühn, Herbert	*Oberleutnant zur See*
Landfermann, Karl-August	*Kapitänleutnant (Ing)*
Lasser, Franz	*Funkmaat*
Laubert, Helmut	*Kapitänleutnant*
Laurenz, Dr. Fritz	*Arzt*
Liebe, Heinrich	*Fregattenkapitän*
Linnenbaum, Franz	*Obermaschinist*
Lüth, Wolfgang	*Kapitän zur See*
Merten, Karl-Friedrich	*Kapitän zur See*
Möllendorff, Goske von	*Kapitänleutnant*
Müller, Hans	*Kapitänleutnant (Ing)*
Nickel, Hans	*Oberleutnant (Ing)*
Peitz, Wilhelm	*Maschinenobergefreiter*
Peters, Fritz	*Obergefreiter*
Peters, Georg	*Korvettenkapitän*
Ratsch, Heinrich	*Kapitänleutnant*
Ratsch, Werner	*Obermechanikermaat*
Reibnitz, Hans	*Kapitänleutnant (Ing)*
Reim, Willi	*Maschinenmaat*
Rosenstiel, Jürgen von	*Kapitänleutnant*
Sander, Paul	*Oberleutnant zur See*
Schmidt, Dietrich	
Schmidt, Erich	
Schmidt, Heinrich	
Schroeter, Karl-Ernst	*Korvettenkapitän*
Schuch, Heinrich	*Fregattenkapitän*
Spitzley, Erich	*Matrosenobergefreiter*
Steinmetz, Ludwig	*Oberleutnant (Ing)*
Thomas, Johannes	*Oberleutnant (Ing)*
Wagener, Hugo	*Obermaschinenmaat*
Wagner, Hugo	*Mechanikerobergefreiter*
Weder, Rolf	*Hauptgefreiter*
Wendt, Emil-Werner	*Matrosenobergefreiter*
Wilshusen, Edmund	*Obermaschinenmaat*
Zander, Helmut	*Oberleutnant (Ing)*
Zesch	*Funkmaat*
Ziesmer, Reimar	*Kapitänleutnant*

Known Crewmembers for the U-68

Adamczack, Stephan	*Oberfunkmaat*
Adelsbach, Helmut	*Maschinenmaat*
Anter, Egon	*Leutnant zur See*
Bade, Karl-Franziskus	*Obersteuermann*
Baumann, Gottlieb	*Maschinenmaat*
Berner, Eberhard	
Betz, Karl	*Oberleutnant zur See*
Beunle, Hermann	
Bonin, Rudolf	*Maschinenobergefreiter*
Brachmann	
Brauweiler, Herbert	*Maschinenmaat*
Brunemann, Ewald	*Obermaschinist*
Buder, Erich	*Matrosenobergefreiter*
Bulla, Wilhelm	*Funkgefreiter*
Bungartz, Dr. Johannes	*Arzt*
Buthge, Walter	*Oberbootsmaat*
Christoph	
Deichmann, Max	*Matrosenobergefreiter*
Deska, Albert	*Oberbootsmaat*
Dingel, Otto	*Maschinenobergefreiter*
Dressel, Walter	*Maschinenobergefreiter*
Durre	*Mechanikerobergefreiter*
Eichel, Wilhelm	*Obermaschinenmaat*
Engelhard, Jürgen von	*Kapitänleutnant (Ing)*
Falkenberg, Karl	
Feilscher	
Fiacre	*Maschinenmaat*
Frech, Ludwig	*Maschinengefreiter*
Freund, Günter	*Leutnant zur See*
Friebe, Artur	*Matrosenobergefreiter*
Gardemann, Heinz	*Obermaschinenmaat*
Geest, Ernst	*Matrosenobergefreiter*
Gerhardt, Christian	*Matrosenobergefreiter*
Gerltzer, Eduard	*Matrosenobergefreiter*
Gerth, Günter	*Obermaschinenmaat*
Grebener	*Maschinenmaat*
Grezian, Gerhard	*Bootsmaat*
Griese, Walter	*Obersteuermann*
Guth	*Mechanikermaat*
Hänert, Klaus	*Kapitänleutnant*
Happe, Werner	*Oberleutnant zur See*
Hedtfeld	*Maschinenobermaat*
Heese, Heinz-Otto	*Leutnant zur See*
Heilborn, Karl	
Hein, Kurt-Ewald	*Maschinenmaat*
Heinz, Herbert	*Maschinenmaat*
Heldt, Heinz	*Mechanikermaat*
Helmig, Herbert	
Herrmann, Konstantin	*Obermaschinenmaat*
Herrmann, Werner	*Mechanikerobergefreiter*
Hertmanni	*Maschinenmaat*
Hinsche, Willi	*Maschinenobergefreiter*

Hölzer, Paul	
Hoffmann	*Matrosenobergefreiter*
Husing, Wilhelm	*Obermaschinist*
Jansky, Alois	*Sanitätsobermaat*
Jepsen, Helmut	*Bootsmaat*
Jünger, Heinz	
Jürgens, Gunther	*Maschinengefreiter*
Kantmann, Johann	*Matrosenobergefreiter*
Kastrup, Hans	*Matrosengefreiter*
Klaunig, Bernhard	*Kapitänleutnant (Ing)*
Klembt, Karl	
Kluth, Wilhelm	*Bootsmaat*
Knoppe, Fritz	*Maschinenobergefreiter*
Köhler, Wilhelm	*Matrose*
König, Hans	*Maschinenmaat*
Koltz, Fritz	*Maschinenobergefreiter*
Konrad, Bruno	*Maschinenobergefreiter*
Kopp, Willi	*Matrosenobergefreiter*
Krahe, Hans	*Oberfunkmaat*
Krebs, Franz	*Maschinenobergefreiter*
Kröck, Heinrich	*Bootsmaat*
Kuczwalski, Heinz	*Mechanikerobergefreiter*
Kult, Wilhelm	
Kurowski, Alex	*Obersteuermann*
Lauzemis, Albert	*Kapitänleutnant*
Lebek, Richard	
Leja, Georg	*Funkobergefreiter*
Lenzen, Hans	*Bootsmaat*
Limbrunner, Max	
Linnenberg, Heinrich	*Maschinenobergefreiter*
Linnenweber, Ferdinand	
Löhr, Josef	*Maschinenobergefreiter*
Lüdmann, Heinrich	*Obersteuermann*
Malm, Hans	*Mechanikermaat*
Mannheller, Wilhelm	*Oberleutnant zur See*
Maus, August	*Kapitänleutnant*
Merten, Karl-Friedrich	*Kapitän zur See*
Meyer, Rolf	*Oberleutnant zur See*
Meyer, Walter	*Oberleutnant zur See*
Nechyba, Wilhelm	*Funkobergefreiter*
Neu, Kurt	*Maschinenmaat*
Nobbe, Karl-Heinz	*Matrosenobergefreiter*
Ossig	*Maschinenmaat*
Ostkop, Erich	*Matrosengefreiter*
Pastofski, Rudi	*Obersteuermann*
Paulnik, Fritz	*Obermaschinenmaat*
Penner, Ludwig	*Oberfunkmaat*
Peters, Silvester	*Leutnant zur See*
Pommerenke, Walter	*Matrosenobergefreiter*
Popp, Friedrich	*Mechanikerobergefreiter*
Preuschopt, Günther	
Rabies, Maximilian	*Matrosenobergefreiter*
Reimund, Alfred	*Maschinenobergefreiter*
Rempel	*Maschinenmaat*
Renner, Walter	*Maschinenobergefreiter*
Rössner, Georg	*Mechanikermaat*
Schaumburg, Hans	*Obergefreiter*
Schendel	*Maschinenmaat*
Scherraus, Ekkehard	*Oberleutnant zur See*
Schmelzle, Alfred	*Stabsobermaschinist*
Schmidt, Lorenz	*Maschinenobergefreiter*
Schmidtke, Max	*Matrosenobergefreiter*
Schneider, Walter	
Schöns, Erich	
Schroller, Alfred	*Maschinenobergefreiter*
Schubert	*Maschinenmaat*
Schuler, Georg	*Maat*
Schuster, Heinrich	*Maschinenmaat*
Schwing	*Matrosenobergefreiter*
Seehausen, Gerhard	*Oberleutnant zur See*
Sendler, Dr. Ulrich	*Arzt*
Sonnenburg, Heinz	*Mechanikermaat*
Stahn, Heinz	*Mechanikerobergefreiter*
Stobbe, Ernst	*Oberleutnant zur See*
Stöhr	*Maschinenmaat*
Szeszka, Manfred	*Matrosengefreiter*
Thomas, Karl	
Uhlending, Anton	*Stabsobersteuermann*
Veit, Karl	*Obermaschinist*
Vogelsang, Hubert	*Bootsmaat*
Vogt, Paul	*Maschinenobergefreiter*
Volmari, Franz	*Oberleutnant (Ing)*
Warner, Richard	*Obermaat*
Weigand	*Matrosenobergefreiter*
Wex, Günter	*Leutnant zur See*
Wiemer, Werner	*Obermaschinist*
Wille, Hans	*Obersteuermann*
Zander, Gerhard	*Maschinenmaat*
Zorbel, Fritz	*Obermaat*

Known Crewmembers for the U-170

Ahnert, Gottfried	*Obermechanikersmaat*
Andre, Thomas-Michael	
Bader, Horst	*Oberleutnant zur See*
Bauer, Fritz	
Beck, Kurt	
Bedey, Wilhelm	
Belgar, Kurt	
Böhme, Hans	
Bossmann, Erhard	
Brat, Walter	
Calmaro, Arthur	*Leutnant (Ing)*
Clausen, Dr. Claus	*Arzt*
Clasussen, Hans	
Danzer, Wolfgang	*Mechanikersmaat*
Dingeldein, Otto	*Kapitänleutnant (Ing)*
Dorn, Heinz	
Dralle, Adolf	
Engel-Emden, Siegfried	
Fessler, Otto	
Frank, Karl-Heinz	
Fuchslocher, Lothar	
Gräber, Willi	
Greiner, Karl	*Obermaschinist*
Groh, Oskar	
Hädel, Gerhard	*Oberbootsmaat*
Hartmann, Curt	*Oberleutnant zur See*
Hauber, Hans-Gerold	*Oberleutnant zur See*
Heber, Emil	
Hemmen, Heinz	*Leutnant zur See*
Höllwerth, Johann	*Maschinist*
Justenhoven, Heinz	
Kaim, Ludwig	
Kalfak, Rudi	

Klausecker, Josef	
Kniep, Albert	*Oberleutnant zur See*
Kurztusch, Erich	
Laube, Dr. Alfred	*Arzt*
Lautz, Rudolf	*Obermaschinist*
Lehnert, Johannes	*Maschinenmaat*
Liss, Horst	
Mahler, Werner	
Manke, Walter	
Mannacher, Hans	
May, Jacob	
Meise, Hermann	
Mertens, Josef	
Methmann, Otto	
Michael, Rolf	
Mühlbauer, Rudolf	*Oberbootsmann*
Müller, Fritz	*Matrosenhauptgefreiter*
Oedekofen, Otto	
Orywol, Kurt	*Maschinengefreiter*
Pazelt, Karl	
Petersen, Peter	*Bootsmaat*
Pfeffer, Günther	*Kapitänleutnant*
Pommering, Fritz	
Prediger, Willi	
Preisendörfer, Richard	
Prestel, Alois	
Quachigroch, Eduard	
Rabbe, Erich	
Rack, Josef	
Rädel, Gerhard	*Bootsmaat*
Radtke, Helmut	
Raulf, Fritz	
Richter, Johannes	*Stabsobersteuermann*
Rogowski, Erwin	
Ruffin, Heinrich	
Schlüter, Achim	*Oberleutnant zur See*
Schmidt, Kurt	*Oberleutnant (Ing)*
Weigel, Felix	*Leutnant zur See*
Wolf, Hermann	
Wörle, Engelbert	
Wüstermann, Karl	
Ziska, Paul	

Known Crewmembers for the U-171

Bart, Walter	
Böhme, Hans	
Borowicz, Herbert	*Matrosenobergefreiter*
Bräutigam, Viktor	*Maschinengefreiter*
Brosch, Wilhelm	*Maschinengefreiter*
Danzer, Wolfgang	*Mechanikersmaat*
Dattenberg, Herbert	*Maschinengefreiter*
Dieter, Wilhelm	*Bootsmaat*
Dingeldein, Otto	*Kapitänleutnant (Ing)*
Dorn, Heinz	
Ebbinghaus, Heinz	*Obermaschinist*
Eisenschmid, Wilhelm	*Maschinenmaat*
Engel-Emden, Siegfried	
Friedrich, Karl	
Geckeler, Rolf	*Steuermann*
Greiner, Karl	*Obermaschinist*
Grützmacher, Johannes	*Maschinenmaat*
Hartmann, Curt	*Oberleutnant zur See*
Heber, Emil	
Hemmen, Heinz	*Leutnant zur See*
Höllwarth, Hans	
Klein, Erwin	*Maschinengefreiter*
Klocke, Herbert	*Maschinenobergefreiter*
Kniep, Albert	*Oberleutnant zur See*
Kraus, Wilhelm	
Kunze, Kurt	*Matrose*
Lau, Kurt	*Oberleutnant zur See*
Manke, Walter	
May, Jacob	
Methmann, Otto	
Müller, Fritz	*Matrosenhauptgefreiter*
Niggemann, Fritz	*Maschinengefreiter*
Nolte, Helmut	*Funkmaat*
Oedekofen, Otto	
Olekers, Heinz	*Maschinengefreiter*
Orywol, Kurt	*Maschinengefreiter*
Pfeffer, Günther	*Kapitänleutnant*
Rädel, Gerhard	*Bootsmaat*
Raulf, Fritz	
Richter, Johannes	*Stabsobersteuermann*
Sass, Werner	*Kapitänleutnant*
Schader, Hans	*Maschinenmaat*
Schertel, Nikolaus	*Maschinenmaat*
Sprick, Heinz	*Maschinenmaat*
Ströhlein, Erich	*Matrosenobergefreiter*
Strohm, Gerhard	*Matrosengefreiter*
Thölke, Herbert	*Maschinengefreiter*
Uschkoreit, Kurt	*Matrosenobergefreiter*
Wagner, Bruno	*Maschinengefreiter*
Wohlfahrt, Gerhard	*Matrosengefreiter*
Wörle, Engelbert	
Wüstermann, Karl	
Ziska, Paul	

Known Crewmembers for the U-437

Atwater	*Bootsmann*
Bade, Karl-Franziskus	*Obersteuermann*
Bald, Helmut	*Matrose*
Bieder, Friedrich-Wilhelm	*Leutnant zur See*
Bubser, Paul	*Mechanikermaat*
Bugl, Josef	*Maschinenobergefreiter*
Busche, Heinz	*Oberleutnant (Ing)*
Dörr, Alois	*Maschinengefreiter*
Falke, Friedrich	*Funkmaat*
Feldmann, Heinrich	*Oberleutnant (Ing)*
Förster, Erich	*Maschinengefreiter*
Gerhardus, Emil	*Bootsmaat*
Heyne, Friedrich-Wilhelm	*Oberleutnant zur See*
Hoffmann, Erich-Michael	*Oberleutnant zur See*
Jeschke, Hubert	*Oberleutnant zur See*
Joukel, Rudolf	*Funker*
Knubbertz, Josef	*Matrose*
Kowalewsky, Fritz	*Obermaschinist*
Lamby, Hermann	*Kapitänleutnant*
Leinemann, Heinrich	*Obermaschinist*
Liermann, Rudolf	*Maschinenobergefreiter*
Loeder, Herbert	*Oberleutnant zur See*
Marx, Eberhard	*Oberleutnant zur See*
Plate, Dr. Karl-Heinrich	*Oberleutnant zur See*
Rettkowski, Heinz	*Matrose*

Riekhoff	*Obersteuermann*
Rohrbeck	*Obermaat*
Romig, Kurt	*Matrosenobergefreiter*
Ruhm, Wilhelm	*Obermaat*
Sambolz, Otto	*Matrose*
Schmich, Helmut	*Mechanikerobergefreiter*
Schneider, Robert	*Funker*
Schultz, Erwin	*Maschinenmaat*
Schulz, Werner-Karl	*Korvettenkapitän*
Schwender, Edgar	*Funkmaat*
Sehl, Walter	*Oberleutnant (Ing)*
Steinschulte, Friedrich	*Oberleutnant (Ing)*
Voss, Wilhelm	*Bootsmaat*
Wichertt, Helmut	*Maschinenobergefreiter*
Wolff, Heinz	*Kapitänleutnant*

Known Crewmembers for the U-3029

Bade, Karl-Franziskus	*Obersteuermann*
Busche, Heinz	*Oberleutnant (Ing)*
Feldmann, Heinrich	*Oberleutnant (Ing)*
Hausen, Paul	*Leutnant (Ing)*
Lamby, Hermann	*Kapitänleutnant*
Niemeyer	*Leutnant (Ing)*
Plate, Dr. Karl-Heinrich	*Oberleutnant zur See*
Reichstein	*Leutnant zur See*
Romig, Kurt	*Matrosenobergefreiter*

Sources, "Jonah:" Clay Blair, *Hitler's U-boat War: The Hunters, 1939-1942*, New York: Random House, 1996, 82, 85, 634, 635, 636, 638; Clay Blair, *Hitler's U-boat War: The Hunted, 1942-1945*, New York: Modern Library, 2000, 317, 358, 407, 563, 621; Jochen Brennecke, *The Hunters and the Hunted*, translated by R. H. Stevens, New York: W. W. Norton and Company, 1957, 152, 153; Manfred Dörr, *Die Ritterkreuzträger der U-Boot-Waffe, Band 1: A-J, Band 2: L-Z*, Osnabrück, FRG: Biblio Verlag, 1988, Band 2 – 82, 83, 84, 114, 115, 116, 117, 136, 376; Michael Gannon, *Operation Drumbeat: The Dramatic True Story of Germany's First U-boat Attacks Along the American Coast in World War II*, New York: Harper & Row, 1990, 32; Georg Högel, *Embleme, Wappen, And Malings Deutscher U-Boote 1939-1945*, Herford, Deutschland: Koehler, 1987, 44, 45; Herbert Ritschel, *Kurzfassung Kriegstagebücher deutscher U-boote 1939-1945, Band 1: KTB U1 – U50*, Norderstedt, Germany: Books on Demand, 239-258; Herbert Ritschel, *Kurzfassung Kriegstagebücher deutscher U-boote 1939-1945, Band 2: KTB U51 – U99*, Norderstedt, Germany: Books on Demand, 163-189; Herbert Ritschel, *Kurzfassung Kriegstagebücher deutscher U-boote 1939-1945, Band 3: KTB U171 – U222*, Norderstedt, Germany: Books on Demand, 5, 6; Theodore P. Savas, Editor, *Silent Hunters: German U-boat Commanders of World War II*, Campbell, CA: Savas Publishing, 1997, 20, 39, 40, 41; Jak Mallmann Showell, *U-boats at War: Landings on Hostile Shores*, Hersham, England: Ian Allan Publishing, 2000, 15, 16, 18; www.ubootwaffe.net; www.uboatarchive.net.

Preparing for war, August 1939, U-38 – (left) Commander Heinrich Liebe, (middle) 1st Watch Officer Wolfgang Lüth, and (right) Chief of the Boat. *Liebe accounted for 187,267 tons of Allied shipping during the war, while Lüth sank 225,204 tons. This photo and most others shown in this chapter are from a collection of pictures taken on the first war patrol of the U-38, August-September 1939, compiled by future German Cross in Gold winner Karl Bade.*

Preparing for war, August 1939, U-38 – 1st Watch Officer Wolfgang Lüth. *Lüth was partial to wearing a checked shirt at sea.*

Preparing for war, August 1939, U-38 – (left) 1st Watch Officer Wolfgang Lüth, (right) Commander Heinrich Liebe.

Preparing for war, August 1939, U-38 – crewmen on the dock.

Preparing for war, August 1939, U-38 – crewmen sitting on the deck of the U-38.

Preparing for war, August 1939 – U-38 and U-39 receiving supplies. *The U-38 departed Wilhelmshaven on August 19 and headed to the Atlantic off Portugal. The U-39 departed the same day for operations off Ireland. She became the first U-boat sunk in the war when attacked on September 14, 1939 by the British destroyers HMS Faulknor, HMS Foxhound and HMS Firedrake.*

Preparing for war, August 1939, U-37 receiving supplies. *The U-37 departed Wilhelmshaven on August 19 for operations in the Atlantic. On the quay is a military motorcycle.*

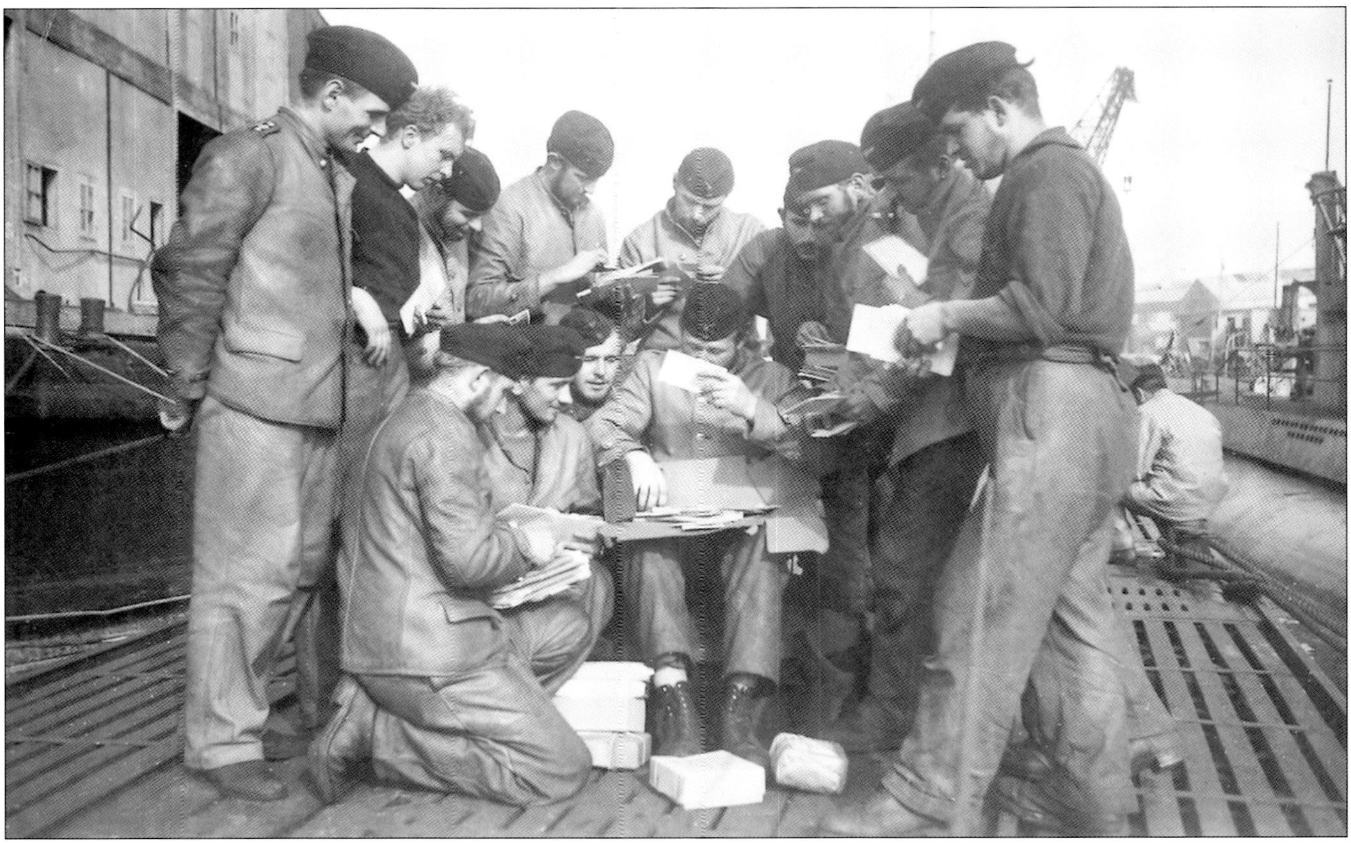

Preparing for war, August 1939, U-38 – crewmen on the deck as a non-commissioned officer passes out mail. *Sailors are wearing two-piece leather U-boat outer garments.*

Preparing for war, August 1939, U-38 – seven crewmen on the deck. *Sailors are wearing cap-band U-boat Flotilla Hundius.*

Preparing for war, August 1939, U-38 – crewmen on the deck in formation in white caps.

Preparing for war, August 1939, U-38 – Chief of the Boat on the bridge.

First War Patrol, August-September 1939, U-38 – First Officer Wolfgang Lüth (second from left) with watch personnel crewmen on the dock.

First War Patrol, August-September 1939, U-38 – Chief Engineer overseeing the helmsmen in the control room.

First War Patrol, August-September 1939, U-38 – 1st Watch Officer Wolfgang Lüth (left) with crewmen on the bridge at sea.

First War Patrol, August-September 1939, U-38 – view from the bridge at sea.

First War Patrol, August-September 1939, U-38 – crewmen scan the horizon with binoculars at sea.

First War Patrol, August-September 1939, U-38 – crew on the bridge in Wilhelmshaven harbor. *White caps got dirty easily.*

First War Patrol, August-September 1939, U-38 – view aft from the bridge at sea. *Anti-aircraft gun mount is visible; the weapon was stored inside the boat when not in use to protect it from the elements.*

First War Patrol, August-September 1939, U-38 – watch crew at dusk. *One crewman wears the physical training uniform.*

First War Patrol, August-September 1939, U-38 – blurred photo of crewman in the control room probably during a dive.

First War Patrol, August-September 1939, U-38 – crewman next to the periscope. *He also wears the U-boat Flotilla Hundius cap-band.*

First War Patrol, August-September 1939, U-38 – boat diving. *View is to the aft of the boat.*

First War Patrol, August-September 1939, U-38 – crewman in foul weather gear keeps watch. *View is foreward including the deck-gun; deck is awash.*

First War Patrol, August-September 1939, U-38 – another view foreward from the bridge. *The boat appears to be beginning to dive.*

First War Patrol, August-September 1939, U-38 – attack periscope viewed from the bridge.

First War Patrol, August-September 1939, U-38 – rough weather. *It is easy to see how crewmen could be swept overboard and how deck-gun was impossible to man in rough seas.*

First War Patrol, September 11, 1939, U-38 – the British 9,456-ton motor tanker Inverliffey carrying 13,000 tons of gasoline.

First War Patrol, September 11, 1939, U-38 – torpedo explosion starts fire on the Inverliffey.

First War Patrol, September 11, 1939, U-38 – view of the destruction of the Inverliffey from the bridge of the U-38. *1st Watch Officer Wolfgang Lüth observes the action.*

First War Patrol, September 11, 1939, U-38 – first torpedo from the U-38 strikes the Inverliffey.

First War Patrol, September 11, 1939, U-38 – Inverliffey burning out of control.

First War Patrol, September 1939, U-38 – lifeboat, probably from the Inverliffey, approaches the U-38.

First War Patrol, September 1939, U-38 – lifeboat nears the U-38 as sailor waves.

First War Patrol, September 1939, U-38 – crewmen from a lifeboat, probably from the Inverliffey, begin to board the U-38.

First War Patrol, September 11, 1939, U-38 – lifeboat from U.S. tanker RG Stewart approaches the U-38. *The U-boat stopped the RG Stewart by a shot fired across her bow about 253 miles west of Ushant, France.*

First War Patrol, September 1939, U-38 – crewmen from a lifeboat, probably from the Inverliffey, prepare to come aboard the U-38. *Officer at the front of the lifeboat appears to be the ship's master, William Trowsdale.*

First War Patrol, September 1939, U-38 – crewmen on the aft of the U-38; facial expressions do not seem to show much apprehension.

First War Patrol, September 11, 1939, U-38 – U.S. tanker RG Stewart.

First War Patrol, September 1939, U-38 – lifeboat off the stern of the U-38.

First War Patrol, September 11, 1939, U-38 – close-up of U.S. tanker RG Stewart. *American flag is prominently displayed on the side of the ship.*

Deck gun on the U-38 in winter weather. *Photo taken in the Jade Bay. In the background appears to be a heavy cruiser.*

U-38 navigating the Kaiser Wilhelm Canal in heavy ice.

Crewmen of the U-38 during winter. *Karl Bade is on the left.*

Conning tower emblem of the U-38 – Cupid drawing his bow while seated on a torpedo. *Design was painted on the boat in the November-December 1939 timeframe.*

Karl Bade (middle) on the bridge of a U-boat.

Karl Bade bundled up for cold weather on watch on the bridge of a U-boat.

Karl Bade with another U-boat sailor relaxing on shore in 1943.

Karl Bade after receiving German Cross in Gold. *Photo taken on May 9, 1944 at St. Nazaire, France. Photo probably a post-war copy of an original.*

Karl Bade (left) and Kapitänleutnant Carl Emmermann (right) Knight's Cross with Oak Leaves winner and Commander, 6th U-boat Flotilla. *Photo taken during award ceremony for the German Cross in Gold to Karl Bade on May 9, 1944 at St. Nazaire. Photo probably a post-war copy of an original.*

Karl Bade (center) with German Cross in Gold. *Photo taken during award ceremony for the German Cross in Gold to Karl Bade on May 9, 1944 at St. Nazaire. Photo probably a post-war copy of an original.*

Heinrich Liebe, commander of the U-38. *Postcard signed during the war.*

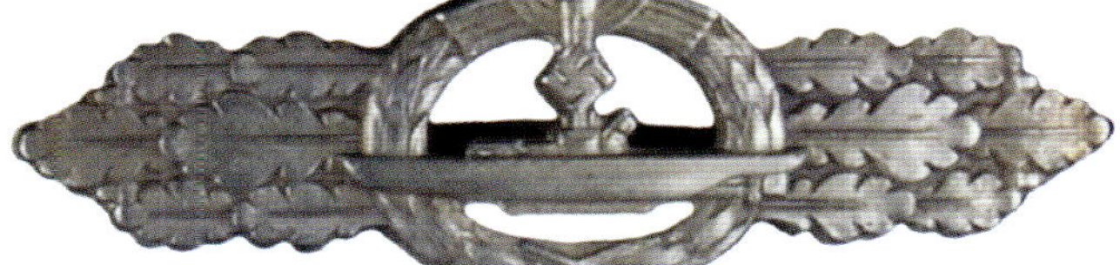

U-boat Front Clasp in Bronze awarded to Johannes Richter of the U-170. *The U-boat Front Clasp was awarded to holders of the U-boat War Badge to recognize continued combat service and valor. It was instituted on May 15, 1944; there were no fixed merits to earn the award, but was based on the recommendations of the U-boat commander and subject to approval by Admiral Dönitz and could include days at sea on war patrols, the number of war patrols completed and outstanding acts of service.*

U-boat Front Clasp in Bronze awarded to Johannes Richter (reverse.) *Wilhelm Ernst Peekhaus designed the award, which was composed of a laurel wreath surrounding a submarine, surmounted by the national emblem. On each side there were three rows of oak leaves; the two crossed swords at the base of the wreath emphasized the military nature of the award. All classes of the badge were manufactured in zinc; this particular award is the relatively rare first variant that was die-stamped (later version was die-cast). On the left side of the reverse of the first version of the badge is the word "ENTW" above the word "PEEKHAUS", which is above the word "BERLIN." On the right hand side are also three lines of words; the top is "AUSF.", the second line is "SCHWERIN" and the third line is "BERLIN SW68."*

Karl-Friedrich Merten, commander of the U-68. *Postcard signed during the war.*

Johannes Richter at sea. *(Photo courtesy of U-boat Archive & Museum, Cuxhaven, Germany.)*

CHAPTER THREE

"The Bull of Scapa Flow"
U-47
1939-1941

The welders, electrical engineers, diesel mechanics and other technicians of the Krupp Germaniawerft AG shipyards at Kiel-Gaarden had no idea that the U-boat they began building in 1937 and would launch on October 29, 1938 – the *U-47* – would become the most famous German U-boat of World War II. Nor did the trainers of the boat's crew, prior to her commissioning on December 17, 1938, realize they were working with men who in just ten months would become the toast of Germany. If anyone had an inkling of greatness ahead, it might have been Karl Dönitz concerning the *U-47*'s skipper, Günther Prien. Born on January 16, 1908 at Osterfeld/Thuringia, Prien was a little older than the other aspiring officers who joined the *Kriegsmarine* in 1933; he had served in the merchant marine fleet for ten years previously – perhaps this additional experience and maturity brought him to the attention of the U-boat chief. In his memoirs, Karl Dönitz summarized his feelings toward Günther Prien:

> "Prien was all that a man should be, a great personality, full of zest and energy and the joy of life, wholly dedicated to his service and an example to all who served under him ... In war, notwithstanding his sudden leap to fame and popularity after the Scapa Flow exploit, he remained a simple, frank and courageous fighting man, intent only on doing his job and adding to his exploits. I held him in great affection and esteem."

Dönitz's Crews
***Korvettenkapitän* Günther Prien**
Born on January 16, 1908 in Osterfeld, Thuringia.
Served as the Commander of the *U-47*.
Awarded the Knight's Cross on October 18, 1939 and the Knight's Cross with Oak Leaves on October 20, 1940.
Spent 238 days at sea on U-boat war patrols.
Killed in action on March 8, 1941 in the Atlantic Ocean south of Iceland.

Prien's march toward "the Scapa Flow exploit" actually started shortly before the war began, when in the small U-boat service he became well-known by the nickname "*Brauseköpfchen*" ("the little blusterer"). He was promoted to *Kapitänleutnant* on February 1, 1939 and continued preparing his boat for possible future combat. On August 19, 1939 the *U-47* – a Type VIIB U-boat – left Kiel under the command of *Kapitänleutnant* Günther Prien for operations in the North Atlantic; the operation became her first war patrol on September 1, 1939, when Germany invaded Poland and World War II began in Europe. The *U-47* would sink three ships on this first war patrol. On September 5, 1939 at 8:15 a.m., northwest of Portugal, the *U-47* sank the British 2,407-ton *Bosnia* carrying sulphur from Licata, Sicily to Manchester; one crewman perished in the attack. The next day, on September 6, 1939 at 2:20 p.m., southwest of Ireland with torpedoes and deck-gun fire, the *U-47* sank the British 4,086-ton *Rio Claro* bound from Sunderland to Montevideo, Uruguay with a load of coal. At 5:47 p.m. on September 7, 1939 the *U-47* sank the British 1,777-ton *Gartavon* with 88-mm deck-gun fire south of Ireland; she was carrying 4,200 tons of sugar from La Goulette, Tunisia to the Clyde, Scotland. Günther Prien arrived back at Kiel on September 15, 1939. For his achievements on the patrol he received the Iron Cross 2nd Class on September 25, 1939, as did his 1st Watch Officer Engelbert Endrass and Chief Engineer Johann Wessels.

From the outset of the war, Admiral Dönitz always had in mind the idea of an operation against the British fleet at Scapa Flow in the Orkney Islands of Scotland. World War I German Imperial Navy U-boat commanders von Hennig and Emsland attempted, but failed in their attempts against the strongly guarded base, due in part to extremely difficult problems in currents. Given that the top submerged speed of a U-boat was about seven knots and that routine currents in the Pentland Firth exceeded that speed, it was obvious that a U-boat entering the area would have severe difficulties – not to mention defeating the nets, minefields, booms, guard-ships and surface patrols that protected the anchorage.

However, a conversation shortly after the outbreak of the war with a B.d.U. staff officer, *Kapitänleutnant* Victor Oehrn, convinced Dönitz an attempt could be made. From there events moved quickly. Roughly a week later, on September 11, 1939 *Luftwaffe* reconnaissance aircraft from the 2nd Air Fleet photographed heavy and light enemy warships in the anchorage. *Kapitänleutnant* Horst Wellner, commander of the *U-14*, reported to Dönitz on the conclusion of his war patrol to the Orkneys on September 29. In addition to providing information on the prevailing currents, lighting and patrol activity, Wellner offered his opinion that a boat could penetrate into Scapa Flow through the Hoxa Sound if the booms were open. Dönitz wasn't quite convinced and requested that the 2nd Air Fleet conduct an additional mission to the area and provide detailed photographs of all the obstacles guarding the various entrances to Scapa Flow. On September 26, Dönitz received a set of excellent photographs, which led him to the following conclusion in the B.d.U. war diary:

> "Holm Sound is completely blocked by two merchant ships, apparently sunk, which lie diagonally across the channel of Kirk Sound, and a third vessel to the north of the other two. To the south thereof and running as far as Lamb Holm is a narrow channel about fifty feet wide, in which the depth is 3 1/2 fathoms and on either side of which are shallows. To the north of the merchant ships is a further small channel. The shore on both sides is practically uninhabited. Here, I think, it would certainly be possible to penetrate – by night, on the surface at slack water. The main difficulties will be navigational."

Having decided on how to conduct the attack, Dönitz had to now select exactly the right commander; his first choice was Günther Prien of the *U-47*. On the submarine tender *Weichsel* at Kiel harbor Dönitz gave Prien the entire file on the operation, asked him to read it carefully and to think it over before volunteering for such a dangerous undertaking. Prien accepted the next day.

On October 4, 1939 Dönitz withdrew all U-boats operating off the Orkneys in order to avoid arousing alarm or suspicion in the target area. On October 8, 1939 at 11:00 a.m., the *U-47* left Kiel under the command of Günther Prien. He submerged the following day south of Dogger Bank, staying out of sight until night when the U-boat surfaced and proceeded toward the Orkney Islands. By October 10 the *U-47* was north of Dogger Bank and again Prien submerged the boat during the day and only surfaced and continued northwest after dark. On October 11, 1939 the *U-47* had reached Devil's Hole; during that day the boat lay submerged off the Orkneys. Prien surfaced that evening and approached the coast in order to fix his exact position. Through October 13 the *U-47* lay submerged in ninety meters of water east of the Orkneys; the crew slept until 4:00 p.m., ate breakfast at 5:00 p.m. Meanwhile, the Chief Engineer Johann Wessels determined that the lubricating oil of the diesel engines contained seawater and had to fabricate a solution – he did after several hours and the mission continued. The war log of the *U-47* continued the account:

> "After warm supper for entire crew, set course for Holm Sound. Everything goes according to plan until 2307 [11:07 p.m.], when it is necessary to submerge on sighting a merchant ship just before Rose Ness. I cannot make out the ship in either of the periscopes, in spite of the very clear night and the bright lights. At 2331 [11:31 p.m.], surfaced again and entered Holm Sound. Following [the] tide. On nearer approach, the sunken blockship in Skerry Sound is clearly visible, so that at first I believe myself to be already in Kirk Sound, and prepare for work. But the navigator, by means of dead reckoning, states that the preparations are premature, while I at the same time realize the mistake, for there is only one sunken ship in the straits. By altering course hard to starboard, the imminent danger is averted. A few minutes later, Kirk Sound is clearly visible."

Prien, who had memorized the charts of the sound, decided to pass the blockships on the northern side. The Northern Lights provide more illumination than Prien desired and he feared being spotted. On the bridge of the surfaced boat were Prien, his 1st Watch Officer Engelbert Endrass and the 2nd Watch Officer Amelung von Varendorff. Below in the control room Wessels and *Obersteuermann* Wilhelm Spahr, the boat's navigator, tracked the U-boat's course. His war log continued:

> "On a course of 270 I pass the two-masted schooner, which is lying on a bearing of 315 in front of the real boom, with 15 meters to spare. In the next minute the boat is turned by the current to starboard. At the same time I recognize the cable of the northern blockship at an angle of 45 degrees ahead. Port engine stopped, starboard engine slow ahead, and rudder hard to port, the boat slowly touches bottom. The stern still touches the cable, the boat becomes free, it is pulled round to port, and brought on to course again with difficult rapid maneuvering, but we are in Scapa Flow."

Once inside the anchorage, Prien began to line up his targets. At 12:58 a.m., Prien gave the command to launch all four torpedoes from the bow tubes, two at the northern target (which he believed was the battleship *HMS Repulse*) and two at the southern (*HMS Royal Oak*). Only three of the four torpedoes launched, as there was a problem with the firing mechanism on tube four. After waiting about three and a half minutes, the crew heard a single explosion. Assuming that the northern target (in reality the old aircraft carrier *HMS Pegasus*) had been struck, Prien gave the command to turn around and fire the stern torpedo; it launched, but missed. Unknown to Prien, the first torpedo had in fact hit the *HMS Royal Oak* at 1:04 a.m.

Unsatisfied with the results and not under pressure by the British defenses, Prien decided to attack again and ordered the bow torpedo crew to reload the tubes. By this time the problems with tube four had been corrected. When three tubes were ready for action, the *U-47* worked itself into a new firing position, now less than 1,500 meters away from the *Royal Oak*. Three torpedoes raced out of the tubes and toward the venerable battleship – at 1:16 a.m. the crew heard two resounding explosions as the hull of the British vessel exploded sending plumes of thick black smoke into the night air. The *Royal Oak* had taken a hit in an aft magazine. In fact, all three torpedoes had found their mark; the concussion was felt by the men of *U-47* standing on the bridge more than a mile away.

As the *Royal Oak* lay dying – along with 833 of her crew – the *U-47* faced the problem of slipping out of Scapa Flow back through the Kirk Sound. Due to the ebbing of the tide, *Obersteuermann* Wilhelm Spahr was forced to thread the boat through the southern channel, between the blockship *Minich* and the coast of the islet of Lamb Holm. The task would have been difficult enough even in perfect weather and conditions, but here it was left to Spahr to guide the U-boat out in one piece through a narrow, shallow channel while both avoiding the enemy and taking on a current running in excess of ten knots.

Despite the current and the narrow channel the *U-47* made it to the open sea, but disaster almost struck when the chief engineer determined that one propeller was losing revolutions. Soon after he gave the bad news to the commander that the coupling joining the starboard diesel engine to the propeller shaft was about to disintegrate. Prien took the boat to near the bottom so no enemy would spot the stricken boat while repairs were being made. Wessels and two senior machinists bore-out the coupling bolts, and after finding that replacement bolts onboard were too large, went back and re-bored the holes themselves. This painstaking task took several hours but at its conclusion the *U-47* headed toward Germany.

1st Watch Officer Endrass then went down on deck with a can of paint and painted a snorting bull – the Bull of Scapa Flow – on the *U-47*'s conning tower; this talisman would become Prien's personal emblem, and ultimately that of the 7th U-Boat Flotilla.

The *U-47* arrived at Wilhelmshaven on October 17, 1939, where Prien and his crew were greeted by an enthusiastic crowd, including a ceremonial honor guard, *Kapitän zur See* Karl Dönitz and *Großadmiral* Erich Raeder, who awarded every crewmember with the Iron Cross 2nd Class. Prien received the Iron Cross 1st Class, as did Endrass and Wessels; Raeder promoted Karl Dönitz to *Konteradmiral* and notified Günther Prien that he would be receiving the Knight's Cross from Adolf Hitler in Berlin. After a short aircraft flight to Kiel, the crew flew to Berlin in three aircraft – Prien traveling in Hitler's personal Ju-52 aircraft. The three aircraft carrying Prien and his crew arrived at Berlin's Tempelhof airfield at 11:00 a.m. on October 18 and were met by more naval officials before proceeding in a motorcade through cheering crowds along the route to the Reichs Chancellery and a meeting with the Führer. After meeting Hitler and making the obligatory opening speeches, Hitler presented Prien with his Knight's Cross. Prien and the crew continued their victory celebration by eating lunch with the German leader, followed by meeting press chief Otto Dietrich and conducting a press conference in the afternoon.

The crew then went to the prestigious Hotel Kaiserhof, where they would stay the night. The day's events were capped off with an evening at the Wintergarten Theatre. During the show the crowd cheered Prien to deliver a speech, which in turn was broadcast to the nation on the radio program "Wunschkonzert." The following day the happy, but exhausted, sailors flew back to Wilhelmshaven.

The *U-47* departed Wilhelmshaven under Günther Prien on October 20, 1939 and arrived at Kiel the next day. The boat remained there almost one month before departing Kiel on November 16, 1939 for her third war cruise around the Orkneys and Norway. The *U-47* sank three ships on this patrol, but missed a bigger prize when on November 28, 1939 a torpedo the boat fired at the British heavy cruiser *HMS Norfolk* exploded prematurely. On December 5, 1939 at 2:40 p.m., the *U-47* sank the British 8,795-ton *Navasota*, sailing in ballast with convoy OB-46 from Liverpool to Buenos Aires, Argentina; thirty-seven crewmen died. The next day at 9:29 p.m., Prien sank the Norwegian 6,214-ton *Britta* bound from Antwerp, Belgium to Curacao; six of her crew perished in the freezing water. Finally on December 7, 1939 at 5:24 a.m., the *U-47* torpedoed the Dutch 8,159-ton *Tajandoen* carrying cement, iron and steel from Antwerp to Batavia, Indonesia; six of her crew died when the ship went down. The boat returned to Kiel on December 18, 1939; she would need extensive repairs and would not return to action for almost three months. During this time 1st Watch Officer Endrass departed the boat for training that would lead him to assume command of the *U-46*.

On February 29, 1940 the *U-47* departed Kiel under Günther Prien and arrived at Wilhelmshaven on March 5, 1940 after problems with the boat's compass repeaters. After a few days, the *U-47* departed Wilhelmshaven on March 11, 1940 – again for operations around the Orkneys and Norway. At 5:40 a.m. on March 25, 1940, the *U-47* sank the Danish 1,146-ton *Britta*, in ballast bound from Kalunborg, Denmark to Liverpool, with two torpedoes; thirteen of her crew went missing in action. The *U-47* returned to Wilhelmshaven on March 29, 1940. It would be the final patrol on the U-boat for Chief Engineer Johann Wessels; he became the flotilla engineer for the 1st U-boat Flotilla and would go on to win his own Knight's Cross.

The *U-47* left Wilhelmshaven on April 3, 1940 for operations off Norway and the Shetlands codenamed "Operation Hartmut" – the U-boat arm's support of the invasion of Norway ("Operation Weserübung") – after Hitler decided that only by securing Norway could he protect the 70% of iron ore Germany imported from Sweden. During this war patrol, the *U-47* suffered from a complete failure of torpedoes, to include an ineffective attack – from pointblank range – against the British battleship *HMS Warspite* on April 19, 1940 near Narvik. The *U-47* also experienced navigation problems within the confines of the fjords; at one point the U-boat became grounded. Prien managed to free the boat, but at that moment a British destroyer attacked the boat with depth charges, damaging the engines. The *U-47* returned to Kiel on April 26, 1940 and again required significant repairs.

On June 4, 1940, with repairs completed, the *U-47* left Kiel under the command of Günther Prien for her sixth war patrol southwest of Ireland. This patrol was much more successful than the foray to Norway; Günther Prien would sink eight ships:

1. On June 14, 1940 at 7:44 p.m., just south of Ireland, the *U-47* sank the British 5,834-ton *Balmoralwood* of convoy HX-47, bound from Sorel, Canada to Falmouth, England; the ship, carrying 8,730 tons of wheat and four aircraft sank, but all her crew survived.
2. On June 21, 1940 at 8:07 p.m., south of Ireland, the *U-47* sank the British 13,056-ton tanker *San Fernando*, part of convoy HX-49 sailing from Curacao to Liverpool, England; 13,500 tons of fuel oil went down with the ship, but again there were no fatalities among her crew.
3. At 2:41 a.m. on June 24, 1940, southwest of Ireland, Prien sank the Panamanian 1,885-ton *Cathrine*, bound from Jacksonville, Florida for London, with 88-mm deck-gun fire.
4. On June 27, 1940 at 3:38 a.m., southwest or Ireland, the *U-47* torpedoed the Norwegian 4,005-ton *Lenda,* carrying timber from Halifax, Nova Scotia to Hull, England; one crewman died as the U-boat finished off the ship with gunfire.
5. At about the same time on June 27, 1940, the *U-47* sank the Dutch 2,580-ton *Leticia*, carrying 2,589 tons of gas oil from Curacao to Falmouth with 88-mm deck-gun fire; two men died.
6. On June 29, 1940, southwest of Ireland, Prien sank the British 4,127-ton *Empire Toucan* with torpedoes and gunfire; the ship was in ballast bound from Garston, England to Port Sulphur, Louisiana – three men perished in the attack.
7. On June 30, 1940 at 2:45 a.m., the *U-47* torpedoed the Greek 4,201-ton *Georgios Kyriakides* carrying 7,243 tons of bagged sugar from Macoris, Dominican Republic to Liverpool; all her crew survived the attack southwest of Ireland.
8. On July 2, 1940 at 7:58 a.m., the *U-47* sank the British 15,501-ton *Arandora Star* bound from Liverpool for Canada; 740 passengers lost their lives, while 868 survived the attack northwest of Ireland.

The *U-47* returned to Kiel on July 6, 1940. Prien calculated in the logbook that the *U-47* sailed 5,150 sea-miles on the surface and 184 sea-miles submerged on the patrol. It would be seven weeks before the *U-47*'s next patrol. The *U-47* departed under Günther Prien from Kiel on August 27, 1940 for operations in the North West (north of Ireland, west of Scotland) Approaches. Günther Prien hit seven ships on this patrol; six of these ships were in convoy:

1. On September 2, 1940 at 4:35 p.m., northwest of Ireland, the *U-47* torpedoed the Belgian 7,463-ton *Ville de Mons* carrying pears, corn and wheat from New York to Liverpool and Glasgow; all her crew survived.
2. On September 4, 1940 at 1:28 a.m., the *U-47* sank the British 9,034-ton *Titan*, from convoy OA-207, in ballast from London to Nova Scotia; six men perished in the attack northwest of

Ireland. Either during that attack or the next day, September 5, 1940 a man on the *U-47* was washed overboard and drowned during action using the 88-mm deck-gun.
3. On September 7, 1940 at 4:04 a.m., northwest of Ireland, the *U-47* sank the British 5,155-ton *Neptunian*, of convoy SC-2, from Nova Scotia to Liverpool; all thirty-six of her crew died – there were no survivors.
4. The same day at 5:15 a.m., the *U-47* torpedoed the British 5,303-ton *José de Larrinaga*, part of convoy SC-2 heading from Nova Scotia to Newport, England with 7,300 tons of steel and linseed.
5. Minutes later at 5:33 a.m., the *U-47* sank the Norwegian 4,211-ton *Gro*, sailing with convoy SC-2 from Montreal to Manchester loaded with 6,321 tons of wheat; eleven sailors perished.
6. On September 9, 1940 the *U-47* sank the Greek 3,840-ton *Possidon*, from convoy SC-2, carrying 5,410 tons of sulphur phosphate from New Orleans, Louisiana to Glasgow, Scotland; seventeen men went to the bottom with the ship west of Scotland.
7. On September 21, 1940 at 3:00 p.m., west of Ireland, the *U-47* sank the British 5,156-ton *Elmbank* with 88-mm deck-gun fire; the ship, sailing with convoy HX-72, was carrying timber and metals from Cowichan, Canada to Belfast, Northern Ireland – one man died.

The *U-47* arrived at Lorient on September 25, 1940 after just over four weeks at sea. As before, she spent the majority of the voyage on the surface; Prien calculated that the U-boat was surfaced for 5,103 sea-miles and submerged for 213 sea-miles. The *U-47* remained in port for three weeks and then departed on her eighth war patrol that would lead to torpedoing six Allied ships in just three and one-half hours. The *U-47* left Lorient under the command of Günther Prien on October 14, 1940. On October 19 she encountered convoy HX-79 northwest of Ireland and the fireworks began:

• At 10:27 p.m., the *U-47* sank the Dutch 6,856-ton *Bilderdijk* carrying 8,640 tons of grain from Baltimore, Maryland to Liverpool; all her crew survived.
• A little more than one hour later, at 11:31 p.m., the *U-47* torpedoed and damaged the British 6,023-ton tanker *Sitirak*; all crew were saved on the ship carrying 7,771 tons of refined petroleum from Aruba to London.
• Fifteen minutes later, at 11:46 p.m., the *U-47* sank the British 4,947-ton *Wandby*, carrying 1,700 tons of lead and zinc and 7,200 tons of lumber from Canada to Tees, England; all her crew survived.
• Just after midnight – now October 20 – at 12:37 a.m., the *U-47* sank the British 5,185-ton *La Estancia* carrying 8,333 tons of sugar from Panama to Tees, England; one crewman went missing in the attack.
• Just over an hour later, at 1:48 a.m., the *U-47* sank the British 5,026-ton *Whitford Point*, enroute from Baltimore, Maryland to London with 7,840 tons of steel; thirty-seven crewman perished and only two survived.
• Fourteen minutes later at 2:02 a.m., the *U-47* torpedoed and damaged the British 8,995-ton *Athelmonarch*, carrying 13,146 tons of molasses from Santiago, Chile to Liverpool; no one perished in this attack.

The *U-47* returned to Lorient on October 23, 1940 after just over one week on patrol; she spent just 34 sea-miles submerged, while sailing 2,113 sea-miles on the surface. Hitler had approved the award of the Knight's Cross with Oak Leaves for Günther Prien on October 20; Prien received this decoration after returning to France. The refit crews turned the boat around in short order and on November 3, 1940 the *U-47* departed Lorient for her ninth war patrol, again deploying to the North West Approaches. On November 8, 1940 at 1:47 p.m., the *U-47* damaged the Portuguese 1,595-ton *Gonçalo Velho* with 88-mm deck-gun fire but did not sink the target. Almost a month then went by before Prien located convoy HX-90 and sunk his teeth into it. On December 2, 1940 he damaged the British 4,393-ton *Penrose* with 88-mm deck-gun fire; again the ship did not sink. The same day at 4:09 a.m., the *U-47* sank the Belgian 7,555-ton *Ville d'Arlon*. Minutes later, at 5:25 a.m., the *U-47* torpedoed and damaged the British tanker 8,376-ton *Conch*, carrying 11,214 tons of fuel oil from Trinidad to Clyde, Scotland (She was sunk three days later by Otto Kretschmer in the *U-99*.) Prien and the *U-47* returned on December 6, 1940 to Lorient. For this patrol the *U-47* remained on the surface for 5,267 sea-miles, while submerging for an additional 132 sea-miles. At Lorient, Watch Officer Amelung von Varendorff was re-assigned and promoted, the last of Prien's original "Scapa Flow" officers.

The crew had a good two-month rest. The start of the next mission was delayed by a few days because the trial run had revealed some minor faults. Finally, on February 20, 1941, the *U-47* departed from Lorient once again for operations in the North West Approaches. Prien sank four ships and damaged two others on this, the tenth war patrol of the *U-47*. In the middle of the night, on February 26, 1941, the *U-47* encountered convoy OB-290 northwest of Ireland with the following results:

• At 12:18 a.m., the *U-47* torpedoed the Belgian 5,254-ton *Kasongo*, carrying ammunition from Liverpool to Freetown; six men died when the ship sank sometime later.
• At 12:25 a.m., the *U-47* torpedoed and damaged the British 8,106-ton *Diala*, in ballast sailing from Avonmouth, England to Curacao; one man died in the attack but the ship survived. (It sank in January 1942 after an attack by the *U-553*.)
• At 1:10 a.m., the *U-47* sank the Swedish 3,197-ton *Rydboholm*, sailing in ballast from Garston, England to Freetown, Sierra Leone.
• At 1:37 a.m., the *U-47* sank the Norwegian 3,636-ton *Borgland*, carrying six aircraft from Liverpool for Takoradi, Ghana.

Two days later, on February 28, 1941 at 1:26 a.m., the *U-47* sank the British 4,223-ton *Holmelea*, part of convoy HX-109 sailing from Rosario to Hull, England; twenty-eight men died when the ship carrying 7,000 tons of grain, linseed and maize went to the bottom of the North Atlantic. Finally at 5:05 a.m., on March 7, 1941 the *U-47* torpedoed and damaged the British 20,638 ton whaling ship *Terje Viken*, from convoy OB-293; her entire 102-man crew was saved.

The exact cause of *U-47* and Prien's demise remained unknown. On March 7, 1941 the B.d.U. war diary reported the following on the boat:

> "*U-47* contacted a north-bound convoy in AM 1452 on the evening of March 6, and maintained contact until 0440. *U-99*, *U-70* and *UA* were detailed to operate on the convoy, also *U-37*, although this boat was some distance away. Only *U-70* reported on request that it had come up to the convoy. Further reports are lacking for the time being. *U-70* and *U-47* have not replied to their call up."

The next day brought no resolution; on March 8, 1941 the war diary reported: "Reports have not come in from *U-70* and *U-47*."

The mood at Dönitz's headquarters was bleak; the war diary reflected this feeling on March 9, 1941:

> "*U-70* and *U-47* were again requested to send a situation report in the evening, but without result. Both boats are causing great anxiety, as they have not yet replied to the request made on the evening of the 7th. There is still hope that this silence is only due to W/T [wireless-radio] breakdown, especially in the case of *U-47*, which had already experienced a breakdown on this trip."

For some time it was thought that *HMS Wolverine* had destroyed *U-47* with depth charges (at that time for a depth charge to fatally damage a U-boat it had to explode within twenty-three feet of the pressure hull; up to fifty feet would cause damage); however, further post-war research has shown that *Wolverine's* attack had been delivered upon a different boat that survived to report it. One source claims that the British corvettes *HMS Camellia* and *HMS Arbutus* may have destroyed the *U-47*. Other sources allege the *U-47* was hit and destroyed by one of her own torpedoes which went awry. All the men on the *U-47*, including Günther Prien and a prospective commander in training, *Korvettenkapitän* Karl-Eglof *Freiherr* von Schnurbein, perished on March 7, 1941 in the area of the North Atlantic southwest of the Faroe Islands.

Günther Prien sank thirty merchant ships, a combined 162,769 tons, and damaged eight additional ships for 62,751 tons. This placed him ninth among the most successful U-boat commanders of the war and the *U-47* the thirteenth most successful boat of the U-boat service. On March 18, 1941 a special promotion for action in the face of the enemy elevated Günther Prien posthumously to *Korvettenkapitän*.

Known Crewmembers for the U-47

Biermann, Heinrich*	*Maschinenobergefreiter*
Bilstein, Karl-Heinz	*Funkgefreiter*
Blank, Heinz*	*Oberfunkmaat*
Bleek, Kurt*	*Obermechanikermaat*
Böhm, Gustav*	*Stabsobermaschinist*
Böhm, Gustav-August	
Bothmann, Hans-Joachim	*Oberleutnant (Ing)*
Brand, Karl	*Matrose*
Brehme, Kurt*	*Maschinengefreiter*
Dittmer, Peter*	*Matrosengefreiter*
Dziallas, Ernst*	*Obersteuermann*
Endrass, Engelbert*	*Kapitänleutnant*
Engelmann, Friedrich	*Bootsmaat*
Eschger	*Obersteuermann*
Esser, Karl-Heinz	*Funkobergefreiter*
Freudig, Ernst	*Oberfunkmeister*
Frings, Dietmar	*Fähnrich zur See*
Göseke, Heinz	*Funkgefreiter*
Gundlach, Karl-Heinz	*Bootsmaat*
Haas, Willy	*Matrosenobergefreiter*
Hänsel, Gerhard*	*Gefreiter*
Hebestreit, Willi*	*Funkobergefreiter*
Heinz, Heinrich	*Maschinenmaat*
Hentrop, Heinrich	*Maschinenmaat*
Herrmann, Herbert*	*Mechanikerobergefreiter*
Herrmann, Herbert	*Obersteuermann*
Heyer, Gerhard	*Maschinenobergefreiter*
Hirtl, Franz	*Maschinenobergefreiter*
Hölzer, Erwin*	*Maschinenhauptgefreiter*
Hönemann, Martin	*Obermaschinist*
Hötzer, Gerhard*	*Maschinenobergefreiter*
Holstein, Kurt*	*Leutnant (Ing)*
Jahnkow, Willi-Friedrich	*Maschinengefreiter*
Kläbisch, Heinz	*Matrosengefreiter*
Kraus, Hans-Werner	*Kapitänleutnant*
Küsel, Ewald-Max	*Maschinengefreiter*
Leidig, Paul	*Matrosenobergefreiter*
Loh, Willi*	*Mechanikerobergefreiter*
Löhr, Heinz	*Maschinenobergefreiter*
Lösch, Andreas	*Matrosenobergefreiter*
Lüddecke, Werner*	*Maschinengefreiter*
Mantyk, Heinrich*	*Matrosenobergefreiter*
Marquard, Herbert*	*Gefreiter*
Meyer, Willi*	*Bootsmaat*
Notsch, Gottfried	*Matrosenobergefreiter*
Oldekop, Iwan	*Fähnrich zur See*
Pauss, Helmut	*Mechanikerobergefreiter*
Prien, Günther*	*Korvettenkapitän*
Radloff, Walter*	*Maschinengefreiter*
Reimann, Josef	*Maschinenmaat*
Renken, Emil	*Mechanikerobergefreiter*
Römer, Kurt*	*Obermaschinist*
Ronshausen, August	*Obermaschinenmaat*
Roth, Ronni*	*Maschinengefreiter*
Rutschmann, Helmut	*Maschinenmaat*
Sammann, Hans*	*Obersteuermann*
Sander, Erich	*Oberleutnant zur See*
Schmalenbach, Werner*	*Maschinenmaat*
Schmidt, Ernst*	*Gefreiter*
Schmidt, Friedrich*	*Obermaschinenmaat*
Schnarchendorf, Kurt	*Funkmaat*
Schnurbein, Karl-Eglof von	*Korvettenkapitän*
Scholz, Hans	*Matrosengefreiter*
Scholz, Werner*	*Maschinenmaat*
Schweizer, Heinz	*Matrosenobergefreiter*
Smyczek, Rudi*	*Gefreiter*
Söllig, Werner*	*Maschinenmaat*
Spahr, Wilhelm*	*Obersteuermann*
Spörer, Karl*	*Maschinengefreiter*
Steinhagen, Karl*	*Funkmaat*
Stephan, Martin	*Leutnant zur See*
Strunk, Otto*	*Oberleutnant (Ing)*
Suhren, Reinhard	*Fregattenkapitän*
Thewes, Peter*	*Mechanikermaat*
Thomsen, Max	*Maschinenobergefreiter*
Varendorff, Amelung von*	*Oberleutnant zur See*
Walz, Friedrich*	*Matrosenobergefreiter*
Weiser, Friedrich	*Maschinenobergefreiter*
Werder, Gustav*	*Obermaschinist*
Wessels, Johann-Friedrich*	*Korvettenkapitän (Ing)*
Wiensczyk, Bruno	*Matrosenobergefreiter*
Winzer, Ernst*	*Obermaschinenmaat*
Witte, Erwin	*Kapitänleutnant*
Zapf, Fritz	*Maschinengefreiter*
Zöller, Albert	*Maschinenobergefreiter*

* indicates individual participated in the Scapa Flow mission.

Sources, "The Bull of Scapa Flow:" Jochen Brennecke, *The Hunters and the Hunted*, translated by R.H. Stevens, New York: W.W. Norton and Company, 1957, 25, 26, 27, 28, 29; Karl Dönitz, *Memoirs: Ten Years and Twenty Days*, translated by R. H. Stevens, Annapolis, Maryland: Da Capo Press, 1997, 67, 68, 69, 175; Manfred Dörr, *Die Ritterkreuzträger der U-Boot-Waffe Band 1: A-J, Band 2: L-Z*, Osnabrück, FRG: Biblio Verlag, 1988, Band 1-60, 61, 62, Band 2 – 183, 184, 185, 331, 332; *F.d.U./B.d.U. War Diary, 1-15 March 1941* (PG30284), 30, 31; Michael Gannon, *Black May: The Epic Story of the Allies Defeat of the German U-boats in May 1943*, New York: HarperCollins, 1998, 61; Herbert Ritschel, *Kurzfassung Kriegstagebücher deutscher U-boote 1939-1945, Band 1: KTB U1 - U50,* Norderstedt, Germany: Books on Demand, 312-328; Jürgen Rohwer, *Axis Submarine Successes 1939-1945*, Annapolis, Maryland: Naval Institute Press, 1983, 1, 4, 7, 8, 16, 19, 20, 21, 22, 27, 28, 29, 34, 37, 44; T. V. Tuleja, *Twilight of the Sea Gods*, New York: W. W. Norton & Company, 1958, 53, 54, 55; David Westwood, *The U-boat War: The German Submarine Service and the Battle of the Atlantic, 1935-1945*, Philadelphia, PA: Casemate, 2005, 75; www.ubootwaffe.net; www.uboatarchive.net; www.u47.org

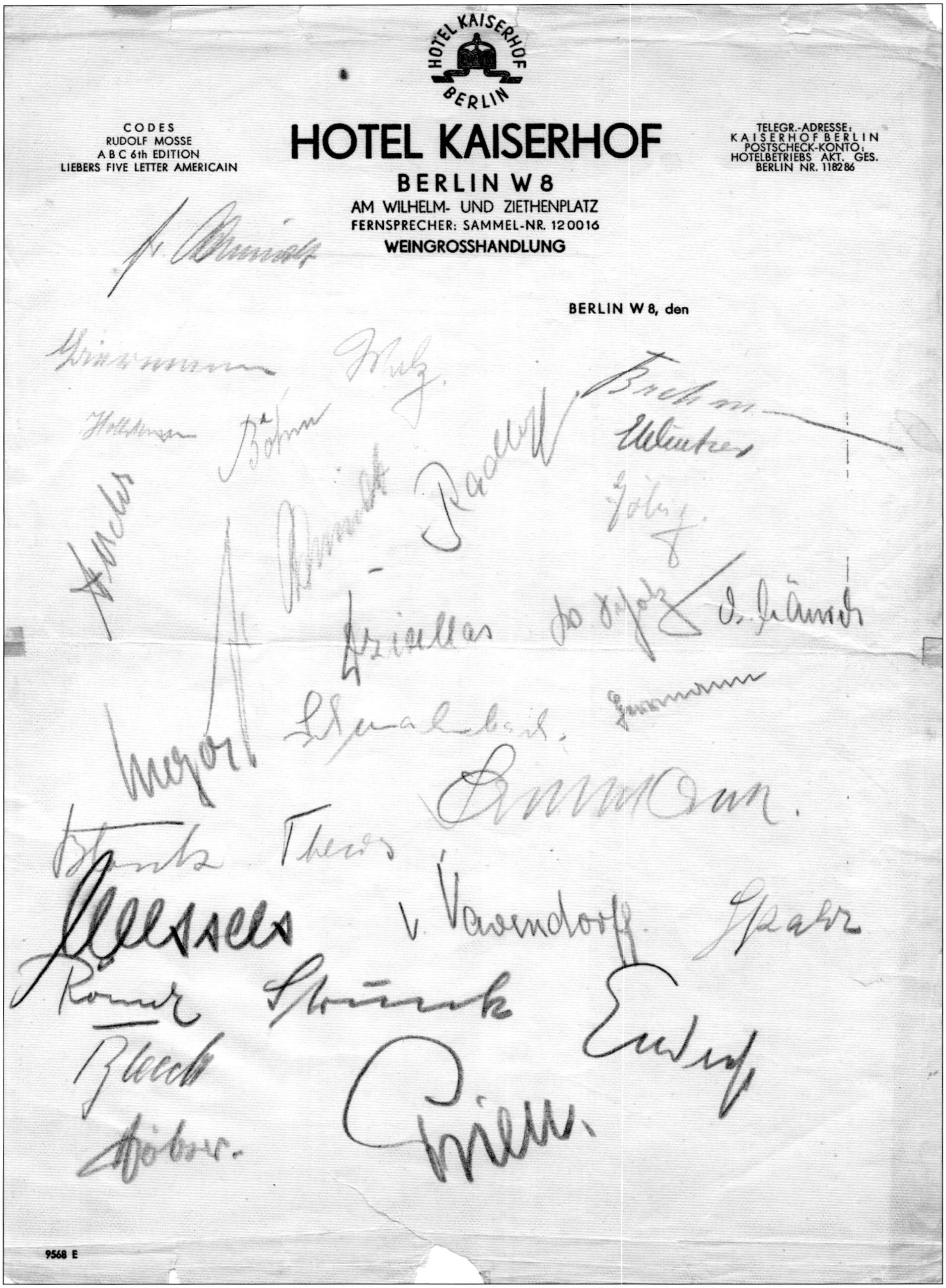

Hotel Kaiserhof stationery with thirty signatures of U-47 crewmen in Berlin, immediately after Prien's success at Scapa Flow. *The entire crew went to Berlin after their return from this war patrol to be personally decorated by Adolf Hitler; they stayed at the Hotel Kaiserhof, where they were besieged by autograph seekers and well-wishers.*

Adolf Hitler congratulating crew of the U-47 after the Scapa Flow mission. *Immediately to Hitler's left is Günther Prien. To the left is the Commander-in-Chief of the German Navy Erich Raeder. Note that many of the men have just been awarded the Iron Cross 2nd Class. Photo is signed in lower right corner by Günther Prien.*

View of the U-47 underway. *The number of crewmen topside indicates that they are not concerned with potential enemy activity.*

View of Günther Prien in white officer's cap.

Opposite
View of Günther Prien, with binoculars, on the bridge of the U-47. *The boat has a conning tower emblem of a raging bull. Staff to the left is a decorative victory pole.*

Inset
Period wartime postcard showing the conning tower design for the U-47, the Bull of Scapa Flow.

View of Günther Prien and two officers of the U-47. *Prien, in white cap, is saluting. Behind him is his 1st Watch Officer Engelbert Endrass.*

Signed photo postcard of Engelbert Endrass. *Endrass served as the 1st Watch Officer for Prien on the Scapa Flow mission; he later commanded his own U-boat and won the Knight's Cross with Oak Leaves. Endrass was killed in action in December 1941.*

View of Günther Prien boarding the U-47 in port. *The narrow boarding plank required a degree of nimbleness to cross.*

Der Stier von Scapa Flow

View of U-47 at the conclusion of her sixth war patrol. *View of Günther Prien, with binoculars and light color leather jacket in port with the U-47. Number "66,587" indicates tonnage claimed.*

View of victory pennants on the raised periscope of the U-47. *U-boats returning from a successful war patrol would display these. Photograph was taken shortly after the U-47 returned from her sixth patrol that lasted from June 4 to July 6, 1940.*

View of Günther Prien with three Luftwaffe crewmen forward of the bridge on the U-47, July 6, 1940. *The U-boat rescued the three on June 6, 1940, when their aircraft was shot down.*

CHAPTER FOUR

"THE OLD GUARD"
U-14, U-109, AND U-28
1939-1942

While Karl Dönitz loved all his boys, there was a special place in his heart for those U-boat commanders who were with the *Kriegsmarine* U-boat arm from the very beginning in the mid-1930s; he felt that they were better trained and more mature than some of the younger commanders who came along later. Immediately after the war, he reflected on these men:

> "They were men who, through years of seafaring in wartime, felt at home in the Atlantic in both summer and winter – a group of bold seamen of outstanding fighting ability."

Dönitz later noted in his memoirs that the great aces of the early part of the war were all "VIIC drivers," swearing by this type of submarine and declining to volunteer to take command of the larger Type IX boats. But this did not always prove true and several of "The Old Guard" U-boat commanders, who thoroughly learned their craft in the 1930s, commanded other types of U-boat with great success.

Dönitz's Crews
***Obersteuermann* Bruno Petersen**
Served as the navigator and quartermaster on the *U-14* and the *U-109*.
Awarded the Iron Cross 2nd Class on January 27, 1940.
Spent 267 days at sea on U-boat war patrols.
Survived the war; lived in Flensburg, Schleswig/Holstein.

Obersteuermann Bruno Petersen saw many of the "Old Guard" skippers during his service as navigator and quartermaster with the *U-14* and *U-109*. His first boat was the *U-14*, a coastal Type IIB craft that were affectionately known by their crews as "canoes," based on their rough handling in choppy surface water. Construction crews laid the boat's keel on July 6, 1935 at the Deutsche Werk AG yard at Kiel-Gaarden; she was launched on December 28, 1935. Three weeks later, on January 18, 1936, she was commissioned with the U-boat Flotilla *Weddigen* at Kiel. In October 1937 the boat transferred to U-boat Flotilla *Lohs*. *Kapitänleutnant* Horst Wellner took command of the boat on October 5, 1937. Born on August 30, 1908 in Zwickau, Saxony, Wellner entered the German Navy in 1929. As soon as the U-boat force was formed, he joined the *U-10* as a watch officer in 1935; clearly he was part of the "Old Guard." The following year he gained more experience on board the *U-16*, again as a watch officer and *Oberleutnant zur See*. Watch officers, although relatively junior, had key responsibilities; the 1st Watch Officer served as the boat's Executive Officer and second in command. Prepared to assume command if the boat's commander was incapacitated, he was in charge of all the boat's weapons systems and conducted torpedo aiming from the conning tower during surface torpedo attacks. The other watch officer, often referred to as the 2nd Watch Officer, was normally junior to the 1st Watch Officer and was responsible for the watch-crew on deck, the deck gun operation and the flak guns. He also supervised the radio room personnel.

As war clouds gathered, the *U-14* left the German port of Memel in the eastern Baltic under the command of Horst Wellner on August 30, 1939 for operations off the Polish coast. The next day Germany invaded Poland and the war began. She became the first German U-boat to attack an enemy vessel during the war when she attempted to torpedo the surfaced Polish submarine *Sep* from a range of 1,000 meters at 10:22 p.m. on September 3, 1939. However, the torpedo exploded prematurely and the intended victim escaped. After one week and the conclusion of her first war patrol, the *U-14* arrived at Swinemünde on September 6, 1939.

On September 13, 1939, the *U-14* left Kiel, still under the command of Horst Wellner, for operations in the North Sea. Although he did not sink any enemy ships, *Kapitänleutnant* Wellner performed an even more valuable service and, arriving on September 17, reconnoitered the Orkneys area and the approaches to Scapa Flow, providing information which would be used for the penetration of Scapa Flow by Günther Prien in the *U-47*. Two days later enemy aircraft dropped six depth charges near the *U-14*, but the U-boat dove quickly and escaped. The U-boat attempted to torpedo an enemy destroyer on September 22 but missed; in return the enemy ship dropped eighteen depth charges near the U-boat. She returned to Kiel on September 29, 1939 after over two weeks on patrol – during which she was subjected to forty-four enemy depth charges – and Wellner conducted a detailed debriefing of his findings with *Kommodore* Dönitz. Because of this achievement, Wellner was given command of another boat, the *U-16* (also a Type IIB) and took his new command on a war patrol on October 12, 1939. Eight days later, on the second day of his patrol, he scored his first victory, sinking the small French steamer *Ste. Clair*. But then his good fortune ran out.

On October 25, 1939 off Goodwin Sands east of Dover the corvette *HMS Puffin* (Lt. Cdr. J.M. Waldegrave) and anti-submarine trawler *HMT Cayton Wyke* (Chief Skipper D.F. Noble) depth-charged the *U-16* sending her to the bottom with her entire 28-man crew.

The loss did not stop the men back on the *U-14* though. The boat departed Kiel at 10:45 p.m. on January 17, 1940 under *Oberleutnant zur See* Herbert Wohlfarth for operations in the North Sea on her third war patrol. On January 25, 1940 at 2:30 a.m., the *U-14* sank the Norwegian 1,752-ton *Biarritz* in the English Channel enroute from Antwerp to Oslo. The ship, loaded with woolen cloth, went down taking twenty-five men with her, but during the encounter the freighter struck the conning tower of the *U-14* causing damage. The *U-14* after just over one week on patrol arrived at Wilhelmshaven on January 26, 1940. The following day several crewmen received awards, including *Obersteuermann* Bruno Petersen – the boat's navigator – who won the Iron Cross 2nd Class for navigating the boat on this short, but successful, mission. Meanwhile, shipyard workers spent almost three weeks repairing the damage to the boat.

Herbert Wohlfarth was an interesting commander and another of the "Old Guard." Born in Kanazawa, Japan on June 5, 1915, he joined the Navy in 1933 and began his career in the surface fleet. Wohlfarth served on the pocket battleship *Graf Spee* in 1935 and 1936 before beginning U-boat training in 1937. On September 26, 1938 he joined the *U-16* as a watch officer, and with that experience took command of the *U-14* on October 19, 1939. His efforts earned Wohlfarth an Iron Cross 2nd Class on October 10, 1939 and the U-boat War Badge on December 20, 1939.

The *U-14* left Wilhelmshaven for her fourth war patrol under the command of Herbert Wohlfarth on February 11, 1940 for operations off Moray Firth, Scotland. One day out, the *U-14* stopped at Helgoland to transfer a sick crewman who required an appendectomy; after this emergency, though, she quickly found success. At 11:55 p.m. on February 15, 1940 off the Orkney Islands he sank the Danish 1,066-ton *Sleipner*, carrying coal, bound from Methil, Scotland to Esbjerg, Denmark. Her crew survived. Minutes later, after midnight, the *U-14* sank the coal-carrying Danish-1,064 ton *Rhone*, killing nine men. At 9:25 p.m. on February 16, 1940 off the Scottish coast Wohlfarth sank the Swedish 1,526-ton coal-carrying *Osmed* bound from Blyth, England to Halmstad, Sweden; thirteen men died in the attack. Ten minutes later the *U-14* sank another ship full of coal, the Swedish 1,646-ton *Liana*; ten men died when she went to the bottom. On February 20, 1940 the *U-14* returned to Wilhelmshaven. She had sailed 1,081 sea-miles on the surface and 132 sea-miles submerged.

The U-boat's fifth war patrol began on March 3, 1940 when the boat left Wilhelmshaven with Herbert Wohlfarth still in command. The German invasion of France and the Low Countries was imminent and the *U-14* sailed for operations off the Dutch coast. Wohlfarth hit four ships on this patrol, the first just four days into the operation. On March 7 at 4:30 a.m., he sank the Dutch 1,965-ton *Vecht*, bound from Rotterdam to Lobito, Angola. Twenty-two Dutch sailors died in the attack. Two days later, at 5:42 a.m. on March 9, the *U-14* sank the British 1,097-ton *Borthwick* steaming from Rotterdam to Leith, Scotland; fortunately all her crew survived the attack. Later, just before midnight of that day, at 11:45 p.m., Wohlfarth sank the British 643-ton *Akeld*, carrying general cargo from Rotterdam to Newcastle with two torpedoes. This attack was not bloodless; thirteen crewmen perished in the attack. Simultaneously the *U-14* sank the British 1,585-ton *Abbotsford*, which was transporting flax from Ghent, Belgium to Grangemouth, Scotland with even bloodier results – all eighteen men on the *Abbotsford* perished. The *U-14* arrived at Kiel on March 11, 1940, completing her mission. Her log reflected sailing 1,000 sea-miles surfaced and 119 sea-miles submerged.

The *U-14*'s sixth war patrol was eventful but unsuccessful. She departed Kiel under Herbert Wohlfarth on April 4, 1940 for operations off the Norwegian coast in support of the German invasion of that country. Wohlfarth's boat was part of Group 3 (of a total of eight groups), operating off Bergen. The thirty German submarines experienced numerous torpedo failures; like the other boats, the *U-14* did not sink any enemy ships, but she had an opportunity when on April 15, 1940 at 8:45 p.m. she spotted a British cruiser of the *Cairo* class and fired two torpedoes at her at a range of 3,000 meters, but missed. The *U-14* returned to Kiel on May 5, 1940.

The *U-14* then went to the training command. Herbert Wohlfarth went on to command the *U-137* and the *U-556*, winning the Knight's Cross on May 15, 1941. When the *U-556* sank six weeks later on June 27, 1941 Wohlfarth became a prisoner of war, spending six years in confinement. Herbert Wohlfarth sank twenty-one merchant ships, a combined 66,032 tons and damaged three additional ships for 20,455 tons. This placed him sixty-sixth among the most successful U-boat commanders of the war.

Meanwhile, *Obersteuermann* Bruno Petersen transferred for service on the *U-109* in December 1940. A Type IXB boat, the U-boat was ordered on May 24, 1938, but engineers at the Deutsche Schiff- und Maschinenbau AG (Deschimag) at Bremen did not lay her keel until March 9, 1940. The boat, under command of Hans-Georg Fischer, was launched on September 14, 1940 and commissioned on December 5, 1940. (The commissioning of new U-boats generally took place at the building yard.) Fischer, born on February 3, 1908 in Rostock, had entered the German Navy in 1926 and served in the surface fleet until April 1940 when he began U-boat training.

For U-boats joining the fleet, Admiral Dönitz ensured that the boat's first crew had adequate time to become a team and learn the nuances of their boat. Twelve weeks before the projected commissioning date, the boat's Chief Engineering Officer (*Leitender Ingenieur* [LI]) and the Chief Petty Officers (CPO) reported in; they would lead the boat. Eight weeks before commissioning the Petty Officers (PO) arrived; they would ensure the orders of the officers and CPOs were carried out quickly and efficiently. Six weeks before the boat was to be commissioned, the crew specialists (radio operators, etc.) would report to the boat. Finally, at the four-week-mark the remainder of the enlisted crew arrived. As the commissioned officers might well still be in individual training or still at sea with other frontline U-boats at this point, the future crew fell under the command of a construction training company, which in turn belonged to the Construction Training Group (*Baubelehrungsgruppe*.)

The *U-109* left the Tirpitz Jetty at Kiel under the command of Hans-Georg Fischer on May 6, 1941 for her first war patrol. Bad weather damaged her decking but the crew repaired the damage. On May 20, 1941 at 2:30 a.m., the *U-109* scored her first victory, the British 5,173-ton *Harpagus*, which was sailing with convoy HX-126 from Halifax, Nova Scotia to Barry Roads, Wales. The *Harpagus* was carrying 8,250 tons of grain; thirty-two crewmen were killed. Hans-Georg Fischer ended his patrol and arrived at Lorient, France on May 29, 1941.

Dönitz was highly dissatisfied with Fischer's performance and made the following entry on the B.d.U. war diary for May 29, 1941 after interviewing Fischer about his patrol:

> "The Commanding Officer of *U-109* made his report: It was the boat's first patrol. The crew was almost entirely new. Result was a 7,000 GRT ammunition ship. The general impression made by the Commanding Officer was one of uncertainty and worry. The boat sank to a great depth during a depth charge hunt and was only just saved by the presence of mind of an

experienced Petty Officer who blew the tanks of his own accord without waiting for orders. There was already considerable doubt about the suitability of this Commanding Officer during his training and this doubt has been confirmed by this general conduct on this patrol. I have therefore found it necessary to relieve him at once."

Fischer was transferred completely out of the U-boat Arm and sent to be the Wargames' Officer for the heavy cruiser *Admiral Scheer*. Replacing Fischer was *Kapitänleutnant* Heinrich Bleichrodt, who was a different kettle of fish altogether. Born on October 21, 1909 in Berga/Sangerhausen in Thuringia, he joined the Navy in 1933 and spent his initial few years on the sail training ship *Gorch Fock* and the heavy cruiser *Admiral Hipper*. In October 1939 Heinrich Bleichrodt began U-boat training. He assumed command of the *U-48* on August 20, 1940 and sank nine enemy ships on his first patrol, earning him a U-boat War Badge on September 24, 1940 and an Iron Cross 1st Class a day later. On his second patrol, Bleichrodt sank seven more ships and earned the Knight's Cross on October 24, 1940. A proven winner, Bleichrodt then transferred out of the *U-48* and undertook a special role of conducting research and development testing of sonar in the Baltic Sea, eventually landing on the *U-109*, when Dönitz needed a combat commander he could trust for the under-performing boat.

It took a while for this transformation to occur. On June 28, 1941, the *U-109* left Lorient under the command of Heinrich Bleichrodt. Remaining on her second war patrol for just over seven weeks, it was one malady after another. In late July Bleichrodt experienced mechanical difficulties and put into Cadiz, Spain on July 21, where he received emergency repairs from the German supply ship *Thalia*. Later, Bleichrodt attempted to attack a convoy heading from Gibraltar to Great Britain but noticed the U-boat had a serious oil leak and returned to Lorient on August 17, 1941 without firing a torpedo. The *U-109* returned to action on October 5, 1941, departing from Lorient for operations off Newfoundland and remaining at sea for over six weeks before returning to Lorient on November 18, 1941. It was a lengthy patrol, but one without confirmed success. Again the *U-109* experienced mechanical problems.

The *U-109's* next war patrol would prove more memorable. Departing the Isere docks at Lorient on December 27, 1941, as part of "Operation Drumbeat" – Dönitz's plan for a simultaneous attack on the same day by several U-boats against the U.S. – Bleichrodt took the *U-109* toward the east coast of the United States to attack Allied shipping in the western Atlantic, a significant navigation challenge for *Obersteuermann* Petersen. The mission began with Bleichrodt receiving orders to patrol the Newfoundland-Nova Scotia area. The *U-109* would hit four enemy ships on this patrol, but it started poorly when Bleichrodt found a 5,000-ton freighter and fired five torpedoes at her from the pointblank range of six hundred yards – all five torpedoes either missed or malfunctioned. The weather was ferocious; temperatures fell to 16°F and ice formed in thick layers on the boat's deck and conning tower. The U-boat's magnetic compass started to "wander" and the gryo became unreliable. Bleichrodt refused to answer B.d.U.'s request for information fearing a lengthy transmission might betray his presence so far west. Finally, at 8:12 a.m. on January 23. 1942 the *U-109* torpedoed the British 4,887-ton *Thirlby*, causing a towering explosion, sinking the ship and killing five crewmen. The freighter, loaded with 7,600 tons of maize, was enroute from New York to Halifax and from there would have sailed to Loch Ewe, Scotland.

A week later at 3:30 a.m. on February 1, while scouting the Bermuda area, the *U-109* was enroute to take on fuel from the *U-130* when she spotted and sank the British 7,924-ton *Tacoma Star*. All eighty-seven men aboard perished as the merchantman, carrying 5,107 tons of refrigerated goods from Hampton Roads, Virginia to Liverpool, went to the bottom. The American destroyer *USS Roe*, on temporary duty with the 5th Naval District defense forces due to the increase in ship sinkings off Cape Hatteras, raced to the scene to rescue survivors, but could find none. At 1:42 a.m. on February 5, 1942, the *U-109* struck again. Spotting the Canadian 11,309-ton *Montrolite*, carrying crude oil from Trinidad to Halifax, he quickly sank the large tanker, killing twenty-eight of her crew. The next day, February 6, 1942, at 2:41 a.m., the *U-109* encountered the Panamanian 3,531-ton *Halcyon* in the Bermuda area, enroute from Halifax to Demerara, British Guiana; the ship was in ballast and not worth a torpedo, so Bleichrodt sank her with 105-mm deck-gun fire. The attack killed three of the *Halcyon's* crew. The *U-109* arrived back at Lorient, after over eight weeks at sea, on February 23, 1942.

With this successful war patrol under their belts, the crew took leave while mechanics overhauled the boat. *Obersteuermann* Bruno Petersen departed the boat, although we are unsure of his later assignments; he survived the war and lived in Flensburg.

On March 25, 1942 the *U-109* departed from Lorient for the east coast of the United States for her sixth war patrol, but for the first four weeks did not register any successful attacks. Finally, at 5:24 a.m. on April 20, 1942, Bleichrodt spotted the British 5,719-ton freighter *Harpagon* several hundred miles east of North Carolina, enroute from New York to Cape Town, South Africa and Bombay, India. The ship was carrying tanks, aircraft and more importantly 2,602 tons of explosives; the attack killed forty-one of her crew. Ten days passed without incident, but at 9:58 a.m. on May 1, 1942 the *U-109* sank the 555-ton *Worden*, some ten miles southeast of Cape Canaveral, Florida. At 11:36 a.m. the same morning the *U-109* damaged the British 6,548-ton *La Paz* bound from Hampton Roads for Valparaiso, Chile. The U-boat's last success on this patrol came at 10:54 a.m. on May 3, 1942 off Florida, when she sank the Dutch 5,825-ton *Laertes*, heading from New York to Cape Town and Bombay. The attack killed eighteen men and deprived the Allies of three aircraft, seventeen tanks and twenty trucks. Heinrich Bleichrodt then returned to Lorient on June 3, 1942 after ten weeks on patrol.

After six weeks in port, the *U-109* left Lorient on July 18, 1942 for her seventh war patrol, one that would earn her captain Heinrich Bleichrodt the Knight's Cross with Oak Leaves. Patrolling off Freetown, Sierra Leone, on August 7, 1942 the *U-109* sank the Norwegian 6,030-ton *Arthur W Sewall* at 9:47 p.m. with torpedoes and gunfire. The ship was in ballast, heading from Freetown to Trinidad; all her crew survived. At 7:13 p.m. on August 11, 1942 in the mid-South Atlantic, Bleichrodt sank the British 5,728-ton *Vimeira*; the ship bound from Curacao and Trinidad to Freetown was carrying 8,100 tons of gas and fuel. The torpedo and gunfire attack killed twenty-three of her crew. On September 3, 1942 off Africa he sank the British 7,173-ton *Ocean Might* carrying 7,000 tons of military stores from Liverpool to Cape Town and the Middle East; four men died in the attack.

Success continued at night several days later when at 11:50 p.m. on September 6 Bleichrodt sank the British 11,449-ton *Tuscan Star*; heading from Santos, Brazil for Freetown, Sierra Leone; 7,840 tons of meat and 5,000 tons of general cargo went to the bottom – along with fifty-two of her crew. Finally, at 1:14 p.m. on September 17, 1942 in the mid-South Atlantic the *U-109* sank the British 5,221-ton *Peterton*. The *Peterton* was carrying 5,758 tons of coal from Oban, Scotland to Buenos Aires; nine men perished when she sank. Perhaps more importantly, the crew of the *U-109* recovered classified papers from the ship that described the sailing routes from Freetown to

Lagos, Nigeria. On September 20, the *U-109* refueled for her return home from the *U-460*. Bleichrodt arrived back at Lorient on October 6, 1942 after eleven and a half weeks on patrol. He had been awarded the Knight's Cross with Oak Leaves on September 23.

Enlisted men on the *U-109* would win prestigious awards as well. *Bootsmaat* Berthold Seidel received the German Cross in Gold on November 11, 1942, while the Navy High Command would approve the German Cross for *Obermaschinenmaat* Karl Reissnauer on August 7, 1943.

Heinrich Bleichrodt took the *U-109* on her eighth war patrol on November 28, 1942. It would be his last combat operation with the boat, but success eluded him. After eight weeks on patrol the boat arrived at St. Nazaire, France on January 23, 1943. Bleichrodt left the boat for an assignment with the 27th U-boat Flotilla; he was promoted to *Korvettenkapitän* on October 14, 1943, and assumed command of the 22nd U-boat Flotilla. He survived the war and died on January 9, 1977 in Munich. Heinrich Bleichrodt sank twenty-four merchant ships, a combined 151,260 tons and damaged two additional ships for 11,684 tons. This placed him fourteenth among the most successful U-boat commanders of the war.

The *U-109* and her remaining crew were not as fortunate. *Oberleutnant zur See* Schramm, the former 1st Watch Officer of the U-boat, took command from Bleichrodt. He successfully completed a war patrol in March and then had a few weeks before deploying again. On April 28, 1943 the *U-109* set sail for her tenth war patrol. At 4:36 p.m. on May 4, 1943 south of Ireland, a very long-range RAF B-24 Liberator (Pilot Officer J.C. Green) caught the *U-109* on the surface and dropped four depth charges from an altitude of eighty feet, which struck the boat. All fifty-two of her crew perished in the attack as floating wooden planking and metal cylinders on the surface marked her demise.

Dönitz's Crews

***Mechanikersmaat* Paul Block**

Born on September 18, 1914 in Görlitz/Saxony.
Served in the torpedo room on the *U-28*.
Awarded the U-boat War Badge on December 18, 1939, the Iron Cross 2nd Class on December 21, 1939 and the Iron Cross 1st Class on September 19, 1940.
Spent 239 days at sea on U-boat war patrols.
Survived the war; lived in Ludwigshafen, Rhineland-Pfalz.

Bruno Petersen was not the only "Old Guard" U-boat man who performed well in the early days of the war. *Mechanikersmaat* Paul Block, who was born on September 18, 1914 in Görlitz in Saxony, entered the German Navy on July 1, 1934 at Wilhelmshaven. A locksmith by trade, Block was identified as a future torpedo specialist; he was promoted to *Mechanikerobergefreiter* on April 1, 1938, to *Mechanikerhauptgefreiter* on July 1, 1938 and subsequently to *Mechanikersmaat* on October 1, 1938. During this period he was assigned to the Torpedo School. He appears to have joined the *U-28* of the U-boat Flotilla *Salzwedel* in 1939.

The *U-28*, a Type VIIA U-boat, was ordered by the *Kriegsmarine* on April 1, 1935. Shipyard workers at the Deutsche Schiff und Maschinenbau AG at Bremen laid her keel at Yard Number 909 on December 2, 1935. She was launched on July 14, 1936; on September 12, 1936 *Kapitänleutnant* Wilhelm Ambrosius commissioned the *U-28* and she immediately joined the U-boat Flotilla *Salzwedel*. By the time that Paul Block joined the crew, *Oberleutnant* Günter Kuhnke had assumed command of the *U-28*. Kuhnke was born at Elbing on September 7, 1912; he joined the Germany Navy in 1931 and like Paul Block received specialized torpedo training. He entered U-boat training in 1935. He assumed command of the *U-28* on October 28, 1938.

As the war drums began to beat in August 1939, Günter Kuhnke and the *U-28* departed Wilhelmshaven on August 19, 1939 for potential operations in the North Atlantic. On September 1, 1939 Germany invaded Poland and the nature of the U-boat's mission changed from potential to actual. On September 14, 1939 at 10:00 a.m., the *U-28* sank the British 4,955-ton *Vancouver City* south of Ireland. The freighter was bringing sugar from Suva, Fiji to Great Britain; three men perished in the attack. But escorts located the *U-28* and at 9:30 p.m. dropped fourteen depth charges in her vicinity. Two days later a British aircraft dropped two more depth charges near the U-boat. Finally, on September 27 the U-boat spent six hours unsuccessfully searching for a downed *Luftwaffe* pilot. The *U-28* returned to Wilhelmshaven on September 29, 1939. Günter Kuhnke received the Iron Cross 2nd Class on the same day; he was promoted to *Kapitänleutnant* on October 1, 1939.

The *U-28* remained in port for over a month, during which time engineers installed a new port diesel engine mount; on November 8, 1939 she departed Wilhelmshaven for her second war patrol. Kuhnke's mission was to circle the British Isles to the north, pass to the west of Ireland and operate southwest of England. Enroute, late on the evening of November 16, some two-hundred miles south of Rockall Banks, the *U-28* stopped the neutral Dutch 5,133-ton tanker *Sliedrecht* carrying 6,600 tons of petroleum products. Finding documents that the ship had been earlier ordered by British authorities in Gibraltar to proceed to Kirkwall, Kuhnke ordered the crew to abandon ship; he then sank the tanker with a torpedo. Five crewmen in one lifeboat were later rescued, but twenty-six men in another lifeboat were never seen again. At 1:19 p.m. on November 25, 1939 south of Ireland, Kuhnke torpedoed the British 5,144-ton freighter *Royston Grange* carrying grain to Liverpool. An enemy destroyer escort pounded the *U-28* for eight hours with depth charges, but Kuhnke escaped and laid twelve anti-shipping mines in Swansea Bay late on December 5, 1939. The *U-28* returned to Wilhelmshaven on December 18, 1939. That day Paul Block received the U-boat War Badge; three days later he was awarded the Iron Cross 2nd Class after the *U-28* made a short journey over to Hamburg where she could be overhauled at the Deutsche Werft shipyard.

After a good two months in port to repair the damages done by the depth charges, the *U-28* departed Wilhelmshaven on February 18, 1940; again it would circle the British Isles. March 7 saw the *U-28* drop eight anti-shipping mines off the Isle of Wight. On March 9, 1940 at 11:17 p.m., Kuhnke fired a torpedo at an illuminated freighter, the Greek 4,979-ton *P Margaronis* sailing in ballast from Antwerp, Belgium to Canada. All thirty crewmen on the ship (which according to the Germans was not flying a flag) perished when she broke in two southwest of Great Britain. Two days later at 3:17 a.m. the *U-28* torpedoed the Dutch 6,236-ton tanker *Eulota* sailing in ballast from Rotterdam, Netherlands to Curacao; all the tanker's crew survived even though the ship broke in two. Kuhnke returned to Wilhelmshaven on March 23, 1940.

Again the *U-28* spent another two months in port, departing Wilhelmshaven on May 20, 1940, but engine problems forced her to pull into Trondheim for emergency repairs. Kuhnke went almost a month before sighting the Finnish freighter *Sarmatia*, sailing in ballast from Liverpool to Nova Scotia. The freighter's crew abandoned ship; the *U-28* fired two torpedoes and the *Sarmatia* quickly sank by the stern southwest of Ireland. The next day at 7:29 p.m., the *U-28* torpedoed the Greek 3,443-ton *Adamandios Georgandis* attempting to reach Cork, Ireland. At 8:00 p.m. Kuhnke fired a coup de grâce that sank the ship. On June 21, 1940 Kuhnke spotted the British 4,443-ton *HMS Prunella*, a special service vessel, and fired a torpedo at noon that struck the target near the bridge. The ship sank several hours later. The *U-28* returned to Wilhelmshaven on July 6, 1940.

On August 11, 1940 the *U-28* departed Wilhelmshaven once again, bound for the North Atlantic. Northwest of Ireland she found the Norwegian 1,599-ton merchant ship *Eva*, a straggler from a convoy, at 4:03 p.m. on August 27, 1940 and stopped her with a torpedo hit. The crew abandoned ship and the *U-28* surfaced and sank the ship, which was carrying 1,750 tons of lumber, with deck-gun fire. The next day, shortly after British aircraft depth-charged the *U-28*, at 8:57 p.m. Kuhnke sank the British 3,946-ton *Kyno* bound from Halifax, Nova Scotia to Hull, England with general cargo; four men on the *Kyno* died in the attack. *Mechanikersmaat* Paul Block was really earning his pay in the torpedo room on this patrol. On September 9, 1940 at 4:47 a.m., one of Block's torpedoes found the British 2,434-ton freighter *Mardinian* carrying 3,500 tons of pitch from Sydney, Nova Scotia to London. The ship went down in thirty minutes with six of her crew some one-hundred miles north-northwest of Bloody Foreland, Ireland.

At 3:26 a.m. on September 11, 1940 Kuhnke got into a convoy and fired two torpedoes. One severely damaged the British 4,678-ton *Harpenden*, while the other sank the Dutch 1,966-ton *Maas*. Twenty men perished when the ship sank west of Ireland. The crew of the *U-28* would not return to Wilhelmshaven after this patrol; the French port of Lorient was now open as a U-boat base and the *U-28* arrived there on September 17, 1940. It was an excellent turn of events; *Mechanikersmaat* Paul Block received the Iron Cross 1st Class two days later. *Kapitänleutnant* Günter Kuhnke received the Knight's Cross on the same day, the thirteenth U-boat man to be so honored. On October 4, 1940 the *U-28* made a short relocation to the U-boat base at St. Nazaire, France, arriving at the new port on October 6.

But her days as a frontline U-boat were numbered. On October 12, 1940 the *U-28* departed St. Nazaire for her sixth and last combat patrol. It would last thirty-five days; at 4:32 a.m. the *U-28* torpedoed the unescorted British 5,389-ton freighter *Matina* carrying 1,500 tons of bananas from Jamaica to Garston, England. The *Matina's* crew abandoned ship and the *U-28* hit the ship with fifteen rounds of 88-mm fire, leaving the ship sinking. Later that day the *U-31* reported sinking the drifting wreck northwest of Ireland; the *Matina's* crew, however, were never seen again. The same fate almost befell the *U-28* on November 13, when at 9:30 p.m. the crew heard two torpedo detonations very close to the stern of the U-boat – the results of an apparent unsuccessful attack by a British submarine. The *U-28* arrived at Wilhelmshaven on November 15, 1940; a week later she sailed to Stettin for a complete overhaul. Her crew then departed and she became a training U-boat until March 17, 1944 when she sank at the Neustadt U-boat pier in an operational accident, while assigned to the 22nd U-boat Training Flotilla.

Günter Kuhnke went on to command the *U-125* for two patrols and then commanded the 10th U-boat Flotilla and the 33rd U-boat Flotilla. He ended the war as a *Korvettenkapitän*. Kuhnke joined the new German Navy in 1955 and retired as a rear admiral. Günter Kuhnke died on October 11, 1990.

Having been identified as a highly skilled torpedo expert, Paul Block was promoted to *Obermechanikersmaat* on May 1, 1941 and was identified as a future commissioned officer in the torpedo branch. He was commissioned a *Leutnant* on April 1, 1944 and an *Oberleutnant* in the torpedo specialties on May 1, 1945 just before the war ended. His last duty assignment was with the Torpedo Arsenal West on the torpedo supply ship *Pelikan*. Paul Block survived the war and settled in Ludwigshafen.

Known Crewmembers for the U-14

Ahme, Joachim	
Bahnsen, Hein	
Bigalk, Gerhard	*Korvettenkapitän*
Bortfeldt, Karl-Hermann	*Oberleutnant zur See*
Brudereck, Rudolf	*Mechanikermaat*
Dierks, Hans-Joachim	*Oberleutnant zur See*
Dies, Seppl	*Bootsmaat*
Dingeldein, Karl	*Bootsmaat*
Ehrlich, Max	*Oberfunkmaat*
Graemer, Heinz	*Obermaschinist*
Gross, Walter	*Bootsmann*
Haar, Emil	*Obersteuermann*
Hartmann	*Leutnant (Ing)*
Heidel, Werner	*Kapitänleutnant*
Hürter, Heinz	
Klaucke, Paul	
Köhntopp, Walter	*Kapitänleutnant*
Könenkamp, Jürgen	*Kapitänleutnant*
Kräth, Hermann	*Maschinenmaat*
Krecht, Anton	
Kressmann, Richard	
Krohn, Otto	*Oberleutnant (Ing)*
Kunze, Erich	
Kühn	*Stabsobersteuermann*
Matz, Joachim	*Korvettenkapitän*
Mielke, Heinz	*Maschinenobergefreiter*
Möller, Erwin	*Maschinenmaat*
Müller, Hans	*Kapitänleutnant (Ing)*
Oehrn, Victor	*Fregattenkapitän*
Petersen, Bruno	*Obersteuermann*
Petersen, Klaus	*Kapitänleutnant*
Purkhold, Hubertus	*Kapitänleutnant*
Schaper, Fritz	*Obermaschinenmaat*
Schönfelder	*Obersteuermann*
Schröder, Gottfried	*Oberleutnant (Ing)*
Skiba, Otto	*Obersteuermann*
Stegu, Stanislaus	
Streubel, Werner	*Oberleutnant (Ing)*
Thöllden, Hans	*Oberleutnant (Ing)*
Wellner, Horst-Joachim	*Kapitänleutnant*
Wenzel, Karl	*Matrosenobergefreiter*
Wittwer, Max	
Wohlfahrt, Herbert	*Kapitänleutnant*
Wohleben, Fritz	

Known Crewmembers for the U-109

Anetzberger, Siegfried	*Obersteuermann*
Arnold, Wolfgang	*Funkmaat*
Bender, Karl	*Maschinengefreiter*
Benzmann, Walter	*Maschinenmaat*
Berkemeier, Friedrich	*Maschinengefreiter*
Bischof, Jürgen	*Funkmaat*
Bleichrodt, Heinrich	*Korvettenkapitän*
Böcker, Gerhard	*Bootsmaat*
Borchardt, Werner	*Bootsmaat*
Boss, Kurt-Albrecht	*Funkobergefreiter*
Braatz, Wilhelm	*Obersteuermann*
Breuckmann, Josef	
Breuer, Matthias	*Mechanikermaat*
Bruns, Helmut	*Leutnant zur See*
Christossek, Günter	*Maschinenobergefreiter*
Detzner, Herbert	*Leutnant zur See*
Eichler, Gustav	*Maschinenmaat*
Engmann, Herbert-Heinz	*Obermaschinist*
Feil, Heinrich	*Mechanikerobergefreiter*
Fischer, Hans-Georg	*Fregattenkapitän*
Flegel, Hans-Jürgen	*Matrosenobergefreiter*
Geisser, Karl	*Maschinenobergefreiter*
Goldbeck, Herbert-Heinrich	*Matrosenobergefreiter*
Gross, Walter	*Bootsmann*
Habicht, Jürgen	*Leutnant zur See*
Hagen, Ferdinand	*Oberfunkmaat*
Heil, Heinz	*Maschinenobergefreiter*
Hengen, Dieter	*Oberleutnant zur See*
Hentschel, Heinz	*Oberbootsmann*
Heyer, Albert	*Leutnant (Ing)*
Hirschfeld, Wolfgang	*Oberfunkmeister*
Hoffmann, Eberhard	*Fregattenkapitän*
Holzapfel, Heinrich	*Maschinenobergefreiter*
Jäckel, Richard	*Matrosenobergefreiter*
Järschel, Werner	*Matrosenobergefreiter*
Jürgensen, Hein	
Keller, Siegfried	*Oberleutnant zur See*
Kindermann, Wilhelm	*Obermaschinist*
Klein, Manfred	*Matrosengefreiter*
Korn, Berthold	*Matrose*
Lechner, Alfons	*Maschinengefreiter*
Lenz, Kurt	*Maschinengefreiter*
Leyes, Aloys	*Maschinenobergefreiter*
Liekefett, Wilhelm	*Mechanikergefreiter*
Lindert, Kurt	*Fähnrich zur See*
Loose, Georg	*Maschinenobergefreiter*
Lusch, Gerhard	*Maschinengefreiter*
Lüttge, Willi	*Matrosenobergefreiter*
Mäck, Karl	*Obermechanikermaat*
Maureschat, Eduard	*Bootsmann*
Monecke, Walter	*Maschinist*
Moritz, Werner	*Obermaschinist*
Morsel, Helmut	
Muck, Kurt	*Obergefreiter*
Nikolai, Anton	*Maschinenmaat*
Peters, Otto	*Maschinenmaat*
Petersen, Bruno	*Obersteuermann*
Pötter, Paul	*Bootsmann*
Reichert, Günter	*Maschinenobergefreiter*
Reissnauer, Karl	*Obermaschinenmaat*
Reiter, Karl	*Matrosengefreiter*
Rieger, Friedrich	*Maschinenobergefreiter*
Salewski, Herbert	*Maschinenmaat*
Sallach, Walter	*Matrosengefreiter*
Salzer, Hans	*Matrosengefreiter*
Schaufel, Gerhard	*Maschinengefreiter*
Schewe	*Obermaschinist*
Schramm, Joachim	*Oberleutnant zur See*
Schwartzkopff, Volkmar	*Kapitänleutnant*
Seidel, Berthold	*Bootsmann*
Seiler, Willy	*Maschinenmaat*
Spenner, Friedrich	*Funkobergefreiter*
Staffeldt, Wolfgang	*Mechanikerobergefreiter*
Strassberger, Max	*Matrosenobergefreiter*
Vetter, Walter	*Obermaschinenmaat*
Wagenhofer, Peter-Alois	*Matrose*
Weber, Martin	*Kapitänleutnant (Ing)*

Wenzel, Karl	*Bootsmann*
Wex, Hans-Dieter	*Oberleutnant zur See*
Wiegele, Walter	*Maschinenmaat*
Will, Karl	*Matrosengefreiter*
Winter, Alfred	
Wissmann, Friedrich-Wilhelm	*Kapitänleutnant*
Witte, Werner	*Kapitänleutnant*
Wittfeld, Herbert	*Matrosengefreiter*
Zank, Karl	*Bootsmann*

Known Crewmembers for the U-28

Ambrosius, Wilhelm	*Fregattenkapitän*
Anderheyden, Willi	*Funkmaat*
Block, Paul	*Leutnant* (T)
Brüller, Ernst-Ulrich	*Kapitänleutnant*
Christiansen, Uwe	*Oberleutnant zur See*
Dannenberg, Wilhelm	
Dietrich, Willi	*Oberleutnant zur See*
Dömkes, Josef	*Bootsmaat*
Eckhardt, Hermann	*Kapitänleutnant*
Exner	*Leutnant (Ing)*
Finger, Arnold	*Obermaschinist*
Gabriel, Bernhard	*Mechanikerobergefreiter*
Gärzke, Friedrich von	*Oberleutnant zur See*
Guggenberger, Friedrich	*Kapitänleutnant*
Hering, Ludwig	*Kapitänleutnant (Ing)*
Heyn, Rudolf	*Obermaschinist*
Kammüller	*Oberleutnant (Ing)*
Kautz, Günter	*Obersteuermann*
Kelling, Hans-Klaudius	*Obersteuermann*
Kelling, Hinrich	*Kapitänleutnant*
Krempl, Erich	*Oberleutnant zur See*
Krieg, Ernst	*Kapitänleutnant*
Kuhnke, Günter	*Korvettenkapitän*
Lange, Helmut	
Lemp, Fritz-Julius	*Kapitänleutnant*
Leuser, Hugo	
Looff, Hans-Günther	*Korvettenkapitän*
Marbach, Karl-Heinz	*Kapitänleutnant*
Meyn, Rudolf	*Obermaschinist*
Niewerth	*Leutnant (Ing)*
Peters, Friedrich	
Poeschel, Wolfgang	*Oberleutnant zur See*
Ranke, Otto	*Oberleutnant (Ing)*
Ratsch, Heinrich	*Kapitänleutnant*
Riehm, Nikolaus	*Obermechanikermaat*
Sachse	*Maschinengefreiter*
Sachse, Dietrich	*Oberleutnant zur See*
Scherer, Andreas	
Simon, Helmut	
Stohwasser, Herald	*Oberleutnant zur See*
Welsch, Paul	*Korvettenkapitän (Ing)*
Werner, Ewald	*Matrosenobergefreiter*
Winter, Alfred	
Zetsche, Hans-Jürgen	*Kapitänleutnant*

Sources, "The Old Guard:" G.H. Bennett, and R. Bennett, *Hitler's Admirals*, Annapolis, Maryland: Naval Institute Press, 2004, 89, 147; Clay Blair, *Hitler's U-boat War: The Hunters, 1939-1942*, New York: Random House, 1996, 293, 327, 336, 374, 441, 471, 473, 533, 671; Clay Blair, *Hitler's U-boat War: The Hunted, 1942-1945*, New York: Modern Library, 2000, 275, 276; Rainer Busch and Hans-Joachim Röll, *German U-boat Commanders of World War II*, translated by Geoffrey Brooks, Annapolis, Maryland: Naval Institute Press, 1999, 68, 275; Karl Dönitz, *Memoirs: Ten Years and Twenty Days*, translated by R.H. Stevens, Annapolis, Maryland: Da Capo Press, 1997, 78; Manfred Dörr, *Die Ritterkreuzträger der U-Boot-Waffe, Band 1: A-J, Band 2: L-Z*, Osnabrück, FRG: Biblio Verlag, 1988, Band 1-60, 61, 62, Band 2 – 349, 350, 351; *F.d.U./B.d.U. War Diary, 16-31 May 1941* (PG30289), 81; *F.d.U./B.d.U. War Diary, 16-30 September 1942* (PG32014), 187; Michael Gannon, *Operation Drumbeat: The Dramatic True Story of Germany's First U-boat Attacks Along the American Coast in World War II*, New York: Harper & Row, 1990, 80; Michael L. Hadley, *U-boats against Canada: German Submarines in Canadian Waters*, Montreal: McGill-Queen's University Press, 1990, 57, 67, 70; Axel Niestlé, *German U-boat Losses during World War II*, Annapolis, Maryland: Naval Institute Press, 1998, 32, 120; Herbert Ritschel, *Kurzfassung Kriegstagebücher deutscher U-boote 1939-1945, Band 1: KTB U1 – U50,* Norderstedt, Germany: Books on Demand, 45, 46, 47, 48, 49, 155, 156, 157, 158, 159, 160, 161, 162, 163; Herbert Ritschel, *Kurzfassung Kriegstagebücher deutscher U-boote 1939-1945, Band 3: KTB U100 – U124,* Norderstedt, Germany: Books on Demand, 185, 194; Jürgen Rohwer, *Axis Submarine Successes 1939-1945*, Annapolis, Maryland: Naval Institute Press, 1983, 1, 3, 6, 7, 10, 11, 14, 16, 19, 20, 26, 27, 28, 35, 53, 74, 75, 77, 91, 92, 113, 115, 120, 124, 214; Jak Mallmann Showell, *U-boats at War: Landings on Hostile Shores*, Hersham, England: Ian Allan Publishing, 2000, 137; War Diary of the U-14, August 23, 1939 – June 12, 1941, PG 30011/1-8; ONI Roll T-297-B, *National Archives Microfilm Publication T1022*, roll 3027, RG 242; www.ubootwaffe.net; www.uboatarchive.net.

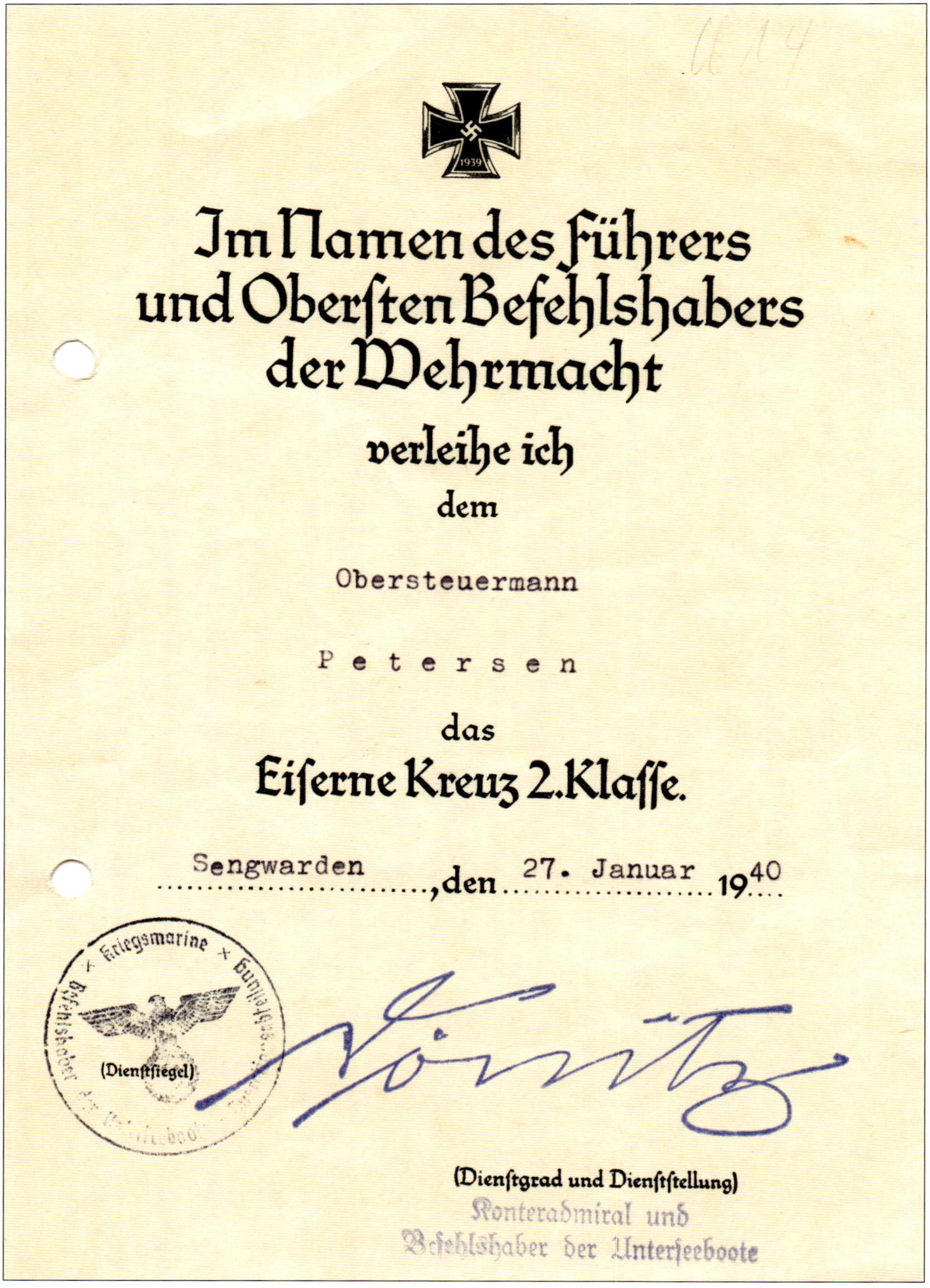

U 14

Im Namen des Führers und Obersten Befehlshabers der Wehrmacht

verleihe ich

dem

Obersteuermann

P e t e r s e n

das

Eiserne Kreuz 2. Klasse.

Sengwarden, den 27. Januar 1940

Kriegsmarine
Befehlshaber der Unterseeboote
(Dienstsiegel)

(Dienstgrad und Dienststellung)

Konteradmiral und
Befehlshaber der Unterseeboote

Iron Cross 2nd Class award document to Bruno Petersen of the U-14 on January 26, 1940. *It was awarded at Wilhelmshaven shortly after the conclusion of a successful third war patrol. Document has a facsimile signature of Konteradmiral Karl Dönitz.*

Im Namen
des Führers und Reichskanzlers

verleihe ich

dem Mechaniker-Obergefreiten
(Dienstgrad)

Paul Block
(Vor- und Zuname)

St.-N.-Nr. N. 1140 / 34 S

Torpedoschule
(Marineteil)

für 4jährige treue Dienste in der Wehrmacht die

Dienstauszeichnung IV. Klasse

Wilhelmshaven, den 1. Juli 1938

Der 2. Admiral der Nordseestation
von Schrader
Konteradmiral

Für die Richtigkeit

(Name)

Kapitän zur See und Kommandeur T.S.
(Dienstgrad und Dienststellung)

Award document for the Armed Forces Service Medal IV Class, dated July 1, 1938 to Paul Block. *Document is signed by Kapitän zur See Kurt Utke, Commander of the Torpedo School.*

Im Namen des Führers
und Obersten Befehlshabers der Wehrmacht

verleihe ich

dem Mechanikermaat
(Dienstgrad)

Paul Block
(Vor- und Zuname)

U.-Flottille "Saltzwedel"
(Marineteil)

die Medaille zur Erinnerung
an den 1. Oktober 1938

Wilhelmshaven, den 16. September 1939

Der Kommandierende Admiral
der Marinestation der Nordsee

Saalwächter
Admiral

Für die Richtigkeit

Friedeburg
Kapitän z. See
u. Chef der Org.Abtlg. B.d.U.

Nr. /

Commemorative Medal of 1 October 1938 (the Annexation of Czechoslovakia) award document to Paul Block of the U-boat Flotilla Salzwedel. *Dated September 16, 1939, it is stamp-signed by Kapitän zur See Hans-Georg von Friedeburg, Chief of the Organization Department, B.d.U.*

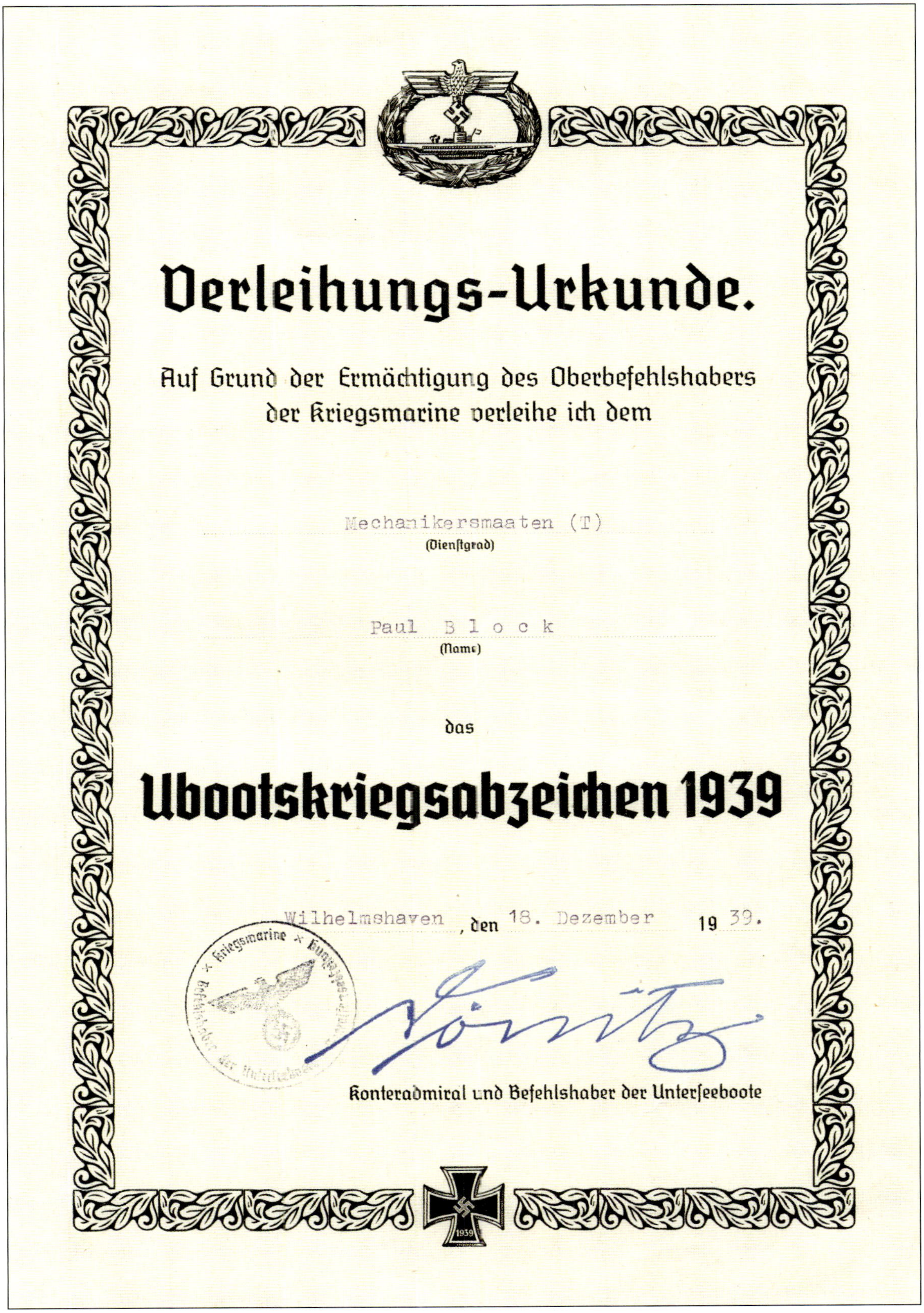

Verleihungs-Urkunde.

Auf Grund der Ermächtigung des Oberbefehlshabers
der Kriegsmarine verleihe ich dem

Mechanikersmaaten (T)
(Dienstgrad)

Paul Block
(Name)

das

Ubootskriegsabzeichen 1939

Wilhelmshaven, den 18. Dezember 1939.

Konteradmiral und Befehlshaber der Unterseeboote

U-boat War Badge award document to Paul Block of the U-28 on December 18, 1939. *The document has a facsimile signature of Karl Dönitz; Block received the award shortly after the conclusion of the boat's highly successful second war patrol. U-boat crewmen generally received the award after their second or third war patrols; in at least one instance award criteria was described as sixty cumulative days at sea on war patrols.*

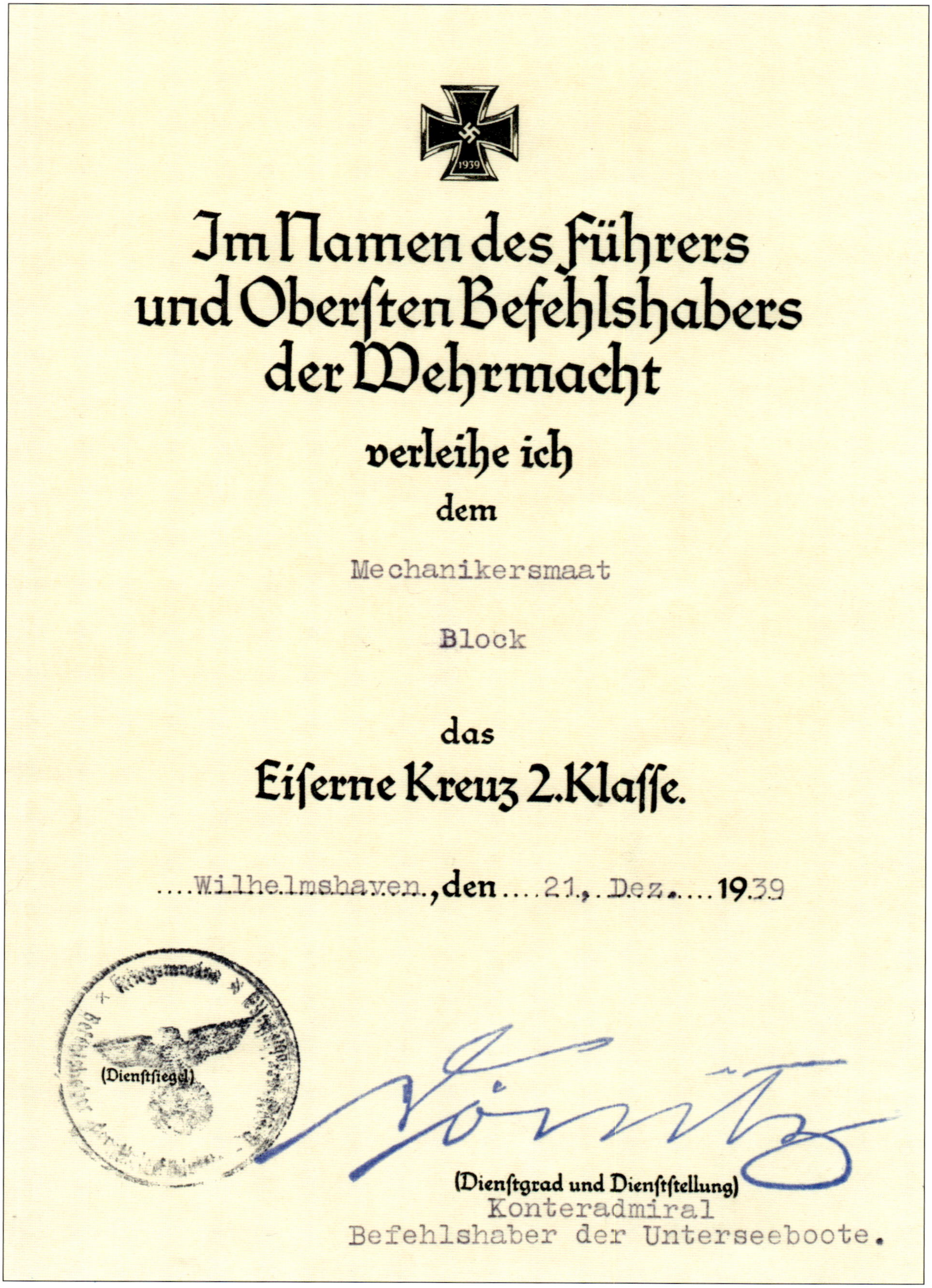

Im Namen des Führers
und Obersten Befehlshabers
der Wehrmacht

verleihe ich

dem

Mechanikersmaat

Block

das

Eiserne Kreuz 2. Klasse.

....Wilhelmshaven., den....21.. Dez.....1939

(Dienstsiegel)

(Dienstgrad und Dienststellung)
Konteradmiral
Befehlshaber der Unterseeboote.

Iron Cross 2nd Class award document to Paul Block of the U-28 on December 21, 1939. *The document has a facsimile signature of Karl Dönitz; it was awarded at Wilhelmshaven, Germany.*

Im Namen des Führers
und Obersten Befehlshabers
der Wehrmacht

verleihe ich

dem

Mechanikersmaaten

B l o c k

das

Eiserne Kreuz 1. Klasse.

Sengwarden, den 19. September 19 40

(Dienstsiegel)

(Dienstgrad und Dienststellung)

Befehlshaber der Unterseeboote

Iron Cross 1st Class award document to Paul Block of the U-28 on September 19, 1940. *The document has a facsimile signature of Karl Dönitz. Inset:* **Post-war photograph of Paul Block.**

CHAPTER FIVE

"DEATH TRAP"
U-25
1940

Most of the different models of German U-boats in World War II were outstanding designs. The Type-VIIs exceeded Dönitz's initial optimism, ranging far wider than the North Sea and eastern half of the North Atlantic for which they were planned. The Type-IXs were indeed U-boat cruisers, operating on both sides of the North Atlantic, the Caribbean, the South Atlantic and even the Indian Ocean.

Such design successes were not always the case, however. The Type-IIs proved to be too small and very rough to handle in the North Sea, where turbulent seas were the norm. The Type-I boats, of which only two were constructed, were also difficult designs. The boats were also difficult to handle, did not dive particularly fast and seemed easy to track by enemy underwater detection gear. While the *Kriegsmarine* learned from these errors – and incorporated improvements into the Type-IX boats – life aboard a Type-I was tenuous at best. Born together in 1934, they died within a month of each other in mid-1940 as the war was in its infancy.

The *U-25* and her sister boat *U-26* were both ordered on December 17, 1934, but progress on the *U-25* soon advanced at a quicker pace. On June 28, 1935 construction workers at Yard Number 903 of the Deutsche Schiff-und Maschinenbau AG yard at Bremen laid her keel and on February 14, 1936 she was launched. The *U-25*'s crew completed her initial trials and the ship was commissioned on April 6, 1936 joining the U-boat School Flotilla based at Neustadt for continued training.

Dönitz's Crews
***Maschinengefreiter* Hans Berg**
Served in the engine room on the *U-25*.
Spent 128 days at sea on U-boat war patrols.
Killed in action on August 3, 1940 in the North Sea.

The *U-25*'s pre-war commanders were quite distinguished in the submarine service. From April 6, 1936 to January 3, 1938 *Korvettenkapitän* Eberhard Godt served in command. A future rear admiral, he later became Dönitz's deputy in charge of all tactical operations for the U-boat arm. Godt died on September 13, 1995 at the ripe old age of ninety-five. Next to command the *U-25* – from January 3, 1938 to December 12, 1938 – was *Kapitänleutnant* Werner von Schmidt. Von Schmidt commanded five other U-boats during the first half of the war before assuming command of the 8th U-boat Training Flotilla in 1943; he survived the war. On December 10, 1938 *Kapitänleutnant* Otto Schuhart became the commander of the *U-25* and remained with the boat until April 3, 1939. A future Knight's Cross winner, he sank the British aircraft carrier *HMS Courageous* in the *U-29* before assuming command of the 21st U-boat Training Flotilla. Schuhart also survived the war; he died on February 26, 1990. The last pre-war commander of the *U-25* was *Kapitänleutnant* Georg-Heinz Michel, who served exactly five months as commander from April 4, 1939 to September 4, 1939. He later commanded the *U-54* and *U-8*, served in various U-boat staff positions and survived the war.

In September 1939 the *U-25* transferred to the combat organization, U-boat Flotilla *Saltzwedel* (later renamed the 2nd U-boat Flotilla) based at Wilhelmshaven. At the same time the man who would become the boat's most distinguished commander, *Kapitänleutnant* Viktor Schütze stepped aboard. Schütze would gain his fame as the skipper of the *U-103*; during his time at the helm of the *U-25* he made three war patrols with this boat, winning the Iron Cross 2nd Class on November 13, 1939 and the Iron Cross 1st Class on February 21, 1940.

The *U-25*'s first war patrol began on October 18, 1939 when she left Wilhelmshaven for operations in the North Atlantic. Among the crew was *Matrosengefreiter* Hans Berg, who as an electrical equipment specialist tended the electric motors in the engine room. A member of the Nazi Party, Berg served in the SA in 1937, winning the SA Sports Badge; he also won one of the grades of the National Sport Badge. He also served in the Hitler Youth.

It was a rough voyage. Three days out, the boat took on water in the stern but the crew repaired her. By October 28 Schütze could see the Spanish coast. Dönitz intended that the boat, with the *U-26* and *U-53*, proceed through the Straits of Gibraltar and operate in the western Mediterranean, but it was not to be. On October 29, the *U-25* experienced rudder difficulties; her damage was not enough to return to port but was enough to abort the mission to the Mediterranean. On October 31, 1939 the *U-25* was more successful, sinking the French 5,874-ton *Baoulé* bound from Kribi, Cameroon to Bordeaux at 5:25 a.m. off La Coruña, Spain. The ship, carrying palm kernels, cotton, cocoa, coffee and rubber, lost two killed when she went down, but Schütze reported to Dönitz that he had four torpedoes that failed during the engagement. Schütze had hoped to be resupplied on the

Spanish coast but Dönitz informed him this would not be possible due to "political difficulties."

Mishaps then began to plague the boat. On November 4, Schütze reported to Dönitz that the crosspiece of the forward torpedo hatch was broken and the boat might not be capable of diving if depth-charged; the commander added he was returning to base. The following day the troubles continued when *Bootsmaat* Wilhelm Lützeler was lost overboard in the Bay of Biscay; an hour-long search failed to produce results. The *U-25* returned to Wilhelmshaven on November 13, 1939. The B.d.U. war diary reported on the boat's troubles:

> "*U-25* entered port. The boat did not have much luck. The C.O.'s task was no easy one. There were torpedo failures, the guns failed at a decisive moment and this boat, parts of which are still rather antiquated, is not easy to handle."

Schütze attempted two patrols in December. The initial patrol commenced from Wilhelmshaven on December 19, destined for the west coast of Portugal. The following day Schütze reported that the *U-25* had a bad leak of oil from one of the tanks; the *U-25* returned to port after just two days. The boat departed Wilhelmshaven a second time that month, on December 31, but the following day again reported an oil leak and returned to base on January 3.

On January 13, 1940 the *U-25* left Wilhelmshaven on its second confirmed war patrol for operations in the North Atlantic, where she would initially operate off the coast of Scotland and then move to the west coast of Spain. Success came swiftly; at 12:55 p.m. on January 17, 1940 the *U-25* hit the British 4,751-ton *Polzella* headed from Narvik, Norway to Methil and Tees in northern England with iron ore, just in front of the bridge as she was north of the Shetland Islands. At 2:10 p.m. the *U-25* sank the Norwegian 1,140-ton freighter *Enid* bound from Trondheim, Norway to Dublin, Ireland with a load of woodpulp. The Norwegian ship was in the process of attempting to rescue survivors of the *Polzella*. While the *Enid* was standing by ready to lower the boats, the *U-25* began shelling her with the deck-gun, hitting her at least six times. *Kapitänleutnant* Schütze then fired a torpedo at his target, striking her in the forward hull and rending the ship in two.

The next day at 4:25 p.m., the *U-25* torpedoed and sank the Swedish 6,873-ton *Pajala*, carrying 9,150 tons of grain and cattle food north of Scotland. Additional success followed and at 11:38 a.m. on January 22, 1940 the *U-25* stopped the Norwegian 2,589-ton *Songa* some two-hundred miles west of the Scilly Isles by firing a shot across her bow. She was carrying barrels, sponges, copper, tires, coffee, cotton and tin from Philadelphia to Rotterdam. After determining the ship was carrying contraband, Schütze ordered her crew to abandon ship and proceeded to sink her at 1:22 p.m. with a torpedo – she slid beneath the waves in eight minutes.

Schütze then moved south. The *U-25* refueled in secret at Cadiz, Spain from the German supply ship *Thalia* on January 30. On February 3, 1940 at 2:32 p.m., the *U-25* sank the British 6,805-ton *Armanistan*, a member of convoy OG-16, off Portugal. The ship was bound from Antwerp to Basra, Iraq carrying 8,300 tons general cargo. During this time the *U-25* resupplied off Spain. The boat then returned north. On February 13, 1940 the *U-25* sank the Danish 5,177-ton *Chastine Mærsk* carrying phosphate fertilizer from Saffi, Morocco for Denmark. The attack, consisting of deck gunfire and torpedoes, occurred at 7:16 a.m. off Norway. The *U-25* returned on February 19, 1940 to Wilhelmshaven from this successful patrol.

The *U-25* departed on April 3, 1940 for her third war patrol under Viktor Schütze from Wilhelmshaven for operations in support of the German invasion of Norway. At 9:27 p.m. on April 9, Schütze radioed B.d.U. stating he had five enemy destroyers in sight. On April 11, the *U-25* reported attacking two British destroyers in the Ofoten Fjord but could not observe the results; it is likely that the torpedoes experienced mechanical failures and detonated early. The *U-25* then moved to the Lofoten area and subsequently to the Shetland Islands. Her contact with B.d.U. headquarters was sporadic as the boat's radio transmitter was out of order. She arrived back at Wilhelmshaven on May 6, 1940 after more than four weeks on patrol.

Viktor Schütze then departed the *U-25* on May 19, 1940 to begin the process of commissioning and commanding the *U-103*. In his place on the *U-25* came *Kapitänleutnant* Heinz Beduhn. Born in Berlin on August 11, 1907 Beduhn was an accomplished submariner. Entering the German Navy in 1926, he served on various surface ships before commencing U-boat training in late 1935. Beduhn served as a watch officer on the *U-10* and *U-16* before commanding the *U-18* and *U-23*. After serving on the *U-23* he moved to the U-boat School Flotilla, where he trained future U-boat men. He was therefore quite qualified to tackle the *U-25*'s challenges.

The *U-25* left Wilhelmshaven under Beduhn's command on June 8, 1940 for operations southwest of Ireland. She hit one enemy ship on this patrol; at 7:16 a.m. on June 13, 1940 the *U-25* torpedoed the British 17,046-ton armed merchant cruiser *HMS Scotstoun*, of the 10th Cruiser Squadron, in the stern some eighty miles west of Barra Island, Outer Hebrides, Scotland. The warship, the converted passenger ship *Caledonia*, sported eight six-inch guns, but was cursed with a slow speed of 15 knots. Six men died in the attack; 346 men evacuated the ship. At 5:29 p.m. the *U-25* fired a coup de grâce, but the torpedo missed. The U-boat crew then fired a second torpedo, which hit aft of the ship's funnel, causing the *HMS Scotstoun* to sink by the stern. Then, more mishaps returned to the boat. On June 19, at 12:30 a.m. the *U-25* was rammed, probably by an enemy destroyer, while making a submerged night attack on a convoy. The collision damaged her bridge and periscope; the boat plunged to a depth of ninety meters but the crew regained control. Unable to remain in his area of operations, Beduhn began to return to Wilhelmshaven. The *U-25* returned to Wilhelmshaven on June 29, 1940. In his out-briefing to Dönitz, Beduhn explained that during the patrol he had also missed engaging a British battle cruiser (either the *HMS Renown* or *HMS Repulse*) because his firing gear had failed during a three-shot fan against the target.

While at port a decision had to be made. The boat sported a lucky mushroom conning tower emblem; after being recently rammed underwater by a freighter, the upper half of the conning tower was destroyed. Should the lucky mushroom be retained? The crew apparently took a vote and the lucky talisman was preserved – but it had lost its magic.

On August 1, 1940 the *U-25* departed Wilhelmshaven; once again, it was bound for the North Atlantic. What happened next was a mystery. Because of recent enemy activity, the B.d.U. considered the northern U-boat transit route through the North Sea was dangerous. Therefore, the *U-25* (and three other U-boats as well) was ordered to use a more southerly route. As Dönitz explained in the war diary:

> "In view of these <u>known</u> dangers on the Northerly route, Route I appears to be the safer. It has not been used for some time. At the time when a change was contemplated, a chart captured from "Seal" [British submarine captured by the Germans] showed 2 circles entered in this route, which led F.O. North Sea Defenses to suspect that there were enemy minefields within these circles. Against this however: the route was several times used by U-boats after the date of issue of "Seal's" chart, and was check-swept by F.O. North Sea Defenses forces;

two sample sweeps were made in the route about a fortnight ago; except for the "Seal" document, which does not give any definite indication of mines, there is no indication at all that the route is fouled. Changes of inward and outward routes, which have always been aimed at and affected, reduce the risk of these routes becoming known. Route I must therefore be considered the safer route at the moment."

But the German calculations were incomplete. On March 3, 1940 the British destroyers *HMS Express*, *HMS Esk*, *HMS Icarus* and *HMS Impulsive* laid Mine Barrage Field No 7 over Route 1. By August 3 two U-boats had safely passed through Route 1 but no reports had been received from the *U-25*. German patrol aircraft reported one new and one older patch of oil in Route 1, an ominous sign. The pilots also reported mine-like objects in the water near the fresh oil patch, another gloomy note. Dönitz dispatched a sea-search party and made the following observation in the war diary on August 4:

"During the search operation for *U-25*, a submarine chaser struck a mine and sank. She had detected a wreck shortly beforehand with her echo ranging gear. *U-25* must be presumed to have been lost in Route 1. There is one small hope, in that the boats transmitter was slightly defective. A dockyard workman repaired it shortly before she sailed, but there is a chance that it may have failed again. The probable loss of this boat led me to reconsider my views set out on August 1 on the subject of outward routes. I am still of the opinion that the decision to use Route 1 was right in the light of information available. One could have reproached oneself with justice if a boat had been lost on the Northern route through the known dangers there. The mines observed in Route 1 were recently laid, as the overgrowth showed they were also outside the periphery of the "Seal" circle. The fact that the boats used this route to a considerable extent after the date of the "Seal" document, without being mined or observing any mines and now suddenly, besides *U-25*, a submarine chaser and a minesweeper have struck mines, shows that this is a new field. It must therefore be assumed that *U-25*, if she is in fact lost, was the victim of a new, hitherto unknown danger."

The *U-25* never reported and her demise claimed the entire crew. Did she strike a British mine, or did mechanical problems cause a catastrophic pressure hull failure? No one would ever know, but she probably met her end on August 3, 1940 north of the Frisian Islands. German authorities found the body of twenty-year-old *Mechanikergefreiter* Alfred Magermanns washed ashore at Helgoland on August 19, 1940. The young man from Nürnberg was buried at the military cemetery at Wilhelmshaven. The other crewmen, including Hans Berg, were never found.

Known Crewmembers for the U-25

Ahlers, Günther	*Steuermann*smaat
Albrecht, Edmund	*Matrosengefreiter*
Arendt, Alfred	*Matrosengefreiter*
Bartel, Johannes	*Matrosengefreiter*
Bauer, Heinrich	*Funkobergefreiter*
Beduhn, Heinz-Günther	*Korvettenkapitän*
Behlau, Fritz	*Maschinenmaat*
Berg, Hans	*Maschinengefreiter*
Bielig, Karl	*Matrosengefreiter*
Braun, Heinz-Wilhelm	*Funkgefreiter*
Brodwolf, Eduard	*Maschinengefreiter*
Damaschke, Rudi	*Matrosengefreiter*
Deckinger, Helmut	*Maschinenobergefreiter*
Diener, Otto	*Maschinenobergefreiter*
Döbereiner, Hans	*Kapitänleutnant (Ing)*
Eisenecker, Jakob	*Maschinenmaat*
Elmenhorst, Hinrich	*Oberleutnant zur See*
Fedde, Franz	*Obersteuermann*
Feutner, Michael	*Maschinenmaat*
Frauenheim, Fritz	*Fregattenkapitän*
Freund, Herbert	
Friedrich, Georg	*Matrosengefreiter*
Fritsche, Heinrich	*Kapitänleutnant (Ing)*
Gerber, Adam	*Maschinengefreiter*
Godt, Eberhard	*Konteradmiral*
Gossler, Kurt von	*Korvettenkapitän*
Gottermeyer, Hans	*Obermaschinist*
Gottwald, Johannes	*Oberleutnant (Ing)*
Gruber, Ernst	*Matrosengefreiter*
Härle, Rudolf	*Obermaschinist*
Heuser, Josef	
Hohmann, Otto	*Bootsmaat*
Jürgens, Ernst	*Maschinenmaat*
Kentrat, Eitel	*Korvettenkapitän*
Kessler, Theodor	*Funkmaat*
Kohlenberger, Alfred	*Maschinenobergefreiter*
Köhler, Walter	*Maschinengefreiter*
Kramer, Walter	*Obermaschinenmaat*
Loh, Willi	*Mechanikerobergefreiter*
Lützeler, Wilhelm	*Bootsmaat*
Magermanns, Alfred	*Mechanikergefreiter*
Marl, Peter	*Oberbootsmaat*
Menzel, Erich	
Metzenauer, Adolf	*Maschinengefreiter*
Meyer, Hans-Georg	*Matrosengefreiter*
Michel, Georg	*Korvettenkapitän*
Müller, Wolfgang	*Bootsmaat*
Noll, Johann	*Mechanikergefreiter*
Norwig, Werner	*Mechanikermaat*
Nothhelfer, Mathias	*Oberbootsmaat*
Nuschke, Horst	*Oberleutnant zur See*
Opelt, Rudolf	*Oberleutnant (Ing)*
Opitz, Herbert	*Korvettenkapitän*
Paulshen, Ottokar	*Kapitänleutnant*
Pinkwart, Albert	*Obermaschinist*
Rählecke, Kurt	*Obermaschinenmaat*
Redlich, Walter	*Maschinengefreiter*
Sander, Paul	*Obersteuermann*
Schlumberger, Heinrich	*Oberleutnant (Ing)*
Schmid, Maximilian	*Maschinenmaat*
Schmidt, Heinrich	*Kapitänleutnant (Ing)*
Schmidt, Werner von	*Korvettenkapitän*
Schöffer, Valentin	*Maschinenhauptgefreiter*
Schollmeyer, Willi	
Schuhart, Otto	*Korvettenkapitän*
Schulz, Werner	*Matrosengefreiter*
Schütz, Erich	*Obermaschinist*

Schütze, Viktor	*Kapitän zur See*
Seidel, Kurt	*Matrosengefreiter*
Seip, Wilhelm	*Maschinenobergefreiter*
Spälter, Werner	*Leutnant zur See*
Spiwoks, Wilhelm	*Funkmaat*
Splettstösser, Hans	*Obermaschinenmaat*
Staffel, Mathias	*Maschinenmaat*
Thiede, Werner	*Mechanikergefreiter*
Wasmuth, Heinrich	*Bootsmann*
Weber, Helmut	*Maschinengefreiter*
Wiebusch, Friedrich	*Maschinengefreiter*

Sources, "Death Trap:" Rainer Busch and Röll, Hans-Joachim, *German U-boat Commanders of World War II*, translated by Geoffrey Brooks, Annapolis, Maryland: Naval Institute Press, 1999, 82, 179, 228, 236; Manfred Dörr, *Die Ritterkreuzträger der U-Boot-Waffe, Band 1: A-J, Band 2: L-Z*, Osnabrück, FRG: Biblio Verlag, 1988, Band 2 – 259, 260, 261; *F.d.U./B.d.U. War Diary, 16-31 October 1939* (PG30250), 41, 48; *F.d.U./B.d.U. War Diary, 1-15 November 1939* (PG30251), 49, 53; *F.d.U./B.d.U. War Diary, 16-31 December 1939* (PG30254), 70, 71; *F.d.U./B.d.U. War Diary, 1-15 January 1940* (PG30255), 74, 76; *F.d.U./B.d.U. War Diary, 1-15 April 1940* (PG30262), 6; *F.d.U./B.d.U. War Diary, 16-30 April 1940* (PG30263), 41; *F.d.U./B.d.U. War Diary, 16-30 June 1940* (PG30267), 81, 84; *F.d.U./B.d.U. War Diary, 1-15 August 1940* (PG30270), 93, 94, 95; Georg Högel, *Embleme, Wappen, Malings Deutscher U-Boote 1939-1945*, Herford, Deutschland: Koehler, 1987, 40, 42; Jürgen Rohwer, *Axis Submarine Successes 1939-1945*, Annapolis, Maryland: Naval Institute Press, 1983, 5, 10, 11, 12, 13, 17, 19, 20; Jak Mallmann Showell, *U-boats at War: Landings on Hostile Shores*, Hersham, England: Ian Allan Publishing, 2000, 136; War Diary of the U-25, September 1, 1939 – August 2, 1940, PG 30022/1-9; ONI Roll T-297-E, *National Archives Microfilm Publication T1022,* roll 3027, RG 242; www.ubootwaffe.net; www.uboatarchive.net; www.volksbund.de.

Crew photograph of the officers and men of the U-25. *Forty-seven men are shown; Hans Berg appears to be the second man to the right of the boat's bell on the lower part of the bridge. Leather jackets and trousers appear to be newly issued; most of the officers and senior non-commissioned officers have added shoulder straps to their jackets. Photo probably taken in 1940.*

Crew at attention on the stern of the U-25. *Civilian dignitaries stand behind; it appears that the national anthem is about to be played.*

Für
Führer, Volk und Vaterland
starb den Heldentod

am 5.8.1940

der Maschinengefreite

Hans Berg

Im Auftrage
des Oberbefehlshabers der
Kriegsmarine ist darüber diese
Urkunde ausgestellt worden.

Im Westen, den 23. Juli 19 42.

Dienststempel

Name

Korvettenkapitän
u. Flottillenchef

Dienstgrad, Dienststellung

Hero's Death Award Document for Maschinengefreiter Hans Berg. *Document is signed by Korvettenkapitän Viktor Schütze, the Commander of the 2nd U-boat Flotilla. Schütze was a former commander of the U-25 and also a Knight's Cross with Oak Leaves recipient. The date of the certificate is almost two years after the U-25 was sunk with all hands.*

Maschinengefreiter Hans Berg. *Cog wheel insignia on upper left arm shows him to be in the engineer specialty. Insignia below rank indicator chevron indicates that Berg attended an electrical equipment specialist course; it was red in color. Below that, the propeller insignia (also in red) denotes that Berg attended a course for motor specialists. From these three insignia we can infer he worked in the engine room, specifically the electrical motors used for submerged propulsion. Berg wears the SA Sports Badge (lowest award on chest). Above that is the German National Sports Badge. Berg also wears a very small oval pin that is not a Navy award. Inset:* **Hans Berg in SA uniform, dated August 6, 1938.**

CHAPTER SIX

"On a Seaman's Grave, No Roses Bloom" U-51 1940

"On a seaman's grave, no roses bloom; on a seaman's grave, no flowers bloom; the single greeting is the white seagulls, and a tear which a small maiden cries," is the mournful refrain of the "U-bootsfahrer Lied" ballad during the war. It was bad enough for so many German families to lose their seafaring loved ones in combat on the high seas; adding insult to injury was the fact that so many of these losses were shrouded in mystery and uncertainty – often until many years after the war. The *U-51* was one such example, a U-boat created in the certainty of final victory and destroyed in much less certain circumstances.

Dönitz's Crews
***Maschinenmaat* Josef Schlander**
Born on January 20, 1917.
Served in the engine room of the *U-51*.
Awarded the Iron Cross 2nd Class on July 8, 1940.
Spent 108 days at sea on U-boat war patrols.
Killed in action on August 23, 1940 in the Bay of Biscay.

The Germany Navy ordered the construction of the *U-51* – a type VIIB boat – on November 21, 1936. Her keel was laid on February 26, 1937 at the F. Krupp Germaniawerft construction yard at Kiel-Gaarden, Germany. The boat was launched on June 11, 1938; she was commissioned two months later on August 6, 1938 under command of Ernst-Günter Heinicke and assigned to the U-boat Flotilla *Wegener* based at Kiel, Germany.

This flotilla was renamed the 7th U-boat Flotilla shortly after the start of the war, but the *U-51* – now under command of *Kapitänleutnant* Dietrich Knorr – did not make her first combat patrol until the beginning of 1940. Knorr, born on February 13, 1912 in Dessau, entered the Navy in 1931, becoming a watch officer on the *U-10* in 1937, and a watch officer for the *U-16* from 1938 to April 1939. On both boats he served under Hannes Weingärtner, one of the earliest *Kriegsmarine* U-boat skippers. The *U-51* was to have made her first war patrol in December 1939, but the crew found sand in her lubricating oil – possibly as a result of sabotage – and her maiden combat patrol was delayed.

U-51 finally left Kiel under the command of Dietrich Knorr on January 17, 1940 on her first combat patrol. Among the crew was *Maschinenmaat* Josef Schlander. Born on January 20, 1917, he likely entered the Navy around 1935; on the *U-51* he served in the engine room. Dönitz directed Knorr to patrol in a low-intensity anti-submarine warfare area west of Ireland to gain some seasoning before going into combat, but Knorr would have none of it. On January 22, 1940 the *U-51* spotted the Swedish 1,640-ton *Gothia* at 9:33 a.m. just west of the Hebrides, Scotland and scored a torpedo hit. The Swedish vessel, carrying sulphate and paper, proved a tough kill, eventually sliding beneath the waves at 4:40 p.m. Twelve crewmen died – the perilous sea took all nationalities of men. Knorr did not report this action to U-boat headquarters immediately; and the B.d.U. diary entry for January 25, 1940 worriedly stated:

> "No news of *U-51* and *U-55*, both on their first patrol west of the English Channel."

At 3:30 p.m. on January 29, 1940 the *U-51* spotted the Norwegian 1,503-ton steamer *Eika* just south of Ireland and sank her with a torpedo. Fourteen crewmen were lost in the freezing water, but the *U-51* rescued two survivors.

The following day Knorr finally reported that the *U-51* was returning to port owing to a technical defect in the bow torpedo tube caps. The boat arrived on February 8, 1940 at Wilhelmshaven, Germany and was again mentioned in the B.d.U. diary:

> "*U-51* entered port, having completed her first patrol. She had to return sooner than would have otherwise been necessary owing to a technical defect which impaired her ability to dive. Her results are therefore small ... Nevertheless the Commanding Officer showed determination. He had the right idea. The second steamer which he sank, a Norwegian whose identity was so unrecognizable that he thought it was an English ship right up to the end, attempted to ram the U-boat when submerged. The Commanding Officer then made a quick decision to fire in spite of the fine inclination. It was only when the steamer was sinking that he identified her as a neutral and saved two members of the crew, who were apparently the only survivors."

On March 11, 1940, the *U-51* left Wilhelmshaven for her second war patrol, again under the command of Dietrich Knorr. Stationed in the Vest Fjord off Narvik, Norway – in support of the German invasion of that country – she spotted five enemy destroyers on April 9. Knorr mounted two attacks against enemy destroyers at night on April 11 but scored no hits, and tried in vain to signal the German surface ships at Narvik of the impending British surprise attack. The *U-51* was then pursued by the destroyers and fired four torpedoes in defense, but none hit, as Knorr reported several torpedo malfunctions to B.d.U. Knorr spotted the British battleship *HMS Warspite* and five destroyers on April 14 and missed the destroyers with two torpedoes. On April 18, the U-boat commander reported firing two torpedoes at a British Southampton class cruiser with no success. Dönitz was furious at the technical failures of the weapons and wrote in the war diary:

> "It is monstrous that B.d.U. should have to be burdened with lengthy discussions and investigations of the causes of torpedo failures and their remedy. This is the business of the technical inspectorates and departments. But as long as these authorities are slow to do what is necessary, I am forced to take action."

Dönitz later concluded that part of the problem lay with U-boats remaining in contact with enemy warships for an extended period of time, which led them to remain submerged for an extremely long period. This in turn caused excess pressure inside the boat which in turn penetrated the depth chamber of the torpedo and thus – unknown to the crew – increased the depth setting of the torpedo, which caused many to run under their intended targets. The B.d.U. modified procedures concerning torpedo detonators, resulting in more hits, and German naval engineers later made better detonators. Admiral Raeder ordered a special investigation of the issue; as a result, several officials in the Torpedo Inspectorate were court-martialed. Little good that did the *U-51*; on April 20 she was attacked by aircraft with depth charges, and after six weeks at sea, at 11:28 p.m. on April 22, 1940 she arrived at Kiel, having encountered much but sunk nothing on this very important patrol. Dönitz summed up his thoughts on May 15, 1940 on the difficulties faced by the *U-51* and the other U-boats:

> "I do not believe that ever in the history of war have men been sent against the enemy with such useless weapons."

The *U-51* departed from Kiel under Dietrich Knorr on June 6, 1940 for its third war patrol, originally to cruise west of the Shetland Islands. He would have much better luck; in fact the U-boat fleet referred to the month as "The Happy Time." On June 12, B.d.U. radioed the *U-51* and ordered it to be prepared to attack convoy HX-48 as part of *Wolf Pack Group Prien*, led by Günther Prien in the *U-47* and also comprised of the *U-32*, *U-28*, *U-25* and *U-30*; B.d.U. ordered the group to keep radio silence. At 3:43 p.m., June 25, 1940 Knorr spotted the British 5,395-ton steam freighter *Windsorwood* southwest of Ireland and sank her with a torpedo. Just thirty-five minutes later, south and west of this position, he found the British 12,049-ton tanker *Saranac*, sailing in ballast to Aruba with convoy OA-172, and sank this ship by torpedo as well; forty men survived the attack but four went missing. On June 29, 1940 at 12:12 a.m., the *U-51* spotted the British 4,724-ton *HMS Edgehill* southwest of Ireland. The *Edgehill* was a decoy ship (Special Service Vessel) armed with nine 4-inch guns and four torpedo tubes. Filled with a buoyant cargo to keep her afloat if hit, the underlying concept of this so-called "Q-ship" was to lure an unsuspecting enemy submarine into a trap and then destroy it before it could react. The first torpedo fired from the *U-51* hit amidships; it stopped the ship but did not sink her due to this buoyant cargo. The *U-51* then surfaced and fired a coup de grâce torpedo at 1:06 a.m. The ship nevertheless remained afloat and Knorr was forced to fire a third torpedo at 1:24 a.m., which caused the vessel to sink slowly by the stern. Fifteen British sailors were killed in the fight, but another twenty-four were later rescued.

The *U-51* began her voyage home on July 1, entering Kiel on July 5. The B.d.U. war diary reported she had sunk five ships totaling 40,311 tons, but this was in error; it was actually two victories. *Maschinenmaat* Josef Schlander received an Iron Cross 2nd Class for his performance on the war patrol, shortly after the *U-51* returned.

The *U-51* left Kiel under the command of Dietrich Knorr on August 9, 1940 for her fourth – and what would prove final – war patrol. On August 15, 1940 west of Scotland he sank the British 5,709-ton tanker *Sylvafield*, a member of convoy HX-62, carrying 7,860 tons of fuel oil from Curacao bound for Clyde. Three of the tanker's crew died in the attack. On August 16, 1940 a flying boat Short Sunderland of the 210th Squadron, 15th Group Coastal Command, Royal Air Force (Flight Officer Ernest Reginald Baker) attacked the *U-51* with depth charges at 2:20 p.m. 180 miles northwest of Bloody Foreland, Ireland, producing oil and air bubbles. One explosion even seemed to blow the boat out of the water and was thought to be a kill; however, the *U-51* survived the attack (although badly damaged) and could only proceed on the surface. Knorr then began to head south toward Lorient, France and made his last desperate radio transmission to the B.d.U. at 7:18 p.m. on August 18, stating he would arrive at Lorient on August 20 at about 7:00 a.m. His position was then south of Ireland, still hundreds of miles from safety and a perilous route it was. U-boat crews frequently referred to the passage through the Bay of Biscay as the "Totenallee" (Death Alley).

Kapitänleutnant Knorr almost made it, but on August 20 the B.d.U. war diary reported ominous news:

> "*U-51* did not arrive at the rendezvous with the escort off Lorient and has not replied to radio signals … The minesweeping flotilla stationed at Lorient immediately checked the inward route for mines, without result. Aircraft sent out from Brest to search flew from square BF14 to Lorient without sighting anything."

It was not mines; it was not depth charges from aircraft; it was not a lurking "Q ship." Incredibly, the *U-51* was torpedoed and sunk as she limped home at 1:16 a.m. on August 20, 1940 in a surface attack by another submarine, the British mine-laying *HM Submarine Cachalot* (Commander David Luce) southwest of Lorient, France. There were no survivors; among the dead was Josef Schlander. On August 23, the B.d.U. war diary had this last communication concerning the boat:

> "Brest Group reported that a large patch of oil was seen in square BF14 during reconnaissance. As *U-51* last reported from this square, the oil patch may have some connection with her."

Another crew met an uncertain fate and an unmarked grave.

Known Crewmembers for the U-51

Budelmann, Hans-Joachim	*Oberleutnant (Ing)*
Burmeister, Franz-Otto	*Matrosenobergefreiter*
Dehmer, Anton	*Obermaschinenmaat*
Durler, Heinz	*Maschinengefreiter*
Ebert, Rolf	*Maschinenobergefreiter*
Ehrhardt, Karl	*Matrosenobergefreiter*
Felger, Werner	*Matrosengefreiter*
Frerk, Karl	*Oberfunkmaat*
Haar, Emil	*Obersteuermann*
Harms, Detlev	*Leutnant zur See*
Heinicke, Ernst-Günter	*Korvettenkapitän*
Hertel, Hellmut	*Kapitänleutnant (Ing)*
Hoffmann, Eberhard	*Korvettenkapitän*
Homann, Joachim	*Oberleutnant zur See*
Hübner, Willi	*Maschinenmaat*
Ites, Otto	*Kapitänleutnant*
Jordan, Heinz	*Maschinenobergefreiter*
Jöster, Franz	*Stabsobersteuermann*
Knorr, Dietrich	*Kapitänleutnant*
Krämer, Kurt-Max	*Matrosengefreiter*
Kuck, Walter	*Obermaschinenmaat*
Lange, Friedhelm	*Matrosenobergefreiter*
Lempert, Johann	*Matrosenobergefreiter*
Marizy, Hans	*Maschinenobergefreiter*
Meister, Hans	*Mechanikergefreiter*
Müller, Ernst	*Bootsmann*
Neufink, Richard	*Mechanikergefreiter*
Nolting, Wilhelm	*Bootsmann*
Nürenberg, Rudolf	*Maschinenmaat*
Nuske, Hans	*Maschinenobergefreiter*
Petermann, Hans	*Maschinenmaat*
Petzold, Otto	*Maschinengefreiter*
Reiprich, Heinz	*Funkobergefreiter*
Rohde, Willi	*Funkgefreiter*
Rosenheinrich, Erwin	*Funkobergefreiter*
Salemka, Wilhelm	*Matrosengefreiter*
Schimming, Ernst	*Maschinenobergefreiter*
Schlander, Josef	*Maschinenmaat*
Schmelcher, Wilhelm	*Maschinenobergefreiter*
Schmitz, Jakob	*Maschinengefreiter*
Schonder, Heinrich	*Kapitänleutnant*
Schulze, Paul	*Oberleutnant (Ing)*
Schwilski, Willi	*Matrosengefreiter*
Seifert, Wilhelm	*Obermaschinenmaat*
Steffen, Hellmut	*Maschinenmaat*
Suhren, Reinhard	*Fregattenkapitän*
Tolck, Hans	*Steuermaat*
Űckert, Andreas	*Maschinengefreiter*
Unsinn, Siegfried	*Mechanikermaat*
Vogel, Hans	*Obermaschinenmaat*
Wehling, Josef	*Maschinenobergefreiter*
Wichmann, Johannes	*Stabsobersteuermann*

Sources, "On a Seaman's Grave, No Roses Bloom:" G.H. Bennett, and R. Bennett, *Hitler's Admirals*, Annapolis, Maryland: Naval Institute Press, 2004, 71; Clay Blair, *Hitler's U-boat War: The Hunters, 1939-1942*, New York: Random House, 1996, 120, 136, 137, 146-152, 167, 179; *F.d.U./B.d.U. War Diary, 16-31 January 1940* (PG30256), 83, 84; *F.d.U./B.d.U. War Diary, 1-15 February 1940* (PG30257), 86; *F.d.U./B.d.U. War Diary, 1-15 April 1940* (PG30262), 2, 3, 6, 7; *F.d.U./B.d.U. War Diary, 16-30 April 1940* (PG30263), 36, 39; *F.d.U./B.d.U. War Diary, 1-15 June 1940* (PG30266), 75, 77, 78; *F.d.U./B.d.U. War Diary, 16-30 June 1940* (PG30267); *F.d.U./B.d.U. War Diary, 1-15 July 1940* (PG30268), 87; *F.d.U./B.d.U. War Diary, 16-31 August 1940* (PG30271), 99, 100; Michael Gannon, *Operation Drumbeat: The Dramatic True Story of Germany's First U-boat Attacks Along the American Coast in World War II*, New York: Harper & Row, 1990, 14; Günter Hessler, *The U-boat War in the Atlantic, 1939-1945, Volume 1-3*, London: Her Majesty's Stationery Office, 1989, 26, 55; Axel Niestlé, *German U-boat Losses during World War II*, Annapolis, Maryland: Naval Institute Press, 1998, 40; Peter Padfield, *Dönitz: The Last Führer*, London: Victor Gollancz LTD., 1984, 211; Herbert Ritschel, *Kurzfassung Kriegstagebücher deutscher U-boote 1939-1945, Band 2: KTB U51-U99,* Norderstedt, Germany: Books on Demand, 5, 6, 7, 8, 9, 10, 11, 12; Jürgen Rohwer, *Axis Submarine Successes 1939-1945*, Annapolis, Maryland: Naval Institute Press, 1983, 11, 12, 20, 21, 25; War Diary of the U-51, December 12, 1939 – August 18, 1940, PG 30048/1-7; ONI Roll T-298-B, *National Archives Microfilm Publication T1022,* roll 3028, RG 242; www.ubootwaffe.net; www.uboatarchive.net.

Opposite
Iron Cross 2nd Class award document to Josef Schlander of the U-51 on July 8, 1940, awarded at Kiel shortly after the conclusion of a successful third war patrol. *Document has a facsimile signature of Konteradmiral Karl Dönitz. Twenty-three-year-old Josef Schlander and forty-two of his comrades would be dead in less than six weeks.*

Inset: ***Narvik Battle Shield award for German Navy personnel.*** *The Narvik Shield was the first Campaign/Battle Shield designed and issued to German military forces in World War II. The design of the shield itself was a motif of elements of all three branches of the Wehrmacht that took part in the campaign: the propeller for the Luftwaffe airmen and paratroopers, the Edelweiss (a white flower found high in the Alpine hills) symbolizing the Army mountain troops and the anchor for the naval and ground troops of the Kriegsmarine. It was worn on the upper left sleeve of the service and dress uniforms of the respective branch of service of the individual and was attached to the uniform using the cloth backing (dark blue for the Navy) issued with each shield.*

1939

Im Namen des Führers und Obersten Befehlshabers der Wehrmacht

verleihe ich

dem

Maschinenmaaten

S c h l a n d e r

das

Eiserne Kreuz 2. Klasse.

Sengwarden, den 8. Juli 1940

Kriegsmarine × Befehlshaber der Unterseeboote

(Dienstsiegel)

(Dienstgrad und Dienststellung)

Kontreadmiral und

Befehlshaber der Unterseeboote

CHAPTER SEVEN

"The Happy Time" U-43, and U-103 1940

Until the fall of France in June 1940, the range of the U-boats had been constrained, as access to the cross-Atlantic convoy routes involved long and risky journeys from Kiel and Wilhelmshaven through the North Sea and around the north of Scotland. However, with the acquisition of the French Atlantic ports of Brest, Lorient, Saint-Nazaire, La Pallice and La Rochelle, Karl Dönitz could take advantage of increased dockyard capacity and proximity to the convoy lanes, which enabled him to extend operations into the central and western Atlantic. Thus, previously thin and sporadic U-boat actions were transformed into more regular and consistent attacks on convoys – a recipe for final success of Dönitz's wolf pack concepts. However, it was not just the acquisition of these new bases on the Bay of Biscay (which flanked Britain to the south) and Dönitz's tactics which explained the rousing success of the U-boats between May and December of 1940 as a post-war history concluded:

> "Numerous factors had contributed to the slaughter: intelligent and intuitive deployment of the few U-boats available, leading to the pack attacks on seven different convoys; boldness, skill and confidence on the part of the two dozen skippers; excellent torpedo performance in night surface attacks; inadequate and inept convoy-escort and ASW measures; and, lastly, not a little luck."

Dönitz's Crews

***Obermaschinist* Friedrich Schirmer**

Born on April 29, 1914 in Datteln/Westphalia.
Served in the engine room on the *U-43*, *U-103*, *U-72* and *U-1170*.
Awarded the Iron Cross 2nd Class on December 13, 1940.
Spent 139 days at sea on U-boat war patrols.
Survived the war; lived in Raisdorf/Kiel.

Whatever the underlying reasons, Dönitz's crews of the time referred to the period as "Die Glückliche Zeit" ("The Happy Time"). And no U-boat seemed happier than the *U-103*.

The *Kriegsmarine* ordered the *U-103* – a Type IXB boat – on May 24, 1938. Shipyard workers laid her keel on September 6, 1939 at the Deutsche Schiff und Maschinenbau AG at Bremen; she was launched on April 12, 1940, commissioned on July 5, 1940 and assigned to the 2nd U-boat Flotilla at Wilhelmshaven. For most of the crew, the *U-103* was their first operational U-boat; the man in charge of the electric motors, *Obermaschinist* Friedrich Schirmer, however, had earlier learned his craft on the *U-43*.

Friedrich Schirmer was born in the town of Datteln (near Recklinghausen,) Westphalia, on April 29, 1914 just before the beginning of World War I. He joined the German Navy on January 1, 1934, trained in the civilian profession of metalworker. After his initial training he served in the boiler room of the light cruiser *Köln* before transferring to a torpedo and escort flotilla. In 1937 Schirmer attended a course to train him as a machinist and further trained to specialize in electric motors. In October 1938 he transferred to the U-boats; he joined the *U-43* on August 26, 1939 and remained with the boat until May 15, 1940. His time on the *U-43* was unforgettable. Under the command of *Kapitänleutnant* Wilhelm Ambrosius, the boat's first war patrol began on November 6, 1939. Departing from Wilhelmshaven, the boat sank three enemy ships. On November 16, 1939 at 2:07 p.m., Ambrosius sank the British 4,915-ton *Arlington Court*, sailing with convoy SL-7A bound from Rosario to Hull with 7,340 tons of maize. Five crewmen died in the attack southwest of Ireland, but British and French destroyers pounded the *U-43* with depth charges. On November 22, 1939 at 4:05 p.m. in the Bay of Biscay, he torpedoed and sank the French 4,374-ton *Arijon*, a member of a convoy headed from Antwerp, Belgium for Buenos Aires, Argentina with steel and paper. Finally, at 9:35 p.m. on November 25, 1939 just west of Portugal, Ambrosius sank the British 2,483-ton *Uskmouth* bound for Sunderland to Monaco with 3,900 tons of coal with torpedo and deck-gun fire. But the damage from the depth charge attack was serious and forced the *U-43* to return to Wilhelmshaven on December 14, 1939.

Repairs to the damaged boat took several months. The *U-43* departed Wilhelmshaven for her second war patrol on March 13, 1940. She did not sink any enemy ships, but experienced an unfortunate event. On March 31, 1940, the 1st Watch Officer Hans-Wilhelm Behrens was washed overboard and drowned. Ambrosius brought the boat back to Wilhelmshaven on April 6, 1940; she had sailed 2,500 sea-miles on the surface and 576 sea-miles submerged. With a new 1st Watch Officer, the *U-43* quickly returned to sea on April 12, 1940 to participate in the German invasion of Norway. She achieved no results and eleven days later on April 23, 1940 returned to that port. Shortly afterward Friedrich Schirmer transferred to a new command and arrived on the *U-103* on August 5, 1940 just as she was finishing her acceptance trials; he was greeted by his new boss, *Oberleutnant* Gerhard Bielig, the boat's Chief Engineer – a man who knew his craft and would later receive the Knight's Cross.

Korvettenkapitän Viktor Schütze served as the commander of the *U-103*. A born leader, he was an excellent skipper and later would rise to be one of the leaders of the entire U-boat force. Born in Kiel on February 16, 1906, he joined the German Navy in 1925 and served in various surface postings until he joined the U-boats on October 1, 1935. Two months later Dönitz thought enough of then-*Kapitänleutnant* Schütze to name him the commander of the *U-19* in the initial operational formation – U-boat Flotilla *Weddigen*. He served in this position for two years and then spent eleven months with the destroyer arm, before returning to the U-boats on August 13, 1938 as the commander of the *U-11*. Schütze assumed command of the *U-25* at the beginning of the war. He made three war patrols with this boat, winning the Iron Cross 2nd Class on November 13, 1939 and the Iron Cross 1st Class on February 21, 1940, before his assignment to bring the *U-103* to operational status, which he did in the first half of 1940.

Friedrich Schirmer's new boat, the *U-103*, departed Kiel under the command of Viktor Schütze on September 21, 1940 for her first war patrol, which certainly turned out to be a "Happy Time" indeed. After initially serving on weather-reporting duty (to indoctrinate new crewmen to the North Atlantic) the *U-103* sank five ships and damaged another. Four of the ships were in convoy: one from convoy OB-227 and three from convoy SC-6:

- On October 6, 1940 at 10:04 p.m. in the mid-North Atlantic, the *U-103* torpedoed and sank the Norwegian 6,123-ton *Nina Borthen* bound from Milford Haven, Wales to Abadan in the Persian Gulf, killing thirty-two crewmen.
- At 10:11 p.m. on October 9, 1940 south of Iceland, the *U-103* sank the Greek 4,407-ton *Zannes Gounaris*, part of convoy SC-6, carrying phosphate rock from Tampa, Florida to Garston/Liverpool; one crewmember died.
- One minute later at 10:12 p.m., the *U-103* damaged the British 3,697-ton freighter *Graigwen*, sailing with convoy SC-6 with 6,160 tons of maize from Montreal, Canada to Barry Roads; seven crewmen perished, but the ship did not sink.
- One minute after that at 10:13 p.m., the *U-103* sank the Greek 3,816-ton *Delphin*, another member of convoy SC-6; the ship, carrying maize and wheat from Montreal to Cork, Ireland sank, but all her crew survived.
- On October 13, 1940 at 8:46 a.m., the *U-103* sank the Estonian 1,186-ton *Nora* off Rockall Banks; the ship was carrying timber from Pugwash, Nova Scotia for Belfast, Northern Ireland.
- On October 15, 1940 at 7:33 p.m., the *U-103* sank the British 4,747-ton *Thistlegarth*, from convoy OB-227, sailing in ballast from Scapa Flow to Father Point, New Brunswick. The ship lost thirty-three men.

The U-103 arrived at Lorient, France on October 19, 1940 after the four-week patrol. Three weeks later, on November 9, 1940, the *U-103* departed Lorient for her second war patrol, which would prove even more successful than her first had been. The *U-103* sank seven ships on this patrol; five were in convoy:

1. On November 21, 1940 at 7:40 a.m. south of Rockall Banks, the *U-103* sank the British 4,768-ton *Daydawn*, sailing with convoy OB-244, from Barry, Wales to Rio Santiago carrying 6,860 tons of coal; two crewmen died in the attack.
2. Ten minutes later, the *U-103* torpedoed and sank the Greek 6,085-ton *Victoria*, a member of convoy OB-244, sailing from Avonmouth, England to Botwood, Newfoundland; she was in ballast and all her crew survived.
3. On November 27, 1940 at 7:56 p.m., the *U-103* sank the British 4,393-ton *Glenmoor*, part of convoy OB-248 bound from Cardiff, Wales to Alexandria, Egypt; her 7,410 tons of coal and her entire thirty-one-man crew went to the bottom west of Ireland.
4. On November 28, 1940 at 8:42 a.m., the *U-103* sank the British 3,578-ton *Mount Athos* carrying 5,250 tons of coal from Barry, Wales to Freetown, Sierra Leone; nineteen of her crew went down with the ship west of Ireland.
5. At 8:24 p.m. the same day, the *U-103* torpedoed and sank the British 4,940-ton *St. Elwyn* carrying coal from Hull, England to Santos, Brazil; twenty-nine of her crew perished in the attack west of Iceland.
6. On December 8, 1940 at 8:58 p.m., the *U-103* torpedoed and sank the British 9,515-ton *Calabria*, from convoy SLS-56. The ship, sailing from Calcutta, India to Clyde, Scotland, was carrying 4,000 tons of iron, 3,050 tons of tea and 1,871 tons of oilcake. More importantly, she had onboard 130 crewmen and 230 passengers, all of whom perished when the ship sank in the frigid water west of Ireland.
7. At 1:32 a.m. on December 9, 1940, the *U-103* sank the British 5,186-ton *Empire Jaguar*, sailing with convoy OB-252, bound from Cardiff, Wales to Philadelphia, Pennsylvania; the ship was in ballast – her entire crew of thirty-seven perished.

Schütze, Schirmer and the rest of the crew with the *U-103* returned to Lorient on December 12, 1940 after more than four weeks on patrol. It was a bloody, successful patrol and Schirmer received an Iron Cross 2nd Class the following day. Viktor Schütze received the Knight's Cross for his successful command of the boat. Friedrich Schirmer then departed the boat for additional training, but for the *U-103* the war continued. On January 21, 1941 the *U-103* sailed from Lorient under the new Knight's Cross winner Viktor Schütze for her third war patrol. She hit four ships on this operation; three of these ships were in convoy. On February 13, 1941 at 4:25 p.m. south of Iceland, the *U-103* damaged the British 10,516 ton tanker *Arthur F Corwin*, a member of convoy HX-106 bound from Aruba to Avonmouth with 14,500 tons of aviation spirits, but the ship survived. Four days later Schütze was more successful; on February 17, 1941 at 6:33 a.m. south of Iceland, the *U-103* torpedoed and sank the British 10,455-ton tanker *Edwy R Brown*, part of convoy HX-107 bound from Aruba to Liverpool with 14,000 tons of oil. The next day on February 18, 1941 at 9:33 p.m. south of Iceland, the *U-103* sank the British 5,459-ton *Seaforth*, which was heading from Monrovia, Liberia to Liverpool. Schütze's last victim on this patrol occurred on February 19, 1941 at 10:22 p.m. west of Scotland, when the *U-103* sank the Norwegian 7,034-ton *Benjamin Franklin* of convoy HX-107, heading from Bermuda to Liverpool with a load of zinc, lead and wood pulp.

Viktor Schütze and the *U-103* returned to Lorient on February 24, 1941 after nearly five weeks at sea and remained in port for over a month. The boat then left Lorient, still under the command of Viktor Schütze on April 1, 1941 for her fourth war patrol, bound for the South Atlantic off Africa. It would prove to be her most successful; the *U-103* sank thirteen ships on this patrol – four of these ships were in convoy:

1. On April 25, 1941 Schütze sank the Norwegian 2,267-ton *Polyana*, sailing with convoy OG-60 from Oban, Scotland to Freetown, Sierra Leone, with a load of coal; all twenty-five of her crew perished in the attack west of Portuguese Guinea.
2. On May 1, 1941 at 6:34 p.m., the *U-103* torpedoed and sank the British 1,494-ton *Samsô* just off the African coast; one crewman died as the ship carrying 1,316 tons of nuts from Bathurst to Freetown went to the bottom.
3. On May 3, 1941 at 10:32 p.m. within sight of the Sierra Leone coast, the *U-103* sank the British 4,253-ton *Wray Castle* carrying 6,900 tons of sugar from Mauritius to Freetown; one crewman died.
4. On May 6, 1941 at 5:17 p.m., the *U-103* torpedoed and sank the British 4,752-ton *Dunkwa*, a member of convoy OB-310, bound from Liverpool to Opobo, Nigeria; eight crewmen perished in the attack off French Guinea.
5. At 5:15 a.m., on May 6, 1941, the *U-103* sank the British 5,529-ton *Surat* carrying 2,500 tons of pig iron and 2,700 tons of peas from Karachi to Britain; three crewmen died in the attack off Sierra Leone.
6. On May 9, 1941 at 11:09 p.m., the *U-103* he sank the British 7,120-ton *City of Winchester*, part of convoy OB-313 sailing from London to Cape Town and Beira, Mozambique; six crewmen died.
7. On May 11, 1941 at 1:48 a.m., the *U-103* torpedoed the British 5,828-ton *City of Shanghai*, from convoy OB-313 bound from Tyne, England to Cape Town. Schütze finished the job with deck-gun fire; eight crewmen died.
8. On May 20, 1941 at 4:38 p.m., the *U-103* sank the Egyptian 3,575-ton *Radames* bound from Vizagapatam, India to Barry Roads with 1,100 tons of iron ore and 4,011 tons of ground nuts; one crewman went missing as the ship sank off Liberia.
9. At 10:52 p.m., on May 22, 1941, the *U-103* sank the British 6,857-ton *British Grenadier* sailing in ballast from Freetown for Aruba.
10. On May 24, 1941 at 3:56 a.m. off Liberia, the *U-103* sank the Greek 4,236-ton *Marionga* carrying government stores from Clyde, Scotland to Takoradi, Ghana; the attack killed twenty-six crewmen.
11. On May 25, 1941 at 10:13 p.m., the *U-103* sank the Dutch 7,789-ton *Wangi Wangi* bound from Sydney, Australia and Durban to Freetown and Clyde with 3,984 tons of steel billets, 1,993 tons of lead and 1,540 tons of general cargo. The attack off Liberia killed one crewman.
12. At 12:34 p.m., on June 8, 1941 off Liberia, the *U-103* torpedoed and sank the British 4,853-ton *Elmdene* carrying 5,000 tons of coal, 1,000 tons of service stores and twenty aircraft from Tyne to Freetown and Alexandria.
13. On June 29, 1941 the *U-103* sank the Italian 6,619-ton *Ernani* west of the Canary Islands.

Schütze refueled at Las Palmas from the German supply ship *Charlotte Schliemann* on July 5. The *U-103* returned to Lorient on July 12, 1941. Two days later he received the Oak Leaves to his Knight's Cross, but his success led to his elevation to become the commander of the 2nd U-boat Flotilla, which led him to turn over command of the *U-103* to another officer. Schütze would hold this operational command until February 7, 1943, when he became the leader of the entire U-boat training command – an organization that comprised eight training flotillas. Promoted to *Fregattenkapitän* on March 1, 1943 and to *Kapitän zur See* on March 1, 1944, Schütze held this key position until the end of the war. Viktor Schütze survived the conflict and died on September 23, 1950 in Frankfurt.

Assuming command of the *U-103* was another excellent officer, *Kapitänleutnant* Werner Winter. Born on March 26, 1912 in Hamburg, Werner Winter joined the *Reichsmarine* on April 9, 1930 serving his first four years in various surface positions. He attended U-boat training in 1935 and as an *Oberleutnant zur See* became the 1st Watch Officer on the *U-17* in the U-boat Flotilla *Weddigen* in 1936. Over the next sixteen months he showed great promise and Dönitz rewarded Werner Winter by giving him command of the *U-22* of the U-boat Flotilla *Lohs* on October 1, 1937. He began the war in this command, leading his boat on two war patrols and winning the Iron Cross 2nd Class on September 18, 1939.

Werner Winter had to wait two months before taking the *U-103* out from Lorient on her fifth war patrol on September 10, 1941. He would sink two ships from convoy SL-87 on September 22. At 11:46 p.m., west of the Canary Islands, Winter torpedoed the British 5,591-ton freighter *Niceto de Larrinaga*. Carrying 3,866 tons of palm kernels, 2,000 tons of manganese and 2,482 tons of nuts from Freetown, Sierra Leone to London, she took three of her crew to the bottom. One minute later, the *U-103* torpedoed the British 5,003-ton freighter *Edward Blyden*, carrying general cargo from Freetown to Liverpool; all on board survived. The *U-103* returned to Lorient on November 9, 1941. The following day *Kapitänleutnant* Winter received the Iron Cross 1st Class.

The crew of the *U-103* now had almost two months to help refit their boat and take a well-deserved leave. Shortly after New Year's Day, on January 3, 1942 Winter took the boat on its sixth war patrol from Lorient, bound for the coast of the United States. On February 2, 1942 at 7:40 p.m. the *U-103* sank the American 6,182-ton tanker *WL Steed* with torpedoes and gunfire east of New Jersey. Sailing from Cartagena, Columbia to New York with 65,936 barrels of crude oil, she went down with thirty-four of her crew. Two days later at 6:43 a.m. on February 4, the *U-103* sank the Panamanian 3,627-ton freighter *San Gil* bound from Santa Marta, Columbia to Philadelphia, Pennsylvania with a torpedo and gunfire, killing two men, just outside Delaware Bay. February 5, 1942 saw two more victories for the *U-103*. At 1:53 a.m. torpedoes from the *U-103* sank the American 8,327-ton tanker *India Arrow* bound from Corpus Christi, Texas to New York, killing twenty-six of her crew. At 6:08 p.m. on the same day, the *U-103* sank the American 8,403-ton tanker *China Arrow*. Her entire crew survived; the ship had been enroute from Beaumont, Texas to New York. After this grave predation of American oil supplies, Winter and the *U-103* returned to Lorient on March 1, 1942 after just over eight weeks on patrol.

The second "Happy Time" was in full swing by now and the *U-103*'s crew was itching to return to the fight. On April 15, 1942 the boat departed Lorient; her destination – the Gulf of Mexico. April transitioned to May without a victory, but aptly on "Cinco de Mayo" (May 5) the *U-103* began a streak of nine sinkings for the month:

1. On May 5, 1942 at 8:30 a.m., the *U-103* torpedoed the British 5,966-ton freighter *Stanbank* carrying 6,488 tons of military stores from New York to Table Bay, South Africa and Alexandria. The ship, which went down northeast of Bermuda, took nine of her crew with her.
2. At 11:00 p.m. on May 17, 1942 off Honduras, the *U-103* sank the American 2,612-ton freighter *Ruth Lykes*, carrying 39,136 bags of Columbian coffee from Barranquilla, Columbia to Houston; six crewmen died in the attack.
3. On May 19, 1942 at 8:24 p.m., the *U-103* torpedoed the American 5,037-ton freighter *Ogontz* carrying canning machinery and nitrates in the Gulf of Mexico.

4. At 3:38 a.m. on May 21, 1942, the *U-103* sank the American 3,372-ton freighter *Clare*, bound from Baltimore to San Juan, Puerto Rico, off the western tip of Cuba.
5. The same day at 4:35 a.m., the *U-103* sank the American 4,727-ton freighter *Elizabeth* with torpedoes and gunfire. Carrying trucks and construction material from Hampton Roads, Virginia to San Juan, the ship went down with six of her crew.
6. On May 23, 1942 at 9:26 a.m. south of Cuba, the *U-103* sank the American 6,625-ton tanker *Samuel Q Brown*, bound from New Orleans for Honolulu, Hawaii, killing two crewmen.
7. The next day on May 24 at 4:40 p.m., the *U-103* torpedoed and sank the Dutch 1,828-ton *Hector* south of Cuba. The freighter, bound from New York to Curacao, took two crewmen with her when she sank.
8. On May 26, 1942 at 4:16 a.m., the *U-103* torpedoed the American 5,588-ton freighter *Alcoa Carrier* bound from Mobile, Alabama to Trinidad, west of Jamaica.
9. At 11:42 a.m., on May 28, 1942 west of Jamaica, the *U-103* sank the American 6,414-ton tanker *New Jersey* with torpedoes and gunfire; the ship was bound from Hampton Roads for Aruba.

Kapitänleutnant Werner Winter and the *U-103* arrived back at Lorient on June 22, 1942 after a very successful nine weeks on patrol. On the return voyage, on June 5, B.d.U. informed Winter that he had been awarded the Knight's Cross for his achievements. This recognition came with a price, and Werner Winter had to relinquish command of the U-boat to become the commander of the 1st U-Boat Flotilla, a position he assumed on July 15, 1942; he survived the war. In his place came *Oberleutnant zur See* Gustav-Adolf Janssen. Born in Blankenese/Hamburg on April 9, 1915, he was an experienced commander having served as the skipper of the *U-151* and *U-37* for a total of eleven months before taking command of the *U-103* on July 14, 1942.

On October 21, 1942, Janssen took the *U-103* from Lorient for her ninth war patrol. At 12:12 a.m. on October 31, 1942 west of Portugal, the *U-103* he sank the British 6,405-ton freighter *Tasmania*, part of convoy SL-125 bound from Freetown to Glasgow, Scotland, with 8,500 tons of foodstuffs and 2,000 tons of pig iron; two men died in the attack. The boat then had a long lull until December 6, when at 11:59 p.m. in the mid-Atlantic the *U-103* sank the British 5,025-ton *Henry Stanley*, from convoy ON-149 headed from Freetown to Liverpool; this attack was bloodier and sixty-three men aboard the ship were killed. Finally, on December 13, 1942 the *U-103* damaged but did not sink the British 13,945-ton *Hororata*. After nearly ten weeks at sea, the *U-103* returned to Lorient on December 29, 1942; she had spent 9,800 sea-miles on the surface and 740 sea-miles submerged.

They were her last victories. The *U-103*, under newly-promoted *Kapitänleutnant* Janssen, conducted five more war patrols over the next twelve months. On four occasions she was attacked by Allied aircraft, but no one was killed and she returned safely each time to port. *Obermaschinenmaat* Alfons Wieser received a German Cross in Gold on February 24, 1944 for his long and excellent service on the boat. Taken out of operational service in March 1944, she was sunk on April 15, 1945 at the dock at Kiel during an Allied bombing raid; one man died in the attack. The *U-103* had certainly experienced a happy time in the war, sinking forty-five ships for a total of 237,596 tons – making her the second-most successful U-boat of the war.

Meanwhile, Schirmer's first boat, the *U-43*, was having a happy time of her own. On May 13, 1940 she left Wilhelmshaven on her fourth war patrol. On June 21, 1940 at 4:30 p.m. off Portugal, the *U-43* sank the British 8,627-ton tanker *Yarraville*, part of convoy 65-X; five crewmen died. Her next victim came at 10:27 p.m. on June 30 south of Ireland, when the *U-43* torpedoed the British 13,376-ton *Avelona Star*, carrying 5,630 tons of frozen meat and 1,000 tons of oranges with convoy SL-36 from Buenos Aires, Argentina to London; six of her crew went missing. Another ship from Buenos Aires slid beneath the waves southwest of Ireland at 9:19 p.m. on July 9, 1940, when the *U-43* torpedoed and sank the British 3,944-ton freighter *Aylesbury* carrying grain and general cargo. Finally, on July 17, 1940 at 10:40 a.m. northwest of Ireland, the *U-43* sank the British 3,509-ton *Fellside*, a straggler from convoy OA-184 from Middlesbrough, England to Sydney, Nova Scotia; twelve men perished beneath the waves, but the *U-43* returned to Wilhelmshaven on July 22, 1940. Battle damage would again force over two months of repairs.

The *U-43* thus remained at Wilhelmshaven until September 9, 1940, when the boat departed for her next war patrol; however, after three days she made for Bergen, Norway due to seawater leaks into the pressure hull. On September 15, 1940 she sailed from Bergen on her sixth war patrol. On September 25, at 1:30 p.m. west of Ireland, the *U-43* encountered the British 5,802-ton freighter *Sulairia*, a member of convoy OB-217, carrying 1,800 tons of general cargo and bricks from Glasgow to Montreal; she torpedoed the freighter, killing one man. After more than four weeks at sea, the *U-43* arrived at Lorient, France on October 18, 1940. Dönitz was uneasy about the performance of the *U-43* and stated so in the B.d.U. war diary:

> "During a patrol lasting five weeks she sank only one medium-sized steamer. The Commanding Officer, who had good peacetime training, is apparently past his job and will be relieved. His previous patrol was also unsatisfactory."

Thus Wilhelm Ambrosius gave up command of the *U-43*; he went on to command the 22nd U-boat Flotilla and survived the war. To the *U-43* came *Oberleutnant* Wolfgang Lüth. Born on October 15, 1913 in Riga, he entered the *Kriegsmarine* in 1933, serving in a variety of surface positions until 1938, when he joined the U-boat service. Lüth briefly served as the 2nd Watch Officer on the *U-27* in 1938 before joining the *U-38* as an *Oberleutnant zur See* and 1st Watch Officer on October 24, 1938 (see previous chapter "Jonah"). He remained in this position for approximately one year before attending U-boat commander's school; he then briefly commanded the *U-13*, *U-9* and *U-138* (during which time he received the Iron Cross 2nd and 1st Class) before coming to the *U-43*.

Lüth arrived to take command of the *U-43* on October 21, 1940; three days later he was awarded the Knight's Cross for his previous achievements with the *U-138*. It was a good omen. On November 10, 1940 the *U-43* sailed from Lorient. On December 2, 1940 at 9:01 a.m., the *U-43* torpedoed and sank the British 7,113-ton freighter *Pacific President*, part of convoy OB-251 from Oban, Scotland to New York; the ship was in ballast, when she went down with her entire crew off Rockall Banks. At 9:41 a.m., the *U-43* torpedoed the British 12,247-ton tanker *Victor Ross* bound from Liverpool to New York. She was in ballast, and her entire crew also perished in the attack. At 10:48 p.m. on December 6 in the mid-Atlantic, the *U-43* sank the Norwegian 1,902-ton freighter *Skrim*, a straggler from convoy OB-252 bound from Aberdeen, Scotland to Sydney, Nova Scotia; all twenty-three crewmen went down when the ship sank in sixty-three seconds. Finally, on December 13, 1940 the *U-43* torpedoed and damaged the British 10,350-ton *Orari*, but she made port. The *U-43* arrived back at Lorient on December 17, 1940, but then ran into misfortune. On February 4, 1941 the U-boat accidentally flooded and sank at the U-boat docks at Lorient after a ballast-tank valve was mistakenly left open. A court of inquiry blamed the 1st and 2nd Watch Officers and ordered them to pay for the repairs out of their salaries!

The *U-43* then remained in Lorient for almost five months during which time Wolfgang Lüth was promoted to *Kapitänleutnant*. On May 11, 1941, Lüth took the *U-43* out on her eighth war patrol and success returned to the boat once again. On May 15, 1941 at 4:15 a.m. Lüth sank the small French 488-ton *Notre Dame du Châtelet* with deck-gun fire southwest of Ireland. On May 24, the boat was part of the trap Dönitz attempted to set south of Greenland during the voyage of the battleship *Bismarck*, but the waiting U-boats spotted no targets. At 8:24 p.m. on June 6, 1941 the *U-43* torpedoed and sank the Dutch 4,802-ton freighter *Yselhaven*, sailing in ballast with convoy OB-328 from Liverpool to St. Lawrence, Canada; twenty-four men went down with the ship east of Newfoundland. The *U-43*'s last victory of the patrol occurred at 3:15 a.m. on June 17, 1941 in the mid-Atlantic when Lüth sank the British 2,727-ton *Cathrine*, a member of convoy SL-76, carrying 3,700 tons of manganese ore from Freetown to Barrow Bay, Ontario; twenty-four crewmen died. The *U-43* returned to Lorient on July 1, 1941.

On August 2, 1941 the *U-43* departed Lorient for her ninth patrol. Attacking an enemy convoy, Lüth fired a salvo of six torpedoes but all six ran erratically and missed their targets. Lüth returned to Lorient on September 23, 1941. The boat was not sea-worthy and required more repairs that took six weeks. Anxious to get on the winning track, the *U-43* sailed from Lorient on November 10, 1941. The crew did not have long to wait and soon ran into convoy OS-12. On November 29, 1941 at 4: 11 a.m., the *U-43* torpedoed the British 5,569-ton *Thornliebank*, north of the Azores, carrying ammunition from Barry, Wales to Freetown, Sierra Leone and the Middle East; the ship exploded in a huge roar – all seventy-eight men in her crew vanished. Escort destroyers attempted to exact revenge and depth-charged the *U-43* for several hours. The following day at 7:26 p.m., the *U-43* sank the British 4,868-ton *Ashby*, in ballast and sailing from Middlesbrough, England to Freetown, Sierra Leone; seventeen men died when the freighter went down. Finally, on December 2 at 9:24 a.m. southeast of the Azores, the *U-43* sank the American 7,542-ton tanker *Astral* carrying 78,200 barrels of gasoline and kerosene from Aruba to Lisbon, Portugal; the ship exploded when struck by two torpedoes and all thirty-seven of her crew perished in the inferno. Lüth also found a destroyer, but missed with his last torpedoes. Running low on fuel as well, the *U-43* returned to Lorient on December 16, 1941.

By now the United States had officially entered the war and it was imperative that the *U-43* quickly return to combat. On December 30, 1941 he departed Lorient. The crew had not lost their touch and on January 12, 1942 at 8:02 a.m. in the mid-Atlantic, the *U-43* sank the Swedish 5,246-ton freighter *Yngaren*, sailing with convoy HX-168 with 4,696 tons of copra, 3,000 tons of manganese ore, trucks and eight aircraft from Bombay, India to Hull; thirty-eight men perished and only two survived the sinking. At 2:54 a.m. on January 14, 1942 the *U-43* sank the British 6,641-ton *Empire Surf*, part of convoy ON-55, bound from Manchester, England for Jacksonville, Florida; the ship was in ballast and went down so swiftly that forty-seven men went with her. The same day at 4:53 a.m. Lüth torpedoed and sank the Panamanian 5,707-ton freighter *Chepo*, also a member of convoy ON-55 bound from Liverpool for Boston and New York; seventeen men went down with the ship in the frigid North Atlantic. Lüth then sailed the *U-43* to Kiel on January 22, 1942, completing the boat's eleventh war patrol.

Wolfgang Lüth remained with the *U-43* until April 11, 1942, but then departed to command the *U-181*. He would go on to win the Oak Leaves, Swords and Diamonds to his Knight's Cross. Shortly after the war ended, a German sentry at the *Kriegsmarine* Officer School at Flensburg-Mürwik mistakenly shot and killed Lüth; he was buried at the Friedhof Adelby. *Oberleutnant zur See* Hans-Joachim Schwantke took Lüth's place on the *U-43* and although he did not have the stature of the former commander, he was a good choice to lead the boat. Born at Hindenburg in Upper Silesia on August 30, 1918, he joined the Navy in 1936. Four years later he entered the U-boat service and served as the 2nd Watch Officer on the *U-43* from January to October 1941. Schwantke then was promoted and selected to be the 1st Watch Officer, a position he held until January 1942 when he left to attend U-boat commander's training. He thus knew the boat and her crew.

Schwantke took the *U-43* out from Kiel on her twelfth war patrol on July 4, 1942 and arrived at Lorient on August 15, 1942; during the voyage, the *U-43* sank no enemy ships, but the U-boat was damaged by destroyer depth charge attacks over several days; both air compressors were broken and two bow torpedo outer doors were jammed half open, making trim difficult. More dockside repairs were needed. On September 23, 1942 the *U-43* tried again and got back on track when on November 18, 1942 at 9:56 a.m. east of Newfoundland she sank the American 9,131-ton tanker *Brilliant*, from convoy SC-109. The *U-43* returned to Lorient on December 9, 1942. After Christmas, on January 1, 1943, the *U-43* went to sea again, and once again she sank a ship. There was a problem, however – it was a German ship. On the evening of March 3, 1943, Schwantke fired three torpedoes at a ship which he identified as a Dunedin Star-type ship. In reality, it was the 5,154-ton German raider *Doggerbank*, close to completing her journey through the Indian Ocean and Atlantic before returning to Germany. The *Doggerbank* had left Yokohama, Japan on December 17, 1942, and she was steaming about 1,000 miles west of the Canary Islands, when she was struck. Only fifteen of her crew made it to a small lifeboat, without water or food. Twenty-six days later, the Spanish tanker *Campoamor* found the boat with only one remaining survivor, Fritz Kürt. According to Kürt, the fifteen men on the raft were quickly reduced to only six after the boat had capsized, including the *Doggerbank's* captain, who committed suicide after shooting four of his crew at their explicit request. The number of fatalities totaled 364.

The *U-43* arrived at Lorient and one disaster followed another. In addition to the *Doggerbank* fiasco, there was battle damage to be repaired. The *U-43* did not return to action until July 13, 1943 but by then the boat was completely cursed. She departed Lorient that day for her fifteenth war patrol – quite an achievement of longevity for the U-boat fleet. Her mission was to lay twelve anti-shipping mines in the Gulf of Guinea off Lagos, Nigeria. On July 30, 1943 southwest of the Azores, the *U-43* ran into the American escort carrier *USS Santee*. Unfortunately for the *U-43*, the *Santee* was a U-boat killer. On July 14 her Avenger aircraft had sunk the *U-160* south of the Azores. On July 15, her aircraft sank the *U-509* northwest of Madeira. Now on July 30 her aircraft spotted the *U-43*, which was on the surface preparing to give some fuel to the *U-403*. The American pilots knew their business and smelled blood again. Launching a Fido homing torpedo, they struck the *U-43* hard and she went down with all fifty-five men. The men of the *U-43* had sailed under excellent commanders; they had also displayed their own level of extraordinary seamanship. *Bootsmaat* Kurt Büttner was posthumously awarded the German Cross in Gold on August 7, 1943. *Obersteuermann* Johann Limbach left the boat in March 1942 and went on to receive a commission and win a Knight's Cross.

Friedrich Schirmer had avoided this fate. After departing the *U-103* he attended an *Obermaschinist* course in 1942 for several months. On August 15, 1943 he joined the crew of the *U-72*, a training boat based in Pillau with the 21st U-boat Training Flotilla, as an *Obermaschinist* in charge of the electric motors and served with the boat until November 10, 1943. On March 3, 1944 Schirmer reported for duty on the *U-1170*; again he was placed in charge of the operation of the electric motors. Another training boat, the *U-1170* was assigned to the 8th U-boat Training Flotilla at Danzig until September 1944 when she transferred to the 33rd U-boat Training Flotilla at Flensburg, where she was at the end of the war. Friedrich Schirmer survived the war also and returned to his pre-war home at Travemünde, before moving to Raisdorf just outside Kiel. Whatever life would throw at him during the rest of his days, he could look back on his "Happy Time" in the *U-43* and *U-103*, two of Dönitz's most proficient U-boats.

Known Crewmembers for the U-43

Adolph, Helmut	*Maschinenobergefreiter*
Albrecht, Frit	*Oberleutnant zur See*
Ambrosius, Wilhelm	*Fregattenkapitän*
Arnold, Hans	*Obermaschinenmaat*
Bär, Kurt	*Maschinengefreiter*
Bauer, Arno	*Obermaschinist*
Bauer, Georg	*Matrose*
Bechstädt, Dr. Georg	*Marinestabarzt*
Becker, Martin	*Obersteuermann*
Becker, Richard	*Kapitänleutnant*
Beckers, Johann	*Obermaschinenmaat*
Behmann, Arno	*Obermechanikermaat*
Behrens, Hans-Wilhelm	*Oberleutnant zur See*
Belusa, Johannes	*Obermaschinenmaat*
Bernbeck, Hinrich-Oscar	*Kapitänleutnant*
Blum, Heinrich	*Maschinenobergefreiter*
Burgheim, Georg	*Mechanikerobergefreiter*
Büttner, Kurt	*Bootsmaat*
Colsmann, Hermann	*Leutnant zur See*
Deeken, Anton	*Maschinenmaat*
Elbeshausen, Günther	*Matrosengefreiter*
Ennöckl, Klemens	*Matrosenobergefreiter*
Evensen, Heinz	*Maschinenmaat*
Fischer, Kurt	*Maschinenmaat*
Flügge, Wilhelm	*Stabsobersteuermann*
Fröhlich, Jann-Friedrich	*Obermaschinenmaat*
Grams, Karl-Rudolf	*Mechanikergefreiter*
Grospietsch, Hans-Dieter	*Leutnant zur See*
Haas, Jakob	*Maschinenmaat*
Hamilton, Ernst	*Maschinenobergefreiter*
Händle, Alfred	*Maschinenobergefreiter*
Hartmann, Rudi	*Maschinengefreiter*
Hauswald, Willi-Gerhard	*Matrosenobergefreiter*
Hefers, Helmut	
Heintel, Otmar	*Matrosenobergefreiter*
Hingsen, Walther	*Oberbootsmaat*
Hintze, Heinz	*Mechanikermaat*
Holtmann, Werner	*Obermaschinist*
Istgenug, Heinz	
Jensem, Walter	*Matrosenobergefreiter*
Kahrs, Heinrich	*Maschinengefreiter*
Kaiser, Max	
Kaschner, Hans	*Korvettenkapitän (Ing)*
Klein, Josef	*Maschinenobergefreiter*
Klinzmann, Otto	*Obermaschinist*
Kluth, Walter	*Matrosengefreiter*
König, Gottfried	*Oberleutnant zur See*
König, Peter-Ewald	*Obermaschinenmaat*
Kördt, Willi	*Maschinenobergefreiter*
Kornbrust, Herbert	*Maschinengefreiter*
Krämer, Horst	*Maschinengefreiter*
Krieger, Heinrich	*Matrosenobergefreiter*
Kröger, Walter	*Maschinenobergefreiter*
Krohn, Otto	*Oberleutnant (Ing)*
Krüger, Hein	
Kruse, Herbert	*Funkmatrosen*
Kugelberg, Wolf-Rüdiger	
Kulzer, Max	*Maschinenobergefreiter*
Kummerfeld, Christian	*Maschinengefreiter*
Landwirt, Georg	
Lange, Heinz	*Maschinenmaat*
Lax, Kurt-Erhard	*Obermaschinenmaat*
Leidfeld, Christian	
Leitsch, Johann	*Maschinenmaat*
Limbach, Johann	*Oberleutnant zur See*
Linne, Hermann	*Mechanikermaat*
Loeser, Paul-Karl	*Kapitänleutnant*
Lüth, Wolfgang	*Kapitän zur See*
Martin, Theodor	*Mechanikergefreiter*
Metzger, Jupp	
Miede, Hein	*Oberbootsmaat*
Mihatsch, Alois	
Möller, Fritz	*Obermaschinist*
Münster, Helmut-Walter	*Kapitänleutnant*
Murkel, Philipp	*Matrosenobergefreiter*
Orywol, Kurt	*Maschinengefreiter*
Ostermann, Fritz	*Matrose*
Petersen, Theodor	*Oberleutnant zur See*
Pfannenschmidt, Heinz	*Bootsmaat*
Pieper, Alfons	*Maschinenmaat*
Pirags, Alfred	*Oberleutnant (Ing)*
Pointner, Rudolf	
Reibnitz, Hans	*Kapitänleutnant (Ing)*
Reif, Karl	*Matrosenobergefreiter*
Reitz, Karl	*Maschinenmaat*
Richter, Kurt	
Ricken, Wilhelm	*Obermaat*
Rosenstiehl, Karl	*Maschinengefreiter*
Ruschkowski, Werner	*Matrose*
Sander, Benno	*Funkgefreiter*
Saxler, Albert	*Matrosenobergefreiter*
Schäfer, Walter	*Bootsmaat*
Schiessl, Helmut	*Oberleutnant (Ing)*
Schindel, Edgar-Adolf	*Maschinenmaat*
Schirmer, Friedrich	*Obermaschinist*
Schlosshause, Georg	
Schmitz, Franz	*Mechanikermaat*
Schnabel, Horst	*Oberbootsmaat*
Schödel, Alfred	*Maschinenobergefreiter*
Scholzen, Hermann	*Maschinengefreiter*
Schraysshün, Richard	*Oberbootsmaat*
Schröder, Reinhold	*Oberfunkmaat*
Schulze, Walter	*Obermaschinist*
Schüz, Eberhard	*Leutnant zur See*
Schwantke, Hans-Joachim	*Kapitänleutnant*

Sochaczewski, Herold	*Matrosenobergefreiter*
Soldau, Werner	
Sorger, Friedrich-Hermann	*Matrosenobergefreiter*
Specht, Herbert-Fritz	*Leutnant zur See*
Steilich, Josef	
Stein, Hans	
Stelich, Josef	*Obermaschinist*
Stemmann, Ernst-John	*Maschinenmaat*
Strahlendorf, Heinz	*Obersteuermann*
Streit, Paul	*Matrosenobergefreiter*
Struck, Friedrich	*Obermaschinist*
Stuhlmacher, Alfred	*Funkobergefreiter*
Tack, Konrad	*Funkmaat*
Teichmann, Herbert	*Obersteuermann*
Toth, Anton	*Matrosenobergefreiter*
Trenz, Andreas	*Maschinengefreiter*
Vollheide, Artur	*Maschinenobergefreiter*
Vollmer, Friedrich-Hermann	*Korvettenkapitän (Ing)*
Waldbüsser, Wilhelm	*Obermaschinenmaat*
Wefers, Helmut	
Welsch, Paul	*Korvettenkapitän (Ing)*
Wernicke, Alfred	*Obermaschinist*
Wevers, Helmut	*Mechanikerobergefreiter*
Wittauer, Georg	*Maschinenmaat*
Witte, Erwin	*Kapitänleutnant*
Wuerzbach, Helmut	
Würdemann, Erich	*Kapitänleutnant*
Zitt, Robert-Rudolf	*Maschinenobergefreiter*

Known Crewmembers for the U-103

Adlig	*Funkobermaat*
Albert, Ludwig	*Obermaat*
Assmann, Siegfried	*Obersteuermann*
Ausserhofer, Egon	*Oberleutnant (Ing)*
Bade, Karl	*Obermaschinist*
Bahnsen, Hermann	*Obermaschinist*
Baumgart, Hans	*Obermaat*
Behlau, Alfred	
Beinert	
Berndt, Erich	
Bernsdorf, Hans	
Besener, Hans	*Obermaschinenmaat*
Bielig, Gerhard	*Kapitänleutnant (Ing)*
Bör, Hermann	*Kapitänleutnant (Ing)*
Borchert, Helmut	
Brauel, Wilhelm	*Kapitänleutnant*
Brückner	
Christ	
Cordes, Ernst	*Kapitänleutnant*
Dabelstein, Herbert	
Decken, Ernst	*Obersteuermann*
Eckstein	
Fehr, Heinrich	*Hauptgefreiter*
Fischer, Gerhard	*Obermaschinenmaat*
Fraatz	
Frank, Heinz	
Freund, Herbert	
Fritz, Karl-Heinz	*Leutnant zur See*
Fuchs, Hans-Joachim	*Maschinenmaat*
Fuchs, Jochen	*Obersteuermann*
Galk, Max	*Obergefreiter*
Gassmann, Helmut	
Gelhaus, Harald	*Kapitänleutnant*
Gissel, Günter	*Maschinenmaat*
Gottermeyer, Hans	*Obermaschinist*
Grenzian, Gerhard	
Günter	
Hecker, Wilhelm	*Obermaat*
Heinke, Max	*Obergefreiter*
Hertel, Georg	*Maschinenobergefreiter*
Himmeter, Heinrich	*Obergefreiter*
Hiort, Jürgen	*Oberfähnrich (Ing)*
Hoffrath, Fritz	
Hollemann, Otto	*Maschinenmaat*
Hormes, Harald	*Bootsmaat*
Hüber	*Mechanikerobergefreiter*
Janssen, Günter	
Janssen, Gustav-Adolf	*Kapitänleutnant*
Kalsuchka, Max	
Karg, Alfons	*Oberbootsmaat*
Kathan	
Katzelberger, Leopold	*Bootsmaat*
Köpping, Hermann	*Obermaat*
Krauss, Walter	
Krumaker, Emil	
Kunze, Alfred	*Bootsmaat*
Kusch, Oskar-Heinz	*Oberleutnant zur See*
Kuschniersch, Paul	*Obermaschinist*
Laszig, Paul	*Obergefreiter*
Lehmann, Franz	*Obersteuermann*
Lehmann, Wolfgang	*Obergefreiter*
Lehnert, Dr. Karl	*Arzt*
Liebetrau, Richard	*Obersteuermann*
Lücking	
Ludwig, Albert	*Obermaschinist*
Luz, Eugen	*Funkobergefreiter*
Mai, Wilhelm	*Obersteuermann*
Maier, Hermann	
Markert, Albrecht	*Oberleutnant zur See*
Markworth, Friedrich	*Kapitänleutnant*
Marl, Peter	*Oberbootsmaat*
Meyer, Georg	
Müller, Walter	
Murl, Heinz	*Oberleutnant zur See*
Nellen, Josef	*Mechanikerobergefreiter*
Nieder, Heinrich	*Obergefreiter*
Ott	*Obermaat*
Papalecca	*Maschinenobergefreiter*
Pich, Helmuth	*Kapitänleutnant*
Pick, Otto	*Obermaschinist*
Poken, Max	
Rabus	
Rappard, Konstantin von	*Kapitänleutnant*
Redack, Georg	*Funkobergefreiter*
Rodeck, Kurt	*Matrosenobergefreiter*
Römer, Wolfgang	*Kapitänleutnant*
Rücker, Claus	
Rudolph, Hans	*Obergefreiter*
Rust, Gottfried	*Obersteuermann*
Sander, Paul	*Obersteuermann*
Sass, Walter	*Leutnant zur See*
Sawatzki, Rudolf	
Schaper, Konrad	*Mechanikerobergefreiter*
Schenk, Wilhelm	

Schildt, Gustav-Adolf	*Obermaschinist*
Schimke, Ernst	*Maschinenobergefreiter*
Schirmer, Friedrich	*Obermaschinist*
Schmidt, Artur	
Schökel, Walter	*Maschinenmaat*
Scholl, Werner	
Schöps	
Schuchardt, Johannes	
Schultz, Günter	*Oberfähnrich (Ing)*
Schunck, Hans-Norbert	*Oberleutnant zur See*
Schütze, Viktor	*Kapitän zur See*
Schwamborn	*Matrosengefreiter*
Stagge, Fritz	*Obermaschinenmaat*
Stecker, Wilhelm	
Stefan, Albert	
Stegmeier, Franz	
Stoldt, Alfred	*Maschinengefreiter*
Strehlow, Otto	*Kapitänleutnant (Ing)*
Theissen, Karl	*Matrosenobergefreiter*
Tiefenbach, Martin	
Trinks, Richard	*Obermaschinist*
Trossina, Wilhelm	
Uhlemann, Helmuth	*Matrosenobergefreiter*
Wacker, Eduard	*Oberleutnant (Ing)*
Wamers, Otto	*Oberleutnant (Ing)*
Warnke	
Wattenberg, Jürgen	*Kapitän zur See*
Wheland, Hans	
Wermuth, Otto	*Oberleutnant zur See*
Wershofen, Anton von	
Wick, Hans	*Obermaschinist*
Wieser, Alfons	*Obermaschinenmaat*
Wiesner, Kurt	
Winter, Werner	*Korvettenkapitän*
Witzel	
Wohlers	
Zimmermann	
Zounek, Horst	

Sources, "The Happy Time:" Clay Blair, *Hitler's U-boat War: The Hunters, 1939-1942*, New York: Random House, 1996, 119, 195, 196, 212, 232, 233, 268, 288, 306, 363, 409, 410, 657, 658; Clay Blair, *Hitler's U-boat War: The Hunted, 1942-1945*, New York: Modern Library, 2000, 199, 397; Rainer Busch and Hans-Joachim Röll, *German U-boat Commanders of World War II*, translated by Geoffrey Brooks, Annapolis, Maryland: Naval Institute Press, 1999, 20, 115, 240; Manfred Dörr, *Die Ritterkreuzträger der U-Boot-Waffe, Band 1: A-J, Band 2: L-Z*, Osnabrück, FRG: Biblio Verlag, 1988, Band 2-92, 93, 94, 259, 260, 261, 340, 341, 342; *F.d.U./B.d.U. War Diary, 16-31October 1940* (PG30275), 120; Herbert Ritschel, *Kurzfassung Kriegstagebücher deutscher U-boote 1939-1945, Band 1: KTB U1 - U50,* Norderstedt, Germany: Books on Demand, 264-285; Herbert Ritschel, *Kurzfassung Kriegstagebücher deutscher U-boote 1939-1945, Band 3: KTB U100 – U124*, Norderstedt, Germany: Books on Demand, 40-71; Jürgen Rohwer, *Axis Submarine Successes 1939-1945*, Annapolis, Maryland: Naval Institute Press, 1983, 6, 7, 20, 22, 23, 30, 31, 36, 37, 38, 39, 42, 43, 50, 51, 52, 53, 55, 57, 58, 67, 72, 73, 77, 93, 96, 97, 98, 99, 131, 138, 140, 141, 153; Jak Mallmann Showell, *U-boats at War: Landings on Hostile Shores*, Hersham, England: Ian Allan Publishing, 2000, 137; www.ubootwaffe.net; www.uboatarchive.net.

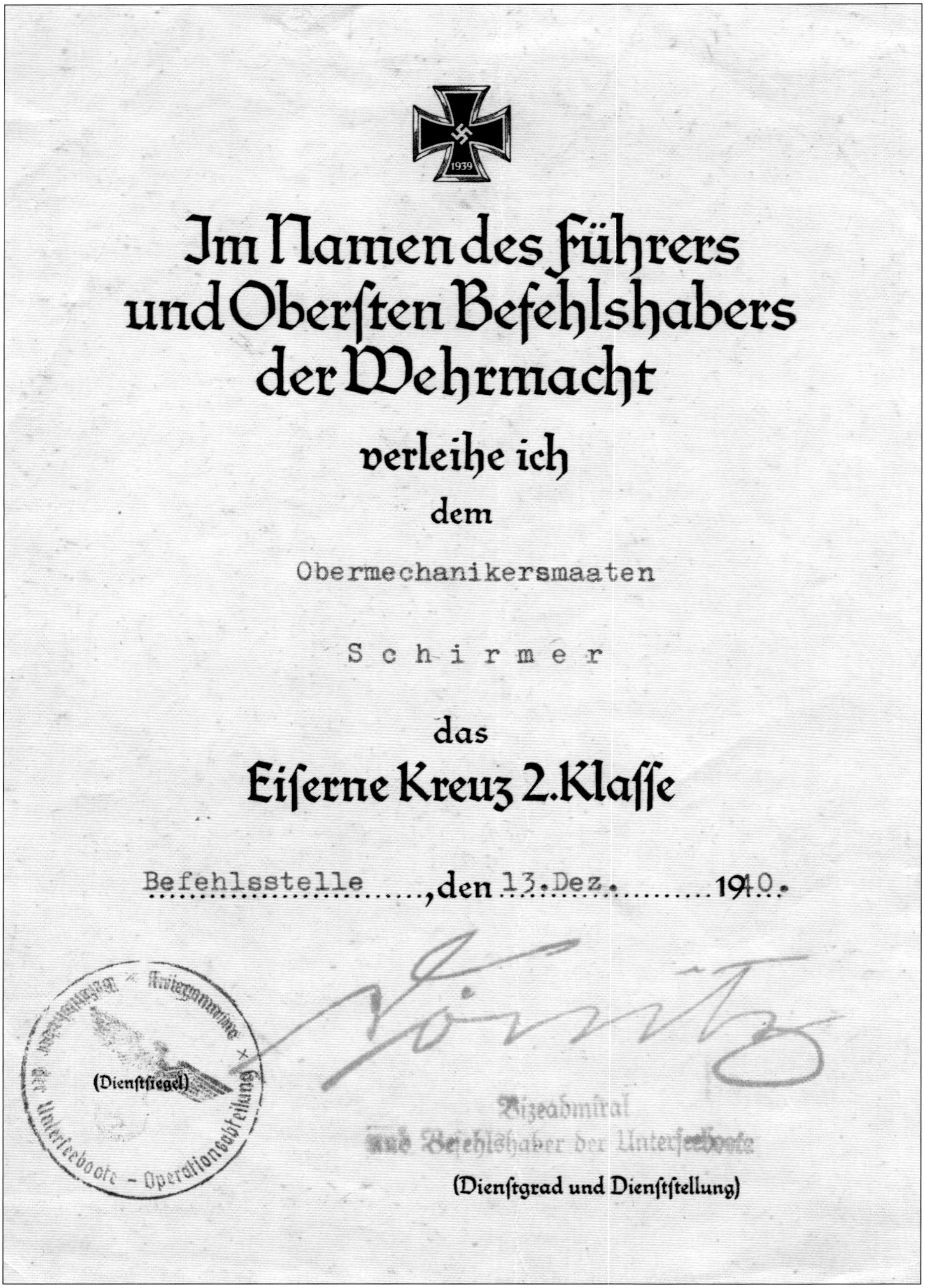

Im Namen des Führers und Oberſten Befehlshabers der Wehrmacht

verleihe ich

dem

Obermechanikersmaaten

S c h i r m e r

das

Eiſerne Kreuz 2. Klaſſe

Befehlsstelle, den 13.Dez. 1940.

(Dienſtſiegel)

Vizeadmiral und Befehlshaber der Unterſeeboote

(Dienſtgrad und Dienſtſtellung)

Iron Cross 2nd Class award document to Friedrich Schirmer of the U-103. *Medal was awarded on December 13, 1940 at Lorient, France, one day after the conclusion of a war patrol. Document has a facsimile signature of Vizeadmiral Karl Dönitz.*

Obermechanikermaat Friedrich Schirmer (left) and comrade on December 13, 1940 shortly after receiving the Iron Cross 2nd Class.

Friedrich Schirmer grabbing a smoke on the bridge midway through a patrol.

Friedrich Schirmer in blue sailor's shirt. *Photo taken at a studio in Wilhelmshaven.*

Officers in discussion next to a U-boat in port.

View from the bridge. *U-boat commander is wearing a white cap.*

Oberleutnant zur See Friedrich Justi, commander of the U-1170, at a banquet. *Photo is a post-war copy of an original.*

Petty Officers of the U-1170 in 1944. *Maschinenmaat on the right wears U-boat War Badge; he probably had at least two war patrols on a submarine. He also has attended a special course for motor specialists. Photo is a post-war copy of an original.*

Chief Petty Officers of the U-1170 in 1944. *Friedrich Schirmer is second from left. All wear Kriegsmarine ceremonial daggers. Photo is a post-war copy of an original.*

View of U-boats under camouflage nets in port.

The U-1170 at Danzig, 1944. *White stripe in the conning tower denotes boat is in a training status.*

Studio portrait photo of Friedrich Schirmer.

Signed photograph of Wolfgang Lüth. *Had the war continued, Dönitz planned to make Lüth the Chief of the U-boats.*

CHAPTER EIGHT

"FAMILY" U-107 1941

Karl Dönitz loved his U-boat sailors like his own family. But in the case of the commander of *U-107*, Günter Hessler, the ties went even further; Hessler was Dönitz's son-in-law. Günter Hessler was born on June 14, 1909 in Beerfelde/Lebus. He joined the Navy on April 5, 1927 and received basic sea training on the sailing training ship *Niobe*. For the next twelve years Hessler served in a variety of surface assignments, gravitating toward more and more torpedo boat postings. He commanded the torpedo boat *Falke* when the war began, winning the Iron Cross 2nd on November 18, 1939. On April 1, 1940 Hessler joined the U-boat service, which would ultimately place Dönitz in an unusual situation, as in November 1937 *Kapitänleutnant* Hessler had married Ursula Dönitz, Karl Dönitz's oldest child and only daughter. For six months Günter Hessler attended various U-boat courses before assuming command of the *U-107* on October 8, 1940. Hessler would have four aces painted on the conning tower as the boat's motif; this decoration would certainly work a special magic for the boat.

> *Dönitz's Crews*
> ***Funkmaat* Bernhard Geismann**
> Born on April 16, 1917 in Düsseldorf.
> Entered Navy on January 1, 1936.
> Served as a radio operator on the *U-107*.
> Awarded the Iron Cross 2nd Class and the U-boat War Badge on July 10, 1941.
> Survived the war; lived at Norderney, East Friesland Islands.

The *U-107* was a Type IXB boat. Built at the Deutsche Schiff- und Maschinenbau AG construction yard at Bremen, the boat was ordered before the war on May 24, 1938. Engineers actually laid the keel on December 6, 1939; the boat was launched on July 2, 1940, commissioned on October 8, 1940 and assigned to the 2nd U-boat Flotilla.

After sea trials, the *U-107* departed Wilhelmshaven on January 24, 1941 for her first war patrol, which proved quite successful. Among the crew was *Funkmaat* Bernhard Geismann, who served in the key position of radio operator on the *U-107*. Hailing from Düsseldorf, he was an electrician by trade. Günter Hessler hit four ships on this patrol to the mid-North Atlantic. On February 3, 1941 at 1:45 a.m., the *U-107* sank the British 4,683-ton *Empire Citizen*, sailing with convoy OB-279 from Liverpool, England to Rangoon, Burma. Seventy-eight men lost their lives on the ship, which was carrying general cargo. At 11:33 p.m. the *U-107* scored her second victory of the day, torpedoing and sinking the British 5,051-ton ocean boarding vessel *Crispin*, also a member of convoy OB-279. The next day an enemy destroyer forced Hessler to dive, but the U-boat was not detected or attacked. At 5:32 p.m. on February 6, 1941 Hessler sank the Canadian 3,388-ton *Maplecourt*, part of convoy SC-20. The entire crew of the ship – thirty-seven men – perished as the load of 3,604 tons of general cargo and 1,540 tons of steel went to the bottom with the vessel. At the end of the month, at 10:42 p.m. on February 23, 1941, the *U-107* struck the British 5,360-ton ocean boarding vessel *Manistee*, from convoy OB-288. The target did not sink immediately and was finally sunk after several additional attacks by the U-boat at 7:58 a.m. the following day. The *U-107* arrived at Lorient, France on March 1, 1941 after just over five weeks at sea; she had sailed 5,420 sea-miles surfaced and 108 sea-miles submerged. For this successful cruise Günter Hessler received the Iron Cross 1st Class.

Hessler and the crew of the *U-107* had the month of March to enjoy their success before departing on their second war patrol – a single patrol that would last thirteen and a half weeks and prove to be more successful than that by any other U-boat in the war. On March 29, 1941, the *U-107* left Lorient under the command of Günter Hessler; on this endeavor Günter Hessler would sink fourteen ships while on patrol off the Canary Islands and lurking west of Freetown, Sierra Leone, Africa in the South Atlantic. Eight of these ships were in convoy: one from convoy OB-309, one from convoy OB-318, one from convoy OB-320, one from convoy OB-323 and four from convoy OG-57. This incredible tally enfolded as follows:

1. On April 8, 1941, at 7:42 a.m., the *U-107* sank the British 3,829-ton *Eskdene* with two torpedoes and 104 rounds of 105-mm deck-gun fire.
2. On April 8, 1941 at 7:40 p.m., the *U-107* sank the British 3,316-ton *Helena Margareta*, sailing in ballast with convoy OG-57 from Tyne to Takoradi, Ghana; twenty-seven men were killed.
3. On April 9, 1941 at 12:37 a.m., the *U-107* sank the British 4,671-ton *Harpathian*, sailing with RAF supplies with convoy OG-57 from Clyde, Scotland to West Africa; four men perished.

4. On April 9, 1941 at 7:20 p.m., the *U-107* sank the British 8,516-ton tanker *Duffield*, carrying 11,700 tons of fuel oil with convoy OG-57 bound from Curacao to Gibraltar; twenty-five men died in the attack.
5. On April 21, 1941 at 2:20 p.m., the *U-107* sank the British 10,305-ton *Calchas* carrying 9,000 tons of wheat, butter, flour and steel from Freetown to Liverpool; thirty-two crewmen died as the ship returned fire attempting to damage the U-boat.
6. On April 30, 1941 at 9:55 p.m., the *U-107* sank the British 7,417-ton *Lassell*, with her 7,000 tons of general cargo, sailing with convoy OB-309 from Liverpool to Rio de Janeiro and Buenos Aires; seventeen men died. The U-boat then refueled from the supply ship *Nordmark* (May 3) and received torpedoes from the supply ship *Egerland* (May 9).
7. On May 17, 1941 at 12:36 a.m., the *U-107* sank the Dutch 8,029-ton tanker *Marisa* sailing in ballast from Freetown to Curacao.
8. On May 18, 1941 at 10:27 p.m., the *U-107* sank the British 8,286-ton *Piako* bound from Albany, New York to Freetown and Liverpool; ten crewmen perished and 7,100 tons of refrigerated goods including 1,500 tons of butter and 1,500 tons of meat went to the bottom.
9. On May 27, 1941 at 1:01 a.m., the *U-107* sank the British 5,108-ton *Colonial* carrying 3,500 tons of general cargo with convoy OB-318 from Liverpool to Freetown; all her crew survived.
10. On May 28, 1941 at 2:42 p.m., the *U-107* sank the Greek 3,748-ton *Papalemos* bound from Montevideo, Uruguay to Freetown; the ship with 5,460 tons of cereals sank, but only two crewmen were lost.
11. On May 31, 1941 at 7:39 a.m., the *U-107* sank the British 5,664-ton *Sire*, which was in ballast bound from Las Palmas, Canary Islands to Pepel, Sierra Leone; three crewmen were killed.
12. On June 1, 1941 at 2:01 p.m., the *U-107* sank the British 5,013-ton "Q-ship" *Alfred Jones*, part of convoy OB-320 from the River Mersey to Freetown with RAF aircraft and trucks; two crewmen died.
13. On June 8, 1941 at 4:42 a.m., the *U-107* sank the British 7,816-ton *Adda*, from convoy OB-323 bound from Liverpool to Freetown with general cargo; nine men died when the ship went to the bottom. Sunderland aircraft forced the U-boat to dive four times during the day.
14. On June 13, 1941 at 11:57 a.m., the *U-107* sank the Greek 4,981-ton *Pandias* carrying 4,894 tons of coal from Milford Haven, Wales to Alexandria, Egypt; eleven crewmen perished.

The *U-107* returned to Lorient on July 2, 1941 to a heroes' welcome after ninety-six days at sea during which the U-boat traveled 15,744 sea-miles on the surface and 173 sea-miles submerged. Hessler received the U-boat War Badge on July 3 as well as a Knight's Cross, which had been officially approved on June 24, 1941. This last award had an interesting twist. Dönitz was initially reluctant to submit Hessler for the honor – which was clearly deserved – due to his personal relationship and by the desire not to appear to show favoritism. Grand Admiral Raeder disagreed and told the U-boat chief that if he did not submit Hessler for the decoration, Raeder would. Dönitz relented and the recommendation was approved up the line with Hitler signing the final approval on June 24.

Others in the crew also received well-deserved awards. *Funkmaat* Bernhard Geismann was awarded both the Iron Cross 2nd Class and the U-boat War Badge on July 10, 1941. In addition to operating the communications equipment, these technical specialists also controlled the underwater listening gear that could pinpoint the location of enemy ships based on sound waves traveling through water – this skill would have been invaluable in locating the fourteen targets sunk on the patrol. The *U-107* remained in port for over two months; technical engineers overhauled the boat and the crew took a well-deserved leave home. In addition, promotions were in order and Hessler was promoted to *Korvettenkapitän*.

Finally, on September 6, 1941 the *U-107* departed Lorient under *Korvettenkapitän* Günter Hessler for her third war patrol. While it would not prove as spectacular as the previous voyage, the *U-107* would hit three ships on this patrol off northwest Africa; all of them were from convoy SL-87 and all were sunk on the same day – in a three-minute period! The patrol did not begin successfully; on September 22, the *U-107* had an engine malfunction that required forty-eight hours of at-sea repairs. That fixed, the *U-107* began the fireworks on September 24, 1941 by sinking the British 4,975-ton *John Holt* at 6:31 a.m. One crewman died as the ship carrying 4,560 tons of West African produce from Duala, Cameroon for Liverpool went to the bottom. Two minutes later the *U-107* sank the British 4,876-ton *Lafian* carrying 6,500 tons of palm products and 1,128 tons of timber from Port Harcourt, Nigeria to Liverpool; all her crew survived. Simultaneously (and probably with the same spread of torpedoes) Hessler sank the British 3,790-ton *Dixcove*. One man perished in the attack. Then the *U-107* hit a protracted fallow period; she arrived back at Lorient on November 11, 1941 after some nine and a half weeks on patrol. Hessler had traveled 10,140 sea-miles on the surface and just 46 sea-miles submerged.

It would be Günter Hessler's last patrol with the *U-107*. Two weeks later, he assumed shore duties at B.d.U. headquarters helping to plan future missions for the U-boat fleet. For these efforts Hessler would receive the German Cross in Gold on November 9, 1944, and a promotion to *Fregattenkapitän* on December 18, 1944. Günter Hessler sank twenty-one merchant ships, a combined 118,822 tons. This placed him twenty-first among the most-successful U-boat commanders of the war.

For the *U-107*, it would mean more combat, but instead of receiving a relatively new commander, the boat's luck held firm when Harald Gelhaus took command. Gelhaus, who was born on July 24, 1915 at Göttingen, was a six-year veteran in the Navy, joining the U-boat arm in early 1940. Prior to assuming command of the *U-107* he served as the 1st Watch Officer on the *U-103* on three war patrols and as the commander of the *U-143* for four war patrols – winning the Iron Cross 2nd and 1st Class and the U-boat War Badge. He would take the *U-107* from Lorient on December 10, 1941 for her fourth war patrol. The *U-107* returned just over two weeks later to Lorient on December 26, 1941 but did not remain in port long; she would be heading far to the west.

For her fifth war patrol the *U-107* departed Lorient on January 7, 1942 under the command of Harald Gelhaus. For three weeks the crew was unable to score a victory, but at 4:45 p.m. on January 31, 1942 they sank the British 7,419-ton tanker *San Arcadio*. Forty-one men died as the ship carrying 6,600 tons of gas oil and 3,300 tons of lubricating oil exploded several hundred miles south of Nova Scotia. At 4:08 p.m. on February 6, 1942 off Cape Hatteras, the *U-107* sank a second ship, the American 3,431-ton *Major Wheeler* bound from Puerto Rico to Philadelphia. On February 21, 1942 at 10:44 a.m., the *U-107* damaged the Norwegian 10,068-ton *Egda* from convoy ON-65 bound from Stanlow, England to Aruba, but the ship, which was in ballast, did not sink. The *U-107* experienced other problems. On February 13 the boat rendezvoused with the *U-564* to transfer fuel, but the boats collided and the pair had to creep to France at one-engine speed. Gelhaus returned to Lorient after eight and a half weeks on patrol on March 7, 1942; he had sailed 7,400 sea-miles on the surface and 252 sea-miles submerged.

The boat remained in Lorient for six weeks – during which time Gelhaus received a promotion to *Kapitänleutnant* – departing port on April 21, 1942 for her sixth war patrol, bound for the Caribbean. It would prove to be a profitable hunting ground. Seven ships would feel the sting of the U-boat's torpedoes and gunfire:

1. On May 29, 1942 at 2:17 a.m., the *U-107* sank the British 2,599-ton *Western Head* between Cuba and Haiti; twenty-four men died as the ship carrying 3,710 tons of sugar sank.
2. On June 1, 1942 at 3:54 a.m., the *U-107* sank the Panamanian 4,536-ton *Bushranger*, carrying bauxite from Paramaribo, Suriname to New York; seventeen men died in the attack west of Jamaica.
3. On June 7, 1942 at 4:08 a.m., the *U-107* sank the 3,910-ton *Castilla* south of Cuba; the ship, carrying flour from Mobile, Alabama to Jamaica, sank with twenty-seven of her crew.
4. On June 8, 1942 at 1:19 a.m., the *U-107* sank the American 3,249-ton *Suwied* off the Yucatan Peninsula; bound from Demerara, British Guiana to Mobile, Alabama with 4,970 tons of bauxite, the ship sank but all her crew survived. Later that day an enemy flying boat forced Gelhaus to keep the boat submerged for several hours.
5. On June 10, 1942 at 5:01 a.m., the *U-107* sank the American 2,606-ton *Merrimack* off the Yucatan Peninsula.
6. On June 19, 1942 at 11:02 a.m., the *U-107* sank the American 35-ton *Cheerio* with 105-mm deck-gun fire north of Aruba; all her nine-man crew survived. Again enemy aircraft forced the *U-107* to run submerged for many hours.
7. On June 26, 1942 at 3:00 p.m., the *U-107* sank the Dutch 10,083-ton *Jagersfontein* near Bermuda; all 165 men aboard were saved.

The *U-107* then refueled on June 27 from the "milk cow" supply U-boat *U-459* and returned on July 11, 1942 to Lorient after eleven and a half weeks on patrol.

The boat's seventh patrol began on August 15, 1942 and this patrol also proved successful. After crossing the Bay of Biscay, Gelhaus radioed to Dönitz at his Kernével headquarters that the boat's Metox radar-detector equipment enabled the *U-107* to successfully avoid attacks by six enemy aircraft. The U-boat's first two victories occurred on September 3, 1942. At 5:52 a.m. the *U-107* sank the British 4,172-ton *Hollinside* off Portugal; three men perished in the attack. Eleven minutes later, at 9:03 a.m., the *U-107* bagged their second ship, the British 4,393-ton *Penrose*; two men died in this attack. Gelhaus then went over a month at sea without another success until shortly after midnight on October 7, 1942 when the *U-107* sank the British 14,943-ton *Andalucia Star* bound from Buenos Aires to the River Mersey. The *U-107* safely returned to Lorient on November 18, 1942; she had gone 14,500 sea-miles on the surface and 731 sea-miles submerged.

The *U-107* departed under Harald Gelhaus from Lorient on January 30, 1943 for her ninth war patrol, which would also prove quite successful. On February 22, 1943 at 7:32 a.m., the *U-107* sank the British 7,801-ton *Roxborough Castle* bound from Glasgow to Buenos Aires; all crew survived. On March 4, an unidentified aircraft attacked the boat southwest of Portugal. The U-boat was moderately damaged by the attack, but Gelhaus determined he could continue his mission. Gelhaus was proven correct in his assessment. On March 13 at 5:30 a.m. the *U-107* went wild, simultaneously sinking the following four ships of convoy OS-44 within minutes:

1. The British 2,352-ton *Oporto*, sailing from Liverpool to Seville, Spain; forty-three crewmen died.
2. The British 4,592-ton *Marcella*, bound from Clyde to Freetown; all forty-four men aboard perished.
3. The Dutch 4,990-ton *Sembilangan*, heading from Liverpool to Alexandria; eighty-six of eighty-seven men went to the bottom with her.
4. The British 5,442-ton *Clan Alpine*, from Liverpool to Port Sudan on the Red Sea; twenty-six men died in the attack.

At 2:35 p.m. on March 22, 1943 the *U-107* again came under attack from an unidentified aircraft but was not damaged by the attack. She arrived back at Lorient after more than seven weeks at sea on March 25, 1943; on her journey she traveled 6,780 sea-miles on the surface – but submerged sea-miles increased to 750. After one month in port the *U-107* departed Lorient under the command of Harald Gelhaus on April 24, 1943 on her tenth – and what would be Gelhaus's last with the boat – patrol. He would score one final victory. On May 1, 1943 at 1:00 a.m., the *U-107* sank the British 12,411-ton *Port Victor* bound from Montevideo to Liverpool. Seventeen of her crew died in the attack north of Portugal. Five days later an enemy destroyer drove the U-boat underwater; depth charges caused no damage though. The *U-107* returned to Lorient on May 26, 1943 after four and a half weeks on patrol. She had gone 4,100 sea-miles on the surface, while submerged miles totaled 450; the *U-107* was now operating over ten percent of the time under water. Gelhaus departed the boat for a key assignment at the Navy High Command Headquarters; he survived the war. Harald Gelhaus sank nineteen merchant ships, a combined 100,373 tons, and damaged an additional ship for 10,068 tons. This placed him thirty-fourth among the most successful U-boat commanders of the war.

Dönitz's Crews

***Obermaschinenmaat* Fritz Stagge**

Served in the engine room of the *U-103*, the *U-107* and the *U-3013*.

Awarded the Iron Cross 2nd Class on April 16, 1940, while serving on the destroyer *Theodor Riedel*.

Survived the war; lived in Worms, Rhineland-Pfalz.

Taking his place was *Oberleutnant zur See* Volker Simmermacher, one of the *U-107*'s own "family." Born on February 1, 1919 in Strasbourg, he joined the Navy in 1937 and served as a watch officer on the battleship *Scharnhorst* through May 1941. He then began U-boat training and joined the *U-107* in November 1941 as a watch officer, serving in this capacity until May 1943 when he was selected for a U-boat commander's course. Simmermacher assumed command of the boat in July. Among the crew was *Obermaschinenmaat* Fritz Stagge, who served in the engine room. Stagge was one of the many U-boat men who transferred to the undersea service during the war from the surface fleet. In April 1940 he served on the destroyer *Theodor Riedel* during the German invasion of Norway. The destroyer landed ground troops at Trondheim on April 9; a week later Stagge received an Iron Cross 2nd Class for his service in the operation. At some later point he left the *Theodor Riedel* and joined the U-boat service.

On July 28, 1943, the *U-107* left Lorient under the command of Volker Simmermacher for her eleventh war patrol. Simmermacher damaged two ships on this patrol; one was from convoy NG-385, but neither ship sank. On August 28, 1943, the *U-107* hit the American 7,176-ton *Albert Gallatin* off Savannah, Georgia. Two weeks later on September 11, 1943, Simmermacher damaged the American 8,246-

ton escort oiler *USS Rapidan*, sailing with convoy NG-385, but the ship made it to Charleston for repairs. The *U-107* arrived back at Lorient on October 3, 1943 after nine and a half weeks on patrol. Submerged operation increased again as she sailed 7,500 sea-miles on the surface and 1,300 sea-miles submerged.

The next four patrols under Simmermacher were unremarkable:

- The *U-107* departed under Volker Simmermacher from Lorient on November 10, 1943 and after two days arrived at St. Nazaire, France on November 12, 1943; the boat encountered no enemy ships.
- The *U-107* left St. Nazaire on November 16, 1943 and arrived at Lorient on January 8, 1944 after seven and a half weeks at sea; the boat fired at an enemy corvette with a homing torpedo but missed and was depth-charged during the war patrol. Surface operations comprised 5,500 sea-miles, while submerged operations accounted for 1,379 sea-miles.
- On April 30, 1944 the *U-107* proceeded from Lorient for a snorkel test and returned to Lorient on May 2, 1944 after just two days.
- The *U-107* departed from Lorient under Volker Simmermacher on May 10, 1944 for operations off New York. Simmermacher hit one last ship on this patrol. He damaged the American 148-ton *Lark* with gunfire off Nova Scotia on June 13, 1944 at 8:30 a.m., but the ship did not sink. The U-boat returned to Lorient on July 23, 1944 after ten and a half weeks on patrol. With her snorkel, the U-boat traveled 4,210 sea-miles on the surface, but more importantly went 2,680 sea-miles submerged.

Simmermacher then departed the ship for an extensive period of training to become a commander of one of the new Type XXI boats. He assumed command of the *U-3013* on November 22, 1944 through the end of the war. Replacing him was *Leutnant zur See* Karl-Heinz Fritz. Born on February 20, 1921 in Hamburg, he joined the Navy in 1941 and became a watch officer on the famous *U-103*, which would become the second most successful boat of the entire war. As a member of the *U-103*'s "family," he was expected to be another successful commander of the *U-107*, but events would prove tragically otherwise.

The *U-107* left Lorient for a short voyage under the command of Karl-Heinz Fritz on August 16, 1944 with a load of snorkels for the U-boats based at La Pallice, France. On August 18, 1944 a British Sunderland aircraft (Flight Lieutenant L.H. Baveystock) of the RAF's 201st Squadron dropped an accurate string of depth charges on the *U-107*; all fifty-nine crewmen perished in the attack southwest of St. Nazaire. She had been a very successful member of the U-boat family. During her career, the *U-107* sank thirty-seven merchant ships, for 207,375 tons, and damaged four ships for 25,638 tons, making the boat the fifth most successful of the U-boat service.

It must have been a bitter blow to Günter Hessler as well. With his father-in-law selected as the last leader of Germany at Hitler's death, Hessler received much attention from the Allies immediately after the war. He served several months as a prisoner of war, and saw his father-in-law receive a ten year sentence at the International Military Tribunal at Nürnberg, even though he testified in his father-in-law's defense. Despite those setbacks, Hessler agreed to write a detailed history of the German U-boat service for the British and American Navy historical offices and completed this work in 1951. He saw Karl Dönitz finally released from Spandau prison in 1956, but he did not outlive his father-in-law. Günter Hessler died at Bochum-Laer on April 4, 1968, two months short of his fifty-ninth birthday.

Known Crewmembers for the U-107

Albert, Ludwig	*Obermaschinenmaat*
Albrecht, Karl	*Maschinenobergefreiter*
Ascherl, Emil	*Maschinenmaat*
Bader, Martin	*Obermechanikermaat*
Bahnsen, Hermann	*Obermaschinist*
Bart, Fritz	*Kapitänleutnant*
Bartels, Gerhard	*Leutnant (Ing)*
Bast, Reinhold	*Oberleutnant zur See*
Baumgart, Hans	*Obermaschinenmaat*
Becker, Willi	*Bootsmann*
Bör, Hermann	*Kapitänleutnant (Ing)*
Buch, Helmut	*Obergefreiter*
Buhrig, Fritz	*Matrosenobergefreiter*
Büttner, Paul-Edoard	*Matrosenobergefreiter*
Dickhaus, Ernst	*Maschinenmaat*
Diekmann, Helmut-Wilhelm	*Matrosenobergefreiter*
Dose, Herbert	*Obermaat*
Ehlers, Walter	*Oberleutnant zur See*
Engler, Ewald	*Kapitänleutnant (Ing)*
Fehr, Heinrich	*Hauptgefreiter*
Fenner, Heinrich	*Maschinenmaat*
Flachmeyer, Hans-Jörg	*Leutnant zur See*
Franz, Werner	*Mechanikergefreiter*
Fritz, Karl-Heinz	*Leutnant zur See*
Fuchs, Hans-Joachim	*Maschinenmaat*
Gaida, Bernhard	
Galk, Max	*Obergefreiter*
Gebhard, Kurt	*Mechanikergefreiter*
Geiger, Hans	*Funkgefreiter*
Geismann, Bernhard	*Oberfunkmaat*
Gelhaus, Harald	*Kapitänleutnant*
Gläsel, Theo	*Oberbootsmaat*
Gutsche, Walter	*Obersteuermann*
Halka, Johann	*Obersanitätsmaat*
Hamm, Rudolf	*Mechanikerobergefreiter*
Hase, Heinz-Dietrich	*Matrosenobergefreiter*
Haustein, Peter	*Obermaschinenmaat*
Hecker, Wilhelm	*Obermaat*
Heidecker, Siegfried	*Obermaschinenmaat*
Heinke, Max	*Obergefreiter*
Hempel, Hans-Joachim	*Obermaschinenmaat*
Herbst, Ernst	*Obergefreiter*
Hertel, Gerhard	*Maschinenhauptgefreiter*
Hessler, Günter	*Fregattenkapitän*
Himmeter, Heinrich	*Obergefreiter*
Hoffrath, Fritz	
Hormes, Harald	*Bootsmaat*
Horn, Gerhard	*Maschinenobergefreiter*
Horster, Johann	*Mechanikerobergefreiter*
Irmschler, Heinz	*Matrosenobergefreiter*
Kaluscha, Max	*Funkmaat*
Kasch, Lorenz	*Kapitänleutnant*
Kirchner, Paul	*Oberbootsmaat*
Klimaschewski, Otto	*Obermaschinist*
König, Josef	*Matrosengefreiter*
Köpping, Hermann	*Obermaat*
Kordt, Heinz	*Maschinenobergefreiter*

Kottysch, Gerhard	*Oberfunkmaat*
Kramer, Ulrich	*Leutnant zur See*
Krause, Alfred	*Obermaschinist*
Krejci, Karl	*Funkgefreiter*
Krumnacker, Emil	*Maschinengefreiter*
Kuschniersch, Paul	*Obermaschinist*
Laszig, Paul	*Obergefreiter*
Lehmann, Franz	*Obersteuermann*
Lehmann, Wolfgang	*Obergefreiter*
Lemke, Otto	*Maschinenobergefreiter*
Liebetrau, Richard	*Obersteuermann*
Lippert, Gerhard	*Maschinenhauptgefreiter*
Mahrl, Peter	*Obermaat*
Mai, Wilhelm	*Obermaschinenmaat*
Makowski, Harry	*Hauptgefreiter*
Markert, Albrecht	*Oberleutnant zur See*
Matthai, Hans	*Maschinenobergefreiter*
Meissler, Helmut	*Obersteuermann*
Mewes, Manfred	*Matrosenobergefreiter*
Meyer, Anton	*Maschinengefreiter*
Möller, Helmut	*Obergefreiter*
Moser, Alfred	*Obergefreiter*
Mrkwa, Paul	*Matrosengefreiter*
Munchow, Max	*Matrosengefreiter*
Neubauer, Edmund	*Matrosenobergefreiter*
Nieder, Heinrich	*Obergefreiter*
Obladen, Wilhelm	*Maschinenobergefreiter*
Ohlsen, Herbert	*Obergefreiter*
Parchen, Herbert	*Mechanikermaat*
Petri, Walter	*Stabsobermaschinist*
Pohlmann, Adalbert	
Popken, Max	*Obermaschinist*
Portofee, Fritz	*Mechanikerobergefreiter*
Quester, Johann	*Matrosenobergefreiter*
Ranzau, Emil	*Oberleutnant zur See*
Rauch, Dietrich	*Kapitänleutnant*
Robbert, Heinz	*Oberleutnant zur See*
Rodeck, Kurt	*Matrosenobergefreiter*
Rudolph, Hans	*Obergefreiter*
Rüggeberg, Rolf	*Fregattenkapitän*
Sack, Fritz	*Maschinenobergefreiter*
Sass, Walter	*Leutnant zur See*
Schenck, Wilhelm	*Oberleutnant (Ing)*
Scherraus, Ekkehard	*Oberleutnant zur See*
Schleewald, Gerhard	
Schmidt, Karl	*Maschinengefreiter*
Schneider, Werner	*Obergefreiter*
Schober, Rudolf	*Matrosenobergefreiter*
Scholz, Karl	*Matrose*
Schwaiger	*Obersteuermann*
Schwartzkopff, Volkmar	*Kapitänleutnant*
Schweigert, Heinz	*Maschinenobergefreiter*
Simmermacher, Volker	*Kapitänleutnant*
Smak, Johann	*Obermaschinenmaat*
Smeets, Peter	*Maschinenobergefreiter*
Städtke, Helmut	*Bootsmaat*
Stagge, Fritz	*Obermaschinenmaat*
Stark, Wilhelm	
Steinmann, Edgar	*Maschinenmaat*
Stenda, Herbert	*Obermaat*
Stephan, Albert	*Obergefreiter*
Theisen, Günter	*Leutnant zur See*
Thelen, Ludwig	
Vogel, Kurt	*Maschinenobergefreiter*
Vowe, Bruno	*Kapitänleutnant*
Wagner, Alfred	*Maschinenmaat*
Wamers, Otto	*Oberleutnant (Ing)*
Wessel, Gerhard	*Mechanikermaat*
Wimber, Hans	Monteur (special engineer)
Windisch, Franz	*Maschinengefreiter*
Witte, Helmut	*Korvettenkapitän*
Wölke, Willi	*Bootsmaat*
Zimmermann, Friedrich	*Oberbootsmaat*
Zündorf, Johannes	*Maschinenmaat*
Zurek, Walter	*Mechanikergefreiter*

Sources, "Family:" Clay Blair, *Hitler's U-boat War: The Hunters, 1939-1942*, New York: Random House, 1996, 268, 269, 297, 301, 381, 382, 502, 582, 671; Rainer Busch and Hans-Joachim Röll, *German U-boat Commanders of World War II*, translated by Geoffrey Brooks, Annapolis, Maryland: Naval Institute Press, 1999, 76, 244; Manfred Dörr, *Die Ritterkreuzträger der U-Boot-Waffe, Band 1: A-J, Band 2: L-Z*, Osnabrück, FRG: Biblio Verlag, 1988, Band 1-92, 93, 133, 134, 135; Axel Niestlé, *German U-boat Losses during World War II*, Annapolis, Maryland: Naval Institute Press, 1998, 119; Herbert Ritschel, *Kurzfassung Kriegstagebücher deutscher U-boote 1939-1945, Band 3: KTB U100 – U124,* Norderstedt, Germany: Books on Demand, 120-156; Jürgen Rohwer, *Axis Submarine Successes 1939-1945*, Annapolis, Maryland: Naval Institute Press, 1983, 42, 43, 49, 50, 52, 53, 54, 55, 56, 67, 76, 77, 99, 100, 101, 102, 106, 120, 127, 150, 156, 164, 171, 181, 182; www.ubootwaffe.net; www.uboatarchive.net.

Verleihungs-Urkunde.

Auf Grund der Ermächtigung des Oberbefehlshabers der Kriegsmarine verleihe ich dem

Funkmaat
(Dienstgrad)

Bernhard Geismann
(Name)

das

Ubootskriegsabzeichen 1939

Im Westen, den 10. Juli 1941

Befehlshaber der Unterseeboote – Operationsabteilung – Kriegsmarine

Vizeadmiral und Befehlshaber der Unterseeboote

U-boat War Badge award document to Bernhard Geismann of the U-107, presented on July 10, 1941. *The document has a facsimile signature of Karl Dönitz; Geismann received the award shortly after the conclusion of the boat's highly successful second war patrol.*

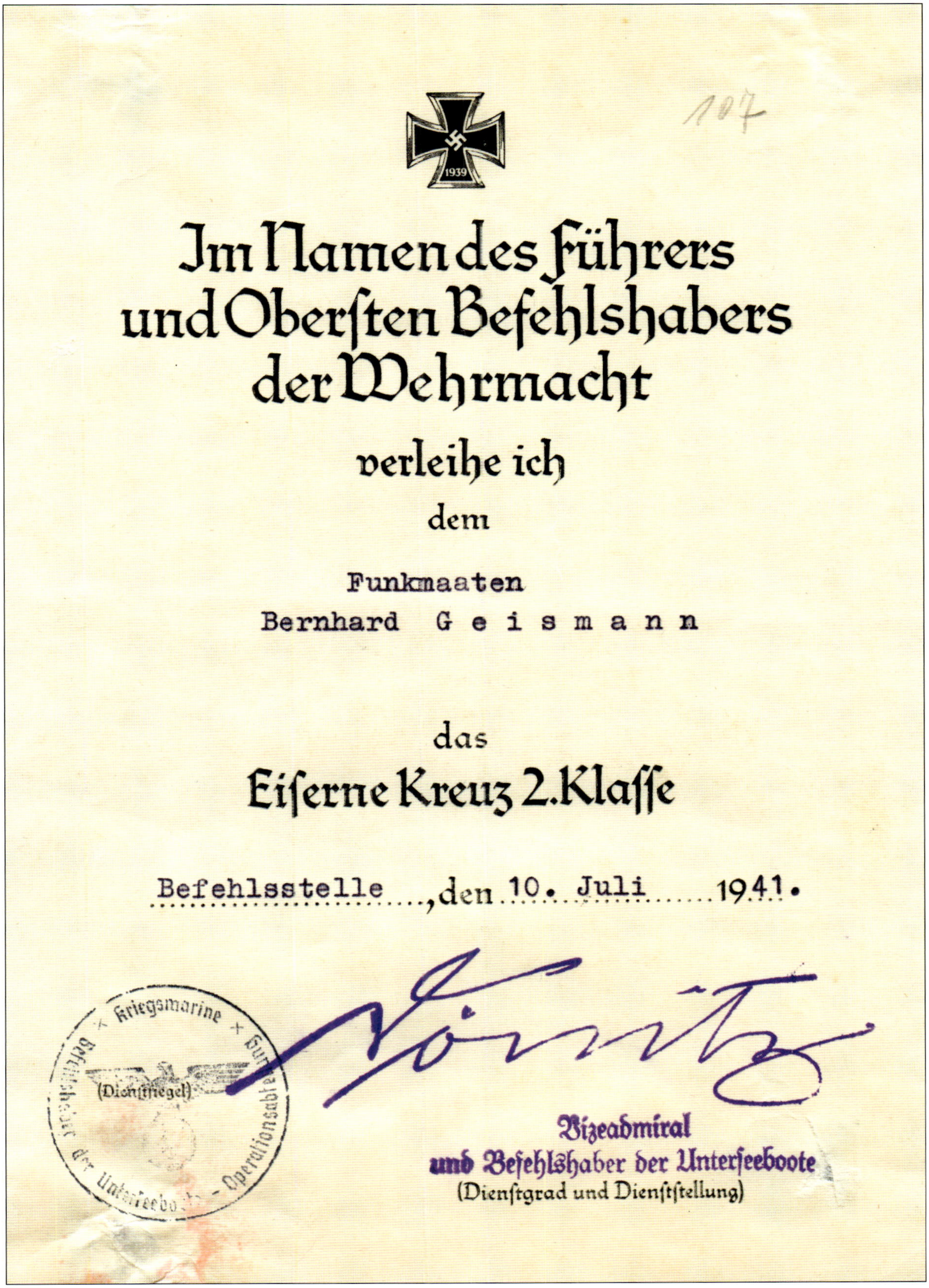
107

Im Namen des Führers
und Obersten Befehlshabers
der Wehrmacht

verleihe ich

dem

Funkmaaten
Bernhard G e i s m a n n

das

Eiserne Kreuz 2. Klasse

Befehlsstelle, den 10. Juli 1941.

Dönitz

Kriegsmarine
Befehlshaber der Unterseeboote - Operationsabteilung
(Dienstsiegel)

Vizeadmiral
und Befehlshaber der Unterseeboote
(Dienstgrad und Dienststellung)

Iron Cross 2nd Class award document to Bernhard Geismann of the U-107, presented on July 10, 1941. *The document has a facsimile signature of Karl Dönitz; it was awarded at Lorient, France.*

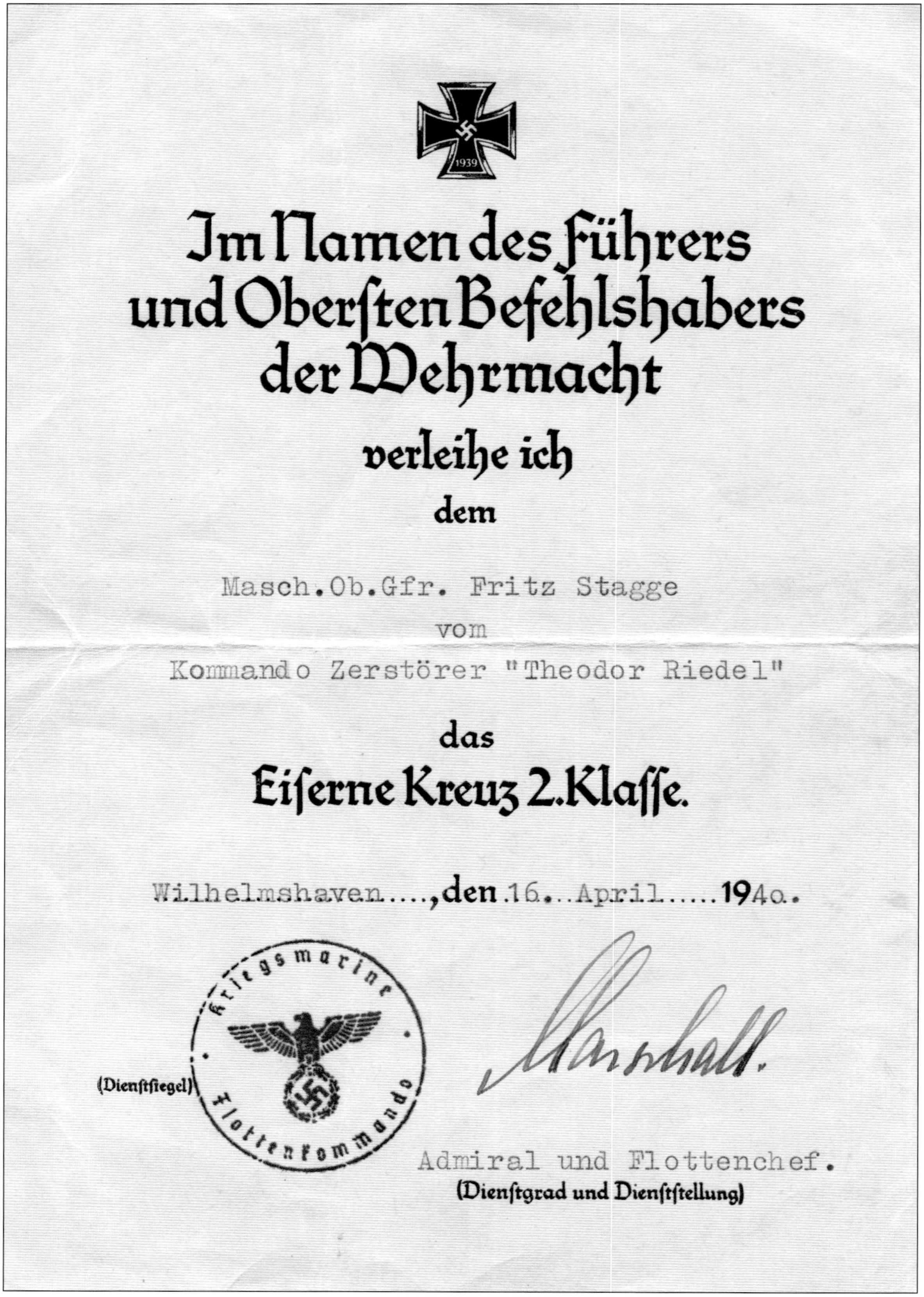

Im Namen des Führers
und Oberſten Befehlshabers
der Wehrmacht

verleihe ich

dem

Masch.Ob.Gfr. Fritz Stagge

vom

Kommando Zerstörer "Theodor Riedel"

das

Eiſerne Kreuz 2.Klaſſe.

Wilhelmshaven....,den.16...April.....1940.

Kriegsmarine Flottenkommando

(Dienſtſiegel)

Marschall.

Admiral und Flottenchef.

(Dienſtgrad und Dienſtſtellung)

Iron Cross 2nd Class award document to Fritz Stagge of the German destroyer Theodor Riedel on April 16, 1940. *The document is signed by Admiral Wilhelm Marschall, Commander of the Fleet; it was awarded at Wilhelmshaven, Germany. Stagge was one of twenty-seven of the crew of the U-107 who also served on the U-103, and six who later served on the U-3013.*

View of the U-107 at her commissioning ceremony on October 8, 1940.

View of the U-107 immediately on her return from her second war patrol during which she sank fourteen ships. *Photo was probably taken July 2 or 3, 1941 at Lorient. Each pennant signifies the estimated tonnage and name of a ship sunk on the patrol. The six pennants fully visible in the photo, from left to right, represent: the Greek 4,981-ton Pandias, the British 5,108-ton Colonial, the British 8,286-ton Piako, the Dutch 8,100-ton (8,029-ton) tanker Marisa, the British 7,816-ton Adda and the British 7,417-ton Lassell.*

One of the U-107's "family" – Chief Engineer Oberleutnant Otto Wamers, shown with U-boat War Badge and Minesweeper Badge. *Wamers also served on the U-451, U-103 and U-3013; he survived the war.*

One of the U-107's "family" – Engine Room sailor Hauptgefreiter Harry Makowski. *Makowski also served on the U-30. Photo taken in December 1942; he survived the war.*

Part of the U-107's "family" enjoys the tropics under an umbrella. *Photo is a post-war copy of an original.*

Three crewmen of the U-107 smile on the bridge at sea. *Photo is a post-war copy of an original.*

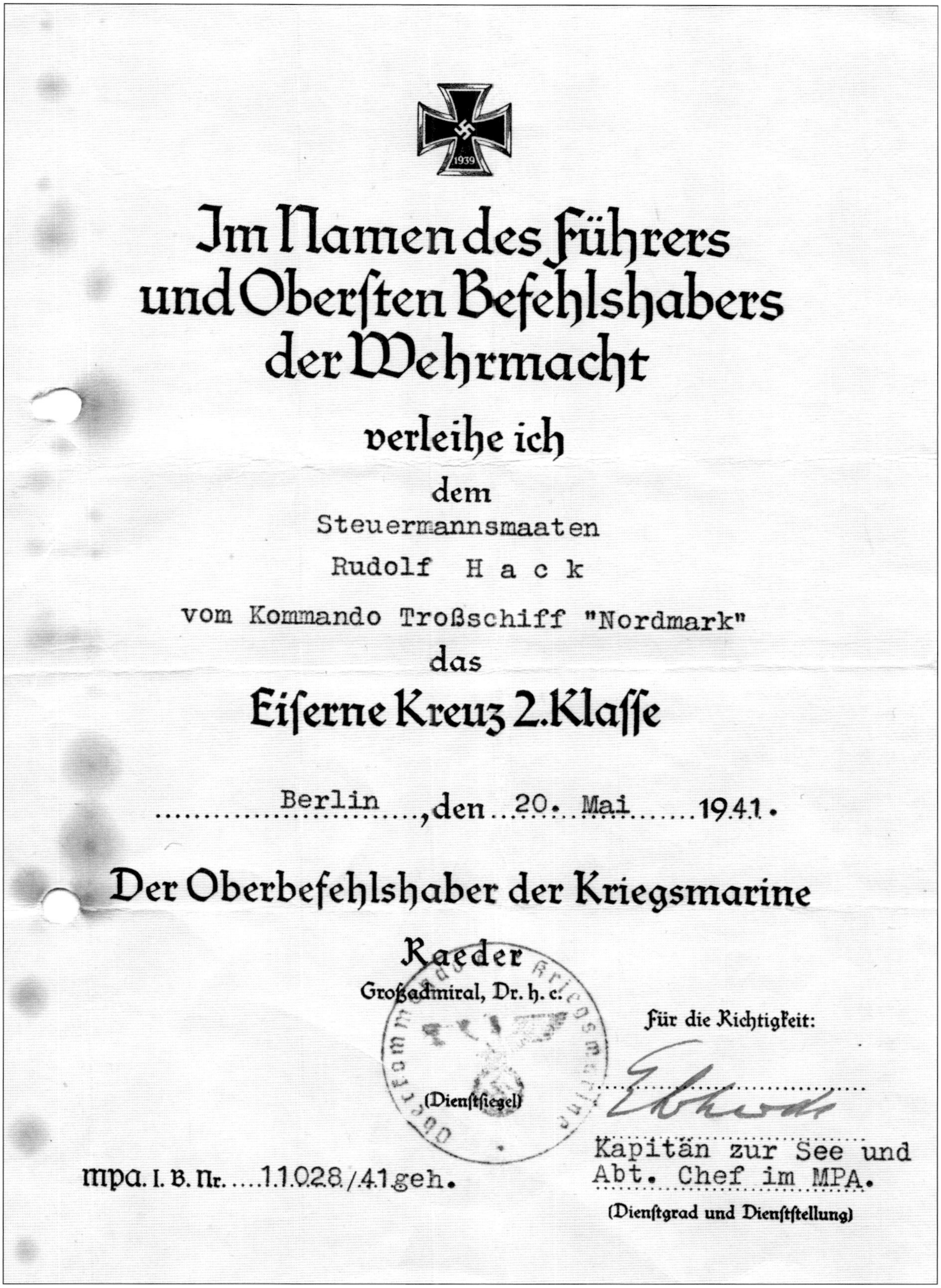

Im Namen des Führers
und Obersten Befehlshabers
der Wehrmacht

verleihe ich

dem

Steuermannsmaaten

Rudolf Hack

vom Kommando Troßschiff "Nordmark"

das

Eiserne Kreuz 2. Klasse

Berlin, den 20. Mai 1941.

Der Oberbefehlshaber der Kriegsmarine

Raeder

Großadmiral, Dr. h. c.

(Dienstsiegel)

Für die Richtigkeit:

Ehrhardt

Kapitän zur See und
Abt. Chef im MPA.

(Dienstgrad und Dienststellung)

MPA. I. B. Nr. 11028/41 geh.

Iron Cross 2nd Class award document to Steuermannsmaat Rudolf Hack on the supply ship Nordmark. *Document is dated May 20, 1941 shortly after the Nordmark resupplied the U-107. Kapitän zur See Werner Ehrhardt in the Navy Personnel Office signed the award in Berlin. The Nordmark was a 22,850-ton tanker converted to a supply ship; she resupplied many Kriegsmarine surface ships and U-boats.*

CHAPTER NINE

"FRUSTRATION" U-204 OCTOBER 1941

Serving in the U-boats was often frustrating. It was frustrating when a skipper lined up a perfect shot and the torpedo malfunctioned somewhere enroute to the target. It was frustrating when a group, or pack, of U-boats could not find a convoy, when by all rights it should be right in front of them. It was frustrating for Dönitz when old commanders failed to keep him informed of ongoing actions, when new commanders lacked the experience needed to be truly aggressive and when excited commanders exaggerated results of their attacks. Almost every U-boat crew experienced frustration; some, like the crew of the *U-204*, experienced it a great deal.

Dönitz's Crews

***Matrosenobergefreiter* Anton Niwczyk**

Born on December 22, 1922 in Castrop/Westphalia.
Served on the *U-204*.
Posthumously awarded the U-boat War Badge on February 2, 1942.
Spent 97 days at sea on U-boat war patrols.
Killed in action on October 19, 1941 in the Atlantic Ocean off Tangier, Morocco.

As with many other wartime requirements, the Navy quickly realized after the start of the war that it needed many more U-boats, and so on September 23, 1939 it ordered construction of the *U-204*, a Type VIIC boat. Construction engineers laid her keel on April 22, 1940 at the F. Krupp Germaniawerft construction yard at Kiel-Gaarden. She was launched on January 23, 1941 and commissioned on March 8, 1941 at Kiel under her first – and what would be her only – skipper, *Oberleutnant zur See* Walter Kell.

Born in Altenwald/Saarland on December 4, 1913, Kell was an interesting character, and was temporarily assigned to the *Luftwaffe* from 1935 to 1939 to become a naval aviator. He would serve as a seaplane pilot on the pocket battleship *Deutschland* in 1939. Kell and his boat were assigned to the 1st U-boat Flotilla commanded by *Korvettenkapitän* Hans Cohausz.

After conducting pre-combat training in the 25th and 27th U-boat Training Flotillas in the Baltic Sea, the *U-204* left Kiel under the command of Walter Kell on May 24, 1941 for her first war patrol. Supporting Kell would be *Oberleutnant zur See* Oskar Wichler as 1st Watch Officer, *Leutnant zur See* Peter Süss as 2nd Watch Officer and *Oberleutnant (Ing)* Eric Reiner, the Chief Engineer. On May 31 at 5:30 a.m. he sank the Icelandic 16-ton steam trawler *Holmsteinn* with deck-gun fire southeast of Greenland. Kell then attempted to refuel from the German 10,000-ton tanker *Belchen*, but the attempt was frustrated when the British cruisers *HMS Aurora* and *HMS Kenya* attacked the supply ship and forced her crew to scuttle the vessel to avoid capture. The *U-204* then was ordered to become part of *Wolf Pack Group West* gathering southeast of the Newfoundland Bank. Fog hampered visibility and the *U-204* experienced diesel engine problems on June 9. On June 10, 1941 Kell finally spotted a target east of Newfoundland at 2:48 a.m.; he subsequently torpedoed the Belgian 7,886-ton *Mercier* carrying mail from Liverpool to Montreal, killing seven crewmen. Kell did not report the sinking to B.d.U. until late on June 22. After being forced to dive by an enemy aircraft on June 26, the U-boat arrived at Brest, France on June 27, where Kell was greeted by the 1st U-boat Flotilla commander. Kell reported to Admiral Dönitz on June 29 to brief him on the patrol; the *U-204* had sailed 6,400 sea-miles on the surface and 90 sea-miles submerged during the 35-day patrol.

An enemy air attack on July 7 damaged the *U-204* at her dock. A few days later a French tugboat accidently struck the U-boat tearing a two-inch gash in her outer hull. With those mishaps behind her, on July 22, 1941, the *U-204* left Brest under the command of Walter Kell on her second war patrol. The very next day a British Sunderland aircraft forced the boat to dive. On July 30, the *U-204* was ordered to patrol due west of Ireland. At 4:45 p.m. on August 2, the *U-204* contacted convoy SL 81 southwest of Ireland. B.d.U. gave her orders not to attack but to transmit beacon signals so that other boats could close in. Kell continued to make shadowing reports but added that, as the dense fog had reduced visibility to one-half mile, he was depending entirely on the boat's hydrophones. At 5:11 p.m. he radioed that he had the convoy escorts in sight. Later, at 6:39 p.m., the boat reported that she had been driven off by convoy escorts. B.d.U. responded at 9:58 p.m. with a radio message to the *U-204* and other boats in the area:

> "This night is decisive, go in and attack! You are more numerous and stronger than the enemy. Always report contact."

At 3:12 a.m. on August 4, the *U-204* reported patrol forces, but heavy rain had reduced visibility to one-hundred meters. After subsequently losing the enemy, the U-boat regained contact with the convoy at 7:00 a.m. On August 5 at 4:16 a.m., Kell reported obtaining a direct hit on a 14,000-ton steamer (possibly the *Abosso*); it does not appear that this ship subsequently sank. Kell then sank the 5,000-ton British freighter *Kumasian*. On August 8, the *U-204* was forced to dive by an enemy aircraft; she later received orders to operate against another convoy. Dönitz was frustrated and wrote in the B.d.U. daily journal:

> "As, at the end of the second year of war, conditions in shadowing convoys have become more difficult, a state of affairs not improved by the inexperience of our many young Captains, there seems little chance of our maintaining contact long enough to make an attack possible. 3-4 times the number of submarines than there were a year ago are necessary now owing to the far stronger air and surface escorts."

Kell was not frustrated eleven days later. *HNoMS Bath* (Lt. Cdr. Fredrik Melsom), a U.S.-built destroyer that was transferred to the Royal Navy and subsequently given to the Norwegians, was escorting convoy OG-71, twenty-two ships bound from England to Gibraltar, as part of the 5th Escort Group, about 400 miles southwest of Ireland. During combat, the *HNoMS Bath* fell behind the convoy. At 2:05 a.m. on August 19, 1941 Kell spotted and hit the Norwegian 1,060-ton destroyer just aft of her midsection. Three minutes later he put another torpedo into the Norwegian ship, killing eighty-three men in a catastrophic explosion. Three hours later he fired a four-torpedo spread against two merchant ships and reported sinking them but this claim has never been verified in post-war records. Kell and the *U-204*, now very low on fuel, returned to Brest on August 22, 1941 after four and a half weeks on patrol. He reported two ships sunk as well as a destroyer; the U-boat had traveled 5,000 sea-miles on the surface and 281 sea-miles submerged. The next day the B.d.U log read:

> "The totals estimated by Captains cannot be regarded as completely reliable, as some of them were made by night from considerable distances."

The *U-204* would get much closer to the enemy on her third war patrol. She departed Brest on September 20, 1941, still under the command of Walter Kell. Among the crew was *Matrosenobergefreiter* Anton Niwczyk. Born in the coal-mining town of Castrop in Westphalia on December 22, 1922, Niwczyk probably joined the Navy in 1939 or 1940; this was likely his first war patrol. On September 23, B.d.U. ordered the U-boat to act as an escort for the outward bound blockade breaker *Rio Grande*; Kell accompanied the vessel on its outward passage to the Azores. The *U-204* then attempted to engage a convoy moving toward Gibraltar with no results. On October 14 the B.d.U. ordered Walter Kell to operate against sea traffic near Gibraltar in the direction of the Madeira Islands. That same day he sank the Spanish 300-ton *Aingeru Guardakoa*. Kell reported he would need to re-fuel soon. On the night of October 14/15, the *U-204* secretly refueled from the German supply ship *Thalia* at Cadiz, Spain, as she would need to remain at sea and not return to base as originally planned. Dönitz had big plans for the many boats clustering near Gibraltar. On October 18 the B.d.U. war diary reported:

> "The next Gibraltar convoy was expected to leave port on the 17th of October. I decided not only to await the convoy during the course of the first day, but also to carry out an attack with all boats directly after the convoy has passed Tarifa. I ordered that the area southeast of Cape Trafalgar was to be the waiting position for *U-206*, *U-563*, and *U-564*, and Cape Spartel the waiting position for *U-204*, *U-71* and *U-83*. The boats received orders to try to remain unnoticed when approaching, and to be submerged by day in the waiting position. If the boats succeed in remaining unnoticed, it will be easy to succeed in picking up the convoy in the night directly after it has left port – perhaps thereby the boats can take full advantage of the carelessness in the convoy during the first hours and the fact that it would not be properly organized."

It was difficult for the *U-204* to remain unnoticed. The convoy, aware of the presence of the hungry wolves, delayed sailing for over a week, but individual ships attempted to run the gauntlet. On October 19, 1941 at 3:00 a.m. Kell sank the British 9,158-ton tanker *Inverlee* off Cape Spartel. She was carrying 13,880 tons of fuel oil; twenty-one men perished in the attack.

But nothing was heard at B.d.U. of the *U-204*. On October 25, the war diary noted frustratingly:

> "*U-204* (Breslau Group) did not report, though it was called several times. It was in the waiting position off Cape Spartel, in an area where, according to reports from *U-71* and *U-83*, an A/S hunt was being carried out. It must be considered lost."

An anti-submarine hunt had indeed occurred, shortly after the attack on the *Inverlee*. The British corvette *HMS Mallow* (Lt. W.R.B. Noall) and sloop *HMS Rochester* (Cdr. C.B. Allen) caught the trail of the *U-204* west of Tangier – in Vichy French Morocco – and proceeded to drop rack after rack of depth charges on their quarry. The U-boat never surfaced and all her crew perished, including *Matrosenobergefreiter* Anton Niwczyk; his family would receive his posthumous award of the U-boat War Badge on February 2, 1942 along with a letter of condolence from the commander of the 1st U-boat Flotilla, *Korvettenkapitän* Hans Cohausz.

But all that remained of the boat off the African coast was an oil slick, and the air and fuel flasks of a torpedo.

Known Crewmembers for the U-204

Ahlgrimm, Karl	*Funkmaat*
Arpe, Richard	*Obermaschinenmaat*
Braun, Erich	*Maschinenmaat*
Braune, Henning	*Fähnrich zur See*
Brockerhoff, Ludwig	*Matrosenobergefreiter*
Delor, Richard	*Bootsmaat*
Deutscher, Fritz	*Matrosengefreiter*
Flammersheim, Christoph	*Obermaschinenmaat*
Fleischmann, Alfred	*Matrosengefreiter*
Frerichs, Erich	*Matrosengefreiter*
Fuchs, Gerhard	*Matrose II*
Furtmann, Theodor-Heinrich	*Matrose II*
Gesellius, Eberhard	*Mechanikergefreiter*
Heinrich, Karl	*Mechanikerobergefreiter*
Hirmer, Helmut	*Fähnrich zur See*
Hirth, Herbert	*Funkmaat*
Holste, Heinrich	*Funkmaat*
Kell, Walter	*Kapitänleutnant*
Krause, Ernst	*Matrosengefreiter*
Kristen, Herbert	*Matrosengefreiter*
Kruel, Alfred	*Obersteuermann*
Lehner, Alfred	*Matrosengefreiter*
Ludwig, Arthur	*Maschinengefreiter*
Mayer, Helmut	*Maschinenobergefreiter*
Mehl, Rudolf	*Maschinengefreiter*
Neumann, Reinhard	*Matrosenobergefreiter*
Niwczyk, Anton	*Matrosenobergefreiter*
Nix, Werner-Hermann	*Matrosengefreiter*
Piegsa, Johann	*Stabsobermaschinist*
Quitta, Bruno	*Funkobergefreiter*
Reiner, Erich	*Oberleutnant (Ing)*
Schillinger, Karl	*Maschinenmaat*
Schneider, Herbert	*Funkobergefreiter*
Schnelle, Oskar-Erich-Willi	*Obergefreiter*
Schulz, Gerhard	*Maschinenmaat*
Schwee, Franz	*Maschinenobergefreiter*
Stechow, Gerhard	*Maschinengefreiter*
Sünder, Kurt	*Maschinenobergefreiter*
Süss, Peter	*Oberleutnant zur See*
Thalhofer, Hans	*Mechanikergefreiter*
Toball, Günter	*Oberleutnant zur See*
Trautmann, Hans	*Maschinengefreiter*
Vogel, Andreas	*Bootsmaat*
Wehner, Herbert	*Bootsmaat*
Wehrle, Franz	*Obermaschinenmaat*
Wichler, Oskar	*Oberleutnant zur See*
Wittmann, Ludwig	*Maschinenhauptgefreiter*
Zierau, Max	*Kapitänleutnant*

Sources, "Frustration:" Chris Bishop, *Kriegsmarine U-boats 1939-45*, London: Amber Books, 2006, 76-77; Clay Blair, *Hitler's U-boat War: The Hunters, 1939-1942*, New York: Random House, 1996, 299, 333-334, 338, 392; Rainer Busch and Hans-Joachim Röll, *German U-boat Commanders of World War II*, translated by Geoffrey Brooks, Annapolis, Maryland: Naval Institute Press, 1999, 123; *F.d.U./B.d.U. War Diary, 16-30 June 1941* (PG30291), 96, 102; *F.d.U./B.d.U. War Diary, 16-31 July 1941* (PG30293), 123; *F.d.U./B.d.U. War Diary, 1-15 August 1941* (PG30294), 128, 129, 130, 132, 136; *F.d.U./B.d.U. War Diary, 16-31 August 1941* (PG30295), 142; *F.d.U./B.d.U. War Diary, 16-30 September 1941* (PG30297), 166; *F.d.U./B.d.U. War Diary, 1-15 October 1941* (PG30298), 178; *F.d.U./B.d.U. War Diary, 16-31 October 1941* (PG30299), 180, 182; Axel Niestlé, *German U-boat Losses during World War II*, Annapolis, Maryland: Naval Institute Press, 1998, 46; Jürgen Rohwer, *Axis Submarine Successes 1939-1945*, Annapolis, Maryland: Naval Institute Press, 1983, 56; Herbert Ritschel, *Kurzfassung Kriegstagebücher deutscher U-boote 1939-1945, Band 3: KTB U171 – U222,* Norderstedt, Germany: Books on Demand, 244-248; War Diary of the U-204, March 8, 1941 – October 25, 1941, PG 30192/1-5; ONI Roll T-308-B, *National Archives Microfilm Publication T1022,* roll 3038, RG 242; www.ubootwaffe.net; www.uboatarchive.net.

Verleihungs-Urkunde.

Auf Grund der Ermächtigung des Oberbefehlshabers
der Kriegsmarine verleihe ich dem
für das Vaterland gefallenen

Matrosenobergefreiten
(Dienstgrad)

Anton Niwczyk
(Name)

als Ehrung für seinen Einsatz

das

Ubootskriegsabzeichen 1939

Befehlsstelle, den 2. Feb. 1942.

Dönitz

~~Vizea~~dmiral und Befehlshaber der Unterseeboote

U-boat War Badge award document to Anton Niwczyk of the U-204, February 2, 1942. *The award was posthumously made some four months after the destruction of the boat. The document has a facsimile signature of Konteradmiral Karl Dönitz. Anton Niwczyk was eighteen years old when he died along with the rest of the crew.*

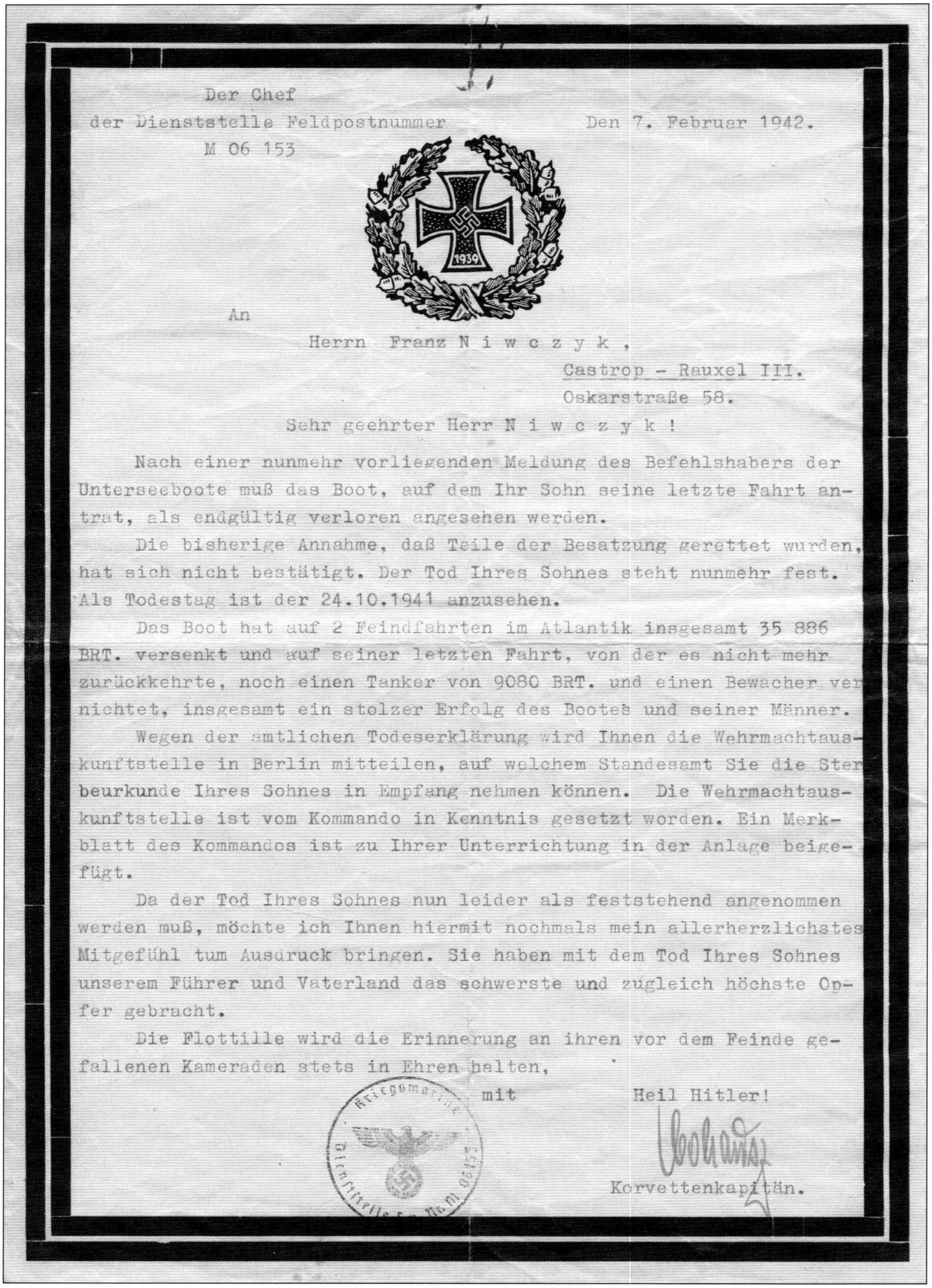

Der Chef
der Dienststelle Feldpostnummer
M 06 153

Den 7. Februar 1942.

An

Herrn Franz N i w c z y k ,
Castrop - Rauxel III.
Oskarstraße 58.

Sehr geehrter Herr N i w c z y k !

Nach einer nunmehr vorliegenden Meldung des Befehlshabers der Unterseeboote muß das Boot, auf dem Ihr Sohn seine letzte Fahrt antrat, als endgültig verloren angesehen werden.

Die bisherige Annahme, daß Teile der Besatzung gerettet wurden, hat sich nicht bestätigt. Der Tod Ihres Sohnes steht nunmehr fest. Als Todestag ist der 24.10.1941 anzusehen.

Das Boot hat auf 2 Feindfahrten im Atlantik insgesamt 35 886 BRT. versenkt und auf seiner letzten Fahrt, von der es nicht mehr zurückkehrte, noch einen Tanker von 9080 BRT. und einen Bewacher vernichtet, insgesamt ein stolzer Erfolg des Bootes und seiner Männer.

Wegen der amtlichen Todeserklärung wird Ihnen die Wehrmachtauskunftstelle in Berlin mitteilen, auf welchem Standesamt Sie die Sterbeurkunde Ihres Sohnes in Empfang nehmen können. Die Wehrmachtauskunftstelle ist vom Kommando in Kenntnis gesetzt worden. Ein Merkblatt des Kommandos ist zu Ihrer Unterrichtung in der Anlage beigefügt.

Da der Tod Ihres Sohnes nun leider als feststehend angenommen werden muß, möchte ich Ihnen hiermit nochmals mein allerherzlichstes Mitgefühl tum Ausdruck bringen. Sie haben mit dem Tod Ihres Sohnes unserem Führer und Vaterland das schwerste und zugleich höchste Opfer gebracht.

Die Flottille wird die Erinnerung an ihren vor dem Feinde gefallenen Kameraden stets in Ehren halten,

mit Heil Hitler!

Cohausz

Korvettenkapitän.

Letter of Condolence to Franz Niwczyk, the father of Anton Niwczyk of the U-204, February 7, 1942. *The document is signed by the 1st U-boat Flotilla commander Korvettenkapitän Hans Cohausz. The letter states that the boat sank a total of 35,886 tons of enemy shipping during its brief career, including a tanker of 9,080 tons on the boat's last war patrol. Cohausz gives the date of the boat's destruction as October 24, 1941 – the best estimate of the B.d.U. – but in reality the U-boat sank on October 19. Hans Cohausz would have written forty-six such letters to the families of Dönitz's boys in the U-204.*

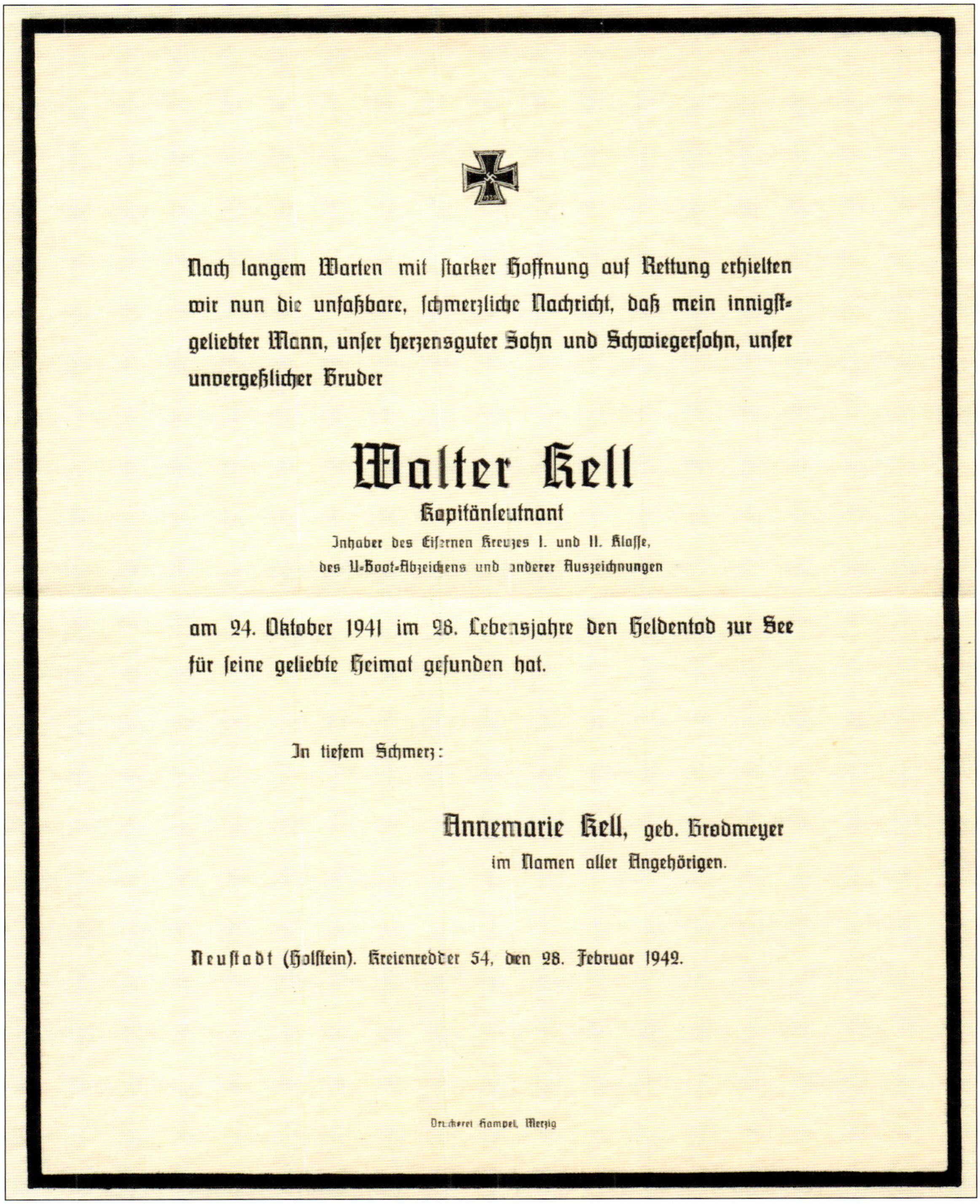

Nach langem Warten mit starker Hoffnung auf Rettung erhielten wir nun die unfaßbare, schmerzliche Nachricht, daß mein innigst-geliebter Mann, unser herzensguter Sohn und Schwiegersohn, unser unvergeßlicher Bruder

Walter Kell

Kapitänleutnant

Inhaber des Eisernen Kreuzes I. und II. Klasse,
des U-Boot-Abzeichens und anderer Auszeichnungen

am 24. Oktober 1941 im 28. Lebensjahre den Heldentod zur See für seine geliebte Heimat gefunden hat.

In tiefem Schmerz:

Annemarie Kell, geb. Brodmeyer
im Namen aller Angehörigen.

Neustadt (Holstein), Kreienredder 54, den 28. Februar 1942.

Druckerei Hampel, Merzig

Death Announcement for Kapitänleutnant Walter Kell of the U-204. *Announcement was sent by his widow Annemarie Kell from Neustadt, Schleswig-Holstein.*

CHAPTER TEN

"Suddenly, There Was a Blinding Flash" U-331 November 1941

In August 1941, Hitler directed that a significant U-boat force transfer from the North Atlantic to the Mediterranean Sea. Initially twenty-one boats made the passage through the dangerous Straits of Gibraltar. Later the High Command ordered this number to increase to thirty-six, but Dönitz successfully reduced that commitment to twenty-five. Dönitz, who had sailed in the Mediterranean at the beginning of World War I, considered the sea to be too calm, and with the water and weather too clear, for submarine activity.

Dönitz's Crews
***Matrosenobergefreiter* Bernhard Gier**
Born on October 7, 1920 in Hillesheim, Rhineland-Pfalz.
Served on the 88-mm deck-gun crew on the *U-331*.
Awarded the U-boat War Badge, the Iron Cross 2nd Class and the Iron Class 1st Class.
Spent 242 days at sea on U-boat war patrols.
Killed in action on November 17, 1942 in the Mediterranean Sea.

The *U-331*, a Type VIIC boat under *Oberleutnant* Hans-Diedrich von Tiesenhausen, was one of these U-boats, and her accomplishments would be immortalized in World War II history by one of the most horrendous photographs of the war – that of the catastrophic explosion of the British battleship *HMS Barham*.

The *U-331*'s history began on September 23, 1939 when she was ordered by the *Kriegsmarine*. Construction engineers at the Nordseewerke at Emden laid her keel on January 26, 1940. The boat was launched on December 20, 1940 and commissioned on March 31, 1941 at the Nordseewerke at Emden. Von Tiesenhausen assumed command; he would be the U-boat's sole commander during her operational life.

Hans-Diedrich von Tiesenhausen was born in Riga, Latvia on February 22, 1913; his family moved to Brandenburg after World War I. Von Tiesenhausen joined the German Navy on April 8, 1934 and spent his first five years serving with the surface fleet, including with the light cruisers *Karlsruhe* and the *Nürnberg* in Spanish waters during the Spanish Civil War. In 1939, von Tiesenhausen received his officer's commission and began U-boat training; he then served four war patrols in 1940 as a watch officer on the *U-23* under the tutelage of Otto Kretschmer, a later Knight's Cross with Oak Leaves and Swords winner. With Kretschmer's boat, von Tiesenhausen earned the Iron Cross 2nd Class on January 30, 1940 and the U-boat War Badge on February 26, 1940. Von Tiesenhausen then underwent additional U-boat training, which prepared him to serve as the 1st Watch Officer on the *U-93*. He served in this capacity for two war patrols in late 1940. Again, he had an excellent commander from which to learn; Claus Korth was also a Knight's Cross winner, and von Tiesenhausen was thus well-prepared to assume his duty on the *U-331*.

The *U-331* underwent the normal training and testing routine over the next several months. Among the crew was *Matrosenobergefreiter* Bernhard Gier. Born in Hillesheim near Daun in the wooded and mountainous German Eifel region on October 7, 1920, Gier most likely joined the German Navy in 1937 or 1938. After receiving artillery training, he joined the *U-331* as part of her 88-mm deck-gun crew.

During a British bombing attack of Kiel on April 7, 1940, a piece of shrapnel penetrated the rear of the U-boat, which required repair. Her work-up training complete, the *U-331* left Kiel on July 2, 1941 for her first war patrol along with the *U-504* and *U-84*. On July 4, the crew spotted the ominous sign of British floating sea mines but the *U-331* avoided them. On July 27, von Tiesenhausen noted in the U-boat's war diary that it was "good, dark attack weather." During the patrol he spotted several enemy ships and attempted attacks; in one, he fired a salvo of four torpedoes, but all missed their intended targets. The *U-331* also underwent depth charge attacks from aircraft and surface escorts – the crew was getting a U-boat education the hard way. She also experienced a mishap when she rendezvoused in mid-ocean to exchange mail and the other boat inadvertently collided with her causing damage to a diving tank.

The boat finally arrived in Lorient, France on August 19, 1941 after almost seven weeks at sea; she sank no enemy ships on this voyage, having refueled from the German supply ship *Thalia* at the Spanish port of Cadiz on August 1 (where they were met by a German Navy officer assigned with the German Navy Attaché in Madrid), and then being driven off three times from successfully attacking a convoy off of Spain. Now assigned to the 1st U-boat Flotilla, commanded by *Korvettenkapitän* Hans Cohausz, this would be her last full patrol in the North Atlantic; on September 24, 1941, von Tiesenhausen and the *U-331* left Lorient bound for Salamis,

Greece in the Mediterranean Sea; after submerging on September 28 after spotting an enemy flying boat, the U-boat passed through the Straits of Gibraltar on September 29. Close to her destination, the *U-331* encountered three enemy barges south of Crete and engaged them in a nighttime artillery duel at 4:00 a.m. on October 10, 1941. Von Tiesenhausen's three torpedoes all missed, but the U-boat's 88-mm gun crew – including *Matrosengefreiter* Bernhard Gier – set the British 360-ton *A-18* aflame. But the *U-331* did not escape unscathed; later that day three enemy fighters attacked the boat, killing one of her anti-aircraft gunners, *Obermaat* Hans Gerstenich. The U-boat arrived at Salamis the next day and was assigned to the 23rd U-boat Flotilla, under the command of *Kapitänleutnant* Fritz Frauenheim. From Lorient to Salamis she had sailed 3,487 sea-miles surfaced and 164 sea-miles submerged.

The *U-331* spent one month in the Greek port, the delay – in part – due to the immature nature of the German refit and repair facilities there. The *U-331* departed Salamis on her third war patrol – and her date with destiny – on November 12, 1941. Von Tiesenhausen first landed a commando party at Gibeisa, Egypt on November 17. The nine men (one commissioned officer – *Leutnant* Kiefer, two senior non-commissioned officers, one junior non-commissioned officer and five enlisted men) were members of the Army's Brandenburg Special Forces' unit and had been training outside Berlin since August. Their mission was to lay explosive charges beneath rail-lines to disrupt the flow of enemy supplies from Egypt to the front lines. Code-named "Operation Shark," the commando party set their charges and returned to the beach, but they could not contact the U-boat and all men were later captured.

On November 25, 1941, off Alexandria, Egypt, the hydrophone operator heard faint noises of approaching ships. Von Tiesenhausen spotted ships on the horizon and attempted to plot a course to intercept. After several course changes, based on the enemy zigzag sailing pattern, he determined the enemy formation to be three British battleships in column: *HMS Queen Elizabeth*, *HMS Barham* and *HMS Valiant*, escorted by destroyers. A witness from the *HMS Queen Elizabeth* painted the scene with the following description:

> "It was just after 4 o'clock in the afternoon, and I had just come off watch. Like most of the watch I had taken a mug of tea on to the upper deck to enjoy the sun and admire the view. It was a beautiful sight – three large battleships steaming in a line ahead and with a screen of twelve destroyers in a "V-shape" ahead and around us. *HMS Queen Elizabeth* was leading, followed by *HMS Barham* which was about 300 yards astern of us, and *HMS Valiant* another 300 yards astern of her."

Von Tiesenhausen quickly took in the panorama, went to battle stations at 4:00 p.m., and the U-boat submerged. Unable to obtain an optimal firing position on the lead *HMS Queen Elizabeth*, at 4:19 p.m. he fired a four-torpedo spread against the second capital ship, which – at only 1,200 yards distance – so filled the periscope that he could not positively identify her. Three of the torpedoes smashed broadside into the 31,100-ton *HMS Barham*. Again we turn to the same Royal Navy eyewitness:

> "Suddenly there was a blinding flash, an enormous explosion and a mushroom of black smoke rose thousands of feet into the air. Debris was hurled into the air, and I saw one of the 15-inch gun turrets lifted up hundreds of feet. We were ordered to take cover because of the falling debris. Apparently a fire aboard the *Barham* caused a small magazine to explode and this in turn blew into the main magazine of the battleship."

The *U-331* avoided retribution, although the crew counted twenty-six depth charge explosions; von Tiesenhausen later signaled that he had torpedoed a battleship and returned to Salamis on December 3, 1941; the U-boat had traveled 2,327 sea-miles on the surface and 677 sea-miles submerged. *Oberleutnant* von Tiesenhausen received the Iron Cross 1st Class on December 7, 1941, while many of his crewmen, including most-likely Bernhard Gier, received the Iron Cross 2nd Class and the U-boat War Badge for completion of their third patrol. Von Tiesenhausen was also promoted to *Kapitänleutnant* on January 1, 1942. It was only some weeks later that the British announced the loss of the *HMS Barham*, and the *Kriegsmarine* then announced on January 27, 1942 that von Tiesenhausen was awarded the Knight's Cross.

Meanwhile, the *U-331* began her fourth war patrol on January 14, 1942 sailing from Salamis. On January 27, 1942 the U-boat ran aground in soft mud off Tobruk, but skillful handling of the boat by von Tiesenhausen – including jettisoning a number of torpedoes to reduce the boat's weight – got the craft off the seabed. As mentioned, on January 27 the B.d.U. radioed the *U-331* concerning the award of the Knight's Cross – in response the crew gave their captain three cheers. Von Tiesenhausen arrived at La Spezia, Italy on February 28, 1942 having sunk no enemy ships but traveling 5,572 sea-miles on the surface and 1,220 sea-miles submerged. The *U-331* was then assigned to the 29th U-boat Flotilla, which was commanded by *Korvettenkapitän* Franz Becker. On April 4, 1942, von Tiesenhausen left La Spezia with the *U-331* for her fifth war patrol. After nine days, on April 13, 1942, the *U-331* crept into the harbor at Beirut under the cover of darkness. After laying a small field of magnetic mines, von Tiesenhausen began his attack by firing a torpedo at a 3,000-ton Norwegian freighter *Lyder Sagen* but it struck a nearby barge that absorbed the explosion. His poor luck continued the following day when he fired another torpedo at a 4,000-ton ship; the torpedo struck its target but failed to explode. Remaining submerged by day, the U-boat continued its surface night attacks for several days sinking three small fishing vessels by gunfire, as well as destroying the Beirut electrical power station by 88-mm deck-gun fire. Bernhard Gier probably earned the Iron Cross 1st Class for these actions. The *U-331* returned to Salamis on April 19. Von Tiesenhausen recorded that the U-boat had gone 2,399 sea-miles on the surface and 315 sea-miles under water.

The boat's sixth war patrol began on May 9, 1942. Von Tiesenhausen sank no enemy ships on this patrol, which ended on May 21 when the *U-331* arrived at Messina, Sicily. The stay on the island proved very short; the *U-331* departed on May 25 for her seventh war patrol. On June 4 at 9:40 p.m., von Tiesenhausen fired a torpedo at a beached steamer on the Libyan coast, believing he hit the target. The patrol ended on June 15, 1942 at La Spezia after diesel problems shortened the voyage. After two months of repairs, von Tiesenhausen departed La Spezia on August 8, 1942 for the boat's eighth war patrol, but ran into difficulties immediately. On August 9, 1942, an Allied aircraft attacked the *U-331*, wounding two crewmen. Von Tiesenhausen was forced to abort the mission and return to La Spezia for repairs on August 10. Transferring the wounded sailors to a hospital, von Tiesenhausen then put to sea with the U-boat on August 12. The *U-331* remained on patrol until September 19, 1942, when she returned to port; once again the boat did not achieve success.

In November 1942, the Allies conducted several amphibious landings in North Africa as part of "Operation Torch." In an attempt to disrupt this operation the *Kriegsmarine* ordered several U-boats to the vicinity. The *U-331*, which had been on patrol since November 7, proceeded to northwest of Algiers – one of the landing sites. At 1:10 p.m. on November 9, 1942, the U-boat fired a torpedo at the *Leedstown*, a 9,135-ton troop transport, off Cape Matifou. The *Leedstown's* captain ordered the ship to be abandoned; the transport sank, but with no fatalities.

On November 17, northwest of Algiers, six aircraft from the 500th Squadron, RAF, and both the 820th Squadron and 893rd Squadron, Royal Navy, attacked the *U-331* with depth charges and aerial torpedoes. The U-boat crew signaled they would surrender, but in the confusion of the moment the British pressed home the attack with depth charges and an aerial torpedo. The boat sank with thirty-two of her crew, while seventeen sailors – including von Tiesenhausen – were rescued and taken prisoner. Bernhard Gier was among the dead.

Von Tiesenhausen would spend the remainder of the war in a prisoner of war camp in Canada. His experiences there were positive and after he returned to Germany in 1947, he applied to immigrate to Canada and arrived there in 1951. Hans-Diedrich von Tiesenhausen died on August 17, 2000 in Vancouver, Canada.

Known Crewmembers for the U-331

Arvidson, Karl	*Matrosengefreiter*
Bernot, Wilhelm	*Funkmaat*
Bieneck, Friedrich	*Maschinengefreiter*
Brings, Hermann	*Maschinengefreiter*
Brunsbach, Hans	*Obermaschinist*
Deltow, Hans	*Maschinengefreiter*
Engelhaupt, Walter	*Matrosenobergefreiter*
Fischer, Manfred	*Funkobergefreiter*
Fliss, Edmund	*Matrosengefreiter*
Flossner, Kurt	*Maschinenmaat*
Franken, Wilhelm	*Korvettenkapitän*
Freudig, Ernst	*Oberfunkmeister*
Fuhrmann, Hermann	*Matrosengefreiter*
Gensch, Richard	*Obermaschinenmaat*
Gerstenich, Hans	*Obermaat*
Gier, Bernhard	*Matrosenobergefreiter*
Götze, Herbert	*Maschinenmaat*
Günther, Rudi	*Maschinengefreiter*
Hardenberg, Hans von	*Leutnant (Ing)*
Hartwig, Erwin-Alfred	*Leutnant zur See*
Helbig, Werner	*Maschinenmaat*
Herb, Fritz	*Maschinenobergefreiter*
Hintereder, Karl	*Matrosenobergefreiter*
Koal, Ewald	*Maschinenmaat*
Koch, Heinz	*Oberleutnant zur See*
Koslowski, Bruno	*Matrosenobergefreiter*
Krischer, Heinrich	*Oberfunkmaat*
Kühn, Herbert	*Oberleutnant zur See*
Laiter, Helmut	*Maschinengefreiter*
Mattert, Ernst	*Matrosenobergefreiter*
Meier, Maximilian	*Bootsmaat*
Nagelhoff, Fritz	*Matrosengefreiter*
Nehls, Friedrich-Karl	*Kapitänleutnant*
Niklas, Karl	*Maschinengefreiter*
Peiseler, Wolfgang	*Maschinengefreiter*
Peitz, Wilhelm	
Richter, Egbert	*Mechanikergefreiter*
Rudeck, Karl	*Maschinengefreiter*
Schmidt, Heinrich	*Bootsmaat*
Schwarz	*Funkobergefreiter*
Seedorf, Egon	*Maschinengefreiter*
Seyda, August	*Funkobergefreiter*
Siebelds, Gerhard	*Bootsmaat*
Siegert, Hans	*Oberleutnant (Ing)*
Stangel	*Obersteuermann*
Stanzel, Franz-Karl	*Oberfähnrich zur See*
Stemmer, Eugen	*Obersteuermann*
Streubel, Werner	*Oberleutnant (Ing)*
Striebe, Walter	*Maschinenmaat*
Szcesny, Paul	*Maschinengefreiter*
Tiesenhausen, Hans von	*Kapitänleutnant*
Tyrtania, Reinhold	*Bootsmaat*
Vogel, Martin	*Mechanikergefreiter*
Wagener, Hugo	*Obermaschinenmaat*
Wagner, Herbert	*Mechanikerobergefreiter*
Walther, Herbert	*Leutnant zur See*
Walther	*Obersteuermann*
Warstat, Willi	*Bootsmaat*
Weber, Heinz	*Obermaschinist*
Weisner, Helmut	*Maschinengefreiter*
Wiessner, Helmut	*Maschinengefreiter*
Wintermann	*Oberleutnant (Ing)*
Zielinski, Helmut	*Maschinengefreiter*
Zizikowsky, Fritz	*Matrosengefreiter*
Zurmühlen, Bernhard	*Kapitänleutnant*

Sources, "Suddenly There Was a Blinding Flash:" G.H. Bennett, and R. Bennett, *Hitler's Admirals*, Annapolis, Maryland: Naval Institute Press, 2004, 120; Chris Bishop, *Kriegsmarine U-boats 1939-45*, London: Amber Books, 2006, 142; Clay Blair, *Hitler's U-boat War: The Hunters, 1939-1942*, New York: Random House, 1996, 332, 336, 396, 399, 488, 646, 648, 650; Clay Blair, *Hitler's U-boat War: The Hunted, 1942-1945*, New York: Modern Library, 2000, 101; Jochen Brennecke, *The Hunters and the Hunted*, translated by R.H. Stevens, New York: W.W. Norton and Company, 1957, 111, 116; Manfred Dörr, *Die Ritterkreuzträger der U-Boot-Waffe, Band 1: A-J, Band 2: L-Z*, Osnabrück, FRG: Biblio Verlag, 1988, Band 2 – 314, 315, 316; Geoffrey Jones, *U-boat Aces*, Cerberus Publishing, Bristol, England, 2005, 71, 72, 73, 80; Axel Niestlé, *German U-boat Losses during World War II*, Annapolis, Maryland: Naval Institute Press, 1998, 55; Herbert Ritschel, *Kurzfassung Kriegstagebücher deutscher U-boote 1939-1945, Band 7: KTB U301 – U374,* Norderstedt, Germany: Books on Demand, 119-133; Jürgen Rohwer, *Axis Submarine Successes 1939-1945*, Annapolis, Maryland: Naval Institute Press, 1983, 227, 231, 232, 237; Jak Mallmann Showell, *German Navy Handbook, 1939-1945*, Thrupp, England: Sutton Publishing, 1999, 148; Jak Mallmann Showell, *U-boats at War: Landings on Hostile Shores*, Hersham, England: Ian Allan Publishing, 2000, 63, 139; War Diary of the U-331, March 31, 1941 – November 21, 1942, PG 30402/1-12; ONI Roll T-312-B, *National Archives Microfilm Publication T1022,* roll 3042, RG 242; www.ubootwaffe.net; www.uboatarchive.net; www.bbc.co.uk/ww2peopleswar/stories/25/a5777625.shtml (*WW2 People's War; an archive of World War II Memories*; testimony of Roland Bundy, aboard the *HMS Queen Elizabeth*.)

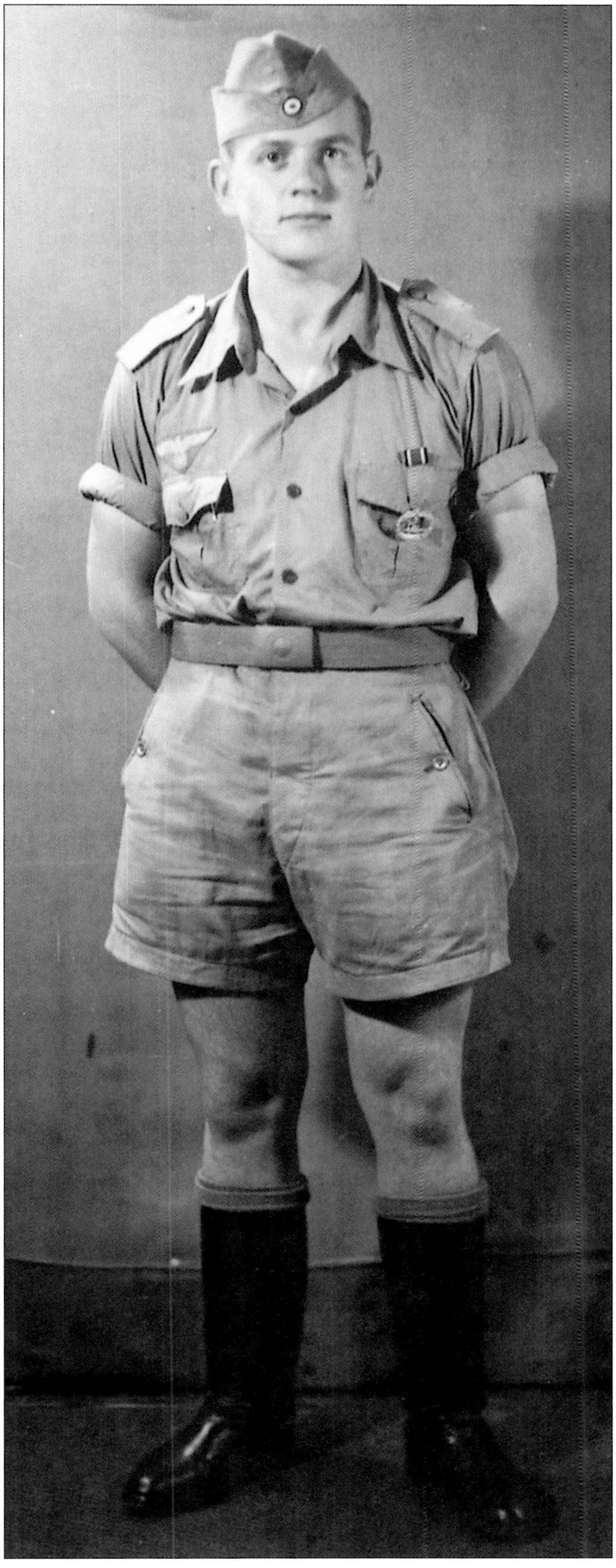

Photo of Bernhard Gier of the U-331 in tan tropical shirt and shorts worn by many U-boat crewmen in the Mediterranean theater. *Gier is wearing the Iron Cross 2nd Class ribbon and the U-boat War Badge.*

Photo of Bernhard Gier in blue pea jacket and trousers. *He is wearing the Iron Cross 2nd Class ribbon in top button-hole, the Iron Cross 1st Class and the U-boat War Badge. Sleeve insignia show him as a Matrosenobergefreiter in the Seaman's Branch. The specialty badge below the rank insignia indicates that Gier was qualified to serve on the boat's deck-gun crew.*

Jesus! Maria! Josef!
Herr, Dein Wille geschehe!

Zum frommen Andenken
an unsern lb. Sohn, guten Bruder, Onkel, Neffen und Vetter,
den Matrosen-Obergefreiten

Bernhard Gier

Inhaber des E.K. 1. u. 2. Kl. u. des U-Boot-Abzeichens

Er fand auf seinem Boot am 17. Nov. 1942 in treuester Pflichterfüllung den Heldentod im jugendlichen Alter von 22 Jahren. Alle, die ihn kannten, werden unsern Schmerz ermessen. Möge er im unendlichen Meer göttlicher Liebe u. Barmherzigkeit ewige Ruhe finden.

Wir empfehlen die Seele des teuren Verstorbenen dem hl. Opfer der Priester und dem Gebete der Gläubigen, auf daß sie

ruhe in Frieden.

In tiefem Schmerz
Eltern, Geschwister u. Anverwandte.
Hillesheim, im Juni 1943.

M. Jos. Goergen, Prüm

Death Announcement in June 1943 by the family of Matrosenobergefreiter Bernhard Gier, U-331. *Information includes his date of death of November 17, 1942 and that he had received the Iron Cross 2nd Class, Iron Cross 1st Class and U-boat War Badge.*

Photo of memorial service for Bernhard Gier in June 1943 in Hillesheim in the Eifel. *Note the deceased's sailor's cap displayed in the floral arrangement. Location appears to be the famous St. Martin's Church.*

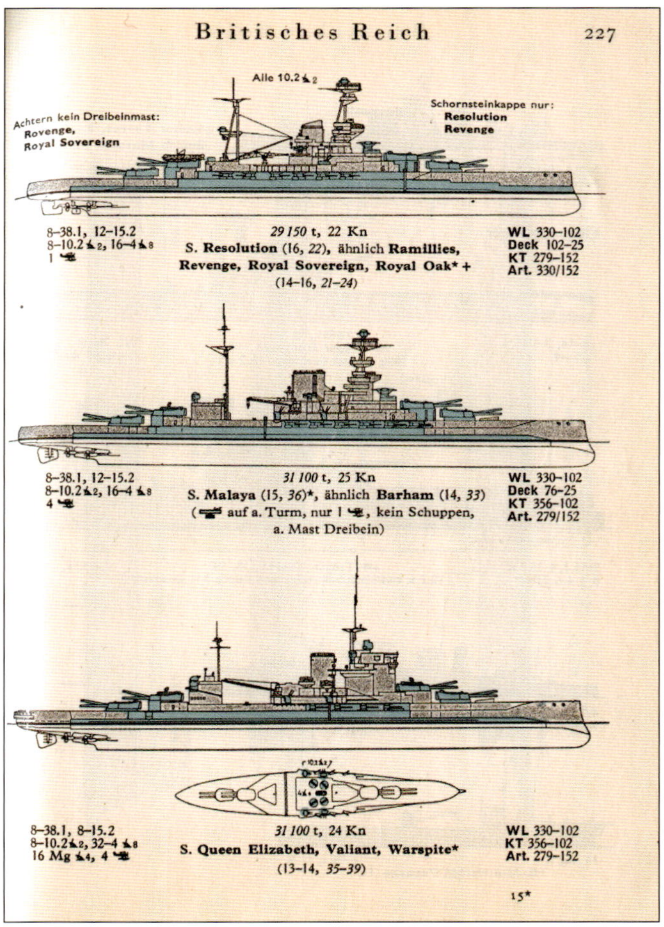

A view of Peter Lohmeyer's ship identification book showing a profile of the HMS Barham (right side, center).

CHAPTER ELEVEN

"AUDACITY" U-751, AND U-668 1941

Audacity is defined in the dictionary as intrepid boldness; it is also a bold or arrogant disregard of normal restraints. Audacity was a good name for a warship; it was also an apt description of an attack by a U-boat against a heavily protected aircraft carrier in December 1941, and the term that highlighted the final moments of this same U-boat crew some seven months later.

The story of audacity in these contexts begins in 1939. On March 29, 1939 German shipbuilders at the bustling Bremer Vulkan shipyards at Vegesack/Bremen on the Weser River finished a 5,537-ton motor merchant vessel for cargo and passenger service with the Norddeutscher Lloyd line at Bremen and christened her the *Hannover*. The same year, on October 9, 1939, the Germany Navy ordered a Type VIIC U-boat, the *U-751*. Ten days later, the British Royal Navy transferred the destroyer *HMS Kempenfelt* to the Royal Canadian Navy, which promptly renamed her *HMCS Assiniboine*. On January 2, 1940, about twenty-five miles away from Vegesack, at the *Kriegsmarinewerft* at Wilhelmshaven, shipbuilders laid the keel of the *U-751* and began the process to construct the U-boat.

Meanwhile, the *Hannover* entered German merchant service; the war had started the previous September and these merchant ships attempted to maintain commerce with neutral nations, bringing vital resources back to Germany as blockade runners. On March 7, 1940, the *HMCS Assiniboine* intercepted the *Hannover* in the Mona Passage, an important shipping route between the Atlantic and Panama Canal that separates the islands of Hispaniola and Puerto Rico. The Canadians ordered to *Hannover* to stop, but the German captain ignored the command and ordered that the ship be set afire and that the sea cocks be opened to flood the lower decks. The British light cruiser *HMS Dunedin* arrived shortly thereafter and a boarding party prevented the German crew from successfully scuttling their ship, but only after battling the fire for four days. The prize was initialing renamed the *Sinbad* by the Ministry of War Transport; the name was changed to the *Empire Audacity* and the ex-*Hannover* fell under new management with the Cunard White Star Line.

But ships were needed for the war effort and on November 11, 1940 the Royal Navy commissioned the *Hannover-Sinbad-Empire Audacity* as an Ocean Boarding Vessel. Meanwhile, on November 16, 1940 the *U-751* was launched and began her sea trials. The British Admiralty then determined that with the ongoing U-boat threat, the Royal Navy could use an escort aircraft carrier for convoy escort duty and the *Empire Audacity* was a good candidate for conversion. On January 22, 1941 the modifications began at the Blyth shipbuilding yard. On the first British escort carrier, the design had no space for a hangar or a lift; her aircraft would be parked on deck. Engineers fitted three arrestor wires and an open conning position on the starboard side, together with a minimal level of anti-aircraft armament. Determining that the principal enemy air threat would be Focke-Wulf Fw 200 "Condor" long-range reconnaissance and bomber aircraft, the carrier's aircraft were all fighters. Experts initially proposed Hurricanes, but this type of aircraft was not available. The designers settled on American Grumman F4F Martlets (known in the U.S. Navy as Wildcats), which were not only available but had been specifically designed for aircraft carrier operations. Eight aircraft would be on deck. The modifications took the displacement of the ship from 5,537 to 11,000 tons.

Nine days after this modification program began, across the North Sea the *U-751* was commissioned on January 31, 1941 and assigned to the 7th U-boat Flotilla at Kiel for further training. Her first commander was *Kapitänleutnant* Gerhard Bigalk. Born on November 26, 1908 at Niederschönhausen near Berlin, Bigalk served in the merchant service before entering the Navy in 1934. He had an early career of varied naval assignments including temporary service with the *Luftwaffe* in the Spanish Civil War as a reconnaissance aircraft pilot with the German Condor Legion, flying thirty-one missions; he was awarded the *Luftwaffe* Observer Badge on November 2, 1936 and the Spanish Cross in Silver with Swords on June 1, 1939. The training came with a cost: on September 19, 1936, while flying in a Junkers W 33, he was involved in a crash along with Reinhard Hardegen (a future U-boat commander and Knight's Cross with Oak Leaves winner), but both men survived. Commissioned a *Leutnant zur See* shortly afterward on October 1, 1936, Gerhard Bigalk was promoted to *Oberleutnant zur See* on June 3, 1938, and *Kapitänleutnant* on June 1, 1939. Married in 1938, he and his wife Charlotte had a daughter Antje-Renate in October 1940. The same year he began U-boat training. While he had no previous combat experience, Gerhard Bigalk did command the *U-14* in a training capacity for two months; he received the Iron Cross 2nd Class on November 30, 1940. Gerhard Bigalk then joined the commissioning effort to bring the *U-751* on line.

> *Dönitz's Crews*
> ***Obermaschinenmaat* Karl-Heinz Götze**
> Born on February 19, 1921.
> Served in the engine room on the *U-751* and the *U-668*.
> Awarded the U-boat War Badge on September 9, 1941; awarded the Iron Cross 2nd Class on December 28, 1941; awarded the U-boat Clasp in Bronze on November 17, 1944.
> Spent 351 days at sea on U-boat war patrols.
> Survived the war; lived in Haiterbach, Baden-Württemberg.

One of the other crewmen was *Maschinenobergefreiter* Karl-Heinz Götze. Born on February 19, 1921, he likely entered the *Kriegsmarine* in 1939. A good athlete, during training he won the German Sports Badge in Bronze that year. The *U-751* was his first boat; he was assigned in the engine room. The *U-751* finished her final preparations and departed Kiel on June 3, 1941 under the command of *Kapitänleutnant* Bigalk for her first war patrol; it would be a long-distance voyage. On June 14, 1941 at 3:46 a.m., the U-boat sank the British 5,370-ton freighter *St. Lindsay* in the mid-Atlantic. Carrying 3,000 tons of general cargo from Glasgow to Trinidad and Buenos Aires, the ship took her entire crew of forty-three with her when she went down. The *U-751* began her return to port on July 1 and arrived at St. Nazaire on July 5, 1941. *Kapitänleutnant* Gerhard Bigalk reported to Dönitz the following day. The B.d.U. war diary summarized the admiral's conclusion:

> "The Commanding Officer of *U-751*, *Oberleutnant* Bigalk, utilized all operational possibilities which arose during his first trip."

Bigalk received the Iron Cross 1st Class on July 7, 1941 for this successful mission. While the *U-751* was at sea, the conversion of the *Empire Audacity* finished and she was commissioned on June 20, 1941. On July 30, 1941 the Admiralty renamed her *HMS Audacity*. Days later, on August 2, 1941, the *U-751* was put to sea again for her second war patrol off southwest Ireland. After five weeks, she began her return to port on September 4 and arrived at St. Nazaire on September 8, 1941. The next day Karl-Heinz Götze and other members of the crew received the U-boat War Badge. Meanwhile, the British Admiralty assigned eight Martletts from the 802nd Squadron of the Fleet Air Arm and assigned the *HMS Audacity* to escort convoys on the route between Britain and Gibraltar. Compared to British and American fleet carriers, the *HMS Audacity* was an undersized pug; she had a top speed of only fifteen knots and carried only six to eight fighter planes, but in the land of the blind, the one-eyed man is king, and these aircraft gave the *HMS Audacity* eyes that could see hundreds of miles away.

Her first escort mission began in September escorting convoy OG-74 from Britain to Gibraltar, during which one of her aircraft shot down a Condor during its bombing run on the convoy rescue ship (designed to rescue survivors from ships which had been attacked) *Walmer Castle* on September 21, 1941. The *U-751* remained in port until October 11, 1941 when she departed St. Nazaire for her third war patrol, but after four weeks off southeast Greenland with the *Wolf Pack Stosstrupp* and *Wolf Pack Schlagetod*, she found nothing and returned to St. Nazaire on November 8, 1941 and remained in the French port for over a month.

On December 14, 1941 thirty-two merchant ships and their escorts departed Gibraltar as part of convoy HG-76. German spies in Spain near Gibraltar reported the departure of the convoy, but erred in describing the escorts as only three destroyers, a submarine, several corvettes and the aircraft tender *HMS Unicorn*. In reality the convoy escort was far more dangerous: three destroyers, four sloops, nine corvettes and the *HMS Audacity*, formed as Escort Group 36, commanded by perhaps the most-proficient U-boat-killer in the Royal Navy, Commander Frederic J. "Johnny" Walker. The discrepancy would prove fatal.

The *U-751* departed St. Nazaire on December 16, 1941 and was vectored to join several other U-boats to attack the convoy; the U-boats made contact with HG-76 the same day. On December 17 a Martlett from the *Audacity* spotted one of the U-boats twenty-two miles ahead of the convoy and forced it to dive. Over the next several days the U-boats and the escorts battled each other in one of the fiercest convoy battles of the war, with the British sinking several German boats. At 11:00 p.m. on December 21, 1941 *Kapitänleutnant* Bigalk spotted the *HMS Audacity* silhouetted by illuminating star-shells fired by the destroyers. There were no surface escorts in sight. The *U-751* fired a spread of three torpedoes from her bow tubes; all three hit and the lightly-armored escort carrier went down in ten minutes – seventy-three men perished in the attack 500 miles west of Cape Finisterre, Spain.

Joachim Hünefeldt, who was on the bridge of the surfaced *U-751* as part of the watch crew, described the event in a post-war memoir:

> "The aircraft carrier traveled constantly in a zigzag course. With a distance calculated at 1500 meters and a position opposite of 110 degrees, we shot a spread of three torpedoes at the target. One of the torpedoes was a dud that hit the stern of the ship. The aircraft carrier made a semicircle turn to port and stopped, unable to maneuver. We submerged to reload our torpedoes. The torpedomen and seamen in the forward torpedo room labored with haste and diligence. Detonations of depth charges were heard in the depths. After reloading the torpedoes, we resurfaced and shot two [more] torpedoes at the *Audacity*. Both torpedoes stuck their target and the *Audacity* sank, with all its aircraft, within ten minutes."

During her brief career, the *HMS Audacity's* planes destroyed five *Luftwaffe* aircraft attempting to shadow convoys; her Martletts also sighted nine U-boats, and assisted in destroying one – the *U-131*. Escort Group 36 responded quickly and in the wild nighttime melee sank the *U-567* under the command of one of Germany's greatest U-boat aces, Engelbert Endrass; there were no survivors.

The *U-751* left the area near the sinking *HMS Audacity* at full speed but two escorting destroyers pursued and depth-charged the U-boat, knocking out the internal lighting and causing several leaks. The next morning the U-boat fired a four-torpedo spread at a group of enemy escorts but achieved no hits. Her torpedoes expended, and with damage, she began her return to base.

On December 22, 1941 Dönitz called off the chase; the U-boats had sunk two merchant ships as well as the *HMS Audacity*, but had lost three of the attacking U-boats. The *U-751* returned to St. Nazaire on December 26, 1941. The daily *Wehrmachtsbericht* (daily dispatches) reported that the *U-751* had sunk the *HMS Unicorn*; despite the confusion Gerhard Bigalk received the Knight's Cross on the same day for his audacious attack. The crew was rewarded as well; *Maschinenobergefreiter* Karl-Heinz Götze received the Iron Cross 2nd Class on December 28, and Joachim Hünefeldt was awarded the Iron Cross 2nd Class and the U-boat War Badge, but the sting of the battle for convoy HG-76 lasted several months throughout the

U-boat force. On March 31, 1942 (three months after his death) the daily *Wehrmachtsbericht* announced:

> "The U-boat under command of *Kapitänleutnant* Endrass, recipient of the Knight's Cross with Oak Leaves, has not returned from patrol. An outstanding U-boat commander is on an eternal patrol with his brave crew."

The war did not stop for the *U-751*, however. On January 14, 1942 the U-boat departed St. Nazaire under *Kapitänleutnant* Bigalk for her fifth war patrol and sailed to Newfoundland. The results were mixed. During several attacks in January off Newfoundland, the *U-751* experienced six torpedo failures. Then on February 2, 1942 in a running gun battle off Halifax, the *U-751* damaged the Dutch 8,096-ton tanker *Corilla* – carrying gasoline from Curacao to Manchester – part of convoy HX-173, but the target began zigzagging and escaped when an escort drove off the U-boat. Then matters improved. On February 4, 1942 at 4:27 a.m., Bigalk torpedoed and sank the British 4,535-ton freighter *Silveray* just off Nova Scotia; she was carrying general cargo from Liverpool to New York. Eight crewmen lost their lives. Royal Canadian Air Force aircraft conducted an extensive search for the *U-751*, but without success. At 5:52 a.m., on February 7, 1942 the *U-751* sank the British 6,952-ton freighter *Empire Sun*. Carrying 9,000 tons of grain from Portland, Maine to Halifax and Great Britain, the ship took one man with her when she sank just off Nova Scotia. Bigalk arrived back at St. Nazaire on February 23, 1942.

The crew of the *U-751* now had a seven-week break before their next patrol. Joachim Hünefeldt left the U-boat for other duties. As a heartfelt remembrance of his service on the *U-751*, *Kapitänleutnant* Bigalk presented him with the tattered remnant of the U-boat's flag with the prescient admonition "You take good care of it." Hünefeldt underwent more U-boat training and assumed duties as the 2nd Watch Officer for the *U-231*; on January 13, 1944 he became a prisoner of war when a British aircraft sank his U-boat north of the Azores Islands.

It is possible that *Maschinenobergefreiter* Karl-Heinz Götze also departed the boat during this time for training and another assignment. On April 15, 1942 the *U-751* departed St. Nazaire for the boat's sixth war patrol, which would take her to the Caribbean. Low on fuel, Bigalk refueled from the *U-459* tanker on May 1, 1942; he also received food supplies and even fresh bread from the *U-459*'s little bakery. At 4:15 a.m., on May 16, 1942, the *U-751* sank the American 1,445-ton freighter *Nicarao* in the Bahamas. Bound from Kingston, Jamaica for Jacksonville, Florida, the *Nicarao* carried charcoal, 21,700 stems of bananas and 1,400 bags of coconuts; eight men died in the attack. It would be a while before the people of Jacksonville had bananas on their Wheaties for breakfast. On May 19, 1942 the *U-751* sank the American 3,110-ton freighter *Isabela* west of Jamaica. The *Isabela* was enroute from New York to San Juan, Puerto Rico with 1,950 tons of general cargo and cars as deck cargo. Bigalk torpedoed her on the starboard side at 10:41 a.m.; the explosion caused the ship to stop. The *U-751* then surfaced and began shelling the *Isabela* with her deck gun from a range of 350 yards; after four hits, the crew abandoned ship and the *Isabela* sank at 10:58 a.m. Three men died in the attack; the surviving crew rowed lifeboats to Cape Briton, Haiti and safety. On the way home, the *U-751* attacked a freighter with three torpedoes but two failed and the other missed its mark. Bigalk arrived at St. Nazaire with the *U-751* on June 15, 1942.

With these successes, B.d.U. planned to send the *U-751* back to the Americas – her mission was to lay magnetic minefields in the harbor at Charleston, South Carolina and at Jacksonville. One month later the *U-751*, still under the command of *Kapitänleutnant* Bigalk, left St. Nazaire on July 14, 1942 for her "lucky seventh" war patrol. It was anything but. The Bay of Biscay was a death trap; on July 16, 1942 the B.d.U. war diary noted the peril:

> "Increased danger from the air in the Bay of Biscay makes an alteration of orders for procedure on approach routes necessary. Danger of mines in waters less than 200 meters in depth is to be regarded as greater than danger from the air as before; boats must, therefore, remain on the surface. But as the danger of unexpected attack from radar-equipped aircraft is greater by night than by day, in the future boats shall proceed by day, and submerge only in the extreme sections when daylight is not sufficient for the whole journey. Increased danger from submarines must be reduced by steering zigzag course, and on the whole taken into account, as also the growing danger as our routes become known to aircraft and submarine."

The warning came too late for Dönitz's crews on the *U-751*. Only three days out of port, on July 17, 1942 northwest of Cape Ortegal, Spain, a Whitley bomber of RAF Coastal command's 502nd Squadron surprised the U-boat on the surface off northwest Spain and dropped six depth charges that, according to the aircrew, literally lifted the *U-751* out of the water. The Whitley doubled back for a second run and *Kapitänleutnant* Bigalk dived and avoided destruction. After several hours he surfaced the boat only to find a Lancaster four-engine bomber of the 61st Squadron orbiting overhead. The Lancaster bore in and dropped ten depth charges, while the *U-751* fired back with all of her flak guns. This massive attack succeeded and the U-boat slid stern first to the bottom. The Lancaster's crew reported that many of the doomed crew made it off the boat into the water, where they shook their fists at the British aircraft in an audacious gesture of final defiance. None were ever seen again. The B.d.U. concluded the boat's fate on July 22:

> "On July 14, *U-751* sailed from St. Nazaire, and up till now has made neither "passing" report nor answered numerous calls. A number of sighting and attacking reports from English aircraft lead to the conclusion that the boat was destroyed by them. The loss cannot be attributed to a mine since the route in question was run over on July 10 and July 15 without result. Loss of boat must be reckoned with."

Maschinenobergefreiter Karl-Heinz Götze had been fortunate and his luck would continue. He transferred to the *U-668*, another Type VIIC that was launched on October 5, 1942 and commissioned on November 16. The U-boat, under the command of *Oberleutnant* Wolfgang von Eichstedt, spent from November 1942 to March 1944 in various training commands of the 5th and 22nd U-boat Flotillas. From April 1, 1944 to April 17, 1945 – operating out of various ports in Norway as part of the 6th and 13th U-boat Flotillas – she conducted eleven war patrols but never sank or damaged an enemy vessel. Götze sailed with her and on November 17, 1944 – with a new rank of *Obermaschinenmaat* – he was awarded the U-boat Clasp in Bronze for his many cumulative patrols during the war. The *U-668* surrendered at Narvik, Norway on May 8, 1945. All her crew survived, with the exception of one man who had earlier transferred to another boat; after their incarceration as prisoners of war Karl-Heinz Götze, Joachim Hünefeldt – who joined the export division of Daimler-Benz – and the other crewmen began to rebuild their lives in post-war Germany, part of the small percentage of U-boat sailors to survive the conflict. On December 24, 1980 Joachim Hünefeldt heard the news that his former U-boat chief, Karl Dönitz had died. He spontaneously made the decision to fly from Stuttgart to Hamburg, where he participated in the funeral for the admiral on January 6, 1981; old U-boat loyalties never die.

Known Crewmembers for the U-751

Abesser, Hermann	*Maschinengefreiter*
Appel, Karl	*Mechanikersmaat*
Bachmann, Helmut	*Matrosenobergefreiter*
Basse, Georg-Wilhelm	*Kapitänleutnant*
Bigalk, Gerhard	*Korvettenkapitän*
Böhme, Kurt	*Kapitänleutnant*
Bolzhauser, Karl-Wilhelm	*Obermaschinenmaat*
Büth, Franz-Josef	*Matrosenobergefreiter*
Damm, Arno	*Oberfunkmaat*
Döhler, Hans-Heinrich	*Oberleutnant zur See*
Emmrich, Edgar	*Maschinengefreiter*
Feike, Friedrich-Wilhelm	*Maschinengefreiter*
Geising, Karl	*Obersteuermann*
Georg, Norbert	*Maschinenmaat*
Gesing, Karl	*Obersteuermann*
Goldbach, Erich	*Mechanikergefreiter*
Gombert, Wilhelm	*Matrosengefreiter*
Götze, Karl-Heinz	*Obermaschinenmaat*
Grassmuck, Karl-Heinz	*Maschinengefreiter*
Grimm, Hugo	*Maschinenobergefreiter*
Haak, Walter	*Maschinenmaat*
Hahnefeldt, Otto	*Obermaschinenmaat*
Hasenschar, Heinrich	*Kapitänleutnant*
Hauck, Joseph	*Obermaschinenmaat*
Hund, Alois	*Matrosengefreiter*
Hünefeldt, Joachim	*Leutnant zur See*
Jacobs, Nikolaus von	*Kapitänleutnant*
Klopfer, Wolfgang	*Bootsmannsmaat*
Kluge, Heinz	*Leutnant (Ing)*
Kochhann, Heinz	*Maschinengefreiter*
Köppe, Helmut	*Kapitänleutnant*
Korinth, Kurt-Walter	*Maschinenobergefreiter*
Kossi, Walter	*Obermaschinist*
Kutschki, Siegfried	*Obermaschinist*
Müller, Helmut	*Mechanikergefreiter*
Müller, Michael	*Maschinenobergefreiter*
Nattermann, Josef	*Funkgefreiter*
Neumann, Helmut	
Niemeyer, Helmut	*Leutnant zur See*
Olrich, Otto	*Fähnrich zur See*
Osswald, Karl-Heinz	*Bootsmannsmaat*
Pflegel, Manfred	*Matrosengefreiter*
Purtz, Hans	*Maschinengefreiter*
Reche, Reinhardt	*Kapitänleutnant*
Reinecke, Karl	*Obermaschinist*
Ruhm, Heinz	*Funkmaat*
Samsen, Egon	*Funkobergefreiter*
Schäfer, Gerhard	*Matrosenobergefreiter*
Schendel, Helmut	*Oberleutnant (Ing)*
Schiprowski, Hermann	*Matrosengefreiter*
Schmaeck, Adolf	*Maschinenmaat*
Schröder, Hermann	*Oberleutnant zur See*
Schröter, Ernst	*Kapitänleutnant*
Schulze, Kurt	*Fähnrich zur See*
Schürmeier, Heinrich	*Maschinenmaat*
Spaeth, Hermann	*Bootsmannsmaat*
Timansky, Walter	*Oberbootsmannsmaat*
Trzewik, Heinz	*Matrosengefreiter*
Urban, Gerhard	*Oberleutnant zur See*
Wall, Walter	*Leutnant zur See*
Weigelt, Erich	*Maschinenobergefreiter*
Wiegand, Ernst	*Matrose*
Wollborn, Fred	*Maschinengefreiter*

Known Crewmembers for the U-668

Ahrens, Wilhelm	*Bootsmaat*
Bauer, Kurt	*Bootsmaat*
Baumelt, Helmut	*Matrosenhauptgefreiter*
Bergerem, Gerd von	*Obersanitätsmaat*
Böhnke, Helmut	*Maschinenobergefreiter*
Brauns, Kurt	*Maschinenobergefreiter*
Breuning, Walter	*Maschinenobergefreiter*
Danigel, Erwin	*Maschinenobergefreiter*
Dienel, Gotthard	*Matrosenobergefreiter*
Dittkrist, Herbert	*Maschinenobergefreiter*
Dostmann, Hans	*Maschinenobergefreiter*
Eggert, Richard	*Obermaschinenmaat*
Eickstedt, Wolfgang von	*Kapitänleutnant*
Engert, Erhardt	*Mechanikerobergefreiter*
Fricke, Walter	*Maschinenobergefreiter*
Fügemann, Heinz	*Maschinenobergefreiter*
Göhre, Gerhard	*Matrosenobergefreiter*
Götz, Günther	*Leutnant zur See*
Götze, Karl-Heinz	*Obermaschinenmaat*
Gross, Hans-Hermann	
Hafner, Hans	*Funkmaat*
Hartenberger, Hugo	*Bootsmaat*
Hartlieb, Kurt	*Mechanikergefreiter*
Heiss, Fritz	*Mechanikergefreiter*
Henning, Fritz	*Kapitänleutnant*
Hirschmüller, Willi	*Maschinengefreiter*
Hoffmann, Gerhard	*Oberbootsmaat*
Hohenstein, Siegfried	*Oberleutnant zur See*
Jersch, Helmut	*Oberleutnant (Ing)*
Kempf, Ferdinand	*Maschinenmaat*
Kettner, Hans	*Obermechanikermaat*
Klausner, Martin	*Oberbootsmaat*
Klinkert, Helmut	*Bootsmaat*
Koch, Paul	*Mechanikergefreiter*
Körner, Uwe	*Funker*
Krieger, Artur	*Maschinenobergefreiter*
Künstler, Herbert	*Matrosengefreiter*
Lehmann, Kurt	*Matrosenhauptgefreiter*
Limper, Werner	*Maschinenobergefreiter*
Mahn, Heinz	*Maschinenobergefreiter*
Menz, Josef	*Funkobergefreiter*
Mohnke, Erwin	*Maschinengefreiter*
Nabenau, Matthias	*Obermaschinist*
Naber, Johann	*Obermaschinist*
Nellesen, Reinhold	
Neugebauer, Helmut	*Funkobergefreiter*
Pannwitz, Ernst	*Obermaschinenmaat*
Pfeiffer, Willi	
Philipp, Karl-Heinz	*Maschinenobergefreiter*
Pilz, Hans	*Maschinengefreiter*
Roth, Anton	*Matrosenobergefreiter*

Russmann, Rudi	*Matrosenobergefreiter*
Schäfer, Günther	*Oberbootsmaat*
Schedler, Friedrich	*Obermaschinist*
Schmidt, Kurt	*Matrosenobergefreiter*
Schulz, Fritz	*Maschinenmaat*
Seuss, Joachim	*Matrosenobergefreiter*
Seybold, Otto	*Oberfunkmaat*
Skeide, Eric	*Maschinenmaat*
Steiger, Ernst	
Themann, Heinrich	
Thörmer, Heinz	*Oberfunkmaat*
Tränkner, Heinz	*Obermaschinist*
Trompter, Heinz	*Leutnant zur See*
Vorhauer, Fritz	*Oberstevermann*
Wagner, Leo	*Oberstevermann*
Wallbrecher, Alfred	*Maschinengefreiter*
Wannisch, Josef	*Matrosengefreiter*
Wethmar, Armin	*Leutnant zur See*
Wildermann, Paul	
Wüstenberg, Wolfgang	*Oberleutnant zur See*

Sources, "Audacity:" Manfred Dörr, *Die Ritterkreuzträger der U-Boot-Waffe, Band 1: A-J, Band 2: L-Z*, Osnabrück, FRG: Biblio Verlag, 1988, Band 1 – 12, 13, 14; *F.d.U./B.d.U. War Diary, 1-15 July 1941* (PG30292), 104, 107; *F.d.U./B.d.U. War Diary, 16-31 December 1941* (PG30301B), 278; *F.d.U./B.d.U. War Diary, 1-15 May 1942* (PG30307A), 45; *F.d.U./B.d.U. War Diary, 16-31 July 1942* (PG30309B), 33, 45; Michael Gannon, *Black May: The Epic Story of the Allies Defeat of the German U-boats in May 1943*, New York: HarperCollins, 1998, 336, 374, 375, 415, 416, 417, 501, 511, 568, 576, 674, 675, 681; Michael Gannon, *Operation Drumbeat: The Dramatic True Story of Germany's First U-boat Attacks Along the American Coast in World War II*, New York: Harper & Row, 229; Joachim Hünefeldt, "The Battle Flag of U-751," translated by William Lehmbeck (US Navy, Retired); Jürgen Rohwer, *Axis Submarine Successes 1939-1945*, Annapolis, Maryland: Naval Institute Press, 1983, 56, 73, 77, 96, 97, 208; Olaf Rose, *U-751: Triumph und Tragödie eines deutschen U-bootes*, Inning am Amersee, Germany: Vowinkel, 2002,7, 8, 9; Gordon Williamson, *Wolf Pack: The Story of the U-boat in World War II*, Oxford, England: Osprey Publishing, 2006, 215; www.ubootwaffe.net; www.uboatarchive.net.

Verleihungs-Urkunde.

Auf Grund der Ermächtigung des Oberbefehlshabers der Kriegsmarine verleihe ich dem

Maschinenobergefreiten
(Dienstgrad)

Heinz G ö t z e
(Name)

das

Ubootskriegsabzeichen 1939

Befehlsstelle , den 9. September 1941

Dönitz

Vizeadmiral und Befehlshaber der Unterseeboote

U-boat War Badge award document to Heinz Götze of the U-751 on September 9, 1941, awarded at St. Nazaire, France. *The document has a facsimile signature of Vizeadmiral Karl Dönitz; Götze received the award one day after the conclusion of the boat's second war patrol.*

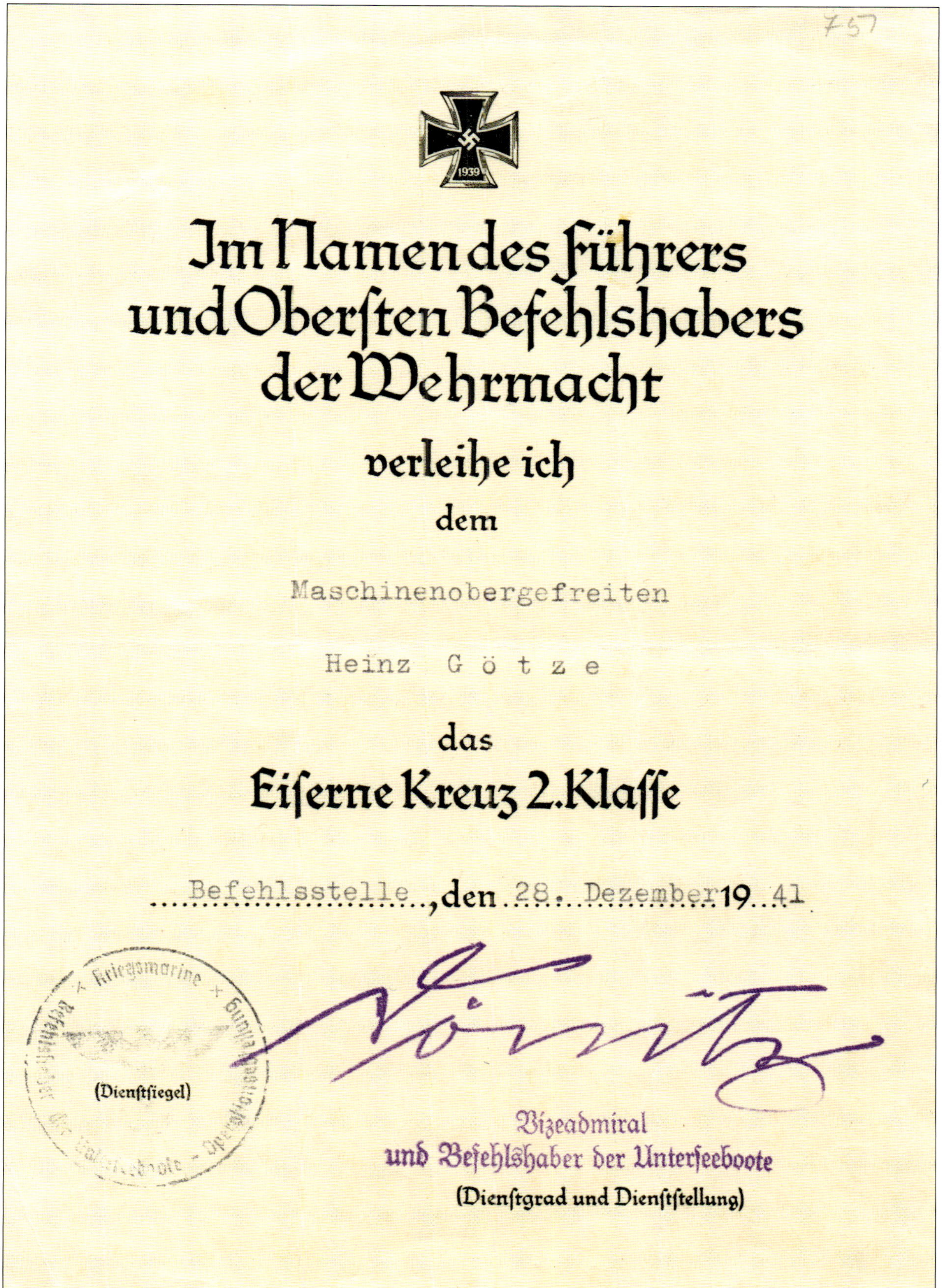

757

Im Namen des Führers
und Obersten Befehlshabers
der Wehrmacht

verleihe ich

dem

Maschinenobergefreiten

Heinz Götze

das

Eiserne Kreuz 2. Klasse

Befehlsstelle, den 28. Dezember 1941

(Dienstsiegel)

Vizeadmiral
und Befehlshaber der Unterseeboote
(Dienstgrad und Dienststellung)

Iron Cross 2nd Class award document to Heinz Götze of the U-751 on December 28, 1941, awarded at St. Nazaire, France two days after the conclusion of a successful fourth war patrol and the sinking of HMS Audacity. *Document has a facsimile signature of Vizeadmiral Karl Dönitz.*

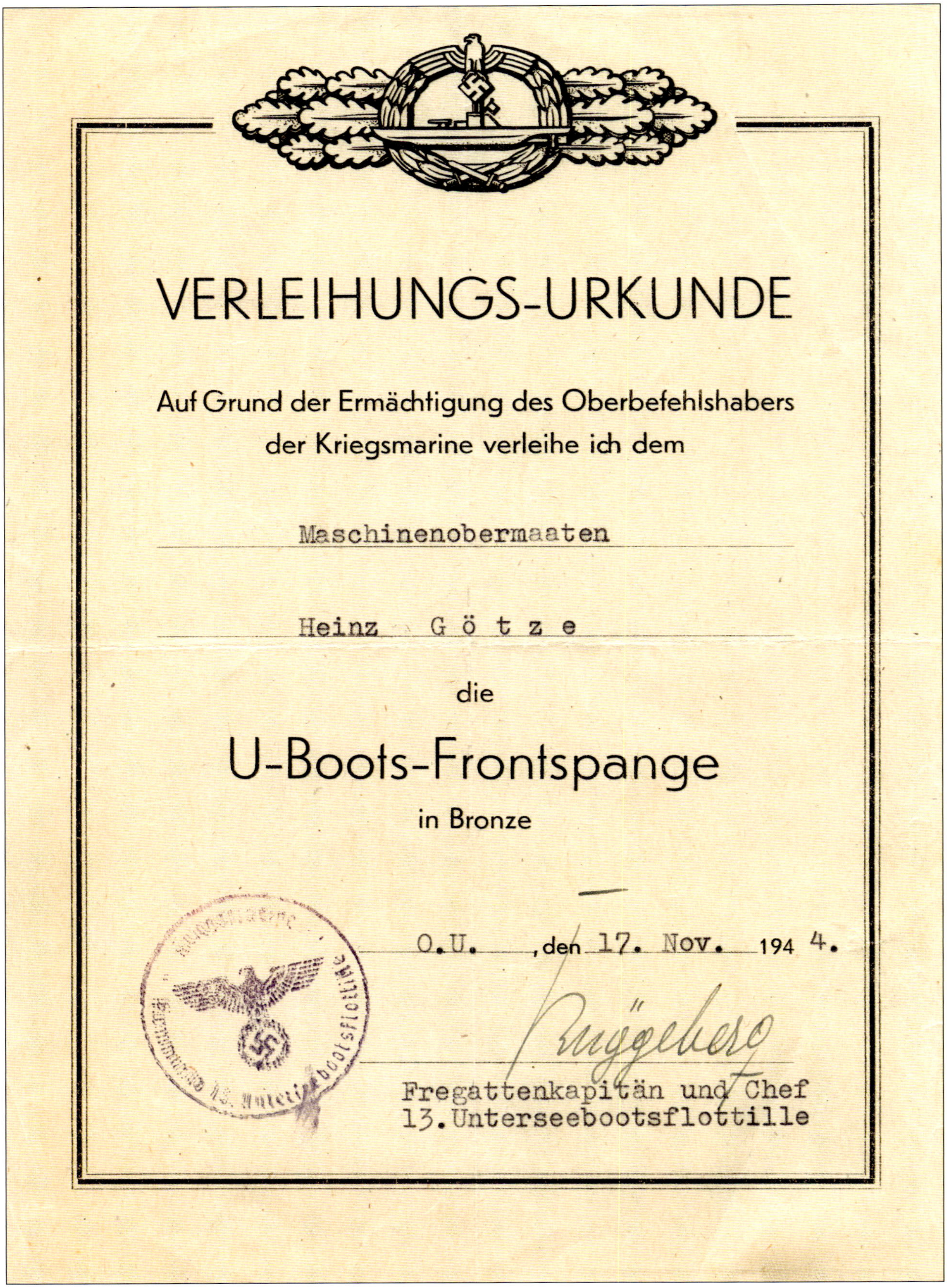

VERLEIHUNGS-URKUNDE

Auf Grund der Ermächtigung des Oberbefehlshabers der Kriegsmarine verleihe ich dem

Maschinenobermaaten

Heinz Götze

die

U-Boots-Frontspange

in Bronze

O.U. , den 17. Nov. 1944.

Fregattenkapitän und Chef
13. Unterseebootsflottille

U-boat Front Clasp in Bronze award document to Heinz Götze of the U-668, on November 17, 1944. *The document is signed by Fregattenkapitän Rolf Rüggeberg, Commander of the 13th U-boat Flotilla in Norway.*

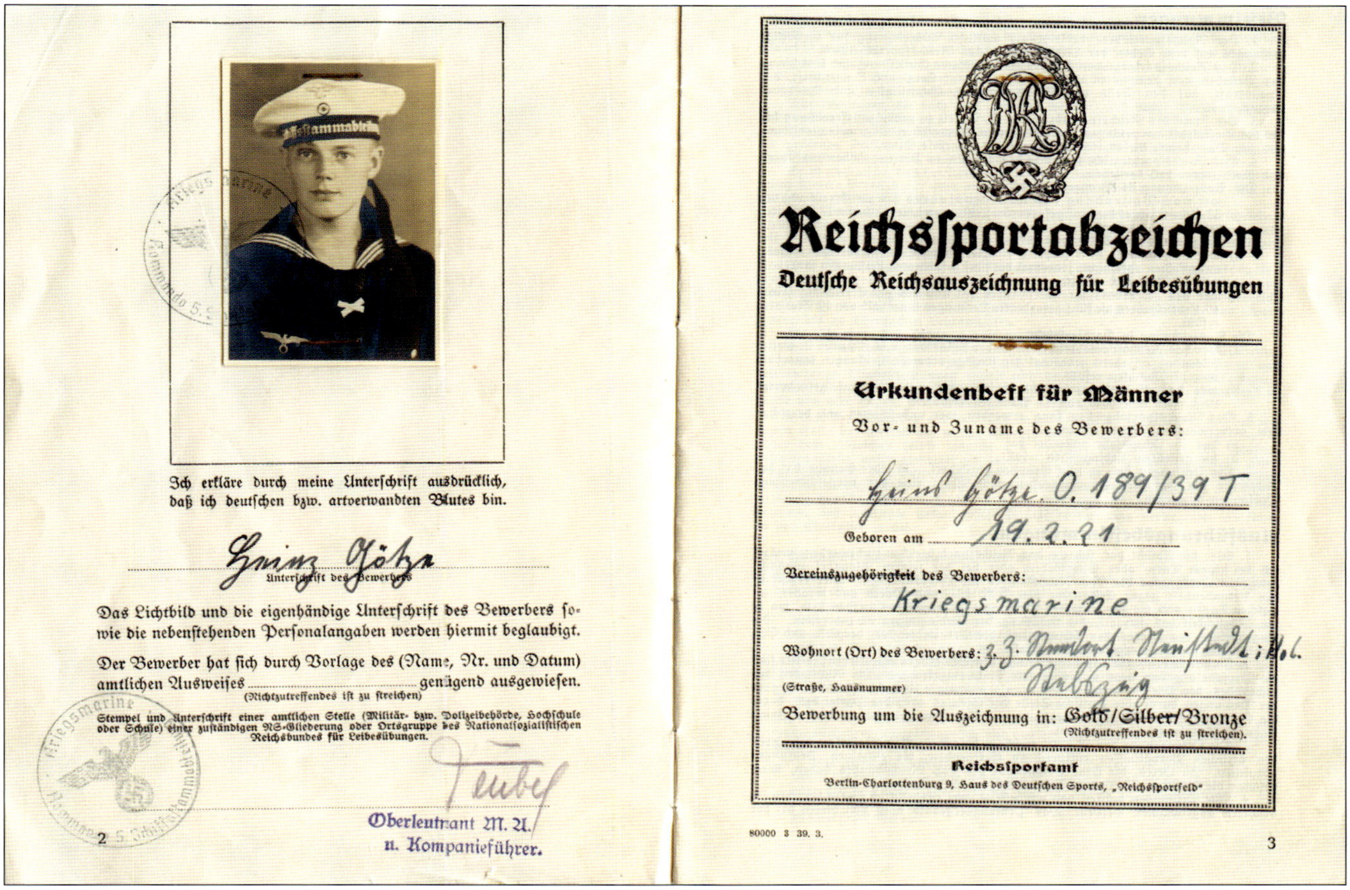

Ich erkläre durch meine Unterschrift ausdrücklich, daß ich deutschen bzw. artverwandten Blutes bin.

Heinz Götze
Unterschrift des Bewerbers

Das Lichtbild und die eigenhändige Unterschrift des Bewerbers sowie die nebenstehenden Personalangaben werden hiermit beglaubigt.

Der Bewerber hat sich durch Vorlage des (Name, Nr. und Datum) amtlichen Ausweises genügend ausgewiesen.
(Nichtzutreffendes ist zu streichen)

Stempel und Unterschrift einer amtlichen Stelle (Militär- bzw. Polizeibehörde, Hochschule oder Schule) einer zuständigen NS-Gliederung oder Ortsgruppe des Nationalsozialistischen Reichsbundes für Leibesübungen.

Oberleutnant M.A.
u. Kompanieführer.

2

Reichssportabzeichen
Deutsche Reichsauszeichnung für Leibesübungen

Urkundenheft für Männer
Vor- und Zuname des Bewerbers:
Heinz Götze 0.189/39 T
Geboren am 19.2.21
Vereinszugehörigkeit des Bewerbers:
Kriegsmarine
Wohnort (Ort) des Bewerbers:
(Straße, Hausnummer)
Bewerbung um die Auszeichnung in: Gold/Silber/Bronze
(Nichtzutreffendes ist zu streichen).

Reichssportamt
Berlin-Charlottenburg 9, Haus des Deutschen Sports, „Reichssportfeld"

80000 3 39. 3.

3

Reich Sports Badge in Bronze award document to Heinz Götze. *Götze competed for the award during naval training in 1940.*

Heinz Götze in full dress uniform with his wife. *Photo was taken after December 28, 1941, when he received the Iron Cross 2nd Class shown on his uniform. Götze survived the war. Photo is a post-war copy of an original.*

Kapitänleutnant Gerhard Bigalk of the U-751, center in white cap and blue uniform, in discussion with another U-boat commander (with flowers) following that commander's successful war patrol. *Photo probably taken at St. Nazaire, France in the summer of 1941. Officer in white uniform wearing the Knight's Cross appears to be Kapitänleutnant Heinrich Lehmann-Willenbrock, commander of the U-96. Both the U-751 and the U-96 were assigned to the 7th U-boat Flotilla at the time. Photo is a post-war copy of an original.*

CHAPTER TWELVE

"From the Caribbean to Cape Town" U-502, U-504, and U-506 1942

Oil. Much like in current times, oil and petroleum products were the life-blood of World War II economies and military forces. The German Wehrmacht needed oil, gasoline and diesel fuel to run the panzer divisions, needed these essentials to keep the *Luftwaffe*'s fighters, Stukas and bombers in the air, and needed this precious commodity to keep the *Kriegsmarine*'s U-boats at sea. Great Britain also needed oil, both for its economy and for the mighty Royal Navy and tenacious Royal Air Force. Karl Dönitz understood this. He also understood one key difference between Germany and Great Britain concerning oil; unlike Germany, all of Britain's oil had to be transported to her by sea from sources that were a great distance away.

And U-boats could stop that flow.

The Type IXC U-boats were not specifically designed to attack these oil tankers, but they were intended to take the undersea fight thousands of miles away from Great Britain, and perhaps equally important, far away from much of the enemy's anti-submarine forces. The Type IXC boats were larger than the more-numerous Type VIIs, displacing 1,540 tons over a length of almost 77 meters and a beam (a ship's/boat's breadth at its widest point) of 6.76 meters. Powered by 4,400 horsepower diesel engines, a Type IXC could hit a top surface speed of 18.3 knots, slightly faster than a Type VIIC. More importantly, by sailing at an optimum fuel consumption speed of ten knots, a Type IXC had a cruising range of 13,450 miles – which could be increased by refueling at sea from supply U-boats. Over this vast distance, a Type IXC could carry twenty-two torpedoes (or forty-four floating mines); for surface attacks a Type IXC was equipped with a larger deck gun – a 105-mm, with 110 rounds. While it took a Type IXC a few seconds longer to submerge than its smaller cousin, the boat could safely dive to a depth of 755 feet.

The *U-502*, *U-504* and *U-506* were Type IXC sister boats, all ordered by the *Kriegsmarine* on September 25, 1939, and all constructed at the shipyards of Deutsche Werft AG at Hamburg-Finkenwärder. Workers laid the keel of the *U-502* at Yard 292 on April 2, 1940. About four weeks later, on April 29 engineers at Yard 294 laid the keel of the *U-504*; on July 11, the engineers laid the keel of the *U-506*. Work continued throughout 1940 at a feverish pace; on February 18, 1941 the *U-502* was launched from her slipway and was commissioned on May 31 of that year by her first – and only – commander *Kapitänleutnant* Jürgen von Rosenstiel. The *U-504* followed closely behind her; after being launched on April 24, 1941, she was commissioned by *Korvettenkapitän* Hans-Georg Friedrich Poske on July 30. Like clockwork the *U-506* kept pace with her slightly older sisters; she was launched on June 20, 1941 and commissioned on September 15, 1941 by *Kapitänleutnant* Eric Würdemann.

The paths of the three boats then slightly diverged, with the *U-502* reporting to the 2nd U-boat Flotilla for several months of training, while the *U-504* and *U-506* joined the 4th U-boat Training Flotilla based at Stettin where the crews received their advanced training. After this training, the *U-502* and *U-504* formally joined the 2nd U-boat Flotilla, while the *U-506* was assigned to the 10th U-boat Flotilla. All three were now set to take the fight to the enemy.

The *U-502* was the first to see action. Her commander Jürgen von Rosenstiel was born in Kiel on November 23, 1912. Entering the Navy in 1933, he served seven years in the surface fleet before beginning U-boat training in 1940. He then served two months as the 2nd Watch Officer on the *U-38* and the 1st Watch Officer for a further three. Among the crew was *Matrosengefreiter* Paul Impertro. Born on July 17, 1921, Impertro was a member of the Hitler Youth, receiving the Hitler Youth Proficiency Badge in Silver. This award designated a certain proficiency level in physical fitness, field craft and political knowledge; Impertro must have been proud of this award as he continued to wear it after joining the Navy, which probably occurred in 1938 or 1939. A surviving photo shows that *Matrosengefreiter* Impertro was qualified as an artilleryman; he almost certainly served on the 105-mm deck-gun on the *U-502*. He may have been from the Ludwigshafen area as this is where he had his studio photo taken.

Dönitz's Crews

***Matrosengefreiter* Paul Impertro**

Born on July 17, 1921.
Served on the 105-mm deck-gun crew on the *U-502*.
Awarded the U-boat War Badge.
Spent 179 days at sea on U-boat war patrols.
Killed in action on July 5, 1942 in the Bay of Biscay.

On September 29, 1941 Jürgen von Rosenstiel departed Kiel with the *U-502* for her first war patrol. On October 7, 1941 he torpedoed and damaged the British 14,795-ton whale factory ship *Svend Foyn*, sailing with convoy HX-152 south of Iceland; although thirty men died in the attack, the ship managed to reach Iceland six days later. Von Rosenstiel and the *U-502* arrived at Lorient, France on November 9, 1941. After settling in, the *U-502* departed Lorient on December 18, but four days later returned to the base after the crew discovered the boat was leaking a discernible trail of oil.

Meanwhile, the *U-504* under the command of Hans-Georg Friedrich Poske entered the fray. Born on October 23, 1904 at Berlin-Schönberg, "Fritz" Poske was a very experienced officer, joining the *Reichsmarine* in 1923. He served in cruisers, torpedo boats and tenders; his surface career culminated in 1939 as the navigation officer on the light cruisers *Nürnberg* and *Königsberg*, winning the Iron Cross 2nd Class on October 2, 1939. He was a member of the *Königsberg* when she was sunk during the Norwegian Campaign in April 1940. Poske began U-boat training in 1941; prior to commissioning the *U-504* he had no frontline U-boat experience. That was about to change on January 6, 1942 when Poske departed Kiel with the *U-504,* for her first war patrol. The *U-504* set a course for Lorient, France; she arrived there on January 20, having seen no action.

Concerning the *U-502*, repairs were made to the boat at Lorient and on January 19, 1942 she departed for her second war patrol bound for the Caribbean and the oil tankers supplying the United States and Great Britain. She would not be alone in this task; Dönitz assigned the *U-67*, *U-156*, *U-129* and *U-161* – their mission was to interdict the flow of oil and bauxite from South America to North America. South American oilfields were concentrated at two places, around the island of Trinidad and under the shallow Lake Maracaibo in Venezuela. Most of the Trinidad oil was refined on the island; Trinidad was also a transfer point for bauxite – the base mineral for aluminum – from small ships heading from the mineral's sources in British Guiana and Dutch Guiana to large craft bound for the United States and Britain. Maracaibo crude oil was shipped from the fields in small shallow-draft tankers to huge refineries on the Dutch islands of Aruba and Curacao; the Lagos refinery on Aruba produced seven million barrels of petroleum products per month – the world's largest output.

The situation led to a difference of strategic opinion between the two major leaders of the *Kriegsmarine*. *Großadmiral* Erich Raeder, the Commander-in-Chief of the Navy, believed the opening of the attack in the oil region, proposed for February 16, 1942, should be initiated by three U-boats shelling the refineries and tank farms on Aruba and Curacao; his reasoning was that the surprise attack would put the massive facilities out of action for months and could be executed without U-boat loss. *Vizeadmiral* Dönitz vehemently disagreed; he believed that not only would such an attack alert enemy shipping to the presence of the U-boats and could result in their loss, but also would be problematic with the employment of just three deck-guns. Raeder held firm and Dönitz, in effect, disobeyed him at least in intent by instructing the U-boat crews to open the campaign by attacking oil tankers and only afterward, if conditions permitted, would they bombard the land facilities.

On February 16, 1942 von Rosenstiel struck oil. At 9:44 a.m. the *U-502* torpedoed and sank the British 2,395-ton tanker *Tia Juana* carrying crude oil from Maracaibo, Venezuela to Aruba. Seventeen crewmen lost their lives in the attack. Additional success followed. At 10:28 a.m. in the Gulf of Venezuela von Rosenstiel torpedoed the Venezuelan 2,650-ton tanker *Monagasa* carrying oil products from Maracaibo to Aruba; fourteen minutes later the *U-502* fired a coup de grâce torpedo which sank the ship, killing five men. The U-boat finished her morning at 11:34 a.m., when von Rosenstiel fired a torpedo at the British 2,391-ton tanker *San Nicolas* carrying crude oil form Maracaibo to Aruba, but the shot missed. At 11:50 a.m. he achieved better results with a second torpedo and the ship burst into flames, sinking with seven of her crew.

On February 22, 1942 the *U-502* sank her teeth into another tanker, the American 9,033-ton *JN Pew* enroute from Aruba to the Panama Canal. At 1:59 a.m. the first torpedo struck amidships on the port side, spraying oil over her length and setting the ship on fire. The tanker, carrying 104,270 barrels of fuel oil, would not go down until the fifth torpedo hit some fifty-five minutes later, taking with her thirty-three men. The next day, February 23, at 9:37 a.m. north of Aruba, von Rosenstiel fired a spread of two torpedoes at the Panamanian 8,329-ton tanker *Thalia* sailing in ballast from Hampton Roads, Virginia to Aruba. At 10:32 a.m. a third torpedo hit the target. Two more torpedoes still did not sink the ship; the *U-502* surfaced and twenty-year-old *Matrosenobergefreiter* Paul Impertro – who given his junior status was probably a loader – and the rest of the 105-mm deck-gun crew went into action. After 103 rounds the tough tanker finally sank; all but one of her crew escaped. Later that day at 4:23 p.m. the *U-502* torpedoed and damaged the American 9,002-ton tanker *Sun*. The tanker, sailing in ballast, was hit amidships about fifty miles north of Aruba. The U-boat departed the area after an aircraft was sighted, but the *Sun* did not sink and the crew managed to sail her to the Venezuelan coast. The *U-502* arrived at Lorient on March 16, 1942.

Dönitz's Crews

***Obermaschinenmaat* Willi Scherhoff**

Born on April 11, 1917 in Wuppertal.
Entered the Navy in 1937.
Served in the engine room on the *U-504*.
Awarded the U-boat War Badge on April 2, 1942; awarded the Iron Cross 2nd Class on December 14, 1942.
Spent 372 days at sea on U-boat war patrols.
Killed in action on July 30, 1943 west of Cape Ortegal, Spain.

Meanwhile, on January 25, 1942 the *U-504* also left Lorient for the coast of Florida for a second war patrol. One of the men in the engine room of the *U-504* was *Maschinenmaat* Willi Scherhoff. Born on April 11, 1917, he joined the Navy in 1937; we have no other details about his service before joining the *U-504*. At 4:44 a.m. on February 22, 1942, just off Florida, Poske torpedoed and sank the American 5,287-ton tanker *Republic*, killing five; the ship had been bound from Philadelphia to Houston. The next day, February 23, at 1:32 a.m. Poske sank the American 10,227-ton tanker *WD Anderson*; only one of her thirty-five men survived when the ship carrying crude oil from Corpus Christi, Texas for Philadelphia went down. On February 26, 1942 at 7:13 p.m. further out to sea off Florida, Poske torpedoed and sank the Dutch 8,245-ton tanker *Mamura* sailing from Houston, Texas for Halifax (and ultimately Belfast). Her entire crew of fifty-six went down with the ship. Poske finished his tally for the patrol on March 16 at 6:24 a.m. when he sank the British 2,802-ton freighter *Manaqui*, sailing with convoy OS-20 from Belfast for Kingston, Jamaica; all forty-one men perished. On April 1, 1942 the *U-504* arrived at Lorient. Willi Scherhoff received his coveted U-boat War Badge the next day as did his commander "Fritz" Poske. Poske also received the Iron Cross 1st Class on April 3, 1942.

Now it was time for the *U-506* to join her sisters in the fight, but her first trip was inauspicious. The *U-506* departed Hamburg on March 2, 1942, but put in to Helgoland the next day. On March 9 the boat departed Helgoland; she arrived at Lorient, France on March 25 without achieving any enemy sinkings. But that was about to change. Erich Würdemann and the *U-506* departed Lorient on April 6, 1942 for a war patrol that would last over two months and result in sinking or damaging eleven enemy ships. One of the crew was *Oberfunkmaat* Robert Rüter who was the radio operator for the U-boat; it was his mission to report to the captain all incoming radio traffic and to send contact and patrol reports back to the B.d.U. so Admiral Dönitz could keep abreast of the fight. Rüter additionally assisted in operating the underwater hydrophones that could detect the sounds of target ships many miles away. Robert Rüter was born in the city of Hamm on April 18, 1915; he joined the Navy in the mid-1930s.

Dönitz's Crews
***Funkmeister* Robert Rüter**

Born on April 18, 1915 in Hamm.
Served as the radio operator on the *U-506* for her first three war patrols.
Awarded the U-boat War Badge and the Iron Cross 2nd Class on June 18, 1942.
Spent 90 days at sea on U-boat war patrols.
Survived the war; died at Soest, North Rhine-Westphalia.

On May 3, 1942 at 8:12 a.m. off Key Largo, Florida, the *U-506* torpedoed and sank the small 567-ton Nicaraguan freighter *Sama* carrying bananas from Baracoa, Cuba to Jacksonville, Florida. Würdemann then proceeded through the Straits of Florida into the Gulf of Mexico. On May 10, 1942 off Louisiana, the *U-506* damaged the American 7,050-ton tanker *Aurora*, sailing in ballast from New York to Beaumont, Texas, with five torpedoes and twenty-two rounds of 105-mm deck-gun fire; with the ship on fire, Würdemann withdrew, but the tanker did not sink. The following day an enemy aircraft dropped a bomb close to the U-boat that damaged a stern torpedo tube.

On May 13, 1942 at 9:38 a.m. five miles from the mouth of the Mississippi River, the *U-506* torpedoed and sank the American 8,862-ton tanker *Gulfpenn*, carrying 90,000 barrels of fuel oil from Port Arthur, Texas for Philadelphia; thirteen men perished in the attack. On May 14, 1942 off Louisiana at 5:47 a.m., the *U-506* torpedoed and fatally damaged the American 6,821-ton tanker *David McKelvy*, carrying 80,000 barrels of crude oil bound from Corpus Christi, Texas to Bayonne, New Jersey; seventeen crewmen perished in the attack. A salvage crew reboarded the burned-out vessel and beached her on the Louisiana coast, but she was declared a total loss.

May 16 was a good day for the *U-506* in the Gulf of Mexico. At 11:01 a.m. the U-boat damaged the American 7,302-ton tanker *William C McTarnahan* with two torpedoes. Sailing in ballast from New York to Port Isabel, Texas the ship survived but eighteen men of her crew died. Minutes later at 11:10 a.m. she damaged the American 9,002-ton tanker *Sun* sailing in ballast from Philadelphia for Beaumont with torpedoes and deck-gun fire. As in the previous attack against her in February by the *U-502*, the *Sun* did not sink. The next day at 5:34 a.m. on May 17, the *U-506* fired two torpedoes that sank the American 5,189-ton tanker *Gulfoil*. The ship was carrying 54,000 barrels of petroleum products from Port Arthur to New York; twenty-one men died when the ship went down. At 8:56 a.m. on May 19, 1942 south of Louisiana, the *U-506* torpedoed and sank the American 4,732-ton *Heredia*, a freighter carrying 1,500 tons of coffee and bananas from Corpus Christi to New Orleans; thirty-six crewmen died in the attack after three torpedoes savaged the ship. On May 20, 1942 at 7:58 a.m. still south of Louisiana, Würdemann sank the American 6,986-ton tanker *Halo* carrying 64,103 barrels of crude oil from Tampico, Mexico to New Orleans. The *U-506* fired two torpedoes at the tanker which ripped her in two, initially killing nineteen men. With the oil from the ship burning on the surface of the water, twenty-three survivors went into the water with only one life raft. Over the next seven days all but three died of injuries and exposure.

The *U-506* then moved out of the Gulf of Mexico and into the Atlantic north of the Bahamas. At 2:15 a.m. on May 28, 1942 the U-boat came across the British 4,457-ton freighter *Yorkmoor* carrying 6,700 tons of bauxite from St. Thomas, Virgin Islands to New York. Running low on torpedoes, Würdemann decided to use deck-gun fire, and after shelling his target for ninety minutes, the *Yorkmoor* finally sank. Würdemann then moved near Bermuda and on May 31, 1942 he sank the British 2,292-ton *Fred W Green* with deck-gun fire. Five crewmen perished when the freighter carrying government stores and some trucks went to the bottom southeast of Bermuda in the attack. After ten weeks at sea far from France, on June 15, 1942 the *U-506* returned to Lorient. On June 18 *Funkobermaat* Robert Rüter was awarded the U-boat War Badge and the Iron Cross 2nd Class.

While the *U-506* was tearing up the Gulf of Mexico, the *U-502* departed Lorient under the command of Jürgen von Rosenstiel on April 22, 1942. He was bound for the Caribbean, but not for a tropical vacation; Dönitz believed that Allied escorts now stretched thin covering the Gulf of Mexico and Atlantic seaboard of the U.S. would permit the *U-502* to duplicate her previous success just north of South America. Dönitz was right; Jürgen von Rosenstiel hit nine ships on this patrol:

- On May 11, 1942 the *U-502* sank the British 4,963-ton freighter *Cape of Good Hope*, northeast of Antigua, with torpedoes and deck-gun fire; the ship was carrying 7,500 tons of military and general cargo from New York to Table Bay, South Africa. Once again *Matrosengefreiter* Paul Impertro and the 105-mm deck-gun crew saw action.
- At 1:15 p.m. on May 24, von Rosenstiel torpedoed and sank the Brazilian 4,996-ton *Gonçalves Diaz* enroute from Rio de Janeiro for New York with coffee; six men died in the attack south of the Dominican Republic. Although the ship was neutral, she did not carry any neutrality markings.
- Four days later on May 28 at 2:00 a.m., the *U-502* torpedoed and sank the American 6,759-ton *Alcoa Pilgrim* south of the Mona Passage of Puerto Rico; thirty-one men perished when the freighter carrying 9,000 tons of bauxite ore and general cargo from Paramaribo, Dutch Guyana for Mobile, Alabama went to the bottom just ninety seconds after the torpedo struck her starboard side below the waterline in the engine room.
- At 4:00 a.m. on June 3, 1942 von Rosenstiel struck again sinking the American 6,940-ton *MF Elliott* off Trinidad; the tanker, sailing in ballast from New York to Caripito, Venezuela sank with fifteen of her crew only six minutes after the torpedo struck her starboard quarter well below the waterline.
- On June 9, 1942 off Trinidad the *U-502* sank two ships: she torpedoed the Belgian 5,085-ton *Bruxelles*, a member of convoy TA-5 carrying general cargo from Trinidad for Kingston, Jamaica; von Rosenstiel also torpedoed the American 6,589-ton tanker *Franklin K Lane*, carrying 73,000 barrels of crude oil from Trinidad to Aruba. The tanker exploded after being hit aft of the bridge but did not immediately sink – fifteen hours later the British destroyer *HMS Churchill* sank her with gunfire, after determining she could not be saved and would be a hazard to navigation in the area until she sank.

• Finally, on June 15, 1942 west of Grenada, the *U-502* had her best day, sinking three ships: going down were the Panamanian 5,010-ton *Cold Harbor* with 6,200 tons of war material including twenty-eight tanks and six aircraft after two torpedoes caused the ammunition in her hold to explode; the American 5,702-ton *West Hardaway* carrying war supplies and coal went down after two torpedo hits; and the American 8,001-ton freighter *Scottsburg* with aircraft, tanks and war stores aboard went down after two torpedo hits, the first of which struck the port side in the engine room.

The *U-502* and her happy crew then turned for home. Undoubtedly there would be decorations for many of the men based on the success of the patrol followed by summer leave for all. Unfortunately a British Wellington bomber from the 172nd Squadron was on patrol west of Nantes. Wellington aircraft, although numerous, had not sunk any U-boats, so the odds of this particular bomber achieving success were small. However, British technicians equipped this Wellington with a device known as the Leigh Light, a 22-million candlepower, 24-inch searchlight. The idea to illuminate enemy submarines at night by powerful searchlight had first been proposed by Squadron Commander Humphrey de Verd Leigh of Coastal Command (he first developed a test device in secret without official permission!); the bomber would approach in total darkness using only its ASV (Air to Surface-Vessel) radar – during the final approach the crew would switch on the searchlight beam giving the bombardier a clear view of the target and not giving the U-boat crew sufficient reaction time to dive.

It looked good in theory; this would be its introduction to actual combat. Dönitz's crews on the *U-502* thus had no inkling what awaited them. During the hours of darkness of July 5 close to safety in the Bay of Biscay, they surfaced the boat to recharge the batteries.

Suddenly out of the darkness swooped the Wellington, piloted by Pilot Officer W.B. Howell; like an exploding sun the Leigh Light flashed on destroying the night vision of every U-boat crewman on the bridge and throwing them into fatal confusion. Moments later the British bomber dropped a series of depth charges on the U-boat immediately sinking her, killing the entire crew, thus keeping secret the existence of the Leigh Light for a while longer. For *Kapitänleutnant* Jürgen von Rosenstiel, *Matrosengefreiter* Paul Impertro and the rest of the crew there would be no medals or leave; for their families only death announcements in local newspapers – fifty-two more men falling for Greater Germany.

In the middle of the *U-502*'s war patrol to the Caribbean, the *U-504* under Hans-Georg Friedrich Poske departed from Lorient on May 2, 1942 for her third war patrol, which was also to the Caribbean. And like von Rosenstiel, "Fritz" Poske was also successful; he sank six ships on this patrol:

• On May 29, 1942 at 9:37 p.m. fifty-four miles south of Grand Cayman Island, the *U-504* sank the British 1,597-ton *Allister* bound from Kingston, Jamaica for Tampa, Florida with five-hundred tons of bananas; fifteen men died in the attack.

• On June 8, 1942 at 6:59 a.m., the *U-504* torpedoed and sank the 3,901-ton freighter *Tela* north of Nicaragua. The ship, bound from New Orleans, Louisiana for Puerto Limon, Costa Rica, sank with thirteen of her crew after being struck by two torpedoes. The same day at 6:09 p.m. the U-boat sank the British 1,512-ton *Rosenborg* by thirty rounds of deck-gun fire (after missing with two torpedoes) east of the Yucatan Peninsula, the freighter bound from Trinidad to Mobile, Alabama with 1,970 tons of bauxite ore went down with four crewmen including her captain.

• At 2:10 a.m. on June 11, 1942 north of Nicaragua, the *U-504* fired three torpedoes and sank the Dutch 4,282-ton freighter *Crijnssen* bound from Curacao for New Orleans. The same day at 6:01 p.m. near the same location the *U-504* sank the American 4,846-ton *American* sailing from Santos, Brazil to New Orleans with 6,500 tons of manganese ore, coffee, gunny sacks, jute and oil.

• North of Nicaragua on June 14, 1942 at 7:12 p.m., the *U-504* torpedoed and sank the 3,280-ton Latvian freighter *Regent* bound from Norfolk, Virginia for Cristóbal, Panama; eleven of her crew went down with the ship.

On July 7, 1942 the *U-504* returned to Lorient, France. Three weeks later the *U-506*, with Robert Rüter still aboard and in the radio room, left Lorient under the command of Erich Würdemann for her fourth war patrol on July 28, 1942 and headed for the waters off West Africa. The men of the *U-506* would sink five ships on this outing. On August 21, 1942 at 10:43 p.m., the U-boat torpedoed and sank the British 5,733-ton *City of Wellington* bringing 500 tons of chrome ore, 2,000 tons of copper ore and 5,000 tons of general cargo from Mossel Bay, South Africa to Freetown, Sierra Leone; seven of her crew perished when the ship went down close to her destination. Two days later at 11:37 p.m. on August 23 off Sierra Leone, Würdemann sank the British 4,416-ton *Hamla* bound from Rio de Janeiro, Brazil to Great Britain with iron ore; all forty-two men went down with the ship. Then, all was calm until 2:33 a.m. on September 5, 1942, when the *U-506* sank the British 6,278-ton freighter *Myrmidon* just north of the equator southeast of Liberia.

On September 13, 1942 off Liberia, the *U-506* sank the Swedish 3,764-ton *Lima* carrying 2,500 tons of manganese ore, 2,500 tons of tea and 1,500 tons of tobacco from Capetown, South Africa to Great Britain; three merchantmen died in the attack. Then events began to turn crazy. Later that evening the *U-156* attacked a large British ocean liner, *Laconia*, between Liberia and Ascension Island. Unbeknownst to the Germans, there were 1,500 Italian prisoners of war onboard. The *U-156* attempted to rescue several hundred and sent a report to U-boat headquarters requesting guidance. Through his headset *Funkobermaat* Robert Rüter heard Dönitz's orders to the *U-506* and several other boats to assist. The *U-506* arrived on the scene at 11:30 a.m. on September 15 and the *U-507* approached a few hours later. Both picked up several hundred more survivors and towed others in lifeboats behind toward the African coast. On September 16 an American B-24 Liberator attacked the U-boats in the confusion; all three U-boats released the tow lines and dove under the surface leaving the *Laconia's* survivors adrift in the ocean – fortunately surface ships were not far away and most of the men in the water survived.

The *U-506* was not damaged in the air attack. On September 30, 1942 she sank the British 6,637-ton *Siam II* carrying cotton and grain from Capetown to Great Britain. Würdemann and his crew returned to Lorient on November 7, 1942. *Funkobermaat* Robert Rüter would then leave the boat and move on to other duties; he would survive the war.

While the *U-506* was on patrol, the *U-504* slipped her berth at Lorient for her fourth war patrol under the command of Hans-Georg Friedrich Poske on August 19, 1942 for a four-month patrol bound for a new hunting ground – South Africa. For the first two months "Fritz" Poske came up with nothing. But at 6:15 a.m. on October 17, 1942, the *U-504* torpedoed the British 5,970-ton *Empire Chaucer* 450 miles south of Capetown, South Africa. The freighter, traveling unescorted from Calcutta, India to Great Britain with 2,000 tons of pig iron and 6,500 tons of general cargo, went down with three of her crew. Six days later, at 11:12 p.m., Poske torpedoed and sank the British 5,669-ton *City of Johannesburg* bound from Calcutta to Great Britain, southeast of East London, South Africa. Two crewmen died and 7,750 tons of general cargo went to the bottom. The victories continued. At 6:13 p.m. October 26, 1942, the *U-504* fatally damaged the American 7,176-ton *Anne Hutchinson* carrying 8,000 barrels of oil from Suez, Egypt to Capetown off East London. Three men died in the attack in which Poske fired three torpedoes and the deck gun. The *U-504* left the scene; Allied tugs attempted to save the ship but the wreck was finally dynamited. Five days later on October 31, the *U-504* sank two ships. At 9:03 a.m. the *U-504* torpedoed the unescorted British 7,041-ton freighter *Empire Guidon* some 180 miles east-southeast of Durban, South Africa. Five personnel went down with the ship, which was carrying 7,032 tons of military stores and coal from Durban to Alexandria, Egypt. Later that day at 5:18 p.m. two torpedoes from the *U-504* slammed into the British 5,113-ton *Reynolds* 210 miles east of Durban. The ship, carrying military stores from Durban to Karachi, India, went down in seconds; her entire crew of forty-seven perished. The *U-504* sank her last ship on the patrol at 4:42 p.m. on November 3, 1942, the Brazilian 5,187-ton *Porto Alegre* off Port Elizabeth, South Africa. The *U-504* returned to Lorient, France on December 11, 1942. During the voyage, on November 6, 1942 Dönitz radioed "Fritz" Poske that he had been awarded the Knight's Cross.

Three days later on December 14, 1942 the *U-506* departed on her fifth war patrol from Lorient still under the command of Erich Würdemann, but without *Funkobermaat* Robert Rüter. The patrol was long but Würdemann sank only two enemy ships. At 3:09 a.m. on March 7, 1943, the *U-506* torpedoed and sank the British 5,212-ton *Sabor* southeast of Mossel Bay, South Africa. Seven men died when the ship, carrying 1,100 tons of salt ballast and sixty-three bags of mail from Capetown to Rio de Janeiro went down. Two days later on March 9, 1943 at 6:13 a.m., the *U-506* torpedoed the Norwegian 4,768-ton freighter *Tabor* southeast of Cape Agulhas, South Africa. The ship would not go down and the *U-506* began shelling the target with her deck gun. The *Tabor* finally sank at 8:57 a.m., taking eleven men with her. The *U-506* returned to Lorient on May 8, 1943; she had been on patrol for more than twenty weeks.

While the *U-506* was on her odyssey, the *U-504* made two war patrols. *Korvettenkapitän* Poske departed the boat on January 5, 1943. He became the commander of the 1st U-boat Training Division (1. *Unterseeboots-Lehrdivision* [ULD]). He finished the war as a *Kapitän zur See*. He died at Wachtberg near Bonn on October 1, 1984. In his place on the *U-504* came *Kapitänleutnant* Wilhelm Luis. Born on December 12, 1915 in Lübeck, Luis was very familiar with the *U-504*; he had served as her 1st Watch Officer from July to December 1942. Prior to this U-boat service, Luis was seconded to the *Luftwaffe* as a naval aviator.

On January 19, 1943 Luis and the *U-504* departed Lorient to patrol southwest of the Azore Islands. She sank no ships on this sixty-five-day patrol but was attacked by an enemy aircraft on January 21 and again on March 12. In both instances the U-boat escaped without damage. Luis returned to Lorient on March 24, 1943. After spending almost a month in port, and exchanging their tropical gear for cold weather clothing, the *U-504* departed Lorient on April 21, 1943 for a patrol off the southern tip of Greenland. Again the *U-504* sank no enemy ships; she arrived at Bordeaux, France on May 29, 1943.

Both the *U-504* and *U-506* remained in port for the month of June. In July the *U-506*, under the command of Erich Würdemann, was the first to go to sea again when she departed Lorient on July 6 for her sixth war patrol. Her journey would be short; and it would be her last. At July 12, 1943 at 3:50 p.m., an American B-24 Liberator bomber from the 1st Anti-Submarine Squadron located the *U-506* with SC137 10-cm radar, a capability that the Germans could not detect. The bomber roared in for the kill, dropping seven depth charges on the U-boat west of Vigo, Spain that broke the U-boat in two. Forty-eight men, including Erich Würdemann, went down with the boat; six crewmen were rescued three days later by a British destroyer. On July 15, 1943 the B.d.U. war diary reported:

> "*U-506* has not reported since she left Lorient on 6.7. She must be presumed lost. There is no information as to whether her loss was caused by aircraft or naval forces."

Then it was the *U-504*'s turn to depart for sea; she left Bordeaux under the command of Wilhelm Luis on July 27, 1943. On July 30, 1943, while heading west through the Bay of Biscay, the *U-504* and two U-tankers (Type XIV) were located by a British B-24 Liberator. The pilot judiciously radioed for help and six additional aircraft subsequently arrived on the scene. The aircraft then attacked, hitting the *U-461* and *U-462* – the two U-boat supply submarines. For the Germans the hell was just beginning. Closing in were five sloops of legendary U-boat killer "Johnny" Walker's 2nd Support Group. All five warships opened fire at the *U-462* and the *U-504*. Luis ordered the crew to crash dive, but Walker in the sloop *HMS Kite* obtained a sonar contact. *Kite* made the first depth charge attack, followed shortly thereafter by the *HMS Wren*. *Kite* then reloaded her launchers and came on for her second attack. *HMS Woodpecker* joined the fray and dropped thirty-two depth charges. Finally, *HMS Woodcock* and *HMS Wild Goose* conducted a depth charge bombardment of the area. The massed attacks brought to the surface "a uniform jacket, a human lung and some well-cured bacon." No man on the *U-504*, including *Obermaschinenmaat* Willi Scherhoff, survived the attack.

Before they were destroyed, the *U-502*, *U-504* and *U-506* sank a total of fourteen of the valuable oil tankers. But the flow of Allied oil went on.

Known Crewmembers for the U-502

Becker, Kurt-Hans	*Maschinengefreiter*
Bergs, Ignatz	*Maschinenobergefreiter*
Bluhm, Kurt	*Obersteuermann*
Blume, Herbert-Werner	*Maschinengefreiter*
Böhme, Horst-Karl	*Matrosenobergefreiter*
Bolte, Horst	*Oberleutnant zur See*
Bühner, Adolf	*Obermaschinist*
Carben, Heinz	*Maschinenmaat*
Christ, Ludwig	*Matrosengefreiter*
Diemer, Willi	*Obersteuermann*
Feige, Walter	*Matrosenobergefreiter*
Gderra, Friedrich	*Oberfunkmaat*
Geiersbach, Karl-Heinz	*Maschinenobergefreiter*
Glaser, Karl	*Maschinengefreiter*
Göring, Heinrich	*Matrosenobergefreiter*
Gross, Hans-Walter	*Maschinengefreiter*
Gruss, Walter	*Maschinenobergefreiter*
Heider, Herbert	*Oberbootsmaat*
Hoffmann, Heinrich	*Obermaschinenmaat*
Impertro, Paul	*Matrosengefreiter*
Kirner, Robert	*Mechanikergefreiter*
Kossky, Hans-Walter	*Mechanikermaat*
Kranefeld, Wilhelm	*Matrosengefreiter*
Kreischer, Friedrich-Wilhelm	*Matrosengefreiter*
Lafrenz, Fritz	*Maschinenmaat*
Lampe, Werner	*Maschinenmaat*
Lucko, Hans	*Oberbootsmann*
Maerken, Kurt von	*Oberleutnant zur See*
Reinicke, Ekkehard	*Leutnant zur See*
Rosenstiel, Jürgen von	*Kapitänleutnant*
Roth, Ludwig	*Funkobergefreiter*
Schlitt, Karl	*Maschinenobergefreiter*
Schwenke, Walter	*Fähnrich (Ing)*
Siegl, Leopold	*Matrosengefreiter*
Simon, Hans	*Maschinenmaat*
Spiertz, Gottfried	*Oberfunkmaat*
Stangiersky, Wilhelm	*Matrosenobergefreiter*
Steimer, Josef	
Stein, Willi	*Matrosenobergefreiter*
Steinaecker, Walter von	*Kapitänleutnant*
Volkmann, Hans	*Matrosengefreiter*
Werther, Klaus	*Matrosengefreiter*
Wohlfart, Johann	*Bootsmaat*
Wörsching, Karl	*Matrosengefreiter*
Zinsser, Friedrich	*Fähnrich zur See*

Known Crewmembers for the U-504

Adamszak, Hans	*Maschinengefreiter*
Becker, Günter	*Maschinengefreiter*
Beckmann, Heinz	*Oberleutnant zur See*
Berrey, Günter-Hans	*Leutnant zur See*
Beuer, Franz	*Bootsmaat*
Biederbach, Heinz	*Maschinenmaat*
Blum, Werner	*Maschinengefreiter*
Böttcher, Hans	*Matrosenobergefreiter*
Bohn, Albert	*Maschinengefreiter*
Breitmoser, Friedrich	*Maschinenmaat*
Buche, Gerd	*Maschinenobergefreiter*
Buchholz, Siegfried	*Maschinenmaat*
Buro, Hans	*Funkobergefreiter*
Cebulla, Günther	*Maschinenobergefreiter*
Dehrmann, Wolf	*Leutnant zur See*
Diergardt, Karl-Heinz	*Funkmaat*
Dörfert, Willi	*Maschinenobergefreiter*
Gausmann, Fritz	*Maschinenobergefreiter*
Griephan, Herbert	*Mechanikerobergefreiter*
Hartung, Otto	*Maschinenobergefreiter*
Hackwitz, Werner	*Funkgefreiter*
Hauser, Wilhelm	*Obermechanikermaat*
Heymann, Wilhelm	*Matrosenobergefreiter*
Hiereth, Franz	*Maschinengefreiter*
Hilsheimer, Helmut	*Maschinenobergefreiter*
Hinz, Leo	*Maschinenmaat*
Jabzinski, Georg	*Matrosenobergefreiter*
Jadwitschack, Karl-Ernst	*Matrosengefreiter*
Jendretzki, Egon	*Maschinenobergefreiter*
Junk, Johann	*Matrosenobergefreiter*
Kaiser, Ernst	*Funker*
Kaletta, Günter	*Oberfunkmaat*
Kallmeyer, Erich	*Matrosengefreiter*
Kasobke, Walter	*Bootsmaat*
Kaufer, Karl-Heinz	*Matrosenobergefreiter*
Kernig, Egon	
Kiepert, Helmut	*Kapitänleutnant (Ing)*
Klauss, Johannes	*Obermaschinist*
Knackstedt, Otto	*Matrosenobergefreiter*
Knaffla, Heinrich	*Maschinengefreiter*
Korzuschnik, Gerhard	*Matrosengefreiter*
Leitner, Walter	*Funkgefreiter*
Liersz, Johannes	*Matrose*
Liminski, Max	*Maschinenobergefreiter*
Lipka, Lothar	*Obermaschinist*
Lipke, Erich	*Maschinenobergefreiter*
Lippka, Helmut	*Bootsmaat*
Luis, Wilhelm	*Kapitänleutnant*
Lutz, Werner	*Leutnant zur See*
Matten, Heinrich	*Maschinenobergefreiter*
Matyssek, Gerhard	*Maschinenobergefreiter*
Mühlfriedel, Franz	*Mechanikergefreiter*
Nordhausen, Dr. Wolfgang	*Arzt*
Obendorfer, Johann	*Matrosenobergefreiter*
Pilz, Günther	*Mechanikergefreiter*
Poske, Hans-Georg	*Kapitän zur See*
Preuss, Ernst	*Matrose*
Quirlin, Hans	*Leutnant zur See*
Rabenau, Georg von	*Kapitänleutnant*
Rausch, Peter	*Maschinenobergefreiter*
Reimann, Willi	*Mechanikergefreiter*
Rode, Karl	*Obermaschinenmaat*
Rosenstiel, Karl	*Maschinenmaat*
Sassenhoff, Günter	*Matrosenobergefreiter*
Scharnhop, Wilhelm	*Obermaschinenmaat*
Scherhoff, Willi	*Obermaschinenmaat*
Schilling, Eberhard	*Leutnant (Ing)*
Schlagowski, Helmut	*Oberfunkmaat*
Schlichtkrul, Kurt	*Matrosengefreiter*
Schmidt, Alfred	*Maschinenobergefreiter*
Schmitt, Peter	*Maschinenmaat*
Schmoeckel, Helmut	*Kapitänleutnant*
Schöps, Willi	*Obersteuermann*
Silberbach, Erwin	*Maschinenobergefreiter*
Sommer, Heinz	*Leutnant zur See*
Spohn, Günter	*Oberleutnant zur See*

Staab, Kurt	*Maschinengefreiter*
Staas, Ewald	*Obersteuermann*
Stache, Heinz	*Funkgefreiter*
Stegk, Hermann	*Oberleutnant zur See*
Stein, Wilhelm	*Maschinengefreiter*
Stein, Willi	*Bootsmaat*
Streit, Richard	*Matrosenobergefreiter*
Strobel, Ernst	*Matrosenobergefreiter*
Wanzek, Bernhard	*Oberbootsmaat*
Weber, Hans	*Matrose*
Widiger, Artur	*Obermaschinist*
Wiese, Walter	*Obermaschinenmaat*
Willaredt, Oswald	*Matrosengefreiter*
Wollschläger, Hans	*Maschinenmaat*

Known Crewmembers for the U-506

Assmann, Bruno	*Maschinenobergefreiter*
Bales, Johann	*Funkgefreiter*
Bätz	*Matrosengefreiter*
Baus, Johann	*Maschinenobergefreiter*
Becker, Erich	*Maschinenobergefreiter*
Beilstein, Willy	*Leutnant zur See*
Bereiter, Walter	*Obersteuermann*
Berger, Alfred	*Leutnant zur See*
Best, Willi	*Bootsmaat*
Brunner, Alfred	*Mechanikergefreiter*
Carl, Werner	*Matrosenobergefreiter*
Christmann, Wilhelm	*Matrosenobergefreiter*
Eberhardt, Otto	*Funkobergefreiter*
Eickhoff, Friedrich	*Matrosenobergefreiter*
Gärner, Theodor	*Matrosenobergefreiter*
Geiger, Kurt	*Matrosengefreiter*
Glasow, Jürgen	*Kapitänleutnant (Ing)*
Gödicki, Hans	*Maschinenobergefreiter*
Grams, Ernst	*Mechanikermaat*
Grap, Wilhelm	*Maschinenmaat*
Groddeck, Günther	*Mechanikergefreiter*
Hager, Hermann	*Matrosenobergefreiter*
Harms, Ernst	*Obermaschinenmaat*
Heinz, Martin	*Maschinenobergefreiter*
Hirsch, Johannes	*Maschinenmaat*
Hofmann, Hermann	*Maschinenobergefreiter*
Jendrusch, Heinz	*Maschinenmaat*
Jödicke, Hans	*Maschinenobergefreiter*
Johannsen, Hans	*Oberleutnant zur See*
Klinner, Josef	*Obermaschinenmaat*
Kobusch, Karl	*Maschinenmaat*
Korte, Alfred	*Maschinenobergefreiter*
Küneke, Rolf	*Leutnant (Ing)*
Langenbeck, Dr. Gerhard	*Arzt*
Legler, Helmuth	*Matrosenobergefreiter*
Maar, Werner	*Mechanikergefreiter*
Mann, Herbert	*Obermaschinist*
Marczewski, Karl	*Oberbootsmaat*
Markgraf, Christian	*Maschinenobergefreiter*
Martin, Heinrich	*Maschinenobergefreiter*
Matz, Heinz	*Maschinenmaat*
Mauch, Bernhard	*Maschinengefreiter*
Michels, Adolf	*Maschinenobergefreiter*
Michels, Willy	*Maschinenobergefreiter*
Moser, Jakob	*Obermaschinenmaat*
Müller, Heinz	*Funkmaat*
Pawel, Otto	*Matrosengefreiter*
Rameil, Adolf	*Maschinengefreiter*
Reike	*Leutnant*
Rhein, Helmut	*Matrose*
Röhler, Martin	*Obermaschinist*
Rüter, Robert	Funkmeister
Rütten, Albert	*Oberbootsmaat*
Schäle, Klaus	*Korvettenkapitän (Ing)*
Schirmacher, Alfred	*Matrosenobergefreiter*
Schmitz, Karl	*Matrosengefreiter*
Scheewind, Fritz	*Kapitänleutnant*
Schult, Hans	*Oberleutnant zur See*
Schurger, Karl	*Maschinenobergefreiter*
Sutmar, Walter	*Maschinenobergefreiter*
Taphorn, Wilhelm	*Oberleutnant zur See*
Thienelt, Joseph	*Maschinengefreiter*
Thoms, Karl	*Matrosenobergefreiter*
Tillessen, Hans	*Kapitänleutnant*
Wäschenfelder	*Maschinenmaat*
Weigang, Kurt	*Matrosengefreiter*
Wiezoreck, Karl	*Bootsmaat*
Winger, Heinz	*Funkmaat*
Wittenberg, Friedrich	*Oberleutnant zur See*
Würdemann, Erich	*Kapitänleutnant*

Sources, "From the Caribbean to Capetown:" Clay Blair, *Hitler's U-boat War: The Hunters, 1939-1942*, New York: Random House, 1996, 367, 368, 369, 371, 374, 438, 441, 499, 500, 504, 505, 507, 578, 579, 580, 584, 585, 586, 587, 610, 615, 654, 671; Clay Blair, *Hitler's U-boat War: The Hunted, 1942-1945*, New York: Random House, 2000, 392; Rainer Busch and Hans-Joachim Röll, *German U-boat Commanders of World War II*, translated by Geoffrey Brooks, Annapolis, Maryland: Naval Institute Press, 1999, 152, 199, 215, 276; Manfred Dörr, *Die Ritterkreuzträger der U-Boot-Waffe, Band 1: A-J, Band 2: L-Z*, Osnabrück, FRG: Biblio Verlag, 1988, Band 2 – 178, 179, 180, 353, 354, 355; *F.d.U./B.d.U. War Diary, 1-15 July 1943* (PG30327), 35; Axel Niestlé, *German U-boat Losses during World War II*, Annapolis, Maryland: Naval Institute Press, 1998, 124; Jürgen Rohwer, *Axis Submarine Successes 1939-1945*, Annapolis, Maryland: Naval Institute Press, 1983, 68, 78, 80, 81, 85, 92, 94, 95, 96, 97, 99, 98, 100, 101, 102, 103, 104, 106, 118, 120, 123, 126, 264, 265, 267; Melanie Wiggins, *Torpedoes in the Gulf: Galveston and the U-boats, 1942-1943*, College Station, TX: Texas A&M University Press, 1995, 17, 25, 26, 27, 28, 41, 43, 45, 46, 48, 51, 52, 53, 54, 69, 74, 78, 83, 84, 85, 97, 231; www.ubootwaffe.net; www.uboatarchive.net.

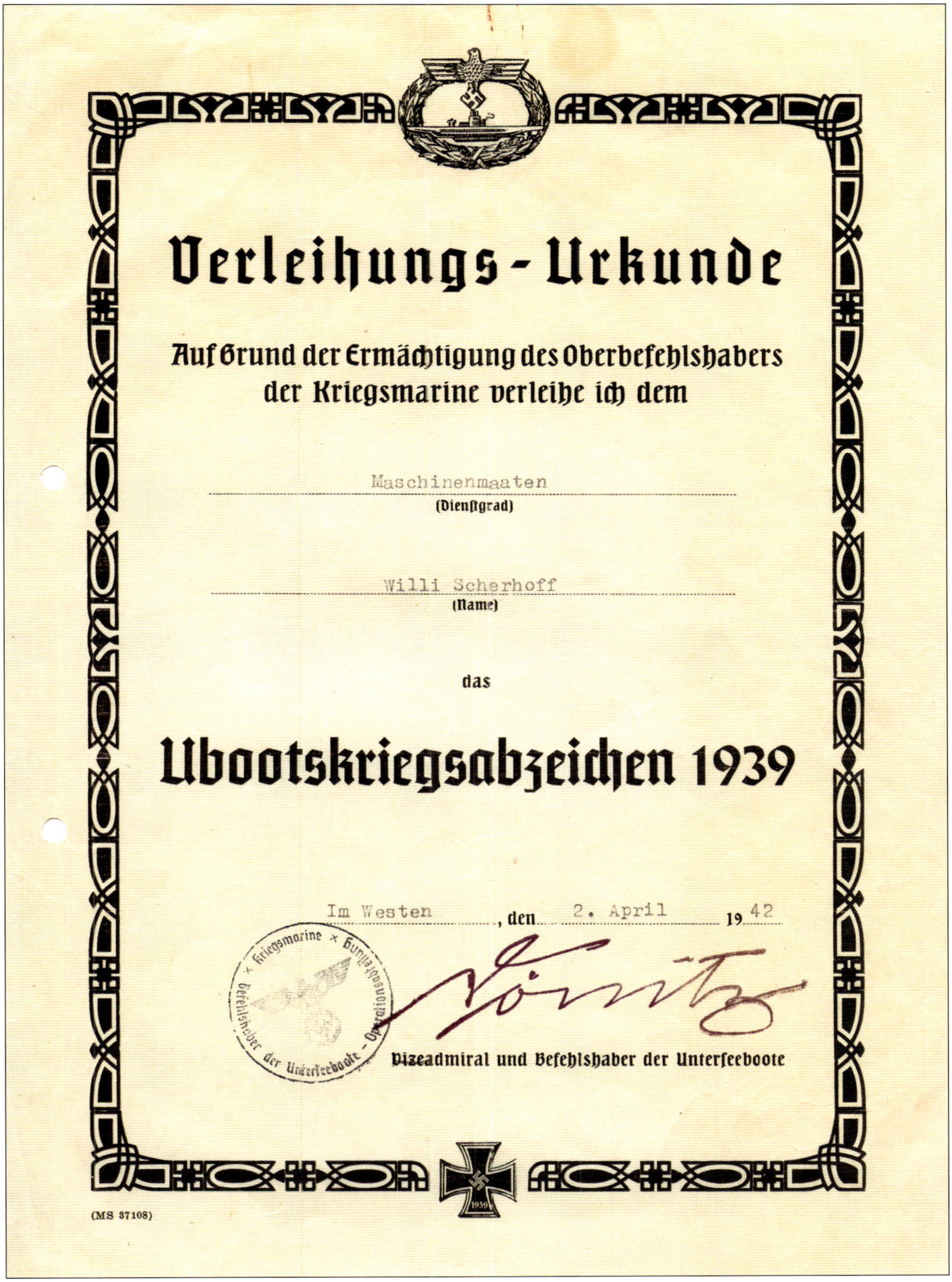

Verleihungs-Urkunde

Auf Grund der Ermächtigung des Oberbefehlshabers der Kriegsmarine verleihe ich dem

Maschinenmaaten
(Dienstgrad)

Willi Scherhoff
(Name)

das

Ubootskriegsabzeichen 1939

Im Westen, den 2. April 1942

Kriegsmarine × Befehlshaber der Unterseeboote – Operationsabteilung

Dönitz

Vizeadmiral und Befehlshaber der Unterseeboote

(MS 37108)

U-boat War Badge award document to Willi Scherhoff, U-504, on April 2, 1942. *The document has a facsimile signature of Vizeadmiral Karl Dönitz; Scherhoff received the award at Lorient, France shortly after the conclusion of the boat's highly successful war patrol off the Florida coast.*

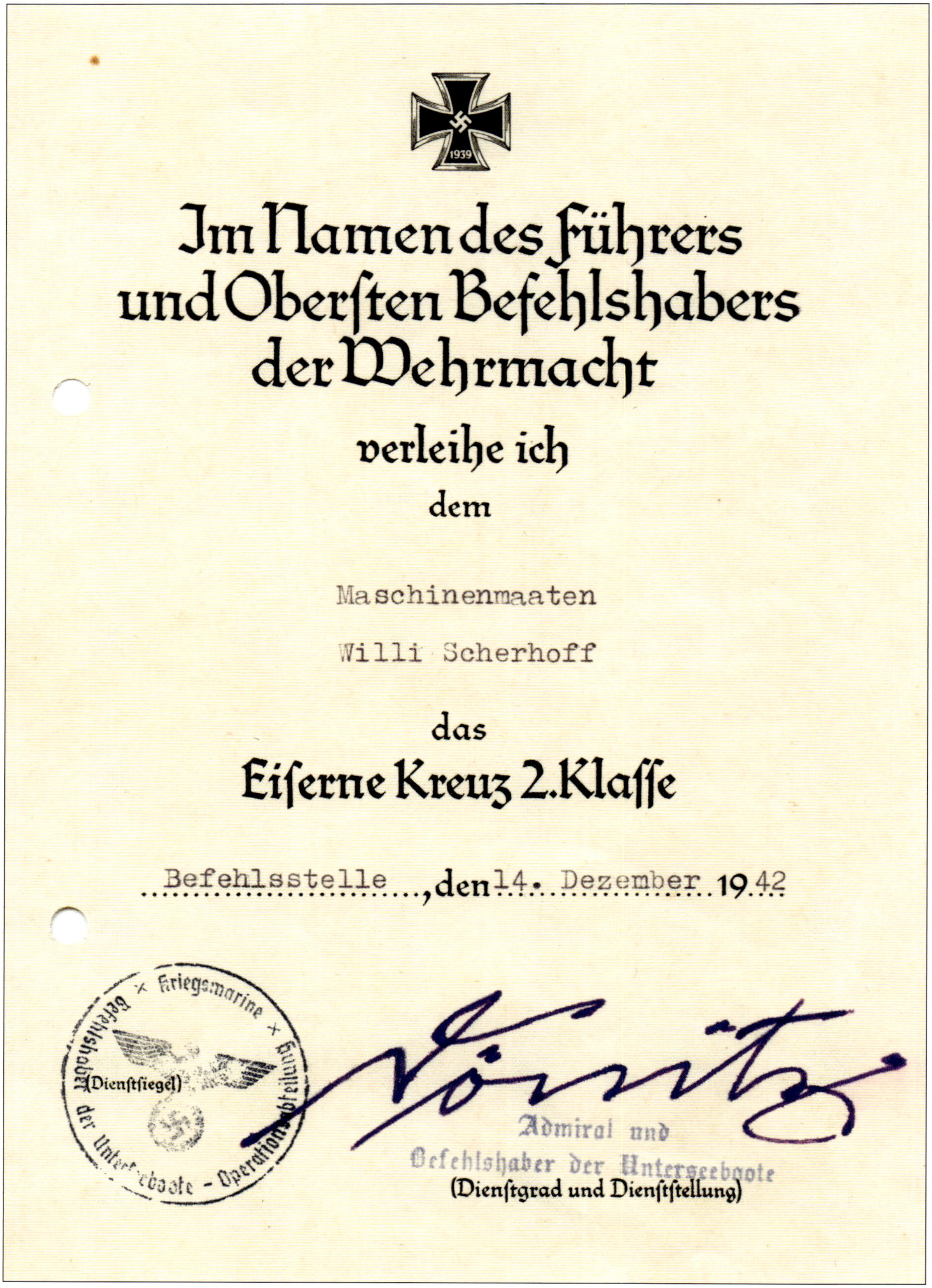

Im Namen des Führers
und Obersten Befehlshabers
der Wehrmacht

verleihe ich

dem

Maschinenmaaten

Willi Scherhoff

das

Eiserne Kreuz 2. Klasse

Befehlsstelle, den 14. Dezember 1942

(Dienstsiegel)

Kriegsmarine + Befehlshaber der Unterseeboote - Operationsabteilung +

Dönitz

Admiral und
Befehlshaber der Unterseeboote
(Dienstgrad und Dienststellung)

Iron Cross 2nd Class award document to Willi Scherhoff, U-504, on December 14, 1942, awarded at Lorient, France shortly after the conclusion of a successful war patrol. *Document has a facsimile signature of Admiral Karl Dönitz.*

Für
Führer, Volk und Vaterland
starb den Heldentod

am 30. Juli 1943

der Obermaschinenmaat

Willi Scherhoff

Im Auftrage
des Oberbefehlshabers der
Kriegsmarine ist darüber diese
Urkunde ausgestellt worden.

Im Westen, den 25. Mai 1944

Kals
Name

Dienststempel

Fregattenkapitän und Flottillenchef
Dienstgrad, Dienststellung

Hero's Death Award Document for Obermaschinenmaat Willi Scherhoff, U-504. *Document is signed by Fregattenkapitän Ernst Kals, the Commander of the 2nd U-boat Flotilla. Kals was a former commander of the U-130 and also a Knight's Cross recipient. The date of the certificate is almost ten months after the U-504 was sunk with all hands.*

Verleihungs-Urkunde.

Auf Grund der Ermächtigung des Oberbefehlshabers der Kriegsmarine verleihe ich dem

Funkobermaat
(Dienstgrad)

R ü t e r , Robert
(Name)

das

Ubootskriegsabzeichen 1939

Im Westen , den 18. Juni 1942

Kriegsmarine
Befehlshaber der Unterseeboote - Operationsabteilung

Dönitz

Admiral und Befehlshaber der Unterseeboote

1939

U-boat War Badge award document to Robert Rüter of the U-506 on June 18, 1942. *The document has a facsimile signature of Admiral Karl Dönitz; Rüter received the award at Lorient, France shortly after the conclusion of the boat's successful war patrol off the American coast in the Gulf of Mexico.*

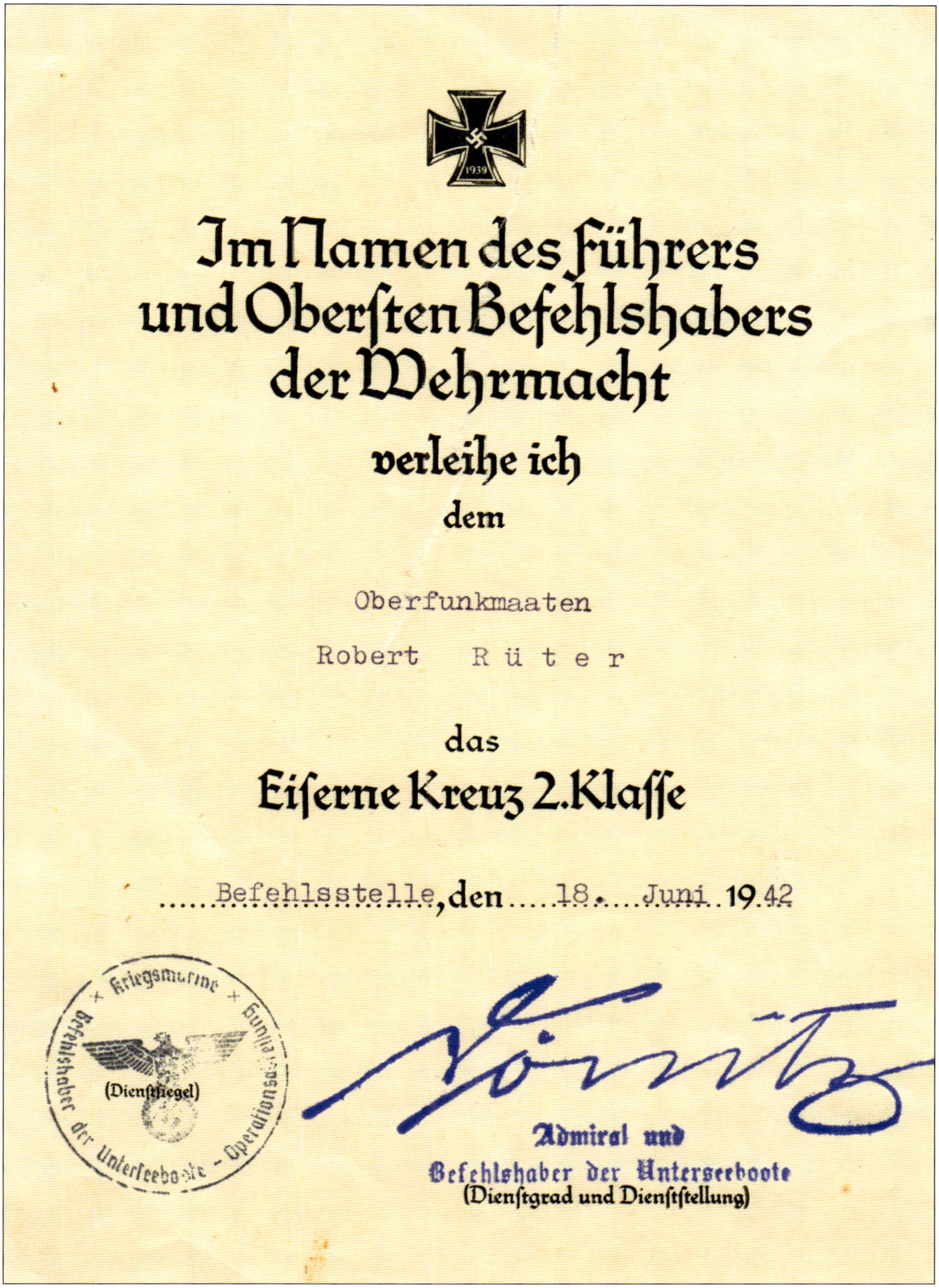

Im Namen des Führers
und Oberſten Befehlshabers
der Wehrmacht

verleihe ich

dem

Oberfunkmaaten

Robert R ü t e r

das

Eiſerne Kreuz 2.Klaſſe

.....Befehlsstelle, den .....18.....Juni..1942

+ Kriegsmarine + Befehlshaber der Unterseeboote – Operationsabteilung
(Dienſtſiegel)

Dönitz

Admiral und
Befehlshaber der Unterseeboote
(Dienſtgrad und Dienſtſtellung)

Iron Cross 2nd Class award document to Robert Rüter of the U-506 on June 18, 1942, awarded at Lorient, France shortly after the conclusion of the same war patrol. *Document has a facsimile signature of Admiral Karl Dönitz.*

Informal marksmanship award document to Robert Rüter. *Competition was on July 29, 1936 at Flensburg-Mürwik in the 150-meter prone position; it is signed by his company commander.*

Photo of Matrosengefreiter Paul Impertro of the U-502. *Photo taken at Ludwigshafen, possibly Impertro's hometown.*

Ach, es ist ja kaum zu fassen,
Daß Du nie mehr kehrst zurück.
So jung mußt Du Dein Leben lassen,
Zerstört ist unser aller Glück.
Ein jeder, der Dich hat gekannt
Und auch Dein treues Herz,
Der drückt uns nur noch stumm die Hand,
In diesem tiefen Schmerz.
Du gutes Herz, ruh' still in Frieden,
Ewig beweint von Deinen Lieben.
Fern der Heimat seiner Lieben,
Ruht er sanft in ewigem Frieden.

Zum ewigen Andenken an unseren lieben, unvergeßlichen Sohn, Bruder, Schwager und Onkel

Paul Impertro Matr.-Obergefr.

geboren am 17. Juli 1921

von Feindfahrt nicht zurückgekehrt am 8. Juli 1942.

Death Announcement for Matrosengefreiter Paul Impertro announcing he did not return from a war patrol on July 8, 1942. *The U-502 was sunk with all hands on July 5.*

U-boat War Badge belonging to Matrosengefreiter Paul Impertro. *U-boat men packed their personnel belongings and left them ashore when they departed on combat missions. These packets were forwarded to next of kin if the sailor was later killed in action or missing. Badge was manufactured by the Schwerin firm of Berlin. This is an early-war high-quality model of tombak; later models were made of zinc. Schwerin badges sometimes had no maker mark.*

Hitler Youth Proficiency Badge in Silver belonging to Matrosengefreiter Paul Impertro.

U-boar War Badge: owner unknown. *Badge was produced by the firm of Funcke & Brüninghaus of Lüdenscheid. Badge was made of zinc and has the maker's mark L/56.*

CHAPTER THIRTEEN

"EAGLE EYE" U-73 AUGUST 1942

Attempting to increase the U-boat force as war clouds began to gather over Europe, the *Kriegsmarine* ordered the construction of the *U-73* on June 2, 1938; construction workers at the Vulkan Vegesack Werft shipyard at Bremen laid her keel on November 5, 1939. Construction went according to schedule and the *U-73* was launched on July 27, 1940. After preliminary trials she was commissioned on September 30, 1940. From that date until January 1941, she underwent various training and work-up exercises before joining the 7th U-boat Flotilla at Kiel. However, during this training the *U-73* was accidentally rammed by the *U-97* severely damaging the outer hull, and the *U-73* was forced to spend several weeks at Danzig undergoing repairs.

> *Dönitz's Crews*
> ***Korvettenkapitän* Helmut Rosenbaum**
> Born on May 11, 1913 at Döblen/Leipzig.
> Served as the commander of the *U-73* and the 30th U-boat Flotilla.
> Awarded the Iron Cross 2nd Class on April 16, 1940; awarded the U-boat War Badge on March 4, 1941; awarded the Iron Cross 1st Class on April 25, 1941; awarded the Knight's Cross August 12, 1942.
> Spent 270 days at sea on U-boat war patrols.
> Killed in an air crash on May 10, 1944 in Romania.

The first commander of the *U-73* was twenty-seven year old Helmut Rosenbaum. The son of a teacher, Rosenbaum was born in Döbeln near Leipzig on May 11, 1913. After graduating primary school, he joined the *Reichsmarine* at age nineteen as a sea cadet. After serving several years as an enlisted man, he was commissioned a *Leutnant zur See* on January 1, 1936; his pre-commissioning training included a world cruise on the German light cruiser *Köln* that stopped in Tsingtau, China. At the port visit, Rosenbaum took a tour of the British aircraft carrier *HMS Eagle*, one of the first true aircraft carriers to be commissioned in any navy.

Thirteen months later Rosenbaum began U-boat training, and two months later joined the U-boat Flotilla *Salzwedel*. He was promoted to *Oberleutnant zur See* on September 15, 1937. One of the well-trained pre-war officers, he served as a watch officer on the *U-35* and *U-27*. From November 1938 to March 1939, Rosenbaum served as the 1st Watch Officer of the *U-26* in Spanish waters during the Spanish Civil War. On March 17, 1939 Rosenbaum assumed command of the *U-2* and commanded her until July 31, 1940. After a promotion to *Kapitänleutnant* on January 24, 1940, during March and April 1940, he took his U-boat on two war patrols but sank no enemy ships. Then he transferred to the almost-finished *U-73* and brought her into the force.

The *U-73* departed Helgoland for her first war patrol on February 8, 1941 for a patrol west of the British Isles. On February 24, 1941 Rosenbaum spotted the 4,260-ton freighter *Waynegate* carrying 6,200 tons of coal from Newport, Wales to Freetown, Sierra Leone as part of convoy OB-288, and torpedoed her at 4:19 a.m. south of Iceland. The *U-73* arrived at Lorient, France on March 2, 1941.

On March 25, 1941 Rosenbaum left Lorient bound for southwest of Ireland for his second war patrol with the *U-73* and on April 3, 1941 he struck paydirt southwest of Iceland when he caught up to convoy SC-26. At 3:28 a.m. the U-boat torpedoed and sank the British 4,313-ton freighter *Alderpool*, carrying 7,200 tons of wheat from New York for Hull, England. At 5:08 a.m. the *U-73* struck again, sinking the British 5,724-ton steam freighter *Westpool* carrying 7,144 tons of scrap iron from Baltimore to Leith, Scotland; thirty-five crewmen went down with her. Four minutes later, at 5:12 a.m., Rosenbaum torpedoed the Belgian 5,409-ton *Indier*. The freighter, bound from Halifax, Nova Scotia to Glasgow, Scotland, took 6,300 tons of steel and forty-two crewmen to the bottom with her when she sank. At 5:32 a.m. Rosenbaum completed the day's carnage by sinking the British 6,895-ton tanker *British Viscount*, carrying 9,500 tons of fuel oil from Curacao to Scapa Flow; twenty-eight men perished when the tanker exploded in flames.

The *U-73* then went until April 20 without another kill, but at 3:52 a.m. that morning Rosenbaum sank the British 8,570-ton *Empire Endurance* destroying much general cargo, as well as two anti-submarine motor launches lashed to her deck as cargo, and killing sixty-five of her crew. The *Empire Endurance* was not unknown to the German Navy; during the invasion of Norway, she was the German transport *Alster* but was captured by the British destroyer *HMS Icarus* and converted for use by the Royal Navy. The *U-73* arrived at St. Nazaire on April 24, 1941 after this successful patrol.

The *U-73* then went through a dry spell. Over the next eight months she made four war patrols with no results as follows:

• May 20, 1941 – June 24, 1941: Her initial mission on the patrol was to support the battleship *Bismarck* by setting an ambush for British naval forces. Rosenbaum closed and was able to see the giant battleship under attack by British destroyers in her final moments, but he could not align a torpedo shot on the enemy. Later, as part of *Wolf Pack Group West* during an unsuccessful attack of a steamer, an enemy destroyer forced the U-boat to dive and damaged her with depth charges.
• July 29, 1941 – August 2, 1941: A diesel engine problem forced the *U-73* back to port.
• August 7, 1941 – September 7, 1941: On August 28 an Iceland-based enemy aircraft depth-charged the *U-73* so severely she had to abort the patrol and return to France.
• October 11, 1941 – November 11, 1941: Southeast of Greenland.

Then Rosenbaum received orders to take his boat through the dangerous Straits of Gibraltar. The *U-73* departed St. Nazaire for this dangerous mission on January 4, 1942, made the passage without incident and arrived at La Spezia, Italy on February 12, 1942; during the trip, on February 3, he fired a spread of torpedoes at an enemy destroyer and heard two subsequent explosions and claimed a victory, but this kill has never been confirmed. Rosenbaum then began to prowl the Mediterranean as part of the 29th U-boat Flotilla. On March 16, 1942 the *U-73* departed La Spezia to interdict British traffic between Alexandria and Malta, but the enemy spotted her not long after. On March 22, 1942, a Bristol Beaufort bomber attacked the U-boat with four bombs, inflicting heavy damage on the U-boat's stern and forcing the U-boat to the surface. Unable to dive, four days later the *U-73* limped into La Spezia for repairs.

Because of damage to her pressure hull and required modifications to her conning tower, she remained in port until August 4, a critical moment in the fight in the Mediterranean theater. Field Marshal Erwin Rommel was on the march into Egypt, with only a tenuous supply line keeping him in check. British air and sea forces based at the island of Malta were barely able to sink enough German and Italian supply ships crossing the Med to keep the issue in doubt, but the *Luftwaffe* began a long-term attack on the island's facilities. To sustain the island, major convoy operations had to be mounted at all costs; the two-pronged effort to resupply Malta during June 1942, known as "Operation Harpoon" [from Gibraltar] and "Operation Vigorous" [from Alexandria, Egypt]) was unsuccessful, with only two merchant ships reaching Malta. The British Admiralty planned a follow-up operation, "Operation Pedestal" for August – there would be no half-measures with two battleships and three aircraft carriers to assist in escorting fourteen fast supply ships from England to resupply Malta.

One of the aircraft carriers was the old *HMS Eagle* that Helmut Rosenbaum visited many years before in China.

On August 10, 1942 British forces bound for Malta passed through the Straits of Gibraltar with British naval leaders erroneously believing that the Germans were unaware of the transit because of the dense fog in the area. They were mistaken; a German agent on the Spanish coast observed the convoy. The next day, seventy miles south of Cape Salinas, Majorca (the Balearic Islands) the U-boat's hydrophone operator detected advancing propeller noises and Helmut Rosenbaum's "eagle eye" subsequently spotted the *HMS Eagle* through the periscope at 11:00 a.m. The aircraft carrier was surrounded by a screen of seven destroyers, was making thirteen knots and was on a zigzag course to make any submarine attack against her more difficult. Through careful maneuvering, Rosenbaum slipped through the defenses undetected closing to within 500 yards of the carrier and at 1:15 p.m. fired a spread of four torpedoes at his target.

Thirty-two seconds later the *HMS Eagle* shuddered with the first of four torpedo hits; eight minutes later, after three boiler rooms flooded and numerous bulkheads collapsed, she sank taking 161 of her crew with her. The *U-73* now had to evade counterattack, which was made more difficult by ongoing mechanical difficulties in the boat including an oil leak, unserviceable direction-finding antenna, a leaking exhaust cut-out, a faulty bilge pump and leaks in the periscope. Undetected, all available crewmen raced to the forward torpedo room to make the boat bow-heavy and the *U-73* dove very deep to 500 feet, remained silent for three hours, slipped away (the U-boat's leaking oil mingled with the oil from the sunken ship masking the Rosenbaum's malady) without damage and reported the success. The following day German radio presented a special report of the sinking and announced that Helmut Rosenbaum had been awarded the Knight's Cross. Rosenbaum's attack was decisive; with less air protection, only five of the fourteen merchant ships of the convoy reached Malta, but the island hung on to remain a thorn in Rommel's side.

A few days later Rosenbaum found the damaged British cruiser *HMS Nigeria*, but was unable to line up a shot. The *U-73* arrived back at La Spezia on September 5, 1942. Helmut Rosenbaum received his Knight's Cross on the deck of the *U-73* after she docked at the quay; he would subsequently receive the Italian Bravery Medal in Silver for the action as well. Rosenbaum then relinquished command of the *U-73*; he had led the U-boat on ten war patrols. He then returned home to Germany for a large reception at Neustadt/Holstein, where his wife and two small daughters, Heidemarie and Ingetraut, were living during the war. On return to the front, he assumed command of the 30th U-boat Flotilla based at Constanza, Romania.

For the next eighteen months Rosenbaum commanded the flotilla, which had the mission to interdict Soviet sea traffic in the Black Sea. In early May 1944 he arranged to fly back to Germany to spend his birthday, May 11, with his family. On May 9 at Mamia, Romania, his men celebrated his birthday two days early; the following morning Rosenbaum boarded a Ju 52 of the Navy's courier squadron for the flight back to Germany. The aircraft refueled at Bucharest and later at Arad. After taking off from Arad, the pilot made for Polet, Romania but four miles northwest of the town the aircraft crashed into a fog-shrouded mountain. Seven men survived; ten died including Helmut Rosenbaum. Two days later, Rosenbaum, and the five other German Navy personnel killed when the flight crashed, were buried at the Orsova German military cemetery twelve miles south of the crash site.

Meanwhile, after Rosenbaum's departure, the *U-73*, under her new commander *Oberleutnant zur See* Horst Deckert, continued in the fight and left La Spezia on October 20, 1942 on her next war patrol. Deckert, who was born on October 11, 1918 in Hannover, was an old hand on the *U-73*, having served as the 2nd Watch Officer on the U-boat from September 1940 to July 1941; he was 1st Watch Officer during the attack on the *HMS Eagle*. For several weeks the boat was unable to successfully find a target, until November 14, 1942. Early that morning Decker torpedoed and damaged the British 7,453-ton *Lalande*, in ballast heading from Algiers to Gibraltar. Seven men went missing but the ship survived the attack. The *U-73* returned to La Spezia on November 19.

With the Allies successfully ashore in North Africa, the *U-73* had a short turn-around time in port and departed La Spezia on December 1. The patrol was a short one; on December 5, an enemy aircraft attacked the boat damaging her so badly that Decker had to return to base on December 8.

Again dockworkers worked around the clock to repair the *U-73* and on December 22, 1942 she departed La Spezia for her next war patrol. On December 27, enemy aircraft struck again; a British Hudson from the 500th Squadron attacked the boat but the U-boat's flak gunners shot down the aircraft. At 2:48 p.m. on January 1, 1943, Decker's luck changed and off the Algerian coast, at a range of only 250 meters, he sent a torpedo from the stern tube into the American 7,176-ton *Arthur Middleton*, from convoy UGS-3. The freighter, bound from New York for Oran, Algeria with a load of explosives and 300 bags of mail (as well as the *USS LCT-21* [255 tons] on her deck) exploded and her entire crew of sixty-six men were lost. The *U-73* escaped the area and later landed French-speaking agents near Oran, but at 1:00 a.m. on January 10, 1943 an enemy aircraft attacked the boat but caused no damage. Two days later on January 13 the *U-73* returned to La Spezia.

The *U-73* remained in port for several months. She finally departed La Spezia on June 12, 1943. Action came quickly; at 9:18 p.m. on June 14 an enemy aircraft attacked the boat, but Deckert was able to continue his mission. On June 21, 1943 at 9:30 a.m. he torpedoed and sank the British 1,598-ton *Brinkburn*, sailing with convoy TE-22 from Gibraltar to Philippeville, Algeria with 2,500 tons of government stores – including 800 tons of ammunition; twenty-two crewmen went down with the ship. Six days later he torpedoed and damaged the British 8,299-ton Royal Navy tanker *Abbeydale*, a member of convoy XTG-2, but the ship did not sink. Convoy escorts then located the U-boat and heavily depth-charged her, forcing Deckert to seek the nearest friendly base. The *U-73* arrived at Toulon, France on July 1, 1943.

On August 2, 1943 the *U-73* went to sea again, departing Toulon still under the command of Horst Deckert. On August 11 off the coast of Sicily, Deckert reported firing two torpedoes at the American light cruiser *USS Philadelphia* and claiming two hits. The *U-73* returned to Toulon on August 29. On October 5, Deckert again led her on patrol; the U-boat landed another special agent on the Algerian coast. The *U-73* returned to Toulon on October 30; as she was just outside the harbor, the British submarine *HM Submarine Ultimatum* spotted the U-boat and fired a torpedo at her, but the torpedo missed.

The *U-73* left Toulon on her final mission on December 4, 1943. During an attack on a convoy on December 13, an enemy destroyer rammed the U-boat damaging a flak gun, but Deckert continued his mission. On December 16, the *U-73* fired a three-torpedo fan and damaged the American 7,176-ton *John S Copley*, part of convoy GUS-24; she managed to limp into port. But retribution came immediately in the form of a hunter-killer group that left the harbor at Mers-el-Kébir, Algeria with the destroyers *USS Woolsey* and *USS Trippe*. The *USS Woolsey* quickly got a good sonar contact and roared in with a depth charge attack. The depth charges cracked the U-boat's pressure hull, causing forward flooding that forced the *U-73* to surface; further gunfire from both destroyers sank the U-boat with sixteen of her crew; thirty-four men survived, including Horst Deckert; the survivors were taken to North Africa and spent the rest of the conflict as prisoners of war.

Known Crewmembers for the U-73

Ahrlich, Karl-Heinz	*Maschinenobergefreiter*
Altmann, Hans-Joachim	*Oberleutnant zur See*
Baum, Heinz	*Maschinenmaat*
Bentin, Werner	*Bootsmaat*
Bentzien, Heinz	*Kapitänleutnant*
Bernt, Karl	*Oberfunkmaat*
Blasche, Kurt	*Funkgefreiter*
Borgmann, Wilhelm	*Obersteuermann*
Böttger, August	*Obermaschinist*
Braune, Erich	*Matrosengefreiter*
Brömmert, Karl	*Oberbootsmaat*
Brüggemann, Alfred	*Maschinenmaat*
Chwoika, Josef	*Maschinenobergefreiter*
Deckert, Horst	*Kapitänleutnant*
Deerberg, Fritz	*Obersteuermann*
Essmann, Theodor	*Funkgefreiter*
Feist, Erhard	*Mechanikergefreiter*
Fenkner, Dr. Max	*Arzt*
Fickeler, Hans	*Maschinenmaat*
Flemming, Fritz	*Matrose*
Freudenthal, Heinz	*Maschinenobergefreiter*
Fritz, Detlef	*Oberleutnant zur See*
Gaedecke, Rudolf	*Maschinenobergefreiter*
Geider, Horst	*Oberleutnant zur See*
Gerlach, Horst	*Bootsmaat*
Glamm, Erwin	*Maschinenobergefreiter*
Gluch, Richard	*Mechanikermaat*
Glück, Erich	*Matrosenobergefreiter*
Götz, Manfred	*Matrose*
Härtling, Heinz	*Maschinengefreiter*
Hartmann, Alfred	*Oberleutnant zur See*
Haskamp, Klemens	*Maschinenmaat*
Heinicke, Hans-Dieter	*Kapitänleutnant*
Herholt, Rudolf	*Bootsmaat*
Heyer, Herbert	*Matrose*
Hölscher, Heinrich	*Obermechanikermaat*
Keller, Karl	*Stabsobermaschinist*
Kinkele, Kurt	*Leutnant zur See*
Kirscht, Erich	*Mechanikergefreiter*
Kloos, Herbert	*Maschinenobergefreiter*
Klose, Kurt	*Matrosenobergefreiter*
Kötter, Heinrich	
Krajer, Fritz	*Obermaschinist*
Krämer, Helmut	*Obermaschinist*
Krieg, Siegfried	*Obermaschinist*
Kruchen, Walter	*Oberleutnant (Ing)*
Kühn, Herbert	*Oberleutnant zur See*
Lepke, Fritz	*Obermaschinist*
Lindemann, Heinz	*Matrose*
Lippert, Ehrenfried	*Oberleutnant (Ing)*
Losch, Walter	*Obermaschinenmaat*
Matejka, Heinz	*Mechaniker*
Mehlich, Walter	*Obermaschinenmaat*
Möller, Wilhelm	*Oberleutnant (Ing)*
Morawietz, Wilhelm	*Matrosengefreiter*
Neu, Gerhard	*Maschinengefreiter*
Nissen, Ude	*Matrose*
Peters, Theo	*Maschinenobergefreiter*
Pohl, Gerhard	*Maschinenobergefreiter*
Porges, Walter	*Maschinenmaat*
Prehn, Otto	*Matrosenobergefreiter*
Pütz, Hans-Willi	*Matrose*
Rachel, Gerhard	*Funkmaat*
Rahe, Heinz	*Kapitänleutnant*
Röpke, Werner	*Mechanikergefreiter*
Rosenbaum, Helmut	*Kapitänleutnant*
Ruf, Hans	*Obermaschinenmaat*

Crew of the U-73. *This and the other photos in this section are from a photo album kept by one of Knight's Cross winner Kapitänleutnant Helmut Rosenbaum's daughters after the conflict.*

Ruf, Konrad	*Mechanikergefreiter*
Schaumlöffel, Hans	*Oberleutnant (Ing)*
Scheffler, Werner	*Maschinengefreiter*
Scheibe, Wilhelm	*Maschinenobergefreiter*
Schmidt, Erich	*Obermaschinist*
Schmidt, Günter	*Oberbootsmaat*
Schmiteckert, Hans	
Schuck, Karl	*Obersteuermann*
Schwertl, Simon	*Maschinengefreiter*
Selbach, Joachim	*Funkmaat*
Sickel, Herbert	*Kapitänleutnant*
Spieler, Helmut	*Bootsmann*
Stadler, Fritz	*Maschinenobergefreiter*
Staeger, Josef	*Funkobergefreiter*
Ulber, Max	*Oberleutnant zur See*
Waldmann, Heinrich	*Matrosenobergefreiter*
Wegener, Helmut	*Matrosenobergefreiter*
Wehling, Kurt	*Matrosenobergefreiter*
Weiser, Emil	*Matrosenobergefreiter*
Wieting, Dietrich	*Oberleutnant zur See*
Ziegner, Heinrich	*Matrosenobergefreiter*
Zimmermann, Horst	*Maschinenobergefreiter*
Zeietasch, Willy	*Mechanikermaat*
Zwoika, Joseph	*Maschinenobergefreiter*

Sources, "Eagle Eye:" Chris Bishop, *Kriegsmarine U-boats 1939-45*, London: Amber Books, 2006, 77, 78, 142, 143, 144, 146; Clay Blair, *Hitler's U-boat War: The Hunters, 1939-1942*, New York: Random House, 1996, 236; 264, 288, 291, 348, 437, 488, 554, 645, 650, 651; Clay Blair, *Hitler's U-boat War: The Hunted, 1942-1945*, New York: Modern Library, 2000, 95, 96, 97, 98, 99, 102, 209, 377, 455, 456, 457; Rainer Busch and Hans-Joachim Röll, *German U-boat Commanders of World War II*, translated by Geoffrey Brooks, Annapolis, Maryland: Naval Institute Press, 1999, 52, 214; Manfred Dörr, *Die Ritterkreuzträger der U-Boot-Waffe, Band 1: A-J, Band 2: L-Z*, Osnabrück, FRG: Biblio Verlag, 1988, Band 2 – 211, 212, 213; Geoffrey Jones, *U-boat Aces*, Cerberus Publishing, Bristol, England, 2005, 92-104; Franz Kurowski, *Knight's Cross Holders of the U-Boat Service*, Atglen, PA: Schiffer Publishing, 1995, 215; Jürgen Rohwer, *Axis Submarine Successes 1939-1945*, Annapolis, Maryland: Naval Institute Press, 1983, 44, 48, 49, 55, 230, 235, 236, 238, 241, 246, 247, 248, 251, 252, 253; www.ubootwaffe.net; www.uboatarchive.net;

Another view of the crew of the U-73. *Helmut Rosenbaum is in the white cap on the left.*

View through a hatch into the control room of the U-73. *Men's uniforms indicate the photo was probably taken in the Mediterranean in 1942.*

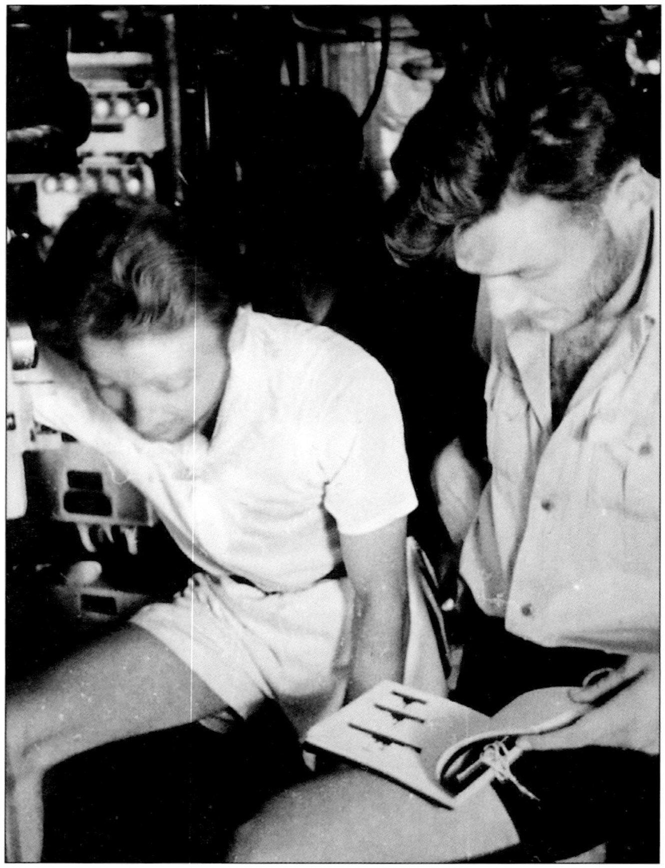

Two crewmen review a ship recognition manual inside the U-73.

Helmut Rosenbaum chats with Luftwaffe trooper. *Given Rosenbaum's officer grade insignia of Oberleutnant zur See, this photo is on the U-2, his first command.*

Helmut Rosenbaum on the bridge of his U-boat.

Formal portrait of Kapitänleutnant Helmut Rosenbaum. *Note U-boat War Badge, Iron Cross 2nd Class ribbon and Iron Cross 1st Class, all of which indicate that the photo was taken between May 1941 and August 1942. Just visible on the left is the Spanish Cross won by Rosenbaum for service in Spanish waters in 1938 while on the U-26.*

Formal close-up photo of Helmut Rosenbaum.

The U-73, probably at her commissioning ceremony on October 31, 1940.

Dignitaries visit the U-73, probably right after her commissioning ceremony.

Helmut Rosenbaum on the reviewing stand at the commissioning ceremony. *Note Spanish Cross on left breast.*

Helmut Rosenbaum in discussions with high-ranking officials.

Four U-boat men drink a toast at St. Nazaire, October 11, 1941. *From left to right are: Gerhard Bigalk (U-751), 7th U-Boat Flotilla Chief Engineer Sattler, Helmut Rosenbaum (U-73) wearing turtleneck sweater under jacket, and Ernst Mengersen (U-101). Bigalk, Rosenbaum and Mengersen would all win the Knight's Cross.*

Portrait of Helmut Rosenbaum about the time of the commissioning of the U-73.

Four U-boat men (in white caps) share a smoke at St. Nazaire, October 11, 1941. *From left to right are 7th U-Boat Flotilla Chief Engineer Sattler, Helmut Rosenbaum (U-73) wearing turtle neck sweater under jacket, Ernst Mengersen (U-101) and Heinrich Schonder (U-77).*

Three U-boat men share a glass of wine. *Gerhard Bigalk is in the middle; 7th U-Boat Flotilla Chief Engineer Sattler is on the right.*

Helmut Rosenbaum with two fellow officers.

Kapitänleutnant Helmut Rosenbaum with two Oberleutnant zur See. *They may be his watch officers assigned to the U-73.*

Helmut Rosenbaum on the bridge of the U-73, St. Nazaire, summer 1941. *Conning tower insignia is the city heraldry of Duisburg, the sponsor-city for the boat.*

Crewmen stand on the deck of the U-73.

Overall view of the conning tower on the U-73, St. Nazaire, summer 1941. *City of Duisburg heraldry is on the side of the boat. In front is a rose tree (in German, Rosenbaum, which is the same name as her commander.) Snorting bull faintly visible to the rear is the insignia of the 7th U-boat Flotilla at St Nazaire.*

A pensive Rosenbaum on the bridge of the U-73.

Helmut Rosenbaum presents his command in formation. *Photo probably taken in conjunction with the presentation of his Knight's Cross at La Spezia in September 1942.*

Helmut Rosenbaum greeting some fellow officers at the ceremony.

Rosenbaum salutes his fellow officers in formation.

Rosenbaum shakes hands with fellow officers.

Children in attendance seem in awe of their latest U-boat hero.

Helmut Rosenbaum troops the line. *Note young German girls in uniform.*

Rosenbaum and fellow officer adjust his uniform.

Helmut Rosenbaum about to receive a large bouquet of flowers from a Hitler Youth.

Helmut Rosenbaum is greeted by children with bouquets of flowers.

Helmut Rosenbaum helping his young daughter, Heidemarie, into a ceremonial carriage after receiving the Knight's Cross. *Reception occurred in his hometown of Neustadt/Holstein.*

Navy men look on as Helmut Rosenbaum gets ready to hoist his young daughter into the carriage.

Helmut Rosenbaum and wife adjust the many bunches of flowers in the carriage.

A happy Kapitänleutnant Helmut Rosenbaum and wife.

The carriage in procession.

Arriving at their quarters with the young Rosenbaums.

Helmut Rosenbaum balancing his daughter and flowers.

Heidemarie apparently wants to go on another ride in the carriage.

Rosenbaum's daughter points down the street as honor guard looks on.

Helmut Rosenbaum holding daughter meets other children.

Rosenbaum comforts his daughter during the meeting with children.

Smiling Helmut Rosenbaum receives more flowers.

Now his daughter must hold flowers as well.

Rosenbaum wonders how many more flowers are coming his way.

The U-boat commander has everything in balance.

Helmut Rosenbaum starts to walk to his quarters before he gets more flowers.

Children greet the U-boat hero and his family. *It appears that he and Frau Rosenbaum have two daughters.*

Helmut Rosenbaum holds his daughter in the window to greet well-wishers.

Crowds gather to welcome the Rosenbaums. *Vehicle in the photo has an armed forces license plate.*

Helmut Rosenbaum greets the crowd from the window.

Helmut and Frau Rosenbaum, with a daughter, say hello to the fans on the street.

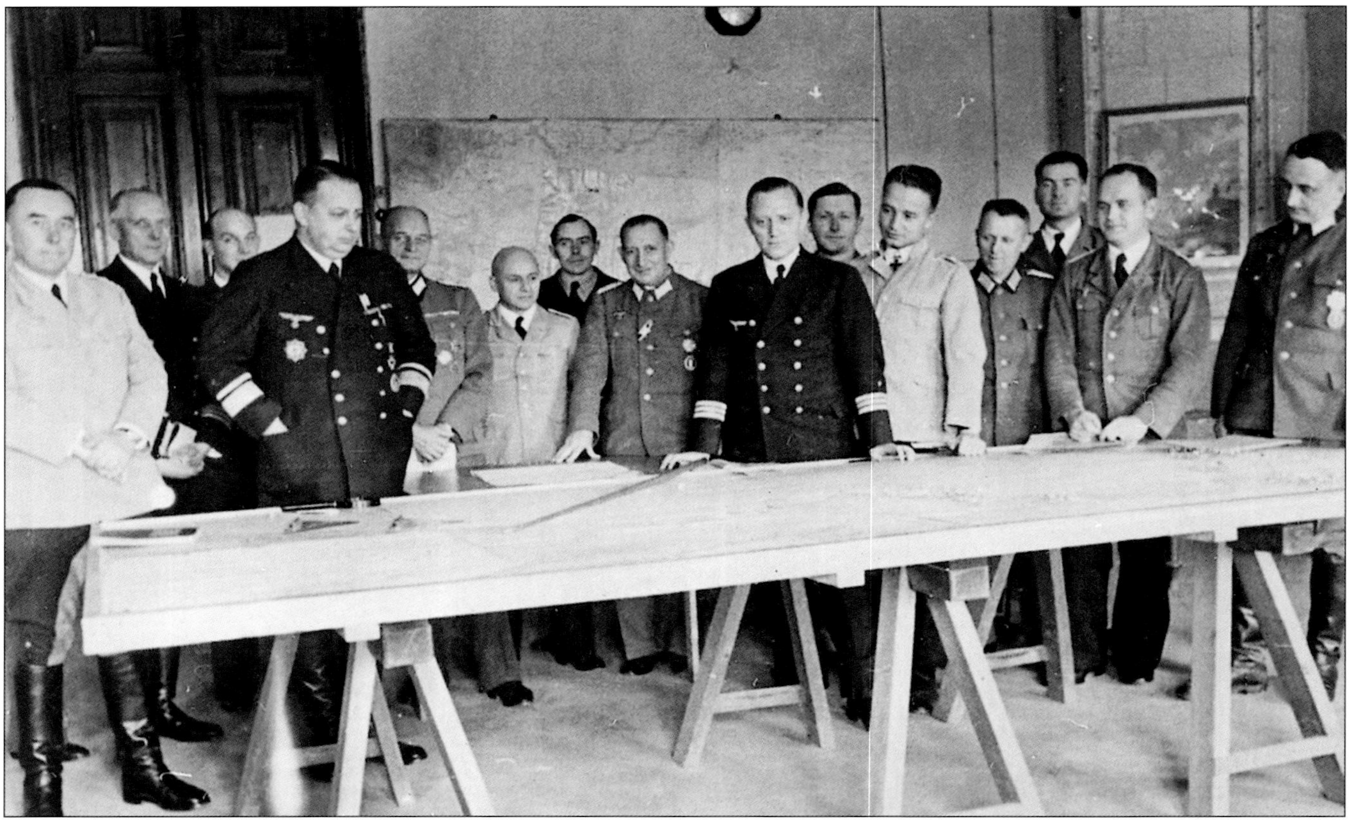

Helmut Rosenbaum (fifth from right) reviews plans with other Navy officials. Admiral with hand in pocket and German Cross in Gold is Konteradmiral Helmuth Brinkmann, Commanding Admiral Black Sea. Photo was taken when Rosenbaum was commander of the 30th U-boat Flotilla in the Black Sea.

Officers examine large photographs with Konteradmiral Brinkmann. *Helmut Rosenbaum is on the far right.*

Brinkmann gets close with a magnifying glass. *Rosenbaum is on the right.*

Brinkmann looking at more details. *Rosenbaum is to his rear.*

The admiral needs one last look. *Note sew-on version of his German Cross in Gold.*

Helmut Rosenbaum, as the 30th U-boat Flotilla commander, boards a U-boat in his command.

Rosenbaum brings a gift of a bottle of champagne on his visit.

Rosenbaum on the left in sunglasses listens to the U-boat commander.

Helmut Rosenbaum on right with another officer in tropical uniform.

U-boat commander on left and Helmut Rosenbaum share an interesting comment. *Note decoration on the white neck-scarf of the commander.*

Helmut Rosenbaum on a launch with another with another officer who appears to have won his Iron Cross 1st Class in World War I.

Helmut Rosenbaum tries his hand at photography.

Helmut Rosenbaum on the right with a fellow officer in Romania.

Clergy read the Gospel at Helmut Rosenbaum's funeral, May 1944. *The location is Orsova in western Romania along the Danube River; this was twelve miles away from where Rosenbaum's flight crashed.*

Fellow officer pay respect at Helmut Rosenbaum's funeral. *Officer on the right wears the Destroyer Badge.*

The priest reading a passage over the flower-draped coffin at Helmut Rosenbaum's funeral.

A Fregattenkapitän makes remarks at Helmut Rosenbaum's funeral.

The Fregattenkapitän adjusts one of the funeral wreaths.

Officer honor guard salute Helmut Rosenbaum's casket.

***An Oberleutnant zur See adjusts the banner on the honor wreath at Helmut Rosenbaum's funeral.** It reads in part – "Our Flotilla Commander."*

Five men united in death; Helmut Rosenbaum's cross is on the left. *Four other men can be identified as: Franz Heger, born March 26, 1901 in Eger; Otto Diederichs, born May 18, 1893 in Wuppertal-Barmen; Otto Schörpf, born December 17, 1899 in Beeskow; and Dr. Werner Drüner, born May 25, 1911 in Gaddersbaum.*

The latest casualties of war among many others.

A final look at Helmut Rosenbaum's last resting place.

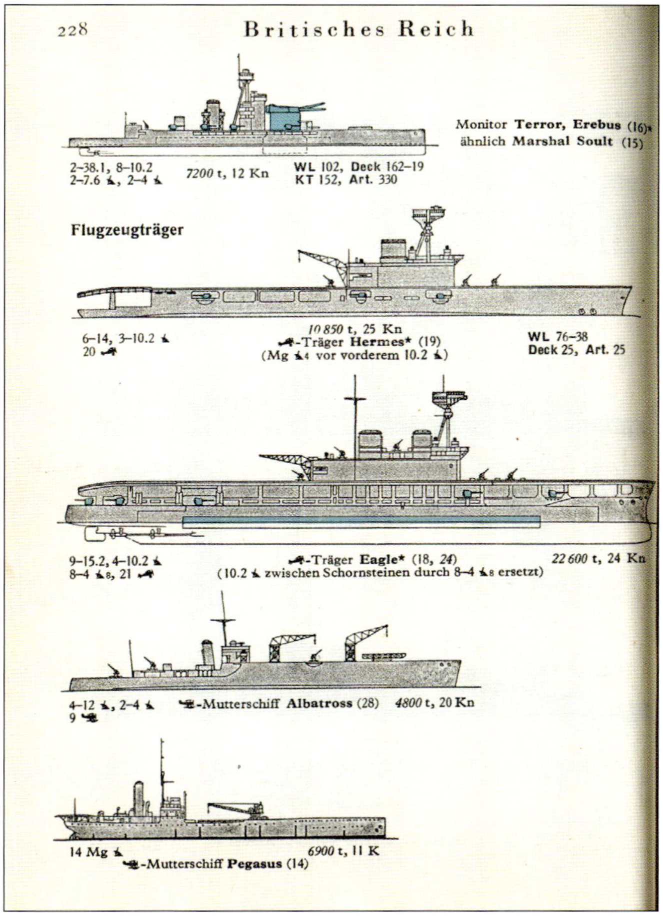

228 **Britisches Reich**

Monitor **Terror, Erebus** (16)
ähnlich **Marshal Soult** (15)
2–38.1, 8–10.2
2–7.6, 2–4
7200 t, 12 Kn
WL 102, Deck 162–19
KT 152, Art. 330

Flugzeugträger

6–14, 3–10.2
20
10 850 t, 25 Kn
-Träger **Hermes*** (19)
(Mg vor vorderem 10.2)
WL 76–38
Deck 25, Art. 25

9–15.2, 4–10.2
8–4, 21
-Träger **Eagle*** (18, *24*)
(10.2 zwischen Schornsteinen durch 8–4 ersetzt)
22 600 t, 24 Kn

4–12, 2–4
9
-Mutterschiff **Albatross** (28)
4800 t, 20 Kn

14 Mg
6900 t, 11 K
-Mutterschiff **Pegasus** (14)

A view of Peter Lohmeyer's ship identification book showing a profile of the HMS Eagle (center).

CHAPTER FOURTEEN

"FRIENDSHIP"
U-60, U-105, U-199, U-201, AND U-847
1939-1943

How could an experienced U-boat veteran, who completed fifteen war patrols during the height of the war, survive every peril the sea or the enemy could throw at him only to be killed in a machinegun training accident? Was it just a matter of time before every one of Dönitz's crews would be killed? Those must have been the questions on every sailor's mind on the *U-847* shortly after she was commissioned in January 1943. The U-boat was to be a special boat, one of six U-cruisers (*U-847* to *U-852*) that would be commanded only by Knight's Cross winners and crewed by skilled veterans. The experienced man of the sea in question was *Maschinenmaat* Artur Netter, born in Gelsenkirchen-Rotthausen, next to the industrial city of Essen, on July 24, 1918; when he died he had been in the U-boat force for four years, but he would never sail with this new boat. The *U-847* had lost a skilled veteran and also a friend.

Dönitz's Crews
***Maschinenmaat* Artur Netter**

Born on July 24, 1918 in Gelsenkirchen-Rotthausen/Ruhr.
Served in the engine room on the *U-60*, *U-201* and *U-847*.
Awarded the U-boat War Badge, Iron Cross 2nd Class and Iron Cross 1st Class.
Spent 400 days at sea on U-boat war patrols.
Seriously wounded in a machinegun training accident and died on March 16, 1943.

We do not know exactly when Artur Netter joined the German Navy, but we do know he began his U-boat service with the engine room crew on the *U-60*, a Type IIC U-boat that was commissioned on July 22, 1939 with U-boat Flotilla *Emsmann* at Kiel and commanded by *Oberleutnant zur See* Georg Schewe. Schewe was born in Ueckermünde, Pomerania on November 24, 1909. He joined the German Navy in October 1928 and after four years began officer training. Commissioned a *Leutnant zur See* on January 1, 1936, Schewe joined the U-boat service the same year. He was promoted rapidly: to *Oberleutnant zur See* on October 1, 1937 and to *Kapitänleutnant* on October 1, 1939. Another sailor on the *U-60* was *Obersteuermann* Johannes Ibelshäuser, who was the navigator/quartermaster of the boat. Ibelshäuser was born on June 16, 1909 at Kiel. He joined the *Reichsmarine* in 1928 and served his first five years as a helmsman on the old battleship *Schlesien*. In 1934 Ibelshauser was promoted to the Petty Officer ranks and transferred to the light cruiser *Köln*. In 1935 he served aboard the light cruiser *Emden* for her cruise to the Indian Ocean; undoubtedly he met his commander on the *Emden* – *Kapitän zur See* Karl Dönitz. Ibelshäuser returned to the *Köln* for another year before several assignments with the new U-boat service in which he served as the navigator on the target ship *Hertha* and minesweeper *M-136*. After commanding the auxiliary minesweeper *R-39*, Ibelshäuser joined the *U-60* as her navigator on July 25, 1939.

The little *U-60* departed Kiel on November 4, 1939 for her first patrol. Sinking no ships on her maiden patrol, on November 21, 1939 the U-boat returned to Kiel. Her time in port would be short; on December 4, the *U-60* sailed from Kiel and arrived at Wilhelmshaven, a move that would put her closer to the North Sea hunting areas.

Dönitz's Crews
***Oberleutnant zur See* Johannes Ibelshäuser**

Born on June 16, 1909 in Kiel.
Served as the navigator/quartermaster on the *U-60* and *U-105*.
Awarded the U-boat War Badge, Iron Cross 2nd Class and Iron Cross 1st Class.
Spent 355 days at sea on U-boat war patrols.
Commissioned; ended the war commanding the U-boat escort ship *Donau*.
Died on February 24, 1983 at Schönkirchen/Kiel.

After eight days at Wilhelmshaven, the *U-60* sailed on December 12, 1939 from the port on a mine-laying mission off the British East Anglian port of Lowestoft. Her mission was a success: on December 19, 1939 the 4,373-ton British freighter *City of Kobe* was sunk by a mine at this location. The same day the *U-60* arrived at Kiel. Georg Schewe received an Iron Cross 2nd Class the next day.

Schewe took the *U-60* on her third war patrol on January 9, 1940, but this too ended in no victories, when he arrived at Wilhelmshaven on January 21, 1940. Along with many of the crew, Schewe was awarded the U-boat War Badge on January 24, 1940. Now under the 1st U-boat Flotilla, the *U-60* departed Wilhelmshaven on February 14, 1940 on her fourth war patrol. Again, she gained no results and she returned to Wilhelmshaven on February 29.

War patrols five and six were just as frustrating. The *U-60* departed from Wilhelmshaven on April 4, 1940 and arrived at Kiel on April 27, 1940 – no results. Schewe and the *U-60* left Kiel next on May 18, 1940 and returned to Kiel on June 11 after three and a half weeks on patrol. Georg Schewe then transferred from the *U-60* to the new *U-105*. Artur Netter remained on the *U-60*, but Johannes Ibelshäuser departed for a one-month stay on the U-boat tender *Lech*; he would rejoin Georg Schewe on the *U-105* on September 10, 1940.

To the *U-60* came Adalbert Schnee, a commander who would achieve even more fame in his career. Born on December 31, 1913 in Berlin, Schnee joined the German Navy in April 1934. After three years of surface duty, to include service on the light cruiser *Leipzig*, he was commissioned a *Leutnant zur See* on April 1, 1937 and joined the U-boat service. In addition to his formal U-boat training, Schnee served for two years on the *U-23* under the command of Otto Kretschmer, one of Dönitz's best commanders. With Kretschmer's boat, Adalbert Schnee (now an *Oberleutnant zur See*) won the Iron Cross 2nd Class on October 21, 1939 and the U-boat War Badge on November 27, 1939. Schnee then earned his own command and skippered the *U-6* for one fifteen-day patrol before coming to the *U-60*.

Adalbert Schnee took the *U-60* on her seventh war patrol departing Kiel on July 30, 1940. On August 13, 1940 at 9:47 p.m., he sank the Swedish 1,787-ton *Nils Gorthon*, sailing with convoy HX-62 from St. John's, Newfoundland for Ridham Dock, England. The freighter, carrying pulpwood, took four of her crew with her when she sank just north of Ireland. The U-boat arrived at Lorient, France on August 18, 1940 to conclude the patrol; Adalbert Schnee received an Iron Cross 1st Class for the voyage. By this time *Leutnant (Ing)* Willi Lechtenbörger had joined the crew as the Chief Engineer; as an engine specialist, Artur Netter would have worked directly for Lechtenbörger, a future Knight's Cross winner (see "Chief Engineers.")

The crew barely had time to catch their wind before the *U-60* departed on her eighth war patrol on August 21, 1940. Ten days later the *U-60* torpedoed and damaged the Dutch 15,434-ton *Volendam*, a member of convoy OB-205, but she did not sink. Schnee had better luck on September 3, 1940 at 3:26 a.m., when he sank the British 1,401-ton freighter *Ulva*, carrying coal to Gibraltar, off Ireland with three of her crew. The *U-60* returned to Lorient on September 6, 1940, but her days as an operational combat U-boat were numbered. On September 16, 1940 the *U-60* departed Lorient for the last time and traveled to Bergen, Norway on October 2. After three days in Norway, the U-boat departed on her ninth and final combat patrol, arriving at Kiel on October 8, 1940.

The *U-60* then transferred to the 21st U-boat Training Flotilla at Pillau where she served for the remainder of the war. But the men of the *U-60* were experienced combat veterans and Dönitz needed many of them to continue the frontline fight. Adalbert Schnee transferred to command the *U-121*, but this was very temporary, lasting only three weeks. Schnee then took command of the *U-201*, a Type VIIC U-boat that was built at the Germaniawerft at Kiel and commissioned on January 25, 1941. It is likely that the *U-60*'s former commander, Adalbert Schnee, and Chief Engineer Willi Lechtenbörger asked for Artur Netter to go with them to Schnee's new boat. Netter likely had eight or nine combat war patrols by this time; Schnee knew the value of "old hands" to steady any jittery new crewmen and Lechtenbörger would know which engine room men truly knew what they were doing. And, as much as their differences in rank would allow, the three men were probably good friends by this time.

After additional training with the 25th and 27th U-boat Training Flotillas, the new boat was ready for combat. On April 22, 1941 the *U-201* departed Kiel under Adalbert Schnee for her first war patrol. It was a good first effort; Schnee ambushed three ships in two different convoys. On May 2, 1941 at 4:15 p.m. south of Iceland, the *U-201* torpedoed and sank the British 8,190-ton tanker *Capulet*, sailing with convoy HX-121 and carrying 11,200 tons of fuel oil from Curacao to Scapa Flow; nine men perished in the explosion. At 2:26 p.m. on May 9, 1941 southeast of Greenland, Schnee sank the British 5,802-ton *Gregalia*, a member of convoy OB-318 in ballast from Glasgow to Buenos Aires. Two minutes later, the *U-201* torpedoed and damaged the British 5,969-ton freighter *Empire Cloud*; five men died but the ship was saved. The *U-201* arrived at Lorient on May 18, 1941. Her 26-day voyage had encompassed 1,594 sea-miles on the surface and 170 sea-miles submerged.

The *U-201* departed from Lorient on June 8, 1941 for her second war patrol. B.d.U. designated the U-boat part of *Wolf Pack Group Kurfürst*. The crew did not sink any enemy ships and arrived at Brest, France on July 19, 1941; she had traveled 6,447 sea-miles surfaced and just 37 sea-miles under water. After roughly a month in port, on August 14 the *U-201* sailed on her third war patrol and although it lasted but eleven days was quite profitable when Schnee ran into convoy OG-71. On August 19, 1941 at 4:06 a.m. just off the Portuguese coast, the *U-201* torpedoed and sank the British 1,809-ton *Ciscar*, carrying general cargo and government stores with convoy OG-71 from Bristol, England to Gibraltar; thirteen men perished in the attack. At almost the same time the *U-201* sank the British 3,255-ton freighter *Aguila*, carrying replacements, general cargo and 397 bags of mail from Liverpool to Gibraltar. The British soldiers at Gibraltar would not get their mail and more tragically, 157 men on the *Aguila* would never see their homes again.

Four days passed before the *U-201* would strike OG-71 again. On August 23, 1941 the *U-201* sank the British 787-ton freighter Stork, at 2:14 a.m. off the Portuguese coast. Nineteen crewmen died when the ship carrying gasoline from Preston, England to Gibraltar exploded. Simultaneously, Schnee torpedoed the British 1,974-ton freighter *Aldergrove*, bound from Cardiff, Wales to Lisbon, Portugal and carrying 2,650 tons of patent fuel (cakes of peat, coal dust and gas tar) and ten tons of German prisoner of war-parcels. The people of Lisbon would be a little cooler that fall and many families in Germany would not hear from their sons as both the fuel and mail were now at the bottom of the Atlantic. The *U-201* returned to Brest on August 25, 1941 with four victory pennants flying from the periscope after sailing 2,409 sea-miles surfaced and 54 sea-miles submerged. The patrol, combined with his previous achievements, earned a Knight's Cross for Adalbert Schnee on August 30, 1941.

The war continued and the *U-201* was needed at sea, so on September 14, 1941 she departed Brest for her fourth war patrol, again under Adalbert Schnee. A week later, Schnee found another convoy – OG-74 – and raced in to the attack:

- On September 21, 1941 at 10:50 p.m., Schnee torpedoed and sank the British 1,575-ton *Runa*, sailing with convoy OG-74, in the mid-Atlantic. Fourteen crewmen and 2,200 tons of coal plunged to the sea bottom.
- At 11:20 p.m. the *U-201* torpedoed the British 1,511-ton freighter *Lissa*. Bound from Milford Haven, Wales to Lisbon with 2,100 tons of coal, the ship took her entire crew of twenty-six men with her to the bottom in the pitch-black darkness of the Atlantic.
- One minute later at 11:21 p.m., the *U-201* sank the British 1,381-ton *Rhineland*. Her entire crew of twenty-six perished,

when the freighter – with 913 tons of coal and 3,566 German prisoner of war parcels bound from Glasgow, Scotland to Lisbon – sank.

• On September 27, 1941 at 2:08 a.m. still in the mid-Atlantic, the *U-201* sank the British 5,155-ton *HMS Springbank*, a fighter catapult ship (she carried a Fulmar fighter of the 804th FAA-Squadron on a cordite powered catapult amidships) sailing with convoy HG-73. Thirty-two men died in the attack

• In the same attack, the *U-201* sank the Norwegian 2,468-ton freighter *Siremalm* carrying iron ore from Almeira, Spain for Barrow, Canada; all twenty-seven men of her crew died.

• Later that evening at 11:03 p.m., after enemy flying boats had driven her underwater, the *U-201* sank the British 3,103-ton *Margareta*, bound from Gibraltar for Glasgow.

Schnee and the *U-201* returned to Brest on September 30, 1941. Schnee logged that the U-boat had sailed 3,364 sea-miles surfaced and 53 sea-miles submerged. After a month, the *U-201* departed Brest on her fifth war patrol but achieved no confirmed successes and returned to Brest on December 9, 1941; on this voyage the *U-201* traveled 118 sea-miles submerged and 6,040 sea-miles surfaced. On December 13, 1941, there was an explosion on the U-boat due to a build-up of battery gases that killed *Maschinenobergefreiter* Josef Zander. The *U-201* remained in port for over three months until March 24, 1942, when she departed Brest; during her time in port Adalbert Schnee was promoted to *Kapitänleutnant* on February 20, 1942. For this sixth war patrol she would go further than the mid-Atlantic; she would now hunt off the American coast. On April 18, 1942 east of North Carolina, Schnee torpedoed the Argentinian 7,417-ton *Victoria* bound from Buenos Aires, Argentina to New York, but the sturdy ship made port.

Schnee received better results a few days later. On April 21, 1942 at 2:36 a.m., the *U-201* sank the Norwegian 2,027-ton *Bris*, carrying asphalt and wheat flower from Baltimore to Pernambuco, Brazil; five men died. The next day, April 22, at 3:29 a.m., Schnee encountered the American 6,069-ton *San Jacinto* bound from New York to San Juan, Puerto Rico. After putting a torpedo into the freighter Schnee finished her off with gunfire; fourteen of the seventy-nine crew and 104 passengers perished in the attack. Later that morning at 9:05 a.m. the *U-201* torpedoed the British 7,217-ton *Derryheen*. The crew survived, but 11,036 tons of general cargo, nitrates and trucks went to the bottom with the freighter. On May 21, 1942 the *U-201* returned to Brest after over eight weeks on patrol that included 8,193 sea-miles surfaced and 602 sea-miles submerged.

The *U-201*'s lucky seventh war patrol began one month later on June 27, 1942 when she departed Brest bound for the Azore Islands. Nine days later, on July 6, Adalbert Schnee encountered his first target and it filled the periscope. The British 14,443-ton refrigerated cargo liner *Avila Star* of the Blue Star Line had started her voyage from Buenos Aires; after stopping at Freetown, Sierra Leone, she was making for Liverpool with 5,659 tons of frozen meat, when the *U-201* torpedoed the ship sending her to the bottom with forty-five crew and seventeen passengers. At 9:00 a.m. on July 11, a decision made on convoy OS-33 gave the U-boat an opportunity. The convoy sailing south from Great Britain had two destinations; some ships were headed for Africa and the others for South America. At that hour the convoy split in two, and six ships turned west. On July 12, 1942 at 12:22 a.m. west of the Canary Islands, the *U-116* torpedoed and damaged the British 7,093-ton *Cortona*, also of convoy OS-33. Minutes later the *U-201* put a torpedo that caused massive damage to her starboard side and set her on fire. Bound from Liverpool to Buenos Aires, she later sank. Thirty-two of her crew in one of the ship's lifeboats pulled away from the ship, but were never seen again. At 2:25 a.m., Schnee torpedoed the British 5,242-ton *Siris*, a member of convoy OS-33 bound from Oban, Scotland for Rio de Janeiro, Brazil. The vessel took on a list of 35°, but when she refused to go under, Schnee surfaced and from a range of two hundred yards finished the task with fifty rounds of gunfire; three men later died after sixteen days in a lifeboat. At 2:21 a.m. on July 13, 1942 the *U-201* struck again sending two torpedoes into the British 6,723-ton *Sithonia*, which broke her back. Seven men died when the ship, bound from Belfast for Montevideo, Uruguay (part of OS-33) with 8,026 tons of coal sank. At 1:46 a.m. on July 15, 1942, the *U-201* continued her rampage, attacking the British 6,990-ton tanker *British Yeoman* with torpedoes and sixty-one rounds of gunfire. Forty-three men died when the tanker carrying fuel from Curacao to the British Navy base at Gibraltar exploded and sank at 12:00 p.m. Finally on July 25, 1942 at 11:05 p.m., the *U-201* torpedoed and sank the British 545-ton anti-submarine trawler *HMS Laertes* (Lt. Patrick Joseph Quinlan) off Freetown. Schnee and the *U-201* returned to Brest on August 8, 1942. For his continued achievements at sea, Adalbert Schnee received the Oak Leaves to the Knight's Cross.

Artur Netter then joined the *U-847*, as did *Oberleutnant (Ing)* Willi Lechtenbörger; it was clear that the Chief Engineer knew he had an excellent engine room comrade and needed his expertise. The *Kriegsmarine* ordered the boat, a Type IXD2, on January 20, 1941 and construction engineers laid her keel at the Deutsche Schiff- und Maschinenbau AG (AG Weser) in Bremen on November 23, 1941. It is likely that Netter arrived at the *U-847* before September 5, 1942 when the U-boat was launched. After sea trials, the *U-847* was commissioned on January 23, 1943, under command of *Kapitänleutnant* Friedrich Guggenberger, an experienced commander who had the Knight's Cross with Oak Leaves and who had sunk the British aircraft carrier *HMS Ark Royal*. Three days later, on January 26, 1943, one man was killed and *Maschinenmaat* Artur Netter was seriously wounded during a machinegun training exercise at Wesermünde. Netter was rushed to a hospital, where he lingered for almost two months until he died of his injuries on March 16, 1943. Artur Netter was buried in his hometown of Gelsenkirchen-Rotthausen.

Unfortunately, it was just a matter of time for his shipmates on the *U-847* also. She would make only one war patrol. The boat had orders to sail to the Indian Ocean to join the *Monsoon Group* of German U-boats operating in the Far East in conjunction with the Japanese. She departed Kiel on this mission on July 6, but struck ice in the Denmark Strait and slid into Bergen, Norway for emergency repairs on July 20. She departed Bergen on July 29 and sailed to the Sargasso Sea area, where she began refueling several U-boats low on fuel. On August 27, aircraft from the U.S. escort carrier *USS Card* spotted the *U-847*, which had been refueling seven U-boats over the previous two weeks. One Avenger and two Wildcat aircraft first strafed the surfaced U-boat, forcing her to dive, and then dropped a Fido homing torpedo just ahead of where they thought the German U-boat would be; they guessed correctly and the *U-847* went down with her entire 62-man crew, including her commander Knight's Cross winner *Kapitänleutnant* Herbert Kuppisch, who had previously commanded the *U-58* and *U-94* with distinction, and who had taken over from Guggenberger.

It was also just a matter of time for the *U-201*. Adalbert Schnee departed the boat after she returned to Brest in July 1942. He went on to serve in various staff positions until 1944 when he volunteered to go to sea again, this time in command of a new Type XXI U-boat. He survived the war and died in Hamburg on November 4, 1982 at age sixty-eight. In his place came *Kapitänleutnant* Günther

Rosenberg. Born in Hamburg on January 17, 1917, he had previously commanded the *U-351*, a training boat, for nine months. Prior to that, he had gone on four war patrols as the 1st Watch Officer on the *U-372*. Rosenberg sank three enemy ships on his first patrol off of South America. Rosenberg took the *U-201* out for a second mission on December 27, 1942 but had to return to Brest two days later with mechanical difficulties.

On January 3, 1943 the *U-201* departed Brest. In mid-February the *U-69* discovered convoy ON-165 and began transmitting its location to several other boats, including the *U-201*. But the British were waiting with Escort Group B-6, which was using high frequency radio detection equipment and radar, which located the U-boats in the atrocious North Atlantic winter weather that had promised to mask the approaching submarines. On February 17, 1943 the *U-201* tangled with the British destroyer *HMS Viscount*. The *Viscount* had experience with U-boats before; on October 15, 1942 she rammed and sank the *U-661* in the North Atlantic, an attack which killed all forty-four men on the U-boat. East of Newfoundland the *HMS Viscount* located the *U-201* and commenced a furious depth charge attack. The attack sank the *U-201* and she took all forty-nine of her crew with her.

Meanwhile, the *U-105* was enjoying a stellar career as well. A Type IXB boat built at the Deutsche Schiff und Maschinenbau AG shipyard at Bremen, she was launched on June 15, 1940 and commissioned on September 10, 1940. Also on the *U-105* was *Obermaschinenmaat* August Bischoff in the engine room. Born on July 12, 1920 he would serve with distinction on three U-boats.

Dönitz's Crews
***Obermaschinenmaat* August Bischoff**

Born on July 12, 1920 in Münster.
Joined the Navy on October 1, 1939 as a trained electrical motor specialist.
Served in the engine room of the *U-105*, *U-188* and *U-3524*.
Awarded the U-boat War Badge on June 13, 1941, Iron Cross 2nd Class, Iron Cross 1st Class, German Cross in Gold on August 3, 1944 and the U-boat Front Clasp in Bronze on September 27, 1944.
Spent 592 days at sea on U-boat war patrols.
Survived the war; lived in Münster.

After three months of pre-combat training, commander Georg Schewe and navigator Johannes Ibelshäuser took the *U-105* on her first war patrol to just south of Iceland, departing Kiel on December 24, 1940. The U-boat sank two ships on her maiden voyage. On January 9, 1941 at 6:14 p.m., Schewe torpedoed and sank the unescorted British 4,843-ton freighter *Bassano* northwest of Rockall Banks. The ship, carrying 5,000 tons of iron and steel and 600 tons of grain from New York to Hull, England, took one crewman with her when she sank. At 2:12 a.m. on January 26, 1941 the *U-105* found the burning and abandoned British 3,564-ton *Lurigethan*, which had been sailing with convoy SL-61 until attacked and heavily damaged by an Fw-200 Condor aircraft three days earlier. Sixteen crewmembers died and 2,459 tons of cottonseed never made it from Port Sudan to Hull, England. The *U-105* finished the patrol by arriving at Lorient, France on January 31, 1941. She had sailed 4,747 sea-miles surfaced and 202 sea-miles submerged.

After just three weeks in port, the *U-105* departed Lorient on February 22, 1941 for the South Atlantic and her most successful war patrol. Georg Schewe would sink twelve ships on this patrol; seven of these ships were in convoy:

1. On March 8, 1941 at 3:41 a.m. northeast of the Cape Verde Islands, the *U-105* torpedoed and sank the British 5,229-ton freighter *Harmodius*, a member of convoy SL-67, carrying 2,000 tons of pig iron and 3,930 tons of general cargo from Kochi, India to London; fourteen men died.
2. On March 18, 1941 at 4:00 a.m., the *U-105* sank the British 4,380-ton *Medjerda*, a straggler from convoy SL-68, north of the Cape Verde Islands; all fifty-four men went down with the ship carrying 6,450 tons of iron ore, when she sank in thirty seconds.
3. At 12:29 a.m. on March 19, 1941, the *U-105* sank the Dutch 7,750-ton *Mandalika*, part of convoy SL-68, near the Cape Verde Islands bound from Batavia, Indonesia to Belfast, Ireland with 9,200 tons of sugar; three men perished in the attack.
4. At 12:46 a.m. on March 21, 1941, Schewe sank the British 5,920-ton *Benwyvis* (convoy SL-68) north of the Cape Verde Islands; the ship carrying 3,500 tons of rice, 500 tons of lead, 1,100 tons of timber and 150 tons of wolfram from Rangoon, Burma to Liverpool, England, took thirty-four men with her to the bottom.
5. Also at 12:46 a.m. on March 21, Schewe sank the British 5,802-ton *Clan Ogilvy*, sailing with convoy SL-68, transporting general cargo, pig iron, ground nuts and tea from Chittagong, India to London; sixty-one men died in the attack.
6. At 9:59 p.m. on March 21, 1941, the *U-105* torpedoed and sank the British 4,038-ton *Jhelum*, from convoy SL-68, five-hundred miles west of French West Africa; eight men died when the ship, carrying 1,400 tons of borax and 1,553 tons of figs from Izmir, Turkey to Oban, Scotland, sank. Following this, on March 29 the *U-105* resupplied from the surface raider *Kormoran*.
7. On April 5, 1941 at 3:38 a.m., the *U-105* sank the unescorted British 5,200-ton *Ena de Larrinaga* east of St. Paul Rocks; the ship, loaded with 5,607 tons of coal and general cargo from Hull, England to Buenos Aires, Argentina, took five of her crew with her. Schewe then resupplied on April 9, 1941 from the supply ship *Nordmark*.
8. Northeast of St. Paul Rocks on May 6, 1941 at 10:52 a.m., the *U-105* he sank the British 4,255-ton *Oakdene*, carrying 6,222 tons of coal from Cardiff, Wales to Buenos Aires, Argentina.
9. On May 13, 1941 at 7:48 a.m., the *U-105* torpedoed and sank the British 6,434-ton *Benvrackie*, dispersed from convoy OB-312, and carrying 5,850 tons of general cargo and aircraft from Loch Ewe, Scotland to Beira, Mozambique, southwest of Freetown, Sierra Leone; twenty-eight crewmen died in the attack.
10. At 8:29 p.m. on May 15, 1941, the *U-105* sank the British 5,920-ton *Benvenue*, from convoy OB-314, loaded with 5,000 tons of general cargo and six aircraft, southwest of Freetown; two men died.
11. At 5:48 a.m. on May 16, 1941, the *U-105* torpedoed the British 11,803-ton *Rodney Star* southwest of Freetown, carrying refrigerated cargo from Uruguay to Scotland. The ship did not sink and Schewe surfaced and began shelling her with his deck-gun. After 113 rounds, a shell exploded in the gun tube wounding six men on the U-boat; at 9:30 a.m. the *Rodney Star* finally sank.
12. On June 1, 1941 at 12:22 a.m., the *U-105* torpedoed and sank the British 4,719-ton *Scottish Monarch* bound from Loch Ewe, Scotland to Freetown, Sierra Leone with 7,000 tons of coal. The ship, which dispersed from convoy OB-319, went down with one man southwest of the Cape Verde Islands.

On May 21, 1941 the *U-105* refueled from the supply ship *Egerland*. After nearly four months at sea, Schewe returned to Lorient on June 13, 1941, having traveled 19,986 sea-miles surfaced and 319 sea-miles submerged. During the patrol B.d.U. radioed the *U-105* on May 23, 1941 that Georg Schewe had been awarded the Knight's Cross; he was formally presented with the award on June 13. August Bischoff, in the engine room, received the U-boat War Badge on this same day. The patrol accounted for 71,450 tons of enemy shipping and was the second most successful patrol of the entire war.

The men had time for a good leave at home; on August 8, 1941 the *U-105* again went to sea, bound for the North Atlantic. Off Greenland at 4:15 p.m. on September 11, 1941, the U-boat fired a spread of four torpedoes that sank the Panamanian 1,549-ton freighter *Montana* bound from Wilmington, Delaware to Reykjavik, Iceland with a load of timber; eighteen men died in the cold sea. That was Schewe's only confirmed victory; the *U-105* returned to Lorient on September 20, 1941; she had logged 6,743 sea-miles surfaced and 463 sea-miles submerged. Georg Schewe would make one final war patrol with the *U-105*; on November 8, 1941 the U-boat departed Lorient, but return to base on December 13, 1941 with no confirmed sinkings. Schewe then left the *U-105* and became a staff officer of the F.d.U. Mediterranean. Promoted to *Korvettenkapitän* on August 1, 1943, he was later assigned to the Navy High Command in Berlin. After the war Schewe spent one year as a prisoner of war; he died on September 16, 1989 in Hamburg.

Life went on in the *U-105*. To the boat came *Kapitänleutnant* Heinrich Schuch as the new commander. Born on August 28, 1906 in Berlin, he was a veteran of the *U-37* and *U-38* with which he made three war patrols. On January 25, 1942 the *U-105* departed Lorient, under Heinrich Schuch; Schuch struck success early finding convoy SL-98 in the North Atlantic. Firing four torpedoes, Schuch heard two huge explosions and believed he had sunk an ammunition ship. He had not, but his torpedoes had blown apart the *HMS Culver*, a former US Coast Guard cutter; 126 men went down with the ship. Schuch returned to Lorient on February 8, 1942. After the patrol, another veteran of the *U-105* departed for other duties. Navigator Johannes Ibelshäuser departed and entered training to become a commissioned officer, very likely after receiving support from his long-time comrade Georg Schewe for this significant career promotion. Ibelshäuser received his commission, was promoted to *Oberleutnant zur See* and ended the war commanding the U-boat escort ship *Donau*. He survived the conflict.

The *U-105* received a new navigator and continued the war. She departed Lorient for Bermuda on February 25, 1942; the U-boat sank two ships on this patrol. At 6:09 a.m. on March 25, 1942 Schuch sank the British 10,389-ton tanker *Narragansett* east of Hampton Roads, Virginia bound from Port Arthur, Texas to Halifax – and then Great Britain – with 14,000 tons of petroleum; all forty-nine men went down with the ship as she exploded in a huge fireball. Two days later at 9:28 a.m. on March 27, 1942, the *U-105* sank another tanker, the Norwegian 7,616-ton *Svenor* carrying 11,410 tons of fuel oil from Curacao to Halifax, Nova Scotia. Eight men died when the ship slid beneath the waves three-hundred miles east of Cape Hatteras, North Carolina. The *U-105* returned to Lorient on April 15, 1942. Heinrich Schuch would make two more patrols with the *U-105* but both resulted in no enemy sinkings. He departed the boat that fall, was promoted to *Fregattenkapitän* in 1943 and survived the war. Departing the *U-105* on December 13, 1941 was August Bischoff, who then was assigned to the *U-188* on August 5, 1942 after further training.

Jürgen Nissen assumed command of the *U-105* on October 29, 1942. He took her to the north coast of Brazil on her next war patrol on November 23, 1943. Nissen started quickly, sinking four ships on this patrol. On December 14, 1942 at 4:14 a.m., the *U-105* sank the British 6,578-ton *Orfor* north of Brazil. The ship, which took twenty-two of her crew with her when she sank, was carrying 7,170 tons of jute fiber from Calcutta, India to the Dominican Republic. In one of the more unusual sinkings in the war, at 1:00 a.m. on January 12, 1943, the U-boat encountered the tiny British 67-ton *CS Flight*, a sailing ship bound from Curacao to Barbados. Nissen first engaged the target with 20-mm flak gun forcing the crew to abandon ship, but there were not enough lifeboats and forty-nine men drowned. The *U-105* then approached close to her quarry and the U-boat men destroyed her with hand grenades. On January 24, 1943 the *U-105* came across the burning British 8,093-ton tanker *British Vigilance*, a former member of convoy TM-1. Some three weeks earlier she had been torpedoed by the *U-514* but had not sunk. After two torpedoes she went to the bottom with the remainder of her 11,000 tons of petroleum.

Finally, at 9:54 a.m. on January 27, 1943, the *U-105* torpedoed the American 5,106-ton *Cape Decision* carrying military supplies – including land mines, ammunition, trucks, two aircraft and two landing craft – from Charleston, South Carolina to Freetown, Sierra Leone. The landing craft, which were on deck, did not sink and once again the U-boat closed and sank the craft with 20-mm gunfire and hand grenades. The *U-105* returned to Lorient on February 14, 1943.

One month later on March 16, 1943, the *U-105* departed Lorient for what would be her final war patrol. Two months passed without success, but on May 15, 1943 the U-boat sank the Greek 4,669-ton *Maroussio Logothetis* carrying 7,024 tons of iron from Rio de Janeiro, Brazil to Great Britain. Twenty-seven men died when the ship went down off the coast of Liberia. But the incredible run of good luck for the *U-105* came to an end. Off the coast of Senegal on June 2, 1943, a French Potez-CAMS 141 flying boat located the surfaced *U-105* and attacked with depth charges. The *U-105* sank with all hands.

Meanwhile the *U-188*, with *Obermaschinenmaat* August Bischoff on board, was beginning her own successful career. A Type IXC/40 U-boat, the *U-188* had her keel laid by shipyard workers at the Deutsche Schiff und Maschinenbau AG at Bremen on August 18, 1941. She was launched on March 31, 1942 and commissioned on August 5, 1942. In command was *Oberleutnant zur See* Siegfried Lüdden. Born on May 20, 1916 at Stargard in Neubrandenburg, Lüdden first served in the surface fleet, was detailed to the *Luftwaffe* for a year and then entered U-boat training in 1940. He then served on the *U-141* and as the aide-de-camp for several U-boat flotilla commanders. In 1941 Lüdden became the 1st Watch Officer on the *U-129*, serving in the South Atlantic and West Atlantic and winning the Iron Cross 2nd Class on December 18, 1941, the U-boat War Badge on December 29, 1941 and the Iron Cross 1st Class on April 8, 1942. After undergoing several months of pre-combat training with the 4th U-boat Training Flotilla, the crew of the *U-188* departed Kiel on their first patrol with the boat on March 4, 1943 for operations off the southern tip of Greenland.

A B-24 Liberator forced the *U-188* to crash-dive on March 18, 1943, on March 21 high seas damaged the deck and on March 27 the starboard diesel experienced problems that took twelve hours to repair. On April 5, B.d.U. designated the *U-188* as part of *Wolf Pack Group Adler*. On April 11, Lüdden made contact with convoy ON-176 and at 5:49 a.m. began the first of several torpedo runs. Two days prior the 1,190-ton *HMS Beverley*, which had been built in 1920 as a U.S. Clemson-class destroyer and transferred to the Royal Navy in 1940, had been seriously damaged in a collision with a merchant ship. Her speed reduced and her sonar inoperative, the *HMS Beverley* took her station at the rear of the convoy. The *U-188*'s torpedoes slammed into the *HMS Beverley*; she went down with 151 men; only four men survived the sinking in frigid conditions. B.d.U. then disbanded the U-boat group, but on April 13, 1943 formed a new concentration *Wolf Pack Group Meise*, which again included the *U-188*. The next day the U-boat again experienced problems with the starboard diesel engine. She received a resupply of fuel from the *U-487* on April 23. On April 30 and May 1, Allied aircraft drove the *U-188* to submerge so frequently that the carbon-dioxide level rose so high that many of the men began to experience severe headaches. The U-boat approached France but shortly before her arrival, on May 2, 1943 at 10:14 a.m., a British Whitely bomber from the RAF's 612th Squadron attacked the surfaced U-boat with bombs and a strafing attack. The gunfire wounded Siegfried Lüdden on the bridge and fatally wounded *Matrosengefreiter* Leo Rupp. Lüdden and the shaken crew of the *U-188* arrived at Lorient on May 4, 1943. During the patrol Lüdden was promoted to *Kapitänleutnant* on April 1, 1943. The U-boat had sailed 7,040 sea-miles on the surface and 496 sea-miles submerged.

After two months in port the crew of the *U-188* set off on a true adventure, bound for Penang, Malaya as part of the *Monsoon Group* of U-boats which was to take the fight to enemy shipping in the Indian Ocean. Departing on June 30, 1943 the *U-188* successfully passed through the Bay of Biscay, North Atlantic, South Atlantic, Cape of Good Hope and Indian Ocean, refueling from the supply ship *KMS Brake* on September 8, 1943. On September 21, 1943 Lüdden spotted the American 7,176-ton *Cornelia P Spencer* three-hundred miles off the coast of Somalia. At 8:03 a.m. he torpedoed the ship; the *U-188* then surfaced to finish the target, but gunners on the freighter drove her back under with their own deck-gun fire. The U-boat fired a final torpedo, killing two men and sending the ship carrying 2,910 tons of steel and 300 tons of gum from Aden to Durban, South Africa to the bottom. Six days later Lüdden had more problems with the pesky starboard diesel engine, but the engine room crew, including August Bischoff, got the engine functioning again. Continuing the mission, on October 5, 1943 east of the Strait of Hormuz, the *U-188* torpedoed and damaged the Norwegian 9,977-ton *Britannia* but the ship made port at Bandar Abbas. The U-boat finally arrived at Penang on October 30, 1943 after sailing 19,331 sea-miles in 122 days. Lüdden reported that at times during the voyage in the Gulf of Aden temperatures in the engine room reached 163°F!

After several months the *U-188* departed under Siegfried Lüdden from Penang, Malaya January 1, 1944. In addition to a mission of sinking enemy ships, the *U-188* was packed with one-hundred tons of wolfram, tin, quinine and even 200 kilos of opium for transport to resource-deprived Germany. Siegfried Lüdden sank seven ships on his return to Germany:

- On January 20, 1944 at 8:39 p.m., the *U-188* sank the British 7,122-ton *Fort Buckingham* with two torpedoes northwest of the Maldive Islands. The ship, sailing in ballast from Bombay to Buenos Aires, went down with thirty-eight of her crew.
- On January 25, 1944 the *U-188* torpedoed and sank the British 7,130-ton *Fort la Maune* northeast of Socotra Island; she was carrying 8,130 tons of general and military cargo from New York to Calcutta, India.
- On January 26, 1944 at 2:25 a.m., the *U-188* sank the unescorted British 7,219-ton *Samouri* sailing in ballast from Bombay, India to New York; she was in the Gulf of Aden northeast of Socotra Island when she went down.
- Later that day at 6:48 p.m., the *U-188* torpedoed and sank the unescorted British 5,427-ton *Surada* northeast of Socotra Island; she went down with 5,000 tons of general cargo from Calcutta, India to Suez, Egypt.
- On January 29, 1944 at 10:07 p.m., the *U-188* sank the Greek 4,677-ton freighter *Olga E Embiricos* just off the coast of Somalia; she took twenty of her crew and 6,900 tons of coal, bound from Durban, South Africa to Massowah on the Red Sea, to the bottom.
- On February 3, 1944 at 11:45 p.m., the *U-188* sank the unescorted Chinese Liberty ship, the 7,176-ton *Chung Cheng*, in the Gulf of Aden; twenty crewmen died and 8,350 tons of ilmenite ore from Calcutta, India never made it to the United States.
- At 7:06 p.m. on February 9, 1944, the *U-188* sank the Norwegian 3,798-ton *Viva* carrying 6,068 tons of general cargo and tea from Bombay, India to Great Britain.

On March 11, 1944 the *U-188* again refueled from the supply ship *KMS Brake*; Lüdden barely avoided catastrophe as later that day British naval units located the *Brake* and sank her. Lüdden refueled from the *U-181* on April 22. In turn he gave fuel to the *U-66* on May 2. On May 6, enemy aircraft attacked the U-boat and drove her under the surface. She arrived at Bordeaux, France on June 19, 1944; during the latter part of the voyage the U-boat's radios became non-operational at the end of April and B.d.U. concluded that she had been sunk. It had been a voyage of 171 days, traveling 20,761 sea-miles, ending when the crew unloaded their special cargo. On August 3, 1944, in recognition for their long and distinguished service on the *U-188*, the following crewmen received the German Cross in Gold: *Kapitänleutnant* Max Kiessling (Chief Engineer), *Obermaschinist* Oskar Kuch, *Obermaschinenmaat* Hans Arnold, *Obermaschinenmaat* August Bischoff and *Mechanikermaat* Max Braun.

The Germans scuttled the *U-188* at Bordeaux on August 20, 1944 to prevent her capture by rapidly advancing Allied ground forces rolling across France. Her crew escaped to safety in Germany. On September 27, 1944 Siegfried Lüdden, August Bischoff and many other crewmen on the *U-188* received the U-boat Front Badge in Bronze for their many days on war patrols at sea. Lüdden became a staff officer to the Commander of U-boats but did not survive the war. On January 13, 1945 he died in a ship fire aboard the *Daressalam*, a U-boat crew accommodation ship berthed at Kiel. On March 18, 1945 the *Kriegsmarine* posthumously promoted Siegfried Lüdden to *Korvettenkapitän*. His comrade August Bischoff transferred to the *U-3524*, a Type XXI U-boat built at Danzig in the F. Schichau shipyard. Knight's Cross winner *Korvettenkapitän* Hans-Ludwig Witt commissioned the U-boat on January 26, 1945, and the *U-3524* trained in the 5th U-boat Training Flotilla until the end of the war, making no war patrols. Her crew scuttled the boat on May 5, 1945 in Gelting Bay near the Danish border. August Bischoff survived the war.

Known Crewmembers for the U-60

Adler	*Maschinenmaat*
Behrens, Kraft	*Mechanikermaat*
Brand, Wilhelm	
Franke, Theodor	*Kapitänleutnant (Ing)*
Giesewetter, Herbert	*Oberleutnant zur See*
Glaser, Heins	*Obersteuermann*
Hackstein, Willi	*Funkmaat*
Hagenbücher, Alfred	*Obermechanikermaat*
Hanke, Heinz	*Obermaschinenmaat*
Hartmann, Karl	*Leutnant zur See*
Holtfreder, Herbert	*Leutnant (Ing)*
Hübschen, Otto	*Oberleutnant zur See*
Ibelshäuser, Johannes	*Obersteuermann*
Kregelin, Ludo	*Oberleutnant zur See*
Lechtenbörger, Willi	*Kapitänleutnant (Ing)*
Leimkühler, Wolfgang	*Oberleutnant zur See*
Lepzy, Viktor	
Lewitz, Konrad	*Oberfunkmaat*
Lückert, Max	*Oberleutnant (Ing)*
Mohs, Hanz	*Kapitänleutnant*
Netter, Arthur	*Maschinenmaat*
Ockein, Werner	*Maschinenmaat*
Pressel, Kurt	*Kapitänleutnant*
Richartz, Willi	*Bootsmaat*
Russ, Albert	
Schewe, Georg	*Korvettenkapitän*
Schnee, Adalbert	*Korvettenkapitän*
Wallas, Georg	*Kapitänleutnant*
Wittwer, Max	
Zink, Herbert	*Leutnant (Ing)*

Known Crewmembers for the U-105

Anderka, Josef	*Maschinenmaat*
Bahner, Rudolf	*Maschinenobergefreiter*
Bähr, Emil	*Obermaschinenmaat*
Barufke, Kurt	*Maschinenmaat*
Bauch, Horst	*Obermaschinist*
Baumeister, Josef	*Maschinenobergefreiter*
Bischoff, August	*Obermaschinenmaat*
Bochmann, Rudolf	*Funkobergefreiter*
Brühn, Helmuth	*Maschinenobergefreiter*
Budde, Kurt	*Funkmaat*
Choroba, Josef-Wilhelm	*Matrosenobergefreiter*
Dewarth, Paul	*Maschinenobergefreiter*
Dewitz, Günther	*Fähnrich zur See*
Dietrich, Johann	*Maschinengefreiter*
Dörenthal, Helmut	*Bootsmaat*
Dornfeld, Helmut	*Matrose*
Dowers, Karl-Heinz	*Mechanikergefreiter*
Dschünke, Harald	
Enthofer, Paul-Gustav	*Funkmaat*
Fassbender, Willi	*Matrosengefreiter*
Feddersen, Günther	*Oberfähnrich zur See*
Fromm, Julius	*Matrosenobergefreiter*
Garn, Heinz	
Gerlich, Gerhard	*Obermaschinenmaat*
Gneiding, Adolf	*Obermaschinenmaat*
Grochowiak, Edmund	*Kapitänleutnant*
Grumpelt, Gerhard	*Obermaschinist*
Haak, Heinz	*Maschinenobergefreiter*
Harländer, Henrich	*Maschinengefreiter*
Hauck, Dr. Friedrich	*Arzt*
Hauptmann, Gerhard	*Maschinenmaat*
Heidel, Heinz	*Maschinengefreiter*
Helms, Rudolf	*Maschinenobergefreiter*
Henschel, Werner	*Maschinenmaat*
Hinrichs, Otto	*Oberleutnant zur See*
Hoffmann, Erich	*Obermaschinenmaat*
Hopf, Otto	*Maschinenmaat*
Hornickel, Alfred	*Obermaschinenmaat*
Ibelshäuser, Johannes	*Oberleutnant zur See*
Ilgner, Fritz	*Maschinenobergefreiter*
Jahns, Adolf	*Obermaschinist*
Janker, Johannes	
Jelten, Helmut	*Obermaschinenmaat*
Jörling, Alfons	
Kellputt, Werner	*Maschinengefreiter*
Kern, Julius	*Maschinenobergefreiter*
Knolle, Heinrich	*Maschinenobergefreiter*
Knorr, Walter	*Matrosenobergefreiter*
Konersmann, Franz-Heinrich	*Matrosenobergefreiter*
König, Wilhelm	*Matrosengefreiter*
Kramer, Kurt-Ernst	*Fähnrich zur See*
Krämer, Gerhard	*Maschinenobergefreiter*
Kröger, Hans-Emil	*Obermaschinenmaat*
Kuhlmann, Heinz	*Maschinenmaat*
Kutschera, Josef	*Maschinenobergefreiter*
Laufs, Hermann	*Kapitänleutnant (Ing)*
Leeling, Gerhard	*Oberfunkmaat*
Lindenau, Willi	*Stabsobermaschinist*
Lüdke, Paul	*Obermaschinist*
Lüdmann, Heinrich	*Obersteuermann*
Mädler, Helmut	*Maschinenmaat*
Makulik, Paul	*Maschinenobergefreiter*
Marschall, Günter	*Funkobergefreiter*
Mehren, Wilhelm	*Obermaschinist*
Meyer, Wolfgang	*Leutnant zur See*
Mielke, Gerhard	*Mechanikergefreiter*
Moll, Willi	*Mechanikermaat*
Moors, Erich	*Maschinenobergefreiter*
Müller, Friedrich-Walter	Korevettenkapitän *(Ing)*
Nagorski, Heinz-Josef	*Bootsmaat*
Nissen, Jürgen	*Kapitänleutnant*
Osthus, Heinz	*Matrosenobergefreiter*
Owsianny, Edmund	*Matrosenobergefreiter*
Palm, Georg	*Matrosenobergefreiter*
Parsen, Walter	
Perschke, Heinz	*Matrosenobergefreiter*
Rave, Ernst-Wolfgang	*Kapitänleutnant*
Reinicke, Fritz	*Oberleutnant (Ing)*
Reith, Hans-Edwin	*Oberleutnant zur See*
Robbert, Heinz	*Obersteuermann*
Sanio, Hans	
Schewe, Georg	*Korvettenkapitän*
Schornborn, Gerhard	*Bootsmann*
Schuch, Heinrich	*Fregattenkapitän*
Schweichel, Hans-Adolf	*Oberleutnant zur See*
Seelisch, Gerhard	*Oberleutnant zur See*
Seelmann, Johann-Anton	*Stabsobersteuermann*
Stahl, Hans	*Kapitänleutnant (Ing)*
Throne, Gerhard	*Mechanikerobergefreiter*
Tusch, Paul	*Leutnant zur See*
Uhlig, Herbert	*Kapitänleutnant*

Uschmann, Wilhelm	*Matrosengefreiter*
Wichner, Willi	
Wiegand, Werner	*Matrosengefreiter*
Wintermeyer, Max	*Kapitänleutnant*

Known Crewmembers for the U-188

Anderer, Richard	*Maschinengefreiter*
Arnold, Hans	*Obermaschinenmaat*
Autenrieth, Wilhelm	*Funkmaat*
Bauer, Karl	*Maschinengefreiter*
Baumann, Gottlieb	*Maschinenmaat*
Beck, Friedrich	*Maschinengefreiter*
Benetschik, Bruno	*Oberleutnant zur See*
Berger, Josef	*Maschinenobergefreiter*
Bernigau, Hubert	*Maschinengefreiter*
Bischoff, August	*Obermaschinenmaat*
Braun, Max	*Mechanikermaat*
Damm, Helmut	*Funkgefreiter*
Effing, Heinrich	*Maschinengefreiter*
Esau, Dr. Ernst-Christian	*Arzt*
Ferdinand, Hans	*Maschinengefreiter*
Göbel, Anton	*Maschinengefreiter*
Götz, Johann	*Bootsmaat*
Hannak, Hermann	*Maschinengefreiter*
Hans, Arnold	*Obermaschinenmaat*
Hausmann, Josef	*Maschinengefreiter*
Heigl, Franz	*Maschinengefreiter*
Heinze, Helmut	*Maschinengefreiter*
Kahlstorff, Otto	*Funkgefreiter*
Kiessling, Max	*Kapitänleutnant (Ing)*
Korn, Heinrich	*Obersteuermann*
Kuch, Oskar	*Obermaschinist*
Landfermann, Karl-August	*Kapitänleutnant (Ing)*
Lüdden, Siegfried	*Korvettenkapitän*
Maus, Herbert	*Matrosengefreiter*
Mäusbacher, Walter	*Obermaschinist*
Meenen, Karl-Heinz	*Oberleutnant zur See*
Möller, Karl	*Maschinengefreiter*
Müller, Albert	*Maschinengefreiter*
Müller, Heinrich	*Maschinenmaat*
Obst, Walter	*Maschinengefreiter*
Olschikowski, Gerd	
Pollner, Wilhelm	*Matrosengefreiter*
Pries, Walter	*Oberbootsmann*
Raduchel, Gerhard	*Maschinenmaat*
Rentsch, Wolfgang	*Maschinengefreiter*
Richartz, Willi	*Bootsmaat*
Rieger, Gerhard	*Mechanikergefreiter*
Rohlfing, Wilhelm	*Matrosengefreiter*
Römhild, Otto	*Matrosengefreiter*
Rötters, Walter	*Matrosengefreiter*
Roy, Willi	*Matrosengefreiter*
Rullang, Johann	*Matrosengefreiter*
Rupp, Leo	*Matrosenobergefreiter*
Sabolewski, Wilhelm	*Matrosengefreiter*
Schröter, Theodor	*Matrosengefreiter*
Schulz, Martin	*Oberfunkmaat*
Schwarzer, Franz	*Matrosengefreiter*
Seibert, Martin	*Maschinengefreiter*
Stahlberg, Gerhard	*Funkobergefreiter*
Staller, Toni	*Maschinengefreiter*
Ständer, Karl	*Maschinengefreiter*
Steimer, Josef	*Bootsmaat*
Storz, Gerhard	*Matrosengefreiter*
Tatomir, Martin	
Urner, Erwin	*Maschinenmaat*
Wolf, Herbert	*Maschinenmaat*

Known Crewmembers for the U-201

Bischoff, Hermann	*Oberbootsmaat*
Boddenberg, Karl	*Oberleutnant zur See*
Bott, Karl	*Maschinengefreiter*
Boyer, Paul	*Maschinenobergefreiter*
Brock, Karl	*Obermaschinenmaat*
Brunke, Heini	*Matrosenobergefreiter*
Buss, Gerhard	*Maschinengefreiter*
Delfs, Hans	*Leutnant (Ing)*
Dierkes	*Obersteuermann*
Drossert, Johannes	*Funkmaat*
Duppel, Martin	*Oberleutnant zur See*
Düpper, Hermann	*Funkobergefreiter*
Endrulath, Karl-Heinz	*Kapitänleutnant*
Erkelenz, Johann	*Matrosenobergefreiter*
Feldmann, Hans	*Obermaschinenmaat*
Gabriel, Horst	*Matrosenobergefreiter*
Gauglitz, Heinz	
Geiger, Adolf	
Gneiser, Heinz	*Mechanikergefreiter*
Gutsche, Herbert	*Funkgefreiter*
Haase, Kurt	
Haueisen, Alfred	*Maschinenobergefreiter*
Hoee, Herbert	*Maschinengefreiter*
Huke, Theodor	*Obermaschinist*
Hülsebus, Friedrich	*Obermechanikermaat*
Hülskath, Wilhelm	*Obermaschinenmaat*
Johannes, Fritz	*Stabsobersteuermann*
Kettner, Kurt	*Maschinenmaat*
Klein, Hermann	
Klepatz, Fritz	*Funkobergefreiter*
Kodura, Ulrich	*Maschinenobergefreiter*
Kröck, Oskar	*Matrosenobergefreiter*
Krumbein, Klaus	*Maschinengefreiter*
Kubitza, Heinrich	*Maschinengefreiter*
Lechtenbörger, Willi	*Kapitänleutnant*
Lehmann, Hans-Kurt	*Maschinengefreiter*
Leimkühler, Wolfgang	*Oberleutnant zur See*
Link, Josef	*Maschinenmaat*
Link, Willi	*Maschinenobergefreiter*
Mantel, Josef	*Fähnrich zur See*
Müller, Josef	*Matrosenobergefreiter*
Muschwitz, Rolf von	*Leutnant zur See*
Nehring, Dietrich	*Fähnrich zur See*
Netter, Arthur	*Maschinenmaat*
Ney, Kornelius	*Matrosenobergefreiter*
Nolte, Herbert	*Mechanikergefreiter*
Oelschlägel, Gottfried	*Maschinengefreiter*
Ostermann, Willi	
Plesiur, Johannes	*Maschinengefreiter*
Richter, Dr. Helmuth	*Arzt*
Rieger, Eberhard	*Oberleutnant zur See*
Rosenberg, Günther	*Oberleutnant zur See*
Schnee, Adalbert	*Korvettenkapitän*
Schramm, Fritz-Peter	*Oberleutnant zur See*
Schütz, Herbert	

Schyns, Peter	*Matrose*
Stemmer, Heinz	*Maschinenobergefreiter*
Stockhaus, Willy	*Maschinenmaat*
Strewe, Gerhard	*Bootsmaat*
Suhr, Georg	*Matrosenobergefreiter*
Wahl, Albert	*Matrosenobergefreiter*
Walking, Erich	*Obermaschinist*
Wienold	
Winters, Carl	*Leutnant zur See*
Wittenbrock, Karl	*Bootsmaat*
Zander, Joachim	*Kapitänleutnant*
Zander, Josef	*Maschinenobergefreiter*
Zeitz, Ernst-Eugen	*Funkmaat*
Zenner, Walter	*Funkmaat*
Zimmerhacke, Johann	*Bootsmaat*

Sources, "Friendship:" Clay Blair, *Hitler's U-boat War: The Hunters, 1939-1942*, New York: Random House, 1996, 124; Clay Blair, *Hitler's U-boat War: The Hunted, 1942-1945*, New York: Modern Library, 2000, 100, 184, 280, 281, 355, 372, 393, 394, 395, 396, 400, 401, 402, 528, 529, 530, 531, 540, 542, 547, 557, 565, 621; Rainer Busch and Hans-Joachim Röll, *German U-boat Commanders of World War II*, translated by Geoffrey Brooks, Annapolis, Maryland: Naval Institute Press, 1999, 214, 225, 228, 229; Manfred Dörr, *Die Ritterkreuzträger der U-Boot-Waffe, Band 1: A-J, Band 2: L-Z*, Osnabrück, FRG: Biblio Verlag, 1988, Band 2 – 50, 51, 89, 90, 91, 227, 228, 233, 234, 235; Herbert Ritschel, *Kurzfassung Kriegstagebücher deutscher U-boote 1939-1945, Band 3: KTB U100 – U124*, Norderstedt, Germany: Books on Demand, 73-94; Herbert Ritschel, *Kurzfassung Kriegstagebücher deutscher U-boote 1939-1945, Band 5: KTB U171 – U222*, Norderstedt, Germany: Books on Demand, 121-129, 201-208; Jürgen Rohwer, *Axis Submarine Successes 1939-1945*, Annapolis, Maryland: Naval Institute Press, 1983, 8, 25, 27, 28; 50, 51, 62, 66, 68, 90, 91, 107, 108, 109, 111, 126, 127; www.ubootwaffe.net; www.uboatarchive.net.

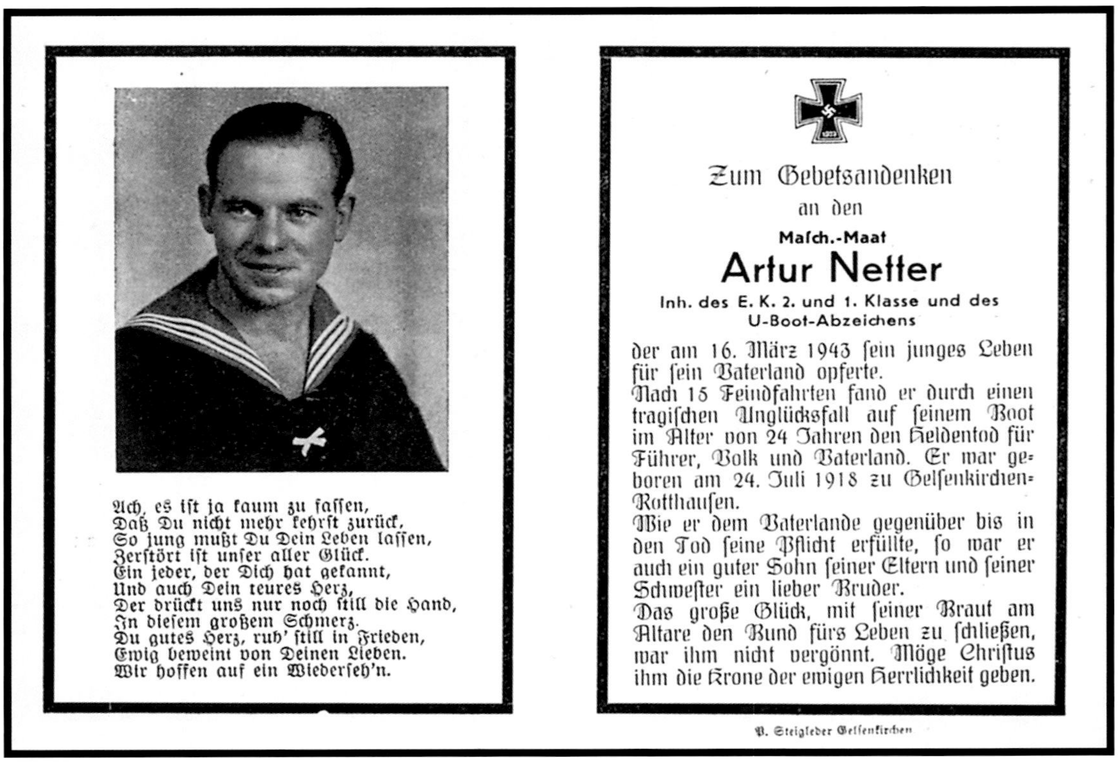

Ach, es ist ja kaum zu fassen,
Daß Du nicht mehr kehrst zurück,
So jung mußt Du Dein Leben lassen,
Zerstört ist unser aller Glück.
Ein jeder, der Dich hat gekannt,
Und auch Dein teures Herz,
Der drückt uns nur noch still die Hand,
In diesem großem Schmerz.
Du gutes Herz, ruh' still in Frieden,
Ewig beweint von Deinen Lieben.
Wir hoffen auf ein Wiederseh'n.

Zum Gebetsandenken
an den
Masch.-Maat
Artur Netter
Inh. des E. K. 2. und 1. Klasse und des U-Boot-Abzeichens

der am 16. März 1943 sein junges Leben für sein Vaterland opferte.
Nach 15 Feindfahrten fand er durch einen tragischen Unglücksfall auf seinem Boot im Alter von 24 Jahren den Heldentod für Führer, Volk und Vaterland. Er war geboren am 24. Juli 1918 zu Gelsenkirchen-Rotthausen.
Wie er dem Vaterlande gegenüber bis in den Tod seine Pflicht erfüllte, so war er auch ein guter Sohn seiner Eltern und seiner Schwester ein lieber Bruder.
Das große Glück, mit seiner Braut am Altare den Bund fürs Leben zu schließen, war ihm nicht vergönnt. Möge Christus ihm die Krone der ewigen Herrlichkeit geben.

W. Steigleder Gelsenkirchen

Death Announcement by the family of Maschinenmaat Artur Netter. *Information includes his date of death of March 16, 1943 and that he had received the Iron Cross 2nd Class, Iron Cross 1st Class and U-boat War Badge. Most important, by knowing from the announcement that Netter had made fifteen war patrols, we can determine with good accuracy the time periods he served on his previous boats.*

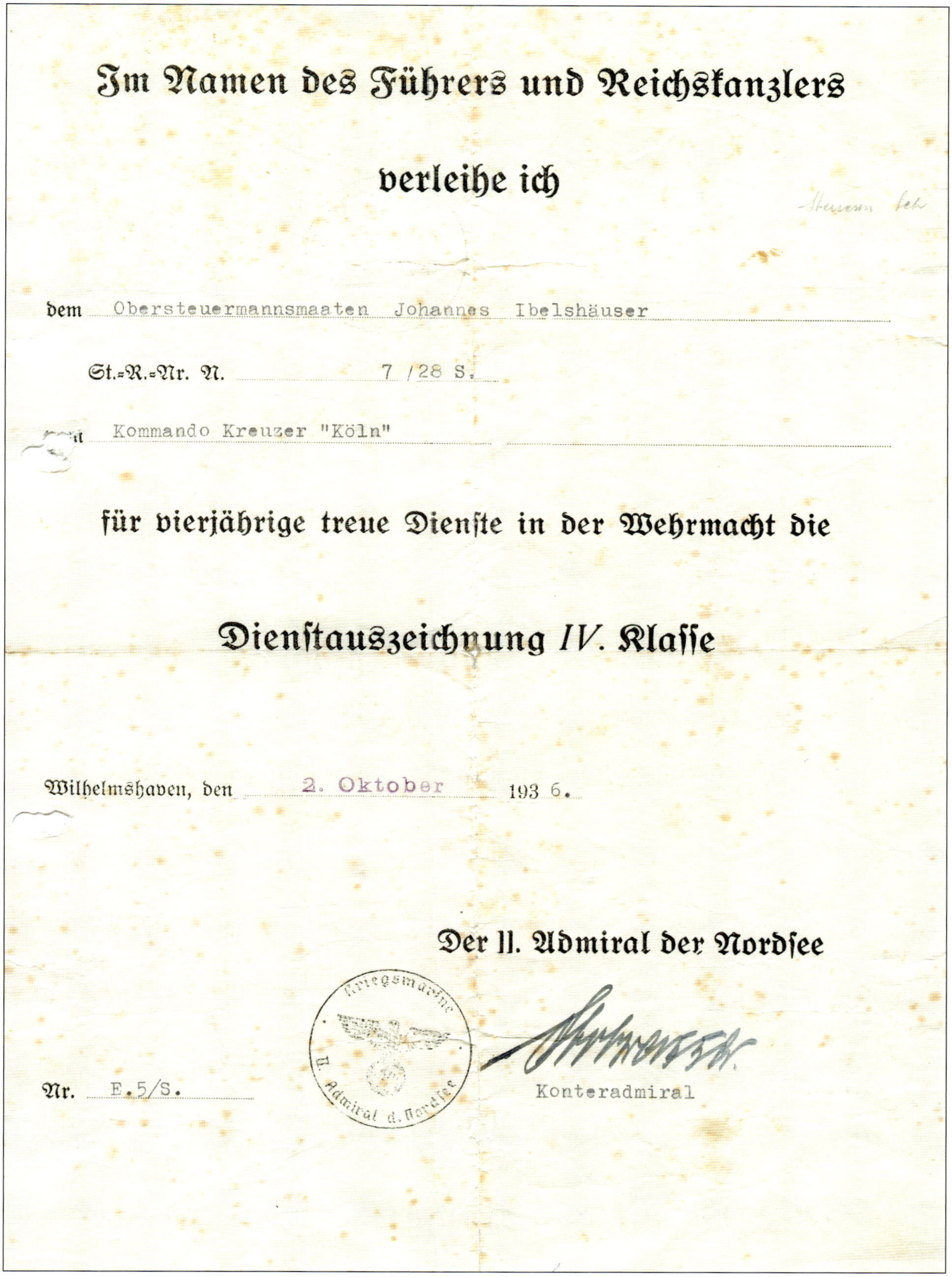

Im Namen des Führers und Reichskanzlers

verleihe ich

dem Obersteuermannsmaaten Johannes Ibelshäuser

St.-R.-Nr. N. 7 /28 S.

Kommando Kreuzer "Köln"

für vierjährige treue Dienste in der Wehrmacht die

Dienstauszeichnung *IV.* Klasse

Wilhelmshaven, den 2. Oktober 1936.

Der II. Admiral der Nordsee

Kriegsmarine II. Admiral d. Nordsee

Konteradmiral

Nr. E.5/S.

Armed Forces Service Medal IV Class, for four years of service, award document to Obersteuermannsmaat Johannes Ibelshäuser, dated October 2, 1936. *Ibelshäuser was assigned to the light cruiser Köln. Document is signed by Konteradmiral Hans-Herbert Stobwasser, 2nd Admiral North Sea. Stobwasser committed suicide in 1946.*

Photo of Navy Cadet Johannes Ibelshäuser, dated 1928.

Wedding photo of Johannes Ibelshäuser and his bride before the war.

Obersteuermann Johannes Ibelshäuser (right) and a Chief Petty Officer comrade before the war.

Kapitänleutnant Georg Schewe just after receiving the Knight's Cross on June 13, 1941. *Photo taken at Lorient, France.*

Kapitänleutnant Georg Schewe receives congratulations from Karl Dönitz just after receiving the Knight's Cross. *Photo taken at Lorient, France on June 13, 1941.*

Georg Schewe with his wife.

Georg Schewe with wife and flowers at a reception.

Official photo of Georg Schewe and his Knight's Cross.

Georg Schewe and family.

Georg Schewe and parents.

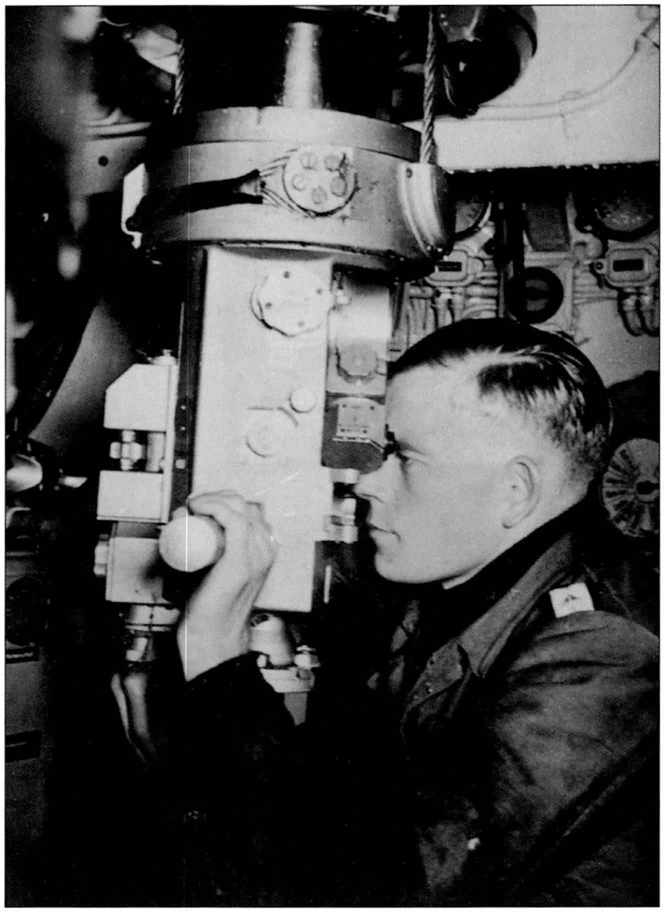

Georg Schewe at the periscope on a U-boat.

Georg Schewe (center, with hands crossed) with visitors on the U-60 shortly before the war. *Photo is a post-war copy of an original.*

Visitors on the U-60. *Photo is a post-war copy of an original.*

Crew on deck of the U-60 shortly before the war. *Crewmen are wearing cap band U-boat Flotilla Emsmann. Photo is a post-war copy of an original.*

Obersteuermann Johannes Ibelshäuser using signal flags on the bridge of the U-60. *After the start of the war the Kriegsmarine removed the national eagle symbol from the bridge-front of all U-boats.*

Obersteuermann Johannes Ibelshäuser on the bridge of a U-boat. *(Photo courtesy of U-boat Archive & Museum, Cuxhaven, Germany.)*

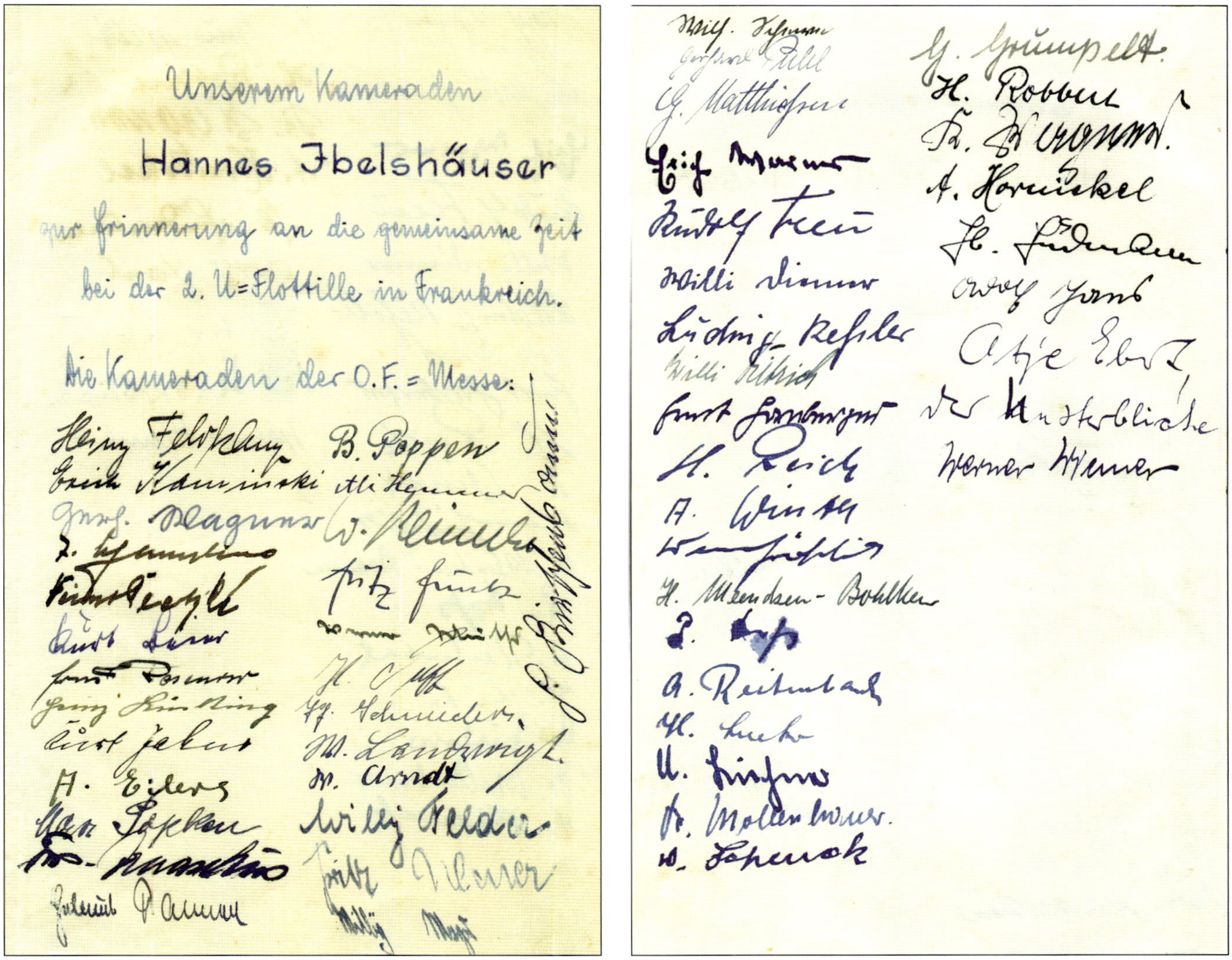

Unserem Kameraden

Hannes Ibelshäuser

zur Erinnerung an die gemeinsame Zeit bei der 2. U=Flottille in Frankreich.

Die Kameraden der O.F. = Messe:

Dedication to Johannes Ibelshäuser on his departure from the 2nd U-boat Flotilla in France to attend officer commissioning training. *Some of the signatures on the multi-page document can be identified as: Alfred Eilers (killed in action August 7, 1943 on the U-117), Gerhard Fuhl (killed in action July 31, 1943 on the U-199), Willi Dietrich (killed in action April 29, 1945 on the U-286), Alfred Reitenbach (killed in action May 6, 1943 on the U-125), Wilhelm Schenck (German Cross in Gold winner on the U-107), Gerhard Grumpelt (U-105), Heinz Robbert (U-105), Alfred Hornickel (U-105), Heinrich Lindmann (U-105) and Adolf Jahns (U-105).*

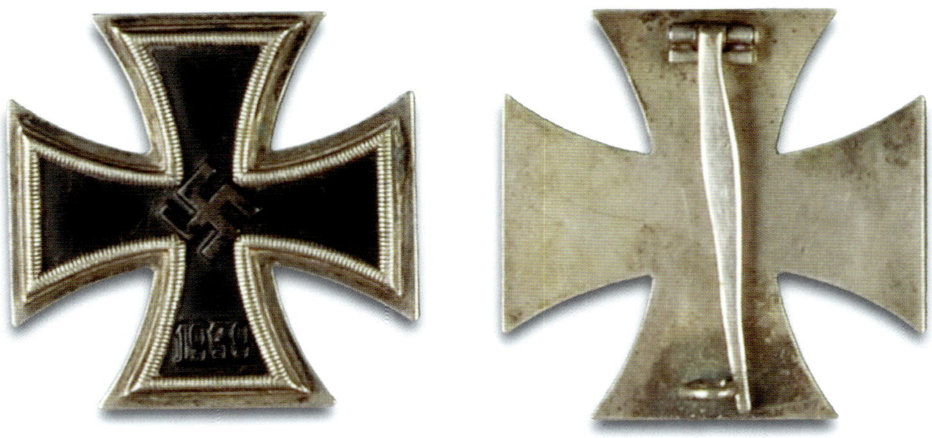

Iron Cross 1st Class belonging to Johannes Ibelshäuser.

Officer's brocade belt and buckle belonging to Johannes Ibelshäuser.

U-boat Front Clasp in Bronze awarded to August Bischoff of the U-188. *The U-boat Front Clasp was awarded to holders of the U-boat War Badge to recognize continued combat service and valor. This is the second version of the award and was die-cast from zinc. The second version was produced from November 30, 1944 to the end of the war. As Bischoff's U-boat Front Clasp in Bronze award certificate was dated on September 27, 1944, this piece was probably a second one he acquired for wear.*

U-boat Front Clasp in Bronze awarded to August Bischoff (reverse.) *Like the first version, the award was composed of a laurel wreath surrounding a submarine, surmounted by the national emblem. On each side there were three rows of oak leaves; the two crossed swords at the base of the wreath emphasized the military nature of the award. On the left side of the reverse of the badge is the word "ENTWURF" above the word "PEEKHAUS". On the right hand side are three lines of words; the top is "AUSF", the second line is "SCHWERIN" and the third line is "BERLIN 68".*

Cloth version of the German Cross in Gold to August Bischoff (front). *Award was made to Bischoff on August 3, 1944. The award document (not shown) was signed by Karl Dönitz. The original award was in metal but U-boat crewmen found that the large badge was too cumbersome to be worn in cramped confines. The badge was then produced in cloth, which was light and did not catch on the myriad of pipes and valves throughout a U-boat. Some versions have a cloth backing covering all the stitching.*

Photograph of two German Cross in Gold winners. *On the left is Mechanikermaat Max Braun; on the right is Obermaschinenmaat August Bischoff. Both men are wearing the original metal version of the German Cross; photo is probably from late 1944 or early 1945. Max Braun died on July 25, 1970.*

August Bischoff (right) with two shipmates and young lady outside a restaurant or hotel in Germany.

Another view of German Cross in Gold winners (left) Mechanikermaat Max Braun and (right) Obermaschinenmaat August Bischoff.

August Bischoff (right) with Luftwaffe sergeant.

CHAPTER FIFTEEN

"The Backbone of the Fleet" U-710 April 1943

U-boat skippers came in all degrees of proficiency; the best ones sank thousands of tons of enemy ships, won various grades of the Knight's Cross and were often beloved by their crews. The worst ones were relieved of command, unless they first really made a critical mistake that destroyed the boat and killed the crew. The engineer officers were often thought of as magicians, exorcising the demons from the massive diesel engines and electric motors so the boat could make it home after a successful cruise, and as ingenious improvisers who could patch up almost any piece of equipment or fixture of broken pipe after a depth charge attack.

Dönitz's Crews
***Stabsobersteuermann* Albert Möbus**
Born on September 15, 1920.
Served as the navigator on the *U-17*, *U-24* and *U-710*.
Awarded the U-boat War Badge on January 20, 1940.
Spent 64 days at sea on U-boat war patrols.
Killed in action on April 24, 1943 in the North Atlantic south of Iceland.

But everyone knew who really ran the boat – the Chief Petty Officers and the Petty Officers.

It was a long, hard road to travel for a man to get to that position. By the end of World War I the German Navy realized that non-commissioned officers (NCOs) required specialist training within a clearly defined system of recruiting and promotion. To ensure a future non-commissioned officer truly understood what it was like to be an ordinary seaman, potential NCOs were selected for specialized training after two or three years of satisfactory service in the ranks, but only if they demonstrated characteristics of self-discipline, dedication and loyalty, and only if they had signed on for a twelve-year enlistment. These selectees would first attend a three-to-ten-month course in their career branch to ensure they had a good technical background. On successful completion of these schools, the graduates would report to the Navy school at Friedrichsort – the NCO Training School. At this school the future NCOs concentrated their training that included: theoretical classroom instruction, nautical studies, sports/physical training and infantry training. As the Navy expanded, requirements for NCOs did as well, and in 1935 the High Command started a second NCO school at Wesermünde, and in 1938 built a new NCO school at Plön.

Every critical area on a U-boat had a Chief Petty Officer (CPO) or Petty Officer (PO) close by because unlike most surface ships with their thick armor and hundreds of compartments if the situation turned badly on a U-boat, it could go catastrophic in a hurry. An *Oberbootsmann* (CPO) was Chief of the Boat; the good ones knew what the commander would order even before the order was given. He was habitually in the control room overseeing how the ship was running but could also quickly run to any threatened area. Often referred to as "Number 1," he was also in charge of the crews' uniforms and equipment and the daily cleaning of the U-boat. The *Obersteuermann* (CPO) had two roles; in port he served as the quartermaster and ensured that all provisions were loaded onboard before sailing. He knew where every spare nook and cranny was on the boat – because he would have to fill every unused space with food and provisions as no one ever actually knew exactly how long a boat would be at sea on a patrol. Once at sea, he would serve as the Navigator, plotting courses on the navigation table off the control room. Two Petty Officers worked for the Chief of the Boat. A *Bootsmannsmaat* (PO), often called "Number 2", was responsible for all the U-boat's munitions. Another *Bootsmannsmaat* (PO) served as the Master at Arms; as "Number 3" he was in charge of all administrative and personal issues regarding the sailors as well as being responsible for quieting a sailor who might lose control during an attack against the boat. The *Oberbootsmann* and his two assistants often served as lookouts on the bridge based on their experience.

In the control room were several *Maschinenmaat* (PO), who operated all the trim controls, ballast controls and the ventilation system gyro-compasses. In the tiny radio room, two *Funkmaat* (PO) would receive and send signals and help decode incoming messages. They would also operate the underwater sound detection gear.

Back in the engine room were up to seven CPOs and POs, all helping to keep the machinery running – port and starboard diesels, electric motors; it was not a room for those averse to continuous loud noise. An *Obermaschinist* (CPO) was in charge of the diesel engines and another *Obermaschinist* was responsible for the electric motors; later in the war both could have an elevated rank of *Stabsobermaschinist* (CPO). An *Obermechaniker* (CPO) and two *Mechanikermaat* (PO) served upfront in the forward torpedo room. They ensured the torpedoes were loaded, set and fired correctly.

An additional Petty Officer served as the chief of the 88-mm deck-gun crew, should the boat surface and use this weapon. Having said all that, every crewman knew that they had to be prepared to help everyone else in case of an emergency.

While commissioned officers received the lion's share of Germany's highest military decorations, such as the Knight's Cross, seven Chief Petty Officers/Petty Officers did as well and they bear noting.

Before he won his own Knight's Cross on November 5, 1940, *Stabsobersteuermann* Heinrich Petersen had spent almost twenty years in the Navy. Born in Hamburg on November 3, 1902, Petersen joined the service at the end of World War I. The post-World War I years saw him serving in various NCO positions in the surface fleet, before leaving the Navy in 1931. He re-joined in 1935 and soon thereafter underwent U-boat training. He joined the *U-23* (a Type IIB coastal boat) as the *Obersteuermann* in 1937. Serving under the famous Knight's Cross with Oak Leaves and Swords winner Otto Kretschmer, Petersen served as Navigator/Quartermaster on the *U-23* for seven war patrols, during which the boat sank eight enemy ships in the North Sea, primarily off the northeast coast of Scotland. Petersen won the Iron Cross 2nd Class on November 19, 1939 and the Iron Cross 1st Class on February 25, 1940. In mid-1940 the *U-23* was transferred to training duties, but Kretschmer and his crew were too valuable to take from combat and they commissioned the *U-99*, a more capable Type VIIB boat. Now a *Stabsobersteuermann*, Petersen navigated the boat to assist in the destruction of a further thirty-six enemy ships – a total of 266,629 tons sunk while in the two boats. Kretschmer received the Knight's Cross with Oak Leaves one day before Petersen won the Knight's Cross. On March 17, 1941 the *U-99* fought a fierce battle southeast of Iceland with the *HMS Walker* (Cdr. D.G. MacIntyre), a British destroyer. Damage from depth charges forced the boat to surface; Kretschmer, Petersen and thirty-eight others were rescued from the frigid water, while three men perished. Heinrich Petersen spent the rest of the conflict in a prisoner of war camp in Canada. He received a promotion while in prisoner of war status to Reserve First Lieutenant. Heinrich Petersen died in Kiel on June 6, 1963.

The second U-boat non-commissioned officer to receive the Knight's Cross was *Obersteuermann* Walter Kaeding on May 15, 1944. Kaeding entered the Navy in 1935 at age nineteen (he was born in Berlin on September 14, 1915). He served in the surface forces for four years before attending U-boat training in 1939. Now a Petty Officer, Kaeding joined the crew of the Type IXB boat *U-123* in which he served for almost four years, rising to *Obersteuermann* (Navigator/Quartermaster). During this period, Kaeding served on thirteen war patrols spending 703 days at sea to include operations in the North Atlantic, off West Africa and along the coast of the United States. Serving for three different commanders, Karl-Heinz Moehle, Reinhard Hardegen and Horst von Schroeter – all of whom won the Knight's Cross – Kaeding and the *U-123* sank fifty-two enemy ships. In addition to the Knight's Cross, Walter Kaeding also won the following awards: Iron Cross 2nd Class and U-boat War Badge, December 11, 1940; Iron Cross 1st Class, August 25, 1941; German Cross in Gold, September 6, 1943; and the U-boat Front Clasp in Bronze, January 9, 1945. He was promoted to *Leutnant zur See* on October 1, 1944. Kaeding was scheduled to take command of the *U-4713* when the war ended. Walter Kaeding died on January 4, 1991 in Bremen.

Horst Hofmann received the Knight's Cross on May 20, 1944 as the *Obersteuermann* on the *U-672*. Born in Cranzahl in the Erzgebirge on January 18, 1919, he joined the Navy at age eighteen in 1937. He soon underwent U-boat training and became a crewmember of the *U-48*, a Type VIIB boat, making five war patrols in this boat under Knight's Cross with Oak Leaves winner Herbert Schultze and sinking sixteen enemy ships in the North Sea and North Atlantic. During this period Hofmann received the Iron Cross 2nd Class on February 25, 1940 and the Iron Cross 1st Class on August 30, 1940; he was also promoted to *Bootsmannsmaat* (PO). Hofmann then attended a series of schools in Germany to include artillery training to prepare him to lead the 88-mm deck-gun crew on his next boat. That assignment came in July 1941 when he transferred to the *U-134*, a Type VIIC boat. The *U-134* sank three Allied ships while Hofmann was part of the crew – although none involved the 88-mm gun; he left the boat in early 1943 to attend Navigator's School and on April 1, 1943 was awarded the German Cross in Gold. Promoted to *Obersteuermann* (CPO), he joined the *U-672* (a Type VIIC) as Navigator/Quartermaster on October 1, 1943. On the *U-672*'s first war patrol, the boat was attacked in the English Channel on July 18, 1944 by the British destroyer escort *HMS Balfour* (Lt. Cdr. C. D. Coventry). After a heavy depth charge attack, the *U-672* surfaced and the entire crew was taken prisoner. He was not released by the British until October 1947. Horst Hofmann died in Lübeck on June 14, 1978.

Stabsobermaschinist Heinrich Dammeier started his Navy career far from the U-boat service. Born February 9, 1914 in Beckedorf near Schaumburg, he joined the Navy as a nineteen-year-old recruit in 1933 and soon found himself on the pocket battleship *Deutschland*. On this ship, he served in the Spanish Civil War as well as an 80-day war patrol at the beginning of World War II, winning the Spanish Cross in Silver with Swords on June 6, 1939 and the Iron Cross 2nd Class on December 2, 1939. Dammeier then went through U-boat training – as did many other surface fleet sailors – being assigned as an *Obermaschinist* (CPO) to the *U-129*, a Type IXC boat in April 1941. A mainstay in the engine room, Dammeier conducted nine war patrols under Nicolai Clausen, Hans-Ludwig Witt and Richard von Harpe (the first two won the Knight's Cross), participating in the sinking of twenty-nine ships – a total of 143,748 tons. During this three-year stint, Heinrich Dammeier spent 721 days at sea and won: the U-boat War Badge on December 29, 1941; the Iron Cross 1st Class on August 18, 1942; the High Seas Fleet Badge (for previous service on the *Deutschland*) on July 15, 1943; and the German Cross in Gold on February 12, 1944. He was also promoted to *Stabsobermaschinist* (CPO) on July 1, 1943. Dammeier transferred to the *U-270* (a Type VIIC boat) on August 1, 1944. His Knight's Cross came through on August 12, 1944. The citation noted that he had saved his boat and crew by his actions in difficult situations. Dammeier would face a difficult situation the very next day as the *U-270* sailed from Lorient to La Pallice, France. At 12:10 a.m. on August 13 a Sunderland aircraft (Flight Officer D. A. Little) of the 461st Squadron, Royal Australian Air Force (RAAF) attacked the *U-270* with depth charges northwest of La Rochelle. Forced to surface, the crew had to abandon ship; seventy-one men were rescued and taken as prisoners of war. Heinrich Dammeier was released from captivity in December 1947. He died in his hometown on May 16, 2001.

Oberbootsmannsmaat Rudolf Mühlbauer received his Knight's Cross on December 10, 1944. Born on March 27, 1919 at Königsbrück, Saxony, he entered the Navy in 1939 and after basic training went into the U-boats. As a junior enlisted man he joined the *U-123* and served with Walter Kaeding. Mühlbauer served with the boat on eight war patrols from September 1940 to May 1942, helping to sink forty-five ships. His efforts earned him an Iron Cross 2nd Class in March 1941 and an Iron Cross 1st Class in June 1942. Promoted to *Bootsmannsmaat* (PO) on August 1, 1942, he joined the *U-170*, a Type IXC-40 boat. Mühlbauer served six war patrols with his boat; during his wartime service he could count 309,500 tons of enemy shipping he helped sink. On January 10, 1944 Rudolf Mühlbauer received the German Cross in Gold. His Knight's Cross citation noted that he saved his boat from certain destruction on two occasions. Rudolf Mühlbauer finished the war as an *Oberbootsmann* (CPO). He died in Laussnitz, Saxony on March 26, 2000.

The sixth CPO/PO to win the Knight's Cross was Heinz Prassdorf, who joined the Navy just short of his nineteenth birthday. Born December 7, 1918 in Rostock, he underwent U-boat training and joined the *U-48* as a *Maschinenobergefreiter* and served with Helmut Hofmann until late 1940 when he transferred to commission the *U-557* and transferred yet again to the *U-558*, a Type VIIC boat. He was promoted to *Obermaschinist* on November 1, 1943. We do not know how long he served on these boats; he must have left the *U-558* before July 20, 1943 when it was sunk in the Bay of Biscay. He joined the *U-1203*, a Type VIIC boat on February 2, 1944 and participated on three war patrols, helping to sink three enemy ships. On April 21, 1945 Prassdorf received the Knight's Cross. The citation noted that in many difficult situations he saved the *U-1203* from destruction during depth charge attacks. Heinz Prassdorf died on November 8, 1993 in Rostock.

The last CPO/PO winner of the Knight's Cross was *Obersteuermann* (CPO) Karl Jäckel, who received his award on May 8, 1945. Born in Gladbeck, Westphalia on December 20, 1913, he entered the Navy in 1937 and appears to have quickly entered U-boat training. He joined the crew of the *U-29* in April 1940 and served on four war patrols with this Type VIIA boat. During this time the boat, under Otto Schuhart (a Knight's Cross winner), sank four enemy ships. Jäckel then transferred to the *U-160* (a Type IXC boat) in October 1941 after the 1st Watch Officer on the *U-29*, Georg Lassen, requested that Karl Jäckel be assigned to his new boat. Lassen would go on to win the Knight's Cross with Oak Leaves. On four war patrols the boat sank 26 enemy ships, some 156, 082 tons. He left the boat, as did Lassen, two months before the boat was sunk in July 1943. Jäckel's next U-boat assignment was with the *U-907*, a Type VIIC. He received the German Cross in Gold on October 28, 1944. His Knight's Cross was approved by Karl Dönitz, who took over leadership of Germany on May 1, 1945 after the death of Adolf Hitler. Karl Jäckel died on December 7, 1984 in his hometown.

Stabsobersteuermann Albert Möbus was not a Knight's Cross winner, nor did he win the German Cross in Gold, but he was emblematic of the German Navy non-commissioned officer corps. Born on September 15, 1920, by 1939 he had completed his U-boat training and was aboard the *U-17*, a Type IIB coastal boat as an *Obersteuermann*. He completed two war patrols with this boat, including one mine-laying mission off Dover, England. He then joined the *U-24* – when the *U-17* transferred to a training flotilla – and may well have participated in the boat's two patrols through April 30, 1940. We do not know what assignment he had over the next two and a half years before he helped commission the *U-710* on September 2, 1942 at Hamburg-Steinwärder; Albert Möbus would be the Navigator/Quartermaster for the boat. He helped guide her through the U.A.K. (U-boat Acceptance Command) tests and the U.A.G. (U-boat Acceptance Group) tests. The U-boat also trained with the 26th U-boat Training Flotilla on gunnery and torpedo skills and with the 25th U-boat Training Flotilla on underwater attack tactics.

The *U-710* left Kiel under the command of *Oberleutnant zur See* Dietrich von Carlowitz on April 15, 1943. It was his first command, although he had been a watch officer for six months on the *U-98*, so he would depend on his NCOs. The U-boat was to head south of Iceland to patrol. B.d.U. transmitted further orders to the *U-710* on April 19, April 26, April 27 and April 28 with no response.

There would never be a response from the *U-710*.

At 5:25 p.m. on April 24, 1943 a British-crewed B-17 Flying Fortress (Flight Officer R.L. Cowey) of the 206th Squadron, 15th Group, Coastal Command, Royal Air Force, while flying cover for convoy HX-234, spotted the submarine south of Iceland. The bomber attacked, and although the surfaced boat fought back with 20-mm flak, six depth charges set for shallow explosion landed very close to the boat and she started to quickly sink.

The aircrew estimated that twenty-five men escaped the U-boat into the freezing water as darkness quickly followed. We do not know if Albert Möbus made it out of the stricken boat, or – if he did – for how long he was able to keep the survivors alive that night, as no member of the crew was ever seen again. Given the tradition of Chief Petty Officer and Petty Officer service in the U-boats, Albert Möbus most certainly gave it everything he had.

Known Crewmembers for the U-710

Bischoff, Gustav-Hinrich	*Oberleutnant zur See*
Carlowitz, Dietrich von	*Oberleutnant zur See*
Decken, Heinz	*Funkmaat*
Eckhardt, Karl	*Maschinenmaat*
Freund, Helmut	*Maschinengefreiter*
Hannuschka, Oskar	*Maschinengefreiter*
Heine, Hubert	*Funkgefreiter*
Hentschel, Bruno	*Obermaschinist*
Hoffmann, Harald	*Maschinengefreiter*
Hümer, Franz	*Maschinenmaat*
Jagla, Wilhelm	*Maschinengefreiter*
Jakob, Heinrich	*Matrosengefreiter*
Janzen, Helmut	*Maschinengefreiter*
Kammerer, Josef	*Matrosengefreiter*
Kämpfe, Rolf	*Maschinengefreiter*
Köck, Josef	*Matrosengefreiter*
Koscholleck, Stanislaus	*Maschinengefreiter*
Krey, Günther	*Maschinengefreiter*
Kroll, Günter-Otto	*Leutnant zur See*
Kroschinski, Gerhard	*Maschinenmaat*
Kunath, Otto	*Maschinengefreiter*
Kunze, Siegfried	*Bootsmannsmaat*
Lay, Alfons	*Maschinenmaat*
Leibig, Paul	*Matrosenobergefreiter*
Lenz, Wilfried	*Oberfähnrich zur See*
Lerch, Max	*Matrosenobergefreiter*
Liebner, Helmut	*Matrosengefreiter*
Lietz, Ernst	*Oberfähnrich (Ing)*
Löchel, Hans	*Matrosengefreiter*
Lottersberger, Otto	*Matrosengefreiter*
Möbus, Albert	*Stabsobersteuermann*
Offenborn, Friedrich	*Obermaschinist*
Reich, Willi	*Matrosengefreiter*
Richter, Herbert	*Maschinengefreiter*
Rosendahl, Egidius	*Maschinengefreiter*
Ruhle, Heinz	*Mechanikermaat*
Schade, Karl-Heinz	*Oberfähnrich zur See*
Schäefer, Gerhard	*Funkobergefreiter*
Schmidt, Gerd	*Maschinenmaat*
Schmoranzer, Fritz	*Maschinengefreiter*
Schönfeld, Heinz	*Bootsmannsmaat*
Seiffert, Fritz	*Leutnant (Ing)*
Simon, Erhard	*Leutnant zur See*
Theves, Hubert	*Mechanikerobergefreiter*
Thies, Paul	*Funkmaat*
Vorwald, Friedrich	*Mechanikerobergefreiter*
Wagner, Rudolf	*Matrosenobergefreiter*
Wasinski, Josef	*Maschinengefreiter*
Willner, Rudolf	*Maschinenmaat*
Wurzer, Josef	*Bootsmannsmaat*

Sources, "The Backbone of the Fleet:" Clay Blair, *Hitler's U-boat War: The Hunted, 1942-1945*, New York: Modern Library, 2000, 275; Rainer Busch and Hans-Joachim Röll, *German U-boat Commanders of World War II*, translated by Geoffrey Brooks, Annapolis, Maryland: Naval Institute Press, 1999, 46; Jean Delize, *U-boote Crews: Daily Life, 1939-1945*, Paris, France: Histoire & Collections, 2007, 75, 76, 77; Manfred Dörr, *Die Ritterkreuzträger der U-Boot-Waffe, Band 1: A-J, Band 2: L-Z*, Osnabrück, FRG: Biblio Verlag, 1988, Band 1-35, 36, 141, 142, 146, 164, 165, 166, 172, 183, 184, 189, 190, 192, 193, 194, Band 2 – 2, 3, 136, 137, 146, 163, 164, 181; Axel Niestlé, *German U-boat Losses during World War II*, Annapolis, Maryland: Naval Institute Press, 1998, 41, 51, 81, 83; Jak Mallmann Showell, *Wolfpacks at War: The U Boat Experience in World War II*, Hersham, England: Ian Allan Publishing, 2002, 17; War Diary of the U-710, September 2, 1942 – April 28, 1943, PG 30717; ONI Roll T-423, *National Archives Microfilm Publication T1022*, roll 3377, RG 242; David Westwood, *The U-boat War: The German Submarine Service and the Battle of the Atlantic, 1935-1945*, Philadelphia, PA: Casemate, 2005, 198; Gordon Williamson, *Wolf Pack: The Story of the U-boat in World War II*, Oxford, England: Osprey Publishing, 2006, 152, 153; www.ubootwaffe.net; www.uboatarchive.net.

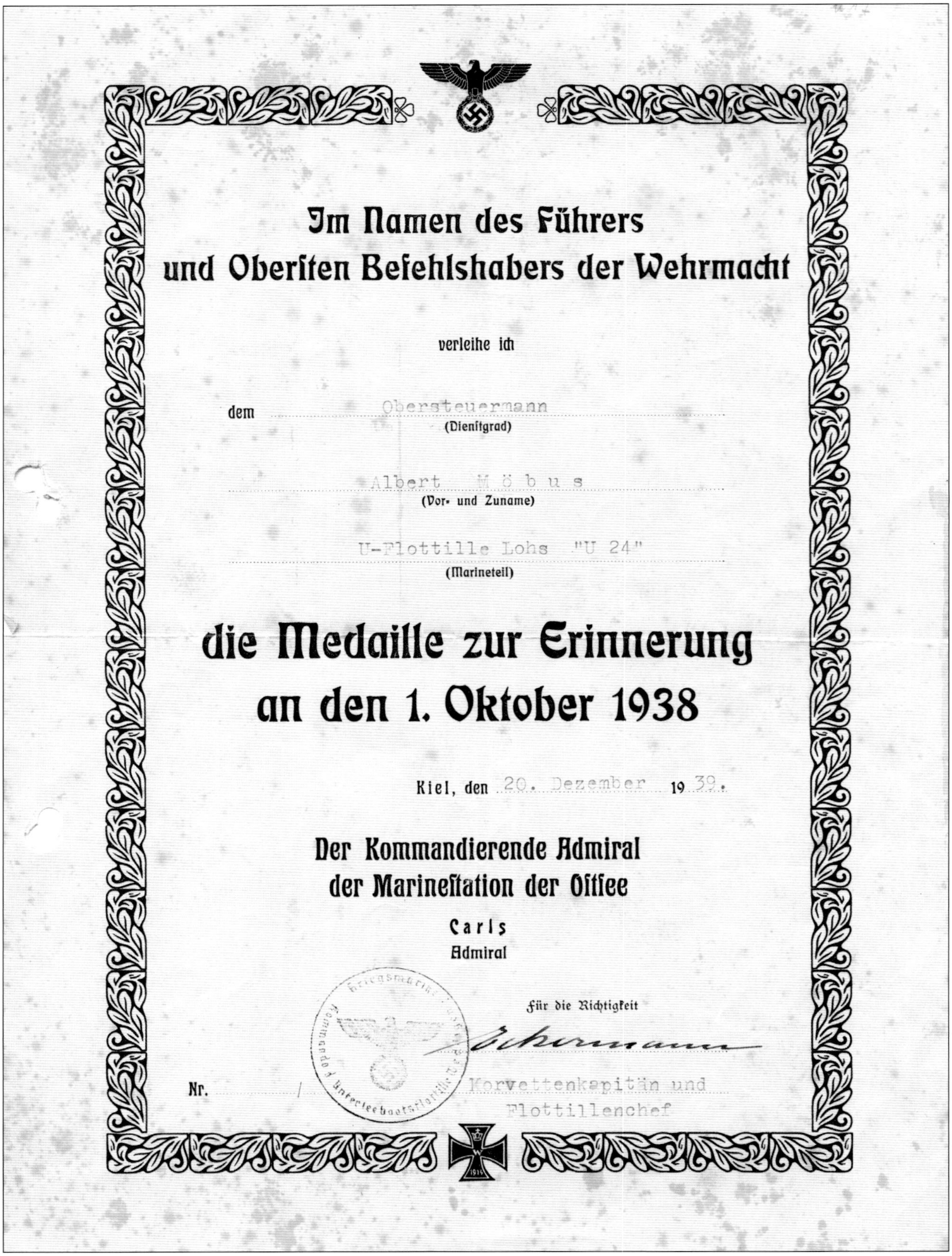

Im Namen des Führers
und Oberſten Befehlshabers der Wehrmacht

verleihe ich

dem Obersteuermann
(Dienſtgrad)

Albert Möbus
(Vor- und Zuname)

U-Flottille Lohs "U 24"
(Marineteil)

die Medaille zur Erinnerung
an den 1. Oktober 1938

Kiel, den 20. Dezember 1939.

Der Kommandierende Admiral
der Marineſtation der Oſtſee

Carls
Admiral

Für die Richtigkeit
Eckermann
Korvettenkapitän und
Flottillenchef

Nr. /

Commemorative Medal of 1 October 1938 (the Annexation of Czechoslovakia) award document to Albert Möbus of the U-24 on December 20, 1939. *Document is signed by Korvettenkapitän Hans Eckermann, Commander U-boat Flotilla Weddigen.*

Verleihungs-Urkunde.

Auf Grund der Ermächtigung des Oberbefehlshabers der Kriegsmarine verleihe ich dem

Obersteuermann
(Dienstgrad)

Albert Möbus
(Name)

das

Ubootskriegsabzeichen 1939

Wilhelmshaven, den 20. Januar 1940

Konteradmiral und Befehlshaber der Unterseeboote

U-boat War Badge award document to Albert Möbus of the U-24 on January 20, 1940. *The document has a facsimile signature of Konteradmiral Karl Dönitz.*

The backbone of the fleet; Oberbootsmann Johann Völz on the bridge of the U-459, a Type XIV supply U-boat. *Born on June 2, 1909, Völz was killed in action on July 24, 1943 when the U-459 was sunk by two British Wellington aircraft off Cape Ortegal, Spain. Photo is from the estate of a former crewmember of the U-459.*

The backbone of the fleet; two Chief Petty Officers of the U-333 after returning from a war patrol. *Photo is from the estate of a former crewmember of the U-333.*

The backbone of the fleet; veteran Chief Petty officer, in his well-worn leather jacket, grabs a smoke on the bridge at sea on the U-459. *Photo is from the estate of a former crewmember of the U-459.*

Rudolf Mühlbauer wearing the Knight's Cross. *On the reverse is a handwritten dedication by Mühlbauer dated April 26, 1945. Photo was taken at the Atelier Fröhlich photo studio in Flensburg.*

The backbone of the fleet; two engineer specialist Chief Petty Officers enjoy some fresh air on the bridge in an unknown harbor, June 1943.

The crew of the U-907; Obersteuermann Karl Jäckel's boat. *Photo taken at Hamburg on May 18, 1944 at the U-boat's commissioning. Jäckel appears to be on the deck, farthest on the right. Photo is a post-war copy of an original.*

Obersteuermann Karl Jäckel (far right) on the deck of the U-907. *Photo taken on May 18, 1944 at Hamburg. Photo is a post-war copy of an original.*

Obersteuermann Karl Jäckel at award of the Knight's Cross on May 8, 1945. *Photo taken at Bergen, Norway. Photo is a post-war copy of an original.*

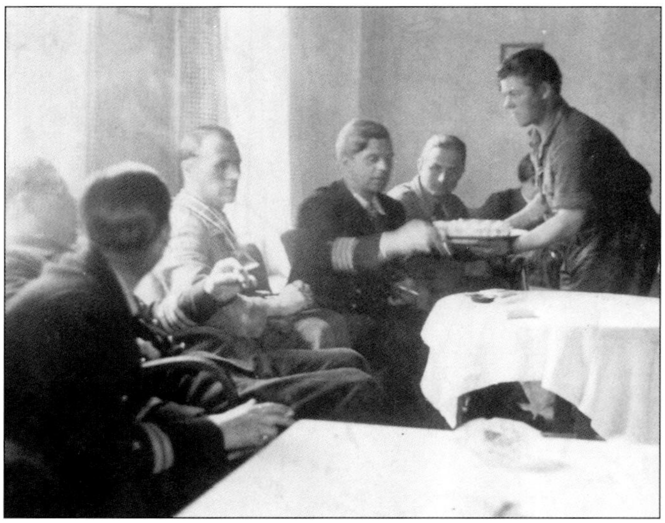

Obersteuermann Karl Jäckel at reception immediately following the award of his Knight's Cross. *Photo taken at Bergen, Norway. Kapitän zur See in center is Hans Rösing, F.d.U. West. Photo is a post-war copy of an original.*

Officers and Chief Petty Officers of the U-907. *All sport excellent beards! Officer in white cap is the commander, Oberleutnant zur See Servais Cabolet; he survived the war and died on May 9, 1976. Photo taken in Norway. Photo is a post-war copy of an original.*

Officers and CPOs of the U-907. *Photo taken in Norway. Photo is a post-war copy of an original.*

Crewmembers of the U-907. *Photo taken in Norway. Photo is a post-war copy of an original.*

Commander of the U-270, Kapitänleutnant Paul-Friedrich Otto, after a successful war patrol. *Hanging from the periscope are two pennants, indicating the U-boat sank two enemy escort vessels during the patrol. Otto actually fatally damaged only one enemy ship, the British frigate HMS Lagan on September 20, 1943. It was the first instance where a German homing torpedo sank an enemy vessel. Twenty-eight men on the Lagan were killed; the British towed the frigate to port but it was declared a total loss, her stern having been blown off. The incident thus dates this photo as being taken at Lorient, France on October 6, 1943. Officer on the right is probably Korvettenkapitän Georg-Wilhelm Schulz, the commander of the 6th U-boat Flotilla.*

Opposite
U-270 returns to port after a successful war patrol. *Just visible at the top is a victory pennant celebrating shooting down an enemy B-17 Flying Fortress aircraft that attacked the U-boat. Note two dual 20-mm flak guns and two dual machineguns on the bridge. On the left with white cap is the U-boat commander Kapitänleutnant Paul-Friedrich Otto. He survived the war. Two Chief Petty Officers stand in the center of the bridge apparently in discussion. The photo was taken at St. Nazaire, France on January 17, 1944.*

Three Chief Petty Officers from the U-270 immediately after returning from a war patrol. *Well-wishers have provided symbolic victory bouquets of flowers and beer. Two men appear to have also received packets of letters from home. Magnification indicates the CPO on the left is Obersteuermann and German Cross in Gold winner Otto Viethsen, CPO in the center is Obermaschinist Kurt Büngener, and CPO on the right is Obermaschinist and German Cross in Gold winner Rudolf Heyn. The photo was taken on January 17, 1944 at St. Nazaire, France. The U-270 sank on August 13, 1944.*

Four Chief Petty Officers from the U-107 in dress uniforms. *Photo is a post-war copy of an original.*

Chief Petty Officers from the U-107 pose for a gag picture somewhere in Germany. *Photo is a post-war copy of an original.*

Three Chief Petty officers at Neustadt marksmanship training in October 1939. *One CPO is Rudi Ellrich, later of the U-99; he survived the war.*

Chief Petty Officer on the bridge of the U-192. *On May 6, 1943 the British corvette HMS Loosestrife sank the U-192 southeast of Cape Farewell. There were no survivors.*

Albert Möbus of the U-24. *(Photo courtesy of U-boat Archive & Museum, Cuxhaven, Germany.)*

CHAPTER SIXTEEN

"OOPS!"
U-404
APRIL 1943

U-boat commanders were not shrinking violets. Highly-motivated and aggressive, they were success-oriented and driven to sink as many enemy ships as humanly possible for both professional (helping the Fatherland win the war) and personal (the attainment of military decorations and distinction) reasons. Like fighter pilots with their air claims, on some occasions U-boat skippers inaccurately reported sinking enemy ships. It wasn't an issue of lying; it was more in believing that the most favorable possible outcome had very likely occurred. However, U-boat commanders had a large disadvantage not present in the air war; in the undersea war there were inherent difficulties in accurately assessing combat results due to light conditions, weather and enemy reaction – it was very difficult to determine target effect when one was being depth-charged at a depth of one hundred feet in heavy seas at night seconds after firing a spread of torpedoes at a convoy. In those times the periscope was withdrawn, depth charge detonations masked hydrophone reception of the sound of torpedo hits, and every man aboard the U-boat was completely absorbed on only one activity – desperately trying to stay alive.

When those inaccuracies involved enemy merchant ships, the mistakes were often not realized until much later, sometimes only after the war, as even in peacetime a certain number of merchant ships sank at sea in uncertain circumstances and surviving crewmen from a torpedo attack almost always had no idea of the identification of the particular enemy submarine that sank them. Warships were another matter; sometimes the Germans believed they sank an Allied warship of one type, when in actuality it was a different ship. On other occasions, a German U-boat skipper believed he had sunk the warship when in fact he had only damaged it and the target made port, damaged but afloat. When those incidents involved a small warship – such as a corvette or destroyer escort – it did not create much consternation. When a capital ship, an aircraft carrier, was claimed to be sunk, when in fact it was not even in the area of the claimed attack, it was a major propaganda defeat. And when that false report only became known after Adolf Hitler had awarded the involved commander with a very high decoration – and after the "victory" was trumpeted by the Nazi Propaganda Ministry – the effect was one large "Oops!"

Otto von Bülow, who would be right in the middle of the arguably most significant inaccurate submarine report to be rendered during the war, was actually an accomplished, professional Navy officer. Born October 16, 1911 in Wilhelmshaven, the son of an Imperial Navy officer, he joined the *Reichsmarine* in 1930 as a Sea Cadet on board a sailing ship, traveling to Africa and Southeast Asia. He was subsequently promoted to Ensign and served on board the pocket battleship *Deutschland*, where he was acting watch officer during the cruise through the Norwegian Fjords carrying Adolf Hitler and Josef Goebbels. Von Bülow was promoted again in 1935 to *Leutnant zur See* and to *Oberleutnant zur See* in 1936 and then served on board the battleship *Schleswig Holstein*, cruising to Africa and the West Indies. He then began a stint in shore duty, was promoted to *Kapitänleutnant* in 1939 and assumed command of the 215th Marine Artillery Flak Battalion at Pillau.

In April 1940, Otto von Bülow was seconded to U-boat training and then took command of the *U-3*, a U-boat used for training officers. In July 1941, he was based in the shipyard at Danzig in Poland, standing by the construction of the *U-404*, a Type VIIC boat. The *U-404* was ordered on September 23, 1939; her keel was laid in the Danziger Werft AG construction yard on June 4, 1941 and she was launched exactly one year later. The U-boat was commissioned on August 6, 1941. She left Kiel, Germany under the command of Otto von Bülow on her first war patrol on January 17, 1942 and arrived at Lorient, France on February 1, 1942 after just over two weeks at sea. She made no attacks on the voyage, but that was about to change.

On February 14, 1942, the *U-404* and Otto von Bülow left Lorient bound for Canada and the United States on her second war patrol as part of "Operation Drumbeat." The boat went three weeks without a victory, but then successes began to accumulate. At 11:35 a.m. on March 5, 1942 off Nova Scotia, von Bülow spotted and sank the American 5,112-ton *Collamer*, sitting stationary outside Halifax, waiting to sail with convoy HX-178 from Halifax bound for Clyde, Scotland and hence to Northern Russia; seven men were killed in the attack. On March 13 off New Jersey at 6:43 a.m., the *U-404* attacked and sank the Chilean 1,858-ton freighter *Tolten* bound from Baltimore to New York; when she plunged beneath the waves, twenty-five men died with her – only one man survived.

The following day at 7:58 a.m. the *U-404* claimed another victim, the American 7,610-ton *Lemuel Burrows*; twenty men perished in the attack off New Jersey. Finally, at 2:16 a.m. on March 17, 1942, von Bülow sank the British 8,073-ton tanker *San Demetrio*; her 4,000 tons of alcohol and 7,000 tons of motor spirits caught fire and nineteen crewmen died as she sank east of the mouth of the Chesapeake Bay. Then the *U-404* headed for home, but encountered what could have been her greatest opportunity yet. At 3:00 p.m. on March 22, von Bülow spotted a convoy of two Boise-class cruisers, six destroyers and five other large ships. The *U-404* fired a spread of torpedoes at one of the cruisers and the hydrophone operator heard two thuds after fifty-two seconds of running time. There were no explosions and the crew assumed that the torpedoes had faulty detonator pistols. Running low on fuel, von Bülow could not track the enemy ships further, and the boat arrived at Brest on April 4, 1942. Two days later the 6th U-boat Flotilla Commander, *Korvettenkapitän* Wilhelm Schulz awarded von Bülow the Iron Cross 2nd and 1st Class.

Von Bülow and the *U-404* waited one month before making her third war patrol. The *U-404* departed from Brest on May 6, 1942, again headed for the American coast and remained at sea almost ten weeks. Otto von Bülow hit seven ships on this patrol. On May 30, 1942 at 10:24 a.m., von Bülow sank the American 5,491-ton *Alcoa Shipper*; heading from Trinidad to New York, seven crewmen died in the torpedo attack. Two days later, at 10:30 a.m. on June 1, 1942 near Bermuda, the *U-404* sank the American 5,492-ton *West Notus*, carrying linseed oil, with its 88-mm deck-gun. The ship was bound from Buenos Aires, Argentina to New York; four men died. On June 3 at 7:30 a.m. von Bülow fired a torpedo – which missed – and then surfaced and sank the Swedish 1,345-ton *Anna*, carrying 1,739 tons of coal, with the 88-mm deck-gun; all her crew survived. The *U-404* then was ordered to proceed to Cape Hatteras but went three weeks without another opportunity to attack. During this time she refueled from the *U-116*, a minelayer. Then, at 9:37 a.m. on June 24, 1942, von Bülow fired three torpedoes and sank the Yugoslavian 3,289-ton *Ljubica Matkovic* off North Carolina, heading from Ciudad Trujillo (Santo Domingo) to New York and then to Britain. Her cargo – 4,100 tons of sugar, 850 tons of fuel oil and 25 tons of wood – sank beneath the waves, but all her crew escaped death. The next day proved even more productive. At 1:16 a.m. on June 25, von Bülow sank the American 4,772-ton freighter *Manuela*, killing two crewmen and sending 26,000 bags of raw sugar and 75,000 bags of refined sugar from San Juan, Puerto Rico to New York to the bottom. Four minutes later, at 1:20 a.m., he sank the Panamanian 3,845-ton *Nordal*; all crew survived, but 6,675 tons manganese, burlap, hides and coffee, bound from Calcutta, India and Bahia, Brazil to Baltimore went down with the ship off North Carolina. Finally on June 27, 1942 at 10:00 p.m., the *U-404* sank the Norwegian 6,827-ton *Moldanger*, enroute from Buenos Aires to New York, killing fourteen, off Delaware. Her patrol a great success, the *U-404* arrived at St. Nazaire, France on July 14, 1942 after nearly ten weeks.

For her fourth war patrol, the *U-404* left St. Nazaire under the command of Otto von Bülow on August 23, 1942. Otto von Bülow hit three ships on this patrol: two were from convoy ON-127 and one was from convoy RB-1. His first two attacks only damaged the target: on September 11, 1942 he damaged the Norwegian 7,417-ton *Marit II*, a member of convoy ON-127, which was sailing in ballast from Shell Haven (London Gateway) to New York and Curacao. At 6:17 a.m. on September 12, 1942, he damaged the Norwegian 9,272-ton *Daghild*, also part of convoy ON-127.

Then things got very bloody. On September 25, 1942 the *U-216* sank the American passenger ship *Boston*; no one died and her crew of sixty-five was picked up by the British 1,120-ton destroyer *HMS Veteran*. Early on the morning of September 26, southeast of Greenland, the U-91 torpedoed and sank the American passenger ship *New York* also sailing in convoy RB-1. Thirty-four men died but thirty others were rescued by the *HMS Veteran*. Later that morning at 10:36 a.m., the *U-404* fired a spread of three torpedoes at the *HMS Veteran*; two hit the ship and she blew apart, sinking immediately south of Iceland. There were no survivors.

The *U-404* returned after her seven-week patrol to St. Nazaire on October 13, 1942. For this patrol and his previous successes, Otto von Bülow received the Knight's Cross on October 20, 1942.

Just before Christmas, on December 21, 1942, the *U-404* left St. Nazaire once again under the command of Otto von Bülow. But the holiday season did not prove lucky for the boat and she arrived back at St. Nazaire more than six weeks later on February 6, 1943, with no sinkings to her credit, after striking a rock on the sea floor that damaged her bow planes on this her fifth war patrol. Six weeks later, the U-boat departed from St. Nazaire on March 21, 1943 and the boat's luck returned. At 9:00 p.m. on March 29, 1943, von Bülow sank the British 8,791-ton *Nagara*, carrying 6,069 tons of refrigerated meat, sailing with convoy SL-126 from Buenos Aires to Cardiff; all her crew survived. The *U-404* then sank the British 7,031-ton *Empire Bowman*, a member of convoy SL-126, sailing from Karachi, Pakistan and Freetown, Sierra Leone to Hull. Four of her crew perished as the ship carrying 2,500 tons of manganese ore went to the bottom on March 30, 1943. Von Bülow claimed his third and last victory of this sixth war patrol for the *U-404*. At 11:30 p.m. on April 12, he sank the British 1,914-ton *Lancastrian Prince*, part of convoy ON-176 heading from Mersey to Boston in ballast; all forty-five crewmen perished. Just as the passengers of the Titanic found out thirty-one years before, victims of ship sinkings east of Newfoundland at 50° North latitude in April did not survive for long in the water.

The *U-404* almost met the same fate. On April 19, 1943 an unidentified aircraft attacked the submarine. But the U-boat was not damaged by the attack.

Six days later, von Bülow encountered the situation that would forever be attached to his name. On April 24 at 4:54 a.m. in the mid-North Atlantic, the *U-404* reported several surface ships heading on a westerly course, subsequently confirmed to be an aircraft carrier and its escorts. The weather was terrible with occasional snowfalls. At 8:17 a.m. on April 25, 1943, von Bülow again spotted what he thought was the *USS Ranger*, an aircraft carrier, with four escorts. He estimated the ship at 14,700 tons and fired two FaT area-searching torpedoes, two G7e electric-powered torpedoes and one electric torpedo with a Pi2 magnetic pistol detonator. Upon hearing four explosions (probably the torpedoes either prematurely exploding or exploding at the end of their run), seeing two tongues of flame and feeling very heavy vibrations during this surface attack, he considered them as hits, and transmitted the message "*Ranger* possible" to the B.d.U.; their answer was to ask him to confirm whether in his opinion he had sunk the carrier. Von Bülow answered with a "sinking assumed" and continued his passage to France, and the B.d.U. war diary logged the aircraft carrier as a "report of success."

On April 25, 1943 German radio announced the sinking of the American flattop, and the following day Adolf Hitler approved that Otto von Bülow receive the Oak Leaves to the Knight's Cross for sinking the *Ranger*. There were two problems with this. First, the *USS Ranger* was not in the area. Second, the crew of the actual intended target, the British escort aircraft carrier, *HMS Biter*, observed the faulty torpedoes exploding some distance away causing no damage. The B.d.U. later disallowed the claim but the damage had been done as Allied media used the incident as another example of Nazi untruthfulness. The *U-404* returned to St. Nazaire on May 3 after just over six weeks on patrol. Promoted to *Korvettenkapitän* on June 1, von Bülow left the *U-404* on July 23, 1943 – one day before she was to depart on patrol – and reported to the training department of the B.d.U. That September he assumed command of the 23rd U-boat Flotilla at Danzig.

The rest of the crew on the U-*404* was not so fortunate. She departed St. Nazaire under the command of *Oberleutnant zur See* Adolf Schönberg on July 24, 1943. Schönberg was born on August 7, 1918 in Babylon, New York. His family returned to Germany after World War I and Schönberg joined the German Navy in 1937. He was seconded to the *Luftwaffe* in 1939 and 1940; on his return he underwent U-boat training and served as the 1st Watch Officer for the *U-404*, under Otto von Bülow, from August 1941 to July 1942. Schönberg then attended a one-month U-boat commander's course and took command of the *U-62*, a command he held until July 19, 1943. His previous experience as a watch officer and commander went for naught; on July 28, 1943 – just four days into her patrol – the *U-404* was on the receiving end of accurate depth charges dropped by two B-24 Liberators (4th Anti-Submarine Squadron) and one British B-24 Liberator (224th Squadron). The *U-404* responded with heavy flak fire that damaged the two attacking aircraft, but the British B-24 took up the attack, dropping seven depth charges. The U-boat sank in the Bay of Biscay northwest of Cape Ortegal, Spain. All hands (fifty-one) were lost.

Von Bülow mourned the loss of his former boat and his friends but continued to command the 23rd U-boat Flotilla, where future U-boat commanders received their training. In March 1945 he joined the new crew of the *U-2545* and commissioned the Type XXI Boat. The boat was commissioned on April 8, 1945, but a few days later von Bülow was appointed to command the 1st Naval Assault Battalion (*Marinesturmbatallion* 1) slated as part of the defense of Berlin and ultimately Hitler's bunker. The unit does not appear to have ever left northern Germany and a few days before the end, von Bülow was placed on the staff of Grand Admiral Dönitz and accompanied him on his way to sign the German surrender in Flensburg. He was taken prisoner on May 24, 1945, and was a prisoner of war for three months.

Otto von Bülow joined the post-war German Navy and retired as a *Kapitän zur See* in 1970. He died on January 5, 2006 at Aumühle. Otto von Bülow sank fourteen merchant ships, a combined 71,450 tons, and damaged two additional ships for 16,689 tons. This placed him sixtieth among the most successful U-boat commanders of the war.

Known Crewmembers for the U-404

Altvater, Gerhard	*Maschinengefreiter*
Besser, Walter	*Maschinenobergefreiter*
Bey, Günter	*Oberfunkmaat*
Bittkau, Paul	*Oberbootsmannsmaat*
Blassen, Hans	*Matrosengefreiter*
Borchardt, Helmut-Paul	*Obermechanikermaat*
Bousonville, Albert	*Matrosengefreiter*
Brakel, Heinrich-Richard	*Obermaschinenmaat*
Bülow, Otto von	*Korvettenkapitän*
Büstrin	*Leutnant zur See*
Erdt, Friedrich	*Matrosenobergefreiter*
Fechtig, Helmut	*Matrosenobergefreiter*
Frank, Walter	*Obersteuermann*
Friedenstab, Alfred	*Matrosenobergefreiter*
Gärtner, Karl	*Matrosengefreiter*
Geisler, Joachim-Friedrich	*Oberleutnant zur See*
Hähle, Karl-Heinz	*Obermaschinenmaat*
Hälbich, Gerhard	*Kapitänleutnant*
Hanusa, Karl	*Mechanikerobergefreiter*
Heckhoff, Karl	*Maschinengefreiter*
Heinrich, Karl-Heinz	*Oberleutnant zur See*
Henke, Heinz	*Matrosenobergefreiter*
Henrich, Karl-Heinz	*Leutnant zur See*
Jäke, Georg	*Obermaschinenmaat*
Janssen, Wilhelm	*Maschinenobergefreiter*
Kinzel, Manfred	*Kapitänleutnant*
Klasen, Franz	*Leutnant (Ing)*
Koch, Heinz	*Funkobergefreiter*
Kohl, Heinz-Günter	*Mechanikerobergefreiter*
Kostrzewa, Wilhelm	*Maschinenobergefreiter*
Kümmet, Willi	*Bootsmann*
Kunze, Walter	*Funkmaat*
Ladwig, Heinrich	*Matrosenobergefreiter*
Lau, Herbert	*Matrose*
Lehnert, Alfred	*Maschinenobergefreiter*
Lorenz, Alfred	*Obermaschinenmaat*
Lowack, Friedrich	*Maschinenobergefreiter*
Magerstädt, Ewald	*Maschinenobergefreiter*
Molka, Horst	*Funkobergefreiter*
Neukirchen, Karl	*Bootsmaat*
Nickol, Werner	*Maschinenobergefreiter*
Ortmann, Ruben	*Matrosengefreiter*
Panitz, Gerhard	*Maschinenmaat*
Pfeifer	*Obersteuermann*
Rademacher, Heinrich	*Matrosenobergefreiter*
Rhein, Werner	*Obermaschinist*
Rickert, Harald	*Matrosenobergefreiter*
Schönberg, Adolf	*Oberleutnant zur See*
Schröter, Kurt	*Maschinenobergefreiter*
Schumann, Heinz	*Maschinenmaat*
Schwager, Erwin	*Kapitänleutnant*
Spättmann, Theodor	*Matrosengefreiter*
Stöhning, Ernst	*Maschinenobergefreiter*
Thelen, Harro	*Leutnant zur See*
Thiele, Heinz	*Maschinenobergefreiter*
Vagt, Dr. Hans-Joachim	Stabsarzt
Wechsler, Hugo	*Matrosenobergefreiter*
Wolf, Helmut	*Maschinenobergefreiter*

Sources, "Oops!:" Chris Bishop, *Kriegsmarine U-boats 1939-45*, London: Amber Books, 2006, 58, 60, 61, 63, 64, 65; Clay Blair, *Hitler's U-boat War: The Hunters, 1939-1942*, New York: Random House, 1996, 517, 605, 606, 607; Clay Blair, *Hitler's U-boat War: The Hunted, 1942-1945*, New York: Modern Library, 2000, 30, 35, 175, 271, 280, 286, 287, 390, 391; Rainer Busch and Hans-Joachim Röll, *German U-boat Commanders of World War II*, translated by Geoffrey Brooks, Annapolis, Maryland: Naval Institute Press, 1999, 43, 230; Manfred Dörr, *Die Ritterkreuzträger der U-Boot-Waffe, Band 1: A-J, Band 2: L-Z*, Osnabrück, FRG: Biblio Verlag, 1988, Band 1-24, 25; *F.d.U./B.d.U. War Diary, 16-31 March 1942* (PG30305b), 138; *F.d.U./B.d.U. War Diary, 16-30 April 1943* (PG30322), 279, 282, 284; Axel Niestlé, *German U-boat Losses during World War II*, Annapolis, Maryland: Naval Institute Press, 1998, 61; Jürgen Rohwer, *Axis Submarine Successes 1939-1945*, Annapolis, Maryland: Naval Institute Press, 1983, 82, 85, 86, 99, 100, 105, 106, 121, 122, 125, 160, 162, 163; Axel Urbanke, Rainer Busch, Manfred Dörr, Andreas Dwulecki, Markus Dyhr, Thomas Huss, Wolfgang Ockert and Walter Storbeck, *U-boot im Focus: U-Boot-Historie von Enthusiasten für Enthusiasten*, Edition 1, Bad Zwischenahn: Luftfahrtverlag-Start, 2007, 11; www.ubootwaffe.net; www.uboatarchive.net.

View of the U-404 at sea from beyond the bow of the boat.

View from the stern of the U-404 over the winter garden at the watch. *Note the men covering all points of the compass to ensure the boat is not surprised by the enemy.*

View of the U-404 off the starboard bow. *The boat appears to be stationary.*

View of the U-404 from the starboard beam. *Again the boat appears stationary.*

View of a burning ship, the victim of the U-404. *The target is most likely the British 8,073 ton tanker San Demetrio hit at 2:16 a.m. on March 17, 1942 east of the mouth of the Chesapeake Bay.*

Another view of the San Demetrio. *Her 4,000 tons of alcohol and 7,000 tons of motor spirits caught fire and nineteen crewmen died as she sank.*

Two U-boats in close proximity to one another. *Crewmen on closest boat are dressed for foul weather.*

Kriegsmarine war photographer Gerhard Garms on the bridge of the U-404 with one of the crewmen. *Garms took all the photos of the U-404 that appear in this book. Gerhard Garms was born January 24, 1917 in Kiel; he died at Kiel on June 16, 2001.*

View of Otto von Bülow (left) and Gerhard Garms (with movie camera) on the bridge of the U-404. *Garms' work regularly appeared in German movie theaters from 1940-1945 in "Die Deutsche Wochenschau."*

U-404 entering a harbor (denoted on the reverse of the photo as Lorient, France). *The boat is displaying four victory pennants denoting enemy ships sunk on the most-recent patrol. Given the history of the U-404, this photograph is likely from April 1942.*

Opposite
Arrival of the U-404 in port after a successful war patrol. *Kriegsmarine war photographer Gerhard Garms is lining up a motion picture shot of a Kapitänleutnant's dog. That officer on the left wears the German Cross in Gold and the Spanish Cross with Swords.*

Close-up view of the crew of the U-404 topside. *The single figure in the middle on the boat's deck appears to be Otto von Bülow. So many crewmen topside indicate the boat is in safe waters as twenty-one men could not safely enter the ship during an emergency dive. Photo is a post-war copy of an original.*

Two crewmen of the U-404 standing watch on the bridge. *Both are prepared for foul weather, which often seemed to follow many U-boats. Photo is a post-war copy of an original.*

View of the U-404 stopped in the North Atlantic in bad weather. *The captain of a Portuguese freighter has approached in the rowboat, prepared to show the men of the U-boat his papers proving his neutrality status. Both U-boat crewmen are wearing life jackets. Photo is a post-war copy of an original.*

View of a U-boat, presumably the U-404, breaking the surface in a staged photograph. *Photo is a post-war copy of an original.*

Crewman preparing to climb to the bridge for his watch duty. *Clad in heavy foul-weather clothing, indicating what awaits him on the bridge, he does not appear to be overjoyed. Photo is a post-war copy of an original.*

Chief Engineer in his domain – the engine room. *It was mostly hot, dirty work, but every man aboard depended on the Chief Engineer's ability. Photo is a post-war copy of an original.*

View of the U-404 from dead ahead.

In port, visitors tour the bridge of the U-404 after a successful war patrol.

Otto von Bülow at an informal celebration following a successful war patrol. *To von Bülow's right is Gerhard Garms, the Kriegsmarine war photographer who presumably accompanied the U-404 on this mission. The officer wearing the Knight's Cross to von Bülow's left (applauding) is the 6th U-boat Flotilla Commander, Korvettenkapitän Wilhelm Schulz. Right:* ***Another view of the gathering.*** *Schulz is opening a bottle of champagne.*

Otto von Bülow, commander of the U-404. *Postcard signed during the war. Von Bülow sent the signed card on July 5, 1944 to a schoolboy.*

Moonlight view of another U-boat at sea from the U-404.

CHAPTER SEVENTEEN

"LUCK"
U-128, AND U-189
APRIL 1943

Plain luck and chance also seemed to play a role on who survived and who perished in the U-boat service. Hellmut Kurrer was an excellent example. Born in Eisleben (the birthplace of Martin Luther in 1483) on February 16, 1916, he began his Navy service in 1935 in the surface fleet that was highlighted in April 1940 when he assumed the leadership position of 1st Watch Officer on the torpedo boat *T6*. Commanded by *Kapitänleutnant* Ralf-Reimar Wolfram, the ship was commissioned on April 30, 1940. German Navy torpedo boats were essentially diminutive fleet destroyers, with the same high speed (34.5 knots/hour) and similar torpedo armament (six torpedo tubes), but with much reduced gun-power (one 105-mm gun, four 37-mm anti-aircraft guns and twelve 20-mm anti-aircraft guns). The primary tasks of torpedo boats were torpedo attacks and fast offensive minelaying; they could also conduct escort and patrol duties. Displacing 853 tons and manned by 119, they were employed more frequently than destroyers.

Dönitz's Crews

***Oberleutnant zur See* Hellmut Kurrer**

Born on February 16, 1916 in Eisleben/Saxony-Anhalt.
Served as the 1st Watch Officer on the *U-128* and the Commander of the *U-189*.
Awarded the Iron Cross 2nd Class on September 10, 1940.
Spent 112 days at sea on U-boat war patrols.
Killed in action on April 23, 1943 southeast of Greenland.

From July to October 1940 the *T6* operated in the Skagerrak, North Sea and English Channel. Hellmut Kurrer performed well, winning the Iron Cross 2nd Class on September 10, 1940. The next month he left the *T6* for good to begin U-boat training, but the *T6* continued in combat operations, moving north from France in the 2nd Torpedo Boat Flotilla to Stavanger, Norway. On November 5, 1940 *Luftwaffe* reconnaissance aircraft spotted two northbound coastal convoys off the British coast. Navy planners computed that both would pass between Kinnaird's Head and Smith's Bank off Scotland at 2:00 a.m. on November 7, an ideal location and time to be attacked by torpedo boats. The 1st and 2nd Torpedo Boat Flotillas left Norway on November 6 and attempted to pass through a gap in a British minefield, which was shown on charts obtained when the Germans captured the *HM Submarine Seal* in May 1940. Just before midnight the torpedo boats approached the ambush area; the night was dark and cloudy with a light north-westerly wind. Just after midnight, the *T6* was rocked by a large explosion on the starboard quarter; ready-use ammunition and signal flares ignited and a serious fire spread aft. The explosion and fire cut telephone lines in the ship and the captain lost awareness of how badly the ship was damaged. As the *T6* listed 10° to starboard, steam and smoke poured out of the ship. Believing the ship to be sinking, Wolfram ordered the crew on deck. The forward turbine room started to flood and the crew began to abandon ship. Minutes later the ship slid beneath the waves and forty-eight men lost their lives. Hellmut Kurrer had been fortunate to have been away at training and was not on the ship when she sank.

Kurrer completed his U-boat training in April 1941 and joined the *U-128*, Type IXC boat of the 2nd U-boat Flotilla, as the 1st Watch Officer. Built at the Deutsche Schiff- und Maschinenbau AG at Bremen, engineers laid her keel on July 10, 1940; she was commissioned on May 12, 1941. Like Kurrer, *Kapitänleutnant* Ulrich Heyse, the *U-128*'s commander had been in the surface fleet – serving as the 1st Watch Officer on the destroyer *Z6 Theodor Riedel* from October 1938 to June 1940. After her commissioning, the *U-128* was scheduled to conduct workup and tactical training exercises in the eastern Baltic, but preparations for "Operation Barbarossa" – the invasion of the Soviet Union – forced these operations to Norway. Enroute to Norway, the *U-128* ran aground and ripped her bottom open. A court of inquiry examined the incident and who might be responsible. Fortunately for the commander Ulrich Heyse and 1st Watch Officer Hellmut Kurrer, the court determined that the rocks had been uncharted and the two retained their positions. However, the U-boat was severely damaged and had to spend months in Kiel undergoing major repairs.

Oberleutnant zur See Hellmut Kurrer served on the *U-128* for three war patrols. For her first, the U-boat left Kiel under the command of Ulrich Heyse on December 9, 1941 and arrived at Kristiansand, Norway on December 10, 1941. One day later, she left Kristiansand for her second war patrol but events halfway around the world would start to affect operations. Japan had attacked the U.S. fleet at Pearl Harbor on December 7 and four days later Germany declared war on the United States. By this time, the *U-128* was west of Ireland; soon she would get new orders.

On December 19, 1941 the B.d.U. diary noted:

"*U-128*, which is at present west of Ireland under way to the area west of Gibraltar, has been ordered to proceed at maximum cruising speed to Lorient. Even though the numbers of boats required by the Naval War Staff have hitherto forced me – in view of the lack of other boats – to send in large U-boats also off Gibraltar, it is nevertheless necessary to release these as soon as possible. This is now possible with medium sized boats. *U-128*'s assignment to Group "Paukenschlag" (Drumbeat) is intended after she has refueled."

The *U-128* arrived at Lorient, France to receive her new orders and resupply on December 24, 1941. Dönitz and his planners would take the fight to the shores of the United States and Canada in what would be known as "Operation Drumbeat." Designed to attack American shipping in coastal waters before they could form into convoys – and before U.S. anti-submarine warfare forces could effectively organize – the offensive would be carried out in the main by Type IX U-boats. The first wave of the operation would begin immediately. *U-128*, part of the second wave, would hunt American ships just off the coast of Florida.

The *U-128* departed under Ulrich Heyse from Lorient on January 8, 1942. She would have a short detour before reaching Florida when on January 16, 1942 the B.d.U. war diary noted:

"*U-128* ordered to Bermuda area to prey on British shipping and to remain outside the 200 meter line because of mines."

But there was some confusion exactly where he was to operate; Bermuda was not Florida. On February 17, 1942 the B.d.U. war diary noted (but did not explain the source of the confusion):

"Apparently *U-128* was in the wrong operations area and will arrive on 19 February in the attack area ordered – 'Straits of Florida.'"

Heyse left Bermuda and moved toward Florida and found the area rich in targets. At 7:45 p.m. on February 19, 1942, the *U-128* sank the American 8,202-ton *Pan Massachusetts* off Daytona Beach, Florida. Twenty-two crewmen died on the tanker carrying 50,000 barrels of gasoline and 50,000 barrels of oil from Texas City to New York. On February 22, 1942 at 11:52 a.m., Heyse sank a second ship – also off Daytona Beach – the American 8,103-ton *Cities Service Empire*, a tanker bound from Port Arthur, Texas to Philadelphia; eleven crewmen were killed in the attack. The B.d.U. war diary entry for that day noted:

"*U-128* reported from operational area in Straits of Florida that he had sunk a tanker (3,000 BRT) in DB 9546 on 19 February, and a fully loaded tanker (12,000 BRT) in DB 9439 on 22 February. Peacetime lights, no air patrol, only destroyers in DB."

"Operation Drumbeat" had achieved surprise, but it was time for the *U-128* to move to fresh killing areas. On March 5, 1942, east of the Bahamas, the U-boat sank the Norwegian 11,007-ton *OA Knudsen*, bound from Port Arthur, Texas to Halifax and hence to Britain; the attack killed one crewman. On March 6 the B.d.U. war diary noted:

"*U-128*: grid DM 33 [Bahamas] lights burning as in peace. Sunk tanker *O.A. Knudsen* (11,517 BRT) all torpedoes fired, return passage. Total: 26,517 BRT sunk."

There were no torpedoes left and other supplies were running low as the *U-128* had been at sea for two months. On March 7, 1942 the B.d.U. war diary noted:

"Consider refueling of *U-332* by *U-128* will not be possible on account of *U-128*'s short food supply."

Heyse managed to ration the remaining food to last until March 23, when the *U-128* arrived back at Lorient after ten and a half weeks on patrol. Kurrer had so proven himself (he probably also won the U-boat War Badge after this patrol) as the 1st Watch Officer that he was selected to attend U-boat commander training and he left the *U-128*. Ulrich Heyse received the U-boat War Badge and the Iron Cross 1st Class. Heyse would command the *U-128* for three more war patrols – winning the Knight's Cross in January 1943 – before leaving the boat in early 1943 for duties in Germany as an instructor. Ulrich Heyse sank twelve merchant ships, a combined 83,639 tons. This placed him forty-third among the most successful U-boat commanders of the war.

Both men were very fortunate. On May 17, 1943 at 8:30 a.m., a U.S. Navy Martin PBM-3C Mariner flying boat from the VP-74 Squadron spotted the *U-128* on the surface in the South Atlantic off Maceió, Brazil and dropped sixth depth charges ahead of the U-boat as she was diving. Forced to the surface by the damage, the U-boat attempted to make a run for the Brazilian coast, but just then another PBM arrived and crippled the surfaced boat with six more depth charges. Then two American destroyers, the *USS Moffett* (Cdr. J.C. Sowell) and *USS Jouett* (Cdr. F.L. Tedder) arrived on the scene and *Kapitänleutnant* Hermann Steinert, the new commander, ordered the boat scuttled. Seven U-boat sailors were killed and forty-seven rescued.

Meanwhile, *Kapitänleutnant* Hellmut Kurrer (he had been promoted on June 1, 1942) assumed command of the *U-189*, a Type IXC/40 U-boat. The *U-189* had been ordered on November 4, 1940; her keel was laid on September 12, 1941 at the Deutsche Schiff- und Maschinenbau AG in Bremen, and she was commissioned on August 15, 1942 at Bremen. She then did her UAK (*U-bootsabnahmekommando* [U-boat Acceptance Command]) tests in August and September, but during them her starboard diesel engine had an explosion; it took a month to repair that problem before the U-boat was accepted as ready for training. At the end of December the *U-189* and her crew began the UAG tests (*U-bootsabnahmegruppe* [U-boat Acceptance Group]) that verified diving capabilities. She completed her Agru Front Training [*Ausbildungsgruppe für Front-U-boote*] in early February that certified that U-boat and crew were ready to join the operational fleet, and then conducted additional pre-combat training with the 25th and 27th U-boat Training Flotillas in the Baltic Sea. Her first war patrol would begin in April 1943 with a key meteorological mission (the meteorologist on board was Kurt Wolf) to report on sea and weather conditions. These missions were critical not only for the U-boats – ice conditions could indicate where convoys would not sail – but also all the services as much of the weather in Western Europe could only be predicted and understood by knowing the weather over the North Atlantic further to the west.

Dönitz's Crews

***Maschinengefreiter* Xaver Ehrensperger**

Born December 1, 1923 in Traidendorf/Bavaria
Served in the engine room on the *U-189*.
Spent 20 days at sea on U-boat war patrols.
Killed in action on April 23, 1943 southeast of Greenland.

Also aboard the U-boat was a young sailor in the engine room, *Maschinengefreiter* Xaver Ehrensperger. Born on December 1, 1923, Ehrensperger hailed from the tiny Bavarian village of Traidendorf nestled between several woods and the Vils River outside the small town of Kallmünz some fifteen miles north of Regensburg. Xaver Ehrensperger probably never saw the sea until he joined the German Navy most likely in 1942.

The *U-189* left Kiel under the command of Hellmut Kurrer on April 3, 1943. After refueling in Norway, on April 5 the U-boat headed west. Five days later, on April 8, the B.d.U. war diary noted:

> "In order to obtain data on ice conditions in the Straits of Denmark *U-189* has been ordered to proceed to AE 22 at increased cruising speed and, after reaching the ice boundary, to proceed along this to the west and report. The boat is prohibited from attacks on unescorted vessels."

Kurrer complied and on April 14, 1943 received new instructions from the B.d.U.:

> "*U-189* will proceed to AK 2810 after passing the Denmark Strait and is to lay a meteorological buoy there."

The *U-189* accomplished this task as well, but conditions were "heating" up as reported in the B.d.U. war diary on April 19, 1943:

> "According to a report from *U-189* the loose drift ice boundary round Iceland runs from AE 2222 via 1665, 1712, AD 4814 to 6880. Permanent ice boundary is not accessible for U-boats. Search for blockade breaker *Regensburg* – possibly iced-up – without success. Land-based aircraft sighted in AE 1575 on 15 April. Surprised by destroyers in AD 2929 on 16 April during snow squalls. 5 depth charges – no damage. Radar locations were not confirmed."

It appears that the *U-189* then took part in a nineteen U-boat pursuit of eastern-bound convoy HX-234. She spotted a destroyer in a heavy snow squall on April 20, but was not observed by the escort. Shortly thereafter Hellmut Kurrer's luck finally ran out. At 4:44 p.m. on April 23 *Oberleutnant zur See* Kurrer radioed to the B.d.U.:

> "Am in contact with escorts."

That evening the *U-189* was sighted east of Greenland by a very long-range B-24 Liberator 'V' (Flight Officer J.K. Moffat) of the 120th Squadron, RAF. Moffat and his crew were enroute to escort convoy HX-234 when they sighted not one but two surfaced U-boats, the nearest being *U-189*. Moffat made his run while taking fire from *U-189*, dropping four depth charges and then coming round for another run. The U-boat's gunners had been silenced by the depth charge explosions, and the boat came to a stop. The Liberator then dropped two more depth charges before flying out to circle for half an hour. Moffat contacted the Senior Naval Officer (SNO) of HX-234, Lt.Cdr. E.C. Day, reporting the boat was down by the stern and that some fifty U-boat men were in the water. The SNO replied that no ships could be spared for any rescue, also citing the presence of other U-boats in the area. Thus, all fifty-four men of the *U-189* died in the icy sea as the cold night descended.

The B.d.U. war diary on April 25 described the convoy fight and mentioned the *U-189*:

> "The England-bound convoy, HX-234, was pursued from the morning of the 21st to the morning of the 25th over a distance of 700 sea miles by altogether 19 boats. 4 boats broke off operations on the second day, so that when the convoy was intercepted with certainty and continuous contact messages were being received, 15 boats were engaged ... The main reason for the failure can be attributed to the extremely changeable visibility experienced during the night. The Commanders, for the most part inexperienced and fresh from home waters, were unable to cope with these conditions. Air activity was so intense on the following day, the 24th, that all boats were beaten off and the convoy lost. On the following morning, the 25th, operations were broken off ... The slight success achieved, in an operation lasting four days and with a fairly large numbers of boats, may be explained as follows: The conditions of convoy warfare are becoming increasingly difficult, above all the case of convoys in the north, where the nights are especially short, and the enemy is able to provide protection with strong air forces from Greenland, and to an even greater extent from Iceland. Boats usually choose a night when a large number of boats are in contact with the convoy, and the not disproportionately strong defense makes success appear likely. The night of 23/24 in this case. Before this, only one boat was in contact and afterwards the air protection was too strong. This night was the only chance. It could not be exploited owing to the very unfavorable weather conditions in conjunction with the inexperience of the large number of new Commanders who were not equal to the situation... One boat, *U-189*, was sunk by the convoy (HX-234) after reporting contact for the last time on the afternoon of the 23rd."

The war diary report came after another U-boat, the *U-413*, reported late on April 23 hearing depth charges and the dreaded sounds of a U-boat breaking up underwater about the time of the attack on the *U-189*.

Known Crewmembers for the U-189

Adam, Emil	*Matrosengefreiter*
Arndt, Gerhard	*Matrosengefreiter*
Ast, Paul	*Obermaschinenmaat*
Blum, Rudolf-Gottfried	*Matrosengefreiter*
Bobe, Arno	*Leutnant zur See*
Böhme, Heinz-Kurt	*Matrosengefreiter*
Bormann, Johannes	*Matrosengefreiter*
Burgenlehner, Sebastian	*Maschinengefreiter*
Dietzmann, Rudolf	*Maschinengefreiter*
Dreher, Günter	*Funkobergefreiter*
Dresky, Gastav von	*Oberleutnant zur See*
Ehrensperger, Xaver	*Maschinengefreiter*
Eichhoff, Herbert	*Maschinengefreiter*
Fichtner, Herbert	*Maschinengefreiter*
Fuchs, Hans	*Matrosengefreiter*
Fuchs, Josef	*Matrosengefreiter*
Garling, Günter	*Funkmaat*
Gaus, Siegfried	*Matrosengefreiter*
Gericke, Erwin	*Maschinenmaat*
Grautstuck, Heinz-Rolf	*Maschinengefreiter*
Gundelach, Rolf	*Leutnant (Ing)*
Günther, Hubert	*Kapitänleutnant (Ing)*
Haupt, Karl	*Maschinenobergefreiter*
Heinicke, Bernhard	*Matrosengefreiter*
Hohenstein, Herbert	*Matrosenobergefreiter*
Hoormann, Willi	*Maschinengefreiter*
Jurtz, Karl-Heinz	*Bootsmannsmaat*
Kaldewey, Hans	*Maschinengefreiter*
Kaufmann, Karl	*Maschinenmaat*
Klockenbusch, Josef	*Oberbootsmannsmaat*
Kopatz, Ernst	*Bootsmannsmaat*
Körtge, Wilhelm	*Obersteuermann*
Künsting, Friedrich	*Maschinengefreiter*
Kurrer, Hellmut	*Kapitänleutnant*
Lindlar, Hubert	*Obermaschinenmaat*
Lübbe, Willi	*Obermaschinist*
Mergen, Helmut	*Funkmaat*
Neumann, Wilhelm	*Obermaschinist*
Ottlewski, Franz	*Maschinengefreiter*
Preuss, Walter	*Maschinenmaat*
Richter, Bruno	*Funkobergefreiter*
Rossbach, Franz Hans	*Maschinengefreiter*
Rudloff, Ernst	*Maschinenmaat*
Ruhland, Josef	*Maschinenmaat*
Schulz, Alfred	*Matrosengefreiter*
Schwanbeck, Berthold	*Mechanikerobergefreiter*
Schwertfeger, Hasso	*Oberfähnrich zur See*
Streich, Richard	*Oberfähnrich zur See*
Szrama, Paul	*Mechanikermaat*
Triebel, Heinrich	*Mechanikergefreiter*
Twistern, Helmut von	*Maschinenmaat*
Waterstraat, Kurt	*Oberleutnant zur See*
Wolf, Kurt	Meterologe
Zenner, Heinz	*Mechanikerobergefreiter*
Zitzler, Josef	*Maschinengefreiter*

Sources, "Luck:" Clay Blair, *Hitler's U-boat War: The Hunters, 1939-1942*, New York: Random House, 1996, 323, 436, 437, 438, 499, 500; Clay Blair, *Hitler's U-boat War: The Hunted, 1942-1945*, New York: Modern Library, 2000, 223, 284; Rainer Busch and Hans-Joachim Röll, *German U-boat Commanders of World War II*, translated by Geoffrey Brooks, Annapolis, Maryland: Naval Institute Press, 1999, 103, 139; Manfred Dörr, *Die Ritterkreuzträger der U-Boot-Waffe, Band 1: A-J, Band 2: L-Z*, Osnabrück, FRG: Biblio Verlag, 1988, Band 1-138, 139; *F.d.U./B.d.U. War Diary, 16-31 December 1941* (PG30301b), 273; *F.d.U./B.d.U. War Diary, 16-31 January 1942* (PG30303), 21; *F.d.U./B.d.U. War Diary, 16-28 February 1942* (PG30304b), 82, 90; *F.d.U./B.d.U. War Diary, 1-15 March 1942* (PG30305a), 115, 116; *F.d.U./B.d.U. War Diary, 1-15 April 1943* (PG30321), 236, 251; *F.d.U./B.d.U. War Diary, 16-30 April 1943* (PG30322), 266, 283; Michael Gannon, *Black May: The Epic Story of the Allies Defeat of the German U-boats in May 1943*, New York: HarperCollins, 1998, 376; Axel Niestlé, *German U-boat Losses during World War II*, Annapolis, Maryland: Naval Institute Press, 1998, 122; Herbert Ritschel, *Kurzfassung Kriegstagebücher deutscher U-boote 1939-1945, Band 3: KTB U171 – U222*, Norderstedt, Germany: Books on Demand, 130; Jürgen Rohwer, *Axis Submarine Successes 1939-1945*, Annapolis, Maryland: Naval Institute Press, 1983, 79, 80, 82; David Syrett, *The Defeat of the German U-boats: The Battle of the Atlantic*, Columbia, South Carolina: University of South Carolina Press, 1994, 44, 50; War Diary of the U-189, August 15, 1942 – April 24, 1943, PG 30176; ONI Roll T-261-A, *National Archives Microfilm Publication T1022,* roll 2886, RG 242; David Westwood, *The U-boat War: The German Submarine Service and the Battle of the Atlantic, 1935-1945*, Philadelphia, PA: Casemate, 2005, 105; M. J. Whitley, *Destroyer! German Destroyers in World War II*, Annapolis, Maryland: Naval Institute Press, 1983, 55, 144, 285; www.ubootwaffe.net; www.uboatarchive.net.

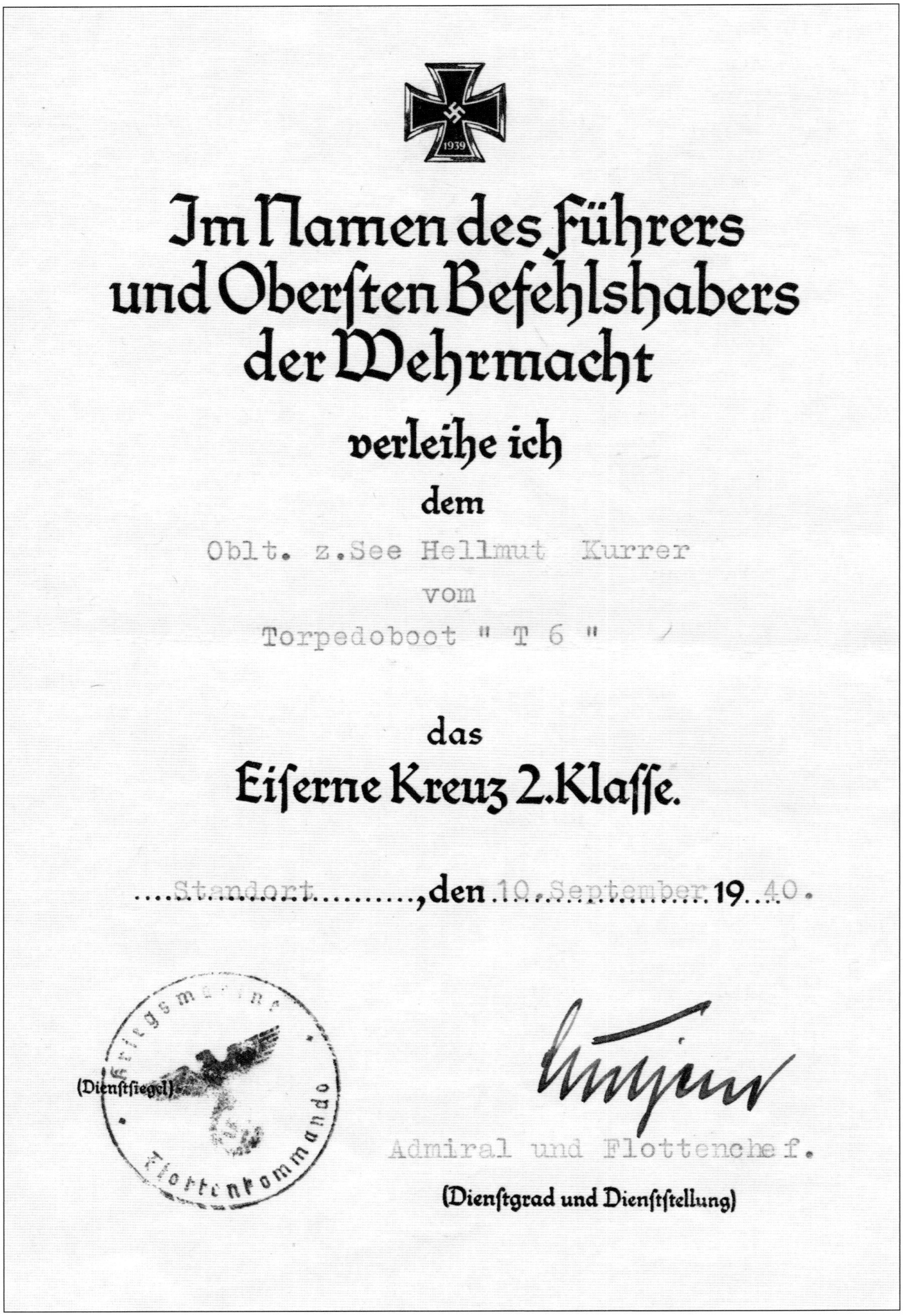

Im Namen des Führers
und Obersten Befehlshabers
der Wehrmacht

verleihe ich

dem

Oblt. z.See Hellmut Kurrer

vom

Torpedoboot " T 6 "

das

Eiserne Kreuz 2.Klasse.

Standort, den 10. September 1940.

(Dienstsiegel)

Kriegsmarine Flottenkommando

Lütjens

Admiral und Flottenchef.

(Dienstgrad und Dienststellung)

Iron Cross 2nd Class award document to Hellmut Kurrer of the Torpedo Boat T6. *Document was signed by Admiral Günter Lütjens Commander of the Fleet on September 10, 1940. Lütjens died in battle on the battleship Bismarck in May 1941. Kurrer went on to command the U-189.*

Destroyer Badge for service on a destroyer or torpedo boat. *This award would have been made to both Hellmut Kurrer and Ulrich Heyse. The award shown is an early war model of tombak manufactured by Schwerin of Berlin.*

Zum frommen Gedenken
im Gebete an
Xaver Ehrensperger
von Traidendorf
Maschinengefr. bei der Kriegsmarine
Den Heldentod gestorben am 24. April 1943 im Alter von 20 Jahren.

Ach es ist ja kaum zu fassen,
Daß Du niemals kehrst zurück.
So früh mußt Du Dein Leben lassen,
Zerstört ist unser ganzes Glück.
So leb' wohl, Du edler Guter,
Du treuer Sohn, lieber Schwager und Bruder.

Mein Jesus, Barmherzigkeit!

Georg Nußstein, Burglengenfeld

Death Announcement for Maschinengefreiter Xaver Ehrensperger, age twenty and on his first patrol, who died with all his boatmates onboard the U-189.

CHAPTER EIGHTEEN

"TAKING CARE OF THEIR OWN" U-262 MAY 1943

Karl Dönitz would do just about anything for his boys. He made sure they received special privileges; he was generous with awards and promotions; he was even prepared to send a valuable U-boat deep into enemy-controlled waters 3,000 miles from Germany to rescue them from a prisoner of war camp. That opportunity first surfaced in 1942 in a daring plan to rescue German U-boat prisoners of war in Canada.

Dönitz's Crews
***Obermaschinist* Friedrich Meyer**
Served on the *U-262* in the engine room manning the electric motors.
Awarded the Iron Cross 2nd Class on February 18, 1943, the U-boat War Badge on May 30, 1943 and the Iron Class 1st Class on May 1, 1944.
Spent 359 days at sea on U-boat war patrols.
Survived the war; lived in Emden.

Admiral Dönitz saw many tangible reasons for attempting to rescue German prisoners of war in addition to fatherly concern. Such a plan would encourage those men behind the wire and improve their morale. Escape attempts would also disrupt enemy security and homeland protection. Successful extraction of U-boat men would serve as a valuable source of crewmembers in a period where losses were high. Finally, such a brazen rescue mission would shine as a valuable propaganda tool.

From the beginning of the war, the U-boat chief anticipated there would be large numbers of U-boat men falling into enemy hands. He also knew that many of those men would have valuable information that, if it could be passed back to Germany, could improve the success of future U-boat operations – information such as the effectiveness of Allied anti-submarine weapons, convoy escort tactics and techniques, and Allied interrogation methods. Dönitz needed a communications system that was immune to Allied censors and intelligence gatherers, who could be expected to carefully examine mail passing through the regular prisoner of war (POW) postal links of the Red Cross. It had to be able to transmit essential data in seemingly innocent correspondence. Finally, he needed a system simple enough that a regular U-boat sailor did not need to be a cryptologist to figure out how to use it.

"Code Irland (Ireland)" was one such U-boat code. Explained to commanding officers prior to their first mission, it established clandestine postal addresses (such as a fictitious home address) in Germany to which the letters could be sent, and also instructions to families to share the contents of letters with the B.d.U. if they noticed stilted or atypical language on the part of their POW sailor (see, "What Really Happened Out There?"). Within the code, the letters of the alphabet represented dots and dashes of the Morse code, a communications system that was taught in the Navy. The letters were written in longhand as usual; back at the B.d.U. these words would "translate" into Morse Code. The B.d.U. staff divided the twenty-six letters of the alphabet into two groups of nine letters (A through I and J through R) and one group of eight letters (S through Z). The code depended on the first letter of each written word in the correspondence. If that letter was an A through I, it signified a dot. If the first letter of the word was a J through R, it signified a dash. Any first letter beginning in S through Z signified a break between Morse letters. As the last letter in Group 1 (A through I) was an "I" and the last letter in Group 2 (J through R) was an "R", the mnemonic "Irland" was used to describe the code so everyone could remember it and its division of groups. So if a U-boat officer incarcerated in a POW camp, for example, were to write "Meine Kameraden und auch ich waren lange in Sorge, denn … " (My comrades as well as I were worried for a long time, for …) the letter would easily pass through the censors, but on the other end in Germany that sequence of first letters from these words (M, K, U, A, I, W, L, I, S, D) would be listed in Morse Code as dash-dash, break, dot-dot, break, dash-dot, break, dot, which equated to **M I N E**, the German word for mine, which the B.d.U. would then know as the type of Allied weapon that sunk the U-boat of that particular officer. Clearly, it would be difficult to send volumes of information in one letter to the B.d.U. But a creative writer or groups of writers could get their message out. A problem that was more difficult to manage concerned delays in the mail system. It took two to three months for a letter to go through the Red Cross system in each direction, so four to six months could pass before the POWs would get a reply to their original message.

Kapitänleutnant Peter-Erich Cremer, temporarily on the B.d.U. staff, put the plan together. He had been seriously wounded in combat in his *U-333* and was on the B.d.U. staff in Berlin as the second staff officer in the operations department in the Hotel am Steinplatz. He was appraised that a large group of U-boat crewmen held at Camp 70 outside of Fredericton, Canada were planning to break out, travel 150 miles north, cross the Northumberland Strait – a narrow channel to Prince Edward Island – and await a rescuing U-boat at the northern tip of that island. Cremer worked out the details including nautical data, meteorological information, location of the pickup, and had that information sent back using "Code Irland" in letters written in longhand appearing to be from family. Cremer selected a primary boat, the *U-376* (Karl-Friedrich Marks) and a backup boat, the *U-262* under command of Heinz Franke. Cremer reckoned that the major difficulty in the operation – assuming the prisoners could escape from the camp – was the difficulty the spring ice flows would present to a U-boat attempting to navigate the narrow Cabot Strait between Newfoundland and Nova Scotia to access Prince Edward Island.

The *U-376* left La Pallice on April 6, 1943, but on April 13 her radio went silent after an attack that night by an aircraft from the 172nd Squadron of the RAF. The *U-262* had departed the same port for the same destination on March 27, but had to return to La Pallice because of a defective air vent. She sailed again on April 7, and at 11:15 a.m. on April 15 B.d.U. directed Franke to open his orders – codename "Elster" (Magpie). Cremer's sealed order to Franke read:

> "As announced by secret letter code, some of our boys, held prisoner in Canada, are planning a breakout from their camp which lies in the area of New Brunswick. They are hoping to be at a certain point on the coast of the western Gulf of St. Lawrence in the first days of May. Your orders are to sail to this sea or coastal area, to attempt to make contact with them at the coastal point indicated, and thereafter to take them on board."

The details, of how to get there and exactly what to do once he got there, were left up to the commander of the *U-262*. Franke later stated:

> "I suddenly found myself faced with a task, the execution of which would most certainly entail a few risks for U-boat and crew. And there were so many unknowns to be considered in my planning, both on the outbound leg as well as the target area."

The *U-262* was a veteran boat. With her keel laid on May 29, 1941 in the Vulkan Vegesack Werft construction yard at Bremen, she was commissioned on April 15, 1942 at Vegesack. *Kapitänleutnant* Günter Schiebusch commanded the boat for her first three war patrols, but he achieved no successes and was replaced by Heinz Franke. He started roughly; in September two British Hudson aircraft dropped eight depth charges near the *U-262* on a war patrol, forcing her to lay up at Bergen, Norway for repairs. On her fourth war patrol out of Narvik, Norway, Franke changed the boat's fortunes and sank the Norwegian 925-ton corvette *HNoMS Montbretia* escorting convoy ONS-144 – killing 47 men – on November 18, 1942. Eight days later, in a surface attack with his last torpedoes, Franke sank the British 7,178-ton *Ocean Crusader*; there were no survivors. On February 6, 1943, on their fifth war patrol, sailing out of La Pallice, France, the crew of the *U-262* sank the 2,864-ton *Zagloba*, sailing with convoy SC-118. This rescue mission would be the U-boat's sixth war patrol.

Franke headed west and almost immediately ran into a large Allied convoy which he reported to B.d.U.; Berlin replied that he could attack convoys east of Newfoundland but that he had to be at the pick-up location on time without fail. Then potential disaster struck; early on April 16, escort destroyers spotted the *U-262* and attacked with depth charges but Franke shook off his pursuers and continued toward Canada. Franke arrived off Cabot Strait on April 26 and began transiting the strait that night on the surface. He immediately encountered ice but initially was able to pass through the thin ice layers at a reduced speed. Still surfaced, the *U-262* then encountered large chunks of ice ten-meters square which stopped the boat. Franke described the situation:

> "I'm held firm in a vast field of drift ice [from which] I have to assume that the ice thickens into a solid layer further to the west."

Franke then submerged and began a blind sixteen-hour run under the ice. The *U-262* was heavily damaged; ice had damaged the forward torpedo ports and the forward torpedo tubes were thus flooded and not operational. Franke tried to surface at the end of this period, but the ice was too thick and damaged the superstructure of the boat. He tried again five minutes later, blowing all tanks to give the boat the maximum surge of buoyancy. The *U-262* hurtled upward, breaking the ice – but a large chunk still blocked the hatch in the conning tower. After several minutes, the crew was able to force the hatch open. What they found was a clear night sky and a damaged net-cutter, a mangled anti-aircraft gun and a damaged 88-mm deck-gun; the *U-262* was now defenseless.

Franke then worked his way slowly toward North Point, Prince Edward Island, traveling submerged by day and surfacing at night. He reached an area four miles from the coast early on May 2. For four days the Germans peered through the periscope hoping for a sign from the shore – perhaps a light at night or some type of signal fire – that aspect had not been discussed in the "Code Irland" letters. Each night Franke would take the boat extremely close to shore hoping to see some signal from his comrades – to no avail. With no signal, on May 6 the *U-262* finally reversed engines and backed away to deeper waters to begin the return trip to France; Franke felt a great sense of disappointment at failing to retrieve his U-boat comrades. And what of the prisoners? An earlier escape attempt had resulted in increased Canadian surveillance of Camp 70 – which made a successful escape impossible – but that information came too late to abort the mission. The *U-262* returned safely to La Pallice, France on May 25, 1943 and participated in several further conventional war patrols (one in which the *U-262* shot down two attacking aircraft), winning the Knight's Cross for Heinz Franke six months later. As for his comrades at Camp 70; they also returned to Germany, but only some four years later. Heinz Franke survived the war and joined the post-war German Navy, retiring as a *Fregattenkapitän* in 1967. He died on April 5, 2003.

Known Crewmembers for the U-262

Arnold, Heinz	*Mechanikerobergefreiter*
Atzinger, Siegfried	
Bartels	*Leutnant (Ing)*
Bense, Willi	*Obermaschinenmaat*
Berns, Werner	*Matrosenobergefreiter*
Bieneck, Franz	*Matrosenobergefreiter*
Bohlsen-Jansen, Bodo	
Bremen, Bernhard	*Matrosenobergefreiter*
Brössel, Georg-Ludwig	*Matrosenobergefreiter*
Brutscher, Hans	
Buksch, Alfred	*Bootsmannsmaat*
Bülow, Bubi	*Matrosenobergefreiter*
Buschmann, Anton	*Obermaschinenmaat*
Clees, Günter	*Maschinenobergefreiter*
Dokter, Karl	*Mechanikerobergefreiter*
Franke, Heinz	*Kapitänleutnant*
Garbe, Jochen	*Leutnant zur See*
Garotzki, Herbert	*Obersteuermann*
Goldmann, Karl-Heinz	*Matrose*
Göthe, Willi	*Oberbootsmannsmaat*
Grasshof, Gerhard	*Matrosenobergefreiter*
Greining, Otto	*Oberbootsmannsmaat*
Gressmann, Walter	*Matrosenobergefreiter*
Grunewald, Ernst	*Obermaschinenmaat*
Hartun, Walter	*Matrosenobergefreiter*
Hellmann, Hans	*Oberleutnant zur See*
Herkath, Christian	*Obermaschinist*
Hertel, Herbert	*Maschinenobergefreiter*
Hindel, Rolf	*Maschinenobergefreiter*
Hösterei, Paul	*Mechanikermaat*
Hübsch, Horst-Dieter	*Oberleutnant zur See*
Kersten, Herbert	*Funkobergefreiter*
Köhler, Werner	*Obermaschinenmaat*
Kopff, Edmund	*Oberleutnant zur See*
Krist, Karl-Heinz	*Obermaschinenmaat*
Laudahn, Karl-Heinz	*Kapitänleutnant*
Lettau, Bruno	*Maschinenobergefreiter*
Machlinski, Max	*Maschinenobergefreiter*
Mak, Friedrich	*Obermaschinenmaat*
Manghardt, Anton	*Sanitätsmaat*
Markwart, Erwin	*Matrosenobergefreiter*
Meyer, Friedrich	*Obermaschinist*
Müller, Alfred	*Maschinenobergefreiter*
Niebuhr, Franz	*Obermaschinenmaat*
Niering, Kurt	*Funkmaat*
Nitschke, Martin	*Funkobergefreiter*
Nussbaum, Karl	*Maschinenobergefreiter*
Palm, Waldemar	*Leutnant zur See*
Roderhuiser, Willy	*Maschinenobergefreiter*
Schiebusch, Günter	*Korvettenkapitän*
Schiller, Heinz	*Oberleutnant zur See*
Sternberg, Siegfried	*Obermaschinenmaat*
Steuernagel, Helmut	*Obermaschinenmaat*
Strack, Erwin	*Maschinenobergefreiter*
Sutholt, Heinz	*Oberleutnant (Ing)*
Thiele, Franz	*Obermaschinenmaat*
Wandel, Franz	*Matrose*
Wieduwilt, Helmut	*Oberleutnant zur See*

Sources, "Taking Care of Their Own:" Clay Blair, *Hitler's U-boat War: The Hunted, 1942-1945*, New York: Modern Library, 2000, 23, 118, 119, 120, 225, 226; Peter Cremer, *U-boat Commander: A Periscope View of the Battle of the Atlantic*, translated by Lawrence Wilson, Annapolis, Maryland: Naval Institute Press, 1984, 114, 115; *F.d.U./B.d.U. War Diary, 1-15 April 1943* (PG30321), 229, 253; *F.d.U./B.d.U. War Diary, 16-30 April 1943* (PG30322), 258; *F.d.U./B.d.U. War Diary, 1-15 May 1943* (PG30323), 340; Michael L. Hadley, *U-boats against Canada: German Submarines in Canadian Waters*, Montreal: McGill-Queen's University Press, 1990, 168-174; Jürgen Rohwer, *Axis Submarine Successes 1939-1945*, Annapolis, Maryland: Naval Institute Press, 1983, 137, 138, 139, 148, 174, 175; War Diary of the U-262, April 15, 1942 – November 5, 1944, PG 30238/1-9; ONI Roll T-261-A, *National Archives Microfilm Publication T1022*, roll 2886, RG 242; www.ubootwaffe.net; www.uboatarchive.net.

Studio portrait of Friedrich Meyer. *Meyer was a Chief Petty Officer in the engine room of the U-262 during the rescue mission, operating the diesel engines and electric motors.*

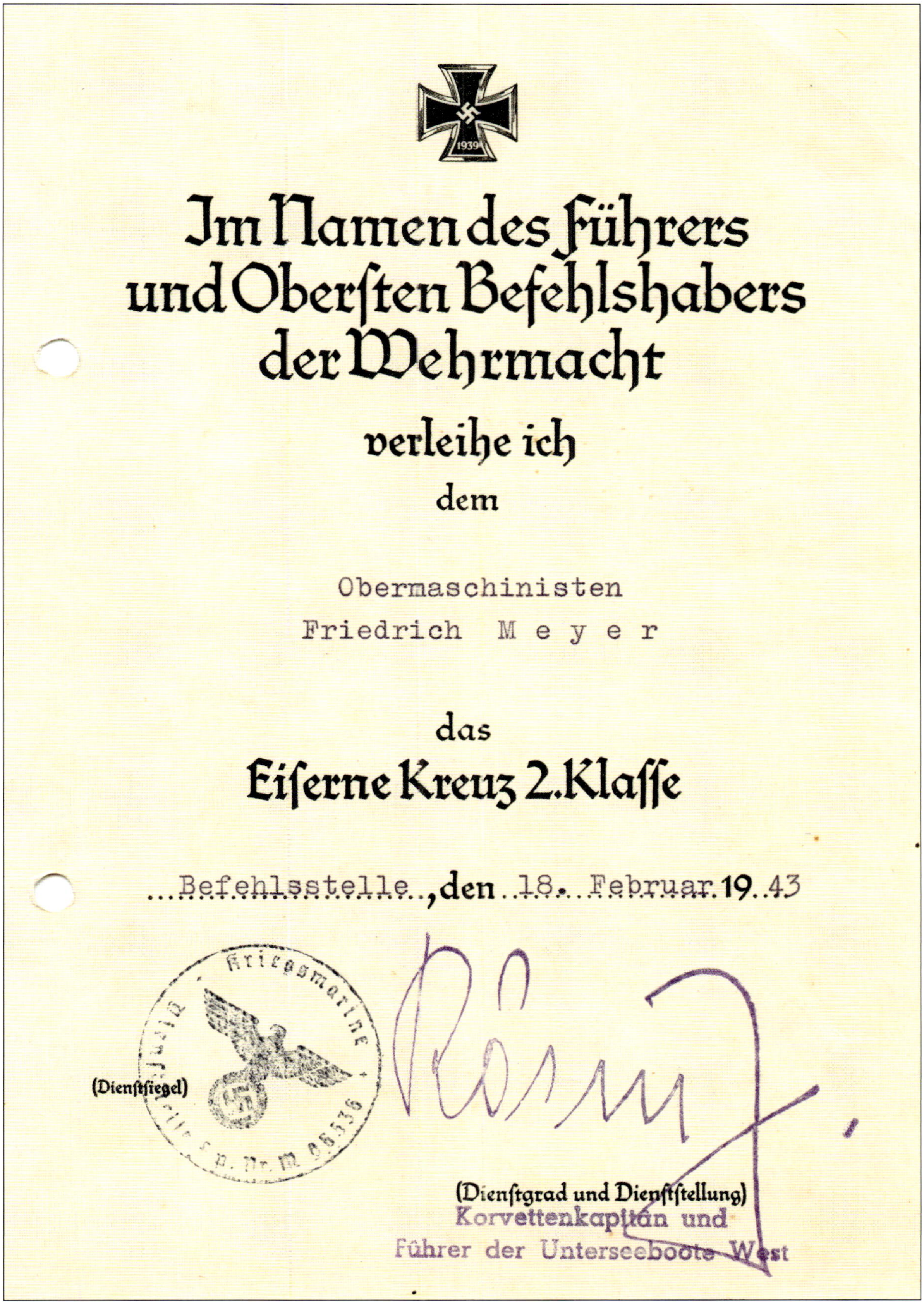

Im Namen des Führers
und Obersten Befehlshabers
der Wehrmacht

verleihe ich

dem

Obermaschinisten
Friedrich Meyer

das

Eiserne Kreuz 2. Klasse

...Befehlsstelle.., den 18. Februar 19 43

Kriegsmarine

(Dienstsiegel)

(Dienstgrad und Dienststellung)
Korvettenkapitän und
Führer der Unterseeboote West

Iron Cross 2nd Class award document to Friedrich Meyer of the U-262 on February 18, 1943. *It was awarded at La Pallice shortly after the conclusion of a successful fifth war patrol. Document has a facsimile signature of Kapitän zur See Hans Rudolf Rösing, Chief of U-boats, West.*

262

Verleihungs-Urkunde

Auf Grund der Ermächtigung des Oberbefehlshabers der Kriegsmarine verleihe ich dem

Obermaschinisten
(Dienstgrad)

Friedrich Meyer
(Name)

das

Ubootskriegsabzeichen 1939

Im Westen, den 30. Mai 1943

Rösing

~~Admiral und Befehlshaber der Unterseeboote~~
Kapitän zur See
und Führer der Unterseeboote West

(MS 37108)

U-boat War Badge award document to Friedrich Meyer of the U-262 on May 30, 1943. *The document has a facsimile signature of Kapitän zur See Hans Rudolf Rösing, Chief of U-boats, West. This award was made shortly after the U-262 returned to France from Canada, her sixth war patrol.*

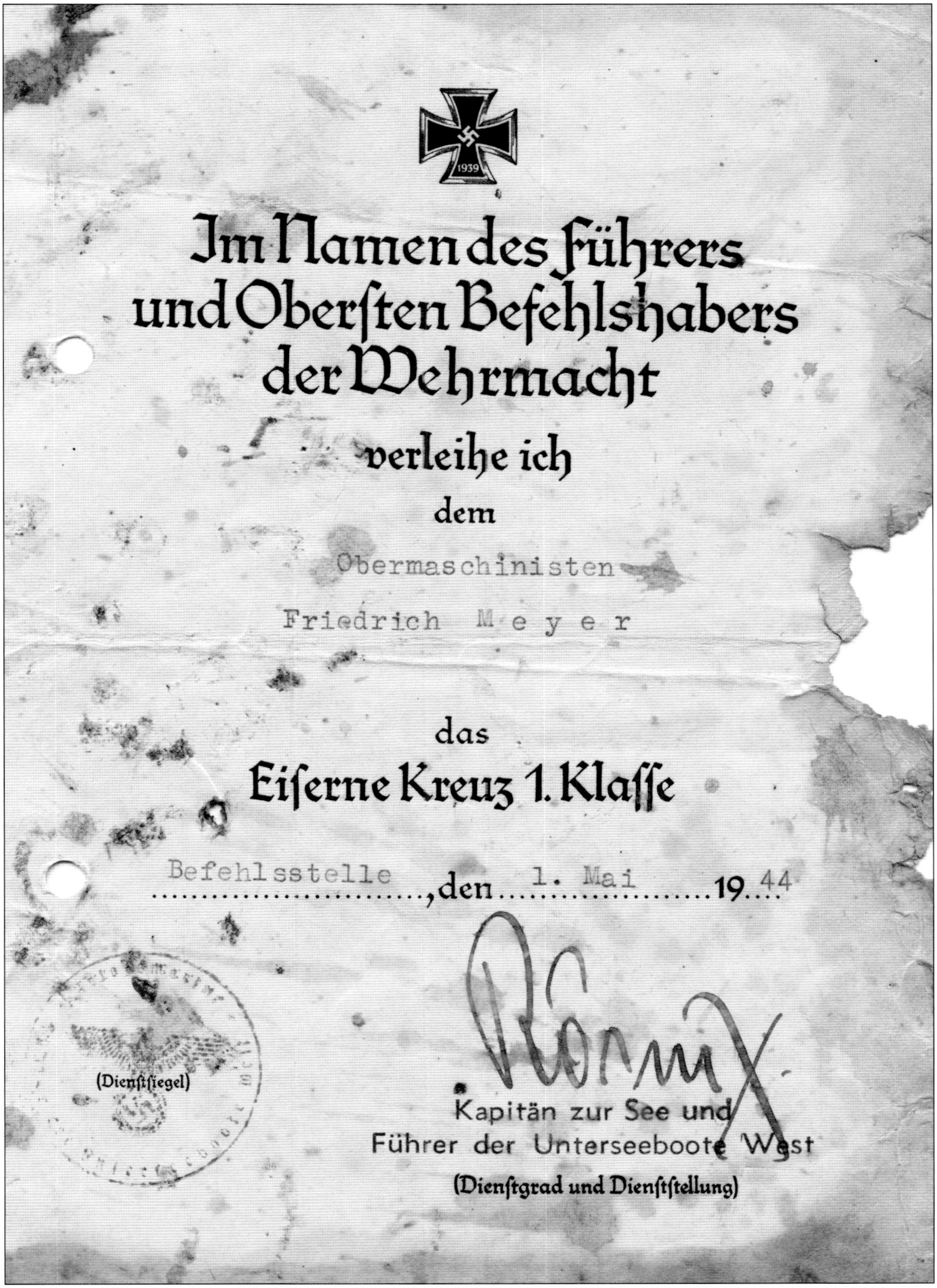

Im Namen des Führers
und Obersten Befehlshabers
der Wehrmacht

verleihe ich

dem

Obermaschinisten

Friedrich Meyer

das

Eiserne Kreuz 1. Klasse

Befehlsstelle, den 1. Mai 1944

(Dienstsiegel)

Kapitän zur See und
Führer der Unterseeboote West

(Dienstgrad und Dienststellung)

Iron Cross 1st Class award document to Friedrich Meyer of the U-262 on May 1, 1944, awarded at La Pallice shortly after the conclusion of a successful ninth war patrol. *Document has an original ink signature of Kapitän zur See Hans Rudolf Rösing, Chief of U-boats, West.*

CHAPTER NINETEEN

"GOLIATH"
U-97
MAY 1943

The keys to successfully executing Dönitz's U-boat strategy were communications and leadership. Learning through experience both in World War I, the mid-war years and the early years of World War II, Dönitz constantly shifted his operational headquarters to be closer to the bulk of his frontline boats and crews. In this manner he could see his charges off to their patrol, monitor their progress at sea, issue awards and decorations to deserving crewmembers and receive timely personal debriefings from returning U-boat commanders, so he could quickly pass their experiences learned to the rest of the U-boat fleet. To facilitate these actions, he moved the headquarters of the B.d.U. to the following wartime locations:

August 1939	Swinemünde
September 1939 – November 1939	Wilhelmshaven (Marine Station)
November 1939 – September 1940	Sengwarden/Wilhelmshaven
September 1940 – October 1940	Paris, France (Boulevard Souchet 18)
October 1940 – March 1942	Kernével/Lorient, France
March 1942 – March 1943	Paris, France (Avenue Maréchal Maunoury)
March 1943 – December 1943	Berlin-Charlottenburg (Hotel am Steinplatz)
December 1943 – February 1945	Bernau near Berlin (Codenamed "Koralle")
February 1945 – April 1945	Sengwarden/Wilhelmshaven
April 1945	Plön
May 1945	Flensburg-Mürwik

From this list, it is obvious that during the first years of the war, Dönitz attempted to get closer to his crews so he could look into the eyes of his boat commanders and their men and judge how well the undersea campaign was going and what he needed to influence events. He came closest to his boys at Kernével, where the B.d.U. appropriated a beautiful mansion formally known as the Villa Kerillon, overlooking the entrance to Lorient. Unofficially, the villa was known as the "Chateau des Sardines," thanks to a previous owner who had made his fortune in the sardine-fishing trade. The U-boat admiral could track his charges in the map room and could also inspect the appearance of every boat entering and exiting the busy Lorient U-boat base through his pair of commander's binoculars. More importantly, he could talk to them at sea. It is not coincidental that this period would prove to be the most successful for the U-boats of the entire war.

At night U-boats surfaced and sent shortwave communications to Dönitz's headquarters at Kernével. Dönitz's communications staff would then key land lines that led to powerful receivers and transmitters (receivers at Villecresnes; transmitters at Sainte-Assise) southeast of Paris – formerly owned by the Compagnie Radio-France and used by the French government for communications with France's far-flung colonies around the world. Now they were under new management.

Dönitz's crews could also communicate with their commander from underwater. At the start of the war, the main German Navy facility for underwater radio communication was a 300-kilowatt transmitter referred to as "Nauen." Then they got really serious. From 1942 to 1945 at Calbe, Germany – forty-three kilometers from Magdeburg – enormous long wave radio antenna (known as the "Goliath" station) communicated with the submarines; the site pumped out 1,800 kilowatts. "Goliath" was, in turn, connected to Kernével by a secure land cable through which the information quickly passed; "Goliath" could contact any German U-boat at sea except those submerged deep in narrow Norwegian fjords to the north.

This underwater radio communication was very useful as the U-boats were able to receive messages from their commands without surfacing. Thus, the U-boats – when communicating from underwater – could not be detected by radar and Allied HF direction finders could not detect the U-boats' positions because the boats were not using their radio transmitters, only receivers. Because the communication was one-way, it was specifically organized by a previously determined method. Messages were marked by serial numbers, each serial number for each U-boat. The messages were transmitted without confirmation of reception, mostly at night, sometimes from several transmitters simultaneously. Each U-boat radio operator knew the time of transmitting. When the designated time window was coming, the radio operator notified the commander who ensured the boat was at the correct depth. Boats in the North Sea, often 600 miles from the transmitter in Germany, would ensure their boat's antenna was at a depth of fourteen to twenty-four meters. Boats in the Mediterranean, some 1,400 miles distant, would be slightly shallower – twelve to seventeen meters deep. Those long-range raiders in the Indian Ocean, 5,000 miles away would best pick up the signal at only seven to fourteen meters under the surface. Reception efficiency was excellent, with an estimated 90% of all messages received successfully.

After the British commando raid on St. Nazaire in March 1942, Donitz reluctantly concluded that he should move his headquarters from Lorient to Paris. In January 1943, Hitler selected Dönitz to replace Admiral Eric Raeder as the Commander-in-Chief of the entire German Navy. Two months later the U-boat chief decided to consolidate naval headquarters in Berlin and B.d.U. moved from Paris (Avenue Maréchal Maunoury) to the Hotel am Steinplatz in Berlin-Charlottenburg. As author Michael Gannon surmised: the effect of Dönitz now not being constantly at the French ports to wish his men well after every mission would be impossible to calculate.

Dönitz's Crews
***Oberfunkmaat* Rolf Teucher**

Born on December 19, 1917 in Chemnitz/Saxony.
Served as a senior radio operator on the *U-97*.
Awarded the U-boat War Badge, the Iron Cross 2nd Class on March 8, 1941, the Iron Class 1st Class on May 6, 1942 and the German Cross in Gold on May 16, 1943.
Spent 314 days at sea on U-boat war patrols.
Survived the war; lived in Flensburg, Schleswig-Holstein.

Oberfunkmaat Rolf Teucher was one of those U-boat radio operators who knew how to communicate effectively with Dönitz and B.d.U. For the *U-97*, he was the link to the outside world. Born in the industrial city of Chemnitz in Saxony on December 19, 1917, he joined the Navy on January 1, 1937. Two personal documents show that as a *Funkobergefreiter* he received the U-boat War Badge in November 1939, although we do not know on which boat he served at that time. He apparently joined the crew of the *U-97* in 1940. The German Navy had ordered the construction of the boat two years previously on May 30, 1938. Shipyard engineers at the F. Krupp Germaniawerft AG at Kiel-Gaarden laid her keel on September 27, 1939. The boat was launched on August 15, 1940 – it is likely that Teucher was on the boat by that time. The Navy commissioned the *U-97* on September 28, 1940 and she underwent extensive work-ups in the Baltic Sea for the next several months under the auspices of the 7th U-boat Flotilla.

The *U-97*'s first commander was *Oberleutnant zur See* Udo Heilmann. Heilmann was one of the old guard U-boat men. Born in Kiel on March 4, 1913, he entered the Navy in 1933 and within three years was in the U-boat fleet, as small as it was at the time. From June 1937 to October 1939, Heilmann served as the 1st Watch Officer for the *U-18*, a small Type IIB boat in U-boat Flotilla *Lohs*, and served on two short war patrols with this boat. He then assumed command of the *U-24*, another Type IIB, and commanded her for four war patrols; the *U-24* sank no ships on these missions. Then the Navy tabbed Heilmann to bring the new *U-97* on line.

Assigned to the 7th U-boat Flotilla, the *U-97* departed Kiel on February 17, 1941 for her first war patrol. The Germans located a convoy and Dönitz ordered Heilmann to move to the action. Fortune came early and Heilmann sank three ships and damaged another of convoy OB-289, all on the same day, but did not send a contact report and was rebuked by Dönitz in the B.d.U. war diary. But the results for the new boat were impressive:

- On February 24, 1941 at 2:12 a.m., the *U-97* torpedoed the British 4,894-ton *Mansepool* between Iceland and Scotland. The ship was in ballast, sailing from Cardiff, Wales to Halifax, Nova Scotia; two crewmen perished in the attack.
- At the same time, the *U-97* torpedoed the British 4,973-ton freighter *Jonathan Holt*, carrying general cargo from Liverpool to the west coast of Africa. She lost fifty men; only three men survived.
- At 6:24 a.m., the *U-97* torpedoed the British tanker 6,894-ton *British Gunner*; the ship, in ballast and sailing from Swansea, Wales to Aruba, lost three men.
- At 8:18 a.m., Heilmann torpedoed the Norwegian 9,718-ton tanker *GC Brovig*. She did not sink.

Out of torpedoes, the *U-97* received instructions on March 1 to serve as a temporary weather station and reported the changing conditions. Heilmann conducted this mission until March 6, when another boat assumed these duties, but it was a costly duty; on March 3, 1941 *Bootsmaat* Artur Mai was lost overboard in the Bay of Biscay. The *U-97* arrived at Lorient, France on March 7, 1941. Awards for the crew were in order and on March 8, *Funkmaat* Rolf Teucher received an Iron Cross 2nd Class. Then the crew had two weeks respite. The *U-97* then departed Lorient on March 20, 1941 for her second war patrol, and again success smiled on the boat. Heilmann sank three ships; but again he failed in assisting other boats to home in on the convoy:

- On March 23, 1941 at 11:26 p.m. southwest of Ireland, the *U-97* sank the British 8,077-ton tanker *Chama*. The tanker, which was in ballast, was bound from Ardrossan, Scotland for New York; her entire crew of fifty-eight perished.
- The next day at 4:43 p.m., the *U-97* torpedoed the Norwegian 4,301-ton freighter *Horda* steaming from Liverpool to Halifax. Again the results were disastrous and all thirty men aboard the *Horda* lost their lives.
- On April 4, 1941 at 6:19 p.m., the *U-97* torpedoed the British 8,132-ton tanker *Conus*, which was on Admiralty service from Swansea to Curacao. The tanker was in ballast, and once again the results were tragic with all fifty-nine of her crew going to the bottom with the ship.

The *U-97* arrived at St. Nazaire, France on April 10, 1941. The U-boat was on a roll and departed St. Nazaire on May 1, 1941. Five days later she made contact and at 2:40 a.m. (after trailing the target for eight hours) on May 6, 1941, the *U-97* torpedoed the British 6,833-ton *HMS Camito*, in the mid-Atlantic. Previously a steam merchant ship, the *Camito* was requisitioned by the Admiralty in August 1940 and converted to an ocean-boarding vessel. At the time of the attack she was escorting the Italian tanker *Sangro*, which had been taken as a prize two weeks before. Heilmann fired three torpedoes that all missed, before registering a hit; the ship sank the next day. Meanwhile at 3:53 a.m. the same morning, the *U-97* sank the 6,466-ton *Sangro*. On May 8, 1941 at 6:13 p.m., the *U-97* achieved another success, sinking the British 4,553-ton *Ramillies*, which was carrying coke from Oban, Scotland to Baltimore, Maryland; twenty-nine men aboard went down with the ship. Although this would be the U-boat's last victim on this patrol, her duties were not complete. On May 24, 1941 Dönitz ordered the *U-97* and three other boats to a location 420 miles west of Lorient to form a trap for British forces pursuing the battleship *Bismarck*, which was heading for France after destroying the battlecruiser and pride of the British Fleet *HMS Hood*. Events overtook the plan and the *Bismarck* was finally cornered – after receiving an aerial torpedo hit that critically damaged her rudder and left her unable to maneuver – some two hundred miles away from the ambush location. Dönitz then ordered the *U-97* and other U-boats to race for the *Bismarck's* location, but only two made it (neither the *U-97*), after the German battleship had sunk. Low on fuel, the *U-97* arrived at St. Nazaire on May 30, 1941.

The *U-97* remained at St. Nazaire until July 2, 1941 when she sailed on her fourth war patrol. She achieved no results and Heilmann brought the boat back to the base on August 8, 1941. Remaining in France for almost six weeks, the *U-97* departed on September 20, 1941 for her fifth war patrol and got back on a successful track. But first she had to pass through the dangerous Straits of Gibraltar as Dönitz reluctantly ordered her to the Mediterranean on direction of the German Navy High Command. She made the passage on the night of September 27. Udo Heilmann scored his first two victories in the Mediterranean on October 17, 1941. At 3:25 a.m., off the African coast, Heilmann torpedoed the 1,208-ton Greek freighter *Samos*, carrying government stores from Alexandria to Tobruk; thirty-one men perished, while only three survived. Shortly after, at 4:00 a.m., the U-boat torpedoed and sank the small British 758-ton tanker *Pass of Balmaha*, carrying gasoline from Alexandria to Tobruk; all eighteen men aboard were killed. Ten days later on October 27, 1941 the *U-97* arrived at Salamis, Greece and was reassigned to the 23rd U-boat Flotilla, under the command of *Kapitänleutnant* Fritz Frauenheim.

Heilmann and the *U-97* then hit a dry spell. From late December 1941 through May 1942, the U-boat conducted five war patrols in the Mediterranean but sank no enemy ships. However, Rolf Teucher continued his outstanding service and received the Iron Cross 1st Class on May 6, 1942. Udo Heilmann then departed the *U-97* and became a torpedo attack instructor in the 26th U-boat Flotilla until March 1943, when he became an advisor to the F.d.U. Training Department for the duration of the war. But the war went on for the *U-97* under the command of *Oberleutnant* Friedrich Bürgel. Bürgel hailed from Düsseldorf, where he was born on October 24, 1916. He entered the German Navy in 1936 and served on the *Admiral Scheer* for two years in the late 1930s; Bürgel began U-boat training in October 1940. As a young officer, he gained valuable experience as the 1st Watch Officer on the *U-565* from April 1941 to January 1942; this service included four war patrols, one of which was in the Mediterranean.

On June 15, 1942 Bürgel and the *U-97* departed La Spezia, Italy for the boat's eleventh war patrol. On June 28, 1942 at 1:16 p.m., the *U-97* encountered the British 1,433-ton freighter *Zealand*, steaming from Port Said, Egypt to Farmagusta, Cyprus and sank her just south of that island. Fourteen of the crew died in the attack. Eight minutes later, Bürgel torpedoed the Greek 1,755-ton freighter *Memas* headed for the same destination; eight crewmen perished. The *U-97* was not finished; on July 1, 1942 at 1:45 p.m., Bürgel sank the British 786-ton freighter *Marilyse Moller* hugging the Egyptian coast, bound from Port Said to Haifa, Palestine. Thirty-one of her thirty-five men died in the attack. The *U-97* arrived at Salamis on July 4, 1942.

Friedrich Bürgel took the *U-97* on her twelfth war patrol from July 22, 1942 to August 4, 1942 but sank no ships. The *U-97* sailed from Salamis on August 20, 1943 for her next patrol, arriving at La Spezia on August 29, 1942. The U-boat sank no ships on this patrol either. Bürgel left the *U-97* to take command of the *U-205*. He would command this boat until February 1943 when he was taken prisoner when the *U-205* was sunk. In his place on the *U-97* came Hans-Georg Trox. Trox was born at Schrotz, West Prussia on January 21, 1916. He had extensive experience in minesweeping ships, but only six months experience as a 1st Watch Officer on the *U-83* in late 1942. But the crew of the *U-97* was experienced and competent. *Obermaschinist* Paul Engelhardt was awarded a German Cross in Gold on March 22, 1943 for his long-term excellence in the engine room. *Bootsmaat* Max Miedza would depart the *U-97* and go on to win the German Cross in Gold on the *U-296* on October 11, 1944. And *Oberfunkmaat* Rolf Teucher, the master of the radio room, was awarded a German Cross in Gold on May 6, 1943.

Oberleutnant zur See Trox took the *U-97* out for two patrols, but we do not know at what precise time Teucher left the *U-97* for a new assignment. On April 10, 1943 the *U-97* sailed from La Spezia, arriving at Pola, Italy on May 3, 1943. The boat engaged no targets on the mission. On June 5, 1943 she departed again for combat. Sinking the Dutch 1,179-ton freighter *Palima* on June 12 and the British 8,995-ton tanker *Athelmonarch* off the Egyptian coast, her days were numbered.

The next day the British dispatched aircraft from Lydda, Palestine to look for the marauding U-boat. Subsequently, a British Lockheed Hudson light bomber of the 459th Squadron, Royal Australian Air Force, piloted by Flying Officer D. T. Barnard, found the *U-97* just off Haifa fully-surfaced with some crew on deck; it was a fatal error. The Hudson made an immediate depth-charge attack. One depth charge exploded on the U-boat's decking, two more exploded in the water alongside. The U-boat's pressure hull was fatally holed and she sank within five minutes, but the Hudson was damaged by the blast and it took all of Barnard's skill to bring her back to base. Trox and twenty-six other crewmen were killed; twenty-one men were rescued and taken prisoner.

Oberfunkmeister Rolf Teucher survived the war and was mustered out of the German Navy in June 1945.

Known Crewmembers for the U-97

Bauer, Josef	*Oberbootsmann*
Bielfeld, Heinz	*Kapitänleutnant*
Büchel, Max	*Leutnant zur See*
Burchartz, Bernhard	*Obersteuermann*
Bürgel, Friedrich	*Kapitänleutnant*
Cassens, Hermann-Georg	*Obermaschinenmaat*
Colsmann, Peter	*Oberfähnrich zur See*
Dietz, Gerhard	*Funkmaat*
Engelhardt, Paul	*Obermaschinist*
Engelke, Gerhard	*Matrosengefreiter*
Ferkel, Johann	*Maschinenobergefreiter*
Fischel, Unno von	*Oberleutnant zur See*
Fischer, Kurt	*Obermaschinist*
Fraumann, Kurt	
Frühwirth, Alfred	*Maschinenobergefreiter*
Goertz, Gerhard	*Bootsmaat*
Golsmann, Peter	
Gorski, Franz	*Maschinenobergefreiter*
Greif, Max	*Oberbootsmann*
Groos, Paul	*Matrosengefreiter*
Hafer, Fritz	*Maschinenobergefreiter*
Hartmann, Otto	*Oberleutnant zur See*
Hauertmann, Bernhard	*Bootsmann*
Heilmann, Udo	*Korvettenkapitän*
Hösel, Albert	*Maschinenmaat*
Hymmen, Reinhard	*Kapitänleutnant*
Jägle, Rudolf	*Matrose*
Kies, Helmut	*Funkobergefreiter*
Kieswalter, Friedrich	*Oberleutnant (Ing)*
Kirsten	*Obermaschinenmaat*
Köhnen, August	*Matrosenhauptgefreiter*
Kophamel, Alexander	*Oberleutnant zur See*
Kroll, Walter Alfons	*Maschinenobergefreiter*
Krumm, Ewald	*Mechanikergefreiter*
Kubo	*Matrosengefreiter*
Lindel, Gerhard	*Obersteuermann*
Lübbers, Erwin	*Funkobergefreiter*
Luchmann, Ignatz	*Matrosengefreiter*
Lüders	*Maschinenobergefreiter*
Mai, Artur	*Bootsmann*
Mende, Moritz	*Maschinenobergefreiter*
Miedza, Max	*Bootsmann*
Mohwinkel	*Maschinenmaat*
Möller	*Leutnant (Ing)*
Müller, Rudi	*Matrosengefreiter*
Nagel, Gerhard	*Mechanikerobergefreiter*
Netz, Wilhelm	*Oberleutnant (Ing)*
Neuberg, Helmut	*Maschinenmaat*
Nonn, Victor-Wilhelm	*Kapitänleutnant*
Pelloth, Günter	*Matrosenobergefreiter*
Perrmann, Joachim	*Oberfunkmaat*
Prehn, Wilhelm	*Oberleutnant zur See*
Raduns, Karl	*Bootsmann*
Reinartz, Martin	*Maschinengefreiter*
Richardt, Walter	*Obermechanikermaat*
Rowold, Otto	*Oberleutnant (Ing)*
Schäfer, Werner	*Maschinenmaat*
Scheffer, Heinrich	*Maschinenobergefreiter*
Schimanski, Walter	
Schmaljohann	*Matrosengefreiter*
Seyda, August	*Funkobergefreiter*
Siegert, Hans	*Oberleutnant (Ing)*
Siemon, Hilmar	*Kapitänleutnant*
Spaude, Adalbert	*Matrosenobergefreiter*
Spiegelberg	*Oberleutnant zur See*
Stampel, Franz	*Leutnant zur See*
Stein, Heinz	
Teucher, Rolf	*Oberfunkmaat*
Tinschert, Otto	*Kapitänleutnant*
Trox, Hans-Georg	*Kapitänleutnant*
Umnus, Heinrich	*Bootsmann*
Urbansky, Stanislaus	
Wagner, Erwin	*Maschinengefreiter*
Weichynik, Roman	*Matrosenobergefreiter*
Weiler, Theo	*Maschinenobergefreiter*
Weinberger, Karl	*Leutnant zur See*
Weiner	*Matrosenobergefreiter*
Winkelmann, Kurt	*Maschinenobergefreiter*
Wolf, Johannes	*Obermaschinist*
Wolf, Josef	*Maschinenobergefreiter*
Wolfram, Konrad	*Bootsmann*
Zimmermann, Heinz	*Matrosenobergefreiter*
Zwarg, Heinz	*Kapitänleutnant*

Sources, "Goliath:" Clay Blair, *Hitler's U-boat War: The Hunters, 1939-1942*, New York: Random House, 1996, 237, 238, 248, 249, 267, 288, 396, 649, 653; Rainer Busch and Hans-Joachim Röll, *German U-boat Commanders of World War II*, translated by Geoffrey Brooks, Annapolis, Maryland: Naval Institute Press, 1999, 44, 94; Michael Gannon, *Black May: The Epic Story of the Allies Defeat of the German U-boats in May 1943*, New York: HarperCollins, 1998, 108; Michael Gannon, *Operation Drumbeat: The Dramatic True Story of Germany's First U-boat Attacks Along the American Coast in World War II*, New York: Harper & Row, 1990, 68; Günter Hessler, *The U-boat War in the Atlantic, 1939-1945, Volume 1-3*, London: Her Majesty's Stationery Office, 1989, 74; Jürgen Rohwer, *Axis Submarine Successes 1939-1945*, Annapolis, Maryland: Naval Institute Press, 1983, 44, 47, 48, 51, 227, 234, 235, 246; www.ubootwaffe.net; www.uboatarchive.net.

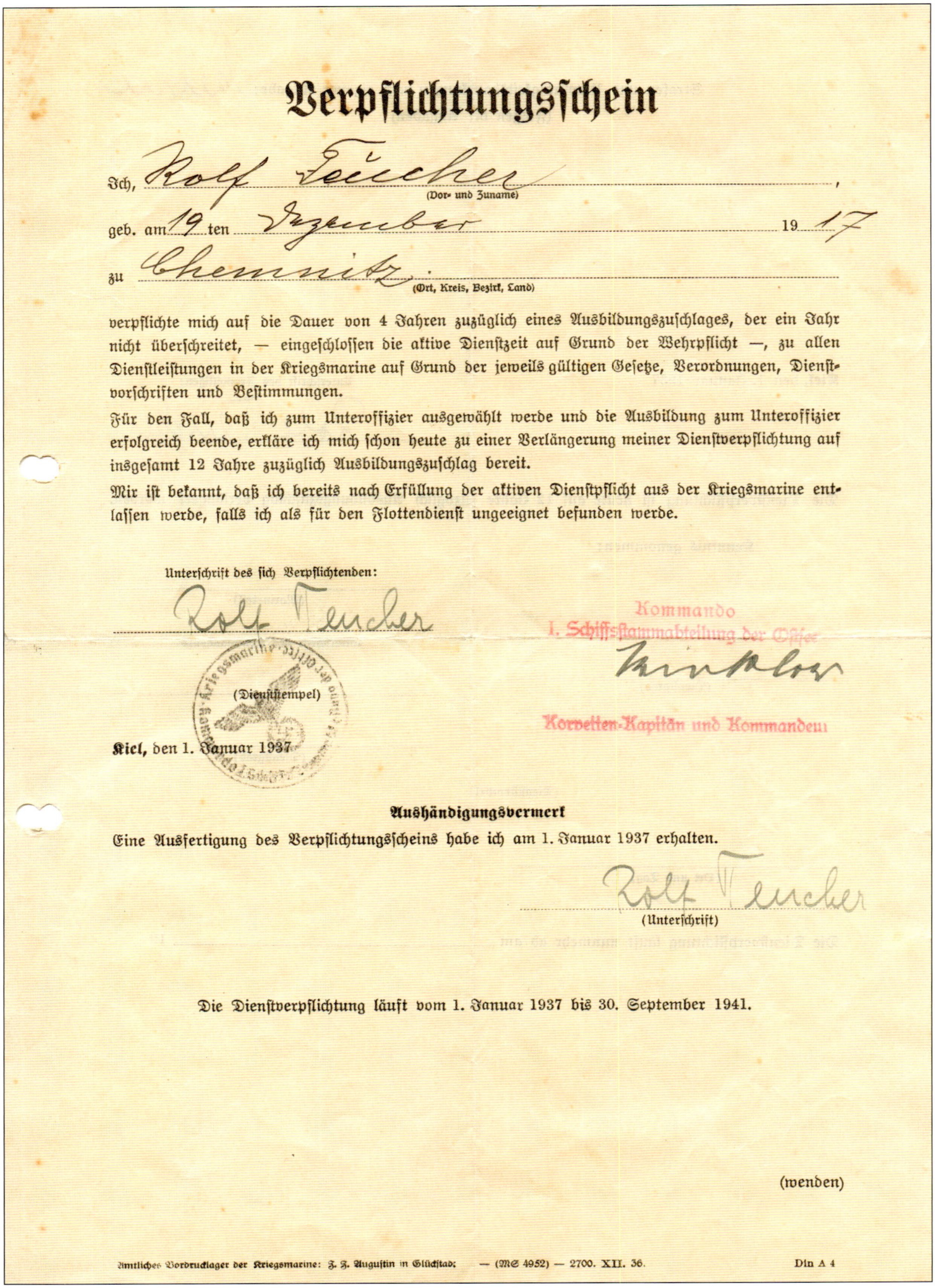

Verpflichtungsschein

Ich, Rolf Teucher,
(Vor- und Zuname)

geb. am 19 ten Dezember 1917

zu Chemnitz.
(Ort, Kreis, Bezirk, Land)

verpflichte mich auf die Dauer von 4 Jahren zuzüglich eines Ausbildungszuschlages, der ein Jahr nicht überschreitet, — eingeschlossen die aktive Dienstzeit auf Grund der Wehrpflicht —, zu allen Dienstleistungen in der Kriegsmarine auf Grund der jeweils gültigen Gesetze, Verordnungen, Dienstvorschriften und Bestimmungen.

Für den Fall, daß ich zum Unteroffizier ausgewählt werde und die Ausbildung zum Unteroffizier erfolgreich beende, erkläre ich mich schon heute zu einer Verlängerung meiner Dienstverpflichtung auf insgesamt 12 Jahre zuzüglich Ausbildungszuschlag bereit.

Mir ist bekannt, daß ich bereits nach Erfüllung der aktiven Dienstpflicht aus der Kriegsmarine entlassen werde, falls ich als für den Flottendienst ungeeignet befunden werde.

Unterschrift des sich Verpflichtenden:

Rolf Teucher

Kommando
I. Schiffsstammabteilung der Ostsee

Winkler

(Dienststempel)

Korvetten-Kapitän und Kommandeur

Kiel, den 1. Januar 1937

Aushändigungsvermerk

Eine Ausfertigung des Verpflichtungsscheins habe ich am 1. Januar 1937 erhalten.

Rolf Teucher
(Unterschrift)

Die Dienstverpflichtung läuft vom 1. Januar 1937 bis 30. September 1941.

(wenden)

Amtliches Vordrucklager der Kriegsmarine: J. J. Augustin in Glückstadt — (MS 4952) — 2700. XII. 36. Din A 4

Enlistment obligation document (Verpflichtungschein) for Rolf Teucher, dated January 1, 1937. *Document is signed by Teucher and a Korvettenkapitän Winkler.*

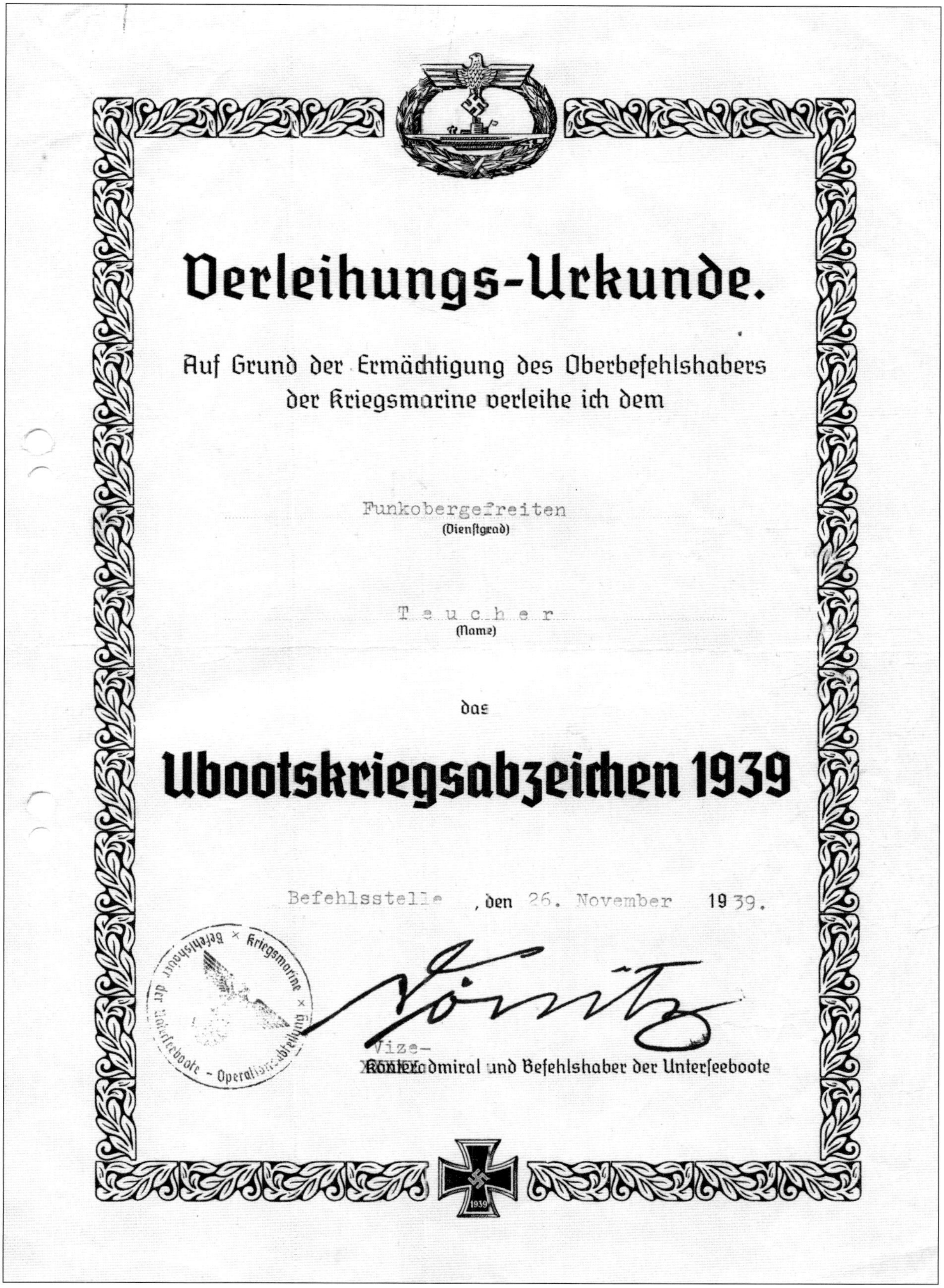

Verleihungs-Urkunde.

Auf Grund der Ermächtigung des Oberbefehlshabers der Kriegsmarine verleihe ich dem

Funkobergefreiten
(Dienstgrad)

T e u c h e r
(Name)

das

Ubootskriegsabzeichen 1939

Befehlsstelle , den 26. November 1939.

Befehlshaber × Kriegsmarine × der Unterseeboote - Operationsabteilung

Dönitz

Vize-
XXXXXadmiral und Befehlshaber der Unterseeboote

U-boat War Badge award document to Rolf Teucher on November 26, 1939. *Document has a facsimile signature of Vizeadmiral Karl Dönitz, which indicates it is probably a backdated award as Dönitz was a Konteradmiral on this date in 1939. The U-97 was not yet in operation in November 1939; it is also possible that Teucher served on another boat before joining the U-97.*

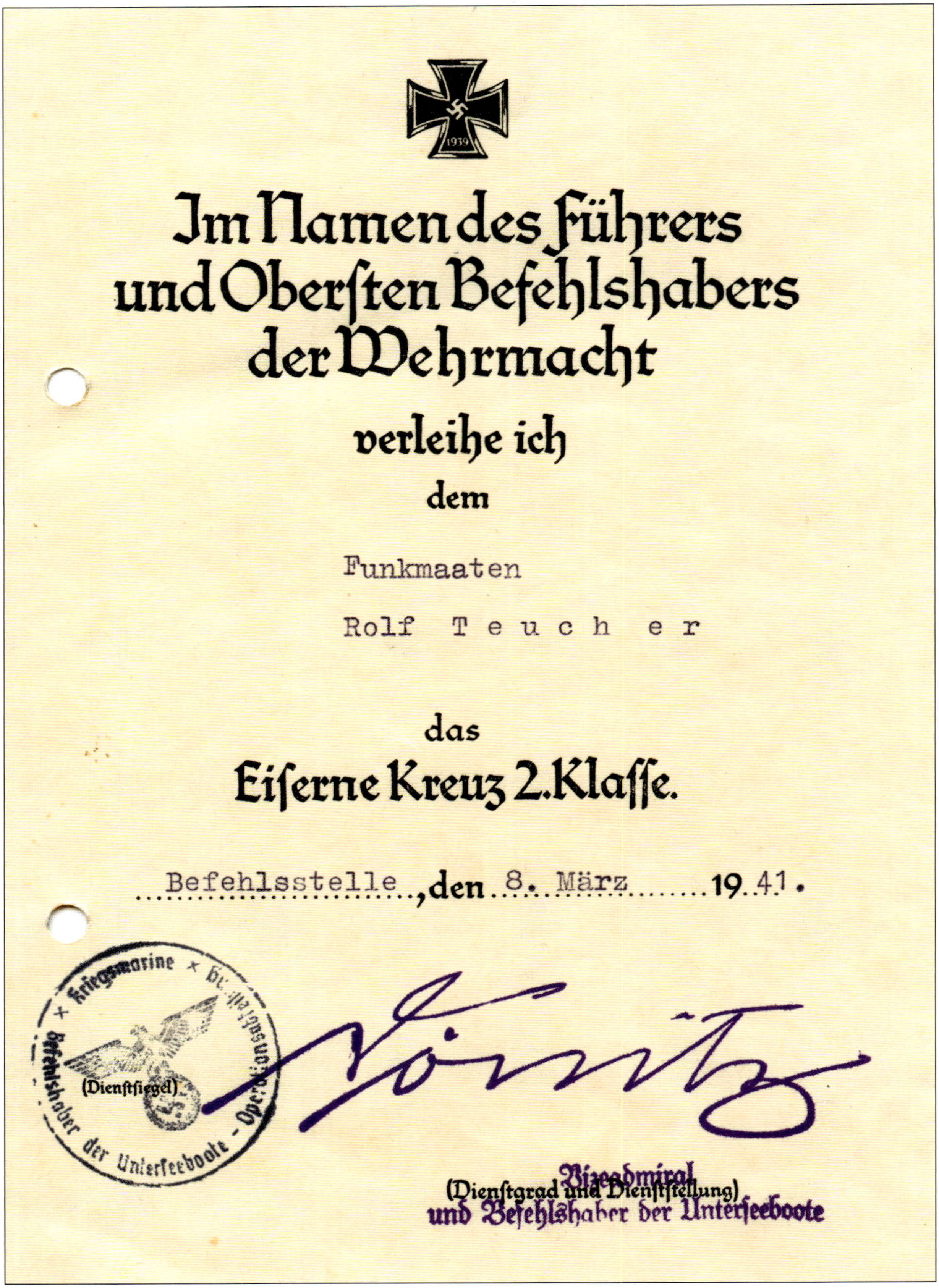
1939

Im Namen des Führers
und Obersten Befehlshabers
der Wehrmacht

verleihe ich

dem

Funkmaaten

Rolf T e u c h e r

das

Eiserne Kreuz 2. Klasse.

Befehlsstelle, den 8. März 1941.

× Kriegsmarine ×

Befehlshaber der Unterseeboote

(Dienstsiegel)

Dönitz

Vizeadmiral
und Befehlshaber der Unterseeboote
(Dienstgrad und Dienststellung)

Iron Cross 2nd Class award document to Rolf Teucher of the U-97 on March 8, 1941, awarded at Lorient, France one day after returning from her first successful war patrol. *Document has a facsimile signature of Vizeadmiral Karl Dönitz.*

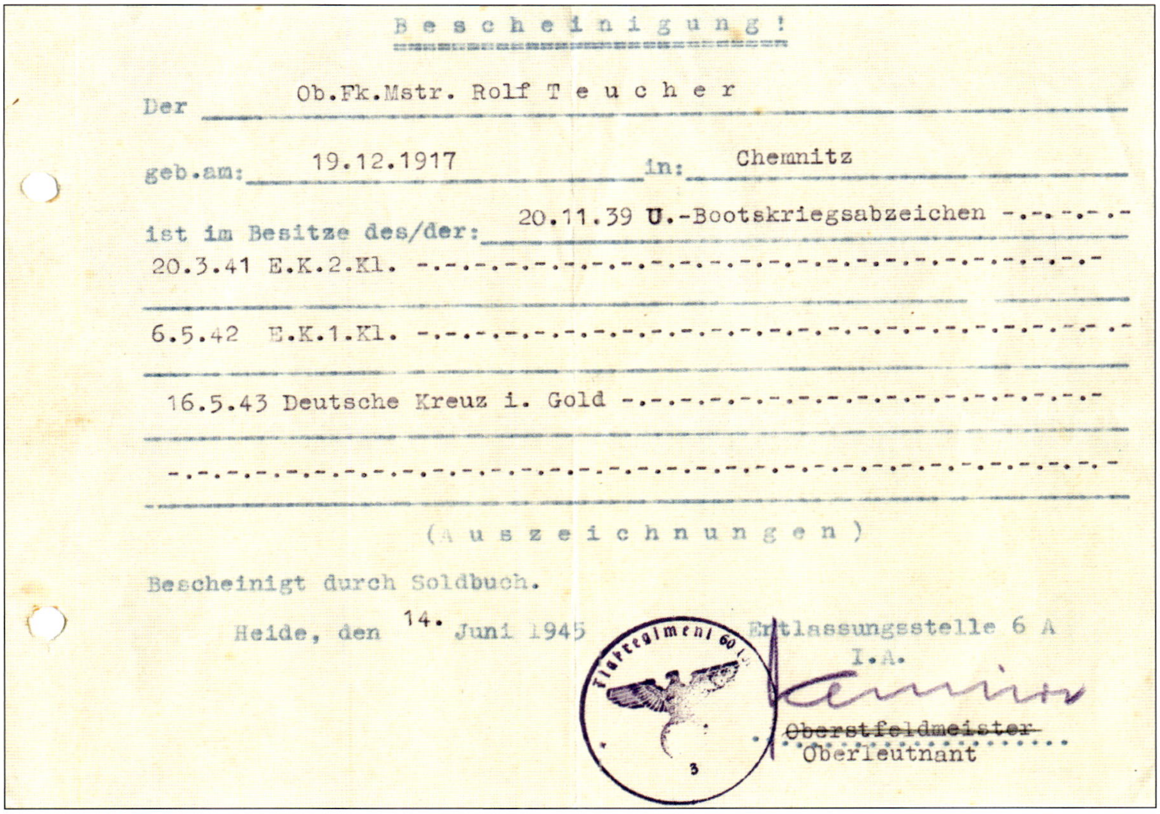

B e s c h e i n i g u n g !

Der Ob.Fk.Mstr. Rolf T e u c h e r

geb.am: 19.12.1917 in: Chemnitz

ist im Besitze des/der: 20.11.39 U.-Bootskriegsabzeichen -.-.-.-.-

20.3.41 E.K.2.Kl. -.-

6.5.42 E.K.1.Kl. -.-

16.5.43 Deutsche Kreuz i. Gold -.-.-.-.-.-.-.-.-.-.-.-.-.-.-.-

-.-

(A u s z e i c h n u n g e n)

Bescheinigt durch Soldbuch.

Heide, den 14. Juni 1945 Entlassungsstelle 6 A

I.A.

~~Oberstfeldmeister~~

Oberleutnant

Post-war discharge summary of awards received by Rolf Teucher, June 14, 1945.

CHAPTER TWENTY

"BRANDENBURGERS"
U-200
JUNE 1943

German U-boats did a variety of important tasks. Most tried to sink enemy warships and merchant vessels. Some served as floating weather stations providing advance meteorological data for the *Kriegsmarine* High Command. Still others supplied other U-boats at sea so they could continue their missions. And a very few transported Special Forces commandos for key sabotage missions behind enemy lines. One of the most significant of these missions, but one that remains relatively obscure, involved the *U-200*.

The story of the *U-200* began almost three years previously, when she was ordered by the German Navy on November 4, 1940. A Type IXD2 boat, her keel was laid by construction workers on November 3, 1941 at the Deutsche Schiff- und Maschinenbau AG (AG Weser) at Bremen. The *U-200* was launched on August 10, 1942; after trials she was commissioned at Bremen on December 22, 1942. Her crew underwent training for the next five months as part of the UAK test program, the UAG validations and the 27th U-boat Training Flotilla at Pillau (for torpedo training), the 24th U-boat Training Flotilla at Gotenhafen (for tactical training) and the 4th U-boat Training Flotilla based in Stettin, before her assignment to the 12th U-boat Flotilla, whose headquarters was in Bordeaux, France.

Dönitz's Crews
***Korvettenkapitän* Georg Schonder**

Born on July 23, 1910 in Erfurt/Thuringia.
Served as the Commander the *U-58*, *U-77* and *U-200*.
Awarded the Iron Cross 2nd Class on October 1, 1939; awarded the U-boat War Badge on December 1, 1939; awarded the Iron Cross 1st Class on July 23, 1940; awarded the Knight's Cross of the Iron Cross on August 19, 1942.
Spent 279 days at sea on U-boat war patrols.
Killed in action on June 24, 1943 in the North Atlantic.

The thirty boats built of this class were large and powerful indeed. They displaced 1,616 tons and could absorb a crew of up to sixty-three men. With 4,400 horsepower diesel engines, the craft could hit a top surface speed of just over nineteen knots an hour. At a more economical twelve-knot speed, the *U-200* had a cruising surface range of 23,700 sea-miles. When under attack, the boat could dive to 755 feet.

The *U-200* would have only one commander during the war. Georg "Hein" Schonder was an experienced U-boat driver, who had previously received the Knight's Cross for his accomplishments on the *U-77*. Born in Erfurt in Thuringia on July 23, 1910, he entered the Navy in 1935. Promoted to *Fähnrich zur See* on July 1, 1935, he served in the surface fleet for three years that included assignments on the old battleship *Schleswig-Holstein* and the torpedo boat *Falke*. Schonder advanced to *Oberfähnrich zur See* on January 1, 1937; three months later he was commissioned a *Leutnant zur See*. In early 1938, Georg Schonder began U-boat training; his first assignment on a boat came on August 6, 1938 as the 1st Watch Officer on the *U-51*, a Type VIIB boat. After another short U-boat course, he became the 1st Watch Officer on the *U-53*, another Type VIIB. He would begin the war in this boat (he was promoted to *Oberleutnant zur See* on April 1, 1939) and participate in two war patrols under *Kapitänleutnant* Ernst-Günther Heinicke. The *U-53* sank two British freighters, and Georg Schonder received the Iron Cross 2nd Class on October 1, 1939 and the U-boat War Badge on December 1, 1939.

Georg Schonder's star was shining and he was reassigned to the *U-9*, a small Type IIB boat, as 1st Watch Officer in early January 1940, days after the arrival of a new commander for the boat, future Knight's Cross with Oak Leaves, Swords and Diamonds winner *Oberleutnant* Wolfgang Lüth. Schonder would sail on four war patrols with the *U-9*, helping to sink three merchant ships. It was clear now that he was commander material and on May 1, 1940 he began the U-boat commander's course. He then assumed command of the *U-58*, a Type IIC boat, and took the boat on a war patrol on July 6, 1940. The *U-58* sank one ship on this patrol; for his effort Georg Schonder received the Iron Cross 1st Class on July 23, 1940. He would command the U-boat for three more war patrols during which he sank a total of two enemy ships.

In late 1940 Georg Schonder transferred to a new Type VIIC U-boat, the *U-77*. With her Schonder sailed on eleven war patrols. His first three were under the 7th U-boat Flotilla out of St. Nazaire, France; the missions were successful and the *U-77* sank three enemy ships. Schonder was promoted to *Kapitänleutnant* on September 1, 1941. In December 1941 the *U-77* departed Lorient, France and made the dangerous passage through the Straits of Gibraltar, sinking one enemy ship, the *Empire Barracuda*, before slipping past Gibraltar on the night of December 16 and arriving at Messina, Sicily on December 19, 1941. While in the Mediterranean, Georg Schonder sank eight enemy ships and on August 19, 1942 he received his Knight's Cross. He left the *U-77* the following month and returned to Germany to begin the process of commissioning the *U-200.*

The *U-200's* primary mission was to sail through the North Sea, transit the South Atlantic, round the Cape of Good Hope, sink any ship she came across in the Indian Ocean and help form a small group of German submarines to be based at Japanese naval bases in Southeast Asia. They also had a secondary, but very important, mission of landing a small team of German special forces troops in South Africa, who would attack key targets – a smaller version of the British raid on St. Nazaire in March 1942. These special forces' men were known as "Brandenburgers."

The Brandenburg commando unit was the brainchild of German Army Captain Theodor von Hippel. Twenty years earlier, von Hippel had served under German *General* Paul von Lettow-Vorbeck, Commander of the East African Theater in World War I. Von Lettow-Vorbeck had conducted a brilliant guerilla war against Allied colonial troops, despite being outnumbered four to one. After that conflict, von Hippel proposed to the *Reichswehr* that small, élite units, highly trained in sabotage and fluent in foreign languages, could operate behind enemy lines and wreak havoc with the enemy's command, communication and logistical elements. The Army rejected his ideas and the persistent captain subsequently approached Admiral Wilhelm Canaris, the commander of the German Intelligence Service (Abwehr). Canaris saw value in von Hippel's ideas and assigned him to the Abwehr's 2nd Department. The unit was formed in 1939 and by December 15 of that year was a battalion in strength. Recruits were highly skilled and trained on foreign languages, small unit tactics, demolitions, parachuting, covert operations, camouflage and physical proficiency. The battalion's 2nd Company was composed of men who had lived in English-speaking territories and who hailed from Africa.

By February 1943 the unit had grown to four regiments in size, plus an additional special coastal operation unit designated the "*Küstenjäger-Abteilung Brandenburg.*" It was to this detachment that the seven commandoes aboard the *U-200* belonged. The unit was based at Langenargen on Lake Constance in southern Germany, where they trained for several weeks on explosives and maneuvering their raft, and was commanded by Rittmeister Conrad von Leipzig. For this mission, the detachment sent nine men; two soldiers became ill and remained behind. The following Brandenburgers, all of whom were born in German South-West and East Africa, boarded the *U-200* in June 1943:

- *Leutnant* Hans Brügmann (b. October 5, 1914)
- *Unteroffizier* Bill Fesq (b. German South-West Africa)
- *Obergefreiter* Otto Hand (b. German East Africa)
- *Obergefreiter* Lehr (b. German East Africa)
- *Feldwebel* Wilfried Moll (b. March 24, 1917 at Gobeon, German South-West Africa)
- *Obergefreiter* Rudolf Otto
- *Obergefreiter* Reinhard Schneider (b. German South-West Africa)

It appears that the Brandenburgers trained in Kiel Bay on deploying their large rubber raft while the *U-200* was surfaced. The seven men had a large amount of special gear they would need to load into the raft at night just off the South African coast and this required practice to reduce the time the *U-200* would have to remain surfaced in such a dangerous area.

And what of their target? What type of Allied facility would warrant the potential loss of a valuable U-boat and these highly trained commandos?

The South African ports of Durban and Cape Town were an important part of the Allied supply lines from India to Great Britain. This was especially significant once the Axis had forced the closure of the Suez Canal, and supplies to Montgomery's 8th Army had to flow around the Cape of Good Hope. Facilities at both ports were extensive, with a well-developed harbor infrastructure. For some time, the Australian-built Prince Edward dry dock in Durban had been of immense strategic importance, being the largest of its kind between Singapore and Gibraltar. But even this graving dock, the second largest in the world in 1925, was insufficient for the number of ships requiring attention, and so work commenced on the Sturrock dry dock in Cape Town, capable of handling (like its counterpart in Durban) battleships and aircraft carriers. The Germans had learned from the British attack at St. Nazaire; the British main target had been the *Forme Ecluse Louis Joubert*, an enormous dry dock capable of holding the largest *Kriegsmarine* warships and the only dock of that size that could accommodate the dreaded battleship *Tirpitz* on the Atlantic coast. With St. Nazaire out of the picture, it would be too risky for the *Tirpitz* to leave her lair in Norway and sail to France. A year later the Germans reasoned: destroy the dry dock at Durban, and the tether on Royal Navy ships might be shortened giving more opportunities for the U-boats.

The *U-200* would transport the Brandenburgers to a section of deserted coast; the commandos would paddle to shore, sabotage the dock and link up with the *Ossewabrandwag* ("Ox-wagon Sentinel"), a nationalist Afrikaner organization in South Africa that opposed South African entry into the war, and continue unconventional warfare activities. Founded at Bloemfontein in 1939, the Ox-wagon Sentinels created a paramilitary group called *Stormjaers* ("storm hunters"), modeled on the Nazi storm-troopers. This organization carried out sabotage against the government; its ethos was made clear in the oath that cadets had to take before they became full-fledged storm troopers:

> "If I retreat, kill me. If I die, avenge me. If I advance, follow me."

With an underground of this nature, the highly-trained Brandenburgers – who spoke the language and knew the customs – might just have a chance of succeeding.

With all preparations made, the *U-200*, her crew and the seven Brandenburgers departed Tirpitz Pier at Kiel on June 12, 1943 in the company of the *U-194* and *U-420*.

"Hein" Schonder had his own motto that he yelled to his many friends on the pier:

> "Fellows, never forget. There are only three kinds of people on this globe: the Living, the Dead and the folks sailing the Seven Seas eternally."

Dönitz's Crews

***Matrosenobergefreiter* Ludwig Wagner**

Born on October 5, 1921 in Mauth/Bavaria.
Served on the *U-200.*
Spent 12 days at sea on U-boat war patrols.
Killed in action on June 24, 1943 in the North Atlantic.

Among the crew was *Matrosenobergefreiter* Ludwig Wagner. Hailing from the small Bavarian town of Mauth nestled in the Bavarian Forest in the Freyung (formerly Wolfstein) district north of Passau, this was his first war patrol on a U-boat; unfortunately it would be his last. By June 14 the three boats were in the Skagerrak between Denmark and Norway; the following day they reached Stavanger, Norway, where they remained through June 15, taking on fuel and allowing the Brandenburgers additional training time. On June 16, the three U-boats were west of Bergen in the Norwegian Sea. By June 17 the trio passed Raudeberg, Norway still heading north. June 18 saw the three turn west into the Atlantic. The next day the U-boats were located north of the Shetland Islands; they travelled still farther north on June 20, with the *U-200* coming under attack by an aircraft of the RAF Coastal Command's 269th Squadron, flying out of Iceland. Schonder took the boat under water and remained hidden for over five hours before surfacing. Pushing ahead with the mission, on June 21 the three U-boats were north of the Faroe Islands, but dispersed after receiving reports of nearby enemy destroyers. The next day saw the U-200 turning west toward Iceland. On June 23 Schonder and the *U-200* were just east of Iceland.

Early on June 24, 1943 it appears that the *U-200* reported her position to B.d.U. as south of Iceland. It was a clear summer's day; and she was making good surface speed. At 4:29 p.m., the crew of a British B-24 Liberator 'H' (Flt. Lt. A. W. Fraser) of the 120th RAF Squadron, which was flying from Reykjavik, Iceland towards a convoy escort rendezvous, spotted the U-boat on the surface and dropped two depth charges that straddled the German boat. Schonder's crew fought back, hitting the bomber with 20-mm flak fire and damaging the aircraft's port wing, fuselage and bomb bay hydraulics. Fraser nursed his aircraft back to base, but the men on the U-boat were not so fortunate. The B-24 crew observed oil and debris on the water and estimated that fifteen U-boat men had survived and were seen swimming in the water. The plane departed and none of the *U-200*'s crew, or the Brandenburgers on board for their special mission, was ever seen again.

Nothing was heard for the following six days. On June 30 the B.d.U. war diary made the following observation:

> "*U-194* and *U-200* were proceeding with *U-420* through the Iceland Passage. The group dispersed in AE 8783 on 21 June after warning of destroyers. *U-420* sent its passage report on 1 July. This was lacking from the other boats, and in spite of numerous requests there was no reply. It is possible that the boats were destroyed by escort forces called up. In this case though, *U-420* should have heard depth charge explosions. There is no information on the loss which must be presumed. Coastal forces of the Brandenburg Division were on board *U-200*."

Flight Lieutenant Fraser himself died one year later in a flying accident looking for more U-boats. The Germans managed to transfer several U-boats to the Far East, a move that spread the U-boat war into the Indian Ocean and even the Pacific. But the spectacular plan to destroy the largest dry dock in Africa died in the North Atlantic with the men on the *U-200*.

Known Crewmembers for the U-200

Benner, Erich	*Matrosenobergefreiter*
Berg, Jakob	*Obersteuermann*
Carduck, Peter	*Funkgefreiter*
Elgert, Walter-Ernst	*Funkgefreiter*
Fährmann, Heinrich	*Matrosenobergefreiter*
Frischmann, Theodor	*Bootsmaat*
Gollan, Kurt	*Matrosenobergefreiter*
Haderer, Emil	*Mechanikergefreiter*
Herbig, Dr. Dietrich	*Arzt*
Jakob, Rudolf	*Maschinenmaat*
Janssen, Hans	*Sanitätsobergefreiter*
Jost, Otto	*Stabsobermaschinist*
Kirsch, Gerhard	*Maschinenobergefreiter*
Körner, Walter	*Maschinengefreiter*
Kroiss, Anton	*Obermaschinist*
Kulas, Richard	*Matrosengefreiter*
Kunde, Walter	*Bootsmaat*
Kunzmann, Karl	*Matrosengefreiter*
Lenges, Clemens	*Matrosengefreiter*
Lenzen, Hermann	*Matrosengefreiter*
Lerch, Hans	*Matrosengefreiter*
Lichtenstein, Heinz	*Maschinenobergefreiter*
Lieske, Herbert	*Matrosengefreiter*
Lohrmann, Georg	*Maschinenobergefreiter*
Lösche, Rolf	*Oberleutnant zur See*
Lundius, Hans	*Matrosengefreiter*
Malek, Engelbert	*Maschinengefreiter*
Mayr, Josef	*Maschinenobergefreiter*
Melbert, Hans	*Maschinengefreiter*
Müller, Hans	*Maschinengefreiter*
Niebecker, Walter	*Obermaschinist*
Olischläger, Arnolf	*Oberleutnant zur See*
Polomski, Karl-Heinz	*Mechanikerobergefreiter*
Puchert, Franz	*Maschinenmaat*
Rahe, Bernhard	*Maschinenobergefreiter*
Räk, Willi	*Maschinenobergefreiter*
Rees, Karl-Eugen	*Leutnant (Ing)*
Reisert, Heinrich	*Maschinengefreiter*
Reuscher, Helmut	*Mechanikergefreiter*
Rieck, Otto	*Maschinenmaat*
Röder, Waldemar	*Oberbootsmaat*
Rohde, Werner	*Maschinenobergefreiter*
Schad, Friedrich	*Maschinenmaat*
Scherf, Rudolf	*Maschinenobergefreiter*
Schonder, Heinrich	*Kapitänleutnant*
Schönfeld, Hans	*Oberfunkmaat*
Schöps, Werner	*Mechanikermaat*
Schubert, Karl-Heinz	*Maschinenmaat*
Schultze, Hartun-Helmut	*Leutnant zur See*
Seise, Karl	*Maschinenmaat*
Sonntag, Otto	*Korvettenkapitän (Ing)*
Stadler, Günther	*Maschinenobergefreiter*
Staufer, Friedrich	*Bootsmaat*
Taut, Siegfried	*Funkmaat*
Treffer, Bruno	*Maschinenmaat*
Umbrecht, Hans	*Maschinenmaat*
Wagner, Karl	*Matrosenobergefreiter*
Wagner, Ludwig	*Matrosenobergefreiter*
Wittke, Heinz	*Maschinengefreiter*
Zander, Gerhard	*Maschinenmaat*
Zapf, Erich	*Maschinengefreiter*

Sources, "Brandenburgers:" Manfred Dörr, *Die Ritterkreuzträger der U-Boot-Waffe, Band 1: A-J, Band 2: L-Z*, Osnabrück, FRG: Biblio Verlag, 1988, Band 2 – 246, 247; *F.d.U./B.d.U. War Diary, 1-15 June 1943* (PG30325), 482, 483; *F.d.U./B.d.U. War Diary, 16-30 June 1943* (PG30326), 494, 502, 503, 505, 506, 507, 508, 509, 512, 514, 525, 526; Peter C. Hansen, *Execution for Duty: The Life, Trial & Murder of a U-boat Captain*, Barnsley, England: Pen & Sword Maritime, 2003, 263; Lawrence Paterson, *Hitler's Grey Wolves: U-boats in the Indian Ocean*, London: Greenhill Books, 2004, 81, 82, 83, 84; Herbert Ritschel, *Kurzfassung Kriegstagebücher deutscher U-boote 1939-1945, Band 3: KTB U171 – U222*, Norderstedt, Germany: Books on Demand, 191; War Diary of the U-200, December 22, 1942 – June 21, 1943, PG 30187; ONI Roll T-307-B, *National Archives Microfilm Publication T1022*, roll 3037, RG 242; www.ubootwaffe.net; www.uboatarchive.net.

Crewmen of the U-200 enjoy watching training. *Brandenburgers' rubber boat is tied down immediately forward of the conning tower. Senior non-commissioned officer wears U-boat War Badge, an experienced veteran. Partially hidden sailor appears to have a lucky horseshoe cap badge.*

U-200; practice embarking the large Brandenburgers' rubber boat from which the sabotage team would depart the U-boat off South Africa. *The photo was probably taken in the Kiel Bay. Officer in white cap is Kapitänleutnant Georg Schonder. This and the other photos in this section are from a group of pictures kept after the war by Georg Schonder's widow.*

Men of the Brandenburgers in Navy fatigue uniforms on the U-200, standing next to a 20-mm anti-aircraft gun. *Man to the far left appears to be Leutnant Hans Brügmann, leader of the Brandenburger sabotage team.*

Kapitänleutnant Georg Schonder (left) with sailor armed with an MP-40 submachine-gun. *This sailor has been awarded an Iron Cross 1st Class, and also has a lucky horseshoe cap badge; given his cap, he appears to be an officer.*

Opposite
U-200 on a calm sea.

U-200 in the Baltic Sea.

Three U-boats at the Tirpitz Pier at Kiel prepare to make way. *The other boats are probably the U-194 and U-420.*

***U-200* crewmen waving to personnel on the pier.**

***U-200* crewmen on deck.**

***U-200* at Kiel on June 12, 1943 before departing on her final mission.** *The other boats are probably the U-194 and U-420.*

U-boat living quarters ship at Kiel.

Well-wishers at pier in front of a U-boat living quarters ship.

Korvettenkapitän Georg Schonder departing what appears to be a medical facility.

Sailors standing formation on the U-200.

Kapitänleutnant Georg Schonder with Knight's Cross.

Kapitänleutnant Georg Schonder on the street.

Kapitänleutnant Georg Schonder salutes next to a machinegun.

Kapitänleutnant Georg Schonder reviewing documents, April 1943.

Kapitänleutnant Georg Schonder; photo is believed to be on his wedding day at Kiel.

Kapitänleutnant and Mrs. Schonder depart a building.

Kapitänleutnant Georg Schonder walking down the street in Kiel with Nazi Party officials.

Georg Schonder (left) earlier in his career with family.

Zum frommen Andenken an den
ehrengeachteten Herrn
Ludwig Wagner
Forstgehilfe von Mauth
Matrosen-Obergefreiter
welcher in treuer Pflichterfüllung am 28. Juni
1943 auf einem Unterseeboot im Alter von
22 Jahren den Heldentod für das Vaterland
starb.

Er ruhe in Frieden!

Buchdruckerei A.G. Passavia, Passau.

Death Announcement for Matrosenobergefreiter Ludwig Wagner of the U-200. *At the age of twenty-one and on his first patrol, Wagner died with all his boatmates onboard the U-200 south of Iceland on June 24, 1943.*

CHAPTER TWENTY-ONE

"The Fastest Target Ever Sunk" U-410, and U-371 February 1944

When Horst-Arno Fenski lined up a torpedo attack against a British light cruiser on February 18, 1944 off the coast of Italy, he did not realize he was making World War II submarine history. The remarkable point of the attack by the *U-410* was that the target – the *HMS Penelope* – was making 28 knots when hit. That is fast, over 32 miles an hour, and as far as can be ascertained, in the history of submarine attacks in any theater of that conflict, no other target ship running at such a high speed was ever successfully attacked.

> *Dönitz's Crews*
> ***Maschinengefreiter* Richard Hauser**
> Born November 9, 1923 in Königsberg.
> Served on the *U-410* and *U-371* in the engine room.
> Awarded the U-boat War Badge on May 14, 1943 and the Iron Cross 2nd Class on August 31, 1943.
> Spent 149 days at sea on U-boat war patrols.
> Taken prisoner on May 4, 1944
> Survived the war; lived in Gerlingen, then Spaichingen, Baden-Württemberg.

Horst-Arno Fenski did not begin his Navy career in the U-boats. Born on November 3, 1918 in Königsberg, he joined the Navy in 1937 and after training joined the crew of the battleship *Gneisenau* in 1939, conducting his first war patrol with this ship from December 1939 to April 1940. Later that year he underwent U-boat training after his commissioning as a *Leutnant zur See*. In May 1941 he joined the crew of the *U-752* as the 1st Watch Officer. In 1941 and 1942 he served four war patrols with this boat, helping to sink eight enemy ships, winning the Iron Cross 2nd Class and the U-boat War Badge and gaining valuable experience. His performance led to his selection for further training as a U-boat commander.

Fenski began his commander's career with the *U-410*, a Type VIIC U-boat, but as her second commander. Ordered on October 30, 1939, her keel was laid at the Danziger Werft AG construction yard in Danzig on the Baltic coast. She was launched on October 14, 1941 and commissioned on February 23, 1942. After train-up, the U-boat joined the 7th U-boat Flotilla. On her first war patrol the *U-410* left Kiel under the command of Kurt Sturm on August 27, 1942. Days turned into weeks as the boat encountered no targets. Finally, at 10:29 a.m. on October 15, 1942 Sturm sank the British 4,212-ton *Newton Pine*, sailing with convoy ONS-136 from Loch Ewe, Scotland bound for Halifax. All forty-seven of her crew perished in the attack. The *Newton Pine* her only success, the *U-410* arrived at St. Nazaire, France on October 28, 1942 after nearly nine weeks at sea.

The *U-410* remained under the command of Kurt Sturm and on December 3, 1942 left St. Nazaire for her second war patrol. It again started slowly, but at 4:33 a.m. on January 3, 1943 the boat came under attack from an unidentified aircraft. Slightly damaged in the incident, the U-boat rescued eighty survivors of the sunken blockade runner *Rhakotis*, and then returned with them to St. Nazaire.

This performance was not satisfactory for Admiral Dönitz who replaced Sturm with Horst-Arno Fenski. Under her new commander the *U-410* departed from St. Nazaire on February 9, 1943. Action began almost immediately. On February 13 an aircraft from the RAF's 202nd Squadron attacked the U-boat west of Portugal, but she was not damaged by the attack. On March 4 west of Gibraltar, an unidentified aircraft attacked the *U-410* a second time, but the U-boat was only slightly damaged in the attack.

Horst-Arno Fenski hit two ships on this patrol; both of them on March 6 and both of them from convoy KMS-10 southwest of Portugal. The *U-410* first damaged, but did not sink, the British 7,134 ton *Fort Paskoyac* with a torpedo, as the target was equipped with overhanging nets that caused a premature detonation. Fenski achieved greater success the same day at 3:20 p.m., when he sank the British 7,133-ton *Fort Battle River*, carrying 3,000 tons of government stores from Liverpool bound for Bougie, Algeria, but Canadian escort ships counterattacked and forced Fenski to withdraw to make repairs. On March 25, north of Portugal, the *U-410* came under attack from an aircraft of the RAF's 172nd Squadron, but the U-boat was not damaged. She arrived at Lorient, France on March 27 after six and a half weeks at sea. Fenski was awarded the Iron Cross 1st Class the following day and was promoted to *Oberleutnant zur See*.

The situation in the Mediterranean was becoming more critical and B.d.U. decided to send Fenski and the *U-410* through the Straits of Gibraltar for operations around Italy. The *U-410* left Lorient on April 26, 1943. She began passage through the Straits on the night of May 5/6, surfacing ten miles off the coast of Spanish Morocco. As she approached Gibraltar, the U-boat dived to a depth of 50-60 meters and continued submerged. On May 8 at 9:43 a.m., Fenski came under attack east of Gibraltar by a Hudson aircraft of the RAF's

500th Squadron. The aircraft came out of the sun and was not spotted by the crew until it was 200 meters away. The plane raked the U-boat with gunfire, while bombs fell nearby. In the confusion, the boat started to dive but three crewmen remained on deck. Fenski rushed to the bridge and manned a machinegun while the crew scrambled below. After the aircraft left, the crew discovered that the pressure hull had been cracked for a distance of five meters between torpedo tubes through which a high-pressure water stream was flooding the boat. Fenski nursed the boat to La Spezia, Italy, arriving on May 13, 1943.

Now part of the 29th U-boat Flotilla and with all repairs finally completed after almost three months in dry dock, on August 7, 1943 the *U-410* left La Spezia for her fifth war patrol; Horst-Arno Fenski would hit two ships on this mission. On August 26, 1943 at 8:30 p.m. north of Tunisia, he sank the American 7,242-ton *John Bell*, carrying general military cargo, from convoy UGS-14 bound from Philadelphia and Hampton Roads for Bandar Shapur in the Persian Gulf. One man died in the attack. Two minutes later the *U-410* sank the American 7,194-ton *Richard Henderson*, carrying general military cargo and high explosives, from the same convoy. Fortunately all seventy crewmen were rescued. The *U-410* then finished her voyage and arrived on August 30, 1943 at Toulon, France.

Despite this success, the situation in the Mediterranean continued to deteriorate and Mussolini was overthrown in Italy On September 12, 1943, still under the command of Horst-Arno Fenski, the *U-410* departed Toulon. Horst-Arno Fenski sank three ships on this patrol: two were from convoy MKS-26 and one was from convoy UGS-17.At 7:00 p.m. on September 26, 1943, he torpedoed the Norwegian 7,176-ton *Christian Michelsen*, a member of convoy UGS-17. The ship was carrying 3,000 tons of bombs, 4,000 tons of ammunition and 3,000 tons of oil and mail in convoy from New York and Hampton Roads to Bizerte, Tunisia and Palermo, Sicily; forty-five of her crewmen died in the attack. On October 1, 1943, Fenski sank the British 3,722-ton *Empire Commerce*, part of convoy MKS-26 enroute from Salerno, Italy to Britain – north of Tunisia. That evening at 10:05 p.m. the *U-410* sank the British 7,133-ton *Fort Howe*, also from convoy MKS-26; two of her crewmen were lost. Fenski returned to Toulon on October 3, 1943. Just outside the harbor, the U-boat rammed a German patrol boat seriously damaging her bow and all forward torpedo tubes. Fortunately for the crew, none of the loaded torpedoes in the tubes detonated. The *U-410* would begin another four-month period of repairs. The next month, on November 26, 1943, *Oberleutnant zur See* Horst-Arno Fenski received the Knight's Cross of the Iron Cross.

The U-boat's seventh war patrol would prove to be her most successful, as well as her last. She departed Toulon under the command of Horst-Arno Fenski on February 3, 1944. At 3:22 p.m. on February 15, 1944 she sank the British 7,154-ton *Fort St Nicolas*, sailing from Naples to Salerno. All crewmen were rescued, an amazing feat considering the ship was carrying 4,000 tons of military stores that included detonators and phosphorous ammunition. An approaching destroyer dropped six to ten depth charges, but the *U-410* did not receive any serious damage.

On February 18, 1944 Horst-Arno Fenski and the *U-410* made their submarine history. A month previously, the *HMS Penelope*, a 5,270-ton British light cruiser, took part in "Operation Shingle," the amphibious assault on Anzio, Italy, providing gunfire support as part of "Force X" in partnership with the *USS Brooklyn*, another light cruiser. The *HMS Penelope* also joined in the bombardments in the Formia, Italy area during the later operations; on February 8, 1944, the ship conducted no less than eight fire missions with her 6-inch guns during the day. Ten days later, early on the morning of February 18, 1944, the light cruiser, under command of Captain G.D. Belben, had left the Anzio support area to return to Naples. Fenski was patrolling at periscope depth in the Gulf of Gaeta and spotted a British cruiser of the Aurora Class at 40.55° N, 13.25° E. Fenski estimated the target was traveling at 28 knots speed, was unescorted, and was executing 40-degree zigzag anti-submarine course changes. He would have one chance and the firing window would be extremely small. But Fenski was close, and at a range of 800 meters, he fired his first torpedo – a T-3 electrical wake-less torpedo – from Tube 4. The torpedo struck the *Penelope* in the after engine room; the ship lost course and power, circling to starboard, while her speed reduced to two knots. Fenski then ordered Tube 1 to fire a FaT torpedo, but it malfunctioned. The crew took immediate action and fired a torpedo from Tube 2, which struck the *Penelope* amidships about fifteen minutes after the first torpedo; she sank two minutes later, accompanied by a large explosion, probably her ammunition detonating. Some 415 of the crew, including the captain, went down with the ship; there were 206 survivors.

The *U-410* was not yet finished on this patrol. At 2:00 a.m. on February 20, 1944, the U-boat sank the American 1,625-ton *USS LST-348*. The *U-410* arrived back at Toulon, France on February 28, 1944 and was greeted by *Kapitän zur See* Werner Hartmann, Commander of the U-boats in the Mediterranean. It would be her last patrol. On March 11, 1944 at the Missiessy Docks in Toulon, a 15th USAAF bombing mission destroyed the boat and on March 28 she was decommissioned. Fenski and the crew of the *U-410* then transferred to the *U-371* whose crew was transferring back to Germany. The *U-371* had served for several years in the Mediterranean off Greece with the 23rd U-boat Flotilla and Italy with the 29th U-boat Flotilla. She was a Type VIIC U-boat, having been commissioned on March 15, 1941 at the Howaldtswerke AG construction yard at Kiel-Gaarden.

On April 23, 1944 the *U-371*, with a new commander and crew departed Toulon and headed south for operations off the coast of Algeria. On the night of May 2, Fenski decided to surface and charge his batteries as he expected to contact a convoy in a few hours. However, when the *U-371* surfaced she found herself almost in the middle of the convoy, and immediately crash-dived to about 100 meters. Fenski surfaced once again in about an hour and headed toward the convoy. Shortly thereafter, Fenski determined that the *U-371* had been detected by surface craft, so he immediately changed course and attempted to escape, hoping to avoid contact until his batteries were fully charged. The U-boat remained on the surface until the destroyer had closed to about 3,000 meters and then fired a T-5 torpedo from her stern tube, and immediately dived to over 100 meters. The torpedo hit the American 1,200-ton destroyer escort *USS Menges* at 1:18 a.m. on May 3; although thirty-one men were killed, she was later able to make port, have a new stern affixed to her and become seaworthy after several months.

Soon after this attack, a very accurate series of depth charges exploded around the U-boat, extinguishing all lights, damaging the hydroplanes, and rupturing the trim tanks. The attacks continued at about 30-minute intervals, each one being more accurate than the one before. Fenski then decided to bottom the boat to make detection by enemy ASDIC (apparatus for detecting submerged objects by listening to the echoes from audible "pings" sent out by a transmitter) more difficult and to save his batteries. Late that night, May 3, the crew heard surface craft in the vicinity, and with air in the boat rapidly getting worse, the emergency lighting system out, and about fifteen tons of water throughout the boat, Fenski decided that his only hope was to surface and attempt to escape in the darkness. After fifteen minutes, surface craft were detected coming up astern and Fenski decided to abandon ship due to the heavy damages. It was a prudent move; the oncoming attackers were the American destroyer escorts *USS Pride* and *USS Joseph E Campbell* and the British destroyer escort *HMS Blankney* and a Free French destroyer escort. In one last defiant act, Fenski fired a T-5 torpedo from the stern tube after most of the crew had left the boat, and a hit was scored at 4:00 a.m. on May 4 on the Free French 1,300-ton destroyer escort *FF Sénégalais*. Back on the *U-371*, the Engineering Officer and a Petty Officer flooded the air tanks and the boat sank rapidly. Both men died, but the rest of the crew, including the commander and Richard Hauser were saved and became prisoners of war. The hunt for the U-boat by Allied escorts had taken twenty-seven hours.

An American interrogation report of the surviving crew of the *U-371* said this of the commander:

> "Fenski was apparently popular with his crew, who regarded him highly. Upon interrogators he made a poor first impression, being arrogant and demanding. But he later proved more pleasant and can be rated one of the better types of U-boat commanders seen by interrogators in this war."

The crew knew their commander and he was indeed one of the "better types," as could be attested to by the crews of the *HMS Penelope* and other ships sunk by the *U-410*. Horst-Arno Fenski died on February 10, 1965 in Hamburg-Wandsbek.

Known Crewmembers for the U-410/371

Beerbaum, Arnold	*Matrosenobergefreiter*
Blum, Walter	
Böhm, Karl	*Oberfunkmaat*
Bressler, Reinhard	*Oberleutnant zur See*
Breun, Gerhard	*Oberleutnant zur See*
Dinges, Hugo	
Döllein, Hans	*Maschinenobergefreiter*
Fenski, Horst-Arno	*Oberleutnant zur See*
Gerisch, Hans	*Obermaschinist*
Gückel, Johannes	*Matrosengefreiter*
Hauser, Richard	*Maschinengefreiter*
Hänel, Rudolf	
Höhnforf, Ernst	*Obermaschinist*
Kölle, Walter	
König, Alois	*Oberleutnant zur See*
Kreff, Willi	
Langohr, Karl-Heinz	*Maschinenobergefreiter*
Linek, Richard	*Mechanikermaat*
Mohndorf, Albert	*Matrosengefreiter*
Müller, Walter	*Leutnant zur See*
Peters, Gerhard	*Oberleutnant zur See*
Puschmann, Hans-Friedrich	*Oberleutnant zur See*
Rachner, Friedrich	*Oberleutnant (Ing)*
Ritschel, Ferdinand	*Oberleutnant (Ing)*
Rose, Josef	*Obermaschinist*
Schneider, Werner	*Oberfunkmaat*
Schulz, Norbert	*Matrosenobergefreiter*
Sperling, Franz	
Stauffer, Friedrich	*Oberbootsmann*
Sturm, Kurt	*Fregattenkapitän*
Ufermann, Friedrich	*Obersteuermann*
Wagner, Erich	*Oberleutnant zur See*
Wohlers, Willi	*Obersteuermann*
Wolff, Willi	*Matrosenobergefreiter*
Zimmermann, Franz	*Matrose*
Zimmermann, Karl	*Matrose*

Sources, "The Fastest Target Sunk, Ever:" Clay Blair, *Hitler's U-boat War: The Hunted, 1942-1945*, New York: Modern Library, 2000, 198, 199; Rainer Busch and Hans-Joachim Röll, *German U-boat Commanders of World War II*, translated by Geoffrey Brooks, Annapolis, Maryland: Naval Institute Press, 1999, 67; Manfred Dörr, *Die Ritterkreuzträger der U-Boot-Waffe, Band 1: A-J, Band 2: L-Z*, Osnabrück, FRG: Biblio Verlag, 1988, Band 1 – 67, 68; Axel Niestlé, *German U-boat Losses during World War II*, Annapolis, Maryland: Naval Institute Press, 1998, 62; Herbert Ritschel, *Kurzfassung Kriegstagebücher deutscher U-boote 1939-1945, Band 7: KTB U301 – U374,* Norderstedt, Germany: Books on Demand, 305-323; Jürgen Rohwer, *Axis Submarine Successes 1939-1945*, Annapolis, Maryland: Naval Institute Press, 1983, 128, 153, 249, 250, 254; Navy Department, Office of the Chief of Naval Operations, "Report on the Interrogation of survivors from *U-371* Sunk 4 May 1944," Washington, DC, August 21, 1944; www.ubootwaffe.net; www.uboatarchive.net.

410

Verleihungs-Urkunde

Auf Grund der Ermächtigung des Oberbefehlshabers der Kriegsmarine verleihe ich dem

Maschinen- Gefreiten
(Dienstgrad)

Richard H a u s e r
(Name)

das

Ubootskriegsabzeichen 1939

Befehlsstelle, den 14. Mai 1943.

Kreisch

~~Vizeadmiral und Befehlshaber der Unterseeboote~~
Konteradmiral und Führer der Uboote
Italien

(MS 37108)

U-boat War Badge award document to Richard Hauser, U-410, on May 14, 1943. *The document is signed by Konteradmiral Leo Kreisch, Chief of U-boats Italy. Hauser received the award the day after the U-410 arrived in La Spezia, Italy after transiting the Straits of Gibraltar.*

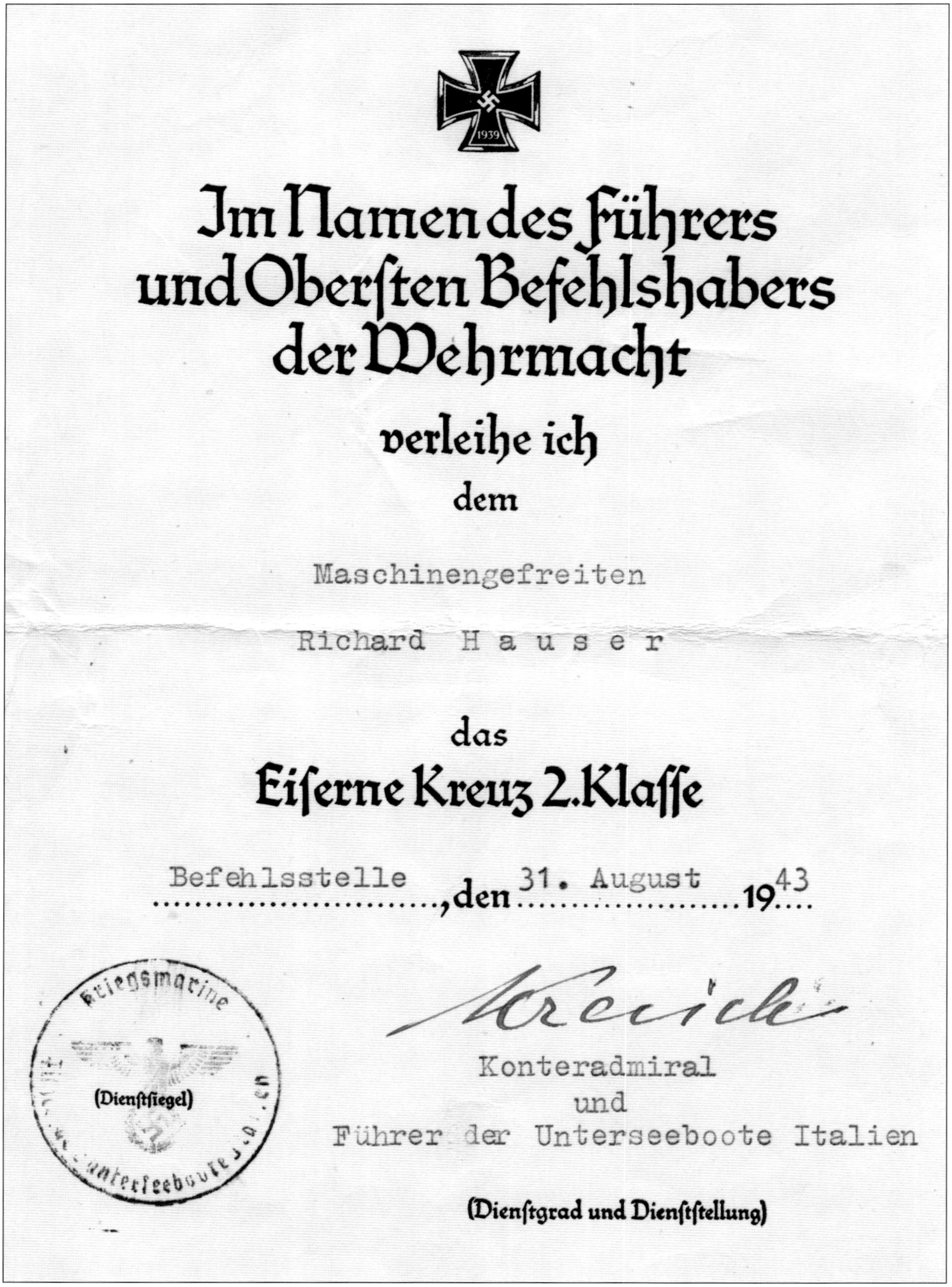

Im Namen des Führers
und Oberſten Befehlshabers
der Wehrmacht

verleihe ich

dem

Maschinengefreiten

Richard H a u s e r

das

Eiſerne Kreuz 2.Klaſſe

Befehlsstelle, den 31. August 1943

Kreisch

Konteradmiral
und
Führer der Unterseeboote Italien

(Dienſtgrad und Dienſtſtellung)

Kriegsmarine (Dienſtſiegel)

Iron Cross 2nd Class award document to Richard Hauser, U-410, on August 31, 1943. *Decoration was awarded at Toulon, France one day after the conclusion of a successful fifth war patrol. The document is signed by Konteradmiral Leo Kreisch, Chief of U-boats Italy.*

Richard Hauser, Christmas 1942.

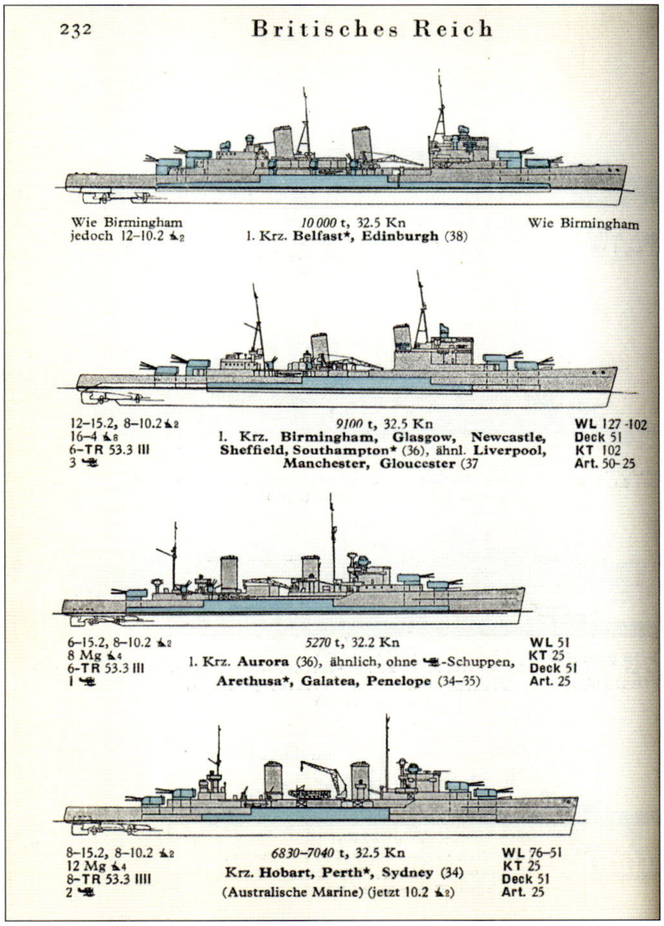

232 **Britisches Reich**

Wie Birmingham
jedoch 12–10.2

10 000 t, 32.5 Kn
1. Krz. **Belfast*, Edinburgh** (38)

Wie Birmingham

12–15.2, 8–10.2
16–4
6–TR 53.3 III
3

9100 t, 32.5 Kn
1. Krz. **Birmingham, Glasgow, Newcastle, Sheffield, Southampton*** (36), ähnl. **Liverpool, Manchester, Gloucester** (37

WL 127-102
Deck 51
KT 102
Art. 50-25

6–15.2, 8–10.2
8 Mg
6–TR 53.3 III
1

5270 t, 32.2 Kn
1. Krz. **Aurora** (36), ähnlich, ohne -Schuppen, **Arethusa*, Galatea, Penelope** (34–35)

WL 51
KT 25
Deck 51
Art. 25

8–15.2, 8–10.2
12 Mg
8–TR 53.3 IIII
2

6830–7040 t, 32.5 Kn
Krz. **Hobart, Perth*, Sydney** (34)
(Australische Marine) (jetzt 10.2)

WL 76–51
KT 25
Deck 51
Art. 25

A view of Peter Lohmeyer's ship identification book showing a profile of the HMS Penelope (third ship down).

CHAPTER TWENTY-TWO

"Sole Survivors" U-413 August 1944

Often a U-boat sank with all hands, and on a few occasions there was but one survivor to later tell what happened. On August 3, 1942, when a British submarine sank the *U-335*, only *Matrosengefreiter* Rudolf Jahnke lived to tell about it. *Matrosengefreiter* Franz Machon was the sole survivor (and spent ten days on a life raft) of the *U-512* when she was sunk by an enemy aircraft on October 2, 1942. When the *U-224* was rammed and sunk by the Canadian corvette *HMCS Ville de Quebec* on January 13, 1943, only *Leutnant zur See* Wolf-Dietrich Danckworth survived. When the *U-301* was sunk by a British submarine in the Mediterranean on January 21, 1943, *Fähnrich zur See* Wilhelm Rahn was the boat's only survivor. *Kapitänleutnant* Klaus Bargsten, the commander of the *U-521*, was the sole survivor when his U-boat was sunk off Maryland on June 2, 1943 by American aircraft. On October 8, 1943, only one man survived on the *U-419* when a British aircraft sank the U-boat. In the Gulf of Oman on October 16, 1943, only *Mechanikergefreiter* Günther Schmidt escaped the *U-533* when she was sunk by a British aircraft; he swam twenty-eight hours to the coast.

Matrosengefreiter Hans Kastrup was the sole survivor when the *U-68* was sunk northwest of Madeira on April 10, 1944 by American aircraft from the *USS Card*. It would appear that just one man, Walter Schmietenknop, survived the sinking of the *U-767* in the English Channel by the British destroyers *HMS Fame*, *HMS Inconstant* and *HMS Havelock* on June 18, 1944 by escaping through a torpedo tube. *Obermechaniker* Erich Stein was the sole survivor on July 5, 1944 when the *U-390* was sunk in the Seine Bay of the English Channel by the British destroyer *HMS Wanderer* and frigate *HMS Tavy*. When the British destroyer *HMS Icarus* and corvette *HMS Migonette* destroyed the *U-1199* with depth charges in the English Channel on January 21, 1945, only *Obersteuermann* Friedrich Claussen avoided the fate of his comrades. On February 17, 1945, only *Matrosengefreiter* Herbert Lochner survived when the British sloop *HMS Lark* and corvette *HMS Alnwick Castle* sank the *U-425* off Murmansk, Russia. Finally, in the Far East, when the American submarine *USS Besugo* torpedoed and sank the *U-183* in the Java Sea on April 23, 1945, only *Obersteuermann* Karl Wisniewski lived to tell about it.

Such a sole survivor was the case with the *U-413*, but her story goes back many years before a fateful morning in August 1944 when only one man knew what really happened in her final moments.

Many U-boat men began their Navy careers in the surface fleet. As the surface ships experienced losses, and since few major ships were built after the war began, this left excess personnel who were valuable sailors and could be utilized in the U-boats. A ship such as the *Königsberg* was one example. The *Königsberg* was a light cruiser of the K-class, a sister ship of the *Köln* and *Karlsruhe*. After a number of foreign port-calls in the 1930s, the ship operated along the Spanish coast from November 1936 to January 1937 during the Spanish Civil War. Her poor hull design and construction rendered her ill-suited to commerce raiding and ocean-going operations; when the war began, she was assigned to duty as a torpedo-training ship in the Baltic and subsequently used for mine-laying operations in the North Sea.

In April 1940, the *Königsberg* participated in the occupation of Norway as part of "Operation Weserübung," transporting troops from Wilhelmshaven to Bergen, Norway, together with the *Köln*, the artillery training ship *Bremse* and the torpedo boats *Wolf* and *Leopard* – as part of the German invasion of that nation. Norwegian 210-mm shore batteries damaged the *Königsberg* and *Bremse* on April 9, 1940, forcing them to remain in Norway, while the other *Kriegsmarine* ships returned to Germany; the Königsberg thus became a classic "target of opportunity."

The next day, fifteen Blackburn Skua dive-bombers of the British Fleet Air Arm's 800th and 803rd Naval Air Squadrons, launched from Hatston, Orkney struck the damaged cruiser. The Germans had only about fifteen minutes warning of the approach of the dive bombers, but of the cruiser's anti-aircraft armament only two 20mm guns on the fore of the ship opened fire, and they were firing almost blind, into the sun. The attackers scored three direct 500-pound bomb hits and several near misses on the *Königsberg*. The ship capsized and sank in Bergen harbor; eighteen of the crew were killed and twenty-three injured in the bombing attack. A portion of the *Königsberg*'s stern was left protruding from the water as she capsized and sank. Light cruisers under water had no need for a crew and the attack thus "freed" some 500 sailors for other pursuits, including one Ernst Hamann; and the U-boats were a growth industry that could use their talents.

Dönitz's Crews
***Obermaschinenmaat* Ernst Hamann**
Born on September 16, 1917.
Entered the Navy in 1938.
Served on the *U-413* in the engine room.
Awarded the Commemorative Medal of 1 October 1938 (the Annexation of Czechoslovakia) on December 20, 1939.
Killed in action on August 20, 1944 in the English Channel.

The Danziger Werft construction yard in Danzig was part of that industry and laid the keel for the *U-413*, a Type VIIC boat, on April 15, 1941 some eight months after she was ordered by the Navy. The U-boat was launched on January 15, 1942 and commissioned on June 3, 1942. The *U-413* left Kiel on October 22, 1942 under the command of *Oberleutnant zur See* Gustav Poel for her first war patrol. She arrived at Marviken, Norway on October 24 after two days. Just four days later, on October 28, 1942 the boat left Marviken on her second war patrol. On November 8, 1942 B.d.U. ordered the *U-413* to the Gibraltar area:

> "To employ a large number of boats first against landing operations on the Moroccan coast. Later to attack ships west of Gibraltar as they approach the Mediterranean with supplies."

B.d.U. also gave this warning to the U-boats in the area:

> "Wariness of the English will already be sharpened in the Straits of Gibraltar by former operations. It can no longer be assumed that all the single ships, which pass through the Straits one after the other, will be unnoticed. The result will be increased watchfulness that will probably lead to losses of ships which are passing through, especially when the boats happen to pass through at an unfavorable phase of the moon. Heavy air patrols will limit freedom of movement of the boats. Warships and transports are unusually strongly protected and the possibility of losses is correspondingly high."

Dönitz urged the crews on in a radio message:

> "The boats operating in the Gibraltar and Morocco areas have received the following radio message: (1) The Führer sends to boats in the Mediterranean 'I expect a completely victorious operation.' (2) I expect the same from boats off Morocco and Gibraltar. We must relentlessly carry out the Führer's will with our tested brutal methods of attack. The sinking of transports will have great significance for the American attack and the French defense."

The *U-413* would do her part. On November 14, 1942, the U-boat sank the 20,107-ton troop transport ship *MV Warwick Castle*. The attack began when at 8:44 AM, the ship in convoy MKF-1X, under Master Henry Richard Leepman-Shaw, was hit by one of two torpedoes fired, about 200 miles northwest of Cape Espichel, Portugal. Thirteen minutes later the *U-413* hit her with two coups de grâce at 8:57 a.m. that caused the ship to sink about one hour later. The master, 61 crewmembers and 34 service personnel died. Two hundred eighty-six men were rescued by several British warships; fortunately the combat troops had already disembarked in Africa, as the ship had been in convoy KMF-1 as part of "Operation Torch." The action was described in the B.d.U. war diary:

> "*U-413* made contact on convoy at 0900 in CG 4556. Convoy included a carrier, course north, speed 10 knots. She sank the troop transport *Warwick Castle*, 20,107 tons. Further action was impossible because of the weather situation."

Five days later, a British Lockheed Hudson aircraft with five bombs attacked the *U-413* and damaged her periscope so severely that she had to put in to Brest, France.

The *U-413* under Gustav Poel departed from Brest on December 27, 1942 for its third war patrol. Gustav Poel hit two ships on this patrol and both of them were in convoy: one from convoy SC-117 and one from convoy SC-118. On January 22, 1943 at 11:53 p.m., Poel sank the Greek 3,556-ton freighter *Mount Mycale* carrying grain and government stores northeast of Newfoundland, a straggler from convoy SC-117 heading from Halifax to Loch Ewe, Scotland; all hands were lost. On February 5, 1943 he sank the American 5,376-ton freighter *West Portal*, a straggler from convoy SC-118 in the mid-Atlantic, bound from Halifax to Liverpool. The U-boat arrived at Brest on February 17, 1943 after seven and a half weeks on patrol.

The *U-413* left Brest, still under the command of Gustav Poel, on March 29, 1943 on her fourth war patrol. On April 21, 1943 south of Greenland with Wolfpack Group *Star*, Poel sank the British 5,486-ton freighter *Wanstead*, from convoy ONS-3 heading from Oban, Scotland to New York. One man from the *Wanstead* was lost. On April 24 at 3:16 p.m., an aircraft of USN VP-84 Squadron attacked the boat, but caused no damage. The British corvette *HMS Loosestrife* depth-charged the U-boat on May 5; again there was no serious damage. The *HMS Spey*, a British frigate, depth-charged the *U-413* on May 20; damage was slight. On May 23 an aircraft from the RAF's 86th Squadron attacked the boat; again there was no damage. Finally, at 7:25 a.m. on May 26, an aircraft attacked the *U-413*. The boat defended itself with flak without destroying the aircraft. Poel returned to Brest on June 13, 1943.

The fifth through seventh war patrols of the *U-413* were uneventful. Gustav Poel's last patrol on the *U-413* began on January 26, 1944, when the boat left Brest. On February 20, 1944 the *U-413* sank the British 1,100-ton destroyer *HMS Warwick* with a FaT torpedo hit to her stern off Trevose Head, north Cornwall, southwest England, killing sixty-seven men. The FaT (Federapperat torpedo – area searching torpedo) was a pattern running torpedo made especially for convoy attacks. The torpedo was pre-set to run in a zigzag pattern; first it went straight, then turned to the left or right and proceeded for 800 or 1600 meters making the next turn opposite. The *U-413* returned to Brest on March 27, 1944 after more than eight weeks at sea. During the voyage, on March 21, 1944 Gustav Poel was awarded the Knight's Cross.

The *U-413* departed Brest under a new commander, *Oberleutnant zur See* Dietrich Sachse on June 6, 1944 as the Normandy landings began. The boat arrived back at Brest just three days later on June 9, 1944, after being attacked from the air. It had been her ninth war patrol. Sachse had been the 1st Watch Officer on board the *U-413* from June 1942 to June 1943. He then attended commander's training, and he took command of the *U-28*. It was a poor start; the boat sank alongside the U-boat mole at Neustadt/Holstein on March 17, 1944; an investigation revealed that the accident was caused by crew error. Despite that verdict, Sachse was given command of the *U-413* on April 20, 1944.

On August 2, 1944 the *U-413* left Brest under the command of Dietrich Sachse. On August 19, 1944 Sachse sank the British 2,360-ton freighter *Saint Enogat*, sailing with convoy ETC-72 bound for

Juno Beach, Normandy. No one was killed in the attack; the *Saint Enogat* would be the *U-413*'s last victim. At 8:17 a.m. on August 20, 1944 the British destroyer *HMS Forrester* (Cdr. G.W. Gregorie), while on an anti-submarine patrol with the British destroyer escort *HMS Wensleydale* (Cdr. W.P. Goodfellow) and the destroyer *HMS Vidette* (Lt.Cdr. G.S. Wooley), made ASDIC contact with a U-boat in the English Channel south of Brighton at position 50.21N, 00.01W. Shortly afterward, the commander of the *U-413* concluded that his boat was being pursued, and took the craft to a depth of about one-hundred feet and proceeded on his electric motors – but at four knots speed he would elude no one. At 9:15 a.m. the *HMS Forrester* attacked the *U-413* with depth charges set to 150 feet; they obtained no result as they fell wide of the target. Making the attack more difficult was a rain squall that brewed up. At 9:34 a.m. the *HMS Vidette* carried out a hedgehog attack; the device threw twenty-four projectiles over the area where the German submarine was believed to be and the deadly bomblets began sinking toward their target and exploding on contact.

Only one man knew what happened next. At least one explosive struck the U-boat and water began flooding the aft of the boat and into the control room. The crew rushed forward to the bow torpedo compartment, entered and closed the watertight door behind them. It was a futile effort and the boat began to sink out of control, interior lights out and the crew already waist-deep in water. *Oberleutnant (Ing)* Karl-Hubert Hutterer, the Chief Engineer, opened the forward hatch and made his escape, only to be taken prisoner when he reached the surface. No one else made it out of the stricken *U-413*. One of the dead was *Obermaschinenmaat* Ernst Hamann, who had been on board the light cruiser *Königsberg* over four years before when she had been sunk off Norway. He survived then, but was not so fortunate now, and died in the English Channel with all but one of his comrades aboard the *U-413*.

Known Crewmembers for the U-413

Altstädt, Werner	*Leutnant zur See*
Baake, Kurt	*Maschinenmaat*
Bäckert, Kurt	*Oberleutnant (Ing)*
Bätz, Rolf	*Marine-Artilleriemaat*
Beckmann, Erwin	*Matrose*
Berger, Walter	*Maschinenobergefreiter*
Bieler, Heinz	*Maschinenobergefreiter*
Birnbaum, Friedrich	*Matrosenobergefreiter*
Bischoff, Karl	*Maschinenobergefreiter*
Böhnke, Helmut	*Maschinenobergefreiter*
Brinkmann, Günter	*Obermechanikermaat*
Brischke, Ernst	*Leutnant zur See*
Brüse, Kurt	*Maschinenobergefreiter*
Bube, Gerhard	*Maschinenmaat*
Dangers, Ewald	*Obersanitätsmaat*
Dembinski, Fritz	*Maschinenobergefreiter*
Externbrink, Heinrich	*Funkobergefreiter*
Feibel, Willi	*Maschinenobergefreiter*
Greul, Karl	*Maschinenmaat*
Hackenbroich, Gottfried	*Maschinenmaat*
Hacker, Karl	*Matrosenobergefreiter*
Hafner, Wilhelm	*Matrosenobergefreiter*
Hamann, Ernst	*Obermaschinenmaat*
Hartung, Wolfgang	*Funkobergefreiter*
Hartwig, Kurt	*Bootsmannsmaat*
Heinicke, Werner	*Funkmaat*
Helme	*Obermaschinenmaat*
Hellmich, Gerhard	*Oberfunkmaat*
Hemmen, Hans	*Matrosenobergefreiter*
Horn, Kurt	*Maschinenobergefreiter*
Hutterer, Karl-Hubert	*Oberleutnant (Ing)*
Just, Willibald	*Matrose*
Krischat, Heinz	*Matrosengefreiter*
Kröner, Helmut	*Maschinenobergefreiter*
Lorenz, Kurt	*Funkobergefreiter*
Malow, Hans	*Maschinenobergefreiter*
Marschner, Helmut	*Oberbootsmann*
Müller, Helmut	*Obergefreiter*
Musiol, Karl	*Obermaschinist*
Mussack, Martin	*Maschinenobergefreiter*
Oster, Walter	*Oberbootsmannsmaat*
Peters, Heinz	*Obergefreiter*
Pfaffinger, Peter	*Obergefreiter*
Pfisterer, Eric	*Oberbootsmannsmaat*
Poel, Gustav	*Kapitänleutnant*
Pölzl, Karl	*Gefreiter*
Regelin, Karl-Heinz	*Maschinenobergefreiter*
Reinhold, Hermann	*Maschinengefreiter*
Roscher, Gerhard	*Obermaschinist*
Sachse, Dietrich	*Oberleutnant zur See*
Schmitz, Friedrich	*Maschinengefreiter*
Schwaiger, Gerhard	*Leutnant zur See*
Schwarzer, Herbert	*Maschinenobergefreiter*
Schwirley, Ernst-Werner	*Oberleutnant zur See*
Serve, Hubert	*Maschinenmaat*
Sock, Josef	*Maschinenobergefreiter*
Tomalla, Theodor	*Obersteuermann*
Ulbrich, Hermann	*Mechanikergefreiter*
Weckop, Heinz	*Mechanikerobergefreiter*
Wüst, Hans	*Maschinenobergefreiter*
Zimmermann, Alfons	*Obermaschinist*
Ziwinsky, Christian	*Maschinengefreiter*

Sources, "Sole Survivors:" Clay Blair, *Hitler's U-boat War: The Hunted, 1942-1945*, New York: Modern Library, 2000, 112, 174, 181; Rainer Busch and Hans-Joachim Röll, *German U-boat Commanders of World War II*, translated by Geoffrey Brooks, Annapolis, Maryland: Naval Institute Press, 1999, 198, 218; Manfred Dörr, *Die Ritterkreuzträger der U-Boot-Waffe, Band 1: A-J, Band 2: L-Z*, Osnabrück, FRG: Biblio Verlag, 1988, Band 2 – 175, 176; *F.d.U./B.d.U. War Diary, 1-15 November 1942* (PG30313A), 97, 99, 105, 115; Geoffrey Jones, *U-boat Aces*, Cerberus Publishing, Bristol, England, 2005, 142, 143; Michael Gannon, *Black May: The Epic Story of the Allies Defeat of the German U-boats in May 1943*, New York: HarperCollins, 1998, 184, 358; Axel Niestlé, *German U-boat Losses during World War II*, Annapolis, Maryland: Naval Institute Press, 1998, 62; Jürgen Rohwer, *Axis Submarine Successes 1939-1945*, Annapolis, Maryland: Naval Institute Press, 1983, 136, 147, 148, 163, 178, 179, 184; Captain James E. Wise, Jr., *Sole Survivors of the Sea*, Baltimore, Maryland: The Nautical & Aviation Publishing Company of America, 1994, 166, 167; www.ubootwaffe.net; www.uboatarchive.net.

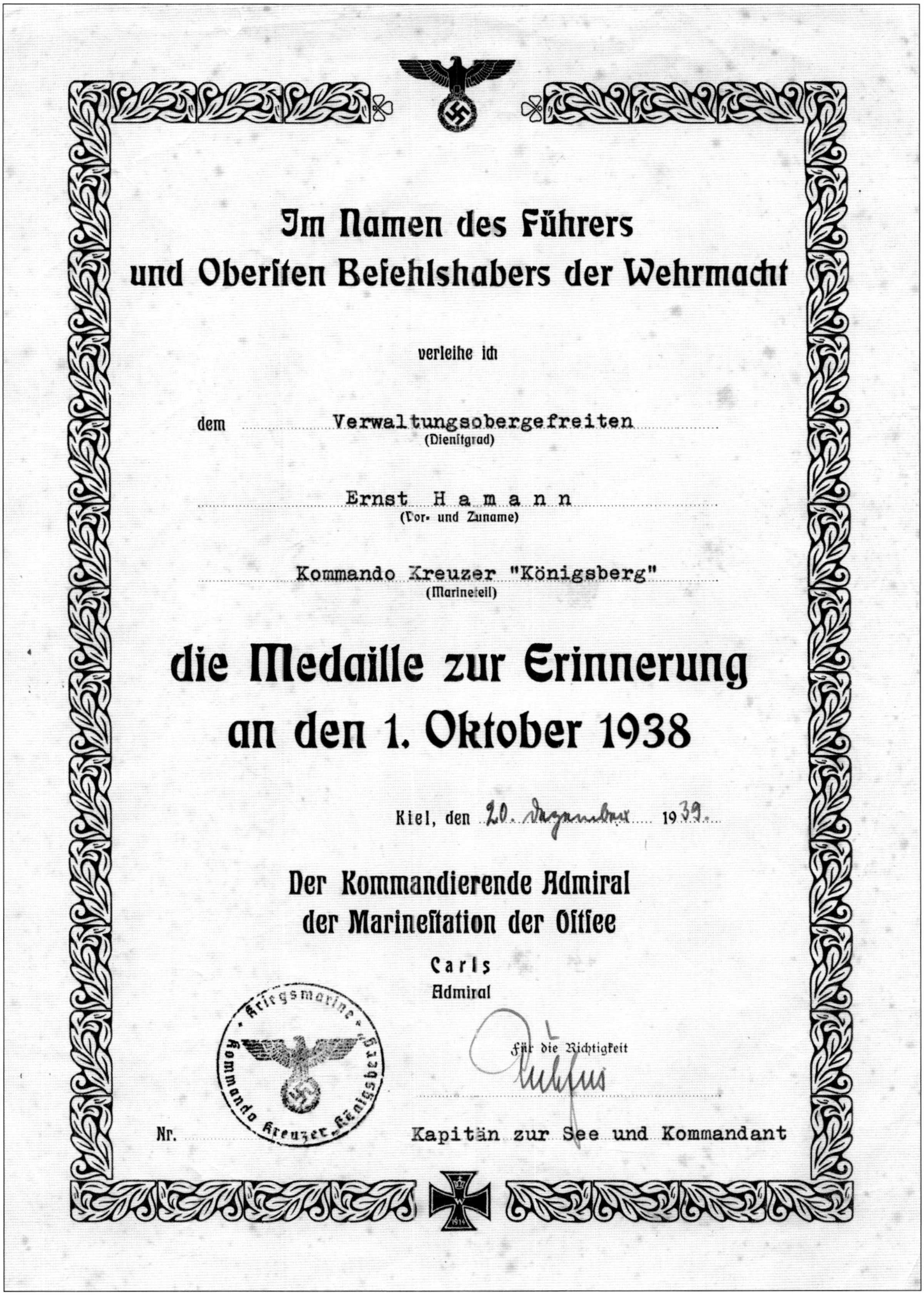

Im Namen des Führers
und Obersten Befehlshabers der Wehrmacht

verleihe ich

dem Verwaltungsobergefreiten
(Dienstgrad)

Ernst Hamann
(Vor- und Zuname)

Kommando Kreuzer "Königsberg"
(Marineteil)

die Medaille zur Erinnerung
an den 1. Oktober 1938

Kiel, den 20. Dezember 1939.

Der Kommandierende Admiral
der Marinestation der Ostsee

Carls
Admiral

Kriegsmarine Kommando Kreuzer Königsberg

Für die Richtigkeit

Ruhfus

Nr.

Kapitän zur See und Kommandant

Commemorative Medal of 1 October 1938 (the Annexation of Czechoslovakia) award document to Ernst Hamann on the light cruiser Königsberg on December 20, 1939. *Document is signed by Kapitän zur See Heinrich Ruhfus, commander of the Königsberg.*

CHAPTER TWENTY-THREE

"Chief Engineers"
U-2, U-387, U-405, U-416, and U-3003
1939-1945

The best U-boat commanders would admit it – the commander did not know where every single pipe and cable in a U-boat was located and what its function was; they did not know how every single gauge worked or what every single valve controlled. They did not know; but their Chief Engineers did – and every sailor on every U-boat knew that next to the commander the Chief Engineer was the most important man on the boat. Officially known as the *Leitender Ingenieur*, translated as Leading or Chief Engineer, they were normally referred to as the "LI." Chief Engineers supervised many men of the engineering technical fields (Techniker), who had a high representation of non-specialized entry-level metal workers. These men had a common vocational experience, were comfortable in an all-metal environment and had a knack to create emergency repairs quickly, often with very few specialized resources. On many boats, for example, the Chief Engineers had little more that basic mechanics tools, steel putty for plugging small leaks and an electrical welder.

The sailors knew of the Chief Engineer's importance as well. When asked the question of who was the most important man on the boat, veteran U-boat man Walter Wittig (*U-518*) unhesitatingly replied, "The LI." And Wittig would know; he spent more than 500 days at sea aboard U-boats and won the prestigious German Cross in Gold.

All the machinists in the engine room worked for the Chief Engineer; but because they were well trained, they could operate without the Chief Engineer standing over their shoulders supervising. Nonetheless, the Chief Engineer was responsible for the smooth functioning of the diesel engines and electric motors; overall he was responsible for everything having to do with the U-boat's propulsion and underwater diving. Instead, the Chief Engineer was often found in the control room, sitting or standing behind the two planesmen who controlled the U-boat's hydroplanes (one operated the bow planes; the other the stern). One of his major tasks as Chief Engineer was to keep the boat in trim so it would neither broach the surface inadvertently nor drift too deep when the commander was at the periscope. Thus, the Chief Engineer could demand silence during these maneuvers and could order the men to instantaneously move to other locations in the boat to keep her stable. This was made doubly difficult when torpedoes were fired or when the boat was being attacked.

Chief Engineers were often the first men to be assigned to a new U-boat before the submarine was completed. Then, when the U-boat went to the UAK for pressure testing, the future Captain and Chief Engineer were present, thus adding to their confidence in the new craft. And, at the end of many a U-boat's life, when faced with potential capture by the enemy, the Chief Engineer had the responsibility for setting the explosive scuttling charges that would sink the U-boat – and his responsibility was not lessened if in doing that he had no chance to personally escape.

From birth to death, Chief Engineers were a constant, reassuring factor for a U-boat and her crew. As one U-boat commander summarized:

> "Without a competent Chief Engineer, the submarine was a sitting duck."

Of the 144 men in the U-boat service who received Germany's highest award for military service and valor – the Knight's Cross – some fourteen were Chief Engineers. Concerning the German Cross in Gold, an award that was below the Knight's Cross – but not a prerequisite for winning the Knight's Cross – 530 U-boat men received this award. Chief Engineers accounted for sixty-six winners of the German Cross in Gold.

Gerd Suhren was the first U-boat Chief Engineer to receive the Knight's Cross. The brother of famed U-boat skipper Reinhard Suhren, Gerd was born on May 16, 1914 in Tafaigata, German Samoa. His family returned to Germany during World War I; Gerd joined the German Navy on April 1, 1933 as a potential engineer officer, first serving on the light cruiser *Karlsruhe*. After several years of rigorous training, Suhren was promoted to *Leutnant (Ing)* on October 1, 1936; six months later he entered the U-boat School for training as a Chief Engineer. Suhren joined his first boat, a Type IIB *U-21*, on October 1, 1937; he remained with this boat for eleven months and then joined the *U-31*. Eight months later Suhren was reassigned to the nearly completed *U-37*, a long-range Type IX boat. He would make seven war patrols with this boat. As with many Chief Engineers who would win the Knight's Cross, Suhren was fortunate to serve under extremely competent commanders. His first wartime skipper was *Korvettenkapitän* Werner Hartmann, a commander who would sink 115,337 tons of enemy shipping and a future Knight's Cross with Oak Leaves winner. Suhren's second wartime commander was Knight's Cross winner Victor Oehrn, responsible for sinking 103,821 tons of shipping.

Gerd Suhren received the Iron Cross 2nd Class and the U-boat War Badge on November 8, 1939. On February 28, 1940 Dönitz personally presented Gerd Suhren with the Iron Cross 1st Class. On October 21, 1940, the day before the end of Suhren's seventh war patrol on the *U-37*, he was awarded the Knight's Cross – the first Chief Engineer to win the award. Dönitz considered Gerd Suhren a valuable asset who could help teach many future Chief Engineers and so reassigned him to be a training officer with the Technical Training Group for Front U-boats for two years. Promoted to *Kapitänleutnant (Ing)* on February 1, 1941, he later served in Berlin but was unhappy being away from the front and volunteered to serve on the *U-2511*, one of the revolutionary new Type XXI U-boats. He joined the project the day the keel was laid on July 7, 1944. Promoted to *Korvettenkapitän (Ing)* on December 1, 1944, Suhren would make one war patrol with the *U-2511*, under the command of Knight's Cross with Oak Leaves winner *Korvettenkapitän* Adalbert Schnee. Unfortunately, at the end of the war Suhren's parents and sister committed suicide in the Sudentenland area of Czechoslovakia during the forced emigration of ethnic Germans out of that region by the Czechs. For two years after the war, Gerd Suhren served in mine-sweeping duty. He died on May 6, 1991.

Erich Zürn was the second Chief Engineer to receive the Knight's Cross; in his case, for service on the *U-48*, the *Kriegsmarine*'s most successful U-boat – which sank 51 ships, a total of 306,875 tons. Erich Zürn was born in Stuttgart on July 23, 1906; he joined the *Reichsmarine* on January 6, 1925 and served for fourteen years as an enlisted man. Zürn began his U-boat training in 1933; he joined the *U-3* as an *Obermaschinist* on August 8, 1935; he also served on the *U-26*, serving in Spanish waters during the Spanish Civil War and winning the Spanish Cross in Bronze without Swords. Rising to the rank of *Stabsobermaschinist*, he began a period of officer training that culminated on November 1, 1939 with his promotion to *Leutnant (Ing)*.

On December 22, 1939 Zürn joined the *U-48* as Chief Engineer; he would make nine war patrols with the U-boat, serving under: *Kapitänleutnant* Herbert Schulze – a Knight's Cross with Oak Leaves winner; *Korvettenkapitän* Hans Rudolf Rösing – a Knight's Cross winner; and *Kapitänleutnant* Heinrich Bleichrodt – a Knight's Cross with Oak Leaves winner. During Zürn's time on the *U-48*, the U-boat sank forty-three enemy ships. He received the Iron Cross 2nd Class on February 25, 1940, the U-boat War Badge on April 20, 1940 and the Iron Cross 1st Class on July 3, 1940. In addition to the boat's successes, she also was hit hard in return on several occasions On April 13, 1940 the *U-48* attempted to attack the British battleship *HMS Warspite* off northern Norway, but was depth-charged by escorting destroyers. On March 22, 1941 British destroyers again found the *U-48* and attacked her with depth charges. Finally, on April 2, 1941 an explosion on the sinking ship *Beaverdale* seriously damaged the surfaced U-boat that was shelling her with its deck-gun. Zürn got the damage under control but the boat was forced to return to base. After two recommendations for the award, on April 23, 1941 Karl Dönitz awarded Erich Zürn the Knight's Cross; one of Zürn's commanders had called him the "soul" of the boat and said that on at least two occasions, without the Chief Engineer the U-boat would have failed to return to base. Zürn left the *U-48* in June and became the Chief Engineer of the 23rd U-Boat Flotilla in Greece. He later served as the Chief Engineer of the 29th U-boat Flotilla in Italy and the 5th U-boat Flotilla at Kiel. He survived the war. Erich Zürn died on August 9, 1965 at Grossholzleute near Isny in southeastern Baden-Württemberg.

Gerhard Bielig was the type of old guard Chief Engineer that Dönitz knew was the key to the success of any U-boat. Born on April 28, 1916 in Berlin, he joined the *Kriegsmarine* in April 1934 as an officer candidate. After three years of intense training, which included practical exercises on the light cruiser *Emden* and light cruiser *Königsberg*, Bielig was commissioned a *Leutnant (Ing)* on April 1, 1937; soon thereafter he began U-boat training. On January 4, 1938 Gerhard Bielig boarded the *U-20*, of the U-boat Flotilla *Lohs*, for duty. He would stay with the boat for two years, being promoted to *Oberleutnant (Ing)* on April 1, 1939, learning how the U-boat fought under *Oberleutnant* zu See Karl-Heinz Moehle, a skipper who would ultimately sink 93,197 tons of enemy shipping and be awarded the Knight's Cross in 1941.

The war began and the *U-20*, a Type IIB U-boat, conducted nine war patrols off the English coast, sinking ten enemy ships in 1939 and 1940. Gerhard Bielig played a key role, keeping the boat operational through many difficult situations as Chief Engineer. He received the U-boat War Badge on October 17, 1939 and the Iron Cross 2nd Class on November 23, 1939. Bielig then transferred on March 28, 1940 to the *U-103* as that Type IXB U-boat was being built. He went on the boat's first war patrol on September 21, 1940 and once again Bielig excelled as the Chief Engineer (see "The Happy Time.") He received the Iron Cross 1st Class on October 21, 1940 and was promoted to *Kapitänleutnant (Ing)* on October 1, 1941. Bielig made five war patrols with the *U-103* to the North and South Atlantic. Once again he was fortunate to serve under two very capable skippers: *Korvettenkapitän* Viktor Schütze, a Knight's Cross with Oak Leaves winner and responsible for sinking 180,073 tons of shipping; and *Kapitänleutnant* Werner Winter, a Knight's Cross winner who sent 79,302 tons of enemy shipping to the bottom.

Karl Dönitz was impressed with Gerhard Bielig's performance and on December 9, 1941 awarded him the German Cross in Gold. Six days later Bielig joined the *U-177*, a Type IXD2, during her construction process; he would make two lengthy war patrols to the South Atlantic and Indian Ocean – a total of 310 days at sea. On February 10, 1943 Karl Dönitz awarded Gerhard Bielig the Knight's Cross, the third Chief Engineer to be so recognized. Specifically, the citation mentioned that on three occasions Bielig saved his boat after it was heavily damaged by enemy depth charges. He spent the rest of the war as an instructor in the 2nd U-boat Training Division and as a training officer with the Technical Training Group for Front U-boats. He survived the war. Gerhard Bielig died at Neuss on September 29, 2004.

Chief Engineer Heinz Krey won his Knight's Cross for bravery. Born in Wiesbaden on December 31, 1921, he joined the *Kriegsmarine* on December 1, 1939 at age seventeen. A few months later Krey became an officer candidate; in 1940 he served on the minesweeper *M-84*. The following year Heinz Krey joined the U-boats, initially serving on the *U-567*. Promoted to *Leutnant (Ing)* on April 1, 1942, Krey joined the *U-703* on July 18, 1942 and served two war patrols on her as a Chief Engineer in training; he received the U-boat War Badge on September 28, 1942. Krey then became the chief Engineer on the *U-752*. On his second patrol with her, on May 23, 1945, enemy Swordfish and Martlet aircraft from the British escort aircraft carrier *HMS Archer* caught the *U-752* on the surface. The U-boat's quad-20-mm flak guns attempted to keep the enemy planes at bay, but the U-boat's commander *Kapitänleutnant* Karl-Ernst Schröter and everyone on the bridge were killed in action. Heinz Krey then took command of the stricken U-boat. As two British destroyers *HMS Keppel* and *HMS Escapade* approached, Krey ordered the crew to abandon ship; remaining behind, he then detonated the U-boat's explosive charges killing himself and destroying the boat to prevent her capture. In the action seventeen men from the *U-752* survived; another twenty-nine were killed in action. Karl Dönitz awarded Heinz Krey the Iron Cross

2nd Class and Iron Cross 1st Class with an effective date of May 22, 1943. On September 4, 1943 Heinz Krey received a posthumous award of the Knight's Cross.

Kapitänleutnant (Ing) Herbert Panknin, on the other hand, received his Knight's Cross as a Chief Engineer for lengthy outstanding service in the U-boat fleet – in his case for a total of 560 days at sea on war patrols during the conflict. Born on December 27, 1913 at Neustettin in Pomerania, Panknin joined the *Reichsmarine* as an engineer candidate on April 8, 1934. After serving in several surface assignments, he began U-boat training in 1937. He was promoted to *Leutnant (Ing)* on April 1, 1937 and became the Chief Engineer on the *U-57* on December 2, 1938 under *Kapitänleutnant* Claus Korth, a future Knight's Cross recipient. Herbert Panknin was promoted to *Oberleutnant (Ing)* on April 1, 1939. Panknin served nine war patrols with the *U-57*, during which time she was credited with sinking nine enemy ships. He left the *U-57* in June 1940 to join the *U-106*, which was being commissioned and was commanded by *Korvettenkapitän* Jürgen Oesten, a future Knight's Cross winner.

Panknin would serve three war patrols in the *U-106*; he was awarded the German Cross in Gold for his service on February 2, 1942. The U-boat commander and his Chief Engineer had forged such a strong team that they were known as the "Firm of Oesten and Panknin." By this time Herbert Panknin had been promoted to *Kapitänleutnant (Ing)* on February 1, 1942 and was serving as the Chief Engineer for the 9th U-boat Flotilla. He received the Knight's Cross on September 4, 1943 for his service on the *U-106*. But Herbert Panknin would go to sea again. He soon joined the forming crew of the *U-861*, which was also commanded by *Korvettenkapitän* Jürgen Oesten. Panknin would serve two lengthy war patrols to the Indian Ocean with the *U-861*. He ended the war helping to bring key war materials from the Japanese at Penang, Malaya to Drontheim, Norway. After the war, Herbert Panknin joined the new German Navy; he retired in 1972. He died on March 15, 2001 in Langen-Sievern in Lower Saxony.

Willi Lechtenbörger was the next Chief Engineer to win the Knight's Cross for heroism. Born at Bottrop in Westphalia on February 2, 1914, he joined the *Reichsmarine* on December 1, 1934. The following year he entered the officer candidate program; he would be commissioned as a *Leutnant (Ing)* on September 27, 1939, shortly after the war began. Willi Lechtenbörger joined the *U-60* on August 1, 1940 then under the command of *Oberleutnant zur See* Adalbert Schnee, a future Knight's Cross with Oak Leaves winner (see "Just a Matter of Time.") Lechtenbörger would serve three war patrols on the *U-60* and would win the Iron Cross 2nd Class and the U-boat War Badge on September 10, 1940. He then transferred to the new *U-201* and served another seven war patrols on this successful U-boat, winning the Iron Cross 1st Class; he was promoted to *Oberleutnant (Ing)* on November 1, 1941. On September 30, 1942 Willi Lechtenbörger received the German Cross in Gold; he left the *U-201* and joined the *U-847*. He would serve only one war patrol with the boat and it ended disastrously. After refueling seven U-boats, and on the way to the Indian Ocean to join the *Monsoon Group* of U-boats, she was in the Sargasso Sea off the Canary Islands on August 27, 1943. Enemy Avenger and Wildcat aircraft from the American escort aircraft carrier *USS Card* found the *U-847* that day and sank her with an air-launched Fido homing torpedo, killing all sixty-two men on board. Willi Lechtenbörger, having been promoted to *Kapitänleutnant (Ing)* on August 1, was posthumously awarded the Knight's Cross on September 4, 1943.

Carl-August Landfermann was born in Dortmund on July 14, 1914; he joined the German Navy on March 1, 1934. For six years he served with the surface fleet, most notably on the light cruiser *Köln*. He left the enlisted ranks on October 31, 1939, when he was commissioned a *Leutnant (Ing)*. On October 30, 1940 Landfermann became the Chief Engineer on the *U-146*, before joining the *U-38* as the Chief Engineer – under the command of Knight's Cross with Oak Leaves winner *Kapitänleutnant* Heinrich Liebe (see "Jonah") on March 24, 1941. Landfermann served three war patrols on the *U-38*, winning the U-boat War Badge on June 24, 1941 and the Iron Cross 2nd Class the following day. He left the *U-38* in January 1942 to join the newly commissioned *U-181,* skippered by the famous *Kapitänleutnant* Wolfgang Lüth, a winner of the Knight's Cross with Oak Leaves, Swords and Diamonds. Winning the Iron Cross 1st Class on January 21, 1943, Landfermann took part in the *U-181*'s 205-day patrol in the summer of 1943. After the U-boat returned to port, Wolfgang Lüth submitted his second recommendation that his Chief Engineer win Germany's highest honor and Carl Landfermann received the Knight's Cross on October 27, 1943. Landfermann became an instructor in 1944; he was promoted to *Kapitänleutnant* on January 1, 1944 and received the U-boat Front Clasp in Bronze on October 12, 1944; he spent 589 days at sea on U-boat war patrols during the conflict. He survived the war and spent four months in a prisoner of war camp. Carl Landfermann died in Hagen on November 18, 2003.

Hellmut Rohweder was born in Hagen on January 17, 1914. He joined the *Reichsmarine* as an engineer officer cadet on April 1, 1935 and attended technical schools at Mürwik, Kiel and Neustadt before being commissioned a *Leutnant (Ing)* on April 1, 1938. On April 1, 1939 Rohweder joined the *U-17* as the Chief Engineer; he would serve three war patrols on the boat, winning the Iron Cross 2nd Class on March 8, 1940 and the U-boat War Badge on May 2, 1940. During his time on the *U-17,* he was promoted to *Oberleutnant (Ing)* on October 1, 1939. On October 1, 1940 Hellmut Rohweder joined the *U-69* as it was going through the building process. When this was completed, he served on four war patrols with the *U-69* under Knight's Cross winner *Kapitänleutnant* Jost Metzler. He proved his competence and won the Iron Cross 1st Class on April 12, 1941. In 1942 Hellmut Rohweder was assigned to the *U-514*, a Type IXC boat; he would serve an additional four war patrols on this boat, fortuitously leaving the boat three months before it was sunk with all hands off Cape Finisterre, Spain. For this service he was promoted to *Kapitänleutnant (Ing)* on December 1, 1942 and received the German Cross in Gold on August 7, 1943 and the Knight's Cross on November 14, 1943, specifically for saving the boat by making emergency damage control in several situations. For the next eighteen months Rohweder served as the Chief Engineer for the 10th U-boat Flotilla, the 12th U-boat Flotilla and the 4th U-boat Training Flotilla; he also received the U-boat Front Clasp in Bronze on October 20, 1944. He went on the *U-673* on a test patrol in 1944 testing a new flak tower. On December 1, 1944 Hellmut Rohweder was promoted to *Korvettenkapitän*. He survived the war, served in the new German Navy and retired as a *Kapitän zur See* in 1972.

To the World War II German public, Chief Engineers were not as widely known as U-boat commanders. But in the case of Johann Wessels, Germans throughout the nation knew the man who was the Chief Engineer on the *U-47* on her daring mission at Scapa Flow (see "The Bull of Scapa Flow"). One of the older Chief Engineers in the U-boat service, Wessels was born in Wilhelmshaven-Rüstringen on May 28, 1904. He entered the *Reichsmarine* in 1923 and for thirteen years served in engine rooms throughout the surface fleet to include the light cruiser *Leipzig* and the pocket battleship *Graf Spee*. On January 1, 1937 Wessels was commissioned a *Leutnant (Ing)* and began U-boat training; his first posting was as the Chief Engineer of the *U-23*; he was promoted to *Oberleutnant (Ing)* on June 1,

1938. On December 17, 1938 Johann Wessels joined the *U-47* as her Chief Engineer. He would serve with the *U-47* on four war patrols, including the famous one to Scapa Flow. Johann Wessels received the Iron Cross 2nd Class on September 25, 1939, the Iron Cross 1st Class on October 17, 1939 (for Scapa Flow) and the U-boat War Badge on December 19, 1939. On January 1, 1940 Johann Wessels was promoted to *Kapitänleutnant (Ing)*.

Johann Wessels left the *U-47* on April 6, 1940 to become the Chief Engineer of the 1st U-boat Flotilla. But the call of the sea beckoned and in June 1942 he volunteered to serve as Chief Engineer on the new *U-198*, a Type IXD2 boat, under the command of *Fregattenkapitän* Werner Hartmann, a Knight's Cross with Oak Leaves winner. The two made a 200-day war patrol to the Indian Ocean, sinking seven ships. On March 9, 1944 Johann Wessels received the Knight's Cross for his performance on this mission; he was promoted shortly thereafter on April 1, 1944 to *Korvettenkapitän (Ing)*. After several months on land, during which time Wessels received the U-boat Front Clasp in Bronze on October 4, 1944, he then joined the *U-870*, a Type IXC/40. Wessels made one patrol with the boat, but it was an important one. The U-boat positioned itself in the North Atlantic off Iceland and transmitted weather reports in support of the German December Ardennes Offensive – the Battle of the Bulge. Wessels survived the war, spending twenty months in an Allied prisoner of war camp. Johann Wessels died on February 9, 1988 at Oldenburg.

Georg Olschewski served on only one U-boat during the war, a Type IXC, boat the *U-66*. But it was a killer boat and during her nine war patrols the U-boat sank thirty-three enemy ships for a total of 200,021 tons. Born in Horstmar near Steinfurt/Westphalia on June 2, 1911, Georg Olschewski joined the German Navy as a recruit on October 31, 1928 just a few months after his seventeenth birthday. Through 1940 Olschewski served as an enlisted machinist in the surface fleet, with assignments on light cruisers *Emden* and *Leipzig* and the destroyer escort *F-10* and *F-8* at the beginning of the war. In early 1941 he began U-boat training and joined the *U-66* as a *Stabsobermaschinist*; he served in this capacity on three war patrols and then was commissioned a *Leutnant (Ing)*. Assuming the post of Chief Engineer, Olschewski served seven additional war patrols on the *U-66*, winning the Iron Cross 2nd Class on February 13, 1942, the U-boat War Badge on June 1, 1942 and the Iron Cross 1st Class on October 2, 1942. During this time he was promoted to *Oberleutnant (Ing)*. On April 23, 1944 *Oberleutnant (Ing)* Georg Olschewski was awarded the Knight's Cross for taking emergency actions that saved the U-boat on several occasions. Later on the same patrol, on May 6, 1944, west of the Cape Verde Islands, Avenger and Wildcat aircraft from the escort carrier *USS Block Island* found the *U-66* and attacked her. Shortly thereafter, the American destroyer *USS Buckley* joined the fight bringing the *U-66* under gunfire and ramming her. Sensing that the boat would be captured, Georg Olschewski kept the U-boat afloat until the crew escaped and then detonated the scuttling charges; twenty-four men died, while thirty-six (including the Chief Engineer) survived to become prisoners of war – the *U-66* went to the bottom. He spent nearly two years as a prisoner of war; he later joined the new German Navy and retired in 1969 as a *Fregattenkapitän*. Georg Olschewski died on September 29, 1996 in Immenstadt/Allgäu in Bavaria.

Karl-Heinz Wiebe served as a Chief Engineer on four different U-boats over thirteen war patrols during a four-year span. Born in Kiel on April 10, 1916, Wiebe joined the German Navy on April 5, 1935, and like Georg Olschewski, he served for several years on surface ships including the artillery training ship *Brummer* and light cruiser *Emden*. Shortly after entering the *Kriegsmarine*, Wiebe entered the officer candidate program; he was commissioned on April 1, 1938 as a *Leutnant (Ing)*. In 1939 Karl-Heinz Wiebe began U-boat training; he was promoted to *Oberleutnant (Ing)* on October 1, 1939. On December 16, 1939 he became the Chief Engineer for the *U-9*, a Type IIB. He would serve six war patrols, sinking nine enemy ships, with this boat that at the time was commanded by future Knight's Cross with Oak Leaves, Swords and Diamonds winner *Oberleutnant* Wolfgang Lüth.

Wiebe was awarded the Iron Cross 2nd Class on February 18, 1940, the U-boat War Badge on March 21, 1940 and the Iron Cross 1st Class on May 30, 1940. In 1941 he joined the *U-67*, serving five more war patrols under *Korvettenkapitän* Günther Müller-Stöckheim, another Knight's Cross winner. He left the boat in 1942 for assignments as an instructor and later as the Chief Engineer for the 1st U-boat Flotilla. In 1943 Wiebe joined the *U-178* and served two more war patrols. Karl-Heinz Wiebe was awarded the Knight's Cross on May 22, 1944 for service as the Chief Engineer on the *U-178* and then served on the B.d.U. Operations Staff. He and other U-boat men were trapped at Bordeaux, France as the Allies advanced, and he was taken prisoner of war in August 1944. He survived the war, joined the new German Navy and retired in 1961 as a *Korvettenkapitän*.

Little did Reinhard König realize in his youth in the central German city of Hanau that he would one day win Germany's highest award for military service and valor and that he would do so as the Chief Engineer of a U-boat. Born on March 30, 1909, he joined the *Reichsmarine* on October 27, 1928. For his first fourteen years of service, König was assigned to various surface ships including the light cruiser *Köln*, before an assignment to the *Kriegsmarine* commerce raider *Atlantis*. Making a twenty-month cruise as an enlisted man with this disguised raider, and winning the Commerce Raider War Badge, Iron Cross 2nd Class and Iron Cross 1st Class, he transferred to the U-boat service in 1942 and was commissioned a *Leutnant (Ing)* on April 22, 1942. On August 1, 1942 König joined the *U-123* and made five war patrols on this U-boat, some 342 days at sea, under *Kapitänleutnant* Horst von Schroeter, a Knight's Cross winner. Promoted to *Oberleutnant (Ing)* on October 1, 1942, König won the Iron Cross 1st Class on March 31, 1943 and the German Cross in Gold on December 12, 1943. On June 18, 1944 Reinhard König transferred to the *U-2506*, but would make no war patrols on this boat. Karl Dönitz awarded Reinhard König the Knight's Cross on July 8, 1944 for his service on the *U-123*, which involved a great degree of bravery. For example, on November 7, 1943 a British "Tsetse" Mosquito aircraft (the first Mosquito to be equipped with a 57-mm cannon) attacked the U-boat, scoring a hit on the conning tower, which killed one man and wounded two others and left the boat unable to dive due to a large hole in the tower. The Chief Engineer stabilized the situation, but during the trip home a large fire erupted in the machine room and at great risk to his life Reinhard König successfully put it out.

For his lengthy U-boat service Reinhard König won the U-boot Front Clasp in Bronze on October 14, 1944 and the U-boat Front Clasp in Silver on March 15, 1945. He spent two years in Allied captivity after the war. Reinhard König died at Bischofsheim on March 28, 1998.

Born the son of a locomotive engineer on September 9, 1908 in Koblenz-Moselweiss, Philipp Lichtenberg joined the *Reichsmarine* on April 1, 1928. After several surface assignments, he joined the clandestine submarine defense school in 1933. By 1935 he was a machinist on the *U-10*, followed by assignments to the *U-16* and *U-18*. At the beginning of the war Lichtenberg made six war patrols on the *U-18* (a Type IIB U-boat), winning the U-boat War Badge and Iron Cross 2nd Class on November 23, 1939 and serving for nine months under future Knight's Cross winner *Oberleutnant zur See* Ernst Mengersen. Lichtenberg then departed for additional training;

on January 1, 1941 Lichtenberg was commissioned a *Leutnant (Ing)*. Philipp Lichtenberg then served as Chief Engineer on the *U-652* (a Type VIIC boat) for five more war patrols, winning the Iron Cross 1st Class on November 11, 1941 and being promoted to *Oberleutnant (Ing)* on October 1, 1941. He became the Chief Engineer for the 29th U-boat Flotilla at the beginning of 1942.

After several assignments as an instructor, Lichtenberg assumed duties as Chief Engineer on the *U-516* (a Type IXC U-boat) on May 10, 1943; he made four war patrols with this boat. On March 25, 1944 Lichtenberg received the German Cross in Gold. He was promoted to *Kapitänleutnant (Ing)* on October 1, 1944; about this time he also received the U-boat Front Clasp in Bronze. On March 31, 1945 Philipp Lichtenberg received the Knight's Cross for his service as Chief Engineer on the *U-516*. In the press release for the award, he was cited as performing bravely when the U-boat was seriously damaged. This occurred on December 19, 1943 near Trinidad when an enemy aircraft attacked and seriously damaged the U-boat; she reached port on February 26, 1944. Philipp Lichtenberg survived the war and spent ten months in British captivity. He later joined the new German Navy and retired as a *Fregattenkapitän*. Philipp Lichtenberg died on December 14, 1993 in Kiel.

Hans Johannsen was the final Chief Engineer to be awarded the Knight's Cross. Johannsen was born in Stadum near Südtondern on January 29, 1913 and joined the German Navy on January 1, 1935. Within a few months he began U-boat training; by 1938 he was a *Maschinenmaat* on the *U-5*. After working with the U-boat School Flotilla at the beginning of the war – during which time he received the Iron Cross 2nd Class on April 20, 1940 – he was promoted to *Obermaschinist* and joined the *U-96* as the *Obermaschinist* in charge of the diesel engines. Johannsen served eight patrols on the *U-96*, winning the Iron Cross 1st Class under the renowned commander *Kapitänleutnant* Heinrich Lehmann-Willenbrock, a Knight's Cross with Oak Leaves winner. During these eight patrols, the *U-96* sank twenty-one enemy ships. In 1942 Johannsen left the boat, was promoted to *Leutnant (Ing)* on October 1, 1942, and received the German Cross in Gold on November 17, 1942. Hans Johannsen then went to several training courses to be a Chief Engineer, a job he assumed on the *U-802* on June 11, 1943. Johannsen served on the *U-802* for three war patrols. He was promoted to *Oberleutnant (Ing)* on October 1, 1943 and received the U-boat Front Clasp in Bronze on November 13, 1944. On March 31, 1945 Hans Johannsen was awarded the Knight's Cross for service as a Chief Engineer on the *U-802*. During the conflict Johannsen spent 582 days at sea on war patrols. He survived the war but spent three years in captivity in a British prisoner of war camp. Hans Johannsen died on March 5, 1961 at Burg on the Baltic island of Fehmarn. In the German novel *Das Boot*, by Lothar-Günther Buchheim, which was the basis for the feature film "*Das Boot*" (The Boat), he was represented by the character of "Johann," a mechanic. However, in the movie Johann suffered a mental breakdown and had to be restrained. In real life, Hans Johannsen kept his calm and successfully guided his boat through many life and death situations.

> *Dönitz's Crews*
> ***Leutnant (Ing)* Waldemar Geschke**
> Born on June 10, 1923 in Berlin.
> Served on the *U-2* as the Chief Engineer.
> Awarded the Iron Cross 2nd Class; named to the Ehrentafel der Deutschen *Kriegsmarine* on January 31, 1945.
> Died when his boat was rammed during a training mission on April 8, 1944 in the Baltic Sea.

Many of the sacrifices by other Chief Engineers were not so well known but were heroic nonetheless; the *U-2* and the *U-416* were two boats blessed with heroic chiefs who personally saved many of their comrades.

The *U-2* was a Type IIA coastal U-boat. Laid down at the Deutsche Werk shipyard at Kiel on February 11, 1935, it was finished in just over five months and was commissioned on July 25, 1935. Primarily a training boat – it made only two war patrols in 1940 – the *U-2* was commanded over the years by four Knight's Cross winners: Heinrich Liebe, Herbert Schultze, Helmut Rosenbaum and Hans Heidtmann, as well as several other very competent skippers. In 1944 the *U-2* was assigned to the 21st U-boat Flotilla, a training organization based at Pillau on the Baltic Sea. In command was *Oberleutnant zur See* Wolfgang Schwarzkopf. Schwarzkopf, twenty-three years old, was in the fourth month of his first command, but he had served as a watch officer since 1941 on the *U-202* and *U-605*.

A very small boat, the *U-2* displaced only 254 tons surfaced and was about forty-one meters long. On April 8, 1944 the boat was on a training mission north of Pillau (today Baltysk). At 7:45 a.m. at position 54°48'N, 19°55'E, the *U-2* collided with the German fishing vessel *Helmi Söhle*. Water flooded the boat, threatening to take her entire thirty-five men to the bottom. *Leutnant (Ing)* Waldemar Geschke was the Chief Engineer for the boat. Born June 10, 1923, and a member of entering class X/1940, he was only twenty years old, but he was a quick thinker with a decisive personality. Seeing the nature of the impending disaster, Geschke remained inside the boat, assisting his fellow crewmen to scramble out of the rapidly sinking craft. By his actions, seventeen men – including the commander – made it to safety, but Waldemar Geschke was not one of them and went down with the boat.

> *Dönitz's Crews*
> ***Oberleutnant (Ing)* Albert Moors**
> Born on March 22, 1923.
> Served on the *U-416* as the Chief Engineer.
> Awarded the Iron Cross 2nd Class; named to the Ehrentafel der Deutschen *Kriegsmarine* on January 31, 1945.
> Died when his boat was rammed during a training mission on December 12, 1944 in the Baltic Sea.

The *U-416* would meet a similar fate. On December 12, 1944 at 5:52 a.m. the boat was also on a training mission. In command was *Oberleutnant zur See* Eberhard Rieger. Rieger was only twenty-one years old; he previously served as the 1st Watch Officer of the *U-390* for eleven months and assumed command of the *U-416* on May 16, 1944.

In the darkness, at position 54°58'N, 19°33'E, northwest of Pillau, the boat was rammed by the German minesweeper *M-203*, commanded by *Oberleutnant zur See* von Caemmerer. The *U-416* was badly damaged and quickly began to sink. Disregarding his own safety, *Oberleutnant (Ing)* Albert Moors – age twenty-one – the Chief Engineer of the *U-416* stayed at his post desperately trying to save the boat. His actions bought enough time for five men to escape, but thirty-six men, including Moors and his commander Eberhard Rieger, were killed.

On January 31, 1945 *Großadmiral* Karl Dönitz signed the following proclamation concerning the two men:

> "In exemplary comradeship having fulfilled their soldierly duty up to the last as a leading engineer of a submarine:

Leutnant (Ing) Waldemar Geschke and *Leutnant (Ing)* d. R. Albert Moors.

Sacrificing their life, they endured death at their post onboard and thereby saved the lives of their companions. For every soldier of the Navy their behavior will be an example and stimulus to the highest devotion to duty. Their names will be in the history of the U-boat service."

This proclamation was for inclusion into the Honor Table (Roll) of the German Navy (*Ehrentafel der Deutschen Kriegsmarine*). In the entire Navy only thirty-seven men received this distinction. It was even rarer in the U-boat arm; only three submariners were so designated. In addition to Albert Moors and Waldemar Geschke, *Korvettenkapitän* Ottokar Paulssen, the commander of the *U-557*, was also honored – a posthumous award as in the case of Moors and Geschke. Since Paulssen had previously received the Iron Cross 1st Class, his family received the Honor Roll Clasp. Moors and Geschke had received the Iron Cross 2nd Class but not the 1st, so their next of kin did not receive Honor Roll Clasps as possession of the higher award was a requirement in regulations. But the sacrifice made by Albert Moors and Waldemar Geschke was emblematic of the sacrifices made throughout the U-boat arm by Chief Engineers – men who played an instrumental role in the incredible successes made throughout the war by Dönitz's crews.

Dönitz's Crews

***Leutnant (Ing)* Günther Koch**

Born on December 11, 1923.

Served on the *U-387* and *U-3003* as an assistant to the Chief Engineer.

Awarded the U-boat War Badge on June 8, 1944.

Spent 91 days at sea on U-boat war patrols; transferred to be an operator of a Seal (*Seehund*), a two-man midget submarine in March 1945.

Survived the war; lived in Lilienthal/Bremen.

Günther Koch was not as decorated as Albert Moors and Waldemar Geschke but he was as typical of the caliber of men who rose to command the engine room. Born on December 11, 1923, he probably joined the German Navy in 1940 or 1941. After initial and specialized training, Koch began his U-boat service on the *U-387* probably in early 1944 when the U-boat was stationed in Norway. On June 8, 1944 Officer Candidate Günther Koch received the U-boat War Badge; he probably had just completed his second or third war patrol with the boat. Koch then departed the *U-387* to finalize his pre-commissioning training.

He was fortunate; in the Barents Sea near Murmansk, Russia on December 9, 1944 the British corvette *HMS Bamborough Castle* depth-charged the *U-387*, sinking her with her entire crew of fifty-one men.

Günther Koch was promoted to *Leutnant (Ing)* and assigned to the *U-3003*, a Type XXI U-boat. Ordered on November 6, 1943, construction workers laid her keel at Bremen on May 27, 1944; *Oberleutnant* Ludo Kregelin commissioned the boat on August 22, 1944. From that time until April 4, 1945 the *U-3003* continued training exercises with the 4th U-boat Training Flotilla, but did not conduct any war patrols. On April 4, 1945 an Allied air attack sank the *U-3003* at Kiel. But by that time Koch had been reassigned to be an operator of a Seal (*Seehund*), a two-man midget submarine used for special operations. Koch survived the war; he then became the technical director for the Gelsenkirchen water works until retiring in 1992 when he settled in Lilienthal near Bremen.

Another Chief Engineer, who did not win the Knight's Cross but exhibited incredible bravery nonetheless, served on the *U-405*. *Oberleutnant (Ing)* Eberhard Dewald, born April 7, 1919, was the son of a police officer. In the late 1930s he entered the German Navy as a cadet in officer training. By that time, his father, Fritz Dewald, had transferred from the police forces to the German Army and was a lieutenant colonel – he would end the war as a brigadier general. The entire family had a military bent; at the same time Eberhard Dewald was beginning his navy career, his brother Hartwig enlisted in the German Army's 14th Infantry Regiment.

Dönitz's Crews

***Oberleutnant* (Ing.) Eberhard Dewald**

Born on April 7, 1919 in Stuttgart.

Served on the *U-405* as the Chief Engineer.

Awarded the U-boat War Badge, Iron Cross 2nd Class and Iron Cross 1st Class.

Killed in action in a fight with the *USS Borie* on November 1, 1943 in the North Atlantic.

It appears that Eberhard Dewald spent his entire U-boat career on the *U-405*, a Type VIIC boat. The *U-405* was commissioned on September 17, 1941; the only commander would be *Korvettenkapitän* Rolf-Heinrich Hopmann, who was born on March 26, 1906 in Kiel. During the war the *U-405* sank the British 7,176-ton freighter *Wade Hampton*, bound from New York to northern Russia with general foodstuffs and war supplies on February 28, 1943. Also on board were two 35-ton motor torpedo boats, which went to the bottom with the ship and nine of her crew. On March 9, 1943 the *U-405* sank the Norwegian 4,665-ton freighter *Bonneville* carrying explosives and invasion barges from New York to Liverpool; a 143-ton LCT (Landing Craft Tank) on board the *Bonneville* went with her as did thirty-six of her crew.

A studio photograph of Eberhard Dewald shows that he earned the U-boat War Badge, the Iron Cross 2nd Class and the Iron Cross 1st Class over the course of the U-boat's first eleven war patrols. On May 4, 1943 the *U-405* was in the Bay of Biscay when a British Halifax bomber of the RAF's 502nd Squadron bombed the boat causing a massive oil leak, but Dewald and Hopmann were able to bring her safely back to port; Dewald probably received his Iron Cross 1st Class for this effort.

From July 1942 to February 1943, the U-boat was assigned to the 11th U-boat Flotilla at Bergen, Norway. She then transferred to the 6th U-boat Flotilla headquartered at St. Nazaire, France.

The *U-405* departed St. Nazaire on October 10, 1943 bound for the central North Atlantic. Three weeks later, the *U-405* began her final battle on October 31, 1943, some 700 miles north of the Azores. That afternoon scout aircraft from the escort carrier *USS Card* spotted a surfaced U-boat about twenty miles north of her task force. The task force commander ordered the destroyer *USS Borie* to race forward of the group, find and kill the U-boat, but the late fall weather conspired against her. Throughout the day the skies were heavily overcast and the sea choppy. Intermittent rain squalls moved in as swells reached 15 to 20 feet. The aging destroyer took the brunt of the pummeling; four portholes on her bridge were smashed by the impact of one wave.

With icy winds and freezing seas making visibility limited, the radar operators on the destroyer finally located two surfaced U-boats just before midnight. Bringing the crew to "General Quarters" the *USS Borie's* commander Lieutenant Charles H. Hutchins reduced speed and began to stalk the enemy. A few minutes later the destroyer had closed to within range and began to shell the *U-256*. Hutchins then raced in and depth-charged the U-boat which had to dive to escape the 4-inch gunfire. Believing he had sunk the enemy U-boat, he radioed the *USS Card* "Scratch one pig boat." But the U-boat, in fact, had escaped.

The *U-405* was attempting to escape as well, but for some reason did not submerge, attempting to flee through the heavy seas and driving rain. For two hours her maneuvering shook off the American destroyer; it is possible that the U-boat had mechanical damage sufficient to prevent her from diving to safety. Just before 2:00 a.m. on November 1, the *Borie's* radar found the U-boat and Hutchins stealthily closed in on his second target. Reaching effective range of his guns, the destroyer commander switched on a high-power searchlight that bathed the U-boat. To the destroyer's surprise (and indicating that the *U-405* was unable to dive) the German gun crews were at their battle stations and immediately began firing. For over an hour both warships maneuvered as best they could in the rough weather, when suddenly the U-boat's deck-gun crew scored two hits, one striking the destroyer's bridge wrecking her radio room and the other penetrating the destroyer amidships. Almost simultaneously the *Borie* hit the *U-405* with a 4-inch round that damaged the U-boat's deck-gun and killed its crew.

The destroyer captain then decided to ram the U-boat. Drawing closer, the *Borie* was seconds away from slicing the U-boat in half with her bow when another huge swell lifted the destroyer in such a manner that the bow actually went over the U-boat and the American destroyer crashed down on the U-boat's deck forward of her bridge, locking both vessels together. For what seemed like an eternity the crews of both vessels conducted a short-range fight against each other. Small arms cracked and a 20-mm gun on the *Borie* raked the deck of the U-boat. Finally, an American sailor fired a flare from a Very pistol that ignited on the U-boat's bridge starting a fire that seemed to kill everyone in that area.

At that moment, another large swell parted the boats and for several minutes the U-boat drew away from the *Borie* which was taking in water and slowly flooding. Unbelievably the U-boat then changed course and headed toward the American destroyer apparently to try her own luck at ramming the enemy. As the *U-405* approached, the destroyer fired as many depth charges as possible to stop the suicide attack; the explosives splashed on both sides of the U-boat, exploded, cracked her hull and the *U-405* began to sink. Twenty Germans were observed dashing topside and entering life rafts, but in the tumultuous seas they were never seen again.

The *USS Borie* continued to sink; hours later rescue ships arrived and rescued all but twenty-seven of her crew. The *Borie's* chief engineer was posthumously awarded a Navy Cross for his valor in attempting to save the ship; Lieutenant Hutchins also received the Navy Cross. As a crewman later wrote:

> "Two gallant crews engaged in a fierce battle using every kind of weapon at their disposal."

No Germans survived the fight so, with the exception of a posthumous German Cross in Gold to *Korvettenkapitän* Rolf-Heinrich Hopmann, none of the U-boat's crew received bravery decorations for the battle; but the bravery of both crews would live on after the war. In 1957 Twentieth Century Fox produced a motion picture entitled "The Enemy Below." Based loosely on a novel that was a fictionalized account of the *USS Borie – U-405* fight, it starred Robert Mitchum as the commander of the *USS Borie* and Curt Jürgens as the skipper of the *U-405*. Austrian actor Theodore Bikel played the U-boat's chief engineer "Heinie Schwaffer." Schwaffer in the movie, like Eberhard Dewald in real life, died trying to save his boat and her crew.

On November 7, 1944 *Oberleutnant zur See* Walter Techand sent a letter of condolence to the father of Eberhard Dewald. The letter read:

> Dear General!
> Being tasked [by the commander of the B.d.U.], it is my sad duty to have to inform you that according to information received from the U-Boat Command your son
>
> *Oberleutnant (Ing)* Eberhard Dewald
>
> with his comrades on the ship has found a heroic death for our People, the Führer and the Fatherland. Our silent hope that everything would still be all right unfortunately did not become reality. We were not able to ascertain how and where he and his comrades have died heroically. Together with his comrades on the ship, in faithful fulfillment of his duties and true to his military oath, he has sacrificed for the future of our people the highest value which he possessed, his young life. I know that it is impossible to express with words in a letter to you, dear General, the condolence for having lost the dearest in your life. For that, the loss and pain which you have suffered is much too great.
>
> For us soldiers, the heroic death of all men is a renewed sacred obligation not to put down our arms until the final victory is achieved. Otherwise, the sacrifice of our comrades would be senseless.
>
> Your son will live in the memory of the community of our soldiers as a particularly good comrade whose remembrance we will always cherish with honor.
>
> Eberhard and I were crew comrades [they went through officer training together], which means that we knew each other very well. For this reason, I have been tasked with expressing to you, dear General, in the name of all crew members, the deeply felt condolence on the occasion of the heroic death of your dear son.
>
> The date of death of your son is November 4, 1943.
>
> The Military Information Bureau for War Casualties and Prisoners of War in Saalfeld, Thuringia has been notified. From there you will receive the information at which Registrar's Office you will be able to obtain the death certificate.
>
> I have not notified additional members of your family.
>
> With deep sympathy, I am taking part in the painful loss which has been visited upon you by the heroic death of your son.
>
> Heil Hitler!
> Your very devoted
> *Oberleutnant zur See* Techand

While not all Chief Engineers were memorialized in books and movies, or were they all rewarded with military decorations they truly deserved, the men in charge of the U-boat's technical performance were well-respected by their crew mates and the epitome of those who came to be known as "Dönitz's crews."

Known Crewmembers for the U-2

Ahnefeld, Ferdinand	
Alberg, Horst	*Maschinenmaat*
Albrecht, Georg	*Funkgefreiter*
Appenroth, Lothar	*Maschinenmaat*
Baghorn, Gerhard	*Oberfähnrich (Ing)*
Barber, Bruno	*Oberleutnant zur See*
Bäsler, Siegfried	*Oberfähnrich (Ing)*
Bauer, Heinrich	*Oberfähnrich (Ing)*
Beinhauer, Paul	*Leutnant zur See*
Bootz, Max	
Botsch, Willi	
Böttcher, Paul-Wilhelm	*Stabsobermaschinist*
Collmann, Herwig	*Kapitänleutnant*
Derr, Berthold-Friedrich	*Matrosengefreiter*
Droeschel, Hans	*Oberleutnant (Ing)*
Düster, Peter	
Eheleben, Fritz	*Maschinenmaat*
Freund, Herbert	
Geschke, Waldemar	*Leutnant (Ing)*
Goldammer, Manfred-Erich	*Maschinengefreiter*
Heidtmann, Hans	*Kapitänleutnant*
Herfurth, Herbert-Richard	*Maschinenobergefreiter*
Herglotz, Helmut	*Oberleutnant zur See*
Hillmann, Jürgen	*Oberleutnant zur See*
Hintze, Heinz	*Mechanikermaat*
Hungeling, Gerhard-Bernhard	*Bootsmaat*
Icke, Martin	*Matrosengefreiter*
Klaunig, Ernst-Adolf	*Kapitänleutnant (Ing)*
Kölzer, Karl	*Kapitänleutnant*
Kötter, Heinrich	
Kreuzinger, Herbert	
Kronenbitter, Willi	*Obersteuermann*
Ksiesyk, Richard	*Maschinenmaat*
Kuppisch, Herbert	*Kapitänleutnant*
Liebe, Heinrich	*Fregattenkapitän*
Maschke, Kurt	
Meth, Franz	*Obermaschinist*
Michahelles, Hermann	*Kapitänleutnant*
Petzokat, Otto	*Obersteuermann*
Pfitzner, Georg	*Maschinenmaat*
Radloff, Karl-Reiner	*Oberleutnant (Ing)*
Rosenbaum, Helmut	*Kapitänleutnant*
Rudolph	*Oberleutnant (Ing)*
Schmidt, Dr. Joachim	*Oberleutnant zur See (Arzt)*
Schneider, Otto	*Obermaschinenmaat*
Schultze, Herbert	*Korvettenkapitän*
Schwaff, Werner	*Kapitänleutnant*
Schwarzkopf, Wolfgang	*Oberleutnant zur See*
Selmer, Josef	*Oberleutnant zur See*
Steiner, Friedrich-Karl	*Oberleutnant (Ing)*
Taubert, Rudolf	*Obermaschinist*
Vollrath, Max	
Wagner, Arno	
Wien, Hermann	*Obermaschinenmaat*
Wilamowitz-Möllendorf, Georg von	*Korvettenkapitän*
Wiskant, Fred	*Bootsmaat*
Wollersheim, Hubert	*Kapitänleutnant (Ing)*
Ziegenhagen, Hans	*Kapitänleutnant (Ing)*

Known Crewmembers for the U-387

Adler, Armin	*Leutnant (Ing)*
Allner, Rudolf	*Matrosenobergefreiter*
Alter, Erich	*Maschinenobergefreiter*
Beilfuss, Paul	*Oberfunkmaat*
Bieler, Artur	*Mechanikergefreiter*
Borowski, Heinrich	*Obermaschinenmaat*
Braner, Hans	*Funkobergefreiter*
Büchler, Rudolf	*Kapitänleutnant*
Christ, Werner	*Matrosengefreiter*
Dopffel, Peter	*Leutnant zur See*
Dörfer, Albert	*Matrose*
Dreyer, Hans	*Obermaschinenmaat*
Drobny, Franz	*Obergefreiter*
Drzymalski, Horst	*Obermechanikermaat*
Ess, Heinrich	*Obermaschinenmaat*
Frühsorge, Herbert	*Obergefreiter*
Heimann, Kurt	*Maschinenmaat*
Hennicke, Hermann	*Maschinengefreiter*
Heyer, Willibald	*Matrosenobergefreiter*
Hildebrandt, Richard	*Matrosenobergefreiter*
Hiller, Hans	*Obersteuermann*
Hug, Heinz	*Matrosenobergefreiter*
Imboden, Hans-Günther	*Maschinengefreiter*
Jacobs, Hans	*Oberleutnant zur See*
Jensen, Hans	*Matrosengefreiter*
Jochim, Albert	*Obermaschinenmaat*
Jonczyk, Paul	*Mechanikerobergefreiter*
Kiehn, Karl-Paul	*Bootsmaat*
Klein, Anton	*Maat*
Koch, Günter	*Leutnant (Ing)*
Komorowski, Heinz	*Oberleutnant zur See*
Kühne, Johannes	*Oberleutnant zur See*
Kurtz, Heinz	*Maschinenmaat*
Lins, Alfred	*Maschinenobergefreiter*
Mangold, Paul	*Obermaschinist*
Mannsfeld, Horst	*Obergefreiter*
Möck, Leo	*Obergefreiter*
Mund, Hans-Werner	*Obergefreiter*
Petras, Heinz	*Obermaat*
Radmacher, Hermann	*Obermaschinist*
Rudat, Wilfried	*Obergefreiter*
Schiemann, Arnold	*Maat*
Schierbaum, Wilhelm	*Obermaat*
Schotteck, Bernhard	*Obergefreiter*
Schulz, Stefan	*Gefreiter*
Stockmann, Werner	*Obergefreiter*
Tank, Günter	*Obergefreiter*
Thiel, Erich	*Gefreiter*
Tolksdorf, Josef	*Gefreiter*
Urch, Herbert	*Gefreiter*
Wilhelm, Alfred	*Obergefreiter*
Witt, Werner	*Gefreiter*
Wortmann, Karl-Heino	*Obergefreiter*

Known Crewmembers for the U-405

Abraham, Paul	*Bootsmann*
Barche, Karl	*Matrosengefreiter*
Bihn, Herbert	*PK*
Blank, Paul	*Obermaschinist*
Clare, Rudolf	*Matrosenobergefreiter*
Czerowski, Erich	*Matrosenobergefreiter*

Dewald, Eberhard	*Oberleutnant (Ing)*
Diekämper, Josef	*Maschinenobergefreiter*
Georgi, Walter	*Oberfunkmaat*
Giese, Otto	*Leutnant zur See*
Groschupp, Hans	*Funkobergefreiter*
Heims, Siegfried-Hans	*Oberleutnant zur See*
Hellwig, Alexander	*Kapitänleutnant*
Henkel, Karl	
Heymuth, Fritz	*Maschinenobergefreiter*
Hof, Ludwig	*Bootsmaat*
Hofmann, Karl	*Obermechanikermaat*
Höhn, Rudi	*Mechanikerobergefreiter*
Hopmann, Rolf-Heinrich	*Korvettenkapitän*
Jarocha, Georg	*Obermaschinist*
Jirowec, Martin	*Matrose*
Krauter, Gotthilf	*Funkobergefreiter*
Kruttke, Dr. Hans-Gerhard	*Arzt*
Likuski, Herbert	*Matrosenobergefreiter*
Manke, Leo	*Maschinenobergefreiter*
Mittenzwei, Fritz	*Mechanikergefreiter*
Monze, Gerhard	*Maschinenobergefreiter*
Müller, Erich	*Maschinenobergefreiter*
Niesta, Alfred	*Oberleutnant zur See*
Peter, Gerhard	*Obermaschinenmaat*
Pies, Helmut	*Mechanikerobergefreiter*
Pütz, Werner	*Maschinenobergefreiter*
Reisewitz, Helmut	*Maschinenobergefreiter*
Rupprecht, Josef	*Matrosenobergefreiter*
Schaffartzik, Paul	*Matrosenobergefreiter*
Schillikowski, August	*Maschinenobergefreiter*
Schlobohn, Fritz	*Stabsobermaschinist*
Schlüter, Heinz	*Maschinenobergefreiter*
Schneider, Bruno	*Maschinenmaat*
Scholz, Walter	*Maschinenmaat*
Schüller, Josef	*Maschinenobergefreiter*
Schweikardt, Julius	*Obersteuermann*
Seessle, Ottmar	*Leutnant zur See*
Siebert, Gerhard	*Matrosenobergefreiter*
Siebert, Herbert	*Funkmaat*
Siegler, Ludwig	*Obermaschinenmaat*
Taubert, Rudi	*Bootsmaat*
Tuschen, Wilhelm	*Matrosengefreiter*
Vennemann, Heinz	*Matrosenobergefreiter*
Weber, Johann	*Matrosenobergefreiter*
Weinkauf, Helmut	
Weisser, Sven	*Leutnant zur See*
Wellmann, Werner	*Maschinenobergefreiter*
Wiendl, Adolf	*Matrosenobergefreiter*
Willner, Horst	*Oberleutnant zur See*
Zurwonne, Ernst	*Matrosenobergefreiter*

Known Crewmembers for the U-416

Andreas, Helmut	*Maschinenmaat*
Arenz, Matthias	*Obermaschinist*
Balz, Fritz	*Obersteuermann*
Berg, Günther	*Oberfähnrich zur See*
Bittner, Ewald	*Maschinengefreiter*
Brilla, Heinrich	*Oberfunkmaat*
Bütow, Heinz	*Maschinengefreiter*
Büttner, Friedrich	*Gefreiter*
Ernst, Hans	*Maschinenmaat*
Foitzik, Norbert	*Maschinengefreiter*
Förster, Siegfried	
Gömmel, Bernhard	*Obersteuermann*
Hanyz, Leo	
Herrmann, Gerhard	*Matrosenhauptgefreiter*
Holldorff, Günther	*Oberfähnrich (Ing)*
Ilchmann, Wilhelm	*Matrosenobergefreiter*
Jina, Siegfried	*Obermaschinenmaat*
Jostes, Karl	*Oberfähnrich (Ing)*
Klarholz, Fritz	*Obersteuermann*
Kresak, Walter	*Funkobergefreiter*
Küber, Anton-Rudolf	*Leutnant (Ing)*
Kühnel, Herbert	*Mechanikerobergefreiter*
Lach, Berthold-Johannes	*Matrosengefreiter*
Laloucek, Franz	*Matrose*
Liedtke, Hans	*Bootsmaat*
Mauerhahn, Eugen	*Maschinengefreiter*
Mehl, Albert	*Maschinenmaat*
Mehnert, Gerhard	*Maschinenmaat*
Moors, Albert	*Oberleutnant (Ing)*
Müller, Georg	*Stabsobermaschinist*
Pollrich, Horst	*Gefreiter*
Reich, Christian	*Kapitänleutnant*
Rieger, Eberhard	*Oberleutnant zur See*
Rohlfing, Friedrich	*Obermaschinist*
Scheibe, Eberhard	*Oberleutnant zur See*
Schilder, Werner-Karl	*Gefreiter*
Schulze, Fritz	*Oberfähnrich (Ing)*
Schürer, Werner	*Obermaschinist*
Thielke, Rudolf	*Gefreiter*
Tuchs, Robert-Vinzenz	*Gefreiter*
Wennhold, Ernst	
Zorn, Rudolf	*Oberleutnant zur See*
Zwarg, Heinz	*Kapitänleutnant*

Known Crewmembers for the U-3003

Flegel, Berthold	
Fleischer, Hannes-Eckart	*Leutnant zur See*
Koch, Günter	*Leutnant (Ing)*
Kregelin, Ludo	*Oberleutnant zur See*
Ploss, Josef	
Reisinger, Rudolf	*Oberleutnant zur See*

Sources, "Chief Engineers:" Chris Bishop, *Kriegsmarine U-boats 1939-45*, London: Amber Books, 2006, 173, 175; Rainer Busch and Hans-Joachim Röll, *German U-boat Commanders of World War II*, translated by Geoffrey Brooks, Annapolis, Maryland: Naval Institute Press, 1999, 211, 241; Jean Delize, *U-boote Crews: Daily Life, 1939-1945*, Paris, France: Histoire & Collections, 2007, 69, 74, 75; Manfred Dörr, *Die Ritterkreuzträger der U-Boot-Waffe, Band 1: A-J, Band 2: L-Z,* Osnabrück, FRG: Biblio Verlag, 1988, Band 1 – 10, 11, 44, 45, 152, 153, Band 2 – 53, 54, 55, 68, 69, 79, 80, 155, 156, 157, 160, 161, 162, 204, 205, 206, 296, 297, 331, 332, 333, 336, 337, 338, 359, 360; Michael Gannon, *Black May: The Epic Story of the Allies Defeat of the German U-boats in May 1943*, New York: HarperCollins, 1998, 37; Michael Gannon, *Operation Drumbeat: The Dramatic True Story of Germany's First U-boat Attacks Along the American Coast in World War II*, New York: Harper & Row, 1990, 102; Franz Kurowski, *Knight's Cross Holders of the U-Boat Service*, Atglen, PA: Schiffer Publishing, 1995, 131, 189, 265, 287, 301; Axel Niestlé, *German U-boat Losses during World War II*, Annapolis, Maryland: Naval Institute Press, 1998, 30, 63; Robert Sinclair Parkin, *Blood on the Sea: American Destroyers Lost in World War II*, New York: Sarpedon, 1996; 178, 179, 180, 181, 182, 183, 184; Lawrence Paterson, *U-boat Combat Missions*, New York: Barnes & Noble, 2007, 95, 113; Jürgen Rohwer, *Axis Submarine Successes 1939-1945*, Annapolis, Maryland: Naval Institute Press, 1983, 200, 153, 155, 174; Horst Scheibert, *Die Träger der Ehrenblattspange des Heeres und der Waffen-SS, Die Träger der Ehrentafelspange der Kriegsmarine, Die Inhaber des Ehrenpokals für Besondere Leistung im Luftkrieg*, Friedberg, FRG: Podzun-Pallas-Verlag, 1986, 129, 130; David Westwood, *The U-boat War: The German Submarine Service and the Battle of the Atlantic, 1935-1945*, Philadelphia, PA: Casemate, 2005, 140; Gordon Williamson, *Torpedo los! The Fascinating World of U-boat Collectibles*, San Jose, CA: R. James Bender Publishing, 2006, 249; Gordon Williamson, *Wolf Pack: The Story of the U-boat in World War II*, Oxford, England: Osprey Publishing, 2006, 180; www.ubootwaffe.net; www.uboatarchive.net; Interview with Walter Wittig, former crewmember on the *U-518* and German Cross in Gold winner at Cuxhaven, Germany on October 21, 2008.

In beispielhafter Kameradschaft haben ihre soldatische Pflicht bis zum Letzten als Leitender Ingenieur eines Unterseebootes erfüllt:

Leutnant (Ing.) Waldemar G e s c h k e,

Leutnant (Ing.) d. R. Albert M o o r s.

Unter Aufopferung ihres Lebens harrten sie bis zum Tode auf ihrem Posten an Bord aus und retteten dadurch ihren Kameraden das Leben. Für jeden Soldaten der Kriegsmarine wird ihr Verhalten Beispiel und Ansporn zu höchster Pflichterfüllung sein.
Ihre Namen werden in die Geschichte der U-Bootswaffe eingehen.

Berlin, den 31. Januar 1945.

Der Oberbefehlshaber der Kriegsmarine

Dönitz

Großadmiral

Official proclamation for inclusion into the Honor Table (Roll) of the German Navy (Ehrentafel der Deutschen Kriegsmarine) for Chief Engineers Leutnant (Ing.) Waldemar Geschke, U-2, and Leutnant (Ing.) d.R. Albert Moors, U-416. *Document is signed by Grossadmiral Karl Dönitz on January 31, 1945. In the entire German Navy only thirty-seven men received this distinction; even rarer in the U-boat arm, only three submariners were so honored.*

Verleihungs-Urkunde

Auf Grund der Ermächtigung des Oberbefehlshabers der Kriegsmarine verleihe ich dem

Ober- Fähnrich (Ing.)
(Dienstgrad)

Günter Koch
(Name)

das

Ubootskriegsabzeichen 1939

An Bord, den 8. Juni 1944

Fregattenkapitän
und
Führer der Unterseeboote Norwegen
~~Admiral und Befehlshaber der Unterseeboote~~

Kriegsmarine
Führer der Unterseeboote Norwegen

(MS 37108)

U-boat War Badge award document for Günther Koch, U-387, on June 8, 1944 just after the U-boat returned from a war patrol. *Document is signed by Fregattenkapitän Reinhard Suhren, Commander of U-boats in Norway and winner of the Knight's Cross with Oak Leaves and Swords.*

Für
Führer, Volk und Vaterland
starb den Heldentod

am 4. November 1943

der Oberleutnant (Jng.)

Eberhard Dewald

Im Auftrage
des Oberbefehlshabers der
Kriegsmarine ist darüber diese
Urkunde ausgestellt worden.

An Bord, den 29. Dezember 1944

Dienststempel

Name
Admiral
u. Kommandierender Admiral
Dienstgrad, Dienststellung
der Unterseeboote

Official Death notice for Oberleutnant (Ing) Eberhard Dewald, Chief Engineer on the U-405. *Document is signed by Admiral von Friedeburg and is dated December 29, 1944. Date of death is given as November 4, 1943.*

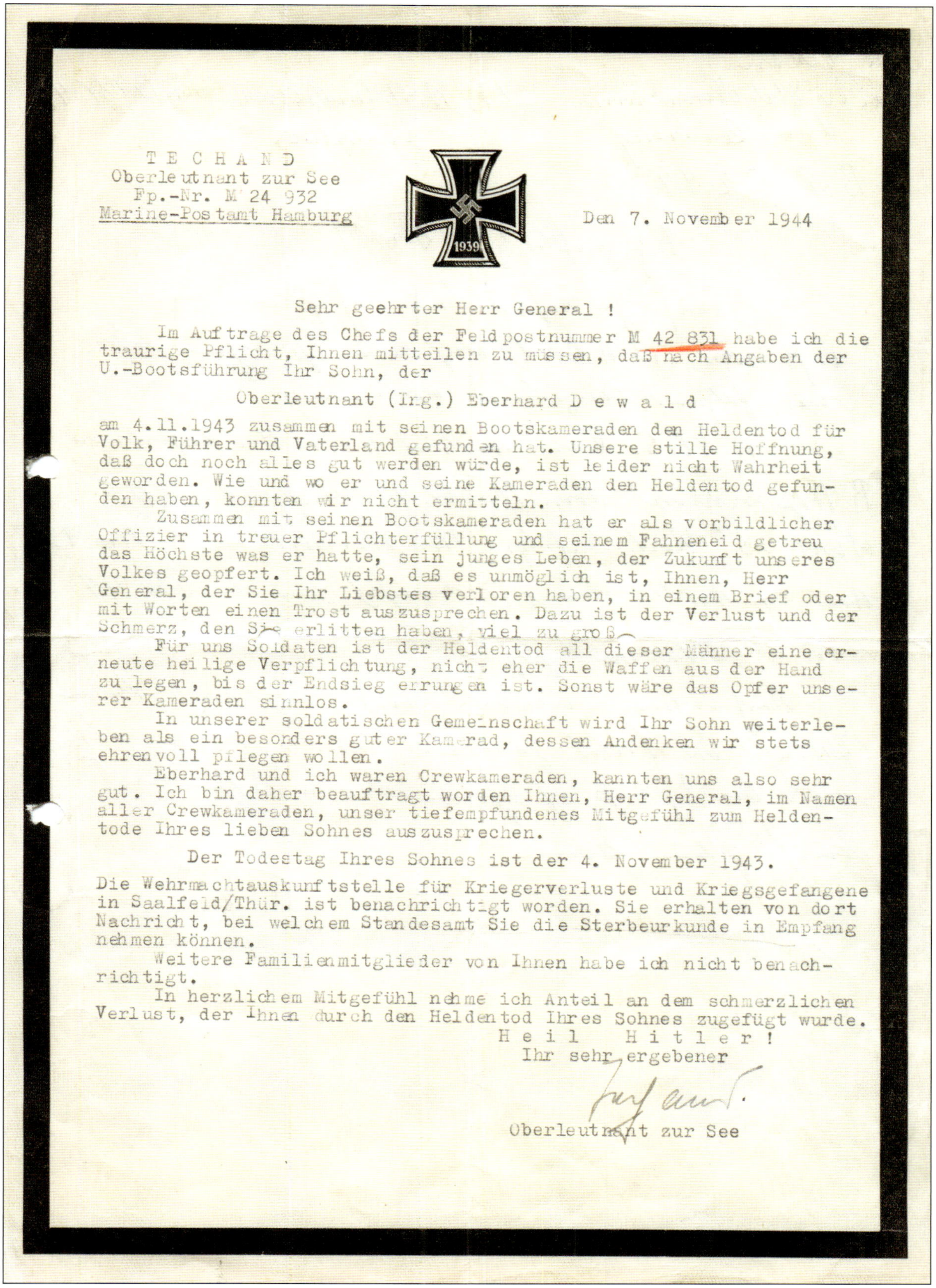

T E C H A N D
Oberleutnant zur See
Fp.-Nr. M 24 932
Marine-Postamt Hamburg

Den 7. November 1944

Sehr geehrter Herr General !

Im Auftrage des Chefs der Feldpostnummer M 42 831 habe ich die traurige Pflicht, Ihnen mitteilen zu müssen, daß nach Angaben der U.-Bootsführung Ihr Sohn, der

Oberleutnant (Ing.) Eberhard D e w a l d

am 4.11.1943 zusammen mit seinen Bootskameraden den Heldentod für Volk, Führer und Vaterland gefunden hat. Unsere stille Hoffnung, daß doch noch alles gut werden würde, ist leider nicht Wahrheit geworden. Wie und wo er und seine Kameraden den Heldentod gefunden haben, konnten wir nicht ermitteln.

Zusammen mit seinen Bootskameraden hat er als vorbildlicher Offizier in treuer Pflichterfüllung und seinem Fahneneid getreu das Höchste was er hatte, sein junges Leben, der Zukunft unseres Volkes geopfert. Ich weiß, daß es unmöglich ist, Ihnen, Herr General, der Sie Ihr Liebstes verloren haben, in einem Brief oder mit Worten einen Trost auszusprechen. Dazu ist der Verlust und der Schmerz, den Sie erlitten haben, viel zu groß.

Für uns Soldaten ist der Heldentod all dieser Männer eine erneute heilige Verpflichtung, nicht eher die Waffen aus der Hand zu legen, bis der Endsieg errungen ist. Sonst wäre das Opfer unserer Kameraden sinnlos.

In unserer soldatischen Gemeinschaft wird Ihr Sohn weiterleben als ein besonders guter Kamerad, dessen Andenken wir stets ehrenvoll pflegen wollen.

Eberhard und ich waren Crewkameraden, kannten uns also sehr gut. Ich bin daher beauftragt worden Ihnen, Herr General, im Namen aller Crewkameraden, unser tiefempfundenes Mitgefühl zum Heldentode Ihres lieben Sohnes auszusprechen.

Der Todestag Ihres Sohnes ist der 4. November 1943.

Die Wehrmachtauskunftstelle für Kriegerverluste und Kriegsgefangene in Saalfeld/Thür. ist benachrichtigt worden. Sie erhalten von dort Nachricht, bei welchem Standesamt Sie die Sterbeurkunde in Empfang nehmen können.

Weitere Familienmitglieder von Ihnen habe ich nicht benachrichtigt.

In herzlichem Mitgefühl nehme ich Anteil an dem schmerzlichen Verlust, der Ihnen durch den Heldentod Ihres Sohnes zugefügt wurde.

H e i l H i t l e r !
Ihr sehr ergebener

Techand.

Oberleutnant zur See

Letter of Condolence for Oberleutnant (Ing) Eberhard Dewald, Chief Engineer on the U-405. *It is written to the fallen officer's father, a German Army general. Document is signed by Oberleutnant zur See Werner Techand on November 7, 1944. Letter says that all crewmen on the boat perished and that the date of death was November 4, 1943. Techand earlier commanded the U-731 before moving to the staff.*

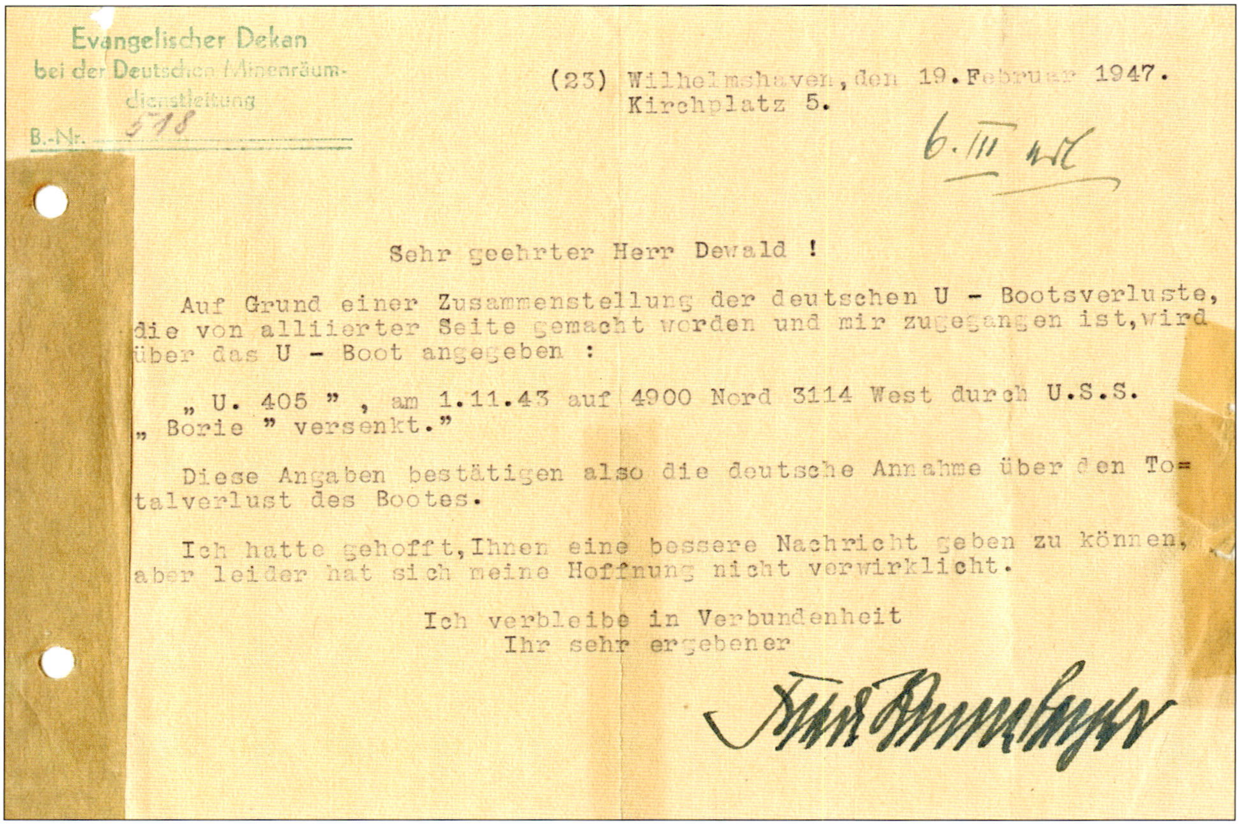

Evangelischer Dekan
bei der Deutschen Minenräum-
dienstleitung
B.-Nr. 518

(23) Wilhelmshaven, den 19. Februar 1947.
Kirchplatz 5.

6. III 47

Sehr geehrter Herr Dewald !

Auf Grund einer Zusammenstellung der deutschen U - Bootsverluste, die von alliierter Seite gemacht worden und mir zugegangen ist, wird über das U - Boot angegeben :

„ U. 405 " , am 1.11.43 auf 4900 Nord 3114 West durch U.S.S. „ Borie " versenkt."

Diese Angaben bestätigen also die deutsche Annahme über den Totalverlust des Bootes.

Ich hatte gehofft, Ihnen eine bessere Nachricht geben zu können, aber leider hat sich meine Hoffnung nicht verwirklicht.

Ich verbleibe in Verbundenheit
Ihr sehr ergebener

Opposite
Letter of Explanation concerning Oberleutnant (Ing) Eberhard Dewald, Chief Engineer of the U-405 to the fallen officer's father. *Letter is dated February 19, 1947 and is from the Protestant deacon for the post-war German Navy de-mining organization. It states that the U-405 was sunk by the USS Borie on November 1, 1943.*

Studio photo of Günther Koch in 1943.

Wartime photo of Oberleutnant (Ing) Eberhard Dewald, Chief Engineer, U-405.

Photo of the brothers Dewald. *Eberhard Dewald (left) is a Kriegsmarine engineer cadet; (right) is his brother Hartwig, who appears to be in the Army's 14th Infantry Regiment.*

Chief Engineer Erich Zürn with his Knight's Cross. *Photo is signed by Zürn and dated April 23, 1941, the day Dönitz presented Zürn with the award.*

Chief Engineer on the U-94.

CHAPTER TWENTY-FOUR

"MILK COW" U-219 1944-1945

The *U-219* was not one of the typical lean gray wolves of Dönitz's attack boats. Compared to a Type VIIC boat, the U-219 was a fat pig, or more accurately, a milk cow. A Type XB U-boat, a category designed in 1938, it could carry up to sixty-six SMA mines in thirty mine shafts and up to fifteen torpedoes. The XB class was special in that they only had two torpedo tubes at the stern; the pair was a defensive measure if approached from the rear as the boat was laying mines in enemy waters. As transport boats (nicknamed "milk cows") – which the *U-219* would become – the boats carried freight containers in the mineshafts, preventing their use for mines. At 2,710 tons submerged and fully loaded, they were the largest German U-boats ever built, but they paid a penalty in diving speed and agility, and six of the eight boats built were sunk during the war (five with all hands.) But the *U-219* was not one of them because the *U-219* was commanded by one of the most-experienced U-boat commanders in the German Navy.

Dönitz's Crews
***Mechanikerobergefreiter* Kurt Helber**
Born on November 11, 1923 in Tübingen/Württemberg.
Served on the *U-219*.
Awarded the U-boat War Badge on January 6, 1944 and the U-boat Front Clasp in Bronze on November 9, 1944.
Spent 183 days at sea on U-boat war patrols.
Survived the war; lived in Bexbach/Saarbrücken.

Korvettenkapitän Walter Burghagen was the only commander the crew of the *U-219* would ever know. The submarine was ordered by the German Navy on August 6, 1940, shortly after Germany captured France ensuring that U-boats operating from the western coast of France could operate far into the Atlantic. Krupp's Germania Werft engineers laid her keel at Kiel-Gaarden on May 31, 1941 and she was launched on October 6, 1942. She was commissioned on December 12, 1942 and with Burghagen at the helm immediately joined the 4th U-boat Flotilla at Stettin for an extensive training period that lasted until July 1943. On the first of that month, the *Kriegsmarine* ordered the transfer of the boat to the 12th U-boat Flotilla at Bordeaux, France.

The *U-219* left Kiel under the command of Walter Burghagen on October 5, 1943 and arrived at Kristiansand, Norway on October 7, 1943 after two days. After refueling, the next day the boat departed Kristiansand and arrived at Bergen, Norway on October 9; Burghagen noticed the U-boat had an oil leak that left a visible trace of her presence – the boat also experienced rudder problems. With these first two sailings under their belt, and after flotilla engineers examined the boat, the crew took the *U-219* from Bergen on October 18 for a much longer, and more important, mission.

The previous summer, the *Kriegsmarine* decided to send several U-boats to operate in the Indian Ocean, an area rich in potential U-boat targets and a region lacking adequate Allied resources for convoy protection. Additionally, Dönitz and *Konteradmiral* Hans-Georg von Friedeburg faced other problems in the Far East. German blockade runners, which had previously transported critical strategic war materials between Germany and Japan, had almost ceased to exist by mid-1943. The B.d.U. was convinced, however, that larger transport Type XB and Type XIV U-boats could pick up the slack and assume the mission of transporting vital goods. They thus developed a plan to send long-range combat submarines and these special transport boats through the Indian Ocean to Japanese territory.

The first packet of German submarines departed Germany and France beginning in June 1943. The group, which did not sail together, included the: *U-200*, *U-487*, *U-462*, *U-188*, *U-168*, *U-509*, *U-514*, *U-532*, *U-183*, *U-506*, *U-533*, *U-516* and *U-847*. Four boats (*U-188*, *U-168*, *U-532* and *U-183*) arrived in the Far East at the end of September 1943, after the tropical monsoon rain period. Perhaps in homage to the forces of nature at sea, the group was named "*Monsun*" (Monsoon). Whatever the motivation for the name, the gesture did not help the *U-200*, *U-487*, *U-509*, *U-514*, *U-506*, *U-533* and *U-847*, which were sunk in the attempt to sail east.

Burghagen departed Bergen on October 18 for the Central Atlantic. His orders were for the *U-219* to be in the second wave of *Monsun* U-boats sent to the Orient. This collection consisted of the: *U-219*, *U-848*, *U-849*, *U-510*, *U-850* and *U-172*. Enroute, Burghagen was to lay mines off Cape Town, South Africa and Colombo, Ceylon. First, however, the *U-219* refueled and re-supplied the *U-91* (November 6), *U-170* (November 29), *U-510* (November 30), and the *U-103* (December 3). On December 11, 1943 the *U-219* was ordered to rendezvous with the *U-172* southwest of the Canary Islands in the South Atlantic (which she did), but Allied intelligence picked up the signals and deciphered them. Grumman TBM Avenger torpedo-bombers of Composite Squadron VC-19 from the escort carrier *USS Bogue* later found and damaged the *U-172*.

On December 13, the *Bogue's* aircraft and destroyers *USS George E. Badger* (Lt. E.M. Higgens), *USS Clemson* (Lt. Cdr. E. W. Yancey), *USS Osmond Ingram* (Lt.Cdr. R.F. Miller) and *USS DuPont* (Cdr. J.G. Marshall) sank the stricken *U-172* with a Fido acoustic homing torpedo and depth charges. Thirteen men on the *U-172* died; the destroyers rescued forty-six others, including the commander *Oberleutnant zur See* Hermann Hoffmann. The U-boat put up a fight, however, and on surfacing for the final time got into a gun battle with the American ships to include Hoffmann himself manning and firing a machinegun, while his crew abandoned ship. The Americans searched for Burghagen's *U-219* for two more days, but the crafty Burghagen shook off his pursuers. The B.d.U. then changed the U-boat's orders and she was recalled to Bordeaux and arrived at U-boat Bunker 3a there on January 1, 1944. During this part of her mission the *U-219* had sailed 6,250 sea-miles on the surface and 1,867 sea-miles under water, indicative of the serious Allied attempts to sink the U-boat.

Konteradmiral Eberhard Godt, the Chief, Operations Section at B.d.U., made the following remark in an addendum to the war diary:

> "The commandant accomplished the task assigned to him with adroitness and excellent adaptability in completely new circumstances for him in the Atlantic."

Mechanikerobergefreiter Kurt Helber, a member of the crew, received the U-boat War Badge on January 6, 1944. Born on November 11, 1923 in the university town of Tübingen, twenty miles southeast of Stuttgart, Helber was not a university type; he liked to work with his hands and was good at visualizing mechanical tasks. He would stay with the *U-219* for the remainder of the war, lending a hand to all mechanical tasks a special boat such as the *U-219* would encounter. The *U-219* then underwent a very lengthy conversion process. Originally designed as a minelayer, at Bordeaux engineers worked to permanently convert the *U-219* to a transport submarine. They additionally fitted the *U-219* with a snorkel so she could proceed underwater using her diesel engines. Cognizant of the overwhelming negative effects of Allied aircraft, dockworkers added a quadruple-mounted 20-mm "Flakvierling" anti-aircraft gun to replace a pair of single-mount 20-mm anti-aircraft guns. This weapon would complement her 37-mm flak gun. During this period the crew went on leave, returned, and continued training at the base including physical training competitions under the watchful eye of Walter Burghagen.

Burghagen was "ancient" by U-boat standards. Born on September 21, 1891 in Dresden, he entered the Navy in 1911 at roughly the same time as the commander of all the U-boats Karl Dönitz. Burghagen initially trained as a telegraph officer and served in this capacity on the battleship *SMS Schlesien* until March 1916. He then underwent U-boat training before becoming a watch officer for the *U-44*, *U-49* and *U-50*. While on the *U-50*, Burghagen was taken prisoner by the British and spent the remainder of the war in England. During the beginning of World War II Burghagen served as a training company commander in the 1st U-boat Training Division and the 2nd U-boat Training Division before coming to the *U-219* at age fifty-one, the oldest active submariner in the German U-boat force.

As modifications were completed, the commander oversaw the loading of supplies aboard the *U-219*. Her mine-chutes had been filled with twenty-four pressurized containers that held a wide variety of supplies. The *U-219* carried an entire radio transmitting station destined for Kobe, Japan. To Penang, Malaya the boat carried diesel engine spare parts and torpedo balancing parts. The craft also was loaded with spare parts for Arado 196 aircraft and hospital supplies and equipment for the German communications station at Singapore. The more exotic cargo included uncut optical glass, crated aluminum bars and mercury stored in the boat's keel. One post-war report indicates that the *U-219* also carried key components for the V-2 rocket for Japan as well.

Ever looking to foresee possible problems, Burghagen ordered the boat to conduct diving and trim tests at La Pallice in April 1944 with this full load. The test almost destroyed the boat; according to the 1st Watch Officer she "sank like a stone" when attempting to submerge. The 12th U-boat Flotilla Chief Engineer was aboard, however, and managed to float her after five hours of trying one potential remedy after another. Burghagen reloaded the U-boat's freight and provisions based on the test.

With Allied ground forces closing in on several German U-boat bases in western France, on August 23, 1944 the *U-219*, still under command of Walter Burghagen, departed Bordeaux bound for Penang, Malaya as part of the second wave of Monsoon boats to head east. British Sunderland and Mosquito aircraft immediately attacked but the U-boat's new anti-aircraft armament drove off the Allied planes. Once free of the coastline, the boat employed the snorkel to proceed submerged, but in mid-September the snorkel raising-gear malfunctioned and the device was rendered non-operational until the engineers on board made makeshift repairs. Burghagen received orders to refuel *Oberleutnant zur See* Karl Albrecht's *U-1062*, Type VIIF in-bound from Penang with 105 tons of strategic supplies for Germany, after herself delivering thirty-nine torpedoes to supply *Group Monsoon*.

Much like the previous December, Allied code-breakers deciphered the Enigma coded traffic, which set up the rendezvous at 11°51'N, 34°45'W in the South Atlantic. At 7:40 p.m. on September 28, 1944 a radar-equipped TBF Avenger of Composite Squadron VC-6 from the escort carrier *USS Tripoli* piloted by Lt. William R. Gillespie reported contact with a surfaced U-boat. Gillespie delivered a low-level rocket attack, but the U-boat's quad 20-mm anti-aircraft guns shot him down. Another Avenger, piloted by Lt. (j.g.) Joseph W. Steere, swooped in and fired eight rockets at the *U-219*, while Lt. (j.g.) Douglas R. Hagwood's Grumman FM-2 Wildcat fighter strafed the U-boat. Steere made another pass and dropped another Mark 24 Fido acoustic homing torpedo and sonobuoys. Burghagen escaped the attack unscathed. However, two days later the *U-1062* was sunk by depth charges from the destroyer escort *USS Fessenden* (Lt.Cdr. W.A. Dobby) southwest of the Cape Verde Islands. All fifty-five men aboard the *U-1062* perished.

The *U-219* attempted to send a report of the air attacks, but was attacked again on October 2 by Allied air and surface forces; for the next three days depth charges, bombs and more Fidos attempted to sink the boat, but the wily Burghagen located a salinity layer upon which the *U-219* could drift with motors turned off – in silence and using the absolute minimum of battery power. The U-boat thus remained submerged for sixty-nine consecutive hours, drifting 120 miles in the current, until she had to surface because of the toxic level of carbon dioxide built-up in the boat. Proving it is better to be lucky than good, Burghagen surfaced in the midst of a sandstorm blowing out of Africa; the harsh conditions prevented Allied anti-submarine forces from regaining radar contact of the *U-219*.

Burghagen continued his mission. With the 12th U-boat Flotilla now disbanded – and its commander *Korvettenkapitän* Klaus Scholtz an American prisoner of war – the *U-219* was administratively reassigned to the 33rd U-boat Flotilla under *Korvettenkapitän* Günter Kuhnke based at Flensburg, Germany. On November 24, 1944 the *U-219* successfully refueled the Type IXC *U-510* west of the Cape Verde Islands and provided radar parts to the *U-181*.

Meanwhile Allied air attacks over the Malay Peninsula rendered Penang untenable as an operational base for submarines. The German U-boats at the base withdrew to Batavia (now Jakarta), Java (now Indonesia) and the Japanese I-boats relocated to Surabaya, Java. The attacks did not stop the *U-219*, which arrived at Tanjong Priok (Batavia's harbor) – the new *Monsoon* U-boat flotilla's base of operations – on December 12, 1944 and her crew began unloading supplies destined for the Japanese. The unloading ended just in time as on December 26, 1944 the 1,135-ton Japanese ammunition ship *Taicho Maru* suddenly – and mysteriously – exploded, wrecking the harbor's facilities and slightly damaging the nearby *U-219*. Life at the base was not a picnic for the U-boat crews. The 1st Watch Officer of the *U-219* recalled that Japanese food did not agree with the U-boat men, who were very distrustful of their Japanese hosts; the uneasiness was also felt by the Japanese toward these European sailors. *Matrosengefreiten* Heinz Engels and Willi Hussong, the U-boat's cooks, had to make do with the change in foodstuffs.

On May 5, 1945, the German naval attaché to Japan sent the code-word signal "Lübeck" to all U-boats in Asia. This signified that Germany had ceased hostilities. At Batavia, *Korvettenkapitän* Hermann Kandeler, commander of the *Kriegsmarine*'s U-boat base, announced to German military personnel that Hitler had died and that Germany had ceased hostilities in the West, but was continuing to resist Soviet forces overrunning Berlin. The *U-219*, ready to return to Europe with a cargo of raw rubber, tin and other war materials, departed Batavia for Surabaya under *Korvettenkapitän* Burghagen and his crew with some Japanese aboard. By agreement between the two countries, the *U-219*, as well as the other *Monsoon* boats, would be turned over to the Japanese. The crew hauled down the German colors; the Japanese raised the Imperial flag and the transfer was complete. At Surabaya the *U-219* was overhauled by the Imperial Japanese Navy's 102nd Repair Unit and commissioned as the *I-505*.

The "new" Japanese asset was assigned to the 2nd Southern Expeditionary Fleet, but no Japanese crew was ever designated because of a lack of submarine personnel in the organization. As a result, she never left her moorings and in September 1945 the *I-505* was surrendered to the British. In February 1946 the British scuttled the *U-219/I-505* off the Sundra Strait at 6°31'S, 104°54'E.

Meanwhile, the *U-219*'s German crew moved to an internment camp – referred to as the "U-Boot Weide" (U-boat Meadow) – at Tjikopo – twenty-five miles south of Jakarta – where they spent the remainder of 1945 before being repatriated to Germany. Walter Burghagen, the old man who led his boat and crew to safety from the Baltic Sea to the Indian Ocean, died in 1971. Kurt Helber also survived and finally settled in the town of Bexbach near Saarbrücken.

Known Crewmembers for the U-219

Assmann, Karl-Heinz	*Leutnant (Ing)*
Awater, Willy	
Bauditz, Lothar	*Leutnant (Ing)*
Bobermien, Martin	*Mechanikergefreiter*
Böhm, Heinz	*Bootsmannsmaat*
Böhm, Heinz	*Obermaschinist*
Böttcher, Heinz	*Oberleutnant (Ing)*
Bürger, Karl	*Maschinenmaat*
Burghagen, Walter	*Korvettenkapitän*
Cords, Hermann	
Cornelsen, Walter	*Obermaschinist*
Dehnrat, Johannes	*Maschinist*
Dietrich, Erich	*Oberbootsmannsmaat*
Duddeck, Horst	*Leutnant (Ing)*
Duerre, Reinhold	*Mechanikergefreiter*
Engels, Heinz	*Matrosengefreiter* (cook)
Felde, Max-Reinhard	*Leutnant zur See*
Feulner, Berthold	*Matrosenobergefreiter*
Gieler, Heinz	*Maschinenmaat*
Haake, Helmut	*Leutnant zur See*
Hahm, Gerhard	*Mechanikergefreiter*
Hastedt, Willi	
Hausberger, Hannes	*Matrose*
Helber, Kurt	*Mechanikerobergefreiter*
Hertel, Kurt	*Maschinenmaat*
Hilgert, Kurt	*Maschinenobergefreiter*
Hinzpeter, Ludwig	*Funkmaat*
Hoffmann, Karl-Heinz	*Maschinenobergefreiter*
Hoppe, Heinz	*Matrosenobergefreiter*
Hussong, Willi	*Matrosengefreiter* (cook)
Klein, Paul	*Maschinenobergefreiter*
Kloh, Heinz	*Matrosengefreiter*
Klump, Franz	*Obersteuermann*
Knaak, Lothar	*Matrosenobergefreiter*
Knopf, Willi	*Matrose*
Knust, Herbert	*Maschinenmaat*
Koch, Werner	*Maschinenmaat*
Kopetzki, Heinz	*Maschinenmaat*
Krause, Alfred	
Kreienbrink, Ernst	*Obermaschinenmaat*
Kreisel, Alois	
Kronacker, Rudolf	*Funkmaat*
Krug, Hans-Joachim	*Oberleutnant zur See*
Kunz, Johannes	*Obersteuermann*
Leistner, Johannes	*Bootsmannsmaat*
Leitsmann, Max	
Loesche, Hans	*Maschinengefreiter*
Loetzen, Kurt	*Matrose*
Lüdke, Paul	*Obermaschinist*
Lukas, Erich	*Funkgefreiter*
Meier, Gottfried	*Bootsmannsmaat*
Mellow, Heinz	*Matrosenobergefreiter*
Meyer, Karl-Heinz	*Maschinenmaat*
Müller, Heinrich	*Maschinenobergefreiter*
Naumann, Fritz	*Maschinenobergefreiter*
Neumeier, Kurt	*Funkgefreiter*
Oelerich, Werner	*Bootsmannsmaat*
Reiners, Helmut	*Maschinist*
Rinkel, Willi	*Maschinenobergefreiter*
Rudzio, Siegfried	*Funkmaat*
Ruehling, Kurt	

Sammer, Ferdinand	*Maschinenmaat*
Sandmann, Heinz	*Matrosenobergefreiter*
Schmuchel, Dr. Günther	*Arzt*
Schomaker, Hermann	
Schottstädt, Helmut	*Maschinenmaat*
Schrein, Herbert	*Kapitänleutnant*
Senftleben, Franz	*Matrosenobergefreiter*
Senker, Walter	*Maschinengefreiter*
Sickel, Hans	*Maschinenobergefreiter*
Slarek, Heinrich	
Sparfeld, Heinz	*Matrosenhauptgefreiter*
Spiwoks, Erich	
Steigleder, Albrecht	*Arzt* (Doctor)
Stöhr, Cornelius	*Leutnant zur See*
Tessner, Hans	*Maschinist*
Thiedemann, Kurt	
Trevisany, Peter	*Maschinist*
Wetzstein, Alfred	
Wycisk, Max	*Maschinenmaat*
Zink, Wilhelm	

Sources, "Milk Cow:" Rainer Busch and Hans-Joachim Röll, *German U-boat Commanders of World War II*, translated by Geoffrey Brooks, Annapolis, Maryland: Naval Institute Press, 1999, 44, 45, 106; Manfred Dörr, *Die Ritterkreuzträger der U-Boot-Waffe, Band 1: A-J, Band 2: L-Z,* Osnabrück, FRG: Biblio Verlag, 1988, Band 1 – 290, 300, Band 2 – 47, 243, 244; Axel Niestlé, *German U-boat Losses during World War II*, Annapolis, Maryland: Naval Institute Press, 1998, 117, 124, 144; Lawrence Paterson, *Hitler's Grey Wolves: U-boats in the Indian Ocean*, London: Greenhill Books, 2004, 91, 138, 148, 149, 212, 220, 240-245, 260, 261, 269-271; Herbert Ritschel, *Kurzfassung Kriegstagebücher deutscher U-boote 1939-1945, Band 3: KTB U171 – U222,* Norderstedt, Germany: Books on Demand, 343, 344, 345, 346, 347; War Diary of the U-219, October 5, 1943 – January 1, 1944, PG 30207; ONI Roll T-94-E, *National Archives Microfilm Publication T1022,* roll 2837, RG 242; Captain James E. Wise, Jr., *Sole Survivors of the Sea*, Baltimore, Maryland: The Nautical & Aviation Publishing Company of America, 1994, 127; www.ubootwaffe.net; www.uboatarchive.net.

Verleihungs-Urkunde

Auf Grund der Ermächtigung des Oberbefehlshabers der Kriegsmarine verleihe ich dem

Mechanikerobergefreiten
(Dienstgrad)

Kurt H e l b e r
(Name)

das

Ubootskriegsabzeichen 1939

Im Westen, den 6. Januar 1944

Kapitän zur See
und Führer der Unterseeboote West

(MS 37108)

U-boat War Badge award document to Kurt Helber of the U-219, January 6, 1944, awarded after the boat arrived at Bordeaux on January 1, 1944. *The document has a facsimile signature of Kapitän zur See Hans-Rudolf Rösing. Kurt Helber was twenty-one years old when he received this award.*

URKUNDE

Der Mech. Ob. Gfr. Helber U 219

errang im Schwimmen – 100 m Brust –

mit der Leiſtung von 1/32/8

den 1. Preis

Jm Westen, den 25. 6. 1944

Korv. Kapt. u. Flott.-Chef

12th **U-boat Flotilla breaststroke competition award document to Kurt Helber at Bordeaux, June 25, 1944.** *The document has a facsimile signature of Korvettenkapitän Klaus Scholtz, commander of the 12th U-boat Flotilla. Helber won the 100-meter breaststroke.*

VERLEIHUNGS-URKUNDE

Auf Grund der Ermächtigung des Oberbefehlshabers der Kriegsmarine verleihe ich dem

Mechanikerobergefreiten

Kurt H e l b e r

die

U-Boots-Frontspange

in Bronze

Plön / Holst. , den 9. Nov. 1944

Kapitän zur See
und Höherer Kommandeur der
Unterseebootsausbildung

U-boat Front Clasp in Bronze award document to Kurt Helber of the U-219, November 9, 1944. *The document is signed by Kapitän zur See Albrecht Schmidt, High Command for U-boat Training.*

Matrosenobergefreiter Kurt Helber. *Photo taken at Tübingen.*

Kurt Helber in tropical uniform. *He wears the U-boat War Badge.*

CHAPTER TWENTY-FIVE

"A Democracy Under the Sea" U-518 1942-1945

Karl Dönitz understood to his core that the U-boat war was extremely difficult on his crews, and from the mid-1930s – when he became the U-boat chief – he implemented many practices of democracy in every-day crew functioning. On a grand scale, this was seen in 1943 – after the disastrous month of May – in his questioning of continuing the U-boat war by putting the measure to a vote by the thousands of U-boat crewmembers under his command. But democracy also came in little steps. Prior to departing on patrol, most crews decided what meals they desired to eat (limited, of course, as to the skill of the boat's cook!) and the quartermaster duly procured the desired victuals from *Kriegsmarine* stores. But the crew's decision-making opportunities did not end with food selection – in some cases they deemed their officers or commanders unfit to lead and had a democratic mechanism to get them replaced. This situation happened on the *U-518*.

Ordered by the German Navy on February 14, 1940, the *U-518*'s keel was laid on June 12, 1941 at the Deutsche Werft AG shipyards at Hamburg-Finkenwärder. Construction took seven months; on February 11, 1942 the U-boat was launched; after a two-month work-up, she was commissioned on April 25, 1942. *Fregattenkapitän* Hans-Günther Brachmann was her first commander and it was at this point that the trouble began.

Brachmann was an old sailor in U-boat terms. Born on February 11, 1914 in Kiel, he entered the post-World War I *Reichsmarine* in 1922 and served in the surface fleet for nineteen years. During this time Brachmann spent nineteen months as the 2nd Gunnery Officer on the battlecruiser *Gneisenau* and subsequently the 1st Gunnery Officer of the light cruiser *Köln* from December 1939 to April 1941. At that point in his career – and for reasons unknown – Brachmann began U-boat training, which lasted for five months before he joined the *U-518* in her pre-launch construction phase.

The summer following her commissioning, the *U-518* and her crew was undergoing her pre-frontline service training, a period that was quite stressful for all concerned. Brachmann was a gunnery officer by trade and gunnery training centered on precise mathematical formulas with no room for improvisation. To the crew the new commander was "too old" and "too strange." Concerning age, the crew noted that during stressful training situations the commander decided to retire to his small quarters and take a nap, leaving decisions to be made by others. He often gave crazy answers to questions; once when informed by the bridge watch that the moon had risen, Brachmann responded with the question "Why?" Concerning food provisions, Brachmann demonstrated he did not understand the selection process. The crew, for example, asked the quartermaster to bring fresh vegetables on board, such as celery, but the commander said that this food would only cause unwanted sexual urges and countermanded the request.

Something clearly had to be done before the boat and crew made their first war patrol, and a delegation of the U-boat's officers and chief petty officers reported to the 4th U-boat Training Flotilla headquarters at Stettin and requested a change in command. The issue was a serious one and would have gone to the flotilla commander *Korvettenkapitän* Heinz Fischer for a decision. Fischer was an "Old Guard" U-boat man, having served in the submarines since 1935. He must have agreed with the *U-518*'s leaders; but replacing a commander was a serious decision and Fischer obtained an interview for the crew delegation with *Konteradmiral* Hans-Georg von Friedeburg in Kiel. Friedeburg agreed with the crew and by the time they returned to their boat, Brachmann had been reassigned, ultimately becoming the commander of the 1st Naval Gunnery School from 1943 to the end of the war.

In his place, B.d.U. assigned *Oberleutnant zur See* Friedrich Wissmann to be the new commander of the *U-518*. Wissmann had served as the 1st Watch Officer on the *U-109* from September 1941 to February 1942, learning his craft under Heinrich Bleichrodt and participating in the "Operation Drumbeat" attack on the coastal United States shipping lanes. The experienced (and decorated) Bleichrodt saw potential leadership qualities in Wissmann and recommended he attend U-boat commander's school, which he did in March 1942. Friedrich Wissmann was affectionately nicknamed by some as "Smart Guy" (a play on words of his last name "Wissmännchen"). He would need every bit of his craftiness in dealing with his unusual crew in the *U-518* and in the wide variety of missions he would undertake over the next several years.

Dönitz's Crews
***Mechanikerobergefreiter* Hans Schillinger**
Born on July 13, 1921 in Mannheim/Baden.
Served on the *U-518* as a torpedo man.
Awarded the U-boat War Badge on December 19, 1942.
Survived the war.

One of the members of the crew was *Mechanikerobergefreiter* Hans Schillinger. A toolmaker by trade, Schillinger was born in the large city of Mannheim, at the confluence of the rivers Rhine and Neckar, on July 13, 1921. He entered the *Kriegsmarine* in 1940 and soon thereafter went to torpedo school at Flensburg. On conclusion of this training, Schillinger reported to Hamburg and assignment to the *U-518*; he would be one of the lucky sailors who had the privilege of trying to sling a hammock in the overcrowded forward torpedo room!

As the tumult aboard the *U-518* began to subside, the war continued. Admiral Dönitz, quite incorrectly as it turned out, was convinced that the Canadian Strait of Belle Isle between Labrador and the northern tip of Newfoundland formed a major entry point into the Atlantic for shipping. As a result, he ordered the *U-518* to transport a covert agent to the area who could monitor and report on Allied shipping traffic back to Germany. In Germany Werner Alfred Waldmar von Janowski, a German citizen who had previously lived in Canada, was selected to be the agent and on September 26, 1942 the *U-518* – with von Janowski aboard – departed Kiel for her first war patrol. Wissmann and the *U-518* – now assigned to the 2nd U-boat Flotilla – initially made for Christiansand, Norway, where the U-boat topped off with water and fuel. On September 28 she left Norway and negotiated the Iceland Passage north of the Faeroes. By October 18 the U-boat reached her initial operational area some sixty miles northeast of Belle Isle. The U-boat remained in this location for ten days but saw no targets of opportunity so Wissmann headed southeast to sail around Newfoundland on the Atlantic side. On November 2, 1942 he conducted a surface torpedo attack at the Wabana anchorage in Conception Bay (near St. Johns) and sank the Canadian freighter *Rose Castle* at 7:03 a.m. (killing twenty-four and sending 10,200 tons of iron ore to the bottom) and three minutes later the British ore carrier *PLM-27*, killing twelve.

The *U-518* also damaged the *Flyingdale* when a torpedo struck the dock where the ship was moored. The attack brought a subsequent Canadian aerial attack forty miles east of Cape Race; the U-boat's lookouts spotted the Canadian bomber at the last instant and Wissmann ordered an emergency dive. Luck was with the boat and the four 250-pound depth charges landed in the swirl of the U-boat's dive, probably just a few feet away from being close enough for a killing blow.

On November 9, Wissmann entered the Baie des Chaleurs and landed the agent near the beach resort of New Carlisle, which was closed for the winter. Unable to blend in with tourists, smelling of "u-boat stink" and attempting to pay for a hotel room with outdated Canadian currency, von Janowski raised suspicions and was apprehended within two days. On November 21, 1942, Hans Schillinger's torpedoes struck three more targets. At 4:16 a.m. the *U-518* damaged two ships, the British 6,997-ton *British Renown* enroute from Liverpool to Curacao, and the British 8,443-ton *British Promise*, heading from Liverpool to New York. Both ships were part of convoy ON-145 and both were sailing in ballast. Just a few minutes later at 4:23 a.m. a torpedo from the *U-518* slammed into the British 6,140-ton *Empire Sailor*, also sailing with convoy ON-145, some two-hundred miles east of Sable Island. The *Empire Sailor* was carrying 2,700 tons general cargo. But much of her cargo was top secret; it included 270 tons of phosgene rocket shells and 26 tons of mustard gas in 68 drums that the British were moving out of Great Britain to preclude any inadvertent release of the lethal chemical weapons should any of the storage sites be struck by *Luftwaffe* air attacks. Three of the crew drowned during the attack, but sixty men were rescued by Canadian corvette *HMCS Timmins* and the Canadian minesweeper *HMCS Minas*. But the crew was not "out of the water" yet; subsequently twenty of the rescued men died as a direct result of inhaling escaping phosgene gas from the rocket shells whose casings had been pierced when the U-boat's torpedo struck them deep in the ship's Number 4 hold.

However, the convoy's escorts were equipped with new forward-throwing Hedgehog mortars that fired barrages of explosive bomblets that exploded on contact with a submarine's hull. At least one scored a direct hit and seriously damaged the *U-518* which was forced to begin her return to port. On November 23, 1942 at 6:36 a.m. Wissmann sank one additional ship, the American 10,172-ton tanker *Caddo* bound from Key West, Florida to Reykjavik, Iceland; fifty-two men perished in the attack. The *U-518* arrived at Lorient, France on December 15, 1942. As a result of his outstanding performance in the torpedo room, *Mechanikerobergefreiter* Hans Schillinger received the U-boat War Badge on December 19, 1942.

The war continued and on January 11, 1943 the *U-518* departed Lorient bound for the South Atlantic and the coast of Brazil. On February 8, 1943, the U-boat crossed the Equator and Hans Schillinger and all other novices to the milestone went through an "appropriate" initiation and received an Equator "Certificate of Baptism" from none other than King Neptune. Those formalities completed, the U-boat's crew got down to more lethal business. On February 14, 1943 an unidentified enemy aircraft attacked the U-boat, but caused no damage. Over the next five weeks it was the *U-518*'s turn to inflict damage and this she did:

- On February 18, 1943 at 3:15 a.m., the *U-518* torpedoed and sank the Brazilian 6,075-ton *Brasiloide* carrying general cargo from Maceio to Bahia, Brazil, off the Brazilian coast; ninety-four men died in the explosion that broke the freighter in two.
- At 2:00 p.m. on March 1, 1943, the *U-518* sank the American 7,176-ton freighter *Fitz-John Porter*, from convoy BT-6. The ship was in ballast and sailing from Bahia to the United States. The *U-518* had previously experienced six missed shots and eight dud torpedoes in her attacks against the convoy.
- On March 20, 1943 at 5:10 a.m., the *U-518* sank the Dutch 7,659-ton *Mariso* with three torpedoes, killing two men. The ship was carrying general cargo from Trinidad to Durban, South Africa when she sank off the Brazilian coast.
- On March 25, 1943, Wissmann hit the Swedish 1,688-ton freighter *Industria* carrying general cargo from Philadelphia, Pennsylvania to Rio de Janeiro, Brazil; the attack off the Brazilian coast killed one man.

His torpedoes expended, most to misses and malfunctions, "Smart Guy" Wissmann returned to port on April 27, 1943 a sadder but wiser commander; no doubt torpedo man Hans Schillinger received an earful of comments due to the poor performance of his torpedoes! He did prove his versatility, however, during the return trip. On April 5, 1943, the *U-167* was badly damaged by an air attack and her skipper scuttled the U-boat in shallow water in the Canary Islands. The crew made it to shore and after negotiations with Spanish authorities for the islands, departed Las Palmas on a tugboat to rendezvous with the offshore *U-455* to arrange for a return to Germany for the men of the stranded *U-167*. However, the fifty men from the *U-167* were too many for one other U-boat to transport and the *U-455* contacted two other U-boats for assistance. Wissmann, who had just refueled from the *U-117*, took about fifteen men from the *U-167* aboard and transported his newly reinforced crew to Lorient.

Dönitz's Crews
***Oberfunkmaat* Walter Wittig**
Born on October 15, 1920 in Greifswald, Mecklenburg.
Volunteered to join the Navy in 1938.
Served on the *U-518* as a radio operator.
Awarded the U-boat War Badge, Iron Cross 2nd and 1st Class, German Cross in Gold, U-boat Clasp in Bronze and the U-boat Clasp in Silver.
Spent 523 days at sea on U-boat war patrols.
Survived the war; lived in Cuxhaven.

Also on the boat was Walter Wittig, a radio operator. Wittig, who was born in Greifswald on October 15, 1920, volunteered to join the Navy in 1938 where he believed he could get technical training for a later civilian occupation. But the Navy would have to wait as Wittig was placed in the Reich Labor Service (Reichsarbeitsdienst) and served in that organization until October 1939 (and actually supported the Army in the Polish Campaign of that year). He got his wish to enlist in the Navy, first becoming a member of the minesweeper *Diana*, which would later patrol the area around Copenhagen for British-laid sea mines. Wittig joined the *U-518* during her construction phase after undergoing U-boat training.

For almost two months the *U-518* remained in port, undergoing refit and allowing the crew to take a well-deserved leave. The *U-518* departed Lorient on June 24, 1943, but soon thereafter disaster struck. On June 27, 1943, in the Bay of Biscay, a British Sunderland aircraft of the RAF's 201st Squadron (piloted by Flight Officer Brian E.H. Layne, RNZAF) attacked the U-boat, badly damaging her and wounding several men. Wissmann made the decision to return to port. The boat was damaged so badly that it had to return to base, but at 11:05 a.m. on June 30 an Australian Sunderland aircraft from the RAAF's 10th Squadron (Flight Lieutenant H.W. Skinner) attacked the U-boat again. The five depth charges missed, and the U-boat's flak fire was so accurate that it badly damaged the wings and rear part of the Sunderland, mortally wounding the rear gunner. The *U-518* limped into Bordeaux on July 3, 1943.

After forty-six days of repair, during which time the U-boat's crew apparently painted the town of Bordeaux red, Wissmann departed France on August 18, 1943 for the Gulf of Mexico. Wissmann patrolled in the area to the Yucatan Channel but sank no enemy ships during his 106-day voyage and returned to Lorient empty-handed on December 1, 1943. This was too much (or more accurately, too little) for B.d.U., and Friedrich Wissmann left command to become a training officer in the 2nd U-boat Flotilla. He survived the war, dying on September 9, 1963. Sometime during this period Hans Schillinger departed the U-boat as well.

Oberleutnant Hans-Werner Offermann joined the *U-518* as her new commander. Born on July 2, 1921 in Offingen, he joined the *Kriegsmarine* in 1939 and had twenty-three months experience as a watch officer on the *U-129*. On January 23, 1944, the *U-518* and her new skipper left Lorient for the U-boat's fifth war patrol. In addition to her regular counter-shipping mission, the *U-518* carried an additional navigator, Naxos radar warning equipment and several Naxos operators for another special mission. Offermann was to rendezvous with the Japanese submarine *I-29* (codenamed "U-Kiefer" or "Pine Tree") and transfer these men and equipment to Germany's ally. Approaching the rendezvous area on February 12, Offermann spotted the American escort carrier *USS Croatan* and fired several torpedoes at his target. He reported three hits, but in actuality all torpedoes missed. After conducting the transfer, the *U-518* headed for the Caribbean, entering through the Mona Passage between the islands of Hispaniola and Puerto Rico.

On March 3, 1944 the *U-518* fired a torpedo at a 4,000-ton freighter but the "eel" missed. At 1:40 a.m. on March 7, 1944, near Aruba off the Colombian coast, the *U-518* torpedoed the Panamanian 3,401-ton tanker *Valera* bound from Aruba to Cristóbal with 35,000 barrels of heavy navy fuel oil. The *U-518* then penetrated the harbor at Colón, Panama; on April 2, Offermann claimed to have sunk a 7,000-ton tanker, but it was never confirmed. The *Valera* was Offermann's only success and the *U-518* returned to Lorient on May 7, 1944. Shipyard workers then fitted the U-boat with a snorkel, while B.d.U. inquired sharply as to why Offermann had failed to sink more targets. The snorkel device enabled U-boats to run on diesel engines even when underwater. A snorkel was quite simple in design; it consisted of a long tube with a valve on one end, which extended above sea level while the boat was submerged. The tube consisted of an intake and exhaust pipe, where outside fresh air was drawn into the U-boat, and poisonous exhaust gases expelled through the exhaust pipe. A safety shutoff valve prevented seawater from entering the intake pipe if the mouth of the tube dipped below the surface. Such a capability gave the *U-518* increased underwater range at a higher speed and also helped the submerged U-boat elude Allied radar.

Offermann departed Lorient on July 4, 1944 for a short test run with the new snorkel and returned to port on July 10. On July 15, the U-boat departed Lorient for the last time for her seventh war patrol; she would hunt for Allied ships in the Caribbean; Offermann changed the location to Cape Hatteras off the coast of North Carolina, when he was informed the *U-518* would finish the patrol in Norway. On August 9, 1944 Allied escort ships attacked a submerged U-boat (which was probably the *U-518*), but Offermann successfully escaped. At 6:14 a.m. on September 12, 1944, the *U-518* damaged the American 7,176-ton *George Ade* headed from Key West, Florida to New York; the ship temporarily survived, but sank the next day in a hurricane. On October 24, 1944 the *U-518* arrived at Kristiansand, Norway having avoided three American hunter-killer groups specifically tracking her in the Atlantic. The following day the *U-518* departed Kristiansand and arrived at Flensburg, Germany four days later.

Hans Schillinger and Walter Wittig departed the boat for other duties; Wittig would attend a non-commissioned officer leadership course. The *U-518* remained in Germany until March 5, 1945 when she sailed from Kiel to Kristiansand. *Oberleutnant zur See* Offermann then departed Kristiansand on March 12, 1945. His last patrol would be to the North Atlantic northwest of the Azore Islands. The war was coming to a close, although exactly how the conflict would come to an end was a mystery to the fifty-six men on the *U-518*. Unfortunately, they would never experience the cessation of hostilities. On April 22, 1945, two American destroyer escorts, the *USS Carter* (LtCdr. F.J. Baker) and *USS Neal A. Scott* (LtCdr. P.D. Holden) located the U-boat and began to depth-charge her. One of the explosive drums found its mark and the explosion crushed the U-boat, killing her entire crew. Hans Schillinger, who became a prisoner of war in August 1944, would finally return to Mannheim, but he would never see his friends from the *U-518* again. Walter

Wittig opened an electrical business after the war, putting his desired technical training to good use. He retired to Cuxhaven and became the leader of the Cuxhaven U-boat Veterans Association, providing a great deal of valuable information to this book

Known Crewmembers for the U-518

Ballert, Rene	*Oberleutnant zur See*
Bennke, Günter-Ernst	*Matrosenobergefreiter*
Benthin, Karl-Dietrich	*Oberleutnant zur See*
Besold, Heinrich	*Oberleutnant zur See*
Bischoff, Goswin	*Leutnant zur See*
Böhm, Karl	*Maschinenmaat*
Bohstedt, Achim	*Oberleutnant zur See*
Brachmann, Hans-Günther	*Kapitän zur See*
Bruckmann, Bruno	*Oberbootsmaat*
Capito, Albert	*Obermaschinist*
David, Ullrich	*Mechanikerobergefreiter*
Dederichs, Adolf	*Mechanikerobergefreiter*
Diefenbach, Martin	*Maschinenmaat*
Diekmann, Heinrich	*Oberleutnant (Ing)*
Dobbratz, Ulrich	Funkmeister
Downar, Helmut	*Maschinenobergefreiter*
Dreiser, Felix	*Maschinengefreiter*
Engler, Heinz	*Maschinenmaat*
Eydeler, Ferdinand	*Maschinenobergefreiter*
Freidel, Alois	*Bootsmaat*
Friedrich, Walter	*Funkhauptgefreiter*
Gawenat, Hans-Egon	*Leutnant zur See*
Gessner, Walter	*Obersteuermann*
Grosser, Walter	*Funkobergefreiter*
Hamann, August	*Obermaschinenmaat*
Heine, Albert	*Obermaschinenmaat*
Hilgers, Johann	*Maschinenobergefreiter*
Hofmeister, Wilhelm	*Matrosenobergefreiter*
Imberg, Albert	*Mechanikermaat*
Kaiser, Heinz	*Funkobergefreiter*
Kaufmann, Johannes	*Matrosenobergefreiter*
Kehm, Robert	*Maschinenobergefreiter*
Kockegei, Albert	*Matrosenobergefreiter*
Kremer, Theodor-Friedrich	*Matrose*
Kronsbein, Rolf-Franz	*Maschinenobergefreiter*
Krull, Siegfried	*Matrose*
Lemke, Paul	*Bootsmaat*
Lemper, Wilhelm	*Maschinenhauptgefreiter*
Lender, Philipp	*Obermaschinist*
Lindner, Alfred	*Matrosenobergefreiter*
Lorenzen, Theodor	*Mechanikergefreiter*
Marschall, Herbert	*Maschinenmaat*
Mühlfeld, Georg	*Maschinenobergefreiter*
Mutz, Josef	*Maschinengefreiter*
Neitzsch, Wilhelm	*Oberleutnant zur See*
Neuert, Heinz	*Maschinenobergefreiter*
Nickel, Fritz	*Oberbootsmaat*
Nuding, Alfred	*Maschinenmaat*
Offermann, Hans-Werner	*Oberleutnant zur See*
Petersen, Peter	*Bootsmaat*
Reichert, Werner	*Matrosenobergefreiter*
Reischl, Ludwig	*Matrosenobergefreiter*
Ridger, Otto	*Oberleutnant zur See*
Rostalski, Rudolf	*Matrosenobergefreiter*
Scherfling, Wolfgang	*Oberleutnant zur See*
Schillinger, Hans	*Mechanikerobergefreiter*
Schmidt, Karl-Heinz	*Matrosenobergefreiter*
Scholz, Hans-Georg	*Obermaschinenmaat*
Schröder, Hans-Joachim	*Oberleutnant zur See*
Seehagen, Rolf	*Mechanikerobergefreiter*
Seehausen, Gerhard	*Kapitänleutnant*
Seipold, Bruno	*Maschinenobergefreiter*
Spiegel, Karl	*Matrosenobergefreiter*
Spring, Ernst	*Funkmaat*
Steinbach, Heinz	*Matrosengefreiter*
Steiner, Roman	*Verwaltungsgefreiter*
Stiller, Günter	*Maschinenobergefreiter*
Taubert, Rudolf	*Obermaschinist*
Tschörch, Heinz	*Sanitätsmaat*
Voll, Hermann	*Obersteuermann*
Weidlich, Paul	*Oberleutnant (Ing)*
Wernz, Gustav	*Maschinenobergefreiter*
Wimmel, Erich	*Matrosenobergefreiter*
Wissmann, Friedrich-Wilhelm	*Kapitänleutnant*
Wittig, Walter	*Oberfunkmaat*
Zwingmann, Werner	*Maschinenmaat*

Sources, "A democracy under the sea:" Clay Blair, *Hitler's U-boat War: The Hunted, 1942-1945*, New York: Modern Library, 2000, 49, 50, 51, 205, 217, 360, 361, 406, 407, 564, 622, 687; Rainer Busch and Hans-Joachim Röll, *German U-boat Commanders of World War II*, translated by Geoffrey Brooks, Annapolis, Maryland: Naval Institute Press, 1999, 38, 68, 192, 272, 273; Michael L. Hadley, *U-boats against Canada: German Submarines in Canadian Waters*, Montreal: McGill-Queen's University Press, 1990, 146, 149, 150, 151, 152, 153, 154, 155, 156, 163, 200; Axel Niestlé, *German U-boat Losses during World War II*, Annapolis, Maryland: Naval Institute Press, 1998, 126; Jürgen Rohwer, *Axis Submarine Successes 1939-1945*, Annapolis, Maryland: Naval Institute Press, 1983, 132, 138, 139, 149, 153, 160, 178, 179, 180, 185; Jak Mallmann Showell, *U-boats at War: Landings on Hostile Shores*, Hersham, England: Ian Allan Publishing, 2000, 37, 41, 95; www.ubootwaffe.net; www.uboatarchive.net; Interview with Walter Wittig, former crewmember on the *U-518* and German Cross in Gold winner at Cuxhaven, Germany on October 21, 2008.

518

Verleihungs-Urkunde

Auf Grund der Ermächtigung des Oberbefehlshabers
der Kriegsmarine verleihe ich dem

Mechanikersobergefreiten (T)
(Dienstgrad)

Hans Schillinger
(Name)

das

Ubootskriegsabzeichen 1939

Im Westen, den 19. Dezember 1942

Kapitän z. See
und Führer der Unterseeboote West

(MS 37108)

U-boat War Badge award document to Hans Schillinger of the U-518. *Document is dated December 19, 1942, awarded three days after the boat arrived at Lorient, France. It has a facsimile signature of Kapitän zur See Hans-Rudolf Rösing.*

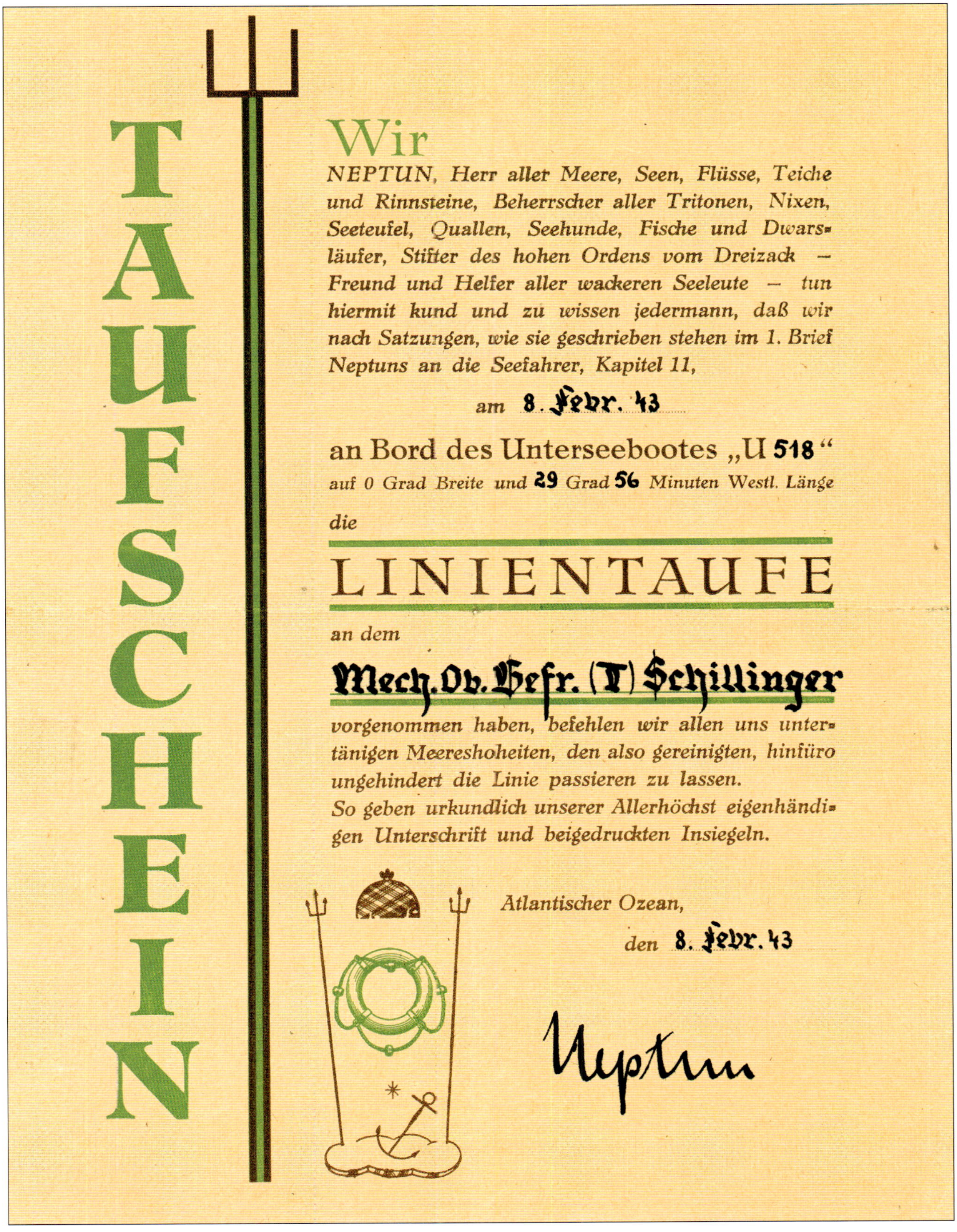

TAUFSCHEIN

Wir

NEPTUN, Herr aller Meere, Seen, Flüsse, Teiche und Rinnsteine, Beherrscher aller Tritonen, Nixen, Seeteufel, Quallen, Seehunde, Fische und Dwarsläufer, Stifter des hohen Ordens vom Dreizack – Freund und Helfer aller wackeren Seeleute – tun hiermit kund und zu wissen jedermann, daß wir nach Satzungen, wie sie geschrieben stehen im 1. Brief Neptuns an die Seefahrer, Kapitel 11,

am 8. Febr. 43

an Bord des Unterseebootes „U 518"

auf 0 Grad Breite und 29 Grad 56 Minuten Westl. Länge

die

LINIENTAUFE

an dem

Mech. Ob. Gefr. (T) Schillinger

vorgenommen haben, befehlen wir allen uns untertänigen Meereshoheiten, den also gereinigten, hinfüro ungehindert die Linie passieren zu lassen.
So geben urkundlich unserer Allerhöchst eigenhändigen Unterschrift und beigedruckten Insiegeln.

Atlantischer Ozean,

den 8. Febr. 43

Neptun

"Certificate of Baptism" document for Hans Schillinger, U-518, February 8, 1943. *These documents were awarded to crewmen who were crossing the Equator for the first time. If conditions permitted, the crew conducted an elaborate ceremony headed by one sailor dressed as Neptune, the sea god.*

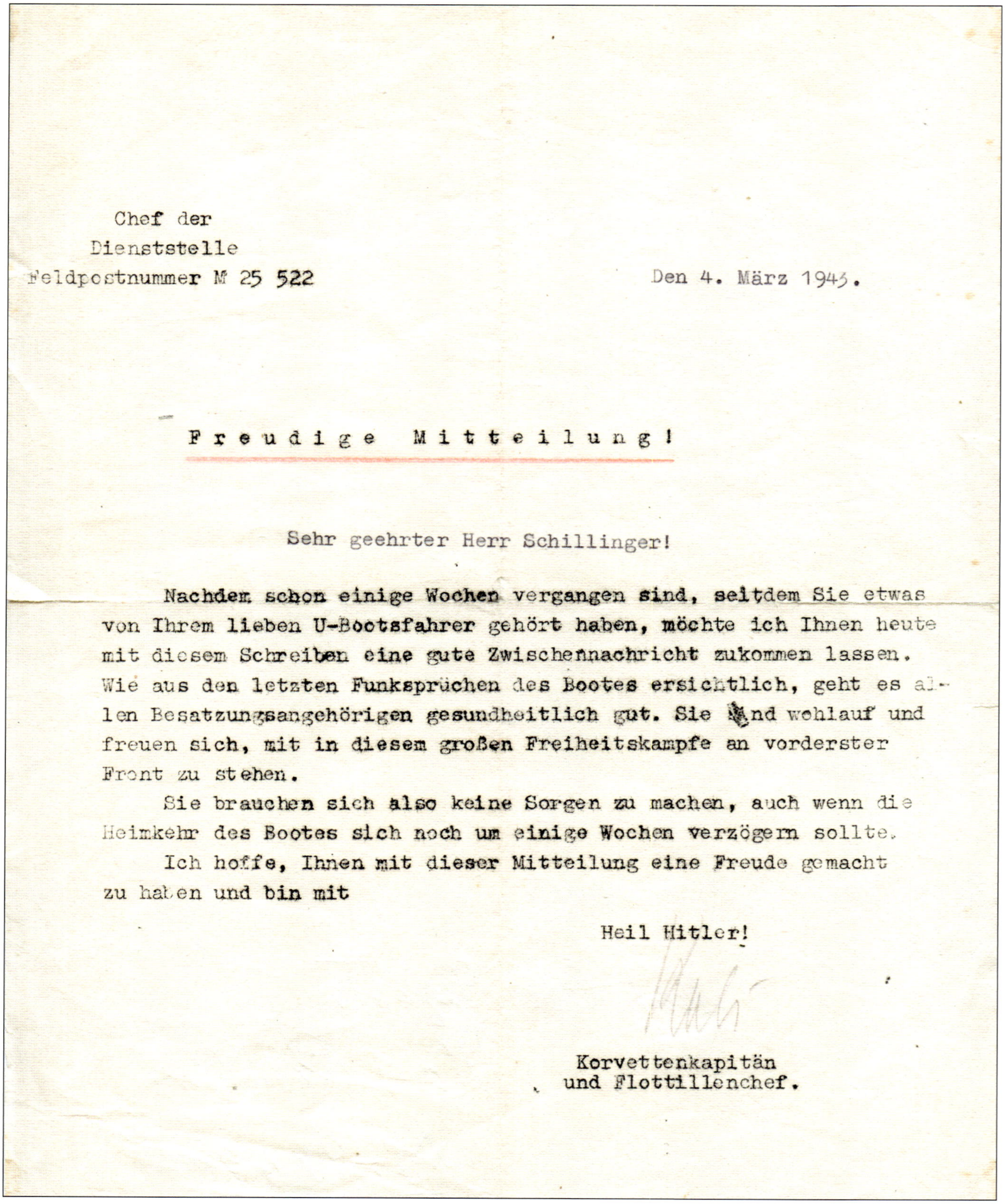

Chef der
Dienststelle
Feldpostnummer M 25 522

Den 4. März 1943.

Freudige Mitteilung!

Sehr geehrter Herr Schillinger!

Nachdem schon einige Wochen vergangen sind, seitdem Sie etwas von Ihrem lieben U-Bootsfahrer gehört haben, möchte ich Ihnen heute mit diesem Schreiben eine gute Zwischennachricht zukommen lassen. Wie aus den letzten Funksprüchen des Bootes ersichtlich, geht es allen Besatzungsangehörigen gesundheitlich gut. Sie sind wohlauf und freuen sich, mit in diesem großen Freiheitskampfe an vorderster Front zu stehen.

Sie brauchen sich also keine Sorgen zu machen, auch wenn die Heimkehr des Bootes sich noch um einige Wochen verzögern sollte.

Ich hoffe, Ihnen mit dieser Mitteilung eine Freude gemacht zu haben und bin mit

Heil Hitler!

Korvettenkapitän
und Flottillenchef.

Letter from U-boat Flotilla to father of Hans Schillinger, dated March 4, 1943. *Letter is signed by Korvettenkapitän Ernst Kals, a Knight's Cross winner and commander of the 2nd U-boat Flotilla.*

Studio portrait photo of Hans Schillinger.

Photo of friends Hans Schillinger (right) and Fritz Keil (left) in tropical U-boat uniform. *Photo taken in Bordeaux, France in July or August 1943. Schillinger wears his U-boat War Badge; Keil appears to have a newly issued Black Wound Badge The U-518 was attacked by a British aircraft in late June; the attack wounded several sailors. On the reverse the sailor describes how the pair had partied hard in Bordeaux – in terms that would have shocked his mother!*

Photo of two comrades from the U-518. *Photo taken in Bordeaux, France in July or August 1943. On the right is Ullrich David; David was killed in action on April 22, 1945. To the left is Fritz Keil.*

Hans Schillinger. *Photo taken in Bordeaux, France in July or August 1943.*

Flensburg-Mürwik torpedo school. *Schillinger attended the school in 1941.*

Sailors cleaning equipment.

Hans Schillinger at torpedo school.

Torpedo school students at Flensburg-Mürwik.

Torpedo mechanics with group leader.

U-boat sailors with nurse. *Hans Schillinger is on the left. The two sailors on the right have been wounded and have been awarded the Black Wound Badge.*

Navy recruits explore a beach.

Navy recruits learn how to break their backs rowing!

Navy sailors celebrate the end of training.

Walter Wittig at the end of the war. *(Photo courtesy of U-boat Archive & Museum, Cuxhaven, Germany.)*

Crew of the U-167, a Type IXC/40 U-boat, in port. *Note camouflage net. After a British depth charge attack, the commander of the U-167 Kapitänleutnant Kurt Sturm scuttled the boat in shallow water near the Canary Islands. Several U-boats rescued the men; the U-518 took about fifteen of the U-167's crew back to France.*

CHAPTER TWENTY-SIX

"What Really Happened Out There?" U-968, and U-615 1944-1945

History is a study in contrasts; an attempt to use what we know to fill in the blanks of what we do not know with what probably happened. The same is true in understanding the U-boat campaign in World War II. On one hand, with the B.d.U. war diary and individual boat diaries, combined with Allied signal intelligence, much is known about the conduct of the undersea struggle. Specialized archives and internet sites, such as the U-Boot-Archive & Museum at Cuxhaven, and the ubootwaffe.net, uboat.net and uboatarchive.net, have made available immense amounts of data for historians, including the names and assignments of over 50,000 U-boat men. Yet much remains unknown. Fifty-two U-boats are still listed as missing in action with no survivors; some of these boats may well have been lost to operational accidents (hull failures, etc.), while others were most probably lost to enemy action that has not clearly been documented. What really happened to these boats? In other cases, we know how the boats met their ends, but with no survivors, we do not know what the boat did in the hours, and in some instances day, leading up to their demise. In just May 1943 alone – one of the pivotal months of the North Atlantic U-boat war – thirty-two U-boats sank with no survivors. Even boats that survived are shrouded in uncertainty as to what went on in combat – one of the best examples is the interesting career of the *U-968*.

Her beginning is known. The *U-968* was ordered by the German Navy on June 5, 1941; the U-boat construction workers at the Blohm und Voss ship-building yard at Hamburg laid her keel on May 14, 1942. Launched on February 4, 1943, she underwent her rigorous trials, before being commissioned on March 18, 1943. The boat then was assigned to the 5th U-boat Flotilla, under command of *Korvettenkapitän* Karl-Heinz Moehle, at Kiel for an additional year of training. Moehle, a Knight's Cross winner, would ensure that the new boats and crews under his command would be ready for anything the enemy could throw at them, as it was an uncertain situation in undersea combat.

Commanding the boat was *Oberleutnant zur See* Otto Westphalen, and much is known about him as well. Born on March 12, 1920 in Hamburg, he joined the Navy in 1938 as an enlisted man and almost immediately entered the officer-commissioning track. He was promoted to *Fähnrich zur See* on December 1, 1939, while serving on the old battleship *Schlesien*; he saw combat early in his career – at the start of the war Westphalen on the *Schlesien* took part in the bombardment of Polish defensive positions on the Hela Peninsula. Westphalen transferred to the torpedo boat *Kondor* in 1940 and advanced to *Oberfähnrich zur See*, while taking part in operations in the North Sea and English Channel. Entering the U-boat training program later in the year, he was commissioned a *Leutnant zur See* on April 1, 1941 and became the 2nd Watch Officer on the *U-566*, commanded by Dietrich Borchert. He was elevated to 1st Watch Officer and sailed on four war patrols with this boat in 1941-42; on his last patrol, the boat sank an enemy merchant ship. *Leutnant zur See* received the U-boat War Badge on October 8, 1941 after his second patrol. Showing promise as a potential U-boat commander, Otto Westphalen attended several U-boat commanders' courses before being placed in command of the *U-121*. For one year he commanded this training U-boat in the 21st U-boat Flotilla based at Pillau. In early 1943 Westphalen transferred to take command of the new *U-968*.

> *Dönitz's Crews*
> ***Mechanikermaat* Willi Lüders**
> Born on June 9, 1918.
> Entered the Navy in 1939.
> Served on the *U-121* and *U-968* in the torpedo room.
> Awarded the Iron Cross 2nd Class and U-boat War Badge on September 11, 1944; awarded the U-boat Clasp in Bronze on February 22, 1945.
> Spent 104 days at sea on U-boat war patrols.
> Survived the war; died on November 13, 1998 at Raisdorf/Kiel.

On the crew was *Mechanikermaat* Willi Lüders. Born on June 9, 1918, he had served on the *U-121* in the 21st U-boat Training Flotilla from 1942 to 1943 and then in the torpedo room on the *U-968*; it appears that Westphalen brought him from the *U-121* to the new boat. In addition to his official duties, Lüders was an excellent cameraman and took many photos of the boat and crew. Toward the end of the *U-968*'s work-up period, Otto Westphalen became involved in one of the U-boat service's most controversial incidents of the entire war. *Oberleutnant zur See* Oskar Kusch was the commander of the *U-154*. Previously a successful watch officer on the *U-103*, he appears to have been easy-going, with a healthy skepticism of Germany's Nazi leadership. Unfortunately for him, several subordinate officers on the *U-154* were of different mind, and at the instigation of the 1st Watch Officer, Ulrich Abel, submitted statements to the effect of accusing Kusch of sedition and cowardice.

A hastily formed court-martial convened at Kiel on January 26, 1944; Otto Westphalen was tabbed as a military judge, one of two non-lawyers designated to sit in judgment with the intent of adding common sense naval experience to the proceedings. The prosecutor demanded a ten-year prison sentence, but to the court's surprise, after secret deliberations, the board – of which Westphalen was a voting member – sentenced Kusch to death by firing squad. Westphalen later remarked that he thought that the chain of command would reduce the sentence; he explained the harsh penalty by saying that the Navy lawyers said the penalty for insulting the *Führer*, which had been shown at trial, would carry a mandatory death penalty in a law that was not yet on the books in the Navy, but that was being developed and would soon be promulgated. Kusch's chain of command did approach Dönitz for him to intercede, and Dönitz seemed to indicate that he would do so, but nothing was ever done and Kusch was executed by firing squad in May 1944.

With Westphalen back on the U-boat after the court-martial, the *U-968* was now ready to go to war and departed Kiel at 8:00 a.m. on March 7, 1944 bound for Norway. The boat reached the 13th U-Boat Flotilla base at Bergen during the night of March 12/13. Here Otto Westphalen topped off the diesel fuel tanks while the quartermaster loaded cold weather clothing for the crew – they would be headed far to the north. Late in the afternoon of March 13, Westphalen and the *U-968* departed Bergen enroute for Narvik. Remaining on the surface of the cold sea to recharge the boat's electric batteries, the crew discovered a serious leak in the conning tower hatch which had not been completely shut due to the presence of the Naxos radar cable. As a result, the inside of the periscope was full of water. The engineer pumped the water out of the tube but the attack periscope retained condensation and the view through it remained clouded. Remaining close to the coastline, the boat headed north, but on March 16 Westphalen received a radio message that attached him to *Wolf Pack Hammer* and ordered him to attack convoy JW-58, a strongly-escorted convoy that would be bound with vital equipment for the Russians at Murmansk. The attack was planned for east of Jan Mayen, an arctic volcanic island 400 miles north of Iceland. A barren place, the Beerenberg volcano glares across the island the Vikings ominously identified as "the cold coast" centuries before.

Crossing the Arctic Circle on March 17, the *U-968* reached the wolf pack's assembly area on March 22 to join the *U-354*, *U-288* and *U-315*. The U-boat command determined that four boats would not be enough to seriously hurt the convoy and ordered two additional packs, *Wolf Pack Thor* (*U-312*, *U-313*, *U-278* and *U-674*) and *Wolf Pack Blitz* (*U-711*, *U-956*, *U-277* and *U-355*) to join the impending fray. Spaced at nine miles between boats to ensure no merchantmen would leak through, the U-boats moved north, traveling submerged by day and surfaced at night. Meanwhile, the Allied convoy departed Liverpool on March 27. On March 30, German aerial reconnaissance reported the presence of a destroyer and two smaller escort ships west of Norway. With the lead elements of the convoy discovered, the German U-boats formed a new picket line on March 31. At about 9:00 p.m., sailing north, the *U-968* surfaced, finding visibility to be mixed – varying from clear and moonlit to as low as 500 meters, when snow squalls passed through. At 2:15 a.m. on April 1, from one of these squalls an enemy destroyer suddenly emerged and headed straight for the *U-968*.

The destroyer captain fired star shells to illuminate his prey, while the *U-968* turned ninety degrees at full speed, transmitting "Destroyer, grid square 8120; *U-968*." The destroyer closed the range; Westphalen fired a single torpedo from the stern tube at 2:31 a.m. and ordered the crew to crash dive. Estimating the range to the target at 2,500 meters, the hydrophone operator heard an explosion nine minutes later and shortly thereafter thought he heard break-up noises of a ship. Westphalen believed he had sunk his pursuer but took no chances and remained submerged until 6:00 a.m. Seeing nothing, he set course north, hoping to find the convoy of which no trace could be seen. Three hours later, the *U-968* was attacked again, this time by a carrier aircraft (identified by Westphalen in his war diary as a Fulmar) which attempted to strafe the U-boat. Rather than submerge, the crew of the *U-968* manned the anti-aircraft guns and kept the "bee" at range with the 37-mm flak gun, but the aircraft continued to shadow the Germans until – in the cover of another snow squall – the *U-968* submerged. At 9:20 a.m. the hydrophone operator detected a destroyer, but in the snow squall neither hunter nor hunted made visual contact.

At about 10:30 a.m. the hydrophone operator again earned his pay by detecting the sound of another approaching destroyer. Westphalen raised the periscope but through the condensation, snow squall and heavy sea swell he could only intermittently see the closing hunter. At 10:40 a.m., when the range had closed to 2,000 meters, Westphalen fired a T5 Wren homing (*Zaunkönig*) torpedo from a bow torpedo tube and apparently lowered the scope, as what happened next was again only known to the hydrophone specialist. After eight minutes and thirty-six seconds the operator again heard the explosion of the torpedo and then break-up and sinking noises, which lasted for five minutes. This time the target was not alone and a few minutes later several destroyers located the submerged *U-968* and proceeded to pound the U-boat for about four hours – dropping an estimated 115 depth charges over a series of five attack passes.

After the second attack run, the *U-968* began taking on water and became extremely stern-heavy. After the third attack run, the commander ordered the compartment doors to be closed as a damaged Battery 1 began to emit gas and the water in the control room reached the upper edge of the rear bulkhead door. To make matters worse, the main bilge pump was out of action; the auxiliary pump was operational, but was unable to cope with the large amount of water entering the boat. With air running out and the boat no longer in trim, the crew turned to hand pumps as the lights went out, the hydrophones went out and diesel fumes spread through the control room. With sparks flying from an electrical panel, the hydrophone operator managed to get his equipment running again and told the captain he could only hear faint noises. Sensing the boat could not remained submerged and survive, Westphalen ordered an emergency surface at about 3:20 p.m. Once topside, Westphalen found that all the enemy destroyers had departed, which was fortunate as the periscope support was damaged, and the boat was incapable of submerging again. Westphalen set a course for Narvik and arrived there at 11:30 p.m. on April 2. The next day Westphalen received the Iron Cross 1st Class and many other men on the *U-968* won decorations as well.

A day later, after some of the damage had been repaired, he set sail south for Trondheim, where more extensive repairs could be made, arriving on April 6. Pulling into the base the *U-968* flew two special warship pennants claiming two destroyers sunk, but post-war records do not indicate that the Allies lost two ships that day. What really happened out there? The *U-968* was definitely attacked. Did Westphalen sink two destroyers or did the hydrophone operator mistake the explosions of the two torpedoes at the end of their runs for hits on the enemy? And what of the break-up noises?

Kapitän zur See Rudolf Peters, the Commander U-boats Norway/North Sea (F.d.U. Norwegen/Nordsee), thought he knew the answer and made the following remark in an addendum to the F.d.U. Norway war diary:

> "The boat was saved by correct, calculated rescue measures in the most difficult situation. I propose the recognition that two destroyers were sunk on April 1, 1944."

The repairs at Trondheim took several months, preventing the U-boat's third war patrol (the short run in April from Narvik to Trondheim was credited as an operational sortie) until July 11, 1944 when the *U-968* departed Trondheim for Narvik, arriving without incident on July 14. On July 17, Westphalen and the *U-968* left Narvik and arrived at Bogen Fjord (near Narvik) on July 21, and again she had a very close call with the enemy. At 11:40 a.m. on July 19, 1944, a B-24 Liberator attacked the boat from astern with five depth charges, killing *Bootsmaat* Werner Hahne (who bled to death from a serious thigh wound) and wounding six other men. The U-boat's flak guns fired back and Westphalen observed several hits on the enemy bomber.

Remaining at the Bogen Fjord for a month (in part to repair the recent attack damage), the *U-968* departed Bogen Fjord on August 20 and headed further north to Hammerfest. Once again, the boat encountered no enemy; this fifth war patrol ended on August 22.

Otto Westphalen's sixth patrol began at Hammerfest on August 29; early on September 4, the *U-968* laid twelve anti-shipping mines far to the east of Murmansk in the White Sea off Kanin Nos on the Nenets Peninsula to hinder the approach to Arkhangelsk. The *U-968* arrived at Hammerfest on September 8, 1944 and then pulled into the Bogen Fjord on September 10.

Fregattenkapitän Reinhard Suhren, the new Commander U-boats Norway, appreciated the mission and noted in the organization's war diary:

> "Well-executed mine operation under the most difficult conditions."

The crew's journey around Norway continued on September 24 when the *U-968* departed Bogen Fjord for a patrol that ended at Narvik on October 3. The U-boat's eighth patrol was longer; departing Narvik on October 14, the *U-968* was detailed to Wolf Pack *Panther*, which was attempting to find and attack convoy PQ-34. Again, she made no attacks and arrived at Ramsund to the north on November 11. Two days later, Westphalen departed Ramsund and arrived at the U-boat bunkers at Drontheim, Norway on November 16. The boat remained here until January 23, 1945 when she undertook a two-day voyage to Narvik – her tenth war patrol. She then underwent snorkel training for four days in the Ofoten Fjord. On February 1, 1945 the *U-968* left Narvik and arrived at Harstad on the same day.

Then things got interesting again, and fortunately for history it was well documented. Westphalen and the *U-968* departed Harstad on February 7, 1945. On February 14, 1945 at 12:30 p.m., the *U-968* penetrated convoy BK-3 and sank the Norwegian 8,129-ton *Norfjell*, sailing in ballast from Archangel to Great Britain, just north of Murmansk. Two crewmen died (a fortunately low number) in the frigid February waters. Westphalen also claimed to have hit three 7,000-ton merchant ships, but there is no record of these sinkings. At 10:15 a.m. on February 17, 1945 off Murmansk, the *U-968* torpedoed the British 1,350-ton sloop *HMS Lark* guarding convoy RA-64 and fresh off of helping to sink the *U-425*. *HMS Lark* did not sink, but was later towed to the Kola Inlet and beached; the Royal Navy later declared her a total loss. At 11:25 a.m. the *U-968* fired another torpedo at a different enemy destroyer and later observed her on fire.

But another U-boat, the *U-425*, was also in the fight and there is confusion as to when she was destroyed. About this time, firing a homing torpedo, the *U-68* observed a hit after six minutes and twenty seconds, but it could have been a torpedo from the *U-425*. The same day at 11:48 a.m., again off Murmansk, the *U-968* sank the American 7,176-ton *Thomas Scott*, also of convoy RA-64. Like the *Norfjell*, she was in ballast when struck by a torpedo on the starboard side. She went out of control and broke in two, but all her crew survived. Now with a total of six ships sunk, the *U-968* arrived at Kilbotn (near Harstad in northern Norway) on February 20, 1945. For his achievements on this war patrol Otto Westphalen received the German Cross in Gold on February 18 (announced while he was still at sea); he received the decoration after arriving at Kilbotn. Enlisted man *Oberfunkmaat* Bruno Aniszewski received a German Cross in Gold as well on March 11, 1945. Reinhard Suhren, F.d.U. Norway, commented on Westphalen's performance in the war diary:

> "In a superior manner, cool understanding in continuous operations, with distinguished shooting ability."

The *U-968*'s thirteenth war patrol was a lucky one; it began on March 12, 1945 when Westphalen departed Kilbotn. On March 20 the *U-968* sank two ships from convoy JW-65. At 1:20 p.m., Westphalen torpedoed the British 1,350-ton sloop *HMS Lapwing* north of Murmansk, killing 158 men, when she sank twenty minutes later. At 2:15 p.m. the *U-968* claimed her second victim, the American 7,210-ton freighter *Thomas Donaldson*, carrying 7,679 tons of general cargo, locomotives and ammunition to Murmansk. The U-boat's torpedo struck the engine room in the starboard side; four crewmen died as the ship sank stern-first three hours later. Westphalen and the *U-968* arrived back at Kilbotn on March 30, 1945 to find that he had been awarded the Knight's Cross on March 23, 1945 for his "triumphant attack" on this supply convoy.

The war was coming to an end when the fourteenth war patrol for the *U-968* began on April 21, 1945. The boat departed Kilbotn on that date and arrived at Harstad on May 6, 1945; during her journey Hitler committed suicide in Berlin and Karl Dönitz assumed a short-lived role as head of the German government. Again, as on her first voyage, uncertainty followed the *U-968*. At 9:00 p.m. on April 29, 1945, she reported sinking the British 1,010-ton corvette, *HMS Alnwick Castle* and the British 1,150-ton destroyer escort *HMS Goodall*, both off Murmansk (the *U-968* claimed the two were destroyers, adding further confusion to the situation). If the *HMS Alnwick Castle* was indeed struck by a torpedo, she did not come close to sinking, surviving the war and being scrapped in 1958. The *HMS Goodall* was sunk on April 29, but possibly not as claimed by the *U-968*. Westphalen had fired a Gnat torpedo at the *HMS Goodall*; some sources state that the torpedo blew off the ship's bow, while other post-war histories postulate that this torpedo apparently missed and the British ship was sunk one hour later by the *U-286*. The men of this U-boat could not clarify the issue; later that day the British frigates *HMS Loch Shin* (Cdr. D.J. de W. Kitcat), *HMS Anguilla*, (Lt. D.J. Jacobsen) and the destroyer escort *HMS Cotton* (Lt.Cdr. I.W.T. Beloe) sank the *U-286* with all hands. In either case, 112 men on the *HMS Goodall* lost their lives in the freezing water.

The following day, May 7, 1945, the *U-968* began her fifteenth and last war mission when she departed Harstad and arrived at Skjomenfjord, Norway. Her war was over; she surrendered on May 16, 1945 to the British at Loch Eriboll, Scotland. After spending some time as prisoners of war, the men of the *U-968* returned to civilian life. Only one man had been killed on the boat; *Bootsmann* Werner Hahne had been buried at the German military cemetery at Narvik, Norway. Torpedo *Mechanikermaat* Willi Lüders wrote a book about his experiences, *Tatsachenbericht eines U-Bootfahrers 1942-45* (*Factual Report by a Submariner 1942-45*); he passed away in 1998 at age eighty. Otto Westphalen was still alive at the time of this book's research.

So what really happened out there in the frigid Arctic water off Narvik and Murmansk in the Norwegian and Barents Seas? How many times did Dönitz's crews on the *U-968* and the equally brave men on the British sloops, destroyers and corvettes tangle with each other and to what result? At war's end, the *U-968* sported six victory pennants bearing silhouettes of escort warships and four pennants that designated merchant sinkings. The *U-968* clearly sank three merchantmen; it is almost certain that she sank the *HMS Lapwing* and *HMS Lark* as well. Concerning the *HMS Goodall*, we simply do not know if it was a torpedo from the *U-968* or the ill-fated *U-286*. On the other hand, no U-boat sank the *HMS Alnwick Castle*. As to the two escort warships claimed by the *U-968* on April 1, 1944, Jürgen Rohwer, who wrote the definitive work *Axis Submarine Successes 1939-1945*, believes that the two explosions heard by the hydrophone operator were end-of-run explosions, not actual target hits. Combined with the fact that no British ships were reported sunk that day in this area, it appears more likely than not that the *U-968* did not sink the pair, but we may never know what really happened.

And what really happened in the closed jury room that January day in 1944 at the court-martial of Oskar Kusch? Were the military judges in confusion over an impending law; did they expect Admiral Dönitz to bail them out in a review process, or did they believe that discipline required the ultimate punishment for a U-boat commander expected to lead his men in difficult situations, where loyalty had to be ironclad? Once again, we may never know.

Similar questions surround the *U-615* and her crew. A Type VIIC boat, the *U-615* was ordered on August 15, 1940; on May 20, 1941 engineers at the Blohm und Voss shipyard #591 laid her keel at Hamburg. The *U-615* was launched on February 8, 1942 and after the normal trials was commissioned on March 26, 1942. In command was *Oberleutnant* Ralph Kapitzky, who was born on June 28, 1916 in Dresden, the son of a banker. Kapitzky entered the German Navy in 1935; he was seconded to the *Luftwaffe* from 1937 to 1940 for aerial navigation and observer training; he also served as the adjutant for the 806th Coastal Flying Group. During the Polish Campaign in 1939, Kapitzky was a flight officer on an He 111 bomber and was shot down and injured. He flew again on a Ju 88 in the Norwegian Campaign in 1940 and flew many missions during the Battle of Britain later that year. In 1941 he returned to his parent service and began U-boat training. During the work-up training after the U-boat's commissioning, Kapitzky was promoted to *Kapitänleutnant* on June 1, 1942. Also on the *U-615* was *Maschinengefreiter* Karl-Heinz Lehr who worked in the engine room.

> *Dönitz's Crews*
> ***Maschinengefreiter* Karl-Heinz Lehr**
> Born on July 14, 1924 in Frankfurt/Main.
> Served on the *U-615* in the engine room.
> Awarded the U-boat War Badge.
> Spent 221 days at sea on U-boat war patrols.
> Survived the sinking of the *U-615* on August 7, 1943 and spent the rest of the war in a U.S. prisoner of war camp; survived the war.

The *U-615* departed Kiel on her first war patrol on September 5, 1942 for operations in the North Atlantic; she initially made for Kristiansand, Norway where she took on additional fuel before heading into the Atlantic. On October 11, 1942 at 7:59 p.m., the *U-615* fired two torpedoes at the Panamanian 4,221-ton *El Lago*, sailing in ballast with convoy ONS-136 from Reykjavik, Iceland to New York, and broke her in two. Fifty-seven men perished in the attack. A British B-24 Liberator attacked the *U-615* on October 15, 1942 in the mid-Atlantic but caused no damage. On October 23, 1942 at 6:52 p.m., the *U-615* fired a spread of four torpedoes and sank the British 12,656-ton *Empire Star* sailing unescorted in the central Atlantic with 10,555 tons of general cargo; forty-two men died in the attack. Several days later the *U-615* refueled from the *U-463*. On October 30, 1942, the *U-615* arrived at La Pallice, France and joined the 3rd U-boat Flotilla. The young crew was given leave in watches over the next three weeks.

On November 25, 1942 the *U-615* departed La Pallice and again patrolled the North Atlantic. However, although she was able to gain and maintain contact with an enemy convoy, after forty-six days and no success, and after refueling from another U-boat, the U-boat returned to La Pallice from her second war patrol on January 9, 1943. The *U-615* remained in port for over a month – due in part to a ruptured forward oil tank when she returned from a short maintenance test-run and inadvertently rammed a corner of the slip – before venturing into combat again. On February 18, 1943, the U-boat departed La Pallice; her war patrol area would be off the southern coast of Greenland and east of Newfoundland. It was a rocky patrol. On February 22, 1943 west of the Bay of Biscay, an unidentified enemy aircraft attacked the *U-615*, but the U-boat was not damaged in the attack. On March 14, 1943 northeast of Newfoundland, another unidentified enemy aircraft attacked the *U-615*; again the U-boat escaped unscathed. Finally, on April 11, 1943, after following his quarry for over a day, Kapitzky fired two torpedoes at the American 7,177-ton *Edward B Dudley*, carrying 4,000 tons of ammunition with convoy HX-232. But the ship remained afloat and Kapitzky closed to eight hundred meters to deliver a coup de grâce. The torpedo struck under the ship's bridge, igniting her cargo and causing a catastrophic explosion that killed all sixty-nine men aboard. A piece of metal from the ship struck Kapitzky in the shoulder as he was standing on the U-boat's bridge. This forced the U-boat to return to La Pallice on April 20, 1943 so the commander could receive required medical attention. On her return, physicians met Ralph Kapitzky at the dock, took him to the airport and flew him to Paris for medical treatment. During his absence, construction workers removed the boat's 88-mm deck-gun and added a second anti-aircraft platform for a new 20-mm flak gun. They also installed a new radar set, a depth charge plotting device and a hydrogen container for inflating radar decoy balloons.

On June 12, 1943 the *U-615* left La Pallice for operations in the eastern Caribbean area. The night before departure, several officers brought a secret ship-detection device to Kapitsky that they called a Nachtfernrohr (night telescope); only Kapitzky would be permitted to remove the device from its locked box and use it. Referred to as the "Seehund Drei" (Seal 3) by the crew, the device was contained in a black case about 18-inches long, 8-inches high and 4-inches thick, with an electric wire that connected the device to a power outlet on the bridge; it was reportedly manufactured by the optical firms of Leitz and Zeiss (one sailor would later state that it operated with infra-red rays while another insisted that they were ultraviolet). The next morning the *U-615* departed her berth and headed west. Two days later the boat came under heavy attack by enemy aircraft in the western Bay of Biscay. At 9:48 a.m. the Royal Air Force struck: a Whitley patrol bomber from the 10th Squadron, one aircraft from the 228th Squadron and one aircraft from the 461st Squadron attacked the surfaced *U-615*, which was traveling with the *U-257* and *U-600*. Later that day at 4:05 p.m. a British aircraft from the 10th Squadron attacked the U-boat again; at 4:49 p.m. another aircraft from the 10th

Squadron attacked the boat. That evening at 8:15 p.m. an aircraft from the 220th Squadron attacked; it was joined at 9:12 p.m. by an aircraft from the 547th Squadron – the sixth enemy aircraft to attack that day. The last attack, by a Wellington bomber, killed 3rd Watch Officer Peter Dittmer who had served on the *U-47* when she sank the *HMS Royal Oak* at Scapa Flow in 1939. During the attacks the flak gunners on the *U-615* exacted their revenge and shot down a Whitely bomber. Two days later at 9:04 a.m. on June 16, an aircraft from the RAF's 59th Squadron attacked the *U-615*; no damage was incurred. Later that day at 4:17 p.m., an aircraft from the RCAF's 422nd Squadron attacked the boat, again with no results. After refueling from the *U-535* and arriving in the Caribbean by passing between Antigua and Guadeloupe on the night of July 27/28, Kapitzky made for the Gulf of Paria and Trinidad. Allied underwater detection picked up the U-boat; Kapitzky, unaware that he had been detected, then made for Curacao. On July 28, 1943 the *U-615* torpedoed and sank the unescorted Dutch 3,177-ton tanker *Rosalia* carrying crude oil from Lake Maracaibo, Venezuela to Curacao. The ship took twenty-three men with her when she sank in flames ten miles south of Curacao. But Kapitzky's orders were to primarily report enemy vessels and only attack when circumstances were absolutely favorable. And circumstances were about to turn just the opposite.

Kapitzky's sinking report of the *Rosalia* to B.d.U. was intercepted by Allied signal intelligence, which then got a clear bearing on the *U-615*'s location. The next day a U.S. Army Air Corps Douglas B-18 *Bolo*, based in Aruba, sighted the *U-615* and attacked, dropping four depth charges and damaging the boat. On August 1, 1943 B.d.U. ordered Kapitzky and the other U-boat commanders then in the Caribbean, to return to France as the resupply U-boats had taken a beating and would not be able to assist the attack boats with extra fuel.

An anti-submarine warfare blimp, the K-68, joined the hunt and over the next week the *U-615* headed east attempting to avoid the closing Allied forces. On August 5, 1943 the destroyer *USS Biddle* located the U-boat and delivered a depth charge attack to no avail. Near midnight that day, a Martin PBM Mariner flying boat attacked the surfaced *U-615* (again with no results). At 2:00 a.m. on August 6, another Mariner showed up in the vicinity, but Kapitzky used a nearby schooner to confuse the enemy radar operator and again escaped. Then, using his previous aviation experience, Kapitzky calculated that before the next round of enemy planes showed on the scene, he could enjoy unopposed surface sailing to the east.

On August 6, 1943 Kapitzky's calculations showed he should submerge soon. The *U-615* was thus making its dive when a Martin PBM Mariner flying-boat patrol aircraft from the U.S. Navy's 204th Squadron attacked her at 3:45 p.m. The aircraft dropped four depth charges that damaged the U-boat considerably: the electric motors and the port diesel engine were put out of action; the lubricating oil gravity tank was damaged and oil began to run into the bilges; and several high-pressure air lines were broken and water entered through some of the glands. The *U-615* surfaced at once and the flak crews manned the two 20-mm anti-aircraft guns. Kapitzky also directed that the portable machine guns be brought to the bridge and that all flak ammunition be brought to the deck – he intended to fight it out. With that, the U-boat opened fire. The plane returned to attack, but was shot down by the heavy barrage laid down by the 20-mm guns. A second PBM attacked the U-boat at 5:35 p.m.; one hour later two additional aircraft joined in the action as damage increased aboard the U-boat.

On one of these attacks, *Kapitänleutnant* Kapitzky was struck in the thigh by a machine-gun bullet and began to bleed to death. Meanwhile during the night of August 6/7, the *U-615* drifted helplessly on the surface. The U-boat's crew gathered on deck awaiting the order to abandon ship. As Kapitzky bade farewell to his men, the entire crew filed by their captain and shook his hand on his last moments on earth; he died at 1:00 a.m. on August 7. The 1st Watch Officer then gave the order to break out the rubber boat, intending to use it to transport the dying captain and a wounded petty officer. In the darkness and confusion, the boat drifted away; the 1st Watch Officer asked for volunteers to swim after the raft, but no one did. He then ordered four men at pistol point to go after the raft; they did, but did not recover the raft. When it became light, American aircraft again attacked the *U-615*, which sank off Curacao at mid-morning on August 7, 1943. After one hour, the American destroyer *USS Walker* picked up the surviving crew including Karl-Heinz Lehr.

For most captured U-boat men such an event meant several years of unremarkable time in an Allied prisoner of war camps before repatriation to Germany. But for several men of the *U-615,* it meant an unusual date with destiny. The survivors of the *U-615* first went to Fort Meade, Maryland to a special compound for initial interrogation and there they would meet an interesting character who had also served on a U-boat.

Several months earlier, on June 12, 1943 American aircraft from the escort aircraft carrier *USS Bogue* bombed and sank the *U-118* west of the Canary Islands. The attacks killed forty men; there were sixteen survivors. One of those who were rescued by the American destroyer *USS Osmond Ingram* was twenty-year-old *Mechanikerobergefreiter* Werner Drechsler. Drechsler was born on January 17, 1923 in Mühlberg, Germany; he grew up in Chemnitz. Growing up, Drechsler was a better-than-average student and had a likeable personality. In public school he learned some French and English before graduating in 1937. From there he attended a trade school to become a mechanic; he began his apprenticeship in this profession in 1938 and left Chemnitz in 1941 to join the German Navy, completing U-boat training and joining the *U-118.*

During the sinking of the U-boat, Drechsler was wounded in the neck and right knee and was operated on at sea during the voyage of the *USS Osmond Ingram* to Norfolk, Virginia. On arrival he spent a further nine days at the base hospital before being transferred to a prisoner of war camp. For reasons that remain unclear even to this day, Werner Drechsler cooperated with interrogators at the Joint Interrogation Center located at Fort Meade, Maryland (just north of Washington, D.C.). For seven months he assumed two false identities (that of U-boat Petty Officer Leimi and Brabant) and was billeted with a number of U-boat prisoners of war as they passed through this camp. Drechsler engaged many of his fellow Germans in conversation on specific U-boat topics at the request of American intelligence officers. One of the men Drechsler befriended at Fort Meade was *Mechanikerobergefreiter* Rolf Wizuy of the *U-615*; in fact, they were roommates until Wizuy experienced appendicitis and had to be hospitalized.

Fort Meade was a transit camp; prisoners stayed there for as little as two or three weeks and as long as nine months. Initially, the inmates were primarily U-boat men; all were held incommunicado in a place where the Geneva Conventions were loosely applied as Allied intelligence attempted to ascertain the evolving nature of the U-boat threat. When American intelligence officers believed a prisoner had told everything he knew, the prisoner was transferred to regular prisoner of war camps elsewhere in the United States and the Red Cross was then notified of their capture.

During this period of uncertainty the command of the 3rd U-boat Flotilla at La Pallice, France wrote several letters to the mother of Karl-Heinz Lehr, who lived in Frankfurt/Main. The first letter, signed by *Korvettenkapitän* Richard Zapp and dated September 1, 1943, read:

> Dear Mrs. Lehr,
> Unfortunately, the reason for me writing to you today is a very painful one. For some time now we have been worried about the destiny of the boat on which your son,
>
> *Maschinengefreiter* Karlheinz Lehr
>
> was assigned. After some time has elapsed, it has unfortunately become a certainty that the boat will no longer return. Due to this, the U-boat Command has declared the boat and its occupants missing, effective August 11, 1943. As so often in the U-boat war, where each boat is fighting by itself, we only know little about it at the present time. The boat had operated successfully in the Caribbean Sea and had sunk a tanker of 6,000 BRT there. The cause of the loss is still unknown at this time.
>
> There is still complete uncertainty regarding the destiny of the brave soldiers.
>
> I know that for you, dear Mrs. Lehr, the difficult time of sorrow and waiting has now begun. Please be aware that everything will be done from our side in order to find a clear understanding about the fate of our comrades.
>
> We are in constant touch with the International Red Cross and all military authorities which may be able to contribute to some clarification, and you will be the first to be informed about everything. Everything which we find out and are able to talk about will immediately be relayed to you.
>
> Should you receive any information from other sources about the missing person, we kindly request that you inform the Command about it.
>
> For all questions of any kind, the military postal number M36094 is now applicable. Of course, we are always fully prepared to be of assistance.
>
> With heart-felt feelings in the uncertainty regarding the fate of your son,
>
> Heil Hitler!

But better news would soon arrive in Frankfurt. On October 25, 1943 another letter from the 3rd U-boat Flotilla arrived which stated:

> Dear Mrs. Lehr!
> It is a pleasure for me to inform you that your son, who had been reported missing,
>
> *Maschinengefreiter* Karl Heinz Lehr
>
> was rescued. According to information received from the International Red Cross, he is a prisoner of war of the Americans, at Camp Stringtown, Oklahoma, USA.
>
> Kindly obtain the regulations for postal contact with German prisoners of war in the USA from the German Red Cross.
>
> Should your son voice any complaints regarding his imprisonment, we request that you inform us about it.
>
> In addition, you are requested that you send to us the first letter he sends after having been taken prisoner for perusal. You will immediately get this letter back.
>
> Heil Hitler!

The letter's last paragraph requesting that U-boat Command review Karl Heinz Lehr's first letter as a prisoner of war reflects Dönitz's anticipation at the beginning of the war that there would be large numbers of U-boat men falling into enemy hands. As the U-boat chief also knew that many of those men would have valuable information that, if it could be passed back to Germany, could improve the success of future U-boat operations, he implemented a code for prisoner of war initial letters (see "Taking Care of Their Own").

It appears that Karl-Heinz Lehr and the men of the *U-615* stayed at Fort Meade until late October 1943 when they were transferred to Camp Stringtown, Oklahoma and U.S. authorities then notified the International Red Cross of their whereabouts, and on November 23, 1943 the German Red Cross provided the Lehr family with an address at Camp Stringtown. It would not remain valid for long as in January 1944 American authorities loaded all the U-boat prisoners of war at Camp Stringtown aboard a train and transferred them to a prisoner of war camp at Papago Park which was inside the city limits of Phoenix, Arizona. The senior German prisoner at the camp was *Kapitän zur See* Jürgen Wattenberg; he hailed from Lübeck where he was born on December 28, 1900 and joined the *Reichsmarine* in 1921. Wattenberg, who had served on the pocket battleship *Graf Spee* and had escaped internment in Uruguay when the ship was scuttled in Montevideo harbor in 1939, returned to Germany and became a U-boat man in 1941, later commanding the *U-162*. On September 3, 1942 the British destroyers *HMS Vimy*, *HMS Pathfinder* and *HMS Quentin* sank the U-boat northeast of Trinidad and Wattenberg began his second period of captivity. Awarded the Iron Cross 2nd and 1st Class and credited with sinking fourteen Allied ships, Wattenberg was a no-nonsense officer, who was promoted to *Kapitän zur See* while in American captivity. He had initially been held at Fort Hunt, Virginia, another special camp for U-boat men (and located just south of Washington, DC) before his transfer to Crossville, Tennessee and a more permanent POW camp. But on January 26, 1944 he also was transferred to Papago Park. Viewed as a hardcore Nazi by camp authorities, he validated their opinion by escaping Papago Park on December 23, 1944; he would remain at large until January 28, 1945 when he was re-captured – but that adventure was well in the future. One of the policies that Wattenberg supported (as it strengthened, the control that could be exerted by the shadow German chain of command) in the camp was that men from the same unit would be billeted together, so it is likely that Karl-Heinz Lehr lived in the same small wooden barracks with the rest of the crew of the *U-615*. The non-commissioned officers (CPOs and POs) had their own barracks, but they were not isolated from the junior enlisted men and communication between the two groups was quite easy.

Drechsler, in his covert assignment meanwhile, remained at Fort Hunt until December 1943 when U.S. Army intelligence determined he was no longer needed at the Joint Interrogation Center and could be sent to a regular prisoner of war camp in a traditional status. U.S. Navy interrogators weighed-in and stipulated that he should never be sent to a prison camp where other German naval prisoners were held in case he should be recognized. But communications between the two services were shoddy and on March 12, 1944, the Army transferred Drechsler to Papago Park.

Unfortunately for Drechsler, camp authorities assigned him to Compound 4; unfortunate in that this was the compound where the men of the *U-615* lived. Compound 4, with about twenty one-story, open-bay barracks – each holding about thirty prisoners – was surrounded by a chain-link fence topped by three rows of stout barbed wire. Drechsler arrived there at 4:00 p.m. on March 12.

By 5:15 p.m., in the close confines of the area, *Mechanikerobergefreiter* Rolf Wizuy, *Funkobergefreiter* Helmut Fischer, *Maschinen-*

obergefreiter Fritz Franke, *Maschinenobergefreiter* Günter Külsen and *Maschinenobergefreiter* Bernhard Reyak (all from the *U-615*), *Matrosengefreiter* Heinrich Ludwig (formerly on the *U-199*) and *Maschinenhauptgefreiter* Otto Stengel (of the *U-352*) spotted the collaborator in the camp, smelled a "rat" and approached him with questions. Drechsler denied any involvement with the Americans or that he had been held at Fort Meade, but the other U-boat men were not convinced and decided to consult with more-senior prisoners.

At 6:15 p.m. the men spoke with *Oberbootsmaat* Werner Reinl, who had been a Petty Officer on Drechsler's boat, the *U-118*, and thus knew the accused, and later *Obersteuermann* Franz Hox, the former navigator on the *U-162* under Jürgen Wattenberg; we can conclude, therefore, that the senior German prisoner of war was aware of the situation. Hox also conferred with *Oberfunkmaat* Friedrich Murza, formerly on the *U-487*, and *Funkmaat* Siegfried Elser, previously of the *U-409* and a German Cross in Gold recipient.

At 8:00 p.m., *Obersteuermann* Hox then called Fischer, Külsen, Franke, Reyak, Wizuy and Ludwig together. Hox told the assembled group:

> "There's nothing I can do personally, you know that. There's no official thing I can tell you to do or have done … Drechsler could be gone from here by the time we got a message to the captain [Wattenberg] … I can't really [suggest to you] on it either. You have to determine that for yourselves. I leave it up to you."

The seven junior enlisted men determined what to do; they were U-boat men and in difficult situations were expected to take the initiative. They went back to the 1st Company orderly room barracks and gathered in the chilly air outside. Word of impending action had flown through the barracks and there may have been as many as twenty-five men in the darkness – either listening or offering their own opinions under the cloak of darkness. One man discussed having the "holy ghost" (a euphemism for a severe, but not fatal, beating) visit Drechsler in the middle of the night. By 8:30 p.m. they had arrived at a decision; there would be no visit by the "holy ghost" that night; it was time for Werner Drechsler to meet "his maker." In the darkness one of the non-commissioned officers, who was never subsequently identified, asked the group:

> "All right, who would like to carry it out?"

Shortly before 10:00 p.m. seven men went to Drechsler's barracks, grabbed him, beat him senseless, tied him up and hanged him from a rafter in the shower room. One source states that several hundred U-boat men later filed through the showers that night, viewing what had happened to a man who broke faith with his other U-boat comrades. Camp guards found his lifeless body several hours later.

American authorities questioned suspects for several months, using a lie detector, but Dönitz's crews seemed to have presented a fairly solid stonewall. Then the interrogations got rough and involved physical duress, exposure to high temperature and the forced wearing of a gasmask filled with freshly cut onions. The sailors started to provide details and on August 15, 1944 a court martial convened at Florence, Arizona. Within two days the verdict was handed down; death by hanging for all seven defendants: Helmut Fischer, Fritz Franke, Günther Külsen, Heinrich Ludwig, Bernhard Reyak, Otto Stengel and Rolf Wizuy. On January 27, 1945 the men were transferred to Fort Leavenworth; after the usual review process (which did not overturn the verdicts based on confessions made under duress) the men were hanged at Fort Leavenworth military prison on August 25, 1945. Shortly before they died, Helmut Fischer said the following:

> "All we can do now is die like good German sailors … We have nothing to be ashamed of."

And as that event passed into history, the questions began concerning the appropriateness of the legal process and verdict in the case; those arguments will never find resolution among the legal community. Questions remain in the historical community as well, and to have an opinion in this realm requires only an inquisitive mind, not a legal degree.

What exactly was the mysterious Nachtfernrohr the *U-615* carried on her final mission? Was it a high-grade optical device or a first-generation infrared sight? What exactly happened at Papago Park among the non-commissioned officers and the senior prisoner of war that led to their non-committal of what should be done, before Werner Drechsler was killed? *Korvettenkapitän* Wattenberg may have known but we cannot ask him; after the war he became the manager of the Lübeck branch of the St. Pauli brewery, and died at the ripe old age of ninety-four on November 27, 1995. Which other crewmen from the *U-615* at Papago Park were involved in the killing of Werner Drechsler? What was Karl-Heinz Lehr's role in the incident? Was he one of the twenty-five men in the darkness when the group decided to kill the collaborator? If so, did he offer an opinion as to what should be done? We may never know.

But we can imagine what happened – both in that jury room and on the Arctic seas in the case of the *U-968* and in the prisoner of war camp in the United States in the case of the men on the *U-615* on a moonlit cloudy night in March 1944 who, in their eyes, upheld the honor of their U-boat service, and that is the beauty of history – history that can come alive in dusty old antique stores off the beaten path in Germany and in the remote stacks of wartime papers in archives and libraries around the world.

Known Crewmembers for the U-968

Ackermann, Walter	*Obermaschinenmaat*
Adamietz, Erich	*Funkobergefreiter*
Altheide, Rudi	*Obermaschinist*
Aniszewski, Bruno	*Oberfunkmaat*
Bartels, Hermann	*Obersteuermann*
Beck, Herbert	*Maschinenmaat*
Bieszk, Paul	*Maschinenobergefreiter*
Bigalke, Gerhard	*Bootsmaat*
Böhm, Gustav	*Maschinenmaat*
Busch, Ernst	*Matrosengefreiter*
Christoffers, Johann	*Mechanikergefreiter*
Coltzau, Helmut	*Bootsmaat*
Dachauer, Josef	*Matrosengefreiter*
Eidam, Hans	*Maschinenmaat*
Feuerstack, Hermann	*Oberleutnant zur See*
Fritz, Erich	*Matrosenobergefreiter*
Galczinski, Erich	*Obersteuermann*
Gaussmann, Ferdinand	*Funkmaat*
Goffrier	*Funkgefreiter*
Görke	*Matrosengefreiter*
Görs, Willi	*Maschinengefreiter*
Gründgens, Richard	*Maschinenobergefreiter*
Günther, Ludwig	*Maschinengefreiter*
Hahne, Werner	*Bootsmaat*
Hähnelt, Richard	*Leutnant zur See*
Herren, Peter	*Maschinengefreiter*
Himmels, Willi	*Matrose*
Hirschbrich, Johann	*Oberleutnant (Ing)*
Hoim, Hagen	*Matrosenobergefreiter*
Hügenell, Willi	*Mechanikerobergefreiter*
Kalecinski, Bruno	*Matrosengefreiter*
Kasper, Franz	*Matrosengefreiter*
Kienscherff, Herbert	*Funkgefreiter*
Klippel, Vinzenz	*Bootsmaat*
Klopp, Helmuth	*Maschinengefreiter*
Krapf, Hans	*Maschinengefreiter*
Kriebel, Paul	*Matrosengefreiter*
Krieg, Siegfried	*Obermaschinist*
Kube, Hans	*Maschinenmaat*
Kucera, Alfred	*Matrosenobergefreiter*
Lankers, Franz	*Maschinengefreiter*
Lehmann	*Maschinengefreiter*
Leue, Fritz	*Obermaschinenmaat*
Ley, Kurt	*Matrosenobergefreiter*
Lüders, Willi	*Mechanikermaat*
Lützkendorf	*Maschinengefreiter*
Mayer, Norbert	*Matrosengefreiter*
Möseler, Leonhard	*Matrosenobergefreiter*
Nebe, Helmut	*Maschinengefreiter*
Nehrbass, Paul	*Maschinengefreiter*
Nelling, Fritz	*Bootsmaat*
Nix, Walter	*Matrosengefreiter*
Oelschlägel, Claus-Dieter	*Oberleutnant zur See*
Oelsner, Rudolf	*Maschinenobergefreiter*
Oschkenat, Willi	*Matrose*
Pablotzki, Bruno	*Matrosengefreiter*
Patzler, Werner	*Maschinengefreiter*
Rahnfeld, Harry	*Matrosengefreiter*
Rasch, Hans	*Matrosenobergefreiter*
Rasche, Günter	*Maschinengefreiter*
Rauch, Günther	*Mechanikerobergefreiter*
Rauschenberg, Walter	*Maschinenobergefreiter*
Rebelein, Fritz	*Bootsmaat*
Ring, Franz	*Maschinengefreiter*
Ritzer, Egon	*Obermaschinist*
Ritzler	*Mechanikergefreiter*
Rohde, Jürgen	*Leutnant (Ing)*
Rojek, Alfred	*Maschinenhauptgefreiter*
Rossum, Heinrich van	*Sanitätsmaat*
Schatteburg, Hans	*Oberleutnant zur See*
Schlosser, Jakob	*Obermaschinist*
Schlott, Heinz	
Schmidt, Reinhold	*Oberleutnant zur See*
Schniecke, Ernst	*Maschinenmaat*
Schoppengerd, Anton	*Maschinenobergefreiter*
Skernewitz, Josef	*Maschinengefreiter*
Stach, Friedrich	*Maschinengefreiter*
Steckmann, Hans-Ulrich	*Artilleriemechaniker*
Stopperka, Rolf	*Obersanitätsmaat*
Storm, Rudolf	*Matrosengefreiter*
Strohm, Gerhard	*Matrosengefreiter*
Sührig, Heinz	*Maschinenobergefreiter*
Teubner, Walter	*Maschinengefreiter*
Trompter, Gerhard	*Maschinengefreiter*
Tscharnke, Günter	*Maschinenobergefreiter*
Voigt, Kurt	*Funkobergefreiter*
Wagner, Josef	
Wenddorff, Horst	*Matrosenobergefreiter*
Wermann, Walter	*Funkmaat*
Westphalen, Otto	*Oberleutnant zur See*

Known Crewmembers for the U-615

Abel, Reinhold	*Maschinenmaat*
Alexander, Kurt	*Matrosenobergefreiter*
Bischof, Erwin	*Maschinengefreiter*
Bluhm, Heinz	*Maschinenmaat*
Brauer, Günter	*Mechanikermaat*
Buhlig, Rudolph	*Obermaschinist*
Daus, Alfred	*Matrosenobergefreiter*
Diesing, Gerhard	*Matrosenobergefreiter*
Dittmer, Hans-Peter	*Obersteuermann*
Drobek, Viktor	*Maschinenmaat*
Egon-Krieger, Klaus von	*Leutnant zur See*
Ehlers, Heinz	*Funkobergefreiter*
Faust, Josef	*Maschinenobergefreiter*
Fischer, Helmut	*Funkobergefreiter*
Fleischer, Helmut	
Franke, Fritz	*Maschinenobergefreiter*
Fricke, Herbert	*Matrose*
Haase, Rolf	*Maschinenobergefreiter*
Hartmann, Johann	*Maschinengefreiter*
Kahlert, Erwin	*Matrosenobergefreiter*
Kapitzky, Ralph	*Kapitänleutnant*
Kögelmeier, Alois	*Matrosenobergefreiter*
Köhler, Heinz	*Matrosengefreiter*
Kotzian, Edmund	*Maschinenmaat*
Krohn, Hans	*Matrosenobergefreiter*
Külsen, Günter	*Maschinenobergefreiter*
Langner, Helmut	*Oberbootsmaat*
Lehner, Stefan	*Maschinenmaat*
Lehr, Karl-Heinz	*Maschinengefreiter*
Mahnke, Rudolph	*Matrosenobergefreiter*
Mamzak, Walter	*Maschinenobergefreiter*

Marx, Otto	*Maschinenobergefreiter*
Meisch, Hans	*Maschinenobergefreiter*
Pruss, Josef	*Maschinenobergefreiter*
Reyak, Bernhard	*Maschinenobergefreiter*
Schlipper, Herbert	*Leutnant zur See*
Schnelle, Martin	*Obermaschinenmaat*
Schrader, Eugen	*Obermaschinist*
Schuhmann, Josef	*Funkmaat*
Schulteiss, Theo	*Funkmaat*
Schulz, Hermann	*Matrose*
Skora, Herbert	*Oberleutnant (Ing)*
Steppat, Fritz	*Matrosenobergefreiter*
Sura, Richard	*Matrosenobergefreiter*
Wilke, Heinz	*Bootsmannsmaat*
Wizuy, Rolf	*Mechanikerobergefreiter*
Zimmermann, Albert	*Bootsmannsmaat*
Zimmermann, Walter	*Mechanikerobergefreiter*

Sources, "What Really Happened Out There?:" Clay Blair, *Hitler's U-boat War: The Hunted, 1942-1945*, New York: Modern Library, 2000, 33, 38, 117, 128, 132, 262, 279, 363, 365; Rainer Busch and Hans-Joachim Röll, *German U-boat Commanders of World War II*, translated by Geoffrey Brooks, Annapolis, Maryland: Naval Institute Press, 1999, 121, 122, 269; Manfred Dörr, *Die Ritterkreuzträger der U-Boot-Waffe, Band 1: A-J, Band 2: L-Z*, Osnabrück, FRG: Biblio Verlag, 1988, Band 2 – 334, 335; Peter C. Hansen, *Execution for Duty: The Life, Trial & Murder of a U-boat Captain*, Barnsley, England: Pen & Sword Maritime, 2003, 123, 124, 125, 126, 127, 128, 129; Axel Niestlé, *German U-boat Losses during World War II*, Annapolis, Maryland: Naval Institute Press, 1998, 53; Jürgen Rohwer, *Axis Submarine Successes 1939-1945*, Annapolis, Maryland: Naval Institute Press, 1983, 206, 211, 212, 213; Theodore P. Savas, Editor, *Silent Hunters: German U-boat Commanders of World War II*, Campbell, CA: Savas Publishing, 1997, 44, 48-73; Axel Urbanke, Rainer Busch, Manfred Dörr, Andreas Dwulecki, Markus Dyhr, Thomas Huss, Wolfgang Ockert and Walter Storbeck, *U-boot im Focus: U-Boot-Historie von Enthusiasten für Enthusiasten*, Edition 1, Bad Zwischenahn: Luftfahrtverlag-Start, 2007, 38, 39, 40; War Diary of the *U-968*, March 7, 1944 – November 11, 1944, PG 30801/1-4; ONI Roll T-408-B, *National Archives Microfilm Publication T1022*, roll 3401, RG 242; War Diary of the *U-968*, September 9, 1944 – February 20, 1945, PG 30801/6-7; ONI Roll T-523, *National Archives Microfilm Publication T1022*, roll 3763, RG 242; Richard Whittingham, *Martial Justice: The Last Mass Execution in the United States*, Annapolis, Maryland: Naval Institute Press, 1997, 29-38, 46-50, 54, 55, 62, 81, 83, 86, 89, 102, 153-180, 206, 213, 219; www.ubootwaffe.net; www.uboatarchive.net; http://www.uboatarchive.net/U-615INT.htm (Office of the Chief of Naval Operations, Navy Department, "Report on the Interrogation of Survivors from *U-615* Sunk on 7 August 1943," Washington, DC, 22 September 1943).

Final victory tally pennants on the U-968, May 1945. *Six pennants to the left are red with warship silhouettes; white pennants on the right are for merchant sinkings. Photo was probably taken at Narvik; Oberleutnant Otto Westphalen is in white cap.*

Close-up view of victory tally pennants on the U-968, May 1945.

Oberleutnant Otto Westphalen receiving the Knight's Cross on March 23, 1945.

First two warship victory tally pennants for the U-968, April 1944. *Pennants are for the action on April 1, when the U-968 claimed two enemy destroyers sunk. Photo taken at either Narvik or Trondheim, Norway. Lower pennant has a black cat silhouette.*

Men of the U-968 stand formation on the deck of the boat in Norway. *Photo from the estate of Willi Lüders.*

Captain of the U-968 with flowers and men of the U-968 after a successful voyage in Norway. *Photo from the estate of Willi Lüders.*

Otto Westphalen, in white cap on boat's bridge, on the U-121 in 1942. *Emblem on the side of the conning tower is that of the U-121; emblem on the front of the tower is that of the 21st U-boat Flotilla. Photo from the estate of Willi Lüders.*

U-968 and crew at the entrance of fortified U-boat pens in Norway. *Photo from the estate of Willi Lüders.*

U-968 at commissioning ceremony on March 18, 1943. *Photo from the estate of Willi Lüders.*

Otto Westphalen, in white cap, is congratulated by a senior officer inside a fortified U-boat pen in Norway. *Photo from the estate of Willi Lüders.*

Otto Westphalen addressing a senior officer at the U-968 commissioning ceremony on March 18, 1943. *Photo from the estate of Willi Lüders.*

Otto Westphalen being awarded the Knight's Cross on the deck of the U-968, March 23, 1945.

Award ceremony for members of the crew of the U-968, 1945. *Fourth man from the left wearing German Cross in Gold is Oberfunkmaat Bruno Aniszewski. Otto Westphalen with Knight's Cross, German Cross in Gold and white cap is on the left.*

Award ceremony for members of the crew of the U-968. *Otto Westphalen is toward the right of the photo in white cap. He appears to be wearing the U-boat Front Clasp in Silver as do some of the other crewmembers.*

Crew of the U-968 in a fortified U-boat bunker in Norway. *Photo from the estate of Willi Lüders.*

Der Chef der Dienststelle M 36094

Im Westen, den 1. September 1943

Sehr verehrte Frau Lehr!

Der Anlaß meines heutigen Schreibens ist leider ein sehr schmerzlicher. Seit einiger Zeit bestand bei uns ernste Sorge um das Schicksal des Bootes, auf dem Ihr Sohn, Maschinengefreiter Karlheinz Lehr, kommandiert war. Nach Ablauf einer angemessenen Zeit ist es leider Gewißheit geworden, daß das Boot nicht mehr zurückkehrt. Daher hat die Ubootsführung Boot und Besatzung mit Wirkung vom 11. August 1943 als vermißt erklärt. Wie so oft im Ubootskrieg, wo jedes Boot auf sich allein gestellt kämpft, wissen wir zunächst nur wenig. Das Boot hat erfolgreich in der Karibischen See operiert und hierbei einen Tanker von 6 000 BRT. versenkt. Die Verlustursache ist zur Zeit noch unbekannt.

Über das Schicksal der braven Besatzung ist noch völlige Ungewißheit.

Ich weiß, daß nun für Sie, sehr verehrte Frau Lehr, die schwere Zeit des Bangens und Wartens beginnt. Seien Sie überzeugt, daß von unserer Seite alles getan wird, um Klarheit über das Schicksal unserer Kameraden zu bekommen.

Wir stehen in ständiger Fühlung mit dem Internationalen Roten Kreuz und allen militärischen Stellen, die zur Aufklärung beitragen können und werden stets als Erste über alles unterrichtet. Alles, was wir erfahren und sagen können, wird Ihnen sofort mitgeteilt.

Sollten Sie von anderer Seite irgendwelche Nachrichten über den Vermißten erhalten, so bitte ich Sie, diese dem Kommando mitzuteilen.

Für alle Fragen irgendwelcher Art ist jetzt die Dienststelle Feldpost-Nr. M 36094 zuständig. Wir stehen Ihnen selbstverständlich jederzeit voll zur Verfügung.

Mit herzlichem Mitgefühl in der Ungewißheit um das Schicksal Ihres Sohnes

Heil Hitler!

Zapp

Korvettenkapitän

Letter from the 3rd U-boat Flotilla to the family of Karl-Heinz Lehr of the U-615. *Letter is dated September 1, 1943 and is signed by Knight's Cross winner Korevettenkapitän Richard Zapp. The letter states that Lehr is missing in action.*

Im Westen, den 1. Oktober 1943

Dienststelle
dpostnummer M 36094

Sehr verehrte Frau Lehr!

Im Anschluß an das Schreiben vom 10.9. teilt Ihnen das Kommando mit, daß die hier vorgefundenen Privatsachen Ihres Sohnes nunmehr an Sie als den Empfangsberechtigten abgeschickt worden sind. Weitere Gegenstände liegen beim Kommando nicht vor. Es besteht jedoch die Möglichkeit, daß Ihr Sohn kleinere Privatsachen auf seiner letzten Fahrt mit an Bord hatte. Ein Inhaltsverzeichnis der übersandten Sachen ist beigefügt.

Die Dienstbekleidungsstücke Ihres Sohnes wurden hier vereinnahmt. Die noch in Ihrem Besitz befindlichen dienstlichen Bekleidungsstücke Ihres Sohnes wollen Sie bitte umgehend an das Marinealtbekleidungslager in Kiel senden. Ein Freifrachtbrief liegt bei.

Die anliegende Empfangsbestätigung wollen Sie bitte nach Erhalt des Gepäcks umgehend dem Kommando übersenden.

Heil Hitler!

Korvettenkapitän.

Second letter from the 3rd U-boat Flotilla to the family of Karl-Heinz Lehr of the U-615. *Letter is dated October 1, 1943 and is signed by a Korevettenkapitän. The letter is about Lehr's personal effects.*

Der Chef der Dienststelle M 36094

Im Westen, den 25. Oktober 1943

Sehr verehrte Frau Lehr!

Es freut mich Ihnen mitteilen zu können, daß Ihr vermißter Sohn,

Maschinengefreiter Karl Heinz Lehr,

gerettet worden ist. Nach Meldung des Internationalen Roten Kreuzes befindet er sich in amerikanischer Gefangenschaft, Camp Stringtown, Oklahoma, USA.

Die Bestimmungen für den Postverkehr mit den deutschen Kriegsgefangenen in USA. bitte beim Deutschen Roten Kreuz einzuholen.

Sollte Ihr Sohn Ihnen aus der Gefangenschaft irgendwelche Beschwerden mitteilen, so darf ich Sie bitten, dieselben anher zu senden.

Außerdem werden Sie gebeten, den ersten Brief aus der Gefangenschaft zur Einsichtnahme mir zu übersenden. Sie erhalten denselben sofort wieder zurück.

Heil Hitler!

Korvettenkapitän.

Third letter from the 3rd U-boat Flotilla to the family of Karl-Heinz Lehr of the U-615. *Letter is dated October 25, 1943 and is signed by a Korvettenkapitän. The letter states that Lehr is a prisoner of war at Camp Stringtown, Oklahoma.*

Ldst. IX

Deutsches Rotes Kreuz
Präsidium
Führungsstab

Aktz.: SW V v.A./Br.
(Bei Beantwortung unbedingt anzugeben)

W 50 f USA

Berlin SW 61, den 23.11.43
Blücherplatz 2
Fernruf: Sammelnummer 66 54 61
Nachtruf: 66 06 56, 66 07 11
Postscheckkonto: Berlin 60 70
Telegrammanschrift: Deutschrotkreuz
RAO US 308

Deutsches Rotes Kreuz-Präsidium
Amt S, Dienststelle Eisenach

Eisenach
Fürstenhof

Betr.: Karl Heinz Lehr, Feld.P.Nr. ?
Bez .:
Anl .: Ausführungsbestimmung 24c, 23 c

Familie
L e h r
Frankfurt a/Main
Gutzkowstr. 40

Das Deutsche Rote Kreuz teilt Ihnen folgendes mit:

Auf Grund einer Meldung des Internationalen Komitees vom Roten Kreuz in Genf, die auf einem amtlichen Kabel aus Washington beruht, befinden sich
Karl Heinz Lehr, geb. 14.7.24
in amerikanischer Kriegsgefangenschaft in den Vereinigten Saaten von Nordamerika. Seine Anschrift lautet:

Kriegsgefangenenpost
Prisoner of War Mail

Karl Heinz Lehr
German Prisoner of War in U.S.A.
Camp Stringtown Oklahoma
Prisoner of War Information Bureau
c/o Provost Marshal General
W a s h i n g t o n / D.C.
U.S.A.

Gebührenfrei
Postage free.

Sobald der Kriegsgefangene eine Kennziffer mit Buchstaben und Zahlen mitteilt, ist sie hinter den Namen einzufügen.

Über den Postverkehr geben die anliegenden Postbestimmungen Auskunft.

Eine weitere endgültige Benachrichtigung auf Grund der amtlichen schriftlichen Bestätigung der Feindseite geht Ihnen vom Arbeitsstab Tunis des zuständigen Wehrkreises zu. Diese Mitteilung erfolgt dann zugleich im Namen des Deutschen Roten Kreuzes.

Um Angabe der Feld.Post Nr. wird gebeten.

Heil Hitler !
Der Sonderbeauftragte
I.A. J. Meyer-Walden

C 0764

Letter from the German Red Cross to the family of Karl-Heinz Lehr of the U-615. *Letter is dated November 23, 1943 and provides an address in the United States to which they can send correspondence to their son.*

Photo of the U-8. *Karl-Heinz Lehr probably trained in this U-boat before reporting to the U-615.*

Photo of Maschinengefreiter Karl-Heinz Lehr.

U-boat stickpin for wear on civilian jacket. *Given the wear, it appears that Karl-Heinz Lehr wore this quite often after the war. Wreath measures 16-mm in width and 13-mm in height.*

APPENDICES

Appendix 1

German *Kriegsmarine* and U.S. Navy World War II Comparative Ranks

Officers

Korvettenkapitän	Lieutenant Commander
Kapitänleutnant	Lieutenant
Oberleutnant zur See	Lieutenant (j.g.)
Oberleutnant (Ing)	Lieutenant (j.g.) – Engineering duties only
Leutnant zur See	Ensign
Leutnant (Ing)	Ensign – Engineering duties only
Arzt	Ship's doctor

Officer Candidates

Oberfähnrich zur See	Senior Midshipman
Oberfähnrich (Ing)	Senior Midshipman – Engineering duties only
Fähnrich zur See	Midshipman
Fähnrich (Ing)	Midshipman – Engineering duties only

Senior Non-Commissioned Officers

Stabsoberbootsmann	Senior Chief Petty Officer/Senior Chief Boatswain
Oberbootsmann	Chief Petty Officer/Chief Boatswain
Bootsmann	Petty Officer 1st Class/Boatswain's Mate 1st Class
Stabsobermaschinist	Chief Senior Machinist
Obermaschinist	Senior Machinist
Maschinist	Machinist
Mechaniker	Torpedoman's Mate 1st Class
Oberfunkmeister	Senior Radioman
Stabsobersteuermann	Senior Navigator/Quartermaster
Obersteuermann	Navigator/Quartermaster
Steuermann	Helmsman

Junior Non-Commissioned Officers (Petty Officers)

Oberbootsmannsmaat	Petty Officer 2nd Class/Boatswain's Mate 2nd Class
Bootsmannsmaat	Petty Officer 3rd Class/Coxswain
Oberfunkmaat	Radioman 2nd Class
Funkmaat	Radioman 3rd Class
Obersignalmaat	Signalman 2nd Class
Signalmaat	Signalman 3rd Class
Obermaschinenmaat	Machinist's Mate 2nd Class
Maschinenmaat	Fireman 1st Class
*Obersteuermann*smaat	Senior Helmsman's Mate
*Steuermann*smaat	Helmsman's Mate
Obermechanikersmaat	Torpedoman's Mate 2nd Class
Mechanikersmaat	Torpedoman's Mate 3rd Class
Sanitätsmaat	Pharmacist's Mate 2nd Class

Enlisted Men

Matrosenhauptgefreiter	Senior Seaman 1st Class
Matrosenobergefreiter	Seaman 1st Class
Matrosengefreiter	Seaman 2nd Class
Funkobergefreiter	Seaman 1st Class (Radio Operator)
Funkgefreiter	Seaman 2nd Class (Radio Operator)
Maschinenobergefreiter	Fireman 2nd Class
Maschinengefreiter	Fireman 3rd Class
Mechanikerobergefreiter	Seaman 1st Class (Artillery or Torpedo)
Mechanikergefreiter	Seaman 2nd Class (Artillery or Torpedo)
Sanitätsobergefreiter	Pharmacist's Mate 2nd Class
Matrose I	Apprentice Seaman
Matrose II	Apprentice Seaman

Appendix 2

German *Kriegsmarine* Pre-War U-boat Organization

Flotilla: U-boat Flotilla *Weddigen*
Named after: *Kapitänleutnant* Otto Weddigen, World War I U-boat commander, who was killed in action on March 18, 1915.
Created: September 27, 1935
Home port: Kiel
U-boats assigned: *U-9*, *U-13*, *U-15*, *U-17*, *U-19*, *U-21* and *U-23*
U-boat tender for the unit: *Donau*
Converted to: 1st U-boat Flotilla, December 1939

Flotilla: U-boat Flotilla *Saltzwedel*
Named after: *Oberleutnant zur See* Reinhold Saltzwedel, World War I U-boat commander, who was killed in action on December 2, 1917.
Created: September 1, 1936
Home port: Kiel (1936), Wilhelmshaven (1936-1939)
U-boats assigned: *U-25*, *U-26*, *U-27*, *U-28*, *U-29*, *U-30*, *U-31*, *U-32*, *U-33*, *U-34* and *U-35*
U-boat tender for the unit: *Saar*
Converted to: 2nd U-boat Flotilla, September 1939

Flotilla: U-boat Flotilla *Lohs*
Named after: *Oberleutnant zur See* Johannes Lohs, World War I U-boat commander, who was killed in action on August 14, 1918.
Created: October 4, 1937
Home port: Kiel
U-boats assigned: *U-12*, *U-14*, *U-16*, *U-18*, *U-20*, *U-22* and *U-24*
U-boat tender for the unit: *Weichsel*
Disbanded: December 1939

Flotilla: U-boat Flotilla *Emsmann*
Named after: *Oberleutnant zur See* Hans Joachim Emsmann, World War I U-boat commander, who was killed in action on October 28, 1918.
Created: December 1, 1938
Home port: Kiel
U-boats assigned: *U-56*, *U-57*, *U-58* and *U-59*
U-boat tender for the unit: *Lech*
Disbanded: December 1939

Flotilla: U-boat Flotilla *Hundius*
Named after: *Kapitänleutnant* Paul Hundius, World War I U-boat commander, who was killed in action on September 16, 1918.
Created: October 1, 1938
Home port: Kiel
U-boats assigned: *U-37*, *U-38*, *U-39*, *U-40* and *U-41*
U-boat tender for the unit: *Isar*
Disbanded: December 1939

Flotilla: U-boat Flotilla *Wegener*
Named after: *Kapitänleutnant* Bernd Wegener, World War I U-boat commander, who was killed in action on August 19, 1915.
Created: June 25, 1938
Home port: Kiel
U-boats assigned: *U-45*, *U-46*, *U-47*, *U-48*, *U-51*, *U-52* and *U-53*
U-boat tender for the unit:
Converted to: 7th U-boat Flotilla, September 1940

Appendix 3
It's Your Turn

OK, it's your turn. We'll walk through the first example together. You come across this first document for sale for the Armed Forces Service Medal IV Class, for four years of service, to a sailor on the pocket battleship *Admiral Scheer*. The document is signed by the commander of the ship with the grade of *Kapitän zur See* and is dated 1 July 1938. The awardee is *Maschinenmaat* Wilhelm Jordt.

We can easily look up the commander of the *Admiral Scheer* at this time; it is future Knight's Cross winner and Admiral Otto Ciliax. Since the award is for four years service and dated in July 1938, we can deduce that Wilhelm Jordt entered the German Navy around 1 July 1934. Simply by knowing all this information, it is a nice document for a collection and can serve as a focal point for a detailed search for the operational history of the *Admiral Scheer*.

But there may be even more to the story. And it may involve U-boats.

Let's go to the *Volksbund Deutsche Kriegsgräberfürsorge* site on the Internet. This organization catalogues German war dead from World War I and World War II and assists in maintaining German military cemeteries throughout Europe and North Africa. This website is: http://www.volksbund.de/

The site is in German, but that will be no problem. When the first page comes up, click on the left-hand side for *Gräbersuche* (graves search). If it is your first time on the site, you may have to register, but you will be able to figure out where to put your name, etc. There is no registration cost. Once you get back to the actual search, after you hit the *Gräbersuche* button, a new screen will come up. Toward the top in the center, click on the words … *zur Onlinesuche* (to the online search). The next screen will have several fields. Start by filling in the top one: *Nachname* (or last name), with the word Jordt and then scroll downward and click *Suche beginnen* (begin search). A new screen will come up with a list of ten names, Jordt, Erich; Jordt, Friedrich, etc. None of the first names match so scroll down and click on … *vor blättern* (next pages). The second (and last) page lists six additional men with the last name of Jordt but once again, none have the first name of Wilhelm (or any derivative such as Willy or Willi). We thus have a pretty good idea that Wilhelm Jordt did not die during the war. While the *Volksbund Deutsche Kriegsgräberfürsorge* does not list every soldier killed (no complex database is 100% accurate), it is recognized as the most complete source of this information.

Are we stuck? No, there is more to search. Very briefly, we know from reading about the *Admiral Scheer* that just before the date of our document, the *Admiral Scheer* was sent to Spain as part of the German contingent to the Spanish Civil War. Beginning in 1939 and lasting through 1942 she served as a surface raider, but then rarely left port. Therefore, it is possible that *Maschinenmaat* Jordt may have served on another ship; thousands of German sailors on surface ships were transferred to the U-boats and maybe that happened to Wilhelm Jordt – let's check for U-boat service.

Go again to the Internet to the site *ubootwaffe.net*: http://www.ubootwaffe.net/

This site is in English. On the first page look to the left and click on the category Crew Lists for World War II. The next screen you see will have an area called Surname; type in Jordt in this block and click on the button search by name. What have we here? Only one name, that of Wilhelm Jordt. It lists him as being born on 30 June 1914 and as having served on the *U-459*, becoming a prisoner of war on 24 July 1943. His last rank was an *Obermaschinist*, a senior chief petty officer. The *ubootwaffe.net* database is very complete, listing over 50,000, but only one is a Jordt and he has a derivative first name of Willy. Could this be the same man that is on our document?

With only this information we cannot be certain, but for many reasons one can reasonably assume that the two men are the same. First, with this date of birth and the entry date into the German Navy, it indicates that Jordt joined the service on about his twentieth birthday, which was frequently when young men enlisted. Second, the rank of *Obermaschinist* is very senior. On most U-boats there were only two such men; one was in charge of the diesel engines and the other oversaw the operation of the electric motors for submerged operations (both under the supervision of the Chief Engineer). A career sailor who was a *Maschinenmaat* in 1936 could later have been promoted to *Obermaschinenmaat*, *Maschinist* and then *Obermaschinist* over the next six years – in fact, this would have been almost his exact career path in this specialty. We also have a reliable source that Wilhelm Jordt was not killed during the war; the fact that Willy Jordt was a prisoner off the *U-459* and survived the conflict supports this.

Lastly, we got lucky with his last name; had that name been Schmidt or Müller, we may have well been stymied. With Jordt, we have only one in the entire U-boat fleet, very probably the same man as is on our document.

Now all that remains is to look up information on the *U-459*. The quickest way is to go back to the *ubootwaffe.net*. Go to the home page and in the upper left corner type in 459 in the window next to U- and hit the search button. Another excellent site you should visit is the *uboat.net*: http://uboat.net/

It is in English also; work your way through the windows to the list of all U-boats and click on *U-459*. It does not list the crew as the other site does, but has a fuller section on what happened to each boat.

After you glean the information in these two sites, you can fill in more details by going to some of the books listed in the annotated bibliography that follows. One simple document can give you days of interesting research. What once was just an old piece of paper is now a window into history.

Here are some helpful reminders. The U-boat War Badge was generally awarded after the sailor completed two or three war patrols. Unusual circumstances could permit the award after the first war patrol in some instances. In at least one instance – on the *U-615* – the award criterion was described as sixty cumulative days on war patrols. A posthumous award could occur if the sailor was killed on the very first war patrol. The award of this badge usually occurred on the day the U-boat returned to port or the following day; therefore, a U-boat War Badge award document dated 7 September 1943 is a good indication that the U-boat to which the sailor was assigned arrived in port on September 6 or 7.

The Iron Cross 2nd Class was generally awarded right after the U-boat returned to port. In many instances the sailor first won the U-boat War Badge and then on a subsequent patrol received the Iron Cross 2nd Class, although legitimate examples exist where the sailor won both awards on the same day, and even some instances when the sailor won the Iron Cross 2nd Class on his first war patrol and the U-boat war Badge on his second patrol. When a sailor received an Iron Cross 2nd Class, it is worth examining what the boat did on that patrol. For example, a sailor in the engine room who won an Iron Cross 2nd Class may well have been on a long patrol or when there were engine problems that he and his crewmates fixed. Another

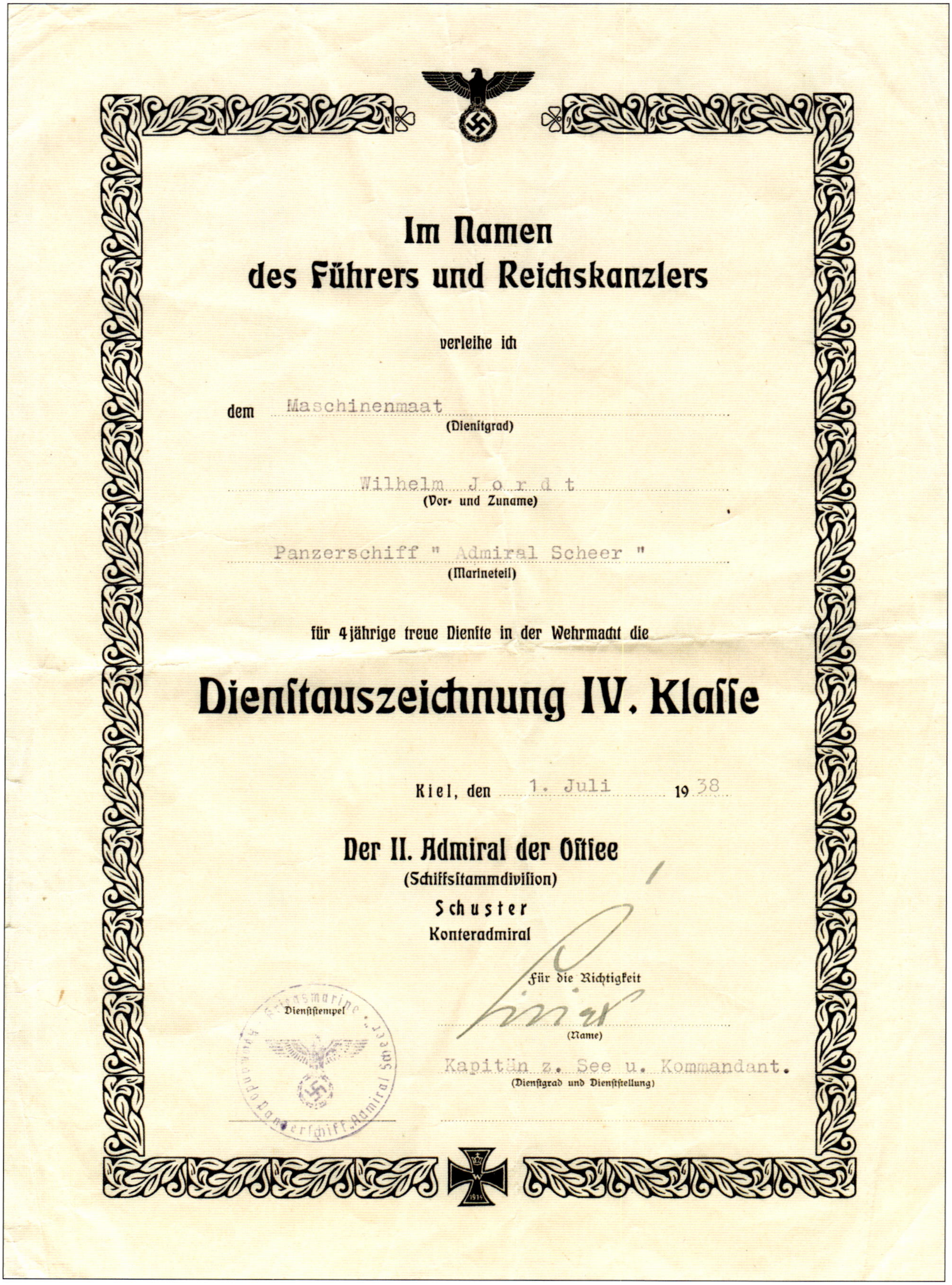

Im Namen
des Führers und Reichskanzlers

verleihe ich

dem Maschinenmaat
(Dienstgrad)

Wilhelm Jordt
(Vor- und Zuname)

Panzerschiff " Admiral Scheer "
(Marineteil)

für 4jährige treue Dienste in der Wehrmacht die

Dienstauszeichnung IV. Klasse

Kiel, den 1. Juli 1938

Der II. Admiral der Ostsee
(Schiffsstammdivision)
Schuster
Konteradmiral

Für die Richtigkeit

(Name)

Kapitän z. See u. Kommandant.
(Dienstgrad und Dienststellung)

Dienststempel

Kriegsmarine
Kommando Panzerschiff Admiral Scheer

Armed Forces Service Medal IV Class award document, for four years of service, to Wilhelm Jordt.

example may be an anti-aircraft gunner who fought off an enemy air attack.

This is not the case with the Iron Cross 1st Class. The dates on the award document rarely are linked to return-to-port dates. Except in extremely rare circumstances – where the Iron Cross 2nd Class and Iron Cross 1st Class were presented on the same day – a sailor almost always received the Iron Cross 2nd Class before he received the Iron Cross 1st Class.

The same information applies to the German Cross in Gold and the U-boat Front Clasp in Bronze and Silver. All three documents were generally not linked to just one patrol so all three were generally not awarded immediately after return from patrol. Concerning the German Cross in Gold, the sailor first had to have been awarded the Iron Cross 2nd Class and Iron Cross 1st Class. He had to receive the U-boat War Badge before receiving the U-boat Front Clasp in Bronze, and the clasp in bronze before the clasp in silver.

• • • • •

Now you are completely on your own. Examine the next three documents. The first document is a *Reichssportabzeichen* (Reich Sports Badge). Looking through it reveals the sailor's name as Günther Gutzeit. It also shows that he was born on 4 October 1924. The second document is an Iron Cross 2nd Class dated 10 September 1943. It is to *Maschinengefreiter* Günther Gutzeit. The third document is for the U-boat War Badge; it is also dated 10 September 1943 and is also to *Maschinengefreiter* Günther Gutzeit. These last documents have a stamped signature of a *Kapitän zur See* who is the *Führer der Unterseeboote West*. You know you have a nice compact set of documents to a U-boat sailor.

Try and answer the following questions:

What U-boat was Günther Gutzeit a member of the crew? Given his rank, where on the U-boat do you think he worked?

Who commanded the U-boat? Was he a successful commander? What awards did this commander receive during the war? What happened to him?

Whose stamped signature is on these last two documents? What did he do in the war?

In which port did Günther Gutzeit receive the U-boat War Badge and the Iron Cross 2nd Class?

Where did the U-boat go on patrol and what did it do on the patrol after which Günther Gutzeit received his U-boat War Badge and Iron Cross 2nd Class?

What was the history of this U-boat? How successful was this U-boat? Did it sink any large enemy warships? Did it participate on any unusual missions? What happened to the U-boat? If it was sunk, did anyone survive?

What happened to Günther Gutzeit? Did he serve on any other U-boats during the war? Was he killed in action or become a prisoner of war? Did he receive any other military awards? Did he survive the war?

As you can see, finding the information for just this one U-boat sailor can give you your own insight into the U-boat war and what Dönitz's crews went through.

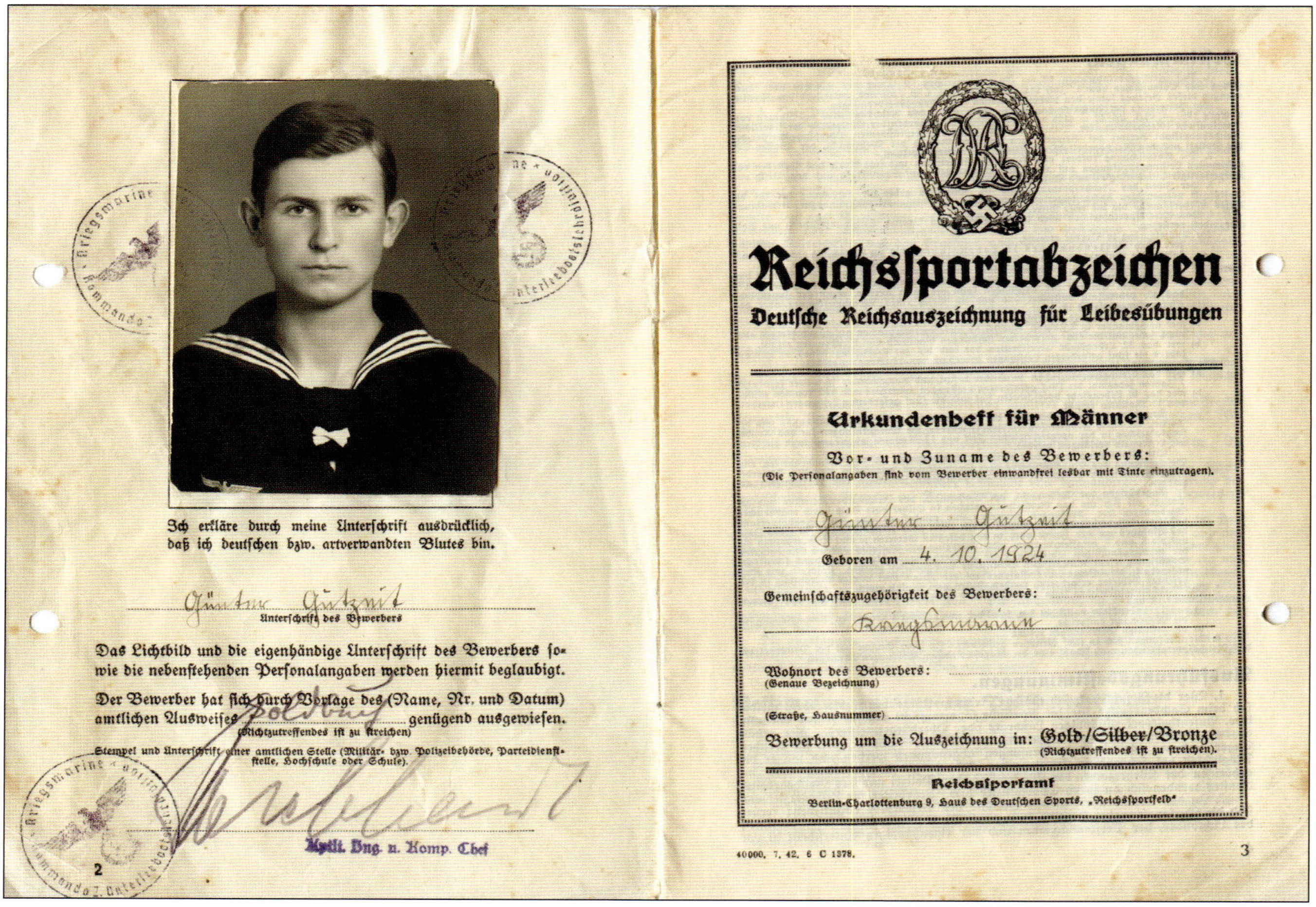

Reich Sports Badge in Bronze award document to Günther Gutzeit.

Verleihungs-Urkunde

Auf Grund der Ermächtigung des Oberbefehlshabers der Kriegsmarine verleihe ich dem

Maschinengefreiten
(Dienstgrad)

Günter Gutzeit
(Name)

das

Ubootskriegsabzeichen 1939

Im Westen, den 10. September 19 43

Kapitän zur See
und Führer der Unterseeboote West

(MS 87108)

U-boat War Badge award document to Günther Gutzeit dated September 10, 1943.

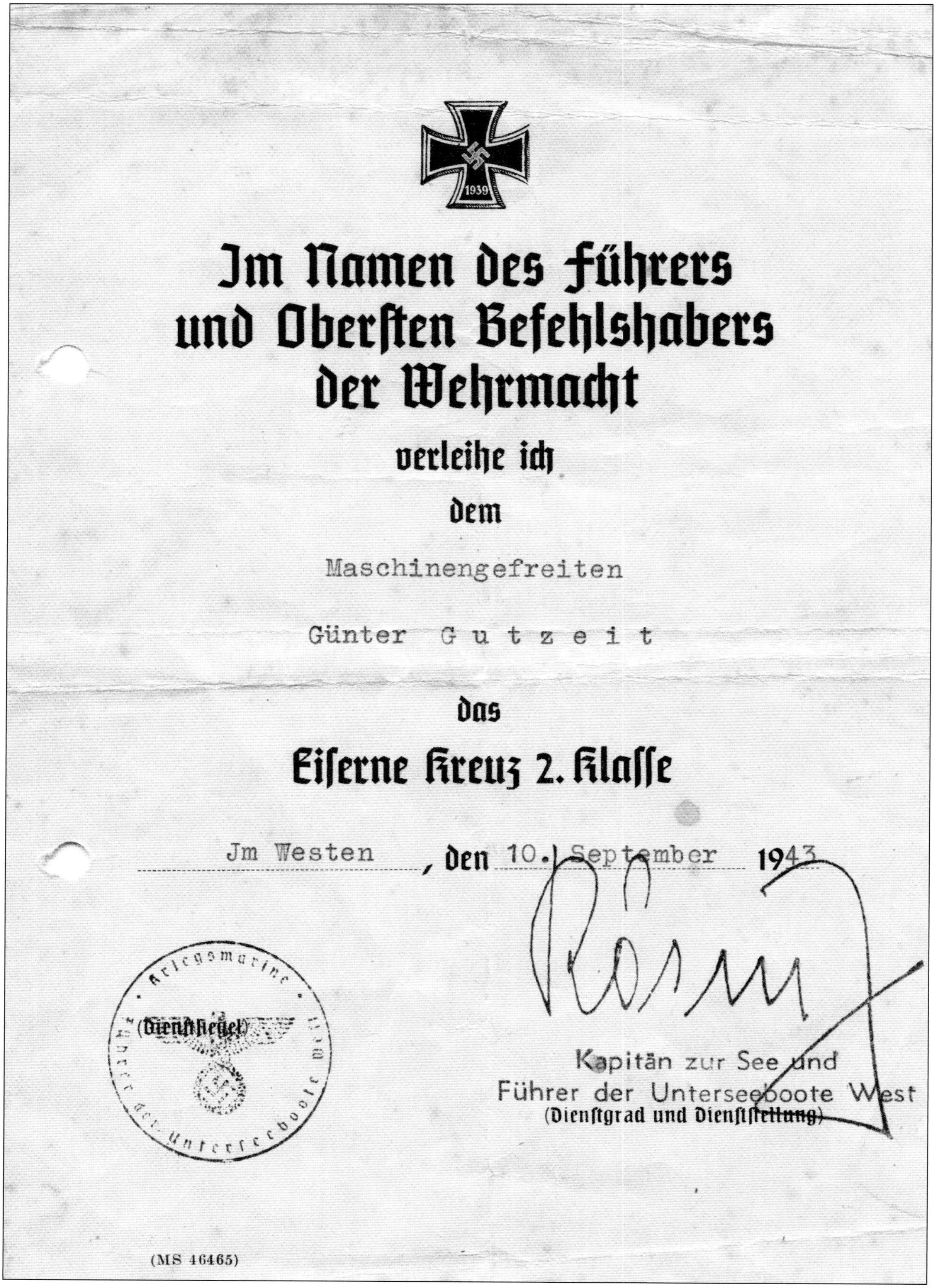

1939

Im Namen des Führers
und Obersten Befehlshabers
der Wehrmacht

verleihe ich

dem

Maschinengefreiten

Günter Gutzeit

das

Eiserne Kreuz 2. Klasse

Jm Westen, den 10. September 1943

Kriegsmarine
(Dienstsiegel)
Führer der Unterseeboote West

Kapitän zur See und
Führer der Unterseeboote West
(Dienstgrad und Dienststellung)

(MS 46465)

Iron Cross 2nd Class award document to Günther Gutzeit dated September 10, 1943.

Appendix 4
Where to Find U-boat Artifacts

OK, let me first put every spouse's and parents' worries at ease, this is not an explanation for how to scuba dive and find artifacts on German U-boat wrecks. One, it is dangerous; second, it is expensive and third, you won't find any personal effects on a submerged wreck that has been subjected to salt water for over half a century. But you can find researchable documents and papers around the world on land with little danger to your personal well being – unless you go over your budget (more on that later).

Having said that, I must first warn you about a danger in U-boat (and other militaria) collecting that is every bit as worrisome to a historical collector as a rip-tide is to a diver – the historical fake. There is no clear equation on how to spot and avoid a fake. I would say there are three techniques you can use to minimize the possibility that you will be stuck with an item that did not originate in World War II.

First, read everything you can on the subject, and obtain for your own personal library the many good sources on the history surrounding the U-boat war (or any other period you are researching). Jak Mallmann Showell puts out some great books (see bibliography). There are several excellent books on the actual items themselves and are also mentioned in the bibliography. Producers and purveyors of fakes generally take great pains to get the material correct from a standpoint of construction, but frequently spend little time getting the actual history-piece correct. Thus, if you come across documents for a specific U-boat that are dated before that boat was commissioned, for example, that would immediately raise suspicions. Or if you find a document signed by a *Korvettenkapitän* Schmidt as the commander of a certain U-boat flotilla and you know that no officer named Schmidt commanded that unit, you should start asking questions. Concerning the items themselves, if you only have the opportunity to obtain one book, get Gordon Williamson's *Torpedo los! The Fascinating World of U-boat Collectibles*. If you intend to obtain all types of German medals, you may want to consider buying Michael Tucker's and Stephen Previtera's *German Combat Badges of the Third Reich, Volume 1* and LTC (Retired) John R. Angolia's *For Führer and Fatherland: Military Awards of the Third Reich*, if you can find it.

Second, try and specialize in one area. The best military antique collectors and dealers have taken decades to learn everything they can on the subject and most would readily admit that they have not seen everything. The more you can specialize, the faster you can get proficient. For me, that specialization is document collecting; any cloth uniform part or insignia that I come across, for example, I need help with.

Third, and this may be the most important, buy from and consult with knowledgeable sources that you trust. This is easier said than done and takes years of building that trust. Added to that, there is always someone, most likely a competitor-dealer who has nothing good to say about specific dealers – in part because they are in competition for your dollar and second, because there is no real body who can adjudicate which dealers are reputable and which are not. Merely by placing a seed of doubt (and it can even be done with an exaggerated facial gesture) may be enough to cause one consternation when considering a purchase from another dealer. I will be listing those dealers with whom I have had positive experiences in just a moment; here are a few basic techniques you may want to consider:

1. Will the dealer give you a return right and for how long? Some dealers give a lifetime return right; others will not accept any return once you walk away with your new purchase; most are somewhere in-between.
2. What is the provenance of the item? It may not be a problem if there is no real chain of custody and the dealer bought it from another collector. Sometimes if a dealer bought the item from a veteran's family it is fine, but sometimes it is not. I generally have found that the wilder the tale is on how the item was originally obtained ("The guy who got this was in the OSS and snuck into Berlin in 1943 and stole it from Hitler's bunker!") the more likely it is suspect. German medals do not have the winner's name engraved on them (such as many British medals) or have a serial number (as many Soviet medals did) so without paperwork such as the actual award documents there is no way you can look at the medals and determine the name of the sailor who won them, unless there is a pretty "airtight" provenance and you ought to get that in writing.
3. Just because four items in a group to one sailor are legitimate does not mean that the fifth is. Unscrupulous dealers have been known to take a perfectly genuine set of items and add a fake piece to significantly increase the value of the set (such as a U-boat Clasp in Bronze.)
4. Has the dealer been honest with you in the past? I would classify dealers into one of four categories: (1) Honest/Expert – this is a dealer who knows his subject area and is also not going to knowingly sell you a fake; (2) Dishonest/Expert – the worst kind as he knows what is genuine and has no problem lying to you and pushing off a fake on you or trying to gouge you on the cost; (3) Honest/Amateur – tries to be a good dealer, and might occasionally even have some good pieces, but his lack of knowledge will end up costing you in the long run; (4) Dishonest/Amateur – Don't even bother talking to him as he won't care what you are saying. When you see the same items in a dealer's inventory year after year, you should ask yourself why no one is buying them.
5. There are thousands of "experts" on the internet. For every item there are those who will say it is a fake and those who will maintain it is genuine. Since they have no financial stake in the piece, it is usually best to stick with experts you personally know.
6. Concerning Ebay auctions, I generally will only buy a photo or perhaps a death announcement. For a substantial item I want to get a dialogue going with a seller that I personally know before I obtain it.

Given all this, here is a list of sources I have found to be very helpful in my collecting over the years, especially recently concerning U-boat items. They are listed by longevity concerning doing business with them; I have always had successful relations with every one over the years:

- Andre Hüsken, Hamburg, Germany: http://www.huesken.com/. Speaks English, large selection, medals/documents/uniforms/photos, updates inventory every few days, have collected from him for 31 years.

- Detlev Niemann, Hamburg, Germany: http://www.detlev-niemann.de/. Fluent English, generally concentrates on medals/documents, updates inventory every Friday (new items go quickly), offers a written certificate guarantee of authenticity for items over a certain price, have collected from him for 27 years.

• Christian Schmidt, Munich, Germany: http://www.christian-schmidt.com/. A tremendous bookstore, not a military antique store; fluent English, specializes in military books (especially those published in Germany), have been a customer for 26 years.

• Helmut Weitze, Hamburg, Germany: https://www.weitze.net/. Fluent English, large selection medals/documents/uniforms/photos, updates inventory every Friday, have collected from him for 26 years.

• Bob Ruman (Articles of War), Silver City, New Mexico: http://www.articlesofwar.com/index.cfm. Another outstanding bookstore, not a military antique store; specializes in military books, have been a customer for 23 years.

• Claus Phillip, Buchholz, Germany: http://www.philipp-militaria.de/. Large selection medals/documents/uniforms/photos, heavier on *Kriegsmarine*, updates inventory generally about once a month, offers a written certificate guarantee of authenticity for items over a certain price, have collected from him for 17 years.

• Thomas Huss, Kiel, Germany: http://www.german-historica.de/. Speaks English, specializes in *Kriegsmarine* medals/documents/uniforms/photos (but has other items), updates inventory generally once or twice a week, have collected from him for 3 years.

• Rick White (Historical-Media), Plymouth, Florida: http://www.historical-media.com/. Specializes in photos, sells from his website and also in Ebay auctions, have collected from him for 2 years.

Now we need to address costs. Military antiques can run from several dollars (sometimes more in an Ebay feeding frenzy) for an original photo, to between $50 and $100 for a death announcement or a photo of a Knight's Cross winner signed after the war, to hundreds of dollars for a medal or a document (or a photo of a Knight's Cross winner that was signed during the war), to $500 to $1,500 for a set of items to one U-boat man, to several thousand dollars to a set of items for a German Cross in Gold winner in the U-boat service, to over $10,000 (sometimes well over) for a set of items including a Knight's Cross for a successful U-boat commander. By developing a relationship with a reputable dealer you can get a fair price, but as you can see it still may be very expensive; that is why you can't afford to get stuck with something that is not genuine. Equally as important, by doing your own research you can actually increase the value of your U-boat artifact if you determine it is to a sailor on a very successful U-boat, a sailor who worked directly for a Knight's Cross winner, or to a sailor/U-boat with a very interesting history.

In fact, in your research you may find something that no historian had ever uncovered before and that will be very satisfying.

Annotated Bibliography

Published Books

Angolia, LTC John R. *For Führer and Fatherland: Military Awards of the Third Reich*, San Jose, California: R. James Bender, 1976. The best old standby for collecting German World War II medals, it covers the medals and the award documents.

Bennett, G. H. and Bennett, R. *Hitler's Admirals*, Annapolis, Maryland: Naval Institute Press, 2004. This is an excellent compilation of debriefings of captured German admirals immediately after World War II by British naval intelligence. The authors re-organize the answers given by the admirals into chronological events through the war; Grand Admiral Dönitz was among those who were part of this study.

Bishop, Chris. *Kriegsmarine U-boats 1939-45*, London: Amber Books, 2006. Organized by U-boat flotilla, if a U-boat enthusiast has room in the library for just one book on the subject, this is that book. Many drawings and photos cover technical details, brief (often single paragraph) histories for many boats and famous commanders.

Blair, Clay. *Hitler's U-boat War: The Hunters, 1939-1942*, New York: Random House, 1996. This is an excellent massive work that ties tactics, technology, personnel and operations together; first of a two-book set.

Blair, Clay. *Hitler's U-boat War: The Hunted, 1942-1945*, New York: Modern Library, 2000. Final volume of Blair's excellent work; this second volume is much harder to find than the first.

Brennecke, Jochen. *The Hunters and the Hunted*, translated by R. H. Stevens, New York: W. W. Norton and Company, 1957. One of the first and best-reading books on U-boats, it is written in an entertaining narrative style; there are no footnotes but it is apparent the author interviewed many significant participants. Unfortunately, it is very difficult to find a copy.

Busch, Rainer and Hans-Joachim Röll. *German U-boat Commanders of World War II*, translated by Geoffrey Brooks, Annapolis, Maryland: Naval Institute Press, 1999. The work contains thumbnail biographical information on 1,411 known German U-boat commanders of the period 1935-1945.

Cremer, Peter. *U-boat Commander: A Periscope View of the Battle of the Atlantic*, translated by Lawrence Wilson, Annapolis, Maryland: Naval Institute Press, 1984. Peter Cremer was a Knight's Cross winner and commander of the U-333.

Delize, Jean. *U-boote Crews: Daily Life, 1939-1945*, Paris, France: Histoire & Collections, 2007. This is an excellent book that describes day-to-day life on a U-boat; richly illustrated.

Dönitz, Karl. *Memoirs: Ten Years and Twenty Days*, translated by R. H. Stevens, Annapolis, Maryland: Da Capo Press, 1997. A view of the U-boat war by the man who led it, it is a must read to understand what Dönitz was trying to achieve and how he saw – or didn't see – Allied counter-measures.

Dörr, Manfred. *Die Ritterkreuzträger der U-Boot-Waffe, Band 1: A-J, Band 2: L-Z*, Osnabrück, FRG: Biblio Verlag, 1988. This is a two-volume set of the extensive Biblio Verlag series on Knight's Cross winners (*Ritterkreuzträger*). Organized alphabetically by last name of the awardee, it has a large number of excellent tables. Written in German, the format is easy to translate key facts with a dictionary.

Edwards, Bernard. *Death in the Doldrums: U-Cruiser Actions Off West Africa*, Annapolis, Maryland: Naval Institute Press, 2005. This quick-reading book focuses on the actions of the *U-68* and *U-505* off West Africa in 1942.

Gannon, Michael. *Black May: The Epic Story of the Allies Defeat of the German U-boats in May 1943*, New York: HarperCollins, 1998. Historian Michael Gannon has produced an extremely detailed account of this pivotal month in the Battle of the Atlantic.

Gannon, Michael. *Operation Drumbeat: The Dramatic True Story of Germany's First U-boat Attacks Along the American Coast in World War II*, New York: Harper & Row, 1990. A well-written and detailed presentation of Dönitz's first offensive in American waters; the endnotes are a treasure-trove of information on their own.

Goebeler, Jans. *Steel Boat, Iron Hearts: A U-boat Crewman's Life aboard U-505*, New York: Savas Beatie, 2006. The author presents an excellent first person account of U-boat life; he also adds an excellent sense of humor to his descriptions.

Hadley, Michael L. *U-boats against Canada: German Submarines in Canadian Waters*, Montreal: McGill-Queen's University Press, 1990. This is a well-written, comprehensive treatment of all U-boat operations in the Canadian theater of operations. Particularly well done are accounts of German special operations involving U-boats.

Hansen, Peter C. *Execution for Duty: The Life, Trial & Murder of a U-boat Captain*, Barnsley, England: Pen & Sword Maritime, 2003. This is the story of the career, trial and execution of Oskar Kusch, commander of the *U-154*.

Hessler, Günter. *The U-boat War in the Atlantic, 1939-1945, Volume 1-3*, London: Her Majesty's Stationery Office, 1989. Authored by the former commander of the *U-107* (and a staff officer for the

B.d.U.) for the British Ministry of Defense in the years immediately following World War II, Hessler was also Karl Dönitz's son-in-law. This is an excellent, detailed account of the German U-boat war in its major theater of operations.

Högel, Georg. *Embleme, Wappen, Malings deutscher U-Boote 1939-1945*, Herford, Deutschland: Koehler, 1987. Written in German, this book describes hundreds of distinctive U-boat emblems, conning tower drawings and boat crests used during the war. An abbreviated format allows non-German readers to understand which boats had particular emblems.

Jones, Geoffrey. *U-boat Aces*, Bristol, England: Cerberus Publishing, 2005. This work provides an excellent collection of U-boat and U-boat commander accomplishments.

Kurowski, Franz. *Knight's Cross Holders of the U-Boat Service*, Atglen, PA: Schiffer Publishing, 1995.

Lohmann, Walter und Hans H. Hildebrandt. *Die Deutsche Kriegsmarine 1939-1945*, Bad Nauheim, FRG: Verlag Hans-Henning Podzun, 1956. Three-volume set lists all ships in the German Navy with technical details, commanders and operational history; it is a veritable who's who of the *Kriegsmarine*, but is very difficult to find.

McKee, Alexander. *Black Sunday: The Royal Oak Tragedy at Scapa Flow*, Bristol, England: Cerberus, 2004. This is an excellent description of the events that unfolded on the *HMS Royal Oak*, although the author does not believe that the *U-47* sank the British battleship.

Niestlé, Axel. *German U-boat Losses during World War II*, Annapolis, Maryland: Naval Institute Press, 1998. Organized as one huge six-column table, it is the latest and best summary of U-boat losses during the war.

Parkin, Robert Sinclair. *Blood on the Sea: American Destroyers Lost in World War II*, New York: Sarpedon, 1996. This work provides a very detailed account of the final battle between the *USS Borie* and the *U-405* in 1943.

Paterson, Lawrence. *Hitler's Grey Wolves: U-boats in the Indian Ocean*, London: Greenhill Books, 2004. Lawrence Paterson is a proven historian of note with respect to all subjects related to Germany's undersea arm. This excellent study covers all U-boat operations in the Indian Ocean and Far East.

Paterson, Lawrence. *U-boat Combat Missions*, New York: Barnes & Noble, 2007. This is perhaps the best book available concerning interior photographs of a Type VII U-boat, the *U-995*. It also provides an excellent description of each compartment and the duties of every crewman aboard.

Paterson, Lawrence. *U-boats in the Mediterranean, 1941-1944*, Annapolis, Maryland: Naval Institute Press, 2007. As the title indicates, this is the story of German U-boats and U-boat operations in the Med.

Ritschel, Herbert. *Kurzfassung Kriegstagebücher deutscher U-boote 1939-1945, Band 1: KTB U1 – U50, Band 2: KTB U51-U99, Band 3: KTB U100 – U124, Band 5: KTB U171 – U222*, Norderstedt, Germany: Books on Demand. This multi-volume set contains the abridged versions of the war diaries (*Kriegstagebücher*, or *KTB*) for every U-boat. Written in German, with the abbreviations list and a dictionary almost any historian or history student can quickly get the hang of what is contained in them.

Rohwer, Jürgen. *Axis Submarine Successes 1939-1945*, Annapolis, Maryland: Naval Institute Press, 1983. This contains key information on every claimed Axis submarine success to include location, submarine, commander, type of weapon, name of target, size of target, etc. It also includes a valuable series of maps of the world's oceans showing German Navy quadrants for reporting and giving movement instructions.

Rose, Olaf. *U-751: Triumph und Tragödie eines deutschen U-bootes*, Inning am Amersee, Germany: Vowinkel, 2002. This is primarily a photo history of the *U-751*.

Savas, Theodore P., Editor. *Silent Hunters: German U-boat Commanders of World War II*, Campbell, CA: Savas Publishing, 1997. This book covers the careers of U-boat commanders: Engelbert Endrass, Karl-Friedrich Merten, Ralph Kapitsky, Fritz Guggenberger, Victor Oehrn and Heinz-Wilhelm Eck.

Scheibert, Horst. *Die Träger der Ehrenblattspange des Heeres und der Waffen-SS, Die Träger der Ehrentafelspange der Kriegsmarine, Die Inhaber des Ehrenpokals für Besondere Leistung im Luftkrieg*, Friedberg, FRG: Podzun-Pallas-Verlag, 1986. The book lists all winners of these awards.

Showell, Jak Mallmann. *Enigma U-boats: Breaking the Code*, Annapolis, Maryland: Naval Institute Press, 2000. This richly illustrated work describes the role of codes and code breaking in the U-boat war. It also presents an excellent description of all U-boats boarded by the Allies during the war.

Showell, Jak Mallmann. *German Navy Handbook, 1939-1945*, Thrupp, England: Sutton Publishing, 1999. General discussion of all *Kriegsmarine* topics, it is especially valuable on midget submarine topics.

Showell, Jak Mallmann. *The German Navy in World War Two*, Annapolis, Maryland: Naval Institute Press, 1979. Overall reference guide to the *Kriegsmarine* from 1935 to 1945, it is an excellent mix of technical subjects, tactics and historical accounts.

Showell, Jak Mallmann. *U-boats at War: Landings on Hostile Shores*, Hersham, England: Ian Allan Publishing, 2000. As the title suggest, this book is a recapitulation of most of the U-boat operations involving landings on enemy territory.

Showell, Jak Mallmann. *U-boat Warfare: The Evolution of the Wolf Pack*, Annapolis, Maryland: Naval Institute Press, 2002. Book presents an interesting point of view on the effectiveness of wolf pack tactics from the beginning of the war until 1943.

Showell, Jak Mallmann. *Wolfpacks at War: The U Boat Experience in World War II*, Hersham, England: Ian Allan Publishing, 2002. A short book, but richly illustrated with excellent discussions on what life was like for a U-boat sailor.

Syrett, David. *The Defeat of the German U-boats: The Battle of the Atlantic*, Columbia, South Carolina: University of South Carolina Press, 1994. This is an excellent coverage of the U-boat war from April 10 to December 7, 1943 when the outcome hung in the balance before shifting permanently to the favor of the Allies. Very well written, it is hard to find.

Tucker, Michael and Stephen Previtera, *German Combat Badges of the Third Reich, Volume 1*, Richmond, Virginia: Winidore Press, 2002. This is an excellent treatment of German World War II Army and Navy badges; there are a few pages devoted to the U-boat War Badge.

Tuleja, T.V., *Twilight of the Sea Gods*, New York: W.W. Norton & Company, 1958.

Urbanke, Axel, Rainer Busch, Manfred Dörr, Andreas Dwulecki, Markus Dyhr, Thomas Huss, Wolfgang Ockert and Walter Storbeck, *U-boot im Focus: U-Boot-Historie von Enthusiasten für Enthusiasten*, Edition 1, Edition 2, Bad Zwischenahn: Luftfahrtverlag-Start, 2007.

Vause, Jordan. *U-boat Ace: the story of Wolfgang Lüth*, Annapolis, Maryland: Naval Institute Press, 1990.

Werner, Herbert A. *Iron Coffins*, New York: Holt, Rinehart and Winston, 1969. The author was a former U-boat commander; the book is about his experiences on several boats.

Westwood, David. *The U-boat War: The German Submarine Service and the Battle of the Atlantic, 1935-1945*, Philadelphia, PA: Casemate, 2005.

Whittingham, Richard. *Martial Justice: The Last Mass Execution in the United States*, Annapolis, Maryland: Naval Institute Press, 1997. History of the murder of German prisoner of war Werner Drechsler and the subsequent court-martial of the perpetrators; several were U-boat sailors from the *U-615*.

Wiggins, Melanie. *Torpedoes in the Gulf: Galveston and the U-boats, 1942-1943*, College Station, TX: Texas A&M University Press, 1995. The book describes U-boat actions in the Gulf of Mexico off the U.S. coast.

Williamson, Gordon. *Torpedo los! The Fascinating World of U-boat Collectibles*, San Jose, CA: R. James Bender Publishing, 2006. Richly illustrated, this book was the inspiration for my own as I saw how pieces of history could be used to personalize a description of the U-boat war.

Williamson, Gordon. *U-Boat Bases and Bunkers 1941-45*, Oxford, England: Osprey Publishing, 2003. Part of the Fortress Series, this well-illustrated book delves into German submarine bases along the Atlantic Coast in World War II.

Williamson, Gordon. *Wolf Pack: The Story of the U-boat in World War II*, Oxford, England: Osprey Publishing, 2006. This is actually a compendium of three previous Osprey books on U-boats; it is an excellent single source on everything from types of U-boat bunkers to torpedoes.

Wise, Captain James E., Jr. *Sole Survivors of the Sea*, Baltimore, Maryland: The Nautical & Aviation Publishing Company of America, 1994. As the title suggests, this is the story of several sole survivors of ships sunk during wartime. There are some excellent prisoner of war accounts of several U-boat men who were sole survivors when their submarine sank. Most helpful to this book was the account of the Chief Engineer of the *U-413*.

Archives Records

National Archives Microfilm Publication T1022, Records of the German Navy, 1850-1945, Washington, D.C.: National Archives and Records Administration (NARA):

War Diary of the *U-14*, August 23, 1939 – June 12, 1941, PG 30011/1-8; ONI Roll T-297-B, *National Archives Microfilm Publication T1022,* roll 3027, RG 242.

War Diary of the *U-25*, September 1, 1939 – August 2, 1940, PG 30022/1-9; ONI Roll T-297-B, *National Archives Microfilm Publication T1022,* roll 3027, RG 242.

War Diary of the *U-51*, December 12, 1939 – August 18, 1940, PG 30048/1-7; ONI Roll T-298-B, *National Archives Microfilm Publication T1022,* roll 3028, RG 242.

War Diary of the *U-189*, August 15, 1942 – April 24, 1943, PG 30176; ONI Roll T-261-A, *National Archives Microfilm Publication T1022,* roll 2886, RG 242.

War Diary of the *U-200*, December 22, 1942 – June 21, 1943, PG 30187; ONI Roll T-307-B, *National Archives Microfilm Publication T1022,* roll 3037, RG 242.

War Diary of the *U-204*, March 8, 1941 – October 25, 1941, PG 30192/1-5; ONI Roll T-308-B, *National Archives Microfilm Publication T1022,* roll 3038, RG 242.

War Diary of the *U-219*, October 5, 1943 – January 1, 1944, PG 30207; ONI Roll T-94-E, *National Archives Microfilm Publication T1022,* roll 2837, RG 242.

War Diary of the *U-262*, April 15, 1942 – November 5, 1944, PG 30238/1-9; ONI Roll T-261-A, *National Archives Microfilm Publication T1022,* roll 2886, RG 242.

War Diary of the *U-331*, March 31, 1941 – November 21, 1942, PG 30402/1-12; ONI Roll T-312-B, *National Archives Microfilm Publication T1022,* roll 3042, RG 242.

War Diary of the *U-710*, September 2, 1942 – April 28, 1943, PG 30717; ONI Roll T-423, *National Archives Microfilm Publication T1022,* roll 3377, RG 242.

War Diary of the *U-968*, September 9, 1944 – February 20, 1945, PG 30801/6-7; ONI Roll T-523, *National Archives Microfilm Publication T1022,* roll 3763, RG 242.

U-boat Archive & Museum, Cuxhaven, Germany.

Unpublished Manuscripts

Hünefeldt, Joachim. "The Battle Flag of *U-751*," translated by William Lehmbeck (U.S. Navy, Retired). This is an excellent mini-memoir of Joachim Hünefeldt, who served on the *U-751* and survived the war. William Lehmbeck met Hünefeldt in Germany and the two men bonded as Mr. Lehmbeck himself had served an extensive career in U.S. submarines after World War II.

Personal Interviews

Interview with Horst Bredow, curator of the U-boat Museum & Archive and former crewmember on the *U-288* at Cuxhaven, Germany on October 22, 2008.

Interview with *Kapitän zur See* (Retired) Peter Monte, former German Navy (Bundesmarine) Attaché to Great Britain and Ireland at Cuxhaven, Germany on October 21, 2008.

Interview with Walter Wittig, former crewmember on the *U-518* and German Cross in Gold winner at Cuxhaven, Germany on October 21, 2008.